THE CAROLINAS & GEORGIA

17th Edition

Where to Stay and Eat
for All Budgets

Must-See Sights
and Local Secrets

Ratings You Can Trust

Fodor's Travel Publications   New York, Toronto, London, Sydney, Auckland
www.fodors.com

FODOR'S THE CAROLINAS & GEORGIA

Editors: Ruth Craig, Mark Sullivan

Editorial Production: Evangelos Vasilakis
Editorial Contributors: Linda Cabasin, Michele Foust, Chris McBeath, Katie McElveen, Leslie Mizell, Lan Sluder, Eileen Robinson Smith
Maps: David Lindroth, *cartographer;* Rebecca Baer and Bob Blake, *map editors*
Design: Fabrizio La Rocca, *creative director;* Guido Caroti, *art director;* Moon Sun Kim, *cover designer;* Melanie Marin, *senior picture editor*
Production/Manufacturing: Angela L. McLean
Cover Photo (Parris Island): Eric Horan

Seventeenth Edition

ISBN 978–1–4000–1741–6

ISSN 1525–5832

SPECIAL SALES

This book is available at special discounts for bulk purchases for sales promotions or premiums. Special editions, including personalized covers, excerpts of existing books, and corporate imprints, can be created in large quantities for special needs. For more information, write to Special Markets/Premium Sales, 1745 Broadway, MD 6-2, New York, NY 10019, or e-mail specialmarkets@randomhouse.com.

AN IMPORTANT TIP & AN INVITATION

Although all prices, opening times, and other details in this book are based on information supplied to us at press time, changes occur all the time in the travel world, and Fodor's cannot accept responsibility for facts that become outdated or for inadvertent errors or omissions. So **always confirm information when it matters,** especially if you're making a detour to visit a specific place. Your experiences—positive and negative—matter to us. If we have missed or misstated something, **please write to us.** We follow up on all suggestions. Contact the Carolinas & Georgia editor at editors@fodors.com or c/o Fodor's at 1745 Broadway, New York, NY 10019.

Be a Fodor's Correspondent

Your opinion matters. It matters to us. It matters to your fellow Fodor's travelers, too. And we'd like to hear it. In fact, we *need* to hear it.

When you share your experiences and opinions, you become an active member of the Fodor's community. That means we'll not only use your feedback to make our books better, but we'll publish your names and comments whenever possible. Throughout our guides, look for "Word of Mouth," excerpts of your unvarnished feedback.

Here's how you can help improve Fodor's for all of us.

Tell us when we're right. We rely on local writers to give you an insider's perspective. But our writers and staff editors—who are the best in the business—depend on you. Your positive feedback is a vote to renew our recommendations for the next edition.

Tell us when we're wrong. We're proud that we update most of our guides every year. But we're not perfect. Things change. Hotels cut services. Museums change hours. Charming cafés lose charm. If our writer didn't quite capture the essence of a place, tell us how you'd do it differently. If any of our descriptions are inaccurate or inadequate, we'll incorporate your changes in the next edition and will correct factual errors at fodors.com *immediately.*

Tell us what to include. You probably have had fantastic travel experiences that aren't yet in Fodor's. Why not share them with a community of like-minded travelers? Maybe you chanced upon a beach or barbecue spot or B&B that you don't want to keep to yourself. Tell us why we should include it. And share your discoveries and experiences with everyone directly at fodors.com. Your input may lead us to add a new listing or highlight a place we cover with a "Highly Recommended" star or with our highest rating, "Fodor's Choice."

Give us your opinion instantly at our feedback center at www.fodors.com/feedback. You may also e-mail editors@fodors.com with the subject line "Carolinas & Georgia Editor." Or send your nominations, comments, and complaints by mail to Carolinas & Georgia Editor, Fodor's, 1745 Broadway, New York, NY 10019.

You and travelers like you are the heart of the Fodor's community. Make our community richer by sharing your experiences. Be a Fodor's correspondent.

Happy traveling!

Tim Jarrell, Publisher

CONTENTS

CLOSEUPS

MAPS

CONTENTS

ABOUT THIS BOOK

Our Ratings

Sometimes you find terrific travel experiences and sometimes they just find you. But usually the burden is on you to select the right combination of experiences. That's where our ratings come in.

As travelers we've all discovered a place so wonderful that its worthiness is obvious. And sometimes that place is so unique that superlatives don't do it justice: you just have to be there to know. These sights, properties, and experiences get our highest rating, **Fodor's Choice**, indicated by orange stars throughout this book.

Black stars highlight sights and properties we deem **Highly Recommended** , places that our writers, editors, and readers praise again and again for consistency and excellence.

By default, there's another category: any place we include in this book is by definition worth your time, unless we say otherwise. And we will.

Disagree with any of our choices? Care to nominate a place or suggest that we rate one more highly? Visit our feedback center at www.fodors.com/feedback.

Budget Well

Hotel and restaurant price categories from ¢ to $$$$ are defined in the opening pages of each chapter. For attractions, we always give standard adult admission fees; reductions are usually available for children, students, and senior citizens. Want to pay with plastic? **AE, D, DC, MC, V** following restaurant and hotel listings indicate whether American Express, Discover, Diner's Club, MasterCard, and Visa are accepted.

Restaurants

Unless we state otherwise, restaurants are open for lunch and dinner daily. We mention dress only when there's a specific requirement and reservations only when they're essential or not accepted—it's always best to book ahead.

Hotels

Hotels have private bath, phone, TV, and air-conditioning unless we specify otherwise. They may operate on the European Plan (aka EP, meaning without meals), the Continental Plan (CP, with a continental breakfast), Breakfast Plan (BP, with a full breakfast), or Modified American Plan (MAP, with breakfast and dinner). We always list fa-

cilities but not whether you'll be charged an extra fee to use them, so when pricing accommodations, find out what's included.

Many Listings
- ★ Fodor's Choice
- ★ Highly recommended
- ⊠ Physical address
- ✛ Directions
- 🕮 Mailing address
- ☎ Telephone
- 🖷 Fax
- ⊕ On the Web
- ✉ E-mail
- 🎟 Admission fee
- ⊙ Open/closed times
- ▭ Credit cards

Hotels & Restaurants
- 🏨 Hotel
- 🛏 Number of rooms
- △ Facilities
- ❡❍❡ Meal plans
- ✕ Restaurant
- ⌂ Reservations
- 🏛 Dress code
- ↘ Smoking
- 🍸 BYOB
- ✕🏨 Hotel with restaurant that warrants a visit

Outdoors
- 🏌 Golf
- ⚠ Camping

Other
- ☺ Family-friendly
- 🄵 Contact information
- ⇨ See also
- ⊠ Branch address
- ☞ Take note

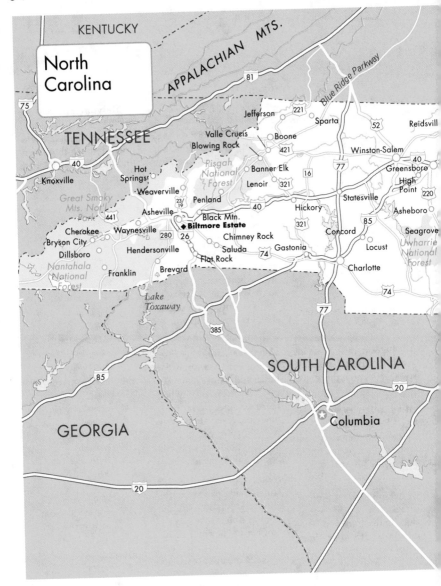

North
Carolina

KENTUCKY

APPALACHIAN MTS.

Blue Ridge Parkway

81

TENNESSEE

75

Jefferson   221   Sparta   52   Reidsvill

Valle Crucis   Boone
Blowing Rock   421   Winston-Salem   40

40   Hot   Pisgah   Banner Elk   16   77   Greensboro
Knoxville   Springs   National   High
            Weaverville   Forest   Lenoir   321   Point   220
Great Smoky   23   Penland   40   Hickory   Statesville
Mts. Nat'l   19   Asheville   Asheboro
Park   441   Black Mtn.   321
        Cherokee   Waynesville   ◆ Biltmore Estate   85
Bryson City   280   26   Chimney Rock   Concord   Seagrove
Dillsboro   Hendersonville   Saluda   74   Gastonia   Locust   Uwharrie
Nantahala   Flat Rock   National
National   Franklin   Brevard   Charlotte   Forest
Forest   74

            Lake
            Toxaway

                        385

                                          SOUTH CAROLINA

85   20

GEORGIA   ★ Columbia

            20

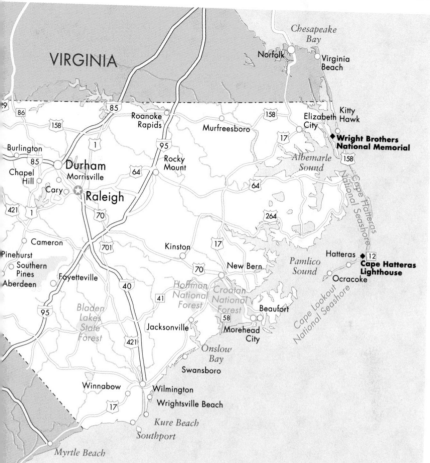

Chesapeake Bay

VIRGINIA

Norfolk

Virginia Beach

86

158

Roanoke Rapids

158

Murfreesboro

17

Kitty Hawk

Elizabeth City

Burlington

1

95

Rocky Mount

◆ **Wright Brothers National Memorial**

Albemarle Sound

158

85

Durham

Chapel Hill

Morrisville

64

Cary

Raleigh

64

Cape Hatteras National Seashore

421

1

70

264

Cameron

701

Kinston

17

Pamlico Sound

Hatteras

◆ 12 **Cape Hatteras Lighthouse**

Pinehurst

Southern Pines

Aberdeen

Fayetteville

70

New Bern

Ocracoke

40

Hoffman National Forest

41

Croatan National Forest

58

Beaufort

Cape Lookout National Seashore

Bladen Lakes State Forest

95

Jacksonville

421

Morehead City

Onslow Bay

Swansboro

Winnabow

Wilmington

17

Wrightsville Beach

Kure Beach

Southport

Myrtle Beach

ATLANTIC OCEAN

0 — 50 miles

0 — 50 km

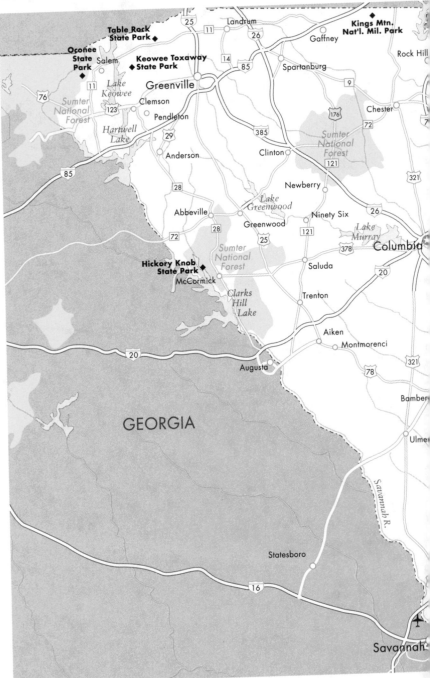

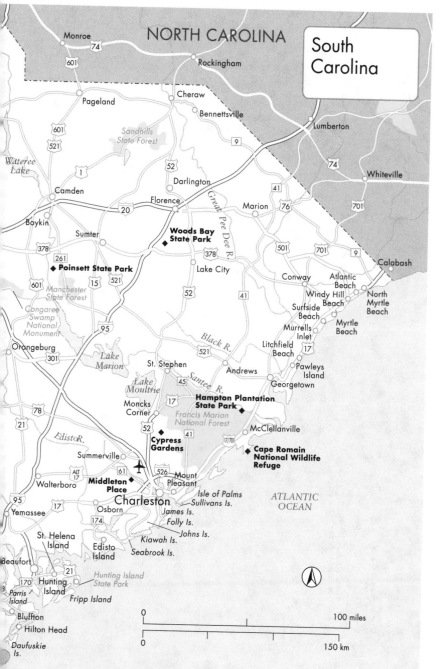

South Carolina

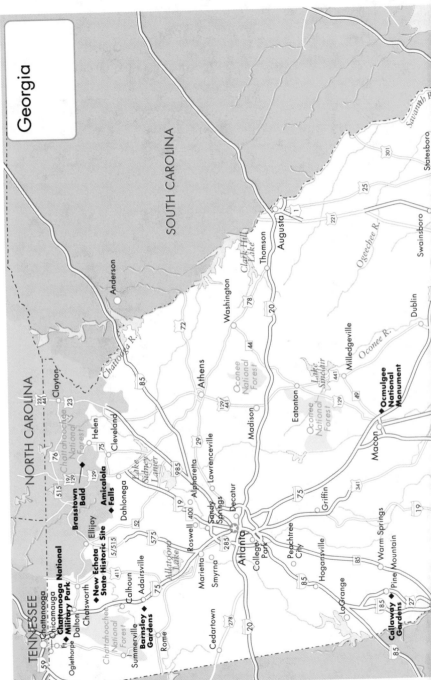

Georgia

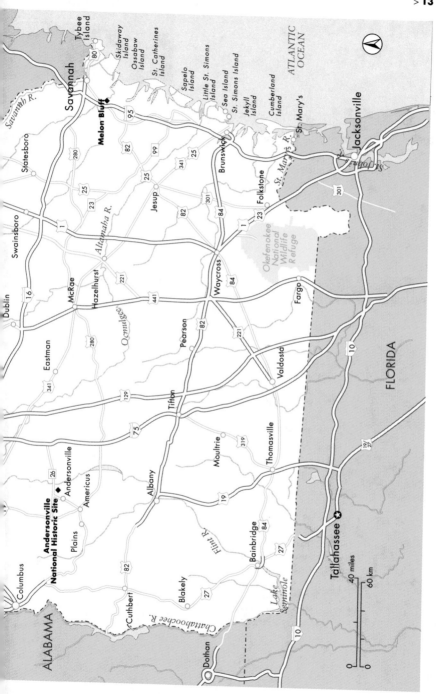

WHAT'S WHERE

THE NORTH CAROLINA COAST	Nothing in the entire region compares with the Outer Banks of North Carolina. This pencil-thin band of barrier islands, with its wind-twisted oaks and gnarled pines, forms a buffer between the mainland and the Atlantic Ocean. Connected by bridges and ferries, these islands have long stretches that are protected from development, thanks to the Cape Hatteras National Seashore, which extended 70 mi from Nags Head to Ocracoke Island, and Cape Lookout National Seashore, running 55 mi from Portsmouth Island to Shackleford Banks. Near Ocracoke Island, on the southern tip of the Outer Banks, are some of the best beaches on the East Coast. Sunny skies warm the rest of North Carolina's 300-mi-long coast most of the year.
THE PIEDMONT & THE SANDHILLS	The New South comes alive in North Carolina's Piedmont, consisting of three major metropolitan centers—Charlotte, the Triad (shorthand for Greensboro, Winston-Salem, and High Point), and the Triangle (Raleigh, Durham, Chapel Hill). The most heavily developed part of the state, the Piedmont sits in the center between the mountains and the coastal plain. Shopping (if you don't mind malls), dining, and nightlife are readily available, especially around the bustling Interstate 40–Interstate 85 corridor, which can get you to almost anywhere you want to go. Sports get top billing here, from college football games to NASCAR races. But you come to know the area best when you explore peaceful country roads leading to gristmills, gold mines, and general stores.
THE NORTH CAROLINA MOUNTAINS	With more than 1½-million acres of stupendous vertical scenery in the Great Smoky Mountains National Park and the Nantahala and Pisgah national forests, western North Carolina is by far the most beautiful part of the state. One of North America's most scenic roads, the Blue Ridge Parkway, winds for 252 mi among the majestic peaks. There are endless opportunities for outdoor adventures, whether it's shooting down white-water rapids, camping in the wilderness, or climbing Mt. Mitchell, the tallest peak east of the Rockies. In Asheville, a resort city for more than a century, you'll find edgy art galleries, sophisticated eateries, and the Southeast's biggest collection of art-deco architecture outside of Miami Beach. The country's largest home, the Biltmore House, sits nearby.

MYRTLE BEACH & THE GRAND STRAND	South Carolina's Grand Strand, a 60-mi-long expanse of white-sand beach, runs south from the North Carolina border. In the center is the carnival-like atmosphere of Myrtle Beach, with its waterslides, amusement parks, outlet malls, and theme shopping centers. Myrtle Beach may be the greatest show on the Strand, but there are other pleasures as well: the quiet refuge of Pawleys Island, with its string of old summer cottages; Brookgreen Gardens, with its magnificent sculptures; and more than 120 golf courses. The Atlantic Ocean is easily accessible nearly everywhere on the Strand, but there are also quiet creeks for canoeing and marshes for crabbing and shrimping. These waterways also offer a unique perspective of the area's history, providing views of some of the plantation houses that were once essential to the local economy.
CHARLESTON	Charleston anchors the Lowcountry (the local term for South Carolina's flat coastal plain) in high style. The harbor town's rich past, dating back to 1670, is evident in the residents' every-day lives: they walk to work on cobblestone streets, live in antebellum mansions, and picnic come festival time at the vast plantations in the shadows of the old "big houses." African- and Caribbean-born Gullah accents can still be heard among the African-American population. Although it's steeped in history, Charleston is very much a town of today. Here you can soak up the latest in music, dance, and theater during the annual Spoleto USA festival, feast at some of the country's leading restaurants, and shop for everything from museum-quality art to one-of-a-kind antiques to the chicest fashions from Kate Spade and Manolo Blahnik. Outdoors lovers are challenged to conquer all of Charleston's outlying beaches and marshes.
HILTON HEAD & THE LOWCOUNTRY	The coastal lowlands that stretch southward from Charleston contain some of the most beautiful landscapes in all of South Carolina. Take U.S. 17 south from Charleston and you will wind through coastal forests with ancient live oaks forming canopies overhead and wide-open marshes that stretch their golden-green pelts out to the horizon. You can discover long stretches of undisturbed beaches, although condos are starting to block the views. Strollable fishing villages with quaint waterfront areas and ornate antebellum homes are other draws. Farther south is Hilton Head Island, a vacation destination dominated by megaresorts, golf courses, tennis courts, and water-sports facilities.

WHAT'S WHERE

THE MIDLANDS & UPSTATE	Radiating out from Columbia, South Carolina's engaging capital city, this region is known for its piney woods, fertile farmlands, and manufacturing plants. Freshwater is in abundance, from the murky swamps and large lakes of the Midlands to the waterfalls and roaring rapids of the hilly Upstate. The small towns of the area each have their own claims to fame: Aiken is one the nation's equestrian centers (Sea Hero and Pleasant Colony were trained here), and Camden is the place to go for well-priced antiques (don't miss the shops along Broad Street). Greenwood and Abbeville are steeped in the Civil War and Revolutionary War history of the region.
SAVANNAH	Georgia's oldest and grandest city, Savannah is still basking in fame from what locals just call "The Book," John Berendt best-seller *Midnight in the Garden of Good and Evil*. But long before *Midnight*, a well-organized historic-zoning effort preserved the mid-19th century heart of downtown. The city has 1,400 restored or reconstructed buildings dating from the time it was founded. Warehouses still line the banks of the Savannah River, where oceangoing vessels haul cargo upstream and tourists line up for beers at local pubs. Although Savannah revels in its well-preserved past and quirky present, city officials are struggling to overcome its high rate of crime, which is well above the national average.
THE COASTAL ISLES & THE OKEFENOKEE	Stretching southward from Savannah, Georgia's coastal isles are "almost Florida," but in some ways they're even more appealing than what you'll find in the state's southern neighbor. Areas like the Cumberland Island National Seashore have become nature reserves, meaning this region remains almost as it was when the first Europeans set eyes on it 450 years ago. Little St. Simons Island and Sea Island cater primarily to those in higher tax brackets, whereas St. Simons Island and Jekyll Island have something for everyone. About 60 mi inland is the wild and mysterious Okefenokee Swamp, one of the nation's largest wetlands.
SOUTHWEST GEORGIA	Some may yawn their way through this quiet corner of Georgia, but there's a lot of history here. The region felt the impact of two presidents: Franklin Delano Roosevelt, who had a summer home in the town of Warm Springs, and Jimmy Carter, a Plains native who returned home to become one of the nation's most active former presidents, engaging in philanthropic and diplomatic work that earned him a Nobel Peace Prize. The brutality of the Civil War is tangible at the Confederate prison

	in Andersonville, and more modern military equipment is on display at the Fort Benning National Infantry Museum near Columbus.
ATLANTA	Long considered a great place to live and work, but the ultimate bore for visitors, Atlanta has succeeded in shaking off that reputation. The whale sharks at the Georgia Aquarium, the memorabilia at the World of Coca-Cola, the modern works at the High Museum of Art, and other newly opened attractions mean that at last there's actually something to do in the capital of the New South. Transplants from other parts of the country have prompted a boom in restaurants, shops, and cultural attractions; the growing population has brought new life to many downtown neighborhoods (and added to the metropolitan area's infamous traffic snarls). Atlanta has always had strong ties to the civil rights movement, and here you can visit the childhood home of Martin Luther King Jr.
CENTRAL GEORGIA	Stretching from Augusta to Macon, Central Georgia lies at the heart of the Old South. You can find plenty of white-columned mansions and shady verandas, evoking a romanticized past. Along the way you'll run across lots of that fabled Southern hospitality, mixed in with run-down trailer parks and rustic barbecue joints. The pace picks up in Athens, a college town that's home to the University of Georgia. The home of '80s and '90s groundbreaking groups like R.E.M., Widespread Panic, and the B-52's still rocks at night.
NORTH GEORGIA	Less than two hours from Atlanta is North Georgia, where you can find the waterfalls and lakes of the southern Blue Ridge Mountains. The peaks are higher and the scenery more dramatic in the nearby North Carolina Mountains, but here you can explore small towns few people (except Georgians) have heard of, like Ellijay, home of the Georgia Apple Festival, and Dahlonega, the site of the first gold rush in America. In the northwestern part of the state you can walk the hallowed ground of Chickamauga, the site of one of the bloodiest battles in the Civil War.

QUINTESSENTIAL CAROLINAS & GEORGIA

Serious BBQ

Don't expect many options if you're invited somewhere for barbecue during your trip to the Carolinas and Georgia. That's because in these parts, barbecue means just one thing: meat, usually pork, that's been smoked over a gentle fire for as long as 12 hours until it falls from the bone in soft, flavorful shreds. The sauce is the source of an unending debate about the merits of ingredients that can include, but are not limited to, ketchup, mustard, vinegar, and hot peppers. Generally, on the coast in all three states, but especially in eastern North Carolina, you can find barbecue served with a thin but flavorful mixture of vinegar, spices, and hot peppers. Central South Carolina is known for its mustard barbecue, a yellowish dish that, for most, is an acquired taste. Richer sauces containing ketchup, molasses, and onion show up in the mountains. Eating barbecue is a social event—even at restaurants, where long tables are set up with squeeze bottles of extra sauce and pitchers of sweet tea.

The Big Game

It's hard not to feel like a local when you're surrounded by thousands of sports fans yelling, screaming, or, in the case of Georgia Bulldog boosters, barking for their favorite college teams. During football season, a party atmosphere takes over the entire region when cars festooned with colorful flags, decals, and bumper stickers stream toward the stadiums. But all the action doesn't take place in fall: basketball is also legendary, with powerhouse teams playing in packed arenas in all three states. Even for games featuring famous rivals—the University of South Carolina and Clemson, the University of North Carolina and North Carolina State University, and the University of Georgia and Georgia Tech—tickets are generally available.

If you want to get a sense of contemporary culture in the Carolinas and Georgia, and indulge in some of the region's pleasures, start by familiarizing yourself with the rituals of daily life. These are a few highlights—things you can take part in with relative ease.

On the Waterfront

The blue ribbons of rivers, creeks, and streams do more than decorate the green landscape of the Carolinas and Georgia. They're among the region's most popular destinations for local outdoor enthusiasts, and you should join them. Jet skis and pontoon boats can be found on the glass-smooth lakes, and canoes and kayaks are always exploring mysterious swamps hung with Spanish moss. In the mountains, roaring rapids promise a wild ride for whitewater rafters, and quieter stretches are perfect for a lazy afternoon in an inner tube. And anglers won't be disappointed, either. Children here don't just learn how to fish; they set crab traps with chicken necks and maneuver nets to bring home a mess of shrimp. The ocean is never far away, and although some beaches get crowded during high season, you can usually find a private strip of sand.

Southern Sounds

Jamaica has reggae and Detroit can lay claim to Motown, but bluegrass, blues, and gospel music can all trace their lineage to the Carolinas and Georgia. Although these genres each have their own distinctive sound, they were all nurtured in the homes, churches, and social clubs of the region, where they were taught, performed, and passed on to future generations. You can hear this distinctive music today at pickin' parlors—where the competition can get fierce—and at local music festivals, county fairs, and in concert halls. For a modern take, head to college towns like Athens, Georgia; Chapel Hill, North Carolina; and Columbia, South Carolina; where bands such as Hootie and the Blowfish, Ben Folds Five, and the B-52's got their start.

IF YOU LIKE

Gourmet Dining

"If you can't fry it, don't buy it," was the mantra of Southern chefs 50 years ago. And although cooking methods may have changed, shrimp, grits, and okra are still staples. Now, however, you can also find them accompanying dishes like benne seed–crusted rack of lamb.

- Like the simple splashes of color that bring the dining room alive at Atlanta's **Bacchanalia**, it's the unexpected touches that make the food sublime. The menu, which changes daily, follows the seasons, with truffle oil scenting cured salmon in fall and fresh figs accompanying seared fois gras come summer.

- Contemporary cuisine with a Southern twist—think okra rellenos and spicy green-tomato soup with crab and country ham—is the star of the show at **Magnolia Grill**, a Durham, North Carolina, hot spot.

- On your way into the Greek-revival mansion that houses Savannah's **Elizabeth on 37th**, you might see the staff snipping the herbs that flavor the remarkable dishes. The other ingredients, like briny oysters, sweet shrimp, heavy summer tomatoes, arrive from just down the road. The biscuits, delivered piping hot, are sublime.

- When he opened Charleston's **Peninsula Grill**, Robert Carter wanted with enough of a drawl to satisfy his Southern roots. He succeeded mightily: the boneless grilled pork chops with andouille-cheddar grits are addictive, as are the 1-pound slabs of coconut cake—his grandmother's recipe—that vanish as if they were petit fours.

Golfing

For those whose vacation has to include a round or two of golf, one of the best reasons to visit the Carolinas and Georgia is that the mild climate allows you to play all year. Even better, you can enjoy the scenery as much as the game. You can hit drivers from a mountaintop, tap in a putt as the ocean crashes all around you, and chip out of a sand trap that sits beside a sapphire-blue marsh dotted with egrets.

- Golf legend Bobby Jones called this resort "the St. Andrews of United States golf." The site of more championships than any other golf resort in the country, **Pinehurst**, in North Carolina, is consistently ranked among the best in the world. Among its eight courses, the Donald Ross–designed Number Two is considered the masterpiece.

- Offering views of the ocean from all 18 holes, Kiawah Island Golf Resort's **Ocean Course** winds through salt marshes and seaside forests are filled with wildlife, including the occasional alligator. It has one of most dramatic last holes in golf.

- In the shadow of the Harbor Town Lighthouse, Hilton Head Island's **Harbour Town Golf Links** is devilishly difficult. Although deceptively short by today's standards, South Carolina's top course leaves no room for error.

- Often called the "granddaddy of golf," **Pine Lakes** has long been a landmark in Myrtle Beach. The columned clubhouse, resembling an antebellum mansion, was built in 1927. The elegant course pitches and weaves through tall pines and, in the spring, glorious azaleas.

Island Hopping

The dozens of islands that hug the coast of North Carolina, South Carolina, and Georgia come in all shapes and sizes, and they have personalities as diverse as their landscapes. Opulent seaside resorts turn a simple vacation into an extravagant getaway. Other islands remain uninhabited, or nearly so, and are accessible only by boat. What they all share is the natural beauty of moss-draped oaks, primeval marine forest, and the ripple of golden sea grass blowing gently in the breeze.

- Best known for chic boutiques, trend-setting restaurants, and world-class golf resorts, **Hilton Head Island** also has a network of trails that let you explore this enclave off the South Carolina coast on foot, by bike or, at the lovely Sea Pines Resort, on horseback.

- It became famous when John F. Kennedy Jr. and Carolyn Bisset held their barefoot wedding on its windswept shore, but locals have always known about the pristine beauty of Georgia's **Cumberland Island**. You won't forget the sight of wild horses running along its shores.

- It's no longer a playground for the Astors and the Vanderbilts, but **Jekyll Island** is still home to many of the sprawling "cottages" that were summer getaways for wealthy families a century ago. This popular Georgia destination also has long stretches of unspoiled beaches.

- The wild ponies that once roamed the rugged scrub forests of North Carolina's **Ocracoke Island** are now safely pastured, but the windswept beaches and whitewashed cottages are as appealing as ever.

Civil War History

The Civil War forever changed the character of the South, particularly the bastions of plantation life in the Carolinas and Georgia. In the many museums in the region, period furnishings offer a glimpse into antebellum life, and heart-wrenching letters illustrate the toll the war took on families, and photographs show the hardships suffered by slaves before and after they were set free.

- A huge painting that encircles the viewer inside the **Atlanta Cyclorama & Civil War Museum** depicts the 1864 Battle of Atlanta in tremendous detail. Inside the museum there's an impressive collection of period weapons, uniforms, maps, and photographs.

- The site of one of the Civil War's worst conflicts, Chickamauga battlefield saw almost 35,000 soldiers killed or injured during a three-day struggle in September of 1863. North Georgia's **Chickamauga & Chattanooga National Military Park and Visitor Center** offers a glimpse into the strategies used by both sides during the campaign.

- Although it was built to protect Charleston after the War of 1812, **Fort Sumter** became a symbol of Southern resistance after it became the site of the first battle of the Civil War. The first shots were fired here on April 12, 1861.

- Near Charleston, **Drayton Hall** is the only plantation along Ashley River Road not destroyed during Gen. William Tecumseh Sherman's march through South Carolina.

GREAT ITINERARIES

SALT & SAND: THE BEACHES OF THE CAROLINAS & GEORGIA

The coastline of the Carolinas and Georgia runs for more than 600 mi and includes some of the superlative stretches of sand on the East Coast. This itinerary includes the region's best beach experiences, from the solitude of the remote barrier islands to the hectic carnival atmosphere of Myrtle Beach.

Day 1: Cumberland Island, Georgia

Start your beach trip on one of the most unspoiled islands on the East Coast. Cumberland Island, off Georgia's southeastern coast, has pristine beaches, high sand dunes, and lovely stretches of marsh. Wild horses roam its shores. If it's in your budget, stay at the island's only lodging, the century-old Greyfield Inn.

Logistics: Leave your car in St. Mary's and cross to Cumberland Island on the ferry called the *Cumberland Queen*. In high season, reserve in advance.

Days 2 & 3: Jekyll Island, Georgia

Once the winter playground of the Rockefellers, Morgans, and Vanderbilts, Jekyll Island now has something for everyone. For a taste of the millionaire's lifestyle, bunk at the 1886 Jekyll Island Club Hotel. To see more of the area, drive to exclusive Sea Island or bustling St. Simons Island.

Logistics: From St. Mary's, drive north on Interstate 95 to the U.S. Highway 17 exit for Jekyll Island.

Day 4: Sapelo Island

Sapelo Island's beaches are uncrowded and undeveloped, but the real reason to visit here is to glimpse the unique culture of the Geechee, direct descendents of slaves who speak a blend of English and West African languages. After a 30-minute ferry ride through the marshes, a local guide will lead you on one of the most interesting tours you'll ever take.

Logistics: Drive north on Interstate 95 to the exit for Darien. Follow the signs to Meridian, where you can take the *Sapelo Queen* across to Sapelo Island. Make reservations in advance.

Day 5: Savannah & Tybee Island

Stay in one of the lovely bed-and-breakfast inns of Savannah. If you must have a little beach time, hit the 1950s-vintage beach resort of Tybee Island, about 18 mi east of downtown.

Logistics: It's an hour's drive, mostly on Interstate 95 north, to Savannah.

Days 6 & 7: Hilton Head Island

On Hilton Head Island, you can try a different golf course every day for more than three weeks, play tennis on any of 300 courts, or look for bargains at outlet malls.

Logistics: It's less than an hour's drive from Savannah north to Hilton Head.

Day 8: Charleston

Take a break from sand and salt to stroll among Charleston's historic homes. To fully appreciate Charleston's charms, you'll want to stay in a B&B or small inn. For a quick dip, Folly Beach and the Isle of Palms are a short drive away.

Logistics: From Hilton Head to Charleston, it's about a two-hour drive north, via U.S. Highway 17.

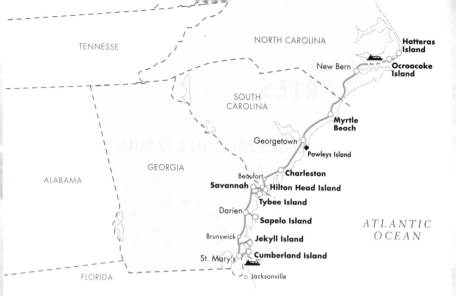

Days 9 & 10: Myrtle Beach & the Grand Strand

Hey, baby, let's do the Shag! The Carolina Shag, best described as "a warm night with a cold beer and a hot date," is virtually synonymous with Myrtle Beach. Along the Grand Strand are quieter destinations like Pawleys Island and Georgetown.

Logistics: It's about a two-hour drive north from Charleston to Myrtle Beach, via U.S. Highway 17.

Days 11 & 12: Ocracoke Island

Ocracoke Island is basically one long beach, with nearly 16 mi of undeveloped national seashore. Don't miss the Ocracoke Lighthouse, the oldest operating lighthouse on the East Coast.

Logistics: This is the longest drive of the trip, about 215 mi, mostly on rural roads. To reach the island, take the Cedar Island–Ocracoke ferry.

Days 13 & 14: Hatteras Island

Hatteras Island, a 33 mi-long narrow ribbon of sandy national seashore, is dotted with seven small villages. You can explore two historic lighthouses or go birding at the Pea Island National Wildlife Refuge.

Logistics: A free ferry runs hourly from Ocracoke Island to Hatteras Island. Arrive early to get a place in line.

TIPS

❶ Be prepared for traffic, especially in summer and on holiday weekends. Interstate 95 can be one big parking lot. U.S. Highway 17, a north–south coastal road, is especially crowded around Myrtle Beach.

❷ Take care when swimming in the Atlantic Ocean. Breakers can come rolling in with tremendous force, creating dangerous rip tides.

❸ Keep a lookout for wildlife. There are wild ponies on Cumberland Island and other islands. Atlantic bottlenose dolphins cavort just off the beach along North Carolina's Outer Banks. Loggerheads and other turtles nest even on the busy beaches of Myrtle Beach.

❹ Always try the local food specialties, such as Lowcountry boil (shrimp, sausage, potatoes, onions, and corn) and she-crab soup in Savannah, shrimp and grits in Charleston, Frogmore stew in South Carolina, and Hatteras-style clam chowder (with a clear broth) on North Carolina's Outer Banks.

WHEN TO GO

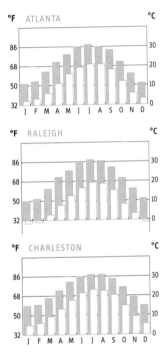

There's really not a bad time to visit the Carolinas and Georgia, but spring is undoubtedly the most attractive season. Throughout the region, the blooming of cherry blossoms is followed by a profusion of azaleas, dogwoods, and camellias in April and apple blossoms in May. Art shows, craft fairs, and music festivals tend to take place in summer, making it a great time to check out the local culture. State and local fairs are held mainly in August and September, although there are a few as early as July and as late as October. Fall can bring spectacular foliage, particularly in the mountains. Don't be surprised if you find yourself sharing the road with a caravan of leaf-peepers. The other spectator sport that draws people to the region every fall is college football. Winter is generally mild, which is why so many "snowbirds" migrate south for the season.

Climate

Spring and fall temperatures are delightful during the day, and at night you usually don't need anything more than a light jacket. Summer can be hot and humid in many parts of the region, but a bit more temperate along the coast and in the mountains. Expect high 70s to the mid-80s and now and then the low 90s. In winter, long periods of mild weather are punctuated by brief bouts of frigid conditions. Temperatures generally average in the low 40s inland and in the 60s by the shore. Thunderstorms are common in spring and summer, but these afternoon downpours generally don't last long. Many locals don't even bother to bring along an umbrella, preferring to wait out the weather. The official hurricane season runs from May to November. Storms occasionally strike the region, either directly from the Atlantic Ocean or moving northward from the Gulf of Mexico. The region is large, so conditions vary; *see* the individual chapters for more information.

Forecasts **Weather Channel Connection** (☎ 900/932-8437 95¢ per minute ⊕ www.weather.com).

ON THE CALENDAR

WINTER	
December	Held in early December, Atlanta's Festival of Trees lets you wander among more than 200 specially decorated Christmas trees. Some of the city's best designers try to outdo each other with eye-popping displays.
	In Albany, Georgia, the annual Mistletoe Market is an arts-and-crafts show that takes place early in the month.
	Highlights among regional holiday celebrations include Winston-Salem's Old Salem Christmas, which re-creates a traditional Moravian Christmas.
	The Tanglewood Festival of Lights, also in Winston-Salem, is one of the country's most spectacular displays of Christmas lights.
	Fantasy in Lights is an outdoor sound and light display at Callaway Gardens in Pine Mountain, Georgia. The highlight is a 5-mi-long roadway lined with 8 million twinkling lights.
January	The new year is marked with family-friendly First Night festivals held in the downtown areas of Athens and Savannah in Georgia; Asheville, Charlotte, and Raleigh in North Carolina; and Charleston and Greenville in South Carolina.
	In Atlanta, Martin Luther King Jr. Week is celebrated midmonth with lectures, exhibits, and rallies.
February	In North Carolina, Asheville hosts the annual Arts and Crafts Conference in the middle of the month.
	Chapel Hill stages the Carolina Jazz Festival, usually at the end of the month. The weekend of lectures, concerts, and jam sessions includes many free events.
	The Battle of Aiken Living History Reenactment, held the last weekend of the month, is a large-scale reenactment of a skirmish that took place late in the Civil War.
SPRING	
March	Spring is celebrated with a midmonth International Cherry Blossom Festival in Macon, Georgia. The city is covered with pink-and-white blooms, since its streets are lined with more than 300,000 trees.
	South Carolina's SpringFest, held on Hilton Head Island, takes place during the entire month.
	The Guilford Courthouse Battle Reenactment takes place on March 15 in Greensboro, North Carolina.
	Savannah has one of the country's most spirited celebrations of St. Patrick's Day. It should, as it has marked the day since 1813.

ON THE CALENDAR

	Aiken, South Carolina, is home to the Aiken Triple Crown, which includes thoroughbred races, steeplechases, and polo matches. It's held on three consecutive Saturdays in March.
April	More than 25,000 people participate in the Cooper River Bridge Run and Walk, usually held the first Saturday in April in Charleston.
	Wilmington, North Carolina, has been holding the North Carolina Azalea Festival since 1948. This colorful display, which culminates with the crowning of the Azalea Queen, is usually the first weekend in April.
	The South Carolina town of St. George, the self-proclaimed "Grits Capital of the World," celebrates the local delicacy with the World Grits Festival, held in the beginning of the month. Locals say they eat more grits per capita than anywhere else in the world.
	In early April, the Masters Golf Tournament attracts thousands of spectators to the Augusta National Golf Club.
	The Biltmore Estate in Asheville, North Carolina, hosts the Festival of Flowers, in early April to late May. This breathtaking display has more than 50,000 tulips, hundreds of varieties of azaleas, and plenty of pink-and-white dogwood and cherry trees.
	Can't get enough jousting? The massive Georgia Renaissance Festival is held weekends from April to early June in Fairburn, not far from Atlanta. A highlight is a market with 150 artisans.
	In Wilkesboro, North Carolina, MerleFest, usually the last weekend in the month, is a celebration of the late musician Merle Watson. Come to hear some great bluegrass picking.
May	In mid-May, the annual Hang Gliding Spectacular takes place in Nags Head, North Carolina.
	Held over Memorial Day weekend in Anderson, South Carolina, Freedom Weekend Aloft is one of the country's largest hot-air balloon rallies.
	The Lake Eden Arts Festival, held midmonth in Black Mountain, North Carolina, features music, crafts, dancing, and poetry, in a hippyish atmosphere.
	In South Carolina, Beaufort's Gullah Festival, held at the end of the month, highlights the fine arts, customs, language, and dress of Lowcountry African-Americans.

		For more than two weeks in May and June, Charleston's Spoleto Festival USA is one of the world's biggest arts festivals. Some of the best-known names in music and theater perform in music halls, auditoriums, theaters, and even outdoor spaces.
SUMMER	June	Summer gets under way in early June at the Sun Fun Festival at Myrtle Beach.
		The Virginia-Highland Summerfest, held in early June, brings art to Atlanta.
		A perennial favorite, the Festival of Flowers has been going strong since 1967. The event, which includes garden tours, is held mid-month in Greenwood, South Carolina.
		Western North Carolina's Brevard Music Center Institute & Festival, which takes place mid-June to early August, showcases everything from chamber music to opera.
		Usually held the last weekend in July, the Atlanta Pride Festival is one of the largest gay-pride events in the country, attracting 300,000 people to a parade, concerts, and an art market.
	July	The renowned American Dance Festival is held in early July in Durham, North Carolina.
		Early July's Highland Games & Gathering of the Scottish Clans takes place on Grandfather Mountain near Linville, North Carolina.
		Clog and figure dancing are part of the Shindig on the Green, held in Asheville from early July to early September. These concerts of bluegrass and string band music start "along about sundown."
		The Georgia Mountain Fair, a crafts and music extravaganza, is held midmonth in Hiawassee, Georgia.
		The last two weeks of the month, Folkmoot USA brings folk music and dance to Waynesville, North Carolina.
		The last weekend of July, Asheville's Bele Chere is the largest free street festival in the Southeast, with lots of music, crafts, and food.
	August	August music festivals include the Mountain Dance & Folk Festival, held annually since 1928, which begins "along about sundown" the first weekend in the month in Asheville.
		The Beach Music Festival is held at the end of the month on Jekyll Island, Georgia.

ON THE CALENDAR

FALL	
September	The Kingsland Catfish Festival in Kingsland, Georgia, on Labor Day weekend, salutes this Southern-fried specialty.
	In early September, the North Carolina Apple Festival brings bushels of these red, yellow, and green orbs to Hendersonville.
	The North Carolina Mountain State Fair is held in Asheville in mid-September.
October	Did somebody say pig-calling competitions? Georgia's Big Pig Jig, held in the town of Vienna over the first weekend of the month, celebrates the glories of authentic Southern barbecue.
	A parade of pigs marks North Carolina's Lexington Barbecue Festival, held in mid-October. Don't ask for barbecue sauce here. Locals call it "dip," and it's made with a special blend of vinegar, ketchup, salt, and pepper.
	Raleigh's North Carolina State Fair and Columbia's South Carolina State Fair are both held midmonth.
	The annual Woolly Worm Festival, where experts predict winter weather by the color of these woolly wigglers, takes place mid-month in Banner Elk, North Carolina. The big event is a woolly worm race, which nets the winner a grand prize of $500.
	The Georgia Apple Festival is held the second and third weekends of the month in Ellijay, Georgia. Vendors sell everything from apple dumplings to apple pies to, well, just plain apples.
	The annual Stone Mountain Highland Games, a celebration of Scottish heritage, is held the third weekend of the month at Georgia's Stone Mountain Park.
	Oktoberfest is celebrated the third weekend of the month in Walhalla, South Carolina.
November	Asheville's Christmas at Biltmore Estate, held early November to December, features candlelight tours of the mansion, decorated with dozens of Christmas trees, 700 poinsettias, and 400 wreaths.
	South Carolina's Society Hill Catfish Festival, held the first Saturday of the month, is known far and wide for the delicious catfish stew. It's so popular, in fact, that organizers sell it by the gallon.
	The Chitlin' Strut, celebrating country music and a certain pork product, is held the Saturday after Thanksgiving in Salley, South Carolina. Don't miss the crowning of the Chitlin' Queen and her court.

The North Carolina Coast

WORD OF MOUTH

"The northern OBX area is great. . . . there is nothing like visiting the Wright Memorial and then the next day, driving down the Outer Banks and experiencing the seclusion, seeing lighthouses (especially Cape Hatteras) and taking the ferry over to Ocracoke, drinking a beer on the small harbor and then going out at night. It is a great escape and in the off-season it is even better."

—Subway_Scoundrel

"Topsail is a place to really relax, read a good book, and enjoy some family time. Buy some local shrimp and fresh vegetables, stock up your drink of choice, and you won't even have to drive anywhere all week. Once you get into the rhythm of the place, you'll never want to leave."

—Devonmcj

www.fodors.com/forums

Updated by
Leslie Mizell

NORTH CAROLINA'S 300-PLUS MI OF COASTLINE are fronted by a continuous series of fragile barrier islands. Broad rivers lead inland from the sounds, along which port cities have grown. Lighthouses, dunes, and vacation homes (often built by out-of-staters) dot the water's edge. There are battle sites from both the American Revolution and the Civil War, elegant golf links, and kitschy putt-putt courses. Aquariums, fishing charters, and museum outreach programs put you up close and personal with the seashore critters. North Carolina's small towns (mostly of 1,000 to 3,000 people) offer genuine warmth and hospitality.

The coast is generally divided into three broad sections that include islands, shoreline, and coastal plains: the Outer Banks (Corolla south through Ocracoke, including Roanoke Island), the Crystal Coast (Core and Bogue Banks, Beaufort, Morehead City, and the inland river city of New Bern), and the greater Cape Fear region (Wrightsville Beach through the Brunswick County islands, including Wilmington). The Outer Banks are actually visible from space, a thin, delicate tracing of white that indicates these barrier islands, which form a buffer between the Atlantic Ocean and the mainland. With just one two-lane road stretching the length of the Outer Banks, locals speak of mile markers instead of street numbers.

Although other states' coasts have turned into wall-to-wall hotels and condominiums, much of North Carolina's coast belongs to the North Carolina Division of Parks and Recreation. This arrangement keeps the coast from being developed, but leaves most of it accessible to the public for exploration, athletic activities, picnicking, and camping. Still, property values have skyrocketed as the dream houses of summer residents gradually replace generations-old beach cottages.

Much of the coast closes down during midwinter, but even the colder season is a special time to visit. You can escape both the crowds and the peak prices, and can still enjoy the seafood, beaches, and museums. Whether you're seeking peace or adventure, you can find it on the coast.

Exploring the North Carolina Coast

The relative isolation that helps preserve the beauty of this area also restricts access and slows travel along its length. Route 12, with the help of the Hatteras Inlet ferry, travels the entire Outer Banks, but to get to it, you must either cross bridges from the mainland on U.S. 158 (from the north) or U.S. 64 (from the west) or take ferries from Swan Quarter or Cedar Island after long mainland drives farther south. Many of the islands and banks of the Crystal Coast and Cape Fear regions are traversed by state routes or U.S. highways, but there's no continuous path along the entire coastline. U.S. 70 is the main route into the Crystal Coast from the west, and Wilmington is the terminus of Interstate 40. The main north–south highway through the Cape Fear region is U.S. 17, which skirts the broadest parts of the rivers and intersects east–west roads as it drops from Virginia to South Carolina.

TOP 5 REASONS TO GO

Water, water everywhere: Rolling waves, sleepy estuaries, rippling inlets, glassy lakes, no-nonsense salt marshes—the landscape variety lets you choose your own adventure, whether it's boating, trekking, sunning, or simply observing.

Pirate lore and hidden booty: The Graveyard of the Atlantic is littered with shipwrecks, many of them popular dive sights. Your imagination will be piqued by tales of hidden treasure chests still lying beneath shifting sands.

Lighting the darkness: North Carolina's seven lighthouses have individual personalities, from the masculine elegance of Currituck's

brick facade to the iconic spiral of Hatteras. You'll want to take time to see them all.

The Lost Colony: In a mystery for the ages, 90 settlers, including the first European baby born in the New World, disappeared without a trace. Their story is presented both in historical context and dramatic entertainment in Manteo.

Don't skimp on the shrimp: You can get fresh seafood of every variety fixed in practically every method—fried, grilled, stuffed, blackened, sautéed, pasta-ed, ka-bobbed, or even raw. And since you're on vacation, the calories don't count, right?

About the Restaurants

Raw bars serve oysters and clams on the half shell; seafood houses sell fresh crabs (soft shells in the early summer season) and whatever local catch—tuna, wahoo, mahimahi, mackerel, shrimp—has been hauled in that day. This is, after all, the coast. Increasingly, though, highly trained chefs are settling in the region and diversifying menus. Fish dishes—broiled, fried, grilled, or steamed—are listed alongside entrées fusing Asian flavors and traditional Southern ingredients such as black-eyed peas.

As the region's tourist season has grown so have the waiting times at many restaurants, especially during the summer months and festival periods. Many places on the coast don't accept reservations. Restaurant hours are frequently reduced or curtailed in winter, and some restaurants in the remote beach communities close entirely for a month or more. Although some of the more upscale, pricey restaurants may require a tie or at least a collared shirt, casual dress (shorts and polo shirts) is acceptable in the majority of area restaurants.

About the Hotels

Hundreds upon hundreds of rental properties are scattered among the towns on the seashore. There are still some small beach cottages to be had. Increasingly, however, it's the so-called McMansions—built by out-of-towners in search of a vacation home and a hefty rental income—that are available. For many people, the motels and hotels clustered up and down the Outer Banks are still the way to go.

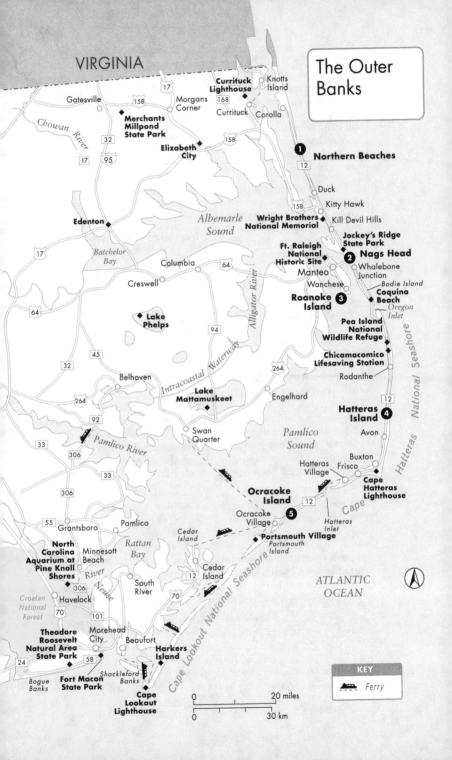

If you're visiting Wilmington and the Cape Fear Coast, or New Bern, Morehead City, and the Central ("Crystal") Coast, the choices are condos, resorts overlooking water—whether it be rivers, sounds, or the ocean—and hotels and motels. Chains hotels have outlets here, but there are a surprising number of small, older, family-run lodgings as well. You might also consider one of the many in-town B&Bs. Most are filled with antiques; many have hosts glad to offer concierge-type services. When planning your trip, always ask about special packages (price breaks on multiple night stays) and off-season rates.

WHAT IT COSTS					
	$$$$	$$$	$$	$	¢
RESTAURANTS	over $22	$17–$22	$12–$16	$7–$11	under $7
HOTELS	over $220	$161–$220	$111–$160	$70–$110	under $70

Restaurant prices are for a main course at dinner. Hotel prices are for two people in a standard double room in high season.

Timing

North Carolina's coast shines in spring (April and May) and fall (September and October), when the weather is most temperate and the water reasonably warm. Traveling during these times means you can avoid the long lines and higher prices associated with peak tourist season.

THE OUTER BANKS

North Carolina's Outer Banks stretch from the Virginia state line south to Cape Lookout. Think of the OBX (a shorthand used on popular bumper stickers) as a series of stepping stones in the Atlantic Ocean. Throughout history the treacherous waters surrounding these islands have been the nemesis of shipping, gaining them the nickname "the Graveyard of the Atlantic." A network of lighthouses and lifesaving stations, which grew around the need to protect seagoing craft, attracts curious travelers, just as the many submerged wrecks attract scuba divers. The islands' coves and inlets, which provided privacy to pirates—the notorious Blackbeard lived and died here—now give refuge to anglers, bird-watchers, and sunbathers.

The region is divided into four coastal sections: the Northern Beaches, beginning with Corolla, followed by Roanoke Island, Hatteras Island, and then Ocracoke Island. For many years the Outer Banks remained isolated, with only a few hardy families making their livings by fishing. Today the islands are linked by bridges and ferries, and much of the area is included in the Cape Hatteras and Cape Lookout national seashores. The largest towns are also the most colorfully named: Kitty Hawk, Kill Devil Hills, Nags Head, and Manteo. Vacation rentals here are omnipresent—there are about 12,000 weekly rental cottages available on the Outer Banks.

You can travel the region from the south end by taking a car ferry to Ocracoke Island or, as in the following route, from the north end. Dri-

First in Flight

DECEMBER 17, 1903, was a cold and windy day on the Outer Banks, but Wilbur and Orville Wright took little notice. The slightly built brothers from Ohio were undertaking an excellent adventure. With Orville at the controls, Wilbur running alongside, and the men of the nearby Lifesaving Service stations acting as ground crew, the fragile *Wright Flyer* lifted off from the Kill Devil Hills dune near Kitty Hawk and flew 120 feet in 12 seconds.

John Daniels, an Outer Banker, photographed the instant the world forever changed: a heavier-than-air machine was used to achieve controlled, sustained flight with a pilot aboard. To prove they were not accidental aviators, the Wrights took two flights each that day, and in Wilber's second attempt, he flew 852 feet in 59 seconds.

Others were attempting—and dying in the attempt of—powered flight as the

Wright brothers opened their Dayton bicycle-repair shop in 1892. Using information on aerodynamics from the Smithsonian Institution and observation of birds in flight, they began experimenting using a box kite roughly shaped like a biplane and a makeshift wind tunnel. The strong, steady winds drew them to the then-remote Outer Banks, where they could test their next phase, manned glider flights, in privacy. In time, they added power to the three-axis control they developed and eventually solved the problems of mechanical flight, lift, and propulsion that had vexed scientists for hundreds of years.

Their success is honored at the Wright Brothers National Memorial in Kill Devil Hills and by the North Carolina boast emblazoned on millions of license plates: FIRST IN FLIGHT.

---

borough Faire Shopping Village, 1177 Duck Rd. #11, Duck ☎ *252/261–6145* ⌕ *Reservations essential* ▭ *AE, D, MC, V* ☉ *No lunch.*

$$$$ ✕ **Nicoletta's Italian Café.** White linen tablecloths, flowers, and a view of the Currituck Beach Lighthouse mean atmosphere with a capital A. There's open-air dining on the porch. For more than a decade, Nicoletta's has been known for fresh seafood and southern Italian pasta dishes. Off-season hours may vary. ⌖ *Corolla Light Village Shops, Rte. 12, Corolla* ☎ *252/453–4004* ▭ *MC, V* ☉ *No lunch.*

★ **$$$–$$$$** ✕ **Blue Point Bar & Grill.** This upscale spot with an enclosed porch overlooking Currituck Sound is as busy as a diner and as boldly colorful—with a red, black, and chrome interior. The menu mixes Southern style with local seafood, including the ever-popular she-crab soup, a thick and rich concoction made with cream, sherry, herbs, Old Bay seasoning, and, of course, female crab. Brunch is served Sunday. ⌖ *1240 Duck Rd., Duck* ☎ *252/261–8090* ⌕ *Reservations essential* ▭ *AE, D, MC, V.*

★ **$$$$** ✕▦ **The Sanderling Resort & Spa.** A remote beach, 5 mi north of Duck, is a fine place to be pampered, go swimming, play tennis, or enjoy a round of golf. A 3-mi nature trail winds through the adjacent Pine Island Bird Sanctuary; the concierge can help arrange kayak tours and other activities. Sanderling has three inn buildings plus villas, all with the mellow look of old Nags Head. Whirling ceiling fans, wicker furniture, and bright tones make the rooms casual and summery. The formal, dinner-only Left Bank restaurant ($$$$) has a wall of windows overlooking Currituck Sound. Crab cakes, roast duckling, or fricassee of shrimp may be on the seasonal menu. The resort-casual Lifesaving Station ($–$$$$), in a restored 1899 lifesaving station, serves breakfast, lunch, and dinner and includes a second-floor lounge. ⊠ *1461 Duck Rd., Duck 27949* ☎ *252/261–4111 or 800/701–4111* 🖷 *252/261–1638* ⊕ *www.sanderlinginn. com* ⇨ *88 rooms, 29 studios, 4 villas* ⚙ *2 restaurants, room service, some in-room hot tubs, some kitchenettes, minibars, microwaves, some refrigerators, in-room VCRs, Wi-Fi, golf privileges, 2 tennis courts, pool, fitness center, hot tub, spa, fishing, bicycles, hiking, racquetball, squash, bar, library, shop, laundry service, meeting room* ▭ *AE, D, MC, V* ⦿I *BP.*

★ **$$–$$$$**   🖾 **Advice 5¢.** A roof with varied pitches and eaves tops this contemporary steely blue-gray beach house with white trim and multipane windows rising from the sandy dunes. Although the name is lighthearted, Advice 5¢ is very serious about guest care. Beds in each room are dressed with crisp, colorful linens. All rooms have private decks, ceiling fans, and baths stocked with thick cotton towels. The suite has a whirlpool bath, sitting area, and cable TV. You have use of the tennis courts, swimming pool, and the beach access at Sea Pines, a nearby resort. From the North Beach area you can easily walk to downtown shops and restaurants. ⊠ *111 Scarborough La., Duck 27949* ☎ *252/255–1050 or 800/238–4235* ⊕ *www.advice5.com* ⇨ *4 rooms, 1 suite* ⚙ *Dining room, fans; no room phones, no TV in some rooms, no smoking* ▭ *MC, V* ⊘ *Closed Dec. and Jan.* ⦿I *BP.*

$$–$$$$ 🖾 **The Inn at Corolla Light.** The inn is a part of the Corolla Light Resort and sits along Currituck Sound, about 10 mi from Duck. The ocean, ¼ mi away, is easily accessed via bikes or open-air trolley service. Even the smaller rooms feel big thanks to the generous use of richly toned fabrics, large beds, and windows with views of the garden, pool, or sound. A special treat are the off-road tours for the inn's guests to the secluded spot where the area's wild horses are now confined. ⊠ *1066 Ocean Trail, Corolla 27927* ☎ *252/453–3340 or 800/215–0772* 🖷 *252/453–6947* ⊕ *www.corolla-inn.com* ⇨ *30 rooms, 13 suites* ⚙ *Restaurant, some kitchenettes, refrigerators, in-room VCRs, golf privileges, 9 tennis courts, 3 pools (1 indoor), wading pool, fitness center, hot tub, boating, jet skiing, fishing, bicycles, hiking, racquetball, volleyball, video game room, shops; no smoking* ▭ *D, MC, V* ⦿I *BP.*

Nags Head

❷ *9 mi south of Kitty Hawk.*

It's widely accepted that Nags Head got its name because pirates would tie lanterns around the necks of their horses to lure merchant ships onto the shoals hoping to wreck them and profit from the cargo. Dubious citizenry aside, Nags Head was established in the 1830s as North Carolina's first tourist haven.

The town—one of the largest on the Outer Banks, yet still with a population of only about 2,800 people—lies between the Atlantic Ocean and Pamlico Sound, along and between U.S. 158 ("the bypass") and Route 12 ("the beach road" or Virginia Dare Trail). Both roads are heavily trafficked in the high season, and the entire area is commercialized. Many lodgings, whether they're dated cottages, shingled older houses, or sprawling new homes with plenty of bells and whistles, are available through the area's plentiful vacation rentals. Numerous restaurants, motels, hotels, shops, and entertainment opportunities keep the town hopping day and night.

> **SIFTING ECOLOGY**
>
> The vegetation on the sand dunes is practically all that's keeping them from blowing away in the wind. Dune conservation is very serious for the survival of the beaches, and the vegetation also provides shelter to turtles, rabbits, snakes, and other wildlife. Please don't disturb it!

Nags Head has 11 mi of beach with 33 public access points from Route 12, all with parking and some with restrooms and showers. ■ TIP→ It's easy to overlook the flagpoles stationed along many area beaches; but if there's a red flag flying from one of them, it means the water is too rough even for wading. These are not a suggestion—ignoring them can mean hefty fines. The first North Carolina Historic Shipwreck Site, the 175-foot **USS *Huron,*** lies in 20 feet of water off the Nags Head Pier and is a favorite with scuba divers. The iron-hulled ship sank in a November storm in 1877, taking all but a handful of her 124-man crew with her. ⊠ *Offshore between MM 11 and MM 12.*

☾ **Jockey's Ridge State Park** has 420 acres that encompass the tallest sand dune on the East Coast (about 90 to 110 feet), although it has lost some 22 feet since the 1930s thanks to the million visitors a year who carry sand away on their shoes and clothes. Walk along the 384-foot boardwalk from the visitor center to the edge of the dune. The climb to the top is a challenge; nevertheless, it's a popular spot for hang gliding, kite flying, and sand boarding. You can also explore an estuary and several trails through the park. In summer join the free Sunset on the Ridge program: watch the sun disappear while you sit on the dunes and learn about their local legends and history. Covered footwear is a wise choice here, as the loose sand gets quite hot in the summer months. ⊠ *U.S. 158, MM 12* ☎ *252/441–7132* ⊕ *www.ils.unc.edu/parkproject* ⊠ *Free* ☾ *Daily 8–sunset.*

Coquina Beach, in the Cape Hatteras National Seashore, is considered by locals to be the loveliest beach in the Outer Banks. The wide-beam ribs of the shipwreck *Laura Barnes* rest in the dunes here. Driven onto the Outer Banks by a nor'easter in 1921, she ran aground north of this location; the entire crew survived. The wreck was moved to Coquina Beach in 1973 and displayed behind ropes, but subsequent hurricanes have scattered the remains, making it difficult to discern. Free parking, public changing rooms, showers, and picnic shelters are available. ⊠ *Off Rte. 12, MM 26, 8 mi south of U.S. 158.*

OFF THE BEATEN PATH

LAKE PHELPS – At 16,600 acres, Lake Phelps, a part of Pettigrew State Park, is a Carolina Bay 5 mi across and about 4 feet deep that has long been considered a treasure by boaters and anglers. In 1985, researchers began to prize it for other reasons. Discovered underneath the sand in the beautifully clear water were ancient American Indian artifacts, including 30 dugout canoes, one of which dates back some 4,400 years. Two are displayed in Pettigrew Park. The park also includes a boat ramp, canoe launch, fishing pier, camping sites, and RV hookups. ⊠ *2252 Lake Shore Rd., 56 mi east of Nags Head via I–64, Creswell* ☎ *252/797–4475.*

Sports & the Outdoors

Bert's Surf Shop (⊠ 103 E. Morning View Pl., U.S. 158, MM 11 ☎ 252/441–1939) rents surfboards, gives private lessons, and runs three- and five-day surf-school programs; it also has a retail shop. There are locations in Atlantic Beach, Emerald Isle, Kitty Hawk, Kill Devil Hills, Surf City, and Wilmington as well.

Nags Head Golf Links (⊠ 5615 S. Seachase Dr., off Rte. 12, MM 15 ☎ 252/441–8073 or 800/851–9404) has a par-71, 18-hole course with ocean views and challenging coastal winds.

Outer Banks Dive Center (⊠ 3917 S. Croatan Hwy. ☎ 252/449–8349) has equipment rental, diving instruction, guided offshore charters, and leads off-the-beach dives to shipwrecks.

Where to Stay & Eat

$$$$
FodorśChoice
★

✕ **Windmill Point.** The menu changes here, but you can always count on the signature seafood trio: a choice of any combination of three fish. You can have it lightly poached or grilled, and topped with roasted red pepper and capers, or shredded cucumber and dill, or a pineapple salsa. Beef, poultry, pasta, and vegetarian selections are always available, and there's a kids' menu as well. Brunch is served weekends from 10 to 4. The restaurant has stunning views of the sound at sunset, eye-catching memorabilia from the luxury liner SS *United States,* and, yes, a real windmill. It's a reproduction of the German-style windmills used in the area a century ago. ⊠ *U.S. 158, MM 16.5* ☎ *252/441–1535* ⊟ *AE, D, MC, V.*

$$–$$$$

✕ **Basnight's Lone Cedar Café.** This is the stomping ground for Marc Basnight, for years North Carolina's most powerful state senator, and his family. Every one of Lone Cedar's long wooden tables has a view of the water. The restaurant is proud to have its own fish-cleaning facility so they can serve the freshest seafood possible. Beef, chicken, pork, pastas, and plenty of locally grown produce are also on the menu. The dining room is relaxed and casual. ⊠ *Nags Head–Manteo Causeway, 7623 S. Virginia Dare Trail* ☎ *252/441–5405* ⌫ *Reservations not accepted* ⊟ *D, MC, V* ⊗ *Closed Jan.*

$$–$$$$
FodorśChoice
★

✕ **Owens' Restaurant.** Inside an old Nags Head–style clapboard cottage, this old-fashioned coastal restaurant has been in the same family and location since 1946. Stick with the seafood or chops, at which they excel. Miss O's crab cakes are ever-popular, as is the filet mignon topped with lump crabmeat and asparagus béarnaise sauce. Pecan-encrusted sea scallops are plump and tender. The 16-layer lemon and chocolate cakes are delicious. In summer arrive early and expect to wait. The brass-and-glass Station Keeper's Lounge has entertainment. ⊠ *U.S. 158, MM 16.5* ☎ *252/441–7309* ⌕ *Reservations not accepted* ▭ *AE, D, MC, V* ⊗ *Closed Jan. and Feb. No lunch.*

$$–$$$$ ✕ **Penguin Isle Soundside Bar & Grille.** The views from Penguin Isle's main dining room and gazebo dining room on Roanoke Sound are panoramic and seductive. The decor is muted as if not to detract from what you're seeing or tasting. Though especially busy in summer, the dining experience here is never uncomfortable, as tables are well spaced. On the dinner menu there's a little of everything: beef tenderloin, yellowfin tuna, pork tenderloin with a pan-fried crab cake, as well as options for the kids. ⊠ *U.S. 158, MM 16* ☎ *252/441–2637* ▭ *AE, D, MC, V* ⊗ *Closed Jan. and Feb.*

$–$$$ ✕ **RV's.** If fiery red sunsets and spicy marinated tuna entice you, head to RV's. It's where locals come to eat, drink, and take in serene views of Roanoke Sound. Portions of everything—from clam chowder to barbecued shrimp to piquant crab cakes and tuna—are huge. You can also get steak, ribs, and chicken. The marvelous turtle cake, with chocolate, pecans, and caramel, is a dieter's nightmare. There's a little pier outside and an attached indoor–outdoor gazebo where you can get a drink. The causeway is between Nags Head and Roanoke Island. ⊠ *Nags Head–Manteo Causeway, MM 16.5* ☎ *252/441–4963* ⌕ *Reservations not accepted* ▭ *MC, V* ⊗ *Closed Dec. and Jan.*

$–$$ ✕ **Don Gato's.** You can't miss the bright-orange building with a surfer on the roof. The interior's bright yellows, reds, and blues are equally intense, but it's the food that holds your attention. The chef draws inspiration from Mexico's Oaxaca region. There's lots of seafood; grilled tuna burritos and shrimp sautéed with onion and cilantro in a garlic sauce are favorites. Mexican beers and made-to-order margaritas get the evening flowing. ⊠ *Rte. 12, MM 11, 3308 Virginia Dare Trail* ☎ *252/441–9330* ▭ *MC, V.*

¢–$ ✕ **Sam & Omie's.** This no-nonsense niche is named after two fishermen who were father and son, and it's the oldest restaurant in the Outer Banks. Fishing illustrations hang on the walls, and Merle Haggard plays in the background. It's open daily 7 to 7, serving every imaginable kind of seafood, and then some. Try the fine marinated tuna steak, Cajun tuna bites, or frothy crab-and-asparagus soup. The chef has been using the same recipe for the she-crab soup for 22 years; locals love it. ■ TIP→ **Diehard fans claim that Sam & Omie's serves the best oysters on the beach.** Dress is beach-casual. ⊠ *U.S. 158, MM 16.5* ☎ *252/441–7366* ⌕ *Reservations not accepted* ▭ *D, MC, V* ⊗ *Closed Dec.–Feb.*

$–$$$　　▦ **First Colony Inn.** Stand on the verandas that encircle this old, three-story,
FodorsChoice　cedar-shingle inn and admire the ocean views. Two rooms have wet
　　★　　bars, kitchenettes, and whirlpool baths; others have four-poster or canopy beds, handcrafted armoires, and English antiques. All rooms contain extras, such as heated towel bars. The story of this landmark's near demolition, its rescue, and the move to the present site is told in framed photographs, letters, and news accounts lining the sunny dining room. In fall and winter Nature Conservancy birding weekends include excursions to the Pea Island Wildlife Refuge. ⊠ *6720 S. Virginia Dare Trail, 27959* ☎ *252/441–2343 or 800/368–9390* ⎙ *252/441–9234* ⊕ *www.*

firstcolonyinn.com ⤷ *26 rooms* ⌂ *Dining room, picnic area, some in-room hot tubs, some kitchenettes, microwaves, some in-room VCRs, pool, croquet, library, business services; no smoking* ⊟ *AE, D, MC, V* ¶⊙¶ *BP.*

$–$$$ 🏨 **The Nags Head Inn.** Being an independent property, not a chain, is not the only thing that makes this motel stand out—the blocky, white stucco exterior with blue accents is in sharp contrast with the cottages that surround it. The five-story hotel has basic, tidy rooms right on the beach. Ask for an oceanside room to get a balcony. Nags Head Inn is especially family-friendly: kids under 12 stay free and cribs and cots are available for $10 extra. ⊠ *Rte. 12, MM 14, 27959* ☎ *252/441–0454 or 800/327–8881* ⊕ *www.nagsheadinn.com* ⤷ *100 rooms* ⌂ *Refrigerators, cable TV, indoor-outdoor pool, hot tub, spa, no-smoking rooms* ⊟ *AE, D, MC, V* ⊙ *Closed late Nov.–Dec.* ¶⊙¶ *EP.*

Shopping

For 35 years, Gallery Row has been a small cluster of art-related businesses that sell everything from beach crafts to oil paintings and from piggy banks to diamond earrings. **Morales Art Gallery** (⊠ 107 E. Gallery Row ☎ 252/441–6484 or 800/635–6035) is the fine-arts store that started it all. Most of the gallery owners live on-site.

The **Tanger Outlet Center** (⊠ U.S. 158 bypass, MM 16 ☎ 252/441–5634 or 800/720–6747) has two dozen stores—including Bass, Coach, Gap Outlet, and Polo Ralph Lauren—selling designer clothes, shoes, casual attire, books, sunglasses, and more.

Roanoke Island

❸ *10 mi southwest of Nags Head.*

On a hot July day in 1587, 117 men, women, and children left their boat and set foot on Roanoke Island to form the first permanent English settlement in the New World. Three years later, when a fleet with supplies from England landed, the settlers had disappeared without a trace, leaving a mystery that continues to baffle historians. Much of the 12-mi-long island, which lies between the Outer Banks and the mainland, remains wild. Of the island's two towns, Wanchese is the fishing village, and Manteo is more tourist-oriented, with sights related to the island's history, as well as an aquarium. You get to the island by taking U.S. 64/264 from U.S. 158.

☾ A history, educational, and cultural-arts complex, **Roanoke Island Festival Park** sits on the waterfront in Manteo. Costumed interpreters conduct tours of the 69-foot ship, *Elizabeth II*, a re-creation of a 16th-century vessel—except when it's on educational voyages. The complex also has an interactive museum and shop, a fossil pit, plays, concerts, arts-and-crafts exhibitions, and special programs. ⊠ *Waterfront, off Budleigh St., Manteo* ☎ *252/475–1500, 252/475–1506 for event hotline* ⊕ *www.roanokeisland.com* ⊡ *$8* ⊙ *Oct.–Dec. and mid-Feb.–Mar., daily 9–5; Apr.–Sept., daily 9–6.*

★ The lush **Elizabethan Gardens** are a 10-acre re-creation of 16th-century English gardens, established as an elaborate memorial to the first Eng-

grilled porkloin on kahlua mashed sweet potatoes. ⊠ *405 Queen Elizabeth Ave., Box 2045, Manteo 27954* 🕾 *252/473–1404 or 800/458–7069* 🖷 *252/473–1526* ⊕ *www.1587.com* ➩ *8 rooms* ⚖ *Restaurant, bicycles, business services, meeting room; no-smoking rooms* ▭ *AE, D, MC, V* ⦿ *BP.*

$–$$$ ⊞ **Island House of Wanchese.** Roy and Jeanne Green purchased the circa-1900 house in 1991 and updated it, turning it into a B&B, but they retained the original wood flooring and wavy glass windows. The wraparound porch is screened in so you can sit and catch the breeze without interference from bugs. Rooms are decorated with antiques, hope chests, and handmade quilts. The resident innkeepers provide evening turn-down service; complimentary beach chairs, towels, and umbrellas; a freezer for your catch; and a full breakfast. ⊠ *104 Old Wharf Rd., Wanchese 27981* 🕾 *252/473–5619* 🖷 *252/473–6163* ⊕ *www.islandhouse-bb.com* ➩ *3 rooms, 1 suite* ⚖ *Cable TV, library; no kids, no smoking* ▭ *AE, D, MC, V* ⦿ *BP.*

¢–$ ⊞ **Scarborough Inn.** Two stories of wraparound porches surround the Scarborough, which is modeled after a turn-of-the-20th-century inn. Outside each room are benches and rocking chairs; inside, each is decorated differently, with family heirlooms as well as modern conveniences, like coffeemakers. Room refrigerators come stocked with ready-made, packaged breakfast items. The property is within walking distance of popular shops and restaurants and about 3 mi from the beach. ⊠ *524 U.S. 64/264, Manteo 27954* 🕾 *252/473–3979* ⊕ *www.scarborough-inn.com* ➩ *12 rooms* ⚖ *Microwaves, refrigerators, cable TV, bicycles, no-smoking rooms* ▭ *AE, D, MC, V* ⦿ *EP.*

Shopping

Manteo Booksellers (⊠ 105 Sir Walter Raleigh St., Manteo 🕾 252/473–1221 or 866/473–1222) stocks an admirable collection of books on the Outer Banks, cuisine, history, nature, lighthouses, shipwrecks, folklore, and related fiction. Local author readings are frequent. The children's section is quite large, too.

CAPE HATTERAS NATIONAL SEASHORE

Longtime visitors to the Outer Banks have seen how development changes these once unspoiled barrier islands, so it's nice to know that the 70-mi stretch of the Cape Hatteras National Seashore will remain protected. Its pristine beaches, set aside as the first national seashore in 1953, stretch from the southern outskirts of Nags Head to Ocracoke Inlet, encompassing three narrow islands: Bodie, Hatteras, and Ocracoke.

Some of the best fishing and surfing on the East Coast are in these waters, which also are ideal for other sports such as windsurfing, diving, and boating. Parking is allowed only in designated areas. Fishing piers are in Rodanthe, Avon, and Frisco.

With 300 mi of coastline, there are plenty of beaches that don't have lifeguards on duty. ▮ TIP➔ **To identify beaches with trained staff, contact the Ocean Rescue in the town, or if you're in a National Park, the Park Service.**

Bodie Island

7 mi south of Nags Head.

Natives pronounce it "Bah-dy" not "Bow-dy," which harkens back to the days when this corner of the Graveyard of the Atlantic was known as "Bodies Island" because of all the dead seafarers who washed onto the shores. The island remains mostly barren, but the boardwalks and observation decks on its marshes offer excellent opportunities to watch wading birds and to kayak or canoe through the inlets.

Bodie Island Lighthouse designer Dexter Stetson is also the brains behind the Cape Hatteras lighthouse, which explains why the two look so much alike. Bodie, with its fat (22-feet tall) black-and-white horizontal stripes, stands 156 feet tall and is capped by a black cast-iron lantern. It's actually the third lighthouse to guard this area of the coast. The first, built in 1847, was simply abandoned because of its shoddy construction. A second, build in 1859, was blown up in 1861 by retreating Confederate soldiers because they feared it would be used as a Yankee observatory tower. The current lighthouse was completed in 1872 and is in the midst of a two-part renovation that won't be complete until 2009. ■ TIP→ Only the lower level, keeper's house, and museum can be toured; visitors will have to make a return trip to climb the 214 steps to the top. ⊠ *1401 National Park Dr.* ☎ *252/473–2111 or 252/441–5711* ⊕ *www.nps.gov/ caha/bdlh.htm* ⊠ *Free* ☉ *Memorial Day–Labor Day, daily 9–6; Labor Day–Thanksgiving, daily 9–5.*

Hatteras Island

❹ *15 mi south of Nags Head*

The Herbert C. Bonner Bridge arches for 3 mi over Oregon Inlet and carries traffic to Hatteras Island, a 42-mi-long curved ribbon of sand jutting out into the Atlantic Ocean. At its most distant point (Cape Hatteras), Hatteras is 25 mi from the mainland. About 85% of the island belongs to Cape Hatteras National Seashore, and the remainder is privately owned in seven small, quaint villages strung along Route 12, the island's fragile lifeline to points north. Among its nicknames, Hatteras is known as the blue marlin (or billfish) capital of the world. The fishing's so great here because the Continental Shelf is 40 mi offshore, and its current, combined with the nearby Gulf Stream and Deep West Boundary Current, create an unparalleled fish habitat. The total population of the towns—Rodanthe, Waves, Salvo, Avon, Buxton, Frisco, and Hatteras Village—doesn't top 3,000.

Pea Island National Wildlife Refuge is made up of more than 5,800 acres of marsh on the Atlantic flyway. To bird-watchers' delight more than 365 species have been sighted from its observation platforms and spotting scopes, including threatened peregrine falcons and piping plovers. Black-billed tundra swans sometimes winter here. A visitor center on Route 12 has an information display and maps of the two trails. ■ TIP→ Remember to douse yourself in bug spray, especially in spring. Guided canoe tours are available for a fee. ⊠ *Pea Island Refuge Headquarters,*

To the Lighthouse

SOONER OR LATER while visiting the coast, you come within sight of one of the "mighty seven": a North Carolina lighthouse. These beacons were once tended by service keepers. But one by one, they've been automated and transferred to the Coast Guard, the National Park Service, or a nonprofit organization.

The last major lighthouse constructed is the first you reach traveling from north to south: Currituck Beach Lighthouse (162 feet, 1875) is an unpainted redbrick tower. Bodie Island Lighthouse (165 feet, 1872) is covered in broad horizontal black and white stripes.

Cape Hatteras Lighthouse is famous as America's tallest lighthouse (198 feet, 1868) and for having been relocated 2,900 feet inland in 1999. Ocracoke Lighthouse (76 feet, 1817), rebuilt after a fire in 1823, is the second oldest lighthouse in the United States still in

continuous service. The bright white exterior was once achieved with a whitewash blend of unslaked lime, glue, rice, salt, and powdered fish.

Cape Lookout Lighthouse (150 feet, 1859) is painted with distinctive black-and-white diamonds—black facing north and south, white facing east and west. Bald Head Island Lighthouse (90 feet, 1817), nicknamed "Old Baldy," is south of Southport; visitors can climb 112 steps to the top of its octagonal weathered gray tower. Far to the south, Oak Island Lighthouse (169 feet, 1958) is the U.S.'s youngest lighthouse and has the last manually operated light in the world. But it lacks the elegance of its older siblings: the completely cylindrical tower has three broad horizontal stripes—black, white, and gray, and its beacon is so bright and hot that workman have to wear protective clothing when working on it.

Rte. 12, 5 mi south of Oregon Inlet ☎ *252/987–2394* ⊕ *http://peaisland.fws.gov* ⛅ *Free* ☉ *June–Aug., daily 9–5; Mar.–May and Sept.–Nov., daily 9–4; Dec.–Feb., hrs vary, call ahead.*

The restored 1911 **Chicamacomico Lifesaving Station** (pronounced "chik-a-ma-*com*-i-co") is now a museum that tells the story of the brave people who manned 24 stations that once lined the Outer Banks. These were the precursors to today's Coast Guard, with staff who rescued people and animals from seacraft in distress. Living-history reenactments are performed June through August. ⊠ *Off Rte. 12 at MM 39.5, Rodanthe* ☎ *252/987–1552* ⊕ *www.chicamacomico.net* ⛅ *$5* ☉ *Mid-Apr.–Nov., weekdays noon–5.*

★ ☉ **Cape Hatteras Lighthouse** was the first lighthouse built in the region, authorized by Congress in 1794 to help prevent shipwrecks. The original structure was lost to erosion and Civil War damage; this 1870 replacement is, at 208 feet, the tallest brick lighthouse in the world. Endangered by the sea, in 1999 the lighthouse was actually raised and rolled some 2,900 feet inland to its present location. It's now the Hatteras Island Visitor Center. In summer the principal keeper's quarters are open for viewing, and you can climb the 257 steps (12 stories) to the viewing balcony. ■ TIP→ **Children under 42 inches in height aren't allowed in the lighthouse.** Offshore lie the remains of the USS *Monitor,* a Confederate ironclad ship that sank in 1862. ⊠ *Off Rte. 12, 30 mi south of Rodanthe, Buxton* ☎ *252/995–4474* ⊕ *www.nps.gov/caha* ⊠ *Visitor center and keeper's quarters free, lighthouse tower $6* ⊘ *Visitor center and keeper's quarters: daily 9–5. Lighthouse tower: Apr.–mid-Oct., daily 10–5.*

A nationally recognized collection of Native American artifacts fills the **Frisco Native American Museum & Natural History Center.** Galleries display native art from across the United States as well as relics from the first inhabitants of Hatteras Island. The museum has been designated as a North Carolina Environmental Education Center. Several acres of nature trails wind through a maritime forest, and a pavilion overlooks a salt marsh. ⊠ *Rte. 12, Frisco* ☎ *252/995–4440* ⊕ *www.nativeamericanmuseum. org* ⊠ *$5* ⊘ *Tues.–Sun. 11–5, Mon. by appointment.*

Where to Stay & Eat

$$$–$$$$ ✕ **Breakwater.** Fat Daddy crab cakes, rolled in potato chips then fried and served with pineapple jalapeño salsa, and oyster stew with grits are two of the more creative signature dishes. You also get more standard seafood options, such as shrimp fried or broiled with white wine and butter. The restaurant sits atop Oden's Dock. Given the casual nature of life here, Breakwater stands out with tables dressed in white linen. The dining room is a bit small, but waiting for a table in comfortable chairs on the deck overlooking Pamlico Sound is not a chore. ⊠ *Waterfront, Rte. 12, Hatteras Village* ☎ *252/986–2733* ▤ *AE, D, MC, V* ⊘ *Closed Sun.–Wed. Labor Day–Memorial Day. No lunch.*

$–$$$ ✕ **Tides.** South of the entrance for the Cape Hatteras Lighthouse, this place is popular for its well-prepared food and homey manner. In addition to offering the usual seafood—try the shrimp gumbo—the menu has chicken and ham. It's also a popular breakfast spot. ⊠ *Rte. 12, Buxton* ☎ *252/995–5988* ▤ *MC, V* ⊘ *Closed Dec.–early Apr. No lunch.*

$–$$$ ▥ **Sea Gull Motel.** When Hurricane Isabel hit Hatteras Island in September 2003, the 1950s-era Sea Gull was leveled. One of the motel's three buildings has been rebuilt with comfort in mind, and the adjacent cottage properties, each of which sleeps up to six and rents by the week during high season, also remain. The 15 rooms, yards from the beach, all have at least a mini-refrigerator and microwave; a two-bedroom suite with a full kitchen is also available. Ask about the corner room with ocean views on two sides. ⊠ *Rte. 12, between MM 70 and 71, Hatteras Village 27943* ☎ *252/986–2550* ⊕ *www.seagullhatteras.com* ⊅ *15 rooms, 1 suite, 2 cottages* ⚠ *Picnic area, some kitchens, refrigerators, microwaves, cable TV, in-room broadband, pool, beach, fishing, no-smoking rooms* ▤ *D, MC, V* ⊙❘ *EP.*

Ocracoke Island

⑤ *Ocracoke Village: 15 mi southwest of Hatteras Village.*

Fewer than 1,000 people live on this, the last inhabited island in the Outer Banks, which can be reached only by water or air. The village itself is in the widest part of the island, around a harbor called Silver Lake. Mandredged canals form the landscape of a smaller residential area called Oyster Creek.

Centuries ago, however, Ocracoke was the stomping ground of Edward Teach, the pirate known as Blackbeard. A major treasure cache from 1718 is still rumored to be hidden somewhere on the island. Fort Ocracoke was a short-lived Confederate stronghold that was abandoned in August 1861 and blown up by Union forces a month later.

Although the island remains a destination for people seeking peace and quiet, they can be hard to find during the summer season, when tourists and boaters swamp the place. About 90% of Ocracoke is part of Cape Hatteras National Seashore; the island is on the eastern flyway for many migrating land and water birds. A free ferry leaves hourly from Hatteras Island and arrives 40 minutes later; toll ferries connect with the mainland at Swan Quarter (2½ hours) and at Cedar Island (15 minutes). Reserve well in advance.

Ocracoke Island **beaches** are among the least populated and most beautiful on the Cape Hatteras National Seashore. Four public access areas have parking as well as off-road vehicle access. ⊠ *Off Rte. 12.*

Look out from the **Ocracoke Pony Pen** observation platform at the descendants of the Banker Ponies that roamed wild before the island came under the jurisdiction of Cape Hatteras National Seashore. The park service took over management of the ponies in 1960 and has helped maintain the population of about 30 animals; the wild herd once numbered nearly 500. All the animals you see today were born in captivity and are fed and kept on a 180-acre range. Legends abound about the arrival of the island's Banker Ponies. Some believe they made their way to the island after the abandonment of Roanoke's Lost Colony. Others believe they were left by early Spanish explorers or swam to shore following the sinking of the *Black Squall,* a ship carrying circus performers. ⊠ *Rte. 12, 6 mi southwest of Hatteras-Ocracoke ferry landing.*

Ocracoke Village Visitor Center and Museum, run by the local preservation society, contains photographs and artifacts illustrating the island's lifestyle and history. "Porch talk" lectures, presentations, and folk stories are regular summer events. The National Park Service office is nearby. ⊠ *Silver Lake Rd., off Rte. 12 and beside Cedar Island ferry dock, Ocracoke Village* ☎ *252/928–7375* ⊕ *www.ocracokepreservation. org* ⊠ *Free* ☼ *June–Aug., weekdays 10–5, weekends 11–4; Easter–May and Sept.–Nov., Mon.–Sat. 11–4.*

Built in 1823, **Ocracoke Lighthouse** is the second oldest operating lighthouse in the U.S. (Sandy Hook, New Jersey, has the oldest). It was first fueled by whale oil, then kerosene, and finally electricity. ■ TIP→ **The squat whitewashed structure, 75 feet tall, is unfortunately not open to the public for climbing—although it's a photographer's dream.** ⊠ *Off Rte. 12, Live Oak Rd., Ocracoke Village* ⊕ *www.nps.gov/caha/ocracokelh.htm.*

On May 11, 1942, the HMS *Bedfordshire,* an armed British trawler on loan to the United States was torpedoed by a German U-boat and sank with all 37 hands lost off the coast of Ocracoke Island. The men were buried on Ocracoke in a corner of the community graveyard. Each year the Queen of England remembers this loss by sending a British flag, via a personal envoy, to the tiny, nicely landscaped **British Cemetery,** which is tended by Ocracoke Coast Guard Station personnel. The wreck was discovered in 1980 and some artifacts were recovered. It's still frequented by divers. ⊠ *Off Rte. 12, British Cemetery Rd., Ocracoke Village* ☎ *252/926–9171.*

**OFF THE
BEATEN
PATH**

MATTAMUSKEET NATIONAL WILDLIFE REFUGE – Hyde County's Lake Mattamuskeet is the largest natural lake in North Carolina. Fed only by rainwater and runoff, the lake is 3 feet below sea level. Although it's been drained for farmland and mined for peat, the reclaimed lake is the centerpiece of a 50,000-acre wildlife refuge that echoes with the calls of some 800 bird species. ⊠ *38 Mattamuskeet Rd., 2½-hr ferry ride and 15-min drive from Ocracoke Island, Swan Quarter* ☎ *252/926–4021, 800/345–1665 for ferry* ⊕ *www.mattamuskeet.org.*

Where to Stay & Eat

$$–$$$$ ✕ **The Pelican Restaurant and Patio Bar.** This 19th-century harborfront home in a grove of twisted oak trees has a patio next to an outdoor bar: many people take a seat here and don't leave for a long while. Jumbo shrimp stuffed with cream cheese and jalapeño peppers and lump crab cakes are two of the most requested food items. "Shrimp Hour," which is really two hours every day (3 to 5), draws crowds because large steamed shrimp sell for 15¢ each. The Pelican also serves breakfast— cereal, egg dishes, biscuits with homemade jelly, and corned beef hash— until 11 AM. Acoustic music plays weekends off season and five nights a week in summer. ⊠ *305 Irvin Garrish Hwy., Ocracoke* ☎ *252/928–7431* ▱ *AE, D, MC, V.*

$$–$$$ ✕ **Back Porch Restaurant.** Seafood is the star here, naturally, but there are some notable beef and chicken dishes, including a stir fry with seasonal vegetables. You have the choice of enjoying your meal indoors or on a screened porch. Enjoy the respectable wine list in the new wine bar. ⊠ *110 Back Rd., Ocracoke* ☎ *252/928–6401* ▱ *MC, V* ⊗ *No smoking* ⊗ *No lunch.*

¢–$$ ✕▣ **Island Inn and Dining Room.** This white clapboard inn on the National Register of Historic Places was built as a private lodge back in 1901. It's starting to show its age a bit, but is full of Outer Banks character. The rooms in the modern wing are good for families. The large rooms in the Crow's Nest, on the third floor, have cathedral ceilings and look out over the island. One- and two-bedroom villas with full kitchens, living rooms, and laundry facilities are also available. The restaurant ($–$$) is known for its oyster omelet, crab cakes, and hush puppies. ⊠ *Lighthouse Rd. and Rte. 12, Box 9, 27960* ☎ *252/928–4351, 877/456–3466 for inn, 252/928–7821 for dining room* 🖷 *252/928–4352* ⊕ *www.ocracokeislandinn.com* ⇱ *28 rooms, 4 villas* ⚐ *Restaurant, cable TV, pool, lobby lounge; no smoking* ▱ *AE, MC, V* ⏣ *EP.*

$ ▣ **Sand Dollar Motel.** The Sand Dollar is small and unassuming, but well-run. A garden and a walkway to a secluded swimming pool give this motel a sense of privacy. It's on a quiet residential street two blocks from Route 12 and the village center. Owner Roger Garrish, an Ocracoke na-

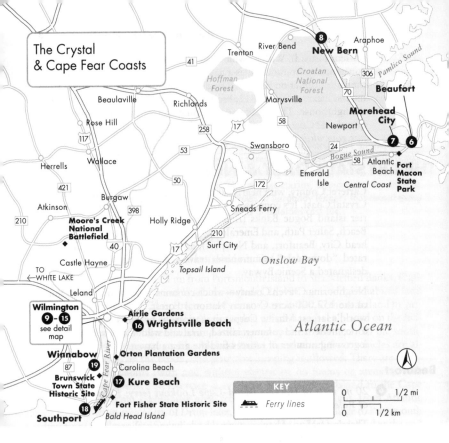

keg; and an English soldier saluting the king is buried upright in his grave. The required tours, either on an English-style double-decker bus or by guided walk, depart from the visitor center. ✉ *130 Turner St.* ☎ *252/728-5225 or 800/575-7483* ⊕ *www.beauforthistoricsite.org* ✆ *$8 tour* ☉ *Mon.–Sat., walking tours at 10, 11:30, 1, and 3:30. Bus tour: Apr.–Oct., Mon., Wed., and Fri. at 11 and 1:30, Sat. at 11. Burying Ground tour: June–Sept., Tues.–Thurs. at 2:30.*

★ **North Carolina Maritime Museum** documents the state's seafaring history. An exhibit about the infamous pirate Blackbeard includes artifacts recovered from the discovery of his flagship, *Queen Anne's Revenge,* near Beaufort Inlet. Other exhibits focus on local fossils and duck decoys. The associated **Watercrafts Center,** across the street, has lectures on boat-building and stargazing, bike tours, birding treks, and fossil hunting tours. ✉ *315 Front St.* ☎ *252/728-7317* ⊕ *www.ah.dcr.state.nc. us* ✆ *Free* ☉ *Weekdays 9–5, Sat. 10–5, Sun. 1–5.*

Where to Stay & Eat

$$$–$$$$ ✕ **Blue Moon Bistro.** Chef Kyle Swain, a Beaufort native, returned home to put into use the lessons he learned apprenticing at some of North Carolina's top caliber restaurants. He pairs classical French technique with creative presentation—shrimp and grits are seasoned with a touch of

North Carolina's Pirates

NORTH CAROLINA'S COAST was a magnet for marauding sea dogs during the Golden Age of Piracy, a period in the first quarter of the 18th century. Among those who visited was Stede Bonnet, the so-called "gentleman pirate." For this successful owner of a sugar plantation, piracy seemed the result of a midlife crisis. He should have stayed on the farm: He was cheated by Blackbeard, captured by authorities, and hanged in 1718.

Of course, the most notorious buccaneer of them all was Blackbeard, whose two-year reign of terror began in 1716. He cultivated fear by strapping on six pistols and six knives, tying his luxuriant beard into pigtails and, legend has it, tucking lighted matches into it during battle.

A polygamist with at least 12 wives, Blackbeard attacked ships in the Caribbean and settlements along the coasts of Virginia and the Carolinas. At least three of his ships sank in North Carolina's waters; archaeologists are studying artifacts from what is likely the flagship, *Queen Anne's Revenge*, which ran aground on a sandbar near Beaufort Inlet in May 1718.

The following November a seafaring posse caught Blackbeard in one his favorite playgrounds, Ocracoke Inlet. The pirate was decapitated and his head was hung from one of the conquering ships. Blackbeard's other lost ships and his reputedly fabulous treasure are still being sought today.

---

lemon and served in a martini glass. Though the emphasis is on local seafood, a meat, poultry, and vegetarian dish is usually among the entrées. The restaurant occupies the 175-year-old Dill House, which has been dressed up with oak woodwork, wainscoting, and suns and moons made of pressed tin. ⊠ *119 Queen St.* ☎ *252/728–5800* ⚑ *Reservations essential* ▭ *D, MC, V* ⊘ *Closed Sun. and Mon. No lunch.*

$$-$$$ ✕ **Clawson's 1905 Restaurant & Pub.** Housed in what was a general store in the early 1900s, Clawson's is stuffed with memorabilia. ■ **TIP→ It gets crowded in summer, so arrive early for both lunch and dinner.** Hearty food such as ribs, steaks, pasta, and local seafood are part of the attraction. Fishtowne Java, the associated coffee bar, opens at 7 AM. The pub has a large selection of North Carolina microbrews. ⊠ *425 Front St.* ☎ *252/728–2133* ▭ *D, MC, V* ⊘ *Closed Sun. Labor Day–Memorial Day.*

$$-$$$ ✕ **The Spouter Inn.** Dining at a shaded table on the Spouter's deck overlooking Beaufort Harbor and Taylor's Creek is one of life's treats. Boats glide by, you see a wild horse or two on Carrot Island just across the way, and a waiter appears with a cool drink and plate of shrimp—caught that day—sitting on a bed of pasta. The prime rib and steak are popular alternatives to seafood; the banana-cream crepe may make you forget all other desserts for a while. Sunday brunch choices include quiche, steak and eggs, and omelets. There's indoor seating as well. ⊠ *218 Front St.* ☎ *252/728–5190* ▭ *AE, MC, V* ⊘ *Closed Mon. and Labor Day–Memorial Day.*

revival, and Victorian styles. Since 1979, $70 million has been spent preserving and revitalizing the downtown area, now a pleasant mix of shops, restaurants, and museums. Sailors and sunseekers enjoy the area, too, as the Neuse and Trent rivers are perfect for such activities as waterskiing and crabbing. The town has four marinas, and, if water sports aren't your thing, five public or semipublic golf courses.

FodorśChoice The reconstructed **Tryon Palace,** an elegant 1770 Georgian building,
★ was the colonial capitol and originally the home of Royal Governor William Tryon. The palace burned to the ground in 1798, and it wasn't until 1952 that a seven-year, $3.5 million effort to rebuild it took place. Today only the stable and one basement wall are original; but the structure and furnishings are so authentic—reconstructed from architect plans, maps, and letters—that 82% of the books in the library are the same titles as were there 200 years ago. It's furnished with English and American antiques corresponding to Governor Tryon's inventory. The stately **John Wright Stanly House** (circa 1783), the **George W. Dixon House** (circa 1826), the **Robert Hay House** (circa 1805), and the **New Bern Academy** (circa 1809) are all part of the 13-acre Tryon Palace complex. You can also stroll through the 18th-century formal gardens. ⊠ *610 Pollock St.* ☎ *252/514–4900 or 800/767–1560* ⊕ *www. tryonpalace.org* ✍ *Self-guided tours $8; tours of garden, kitchen, office, and stables $8; tour of all buildings and gardens $15* ☉ *Mon.–Sat. 9–5, Sun. 1–5.*

In honor of the soda's 100th anniversary, the local bottling company opened the **Birthplace of Pepsi Cola** in the same corner store where teacher-turned-pharmacist Caleb Bradham brewed his first batch of "Brad's Drink." He later renamed it Pepsi-Cola, began marketing the syrup to other soda fountains, and a conglomerate was born. The museum includes a reproduction of Bradham's fountain and exhibits of memorabilia and gift items. ⊠ *256 Middle St.* ☎ *252/636–5898* ⊕ *www. pepsistore.com* ☉ *Mon.–Sat. 10–6.*

Where to Stay & Eat

★ $$$–$$$$ ✕ **Captain Ratty's Seafood & Steakhouse.** The storefront of this local favorite is draped in fish netting and colorful pennants listing the names of patrons' boats. Sandwiches and generous salads are popular lunch items; seafood and steaks are the prime choices for evening meals. The price of oysters depends on whether you do the shucking or have the Ratty's staff do it for you. Kid's menus, takeout, and delivery are available. The upstairs bar features live entertainment Thursday through Saturday. ⊠ *202 Middle St.* ☎ *252/633–2088* ⊟ *MC, V.*

$$–$$$$ ✕ **The Chelsea.** This two-story restored 1912 structure, originally the second drugstore of the pharmacist who invented Pepsi-Cola, retains some fine architectural details, such as its tin ceiling. It's a magnet for weekenders, who look forward to selecting from sandwiches (wraps, pitas, and burgers), large salads, and entrées such as shrimp and grits. The bar is well stocked, and Pepsi products are, as might be expected, the nonalcoholic drinks of choice. ⊠ *335 Middle St.* ☎ *252/637–5469* ⊟ *AE, D, MC, V.*

\$\$–\$\$\$ ✕ **The Flame.** The considerate staff at this dark, woodsy steak house with furnishings vaguely reminiscent of the Victorian era, helps make dinners special. Steak, lobster, grilled shrimp, and teriyaki chicken are all good bets. All-you-can-eat crab legs are served on Monday and Thursday. Sunday brunch with fried turkey and seafood newburg (crab and shrimp in a cream sherry sauce topped with bread crumbs) is popular. ✉ 2303 Neuse Blvd. ☎ 252/633–0262 🖃 AE, D, MC, V ☾ No dinner Sun. No lunch Mon.–Sat.

\$–\$\$\$ ✕ **BearTown French Bakery & Bistro.** You'll likely be so entranced by the selection of breads and sweets that you forgo crab-stuffed mushrooms or mozzarella-stuffed turkey meat loaf in favor of flaky croissants, fruit tarts, scones, triple-berry strudel, bread pudding, eclairs, and slices of white-chocolate rum or grand marnier–truffle cake. The bistro serves breakfast, lunch, dinner, and weekend brunch. There's live music 6 to 9 on Saturday and often during the week as well. ✉ 1905 S. Glenburnie Rd. ☎ 252/634–2327.

¢–\$ ✕ **Pollock Street Deli.** Good-size crowds gather in the tiny rooms of this historic district colonial house—and at its riverfront sidewalk tables—for classic deli treats (the Reuben is renowned; the chicken salad a winner) and Sunday brunch (consider eggs Benedict). Service can be leisurely, but it's also friendly. ✉ 208 Pollock St. ☎ 252/637–2480 🖃 AE, MC, V ☾ No dinner Sun. and Mon.

\$\$–\$\$\$ ▦ **Sheraton New Bern Hotel & Marina.** At the confluence of the Neuse and Trent rivers, this Sheraton—with marina facilities—is actually two properties in one. A hotel has guest rooms overlooking the Trent River, and rooms at the inn have either waterfront or city views. ✉ 100 Middle St., 28560 ☎ 252/638–3585 or 888/625–5144 🖷 252/638–8112 ⊕ www.sheraton.com/newbern ⇨ 150 rooms, 21 suites ♨ Restaurant, room service, some in-room hot tubs, some refrigerators, cable TV, in-room broadband, pool, exercise equipment, marina, 2 bars, nightclub, concierge, business services, meeting room, airport shuttle, no-smoking rooms 🖃 AE, D, DC, MC, V ℺ EP.

★ **\$–\$\$\$** ▦ **Harmony House Inn.** This old 8,000-square-foot home has a curious past—at one point, two brothers sawed the house in half to install a large Victorian staircase. Today the house is 9 feet wider, and you sleep in spacious rooms that lodged Yankee soldiers during the Civil War. Crafty wreaths, quilts, and embroidery complement the mix of antiques and reproductions in guest rooms. White and dessert wines are served in the evening. ✉ 215 Pollock St., 28560 ☎ 252/636–3810 or 800/636–3113 🖷 252/636–3810 ⊕ www.harmonyhouseinn.com ⇨ 7 rooms, 3 suites ♨ Dining room, fans, some in-room hot tubs, cable TV, shop, business services, airport shuttle; no smoking 🖃 AE, D, MC, V ℺ BP.

\$ ▦ **Hanna House.** Camille and Joe Klotz moved here from "up North" and renovated the Rudolph Ulrich House (circa 1896), incorporating the latest in plumbing and bath fixtures into antique-filled rooms. In so doing, they made a home not just for themselves, but for other visitors to this river city. Regulars return again and again to the small B&B, where lush robes hang in closets. Breakfast, with customized coffee blend, is served at the time of your preference, and may include eggs Florentine with hollandaise sauce, apple pancakes, or poached grey trout in remoulade sauce. ⊠ *218 Pollock St., 28560* ☎ *252/635–3209 or 866/830–4371* ⊕ *www.hannahousenc.net* ↬ *3 rooms* ☖ *Dining room; no room phones, no room TVs, no smoking* ⊟ *MC, V* |⊙| *BP.*

$ ⬚ **New Berne House.** Just around the corner from Tryon Palace, owner Barbara Pappas has turned the three floors of a 1922 brick house into a tasteful, albeit eclectic, showcase for her collections. Breakfast is served on vintage dishes, books fill built-in shelves, art covers the walls, and a funky set of hats hang on the 2nd-floor landing. A 3rd-floor bedroom has a brass bed that was reportedly not only saved from a brothel fire in 1897, but was also once owned by U.S. Senator Barry Goldwater. Pappas, soft-spoken and genial, keeps a refrigerator stocked with drinks. Her popular mystery weekends (advance reservations a must) involve scavenging the town's nearby historic district for clues. ⊠ *709 Broad St., 28560* ☎ *252/636–2250 or 866/782–8301* ⊕ *www. newbernehouse.com* ↬ *7 rooms* ☖ *Bicycles, library, piano; no room phones, no room TVs, no smoking* ⊟ *MC, V* |⊙| *BP.*

Shopping

The success of the downtown revitalization process is obvious in the variety of businesses in these old buildings. **Art of the Wild** (⊠ 218 Middle St. ☎ 252/638–8806) features wildlife sculptures carved from wood, stone, horn, and driftwood as well as other gifts and prints. **Bear Essentials** (⊠ 309 Middle St. ☎ 252/637–6663) specializes in earth-friendly products ranging from cosmetics to lotions. A selection of 100% cotton baby clothes and women's wear made from hemp are also sold. **The Four C's** (⊠ 252 Middle St. ☎ 252/636–3285) is the Coastal Casual Clothing Co. and the best place to pick out sportswear and camping gear. **Fraser's Wine & Cheese Gourmet Shoppe** (⊠ 210 Middle St. ☎ 252/634–2580), a specialty food shop, has an enviable international wine selection and imported chocolates.

Regional artists of every genre are represented at **Carolina Creations** (⊠ 317A Pollock St. ☎ 252/633–4369) art gallery and gift shop. You can find blown glass, pottery, jewelry, wood carvings, and all manner of paintings and prints.

WILMINGTON & THE CAPE FEAR COAST

The greater Cape Fear region stretches from Topsail Island north of Wilmington south to Southport. The Cape Fear River Basin begins in the Piedmont region and meanders several hundred miles before spilling into the Atlantic Ocean about 30 mi south of downtown Wilmington.

Miles and miles of sand stretch northward to the Outer Banks and southward to South Carolina. The beaches offer activities from fishing to sunbathing to scuba diving, and the towns here have a choice of accommodations. Approximately 100 points of public access along the shoreline are marked by orange-and-blue signs.

First settled in 1729, Wilmington is one of two deepwater ports in the state. It also has a 300-block historic district and a picturesque riverfront listed on the National Register of Historic Places. South of Wilmington, there are three distinct island communities that are an easy day trip: Wrightsville Beach, Kure (pronounced "*cure*-ee") Beach, and Carolina Beach. Southport, which sits along the west side of the Cape Fear River's mouth, has a revitalized waterfront, shaded streets, grand homes, and year-round golf. Such is the personality of the region that it has something for artists, sportspeople, history buffs, naturalists, shoppers, sunbathers, and filmmakers alike. EUE/Screen Gems Studios, the largest full-service motion-picture facility in the United States east of California, is headquartered in Wilmington.

Wilmington

89 mi southwest of New Bern via U.S. 17 and 117; 130 mi south of Raleigh via I–40.

The city's long history, including its part in the American Revolution and its role as the main port of the Confederacy, is revealed in sights downtown and in the surrounding area. Chandler's Wharf, the Cotton Exchange, and Water Street Market are old buildings now used as shopping and entertainment centers. *Henrietta II,* a paddle-wheeler similar to those that plied the waters of the Cape Fear River, has been put into service as a tourist vessel. Wilmington, also a college town, hosts special annual events such as the Azalea Festival, North Carolina Jazz Festival, Christmas candlelight tours, and fishing tournaments.

Doing justice to all the sights and experiences offered by this scenic old city requires several days. The downtown historic district along the riverfront is very walkable. As you move away from this immediate area, however, a car becomes necessary for visits to places such as the Louise Wells Cameron Art Museum, Airlie Gardens, and the USS *North Carolina* Battleship Memorial. In summer the major thoroughfare can be fairly busy so allow more time than the distance would indicate. Route 132, the main north–south road through town, continues south where Interstate 40 leaves off. U.S. 76 runs from downtown east to Wrightsville Beach; U.S. 421 goes south to Carolina and Kure beaches.

Main Attractions

❿ **Burgwin-Wright Museum House.** The house General Cornwallis used as his headquarters in April 1781 was built in 1770 on the foundations of a jail. After a fine, furnished restoration, this colonial gentleman's town house was turned into a museum that includes seven distinct period gardens. ■ TIP→ One Saturday a month you can see open-hearth cooking demonstrations. ⊠ *224 Market St., Downtown* ☎ *910/762–0570* ⊕ *www. geocities.com/picketfence/garden/4354/* ⊡ *$7* ☉ *Tues.–Sat. 10–4.*

❾ **Cape Fear Museum of History and Science.** Trace the natural, cultural, and social history of the lower Cape Fear region from its beginnings to the present. One exhibit follows the youth of one of Wilmington's most famous native sons, basketball superstar Michael Jordan. Another is about the fossilized skeleton of an ancient (1.5 million years old), giant (20 feet long, 6,000 pounds) sloth discovered in 1991 during the construction of a Wilmington dam. ⊠ *814 Market St., Downtown* ☎ *910/341–4350*

nolia and patio gardens, a salt-spray garden, and a children's garden with a maze. ⌧ *6206 Oleander Dr., 6 mi east of downtown via U.S. 76, Midtown* ☎ *910/452–6393* ⊕ *www.arboretumnhc.org* ✉ *Free* ⊙ *Daily dawn–dusk.*

Poplar Grove Historic Plantation. Take a tour of what was once the first major peanut farm in North Carolina, the 1850 Greek-revival manor house, and its outbuildings. You can also see blacksmith and weaving demonstrations, shop in the country store, and pet the farm animals (goats, sheep, horses, and poultry). At this writing, the 67-acre Abbey Nature Preserve was scheduled to open in fall 2006. ⌧ *10200 U.S. 17, 9 mi northeast of downtown, North Metro* ☎ *910/686–9518* ⊕ *www. poplargrove.com* ✉ *Guided tours $8* ⊙ *Mid-Feb.–mid-Dec., Mon.–Sat. 9–5, Sun. noon–5.*

OFF THE BEATEN PATH

WHITE LAKE – The white, sandy bottom at this Carolina bay in Bladen County is clearly visible. Because the lake has no currents, tides, or hidden depressions, it has a reputation as the "nation's safest beach." Although White Lake has only 500 year-round residents, the lake draws 200,000 people each summer because of its swimming, boating, wake boarding, jet skiing, and waterskiing opportunities. Other attractions include an amusement park and tent and RV–camping accommodations. ⌧ *1879 Lake Dr., 58 mi northwest of Wilmington via U.S. 74 and Rte. 87, White Lake* ☎ *910/862–4800* ⊕ *www.whitelakenc.com.*

⑪ Zebulon Latimer House. Built in 1852 in the Italianate style, this home museum, with 600 Victorian items in its collection, is a reminder of opulent antebellum living. The Lower Cape Fear Historical Society is based here; it leads 2-hour, 12-block guided walking tours of the downtown historic district. ⌧ *126 S. 3rd St., Downtown* ☎ *910/762–0492* ⊕ *www.latimerhouse.org* ✉ *$8* ⊙ *Weekdays 10–4, Sat. noon–5.*

Sports & the Outdoors

Wrecks such as the World War II oil tanker *John D. Gill,* sunk by Germans in 1942 on her second-ever voyage, make for exciting scuba diving off the Cape Fear Coast. **Aquatic Safaris** (⌧ *5751–4 Oleander Dr., Wilmington* ☎ *910/392–4386* ⊕ *www.aquaticsafaris.com*), the only dive shop in Wilmington, leads trips to see them and rents scuba equipment.

From April through December, **Cape Fear Riverboats, Inc.** (⌧ *301 N. Water St., Downtown* ☎ *910/343–1611 or 800/676–0162* ⊕ *www.cfrboats. com*) runs nearly a dozen types of cruises aboard a 3-deck, 156-foot riverboat, the *Henrietta III,* which departs from Riverfront Park.

Where to Eat

$$–$$$$ ✕ **Caprice Bistro.** White-lace curtains at the windows, tables dressed in white, and plain white plates serve as an unobtrusive backdrop for the food here, which is all French, all the time. Chef Thierry is proud of his "solid bistro cooking"—onion soup, *pommes frites* (fries) served with aioli, classic steak *au poivre,* and crisped duck confit. The wine list has American labels as well as French. Although there's no smoking allowed downstairs, you can smoke upstairs in the art-filled sofa bar, which stays open until 2 AM. ⌧ *10 Market St., Downtown* ☎ *910/815–0810* ▭ *AE, MC, V* ⊙ *No lunch.*

$–$$$ ✕ **Water Street Restaurant & Sidewalk Café.** A restored two-story brick waterfront warehouse dating from 1835 holds an eclectic restaurant and outdoor café. Enjoy Greek, Mexican, and Middle Eastern dishes, as well as salads, pitas, burgers, and pasta. Seafood chowder is made daily on the premises. Sidewalk and balcony diners are right on the waterfront. ■ TIP→ There's occasional live music, including a popular jazz Sunday brunch. ✉ *5 Water St., Downtown* ☎ *910/343–0042* ▤ *AE, MC, V.*

$–$$ ✕ **Caffé Phoenix.** First there's the scene: an old, glass-front building (a former dry-goods store), high ceilings, an interior balcony, recorded classical or jazz music playing, area artists' work on the walls. Then comes the service: friendly, attentive. Finally the food: eclectic (Mediterranean, Italian, French, Spanish), in generous portions. The salads—think pear, fennel, and walnuts—and daily specials are especially inventive. Because of the number of wines, coffees, and homemade desserts, the café draws a large after-hours crowd. On Sunday morning a line forms for brunch with Bloody Marys, thick-cut French toast, eggs, and lunch selections. ✉ *9 S. Front St., Downtown* ☎ *910/343–1395* ▤ *AE, D, MC, V.*

¢–$$ ✕ **K38 Baja Grill.** Named for a popular surfers' side road in Baja, Mexico, where some friends once shared memorable roadside fish tacos, the K38 menu heavily references Baja culinary traditions. You won't find Americanized Mexican fare here; instead, sample tricolor corn tortillas with shrimp, scallops, and crab with cheese and roasted garlic cream, tortilla lasagna, and chicken breast baked with artichokes, sun-dried tomatoes, green-chili pesto, and goat-cheese cream. Some dishes have an interesting Asian spin, such as the Sante Fe roll made from tuna, black beans, jack cheese, and wasabi. Rice, grilled vegetables, and fresh fruit accompany many dishes. This restaurant is especially popular with people in their twenties. ✉ *5410 Oleander Dr., Midtown* ☎ *910/395–6040* ▤ *AE, D, MC, V.*

Where to Stay

$$–$$$$ ⬚ **Graystone Inn.** Less B&B than elegant country manor, Graystone is downtown, but feels as quiet and remote as the countryside. The turn-of-the-20th-century home was built by the widow of a successful merchant, and she wasted no expense when it came to architectural detail—it's rich with ceiling coffers, columns, moldings, fireplaces, and other decorative touches. A covered veranda is inviting even if the weather doesn't cooperate for a stroll through the gardens. Bedrooms are stately and comfortable without being overdone. Suite bathrooms are unusually modern and roomy. Continental breakfast items are available for those who can't make the 8:30 to 9 cooked meal. ✉ *100 S. 3rd St., Downtown, 28401* ☎ *910/763–2000 or 888/763–4773* 🖷 *910/763–5555* ⊕ *www.graystoneinn.com* ⇆ *6 rooms, 3 suites* ⌂ *Dining room, some fans, cable TV, Wi-Fi, library; no kids under 12* ▤ *AE, D, MC, V* ⦿ *BP.*

★ **$$–$$$$** ⬚ **The Wilmingtonian.** Members of the entertainment industry often frequent the Wilmingtonian. Luxurious suites each have a different theme—classic movies, nautical heritage, country French, and so on. The Cupola Suite, in the 1841 de Rosset House, is great fun: decorated in soothing blue and cream, it has a spiral staircase leading to a sitting room with views of the city's rooftops. Rooms are spread throughout five buildings set in gardens, including an antebellum home and a convent. Many have gas fireplaces and large whirlpool tubs. Staying here you get dining privileges at the City Club, a private restaurant. ■ TIP→ Request ground-floor accommodations if stairs are a problem; there are no elevators. ⌧ *101 S. 2nd St., Downtown, 28401* ☎ *910/343–1800 or 800/525–0909* 🖶 *910/251–1149* ⊕ *www.thewilmingtonian.com* ➦ *40 suites* ⚫ *Restaurant, room service, some in-room hot tubs, some kitchens, microwaves, refrigerators, cable TV, in-room VCRs, Wi-Fi, library, laundry facilities, business services, meeting rooms, some pets allowed; no kids under 12, no smoking* ⊟ *AE, D, MC, V* ⦿ *BP.*

$–$$ 🏨 **Jameson Inn.** Midway between downtown Wilmington and Wrightsville Beach, this small hotel with large rooms offers all the comforts of home, including in-room recliners. Across the street from a Target-anchored shopping center, there are plenty of restaurant choices within walking distance. Jameson's deluxe continental breakfast includes make-your-own Belgian waffles. ⌧ *5102 Dunlea Ct, Market, 28405* ☎ *910/452–5660 or 800/526–3766* 🖶 *910/794–9251* ⊕ *www.jamesoninns.com* ➦ *67 rooms* ⚫ *Microwaves, refrigerators, cable TV, in-room data ports, pool, gym, business services, some pets allowed; no smoking* ⊟ *AE, D, MC, V* ⦿ *BP.*

Nightlife & the Arts

The city has its own symphony orchestra, oratorio society, civic ballet, community theater, and concert association. The North Carolina Symphony makes four appearances here each year. The old riverfront area, with its restaurants and nightclubs, strolling couples and horse-drawn carriages, really jumps on weekend nights.

Cape Fear Blues Festival (☎ 910/350–8822), held for three days in July, culminates in an all-day blues jam. There are also concerts in nightclubs and on paddle wheelers, and festival parties and workshops.

Level 5 at City Stage (⌧ 21 S. Front St., Downtown ☎ 910/342–0272). Part bar, part theater, Level 5 is all entertainment. At the top of an old Masonic temple, the facility includes a 250-seat venue for off-beat productions and comedy troupes as well as a rooftop bar with live music.

Since 1979 the **North Carolina Jazz Festival** (☎ 910/350–0250) has heated up a chilly February weekend with nightly sets in the Hilton Wilmington Riverside. World-famous musicians perform in a variety of styles, such as swing and Dixieland.

Campy, good fun is the order of the night at **Rum Runners: Dueling Piano Bar** (⌧ 21 N. Front St., Downtown ☎ 910/815–3846), a 6,000-square-foot tiki bar where embarrassingly fruit-filled punches and margaritas are mandatory. When the dueling pianists take the stage and demand you sing along to hits from the past 40 years, you just have to go with the flow.

Thalian Hall Center for the Performing Arts (⌧ 310 Chestnut St., Downtown ☎ 910/343–3664 or 800/523–2820), a restored opera house in continuous use since 1858, hosts more than 250 theater, dance, stand-up comedy, cinema society, and musical performances each year.

Wrightsville Beach

⑯ *12 mi east of Wilmington.*

Wrightsville Beach is a small (5-mi-long), upscale, quiet island community. Many beach houses have been in the same families for generations. Increasingly, however, they're being razed in favor of striking contemporary homes.

The beaches are havens for serious sunning, swimming, surfing, and surf fishing; and the beach patrol is vigilant about keeping ATVs, glass containers, alcohol, pets, and bonfires off the sands. In summer when the population skyrockets, parking can be a problem if you don't arrive early, and towing is enforced.

Where to Stay & Eat

$-$$$ ✕ **Oceanic Restaurant and Grill.** Thanks to three floors of seating with large windows all over, you have a panoramic view of the Atlantic for miles around—a great backdrop for the fresh seafood, steaks, and chicken. The catch of the day can usually be ordered four different ways. Dinner on the pier at sunset is a treat. ⊠ *703 S. Lumina St.* ☎ *910/256–5551* ▤ *AE, MC, V.*

★ ¢-$ ✕ **Causeway Café.** Sipping coffee supplied by the efficient staff, patrons waiting to be seated contemplate what to order this time—malted pancakes? Eggs Benedict? A country ham sandwich? Cinnamon-raisin-sourdough French toast? Shrimp and grits? Though the lunch menu is perfectly respectable, breakfast (served all day) is what packs 'em in at Causeway, which is less than ¼ mi from the bridge separating Wilmington from Wrightsville Beach Island. ⊠ *114 Causeway Dr.* ☎ *910/256–3730* ⌕ *Reservations not accepted* ▤ *No credit cards* ☉ *No dinner.*

$$$-$$$$ ⊡ **Holiday Inn SunSpree Resort Wrightsville Beach.** If you like to be pampered, this is the only place on Wrightsville Beach to fit the bill—but you'll pay a premium for the amenities. Supervised children's activities (ages 4 to 12) give mom and dad a chance to sneak away for a bit, perhaps for a massage. The rooms are standard, although the ocean views are anything but; don't overlook the 3rd-floor oceanview terrace. The restaurant is missable, but live music in the lounge (Tuesday through Sunday in summer) is a nice end to the day. ⊠ *1706 N. Lumina Ave., 28480* ☎ *910/256–2231 or 877/330–5050* ⎙ *910/256–9208* ⊕ *www.wrightsville.sunspreeresorts.com* ⌑ *168 rooms, 16 suites* ⌂ *Restaurant, café, microwaves, refrigerators, cable TV with movies, in-room data ports, Wi-Fi, 5 pools (1 indoor), gym, massages, horseshoes, volleyball, lounge, video game room, shop, playground, laundry facilities, concierge, business services, airport shuttle, no-smoking rooms* ▤ *AE, D, MC, V* ⍾Ⅰ *EP.*

$$-$$$ ⊡ **Silver Gull Motel.** This 30-year beach mainstay might be showing its age a little, but the rooms are clean and reasonably priced and the kitchens were renovated in 2006. The location, right next to Johnny Mercer Pier, is terrific. Movie fans should ask for #327, where scenes from *Divine Secrets of the Ya-Ya Sisterhood* were filmed. ⊠ *20 E. Salisbury St., 28480* ☎ *910/256–3728 or 800/842–8894* ⌑ *32 rooms* ⌂ *Refrigerators, microwaves, cable TV, Wi-Fi* ▤ *AE, D, MC, V* ⍾Ⅰ *EP.*

Kure Beach

⑰ *17 mi southwest of Wrightsville Beach; 21 mi southwest of Wilmington via U.S. 421.*

A resort community with rocketing construction, Kure Beach contains Fort Fisher State Historic Site and one of North Carolina's three aquariums. In some places twisted live oaks still grow behind the dunes. The community has miles of beaches; public access points are marked by orange-and-blue signs. ■ TIP→ **A stroll down the boardwalk, lighted at night, is the romantic cap to an evening.**

Fort Fisher State Historic Site marks one of the South's largest and most important earthworks fortifications from the Civil War, so tough it was known as the Southern Gibraltar. A reconstructed battery, Civil War relics, and artifacts from sunken blockade-runners are on-site. The fort is part of the Fort Fisher Recreation Area, with 4 mi of undeveloped beach. It's also known for its underwater archaeology sites. At least two guided tours are available daily. ⊠ *U.S. 421, Kure Beach* ☎ *910/458–5538* ⊕ *www.ah.dcr.state.nc.us/Sections/HS* ⊠ *Free* ☉ *Apr.–Oct., Mon.–Sat. 9–5, Sun. 1–5; Nov.–Mar., Tues.–Sat. 10–4.*

☙ The oceanfront **North Carolina Aquarium at Fort Fisher** features a 235,000-gallon saltwater tank that's home to sharks, stingrays, moray eels, and other fish from nearby waters. Twice a day, scuba divers enter the multistory tank and answer questions from the onlookers. New exhibits feature creatures of the deep from every undersea corner of the earth. There's a touch tank, a tank with glowing jellyfish, and alligator and turtle ponds. ⊠ *900 Loggerhead Rd., off U.S. 421, Kure Beach* ☎ *866/301–3476* ⊕ *www.ncaquariums.com* ⊠ *$8* ☉ *Daily 9–5.*

Carolina Beach, a town established in 1857, has a boardwalk with a Ferris wheel and an arcade. Bars and marinas line a lively central business district. Its popularity with young people once earned it the nickname Pleasure Island, but affluent families snapping up waterfront property are changing the demographics. Fishing is a major activity and anglers can test their skill on the pier, in the surf, and on deep-sea charter excursions. You can also take a nightly party cruise. ⊠ *3 mi northeast of Kure Beach via U.S. 421.*

Where to Stay & Eat

$$–$$$ ✕ **The Cottage.** Cypress shingles complement yellow trim on Carolina
Fodor's Choice Beach's oldest bungalow (1916). An updated interior, with a series of
★ small dining rooms, is spare but not monastic—wood-plank floors, white walls, Japanese-style screens, and uncovered tables. The Cottage is a refuge of calm, and has some of the best dining around. Seafood specialties include Fish in Foil and salmon cooked on a cedar plank. The black-eyed pea cakes are seasoned to perfection and given some zing thanks to a drizzle of citrus sauce. ■ TIP→ **For dessert, don't pass on the key lime pie.** ⊠ *1 N. Lake Park Blvd., Carolina Beach* ☎ *910/458–4383* ▭ *AE, D, MC, V* ☉ *Closed Sun.*

$–$$$ ✕ **Big Daddy's.** You can't miss this 30-year-old institution—the huge sign sits next to the only stoplight in town. Inside, the enormity continues:

Operation Bumblebee

TOPSAIL (PRONOUNCED "*TOP*-SUHL") was the first barrier island south of Bogue Inlet subject to commercial development. But before there was commerce—and definitely before there were tourists—there was a secret.

The island, 26-mi long and only about ½-mi wide, is still home to eight evenly spaced, reinforced-concrete towers. These lookouts are all that's left of Operation Bumblebee, a U.S. Navy rocket program that was the precursor to NASA. In the 1940s, Topsail, an isolated place that had experienced some military buildup during World War II, was selected as the top-secret site for the development and testing of defense missiles—the granddaddies of supersonic missiles.

These first rockets were put together in the large Assembly Building; they were then transferred via underground tunnels to a seaside launching pad that currently serves as a patio at the Jolly Roger Motel. Observers stationed in either the concrete watchtowers or safer underground bunkers would track the flight of the guided missiles and measure their speed. Between 1947 and 1948, some 200 two-stage rockets blasted out over the ocean. The experiments made Topsail as significant to jet flight as Kitty Hawk was to propeller flight.

Ultimately, salt air, humidity, and increased traffic within the 20-mi firing range did the project in. Many of the buildings and much of the equipment associated with the operation were donated or sold, and two years after the military moved out, Topsail Island had its first incorporated town, Surf City. You can find out more about Operation Bumblebee at the **Missiles & More Museum.** ⊠ *720 Channel Blvd., off Rte. 50, Topsail Beach* ☎ *910/328-8663* ⊕ *www.topsailmissilesmuseum.org* ⊞ *Free* ☉ *Apr.–mid-Oct., Mon., Tues., and Thurs.–Sat. 2–4 or by appointment; mid-Oct–Mar. by appointment only.*

---

three noisy, dimly lighted dining areas seat nearly 500 people. The menu is substantial; although some chicken, steak, and prime rib are listed, seafood stars. It comes prepared almost any way you could want it, and portions are large. An all-you-can-eat salad bar is equally filling. The gift shop at the entrance, which sells beach kitsch and candy, is a magnet for children. ⊠ *202 K Ave., Kure Beach* ☎ *910/458–8622* ⊟ *AE, D, MC, V* ☉ *Closed late Nov.–Feb.*

$$–$$$ ⌂ **Beacon House Inn.** Back in the 1950s, these pine-panel rooms were a boarding house, and Beacon House is filled with reminders of those days. In the morning enjoy a full Southern breakfast (requests taken) and borrow beach towels and umbrellas before heading across the street for a day at the beach. The rooms aren't particularly large, but all except one have an en suite bathroom, and suite bathrooms are luxurious with a hot tub or multihead shower. Three cottages with full kitchens give families—and pet owners—a vacation alternative. ⊠ *715 Carolina Beach Ave. N, Carolina Beach 28428* ☎ *910/458–6244 or 877/232–2666*

⊕ *www.beaconhouseinnb-b.com* ↝ *5 rooms (4 with bath), 2 suites, 3 cottages* ⌂ *Some fans, some cable TV, some in-room VCRs, Wi-Fi, some pets allowed; no kids under 12, no smoking* ▭ *D, MC, V* ⭤ *BP.*

Southport

⑱ *10 mi southwest of Kure Beach via U.S. 421 and ferry; 30 mi south of Wilmington via Rte. 133.*

This small town, which sits quietly at the mouth of the Cape Fear River, is listed on the National Register of Historic Places. An increasingly desirable retirement spot, Southport retains its village charm and character. Stately and distinctive homes, antiques stores, gift shops, and restaurants line streets that veer to accommodate ancient oak trees. The town, portrayed in Robert Ruark's novel *The Old Man and the Boy*, is ideal for walking; it's also popular with moviemakers—*Crimes of the Heart* was filmed here.

If you're approaching the town from Kure Beach and Fort Fisher via U.S. 421, the **Southport–Fort Fisher Ferry,** a state-operated car ferry, provides a river ride between Old Federal Point at the tip of the spit and the mainland. Old Baldy Lighthouse on Bald Head Island is seen en route, as well as the Oak Island Lighthouse and the ruins of the Price's Creek Lighthouse—in fact, this is the only point in the United States where you can see three lighthouses at the same time. It's best to arrive early (30 minutes before ferry departure), as it's first-come, first-served. ☎ *910/457–6942 or 800/368–8969* ⊕ *www.ncdot.org/transit/ferry* ⛴ *$5 per car, one-way* ☉ *Sept.–mid-May, daily every 45 min 6:15 AM–7 PM; mid-May–Aug., daily every 45 min 6:15 AM–8:30 PM.*

Where to Stay & Eat

¢ ✕ **Trolly Stop.** An institution in the Cape Fear region (there are also locations in Wrightsville Beach, Carolina Beach, and Wilmington), this long, narrow hot-dog joint is known for a unique selection of weiners, all with individual names. The North Carolina comes with chili, slaw, and mustard, and the Surfer Dog is topped with bacon bits and cheese. Those who are more health conscious can get vegetarian or fat-free dogs and other sandwiches, too. ⊠ *111 S. Howe St.* ☎ *910/457–7017* ▭ *No credit cards.*

★ **$–$$** ▦ **Bald Head Island Resort.** Reached by ferry from Southport, this entire island bills itself as a resort. It's a self-contained, carless community, complete with a grocery store, restaurants, two inns, and ample rental properties from shingled cottages to luxury homes. You can explore the semitropical island on foot, by bicycle, or in a golf cart. Climb to the top of the quaint "Old Baldy" lighthouse, watch the loggerhead turtles, or take a guided tour through the maritime forest. The entire island will gather for a concert or to watch a movie projected on the 1817-era lighthouse. The 20-minute ferry ride costs $15 per person round-trip; for most of the year, it leaves Southport on the hour and BHI on the half hour. Discounted tickets are available for same-day trips originating on the island. Advance reservations are necessary for the ferry and resort. ⊠ *Bald Head Island, 28461* ☎ *910/457–5000 or 800/432–*

7368, 910/457–5003 for ferry reservations 📠 *910/457–9232* ⊕ *www.*
baldheadisland.com ⇨ *195 condos, villas, and cottages; 25 rooms in*
2 B&Bs ♻ *5 restaurants, grocery, some kitchens, 18-hole golf course,*
4 tennis courts, pool, boating, fishing, bicycles, croquet, marina, babysit-
ting, concierge, business services, children's programs, no-smoking
rooms ▤ *AE, MC, V* ⫶○⫶ *EP.*

Winnabow

⓳ *12 mi north of Southport; 18 mi southwest of Wilmington via U.S. 17.*

On your way along Route 133 between Southport and Wilmington,
Winnabow is more of a crossroads than a town to visit; but there are
gardens and a historic site, both near the Cape Fear River, worth seeing.

The house at **Orton Plantation Gardens** is not open to the public, but the
20 acres of beautiful, comprehensive gardens, begun in 1910, are great
for strolling. The former rice plantation holds magnolias, ancient oaks,
and all kinds of ornamental plants; the grounds are also a refuge for
waterfowl. Thirty-five movies have had scenes shot here. Visitors can
buy plants and seeds from the extensive greenhouses. ⊠ *9149 Orton*
Rd. SE, off Rte. 133 📞 *910/371–6851* ⊕ *www.ortongardens.com*
💵 *$9* ⊙ *Mar.–Aug., daily 8–6; Sept.–Nov., daily 10–5.*

At **Brunswick Town State Historic Site** you can explore the excavations of
a colonial town, see the Civil War earthworks Fort Anderson, and have
a picnic. Special events include reenactments of Civil War encamp-
ments. ⊠ *8884 St. Phillip's Rd., off Rte. 133* 📞 *910/371–6613* ⊕ *www.*
ah.dcr.state.nc.us/Sections/HS 💵 *Free* ⊙ *Tues.–Sat. 10–4.*

THE NORTH CAROLINA COAST ESSENTIALS

Transportation

BY AIR

AIRPORTS   The closest large, commercial airports to the Outer Banks are Raleigh-
Durham, a 5-hour drive, and Norfolk International in Virginia, a 1½-
hour drive. Craven County Regional Airport in New Bern has charter
service and car rentals available. Wilmington International Airport
serves the Cape Fear Coast.

🛈 **Craven County Regional Airport** ⊠ U.S. 70, New Bern 📞 252/638-8591 ⊕ www.
newbernairport.com. **Dare County Regional Airport** ⊠ 410 Airport Rd., Manteo 📞 252/
473-2600 ⊕ www.fly2mqi.com. **Norfolk International** ⊠ 2200 Norview Ave. 📞 757/
857-3351 ⊕ www.norfolkairport.com. **Wilmington International Airport** ⊠ 1740 Airport Blvd. 📞 910/341-4125 ⊕ www.flyilm.com.

CARRIERS   Outer Banks Airways provides charter service between the Dare County
Regional Airport and major cities along the East Coast, as does Flight-
line Aviation, which flies into the First Flight depot, at the Wright
Memorial in Kill Devil Hill. US Airways Express and Midway fly into
Craven County Regional Airport in New Bern. US Airways, Atlantic

Southeast Airlines, and Midway serve the Wilmington International Airport.

🛩 Atlantic Southeast Airlines ☎ 800/221-1212 ⊕ www.flyasa.com. **Flightline Aviation** ☎ 800/916-3226 ⊕ www.flightlineair.com. **Midway** ☎ 800/446-1392 ⊕ www. midwayair.com. **Outer Banks Airways** ☎ 252/441-7677. **US Airways Express** ☎ 800/428-4322 ⊕ www.usair.com.

TRANSFERS Beach Cabs, based in Nags Head, runs 24-hour service from Norfolk to Ocracoke and towns in between; a ride to the Norfolk airport runs about $225. The Connection is a shuttle service with passenger vans large enough to handle families, camping gear, surfboards, and bikes. It's a bargain at $135 from Nags Head to Norfolk. The Outer Banks Limousine Service, headquartered in Kill Devil Hills, serves the entire area and Norfolk International Airport and runs around the clock; getting to the airport costs about $160 from Nags Head for two people, with $10 for each additional person.

🛩 Beach Cabs ☎ 252/441-2500 or 800/441-2503. **The Connection** ☎ 252/449-2777 ⊕ www.calltheconnection.com. **Outer Banks Limousine Service** ☎ 252/261-3133 or 800/828-5466.

BY BOAT & FERRY

Seagoing folks travel the Intracoastal Waterway through the Outer Banks and the Albemarle region. Boats may dock at nearly 150 marinas, including Elizabeth City, Manteo Waterfront Docks, and National Park Service Silver Lake Marina, in Ocracoke. From Ocracoke there are car ferries to Cedar Island and Swan Quarter on the mainland. You need to reserve the ferry by calling the terminal.

The Intracoastal Waterway provides access to many Central Coast destinations, including Beaufort, Morehead City, and Emerald Isle. Beaufort has plentiful anchorage and more than 35 marinas, including the Beaufort Town Docks and the Morehead City Yacht Basin. New Bern can be reached via the Neuse River from Pamlico Sound. Several marinas are available here, including the Sheraton Grand Marina. You can dock for the day (but not overnight) at the public docks of Union Point Park.

The Wilmington area has public marinas at Carolina Beach State Park and Wrightsville Beach and a number of hotels provide docking facilities for guests. A state-run car ferry connects Fort Fisher, south of Kure Beach, with Southport on the coast. For information about the state-run ferry system and its schedules and costs, call the North Carolina Department of Transportation's ferry information line.

🛩 Fares & Schedules **Beaufort Town Docks** ☎ 252/728-2053. **Carolina Beach State Park** ☎ 910/458-7770. **Cedar Island Ferry Terminal** ☎ 252/225-3551 or 800/856-0343. **Elizabeth City** ☎ 252/338-2886. **Manteo Waterfront Docks** ☎ 252/473-3320. **Morehead City Yacht Basin** ☎ 252/726-6862. **National Park Service Silver Lake Marina** ☎ 252/928-5111. **North Carolina Department of Transportation Ferry Information** ☎ 800/293-3779. **Ocracoke Island Ferry Terminal** ☎ 252/928-3841 or 800/345-1665. **Outer Banks Ferry Service** ☎ 252/728-4129. **Sheraton Grand Marina** ☎ 252/638-3585. **Swan Quarter Ferry Terminal** ☎ 252/926-1111 or 800/773-1094. **Union Point Park** ☎ 252/636-4060. **Wrightsville Beach** ☎ 910/256-6666.

BY BUS

Although there's no bus service to the Outer Banks, there are stops in the nearby mainland towns of Edenton and Elizabeth City. The Central Coast has bus service in Greenville and New Bern, and Cape Fear has service in Wilmington.

🔢 Greyhound/Carolina Trailways ☎ 800/231-2222 ⊕ www.greyhound.com.

BY CAR

On the one hand, navigation in the Outer Banks is a snap because there's only one road—Route 12. On the other, traffic can make that single road two lanes of pure frustration on a rainy midsummer day when everyone is looking for something besides sunbathing. Low-lying areas of the highway are also prone to flooding.

Highways into the other areas along the coast—U.S. 158 into Kitty Hawk and Nags Head; U.S. 64/264 around Nags Head and Manteo; Interstate 40, which can take you from Wilmington all the way to Las Vegas or California if you desire, or Raleigh if you're catching a plane; and Highway 17, which services Wilmington and New Bern—run smoothly during all but the busiest days of high season. Any road work is saved for the off-season so you may occasionally run into construction from Labor Day to Easter.

Driving on the beaches is occasionally allowed, but only in designated areas, and permits are sometimes required. The speed limit on the beaches is a strictly enforced 25 mph and pedestrians always have the right of way. Driving on sand can be tricky, so be careful.

BY TRAIN

Amtrak connects to Norfolk, Virginia, about 75 mi to the north of the Outer Banks, but it does not serve the North Carolina coast.

🔢 Amtrak ☎ 800/872-7245 ⊕ www.amtrak.com.

Contacts & Resources

BANKS & EXCHANGE SERVICES

Although there should never be any trouble finding a bank branch or an ATM in the larger cities, many of the smaller towns in the Outer Banks don't have such services. Area banks with good coverage include BB&T, East Carolina Bank, First Citizens, and Wachovia. Normal operating hours are Monday to Thursday 9 to 5 and Friday 9 to 6.

EMERGENCIES

The Healtheast/Outer Banks Medical Center, Beach Medical Care, and Outer Banks hospital all provide around the clock care or emergency services in the Outer Banks region. Carteret General Hospital in Morehead City, and Craven Regional Medical Center in New Bern handle emergencies on the Central Coast. For emergency medical attention in Wilmington contact the Cape Fear Memorial Hospital or the New Hanover Regional Medical Center, a trauma center.

🔢 Emergency Services **Ambulance, police** ☎ 911. **Coast Guard** ☎ 910/343-4881.

🔢 Hospitals **Beach Medical Care** ✉ 5200 N. Croatan Hwy., MM 1.5, Kitty Hawk ☎ 252/

261–4187. **Cape Fear Memorial Hospital** ⊠ 5301 Wrightsville Ave., Midtown, Wilmington ☎ 910/452-8100. **Carteret General Hospital** ⊠ 3500 Arendell St., Morehead City ☎ 252/247-1616. **Craven Regional Medical Center** ⊠ 2300 Neuse Blvd., New Bern ☎ 252/633-8111. **Healtheast/Outer Banks Medical Center** ⊠ 2808 S. Croatan Hwy., Nags Head ☎ 252/441-7111. **Island Medical Center** ⊠ 715 U.S. 64, Manteo ☎ 252/473-2500. **New Hanover Regional Medical Center** ⊠ 2131 S. 17th St., South Metro, Wilmington ☎ 910/343-7000. **Outer Banks Hospital** ⊠ 4800 S. Croatan Hwy., Nags Head ☎ 252/449-4500. **Tarheel Internal Medicine Associates** ⊠ 1123 Ocean Trail, Corolla ☎ 252/453-8616.

INTERNET, MAIL & SHIPPING

The Carolina coast is built for relaxation, not business. You're not as likely to find hotels here with Wi-Fi access as in Raleigh or Charlotte or a 24-hour FedEx drop-off point should you need to send that proposal back to the office ASAP.

Cybercafés and coffeehouses pick up some of the slack and are another way to socialize and kick back on vacation. Places like the Grind or Cravings Coffee House offer free Wi-Fi along with a caffeine jolt. The entire city of Manteo has Wi-Fi access thanks to an education project begun by famous resident Andy Griffith that provides computers to all its schoolkids.

Larger hotels will probably have stamps for letters and postcards for sale at the front desk or gift shop, but if you need to mail a package, you're not out of luck: there are 200 United States Postal Service (USPS) branches within a 100-mi radius of Wilmington. Overnight deliverers are tougher to find, but there are a few FedEx and UPS outfits.

🚩 **Cravings Coffee House** ⊠ 1211 Duck Rd., Duck ☎ 252/261-0655. **FedEx** ⊠ 321 E. 10th St., Greenville ☎ 252/752-0875 ⊠ 4700 Oleander Dr., Wilmington ☎ 910/793-4611. **The Grind** ⊠ 308 S. Lake Park Blvd., Carolina Beach ☎ 910/458-6033. **Mailbox Express** ⊠ Landfall Shopping Center, Wrightsville Beach ☎ 910/ 256-9999. **UPS** ⊠ 5561 N. Croatan Hwy., Kitty Hawk ☎ 252/255-3397 ⊠ 4915 Arendell St., Morehead City ☎ 252/726-4433 ⊠ 2236 S. Croatan Hwy., Suite 6, Nags Head ☎ 252/441-8891 ⊠ 1822 S. Glenburnie Rd., New Bern ☎ 252/637-7500 ⊠ 310 N. Front St., Suite 4, Wilmington ☎ 910/762-2150. **USPS** ⊠ 3553 Cedar Island Rd., Atlantic ☎ 252/225-2131 ⊠ 1903 Live Oak St., Beaufort ☎ 252/322-4041 ⊠ 302 S. Croatan Hwy., Kill Devil Hills ☎ 252/441-5666 ⊠ 212B Hwy. 64/264, Manteo ☎ 252/473-2534 ⊠ 706 Arendell St., Morehead City ☎ 252/726-6848 ⊠ 100 Deering St., Nags Head ☎ 252/441-7387 ⊠ 1122 Irvin Garris Hwy., Ocracoke ☎ 252/928-4771 ⊠ 8207 Market St., Wilmington ☎ 910/686-5192.

MEDIA

Beach books are a must while you're relaxing in the sun or on a shady porch. Unlike most big cities in North Carolina, big chains haven't yet usurped the independent bookshops, where browsing is a lazy pleasure.

Most people on the coast rely on Raleigh's *News & Observer* or Wilmington's *Star-News* to supplement the weekly or semiweekly coverage their own smaller city papers provide. The national news you can get anywhere, but the elaborate wedding write-ups and photos of big vegetables and street festivals are reminders of a slower pace of life.

1

📕 **City News Cards & Book Store** ✉ 514 Arendell St., Morehead City ☏ 252/726-6320. **The Coastland Times** ✉ Manteo ☏ 252/473-2105. **Fort Macon Book Store** ✉ 901 Fort Macon Rd. A, Atlantic Beach ☏ 252/726-8598. **Island Bookstore** ✉ 1177 Duck Rd. #21, Kitty Hawk ☏ 252/261-8981. **The Island Gazette** ✉ Carolina Beach ☏ 910/458-8156. **Manteo Booksellers** ✉ 105 Sir Walter Raleigh St., Manteo ☏ 252/473-1221. **New Bern Sun Journal** ✉ New Bern ☏ 252/638-8101. **North Carolina Books, Inc.** ✉ 1500 N. Croatan Hwy., Kill Devil Hills ☏ 252/441-2141. **Outer Banks Books** ✉ 5000 S. Croatan Hwy. # 34A, Nags Head ☏ 252/441-2682. **The Outer Banks Sentinel** ✉ Nags Head ☏ 252/480-2234. **Rocking Chair Book Store** ✉ 400 Front St. #400, Beaufort ☏ 252/728-2671. **Star-News** ✉ Wilmington ☏ 910/343-2000. **The Topsail Voice** ✉ Hampstead ☏ 910/270-2944. **Two Sisters Bookery** ✉ 318 Nutt St., Manteo ☏ 910/762-4444.

VISITOR INFORMATION

In the Outer Banks, Dare County Tourist Bureau operates three information centers: the Aycock Brown Welcome Center in Kitty Hawk; the smaller, seasonal Hatteras Island Welcome Center near Bodie Island; and the Outer Banks Welcome Center on Roanoke Island, in Manteo.

The National Park Service's group headquarters, at the Fort Raleigh National Historic Site in Manteo, has a 24-hour general information line about Cape Hatteras National Seashore, or you can write the superintendent. The National Park Service at the Cape Lookout National Seashore has information about visiting Cape Lookout.

The Carteret County Tourism Development Bureau operates two visitor centers on the Central Coast: one in Morehead City and one on Route 58 north of the Cameron Langston Bridge to Emerald Isle. Craven County Convention and Visitors Bureau has information about New Bern.

You can find out more about Wilmington and the Cape Fear Coast at the Cape Fear Coast Convention and Visitors Bureau. Southport is part of the area covered by the South Brunswick Islands Chamber of Commerce.

📕 **Aycock Brown Welcome Center** ✉ U.S. 158, MM 1.25, Kitty Hawk 27949 ☏ 252/261-4644. **Cape Fear Coast Convention and Visitors Bureau** ✉ 24 N. 3rd St., Wilmington 28401 ☏ 910/341-4030 or 800/222-4757 ⊕ www.cape-fear.nc.us. **Carteret County Tourism Development Bureau** ✉ 3409 Arendell St., Morehead City 28557 ☏ 800/786-6962 ✉ 263 Rte. 58, Swansboro 28584 ☏ 252/393-3100 ⊕ www.sunnync.com. **Craven County Convention and Visitors Bureau** ✉ 314 S. Front St., New Bern 28560 ☏ 252/637-9400 or 800/437-5767 ⊕ www.visitnewbern.com. **Dare County Tourist Bureau** ✉ 704 S. U.S. 64/264, Box 399, Manteo 27954 ☏ 252/473-2138 or 800/446-6262 ⊕ www.outerbanks.org. **Hatteras Island Welcome Center** ✉ Rte. 12, Buxton ☏ No phone. **National Park Service, Cape Lookout National Seashore** ✉ 131 Charles St., Harkers Island 28531 ☏ 252/728-2250 ⊕ www.nps.gov. **National Park Service's Group Headquarters** ✉ 1401 National Park Dr., Manteo ☏ 252/473-2111 24 hrs ⊕ www.nps.gov. **National Park Service Superintendent** ✉ Rte. 1, Box 675, Manteo 27954. **Outer Banks Welcome Center on Roanoke Island** ✉ 1 Visitors Center Circle, Manteo 27954 ☏ 877/298-4373. **South Brunswick Islands Chamber of Commerce** ✉ 4948 Main St., Box 1380, Shalotte 28459 ☏ 910/754-6644 or 800/426-6644 ⊕ www.ncbrunswick.com.

The Piedmont & the Sandhills

WORD OF MOUTH

"Duke has an absolutely gorgeous campus, more compact [than University of North Carolina's] although split between West and East Campuses, but almost a Hollywood set for a neo-Gothic campus. Duke Chapel and Duke Gardens are don't-misses—just spectacular."

–Cassandra

"April will be azalea time in the Southeast. Charlotte can be absolutely drop-dead gorgeous if all the gods come together properly with azaleas and dogwood blooming."

–Gretchen

By Lisa H. Towle

Updated by Leslie Mizell

THE GENTLY ROLLING HILLS of the Piedmont make up the central third of North Carolina. This region, wedged between the mountains and the coastal plain, gradually rises from 300 to 1,500 feet above sea level. Long ridges, meandering rivers, and large human-made lakes characterize this area, the most heavily developed region of the state. The Piedmont includes the state's three major metropolitan centers—Charlotte, the Triad (Greensboro, Winston-Salem, High Point), and the Triangle (Raleigh, Durham, Chapel Hill).

This area was once mostly farmland, but development has made the Piedmont a center of commerce, education, and manufacturing. For the sake of verbal convenience, North Carolinians group six of the area's urban centers into two threesomes: the Triad and the Triangle. The Triad is short for Greensboro, Winston-Salem, and High Point; the Triangle refers to the shape traced by Raleigh, Durham, and Chapel Hill, in whose center sits Research Triangle Park—a renowned complex of international companies and public and private research facilities. These urban centers have brought world-class museums, shopping, sophisticated restaurants, and professional sporting venues to the region. And one of the beauties of the Piedmont's cities—including Charlotte, which has the state's most dramatic skyline—is that they're characterized by canopies of hardwoods and pines.

South of the Piedmont is the Sandhills region, famous for its clay and its grass: the pottery made by generations of craftsmen and the golf courses that attract players from all over the world. Although vacationers might not have the sightseeing opportunities visiting this part of the state, they can relax in the lap of luxury, as some of the state's best resorts are here.

Exploring the Piedmont & the Sandhills

A visit to the Piedmont might mean catching a Carolina Panthers football game, wandering through the halls of the North Carolina Museum of Art, taking in a performance of the North Carolina Shakespeare Festival, or tapping your toes at the Old Time Fiddlers & Bluegrass Convention. Want to spend all your time on the links? No problem—the Sandhills have courses even Scotland's St. Andrews members envy. Prefer to shop and take in a show? Take your pick of comedies, dramas, and musicals. Or you can pack your tent and explore the mysteries of the Uhwarrie National Forest, High Rock Lake, or the Cape Fear River.

As far as getting there is concerned, you'll need a car. Luckily, you can travel among the Piedmont's cities by nicely maintained highways. Road construction is a fact of life in Charlotte, so it's the only place in the region where you're likely to hit non-rush-hour traffic.

About the Restaurants

In the Piedmont, it's as easy to grab a bagel, empanada, or spanikopita as a biscuit. The region is still the home of barbecue: wood-fired, pit-cooked, chopped or sliced pork traditionally served with coleslaw and hush puppies. Southern dishes such as catfish, fried green tomatoes, grits, collard greens, fried chicken, sweet potatoes, and pecan pie are also fa-

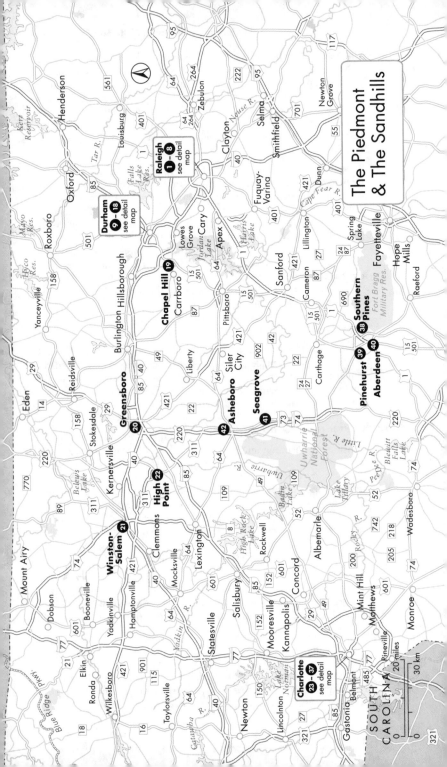

TOP 5 REASONS TO GO

Raleigh museums: Some 20 museums—many within an easy walk of one another—cover every aspect of North Carolina life, from its prehistoric roots to its arts achievements to its sports heroes.

Old Salem: Costumed guides fill this quaint restored village in the heart of Winston-Salem, founded by the Moravians in the mid-18th century.

Seagrove: This Sandhills town has been renowned for its pottery for two centuries. A dozen or more potters provide the wares, from

charmingly ugly face jugs to mugs, plates, and other treasures.

College sports: Home to four of the original Atlantic Coast Conference teams—Duke University, North Carolina State University, University of North Carolina at Chapel Hill, and Wake Forest University—even visitors to the region have to pick sides.

Wineries: North Carolina has nearly 50 wineries, and many of the finest are in the Piedmont. Sample a few fine vintages in their tasting rooms.

vorites. Beware! You'll label yourself a tourist if you pick at your grits, fail to order sweet tea, or ask for the gravy on the side.

Unless your visit coincides with a major basketball tournament, college graduation, or the International Home Furnishings Market, you rarely wait long for a table on a weeknight, even if you don't have reservations. Weekends are a different story, but many restaurants offer a "call ahead" service so you're placed on the waiting list even before you get there.

About the Hotels

Accommodations in the Piedmont include everything from roadside motels to sprawling resorts to lovely bed-and-breakfasts. Most major chains are represented, and some offer great weekend packages with perks like theater tickets. During the International Home Furnishings Show, held in spring and fall in High Point, tens of thousands of people descend on the region, making hotel rooms almost impossible to find. May is graduation time for the region's colleges and universities. If you're planning on visiting the Triangle, book well in advance.

Most lodging options in the Sandhills fall into the resort category; pricing plans and options are multitudinous and can be confusing. Many of the prices quoted are for golf packages. However, there are some chain motels in Southern Pines and Aberdeen, as well numerous B&Bs. The high seasons for golf, which bring the most expensive lodging rates, are from mid-March to mid-May and from mid-September to mid-November.

WHAT IT COSTS				
	$$$$	**$$$**	**$$**	**$**	**¢**
RESTAURANTS	over $22	$17–$22	$12–$16	$7–$11	under $7
HOTELS	over $220	$161–$220	$111–$160	$70–$110	under $70

Restaurant prices are for a main course at dinner. Hotel prices are for two people in a standard double room in high season.

Timing

North Carolina's Piedmont and Sandhills regions shine particularly in spring (April and May) and fall (September and October), when the weather is most temperate and the trees and flowers burst with color.

THE TRIANGLE

The cities of Raleigh, Durham, and Chapel Hill are known collectively as the Triangle, with Raleigh to the east, Durham to the north, Chapel Hill to the west, and, in the center, Research Triangle Park—a cluster of public and private research facilities set in 6,800 acres of lake-dotted pineland—attracts scientists, academics, and businesspeople from all over the world. Throughout the Triangle, an area that has been characterized as "trees, tees, and PhDs," politics and basketball are always hot topics. The NCAA basketball championship has traded hands among the area's three major universities.

Raleigh

85 mi east of Greensboro; 143 mi northeast of Charlotte.

Raleigh is Old South and New South, down-home and upscale, all in one. Named for Sir Walter Raleigh, who established the first English colony on the coast in 1585, it's the state capital and one of the country's fastest growing cities. Many of the state's largest and best museums are here, as are North Carolina State University and six other universities and colleges.

What to See

8 **Artspace.** A nonprofit visual-arts center, Artspace offers open studios where the artists are happy to talk to you about their work. The gift shop showcases the work of the resident artists. ⊠ *201 E. Davie St., Downtown* ☎ *919/821–2787* ⊕ *www.artspacenc.org* ⊑ *Free* ☾ *Tues.–Sat. 10–6.*

7 **City Market.** Specialty shops, art galleries, restaurants, and a small farmers' market are found in this cluster of cobblestone streets. A free trolley shuttles between City Market and other downtown restaurant and nightlife locations from 6:40 PM

HOOFING IT

It's easy to get around downtown Raleigh, as the streets are laid out in an orderly grid around the State Capitol. A good place for a stroll is the Oakwood Historic District, a 19th-century neighborhood with dozens of restored homes.

to 12:40 AM Thursday through Saturday. ⊠ *Martin and Blount Sts., Downtown* ☎ *919/821–1350* ☉ *Most stores Mon.–Sat. 10–5:30; most restaurants Mon.–Sat. 7 AM–1 AM, Sun. 11:30–10.*

❷ **Executive Mansion.** Since 1891, this 37,500-square-foot brick Queen Anne–style structure with elaborate gingerbread trim and manicured lawns has been the home of the state's governors. Reservations for tours must be made at least two weeks in advance. ⊠ *200 N. Blount St., Downtown* ☎ *919/807–7948* 🔄 *Free.*

GETTING AROUND

You can board a trolley run by **Historic Raleigh Trolley Tours** (☎ 919/857–4364) for a narrated hour-long tour of historic Raleigh. Between March and December, the trolley runs Saturday from 11 AM to 3 PM. Although the tour starts and ends at Mordecai Historic Park, you can hop aboard at any stop along the route, including the Capital Area Visitor Center, State Capital Bicentennial Plaza, the Joel Lane House, and City Market. The cost is $8 per person.

❺ **North Carolina Museum of History.** Founded in 1898, the museum is now in a state-of-the-art facility on Bicentennial Plaza. It houses the N. C. Sports Hall of Fame, which displays memorabilia from 230 inductees, from collage heroes to pro superstars to Olympic contenders. You can see Richard Petty's race car, Arnold Palmer's Ryder cup golf bag, and Harlem Globetrotter Meadowlark Lemon uniforms. ■ TIP→ **The Capital Area Visitor Services, in the museum's lobby, is a great place to plan your itinerary, pick up brochures, or arrange area tours.** ⊠ *5 E. Edenton St., Downtown* ☎ *919/807–7900* ⊕ *www.ncmuseumofhistory.org* 🔄 *Free* ☉ *Tues.–Sat. 9–5, Sun. noon–5.*

★ ☾ ❹ **North Carolina Museum of Natural Sciences.** At 200,000 square feet, this museum is the largest of its kind in the Southeast. Exhibits and dioramas celebrate the incredible diversity of species in the state's various regions. There are enough live animals and insects—including butterflies, hummingbirds, snakes, and a two-toed sloth—to qualify as a small zoo. One display contains rare whale skeletons. The pièce de résistance, however, is the "Terror of the South" exhibit, featuring the dinosaur skeleton of "Acro," a giant carnivore that lived in the region 110 million years ago. ⊠ *11 W. Jones St., Downtown* ☎ *919/733–7450 or 877/462–8724* ⊕ *www.naturalsciences.org* 🔄 *Free* ☉ *Mon.–Sat. 9–5, Sun. noon–5.*

❶ **Oakwood Historic District.** Several architectural styles—though the Victorian structures are especially notable—can be found in this tree-shaded 19th-century neighborhood. Brochures for self-guided walking tours of the area, which encompasses 20 blocks bordered by Person, Edenton, Franklin, and Watauga–Linden streets, are available at the Capital Area Visitor Center, on Blount Street. Adjacent to historic Oakwood is **Oakwood Cemetery** (⊠ 701 Oakwood Ave., Downtown ☎ 919/832–6077). Established in 1869, it's the resting place of 2,800 Confederate soldiers, Civil War generals, governors, and numerous U.S. senators.

❻ **State Capitol.** This beautifully preserved example of Greek-revival architecture from 1840 once housed all the functions of state government.

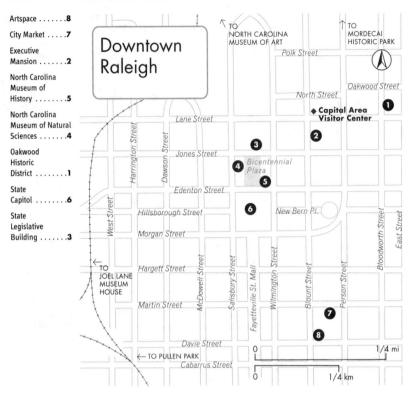

Downtown
Raleigh

Today it's part museum, part executive offices. Under its domed rotunda, the capitol contains a copy of Antonio Canova's statue of George Washington depicted as a Roman general with tunic, tight-fitting body armor, and a short cape. ⊠ *Capitol Sq., 1 E. Edenton St., Downtown* ☎ *919/ 733–4994* ⊕ *www.ah.dcr.state.nc.us* ⬚ *Free* ☉ *Weekdays 8–5, Sat. 10–4, Sun. 1–4.*

❸ **State Legislative Building.** One block north of the State Capitol, this complex hums with lawmakers and lobbyists when the legislature is in session. It's fun to watch from the gallery. A free guided tour is also available through the Capital Area Visitor Center. ⊠ *Salisbury and Jones Sts., Downtown* ☎ *919/733–7928* ⬚ *Free* ☉ *Weekdays 8–5, Sat. 9–5, Sun. 1–5.*

Other Area Attractions

The city is spread out so a car is necessary for visits to museums and parks beyond downtown.

Ava Gardner Museum. In the hometown of the legendary movie star is this museum with an extensive collection of memorabilia tracing her life from childhood on the farm to Hollywood glory days. It's about 30 mi southeast of Raleigh in downtown Smithfield. ⊠ *325 E. Market St., Smith-*

field ☎ *919/934–5830* ⊕ *www.avagardner.org* 🖼 *$4* ☉ *Mon.–Sat.*
9–5, Sun. 2–5.

Joel Lane Museum House. Dating to the 1760s, the oldest dwelling in Raleigh
was the home of Joel Lane, known as the "father of Raleigh" because
he once owned the property on which the capital city grew. Costumed
docents lead tours of the restored house and beautiful period gardens.
⊠ *728 W. Hargett St., at St. Mary's St., Downtown* ☎ *919/833–3431*
🖼 *$4* ☉ *Mar.–mid-Dec., Tues.–Fri. 10–2, Sat. 1–4.*

Mordecai Historic Park. You can see the Mordecai family's Greek-revival
plantation home and other historically significant structures that have
been moved onto the 5,000-acre property, including the house where
President Andrew Johnson was born in 1808. Guided tours begin every
hour. Moses Mordecai, a well-respected lawyer, married two granddaugh-
ters of Joel Lane, the "Father of Raleigh." Mordecai's descendants lived
in the house until 1967. Guided tours are at 10 to 3 Tuesday to Saturday, 1 to 4 on Sunday. ⊠ *1 Mimosa St., at Wake Forest Rd., Downtown* ☎ *919/857–4364* ⊕ *www.raleighnc.gov/mordecai* 🖼 *Free; guided
tour $5* ☉ *Tues.–Sat. 1 hr after sunrise–1 hr before sunset.*

★ **North Carolina Museum of Art.** On the west side of Raleigh, the NCMA
houses 5,000 years of artistic heritage, including one of the nation's largest
collections of Jewish ceremonial art. The museum hosts touring exhibitions of works by such artists as Caravaggio and Rodin. There are tours
at 1:30 Wednesday to Sunday. The in-house restaurant, Blue Ridge, looks
out on mammoth modernistic sculptures that, when viewed from above,
spell the words PICTURE THIS. ⊠ *2110 Blue Ridge Rd., Northwest/Air-
port* ☎ *919/839–6262* ⊕ *www.ncartmuseum.org* 🖼 *Free* ☉ *Tues.–Thurs.
and Sat. 9–5, Fri. 9–9, Sun. 10–5.*

☾ **Pullen Park.** Attracting more than 1 million visitors annually, the park
near North Carolina State University draws folks who come to ride the
train, the paddleboats, or the 1911 Dentzel carousel. You can swim in
a large indoor aquatic center or in an outdoor pool, play a game of tennis, or, if the timing is right, see a summer play at the Theater in the
Park. ⊠ *520 Ashe Ave., University* ☎ *919/831–6468 or 919/831–6640*
🖼 *Free* ☉ *Mar., Mon.–Sat. 10–5:30, Sun. 1–5:30; Apr., weekdays
10–5:30, Sat. 10–6:30, Sun. 1–6:30; May–Aug., weekdays 10–6:30,
Sat. 10–7:30, Sun. 1–7:30; Sept. and Oct. weekdays 10–4, Sat. 10–6:30,
Sun. 1:30–6:30; Nov., Fri. and Sat. 10–5, Sun. 1–5.*

Sports & the Outdoors

BASKETBALL   Raleigh's Atlantic Coast Conference entry is the North Carolina State
University **Wolfpack** (☎ 919/515–3050 ⊕ gopack.cstv.com). The team
plays basketball in the RBC Center, also home to the Carolina Hurricanes.

GOLF   **Hedingham Golf Club.** Designed by architect David Postlethwait, this semiprivate course has water hazards on eight holes. Watch out for hole 9,
where a large pond affects your play three times. ⊠ *4801 Harbour Towne*

Dr. ☎ *919/250–3030* ⊕ *www.hedingham.org* 🏌 *18 holes. 6609 yds. Par 72. Green Fee: $20–$49* ☞ *Facilities: Golf carts, golf academy/lessons.*

Lochmere Golf Club. Designed by Carolina PGA Hall of Famer Gary Hamm, this course meanders through the tree-lined links, challenging players with several different types of water hazards. A tiered green makes hole 3 a difficult par 3. ✉ *2511 Kildaire Farm Rd., Cary* ☎ *919/250–3030* ⊕ *www.lochmere.com* 🏌 *18 holes. 6136 yds. Par 71. Green Fee: $20–$49* ☞ *Facilities: Driving range, putting green, golf carts, rental clubs, pro shop, golf academy/lessons, restaurant.*

Neuse Golf Club. About 20 minutes from downtown Raleigh, this semi-private course feels far from the city's hustle and bustle. The 1993 John LaFoy–designed course follows the Neuse River and is characterized by rolling fairways and rock outcroppings. ✉ *918 Birkdale Dr., Clayton* ☎ *919/550–0550* 📠 *919/550–0553* ⊕ *www.neusegolf.com* 🏌 *18 holes. 7010 yds. Par 72. Green Fee: $59–$79* ☞ *Facilities: Driving range, putting green, rental clubs, pro shop, golf academy/lessons.*

Where to Stay & Eat

$$$$ ✕ **Angus Barn.** A huge rustic barn houses this local institution. The dimly lighted, always-busy restaurant is known for its steaks, baby back ribs, prime rib, and fresh seafood. The astonishing wine-and-beer list at the clubby Wild Turkey Lounge is 35 pages long. The oversize desserts are freshly made; on your way out, you can purchase pies at a small stand near the front door. Reservations aren't accepted for Saturday dinner. ✉ *4901 Glenwood Ave., at Aviation Pkwy., Northwest/Airport* ☎ *919/781–2444* ⊕ *www.angusbarn.com* 🖃 *AE, D, MC, V* ⊗ *No lunch.*

★ $$$$ ✕ **Second Empire.** Wood paneling, muted lighting, and well-spaced tables make for a calming and elegant dining experience in this restored 1879 historic house. The menu, which changes monthly, has a regional flavor; the food is best intricately styled so that colors, textures, and tastes fuse. For an entrée you might order pan-roasted sea scallops served with grits and applewood-smoked bacon, or five-spiced duck confit with green lentils and orzo. A brick tavern on the lower level has a less-expensive menu that includes spare ribs and grilled trout. ✉ *330 Hillsborough St., Downtown* ☎ *919/829–3663* ⊕ *www.second-empire.com* 🖃 *AE, D, MC, V* ⊗ *Closed Sun. No lunch.*

$$$–$$$$ ✕ **Enoteca Vin.** As the French–Italian name indicates, wine takes center stage at this sophisticated but unpretentious restaurant. The sleek interior—part of the old Pine State Creamery—consists of warm maple, stainless steel, exposed brick, and leather club chairs. The eclectic menu emphasizes organic ingredients that are local (flounder, goat cheese) and seasonal (okra, peaches), complemented by food-friendly wines from all over the world. The ever-changing Sunday brunch menu might include French toast with fresh strawberries or shrimp with goat cheese, papaya, avocado, and cherry tomatoes in a red-pepper vinaigrette. ✉ *410 Glenwood Ave., Suite 350, Downtown* ☎ *919/834–3070* ⊕ *www.enotecavin.com* 🖃 *AE, D, MC, V* ⊗ *Closed Mon. No lunch.*

$$–$$$ ✕ **Irregardless Café.** This café's menu—a combination of dishes for meat eaters as well as vegetarians and vegans—changes daily. You might find

Taking Your 'Cue

WANT A GUARANTEED one-word conversation starter in any gathering of North Carolinians? Say "barbecue." John Shelton Reed, a Southerner, a sociologist, and a former director of the Odum Institute for Research in Social Science at the University of North Carolina-Chapel Hill, has called barbecue "the most southern meal of all." But just as there are a myriad of southern accents, there are many types of barbecue. Understanding the distinctions is key to understanding a culinary and cultural phenomenon in North Carolina, where barbecue begins with pork (banish all thoughts of beef) and is not so much a verb as a noun (that is, a dish or an event known as a pig-pickin').

The state's barbecue tradition, variously linked to the cooking techniques of Native Americans, African slaves, and Scottish-Irish settlers, has been immortalized in song, prose, poetry, and the electronic media. So revered is the moist and tangy meat that it has inspired place names such as Barbecue Presbyterian Church, which rises beside Barbecue Creek in the Piedmont's Harnett County. Everyone from firefighters to high school bands offer barbecue at fund-raisers, and it's often featured at receptions and reunions of all sorts. Versions of it are served in eateries ranging from top-drawer to lunch counter, though many argue the most authentic barbecue is found in small-town cinder-block restaurants with on-site smokehouses.

And right there is the, ah, meat of the matter: taste. The method of cooking the meat and the ingredients of the sauce that coats it spark a passion that cuts across lines of age, class, and race. One hundred years or more of tradition have dictated that either whole hogs or shoulders be slow-roasted over a wood or charcoal fire to imbue the meat with an appropriate smoky flavor. Over the past few decades, however, an increasing number of barbecuers have switched to cleaner propane flames.

The real fault line, though, is geography. In eastern North Carolina (that's east of Interstate 95), the entire hog is cooked and the meat is "pulled" (off the bone) or coarsely chopped and then heavily seasoned with a vinegar-and-pepper-based sauce. This concoction, whose exact ingredients are jealously guarded by each owner, has a definite kick. West of Interstate 85, the meat, which usually includes just the pork shoulders, can be sliced or chopped. It's then mixed with a somewhat sweeter sauce made of vinegar, ketchup, brown sugar, and perhaps Worcestershire sauce. Serving as a buffer between these two regions is the Research Triangle area, where you'll find both types of barbecue.

No matter where North Carolinians stand on the barbecue debate, both sides agree that the line of good taste has to be drawn somewhere. In this case, it's at the mustardy sauce used in the state just south of the border.

chicken breast coated with crushed cashews and marinated in a lemon-tahini dressing, for example, or mushroom ravioli in a smoked tomato cream sauce. Salads are amply portioned, and the breads, soups, and yogurts are made on the premises. There's live music every night, and dancing on Saturday, and brunch on Sunday spice things up. The blond wood, brightly hued contemporary art, sunny dining areas, and well-spaced tables all add to the relaxing vibe. The restaurant is midway between North Carolina State University and downtown. ⊠ *901 W. Morgan St., University* ☎ *919/833–8898* ⊕ *www.irregardlesscafe.com* ⊟ *AE, D, MC, V* ⊙ *No lunch Sat. No dinner Sun.*

★ **$$–$$$**   ✕**Margaux's.** Eclectic is the best way to describe the cuisine at this North Raleigh fixture. A blackboard lists the specials, which might include peppercorn-crusted beef fillet with crispy fried oysters or phyllo-wrapped salmon with brie, cranberry jam, and asparagus. A stone fireplace warms the room in winter, and modern sculpture stands and hangs here, there, and everywhere. ⊠ *Brennan Station Shopping Center, 8111 Creedmoor Rd., North Hills* ☎ *919/846–9846* ⊕ *www.margauxsrestaurant.com* ⊟ *MC, V.*

$–$$ ✕**La Shish.** Almost everything in this Greek–Lebanese eatery is made in-house—even the rosewater-infused lemonade. Getting your food may take a while, but, it's worth the wait. The husband-and-wife team of Nawwaf and Dayan Said turn out savory marinated kebabs, falafel, moussaka, and *shawarma* (thinly sliced marinated meat). Save room for baklava and tiramisu, the trademark desserts that come in several different flavors. ⊠ *908 N.E. Maynard Rd., Cary* ☎ *919/388–8330* ⊟ *AE, D, MC, V* ⊙ *Closed Sun.*

¢–$ ✕**Big Ed's City Market Restaurant.** This place was founded by Big Ed Watkins, who claims some of the recipes were handed down from his great-grandfather, a Confederate mess sergeant. Southern cooking doesn't get much more traditional than this place; make sure you indulge in the biscuits. The restaurant is filled with antique farm implements and political memorabilia, including snapshots of presidential candidates who have stopped by. Every Saturday morning a Dixieland band plays. ⊠ *220 Wolfe St., City Market, Downtown* ☎ *919/836–9909* ⌕ *Reservations not accepted* ⊟ *No credit cards* ⊙ *Closed Sun. No dinner.*

$$–$$$ ▣ **Oakwood Inn.** This 1871 Victorian B&B, one of the first to be built in what is now the Oakwood Historic District, is listed on the National Register of Historic Places. Each of the individually decorated guest rooms has a working fireplace. Rosewood antiques fill one room; another has a queen-size sleigh bed as its centerpiece. Afternoon refreshments are served on the front porch overlooking a yard filled with irises and star magnolias. ⊠ *411 N. Bloodworth St., Downtown, 27604* ☎ *919/832–9712 or 800/267–9712* ⊟ *919/836–9263* ⊕ *www.oakwoodinnbb.com* ⌕ *6 rooms* ⌂ *Cable TV, in-room data ports, Wi-Fi* ⊟ *AE, D, MC, V* ⦿ *BP.*

★ **$$–$$$**   ▣ **William Thomas House.** On the edge of downtown is this stately, but not stuffy, Victorian B&B. Guest rooms, each named for family members, are traditionally and elegantly decorated and have oversize windows and 12-foot ceilings. The richly hued common rooms are filled with heirlooms, including a grand piano from 1863. The dining room is filled with china passed down through the generations. ⊠ *530 N. Blount*

St., Downtown, 27604 ☎ *919/755–9400 or 800/653–3466* 🖷 *919/755–3966* ⊕ *www.williamthomashouse.com* 🗐 *4 rooms* 🖒 *Fans, refrigerators, in-room data ports, Wi-Fi, library* 🖃 *AE, D, MC, V* ⭥ *BP.*

$$ 🏨 **Raleigh Marriott Crabtree Valley.** Fresh floral arrangements adorn the elegant public rooms of one of the city's most comfortable hotels. The guest rooms have nice touches like extra-thick mattresses covered with 300-thread-count linens and cozy down comforters. You can dine in the Crabtree Grill and in Quinn's at 4500, a lounge that serves light fare. ⊠ *4500 Marriott Dr., U.S. 70 near Crabtree Valley Mall, University, 27612* ☎ *919/781–7000 or 800/909–8289* 🖷 *919/781–3059* ⊕ *www.marriotthotels.com/rdunc* 🗐 *371 rooms, 4 suites* 🖒 *Restaurants, cable TV, in-room broadband, Wi-Fi, pool, hot tub, fitness room, lounge, laundry service, concierge, business services, meeting room, airport shuttle* 🖃 *AE, D, MC, V* ⭥ *EP.*

$–$$ 🏨 **North Raleigh Hilton.** This is a favorite spot for corporate meetings. Large rooms invite you to kick back on the sofa for some TV or soak in the extra-deep tub, but if you need to work, the ergonomic desk chair is quite accommodating. Lofton's Cafe is open for breakfast, and the Skybox Grill & Bar has several dozen flat-screen televisions so fans won't miss a second of the action. The fitness center has exercise bikes, treadmills, and a whirlpool. ⊠ *3415 Wake Forest Rd., North Hills, 27609* ☎ *919/872–2323 or 800/445–8667* 🖷 *919/876–0890* ⊕ *www.hilton.com* 🗐 *339 rooms, 7 suites* 🖒 *Restaurant, room service, cable TV with video games, in-room broadband, Wi-Fi, indoor pool, gym, 2 bars, laundry service, concierge, business services, meeting rooms, airport shuttle* 🖃 *AE, D, MC, V* ⭥ *EP.*

CAMPING The 5,439-acre **William B. Umstead State Park** (⊠ 8801 Glenwood Ave. ☎ 919/571–4170), between Raleigh and Durham, has 28 campsites. It's open Thursday to Sunday.

Nightlife & the Arts

THE ARTS The **Alltel Pavilion at Walnut Creek** (⊠ 3801 Rock Quarry Rd., Southeast Metro ☎ 919/831–6666 ⊕ www.alltelpavilion.com) accommodates 20,000 fans. Headliners at this amphitheater range from Nine Inch Nails to Counting Crows to Chicago.

The **Progress Energy Center for the Performing Arts** (⊠ 2 E. South St., Downtown ☎ 919/831–6011 ⊕ www.raleighconvention.com/pe.html) has several different performance spaces. The 2,277-seat **Memorial Auditorium** (☎ 919/831–6061) is home to the North Carolina Theatre. The 1,700-seat **Meymandi Concert Hall** hosts the North Carolina Symphony. The 600-seat **Fletcher Opera Theater** provides a showcase for the nationally acclaimed Carolina Ballet and the A. J. Fletcher Opera Institute. The 170-seat **Kennedy Theater** stages shows by smaller, more alternative theater groups.

NIGHTLIFE The **Berkeley Café** (⊠ 217 W. Martin St., Downtown ☎ 919/821–0777) is one of the hottest gathering places for live music, including rock and roll, metal, and electronic. **Charlie Goodnight's Comedy Club** (⊠ 861 W. Morgan St., University ☎ 919/828–5233) combines dinner with a night of laughs. Past performers include Jerry Seinfeld, Chris Rock, and Ellen

Degeneres. There are 18 beers on taps at **Tir Na Nog** (✉ 218 S. Blount St., Downtown ☎ 919/833–7795), a congenial Irish pub. There's Irish music on weekends and classes to teach you that cool step dancing.

Shopping

SHOPPING
CENTERS
Raleigh's first shopping center, **Cameron Village Shopping Center** (✉ 1900 Cameron St., Downtown ☎ 919/821–1350) is an upscale assemblage of boutiques and restaurants. The **Triangle Town Center** (✉ 5959 Triangle Park Blvd., North Raleigh ☎ 919/792–2222) contains some 165 stores, including are Abercrombie & Fitch, Coldwater Creek, Lindt Chocolates, Saks Fifth Avenue, and Williams-Sonoma.

ANTIQUES
The merchandise changes daily at **Carolina Antique Mall** (✉ Cameron Village Shopping Center, 2050 Clark Ave. ☎ 919/833–8227), where 70 dealers stock the 17,000-square-foot floor.

FOOD
Open year-round, the 60-acre **State Farmers' Market** (✉ 1201 Agriculture St., Southwest Metro ☎ 919/733–7417) is the place to go for locally grown fruits and vegetables, flowers and plants, and North Carolina crafts. The cavernous down-home restaurant is a great place to grab a bite.

Durham

23 mi northwest of Raleigh.

Although its image as a tobacco town lingers, Durham is now also known for the medical facilities and research centers associated with the city's prestigious Duke University. With more than 20,000 employees, Duke is the largest employer in this city of 188,000, and residents and visitors alike can take advantage of the lectures, art activities, and sports events associated with the university. Durham has more than a dozen historic sites, including several of North Carolina's 38 National Historic Landmarks.

What to See

⑮ Bennett Place State Historic Site. In April 1865 Confederate General Joseph E. Johnston surrendered to U.S. General William T. Sherman in this house, 17 days after Lee's surrender to Grant at Appomattox. The two generals then set forth the terms for a "permanent peace" between the South and the North. Historical reenactments are held each April; demonstrations show how Civil War soldiers drilled, lived in camps, got their mail, and received medical care. ✉ *4409 Bennett Memorial Rd., Downtown* ☎ *919/383–4345* 🎫 *Free* ☉ *Tues.–Sat. 10–4.*

⑪ Brightleaf Square (✉ Main and Gregson Sts., Duke University ☎ 919/682–9229), in the former Watts and Yuille warehouses, is named for the tobacco that once filled these buildings. The two long buildings—filled with stores like James Kennedy Antiques, Offbeat Music, Shiki Pottery, and Wentworth and Leggett Rare Books and Prints—sandwich an attractive brick courtyard.

 ⑬ Duke Chapel. A Gothic-style gem built in the early 1930s, this chapel is the centerpiece of Duke University. Modeled after England's Canterbury

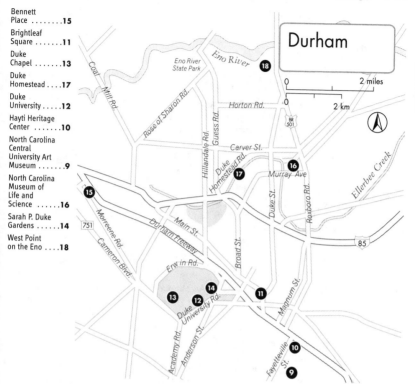

2

Cathedral, it has a 210-foot-tall bell tower. Weekly services are held in Sunday at 11 AM. ☒ *Chapel Dr., West Campus, Duke University* ☎ *919/ 681–1704* ⊕ *www.chapel.duke.edu* ☽ *Sept.–May, daily 8 AM–10 PM; June–Aug., daily 8–8.*

⑰ Duke Homestead. Washington Duke, patriarch of the now famous Duke family, moved into this house in 1852. It wasn't until he heard how the Union soldiers were enjoying smoking his tobacco that he decided to market his "golden weed." Explore the family's humble beginnings at this State Historic Site, which includes the first ramshackle "factory" as well as tour the pack house and curing barn. Guided tours demonstrate early manufacturing processes; the visitor center exhibits early tobacco advertising. ☒ *2828 Duke Homestead Rd.,*

GLASS HALF FULL

They've stood up to 75 years of inclement weather, including barrages by hurricanes Hazel and Fran. But when Duke Chapel's 77 stained-glass windows—the largest measuring 17 by 38 feet—began to weaken, steps had to be taken. The painstaking restoration is being carried out by German-born Dieter Goldkuhle, an artisan who has saved the windows in many houses of worship, including in Washington's National Cathedral. In the meantime, you'll see scaffolding both inside and outside of Duke Chapel.

Downtown ☎ *919/477–5498* ⊕ *www.ah.dcr.state.nc.us* ▨ *Free*
⊙ *Tues.–Sat. 10–4.*

⑫ Duke University. A stroll along the tree-lined streets of this campus, founded in 1924, is a lovely way to spend a few hours. The university, known for its Georgian and Gothic-revival architecture, encompasses 525 acres in the heart of Durham. A highlight of any visit is the **Nasher Museum of Art** (⊠ 2001 Campus Dr., Duke University ☎ 919/684–5135 ⊕ www.nasher.duke.edu), which displays African, American, European, and Latin American artwork from various eras. The collection includes works by Rodin, Picasso, and Matisse. Tours of the campus, available during the academic year, can be arranged in advance. ⊠ *Visitors Center, 418 Anderson St.* ☎ *919/684–3710* ⊕ *www.duke.edu.*

⑩ Hayti Heritage Center. One of Durham's oldest ecclesiastical structures, St. Joseph's AME Church, houses this center for African-American art and culture. In addition to exhibitions of traditional and contemporary art by local, regional, and national artists, the center hosts events like the Bull Durham Blues Festival and the Black Diaspora Film Festival. ⊠ *804 Old Fayetteville St., Downtown* ☎ *919/683–1709* ⊕ *www. hayti.org* ▨ *Free* ⊙ *Weekdays 9–7:30, Sat. 10–3.*

⑨ North Carolina Central University Art Museum. African-American art is showcased at the 1910 North Carolina Central University, the first publicly supported liberal-arts college for African-Americans. The permanent collection includes 19th-century masterpieces and 20th-century works created during the Harlem Renaissance; also on display is artwork by students and local artists. ⊠ *Lawson St., between fine arts and music buildings, South/NCCU* ☎ *919/560–6211* ⊕ *www.nccu.edu/artmuseum* ▨ *Free* ⊙ *Tues.–Fri. 9–5, Sun. 2–5.*

★ ☺ ⑯ North Carolina Museum of Life and Science. Here you can create a tornado, encounter dinosaurs on a prehistoric trail, view artifacts from space missions, and ride a train through a wildlife sanctuary. The nature center contains such native North Carolina animals as flying squirrels. The three-story Magic Wings Butterfly House lets you walk among tropical species in a rain-forest conservatory. In the Insectarium, you can see and hear live insects under high magnification and amplification. ⊠ *433 Murray Ave., off I–85, Downtown* ☎ *919/220–5429* ⊕ *www.ncmls.org* ▨ *Museum $9.50, train ride $2* ⊙ *Mon.–Sat. 10–5, Sun. noon–5.*

★ ⑭ Sarah P. Duke Gardens. A wisteria-draped gazebo and a Japanese garden with a lily pond teeming with fat goldfish are a few of the highlights of these 55 acres in Duke University's West Campus. More than 5 mi of pathways meander through formal plantings and woodlands. The Terrace Café serves lunch Tuesday through Sunday. ⊠ *Anderson St., at Campus Dr., West Campus, Duke University* ☎ *919/684–3698* ⊕ *www.hr.duke.edu/dukegardens* ▨ *Free* ⊙ *Daily 8–dusk.*

⑱ West Point on the Eno. In a city park on the banks of the Eno River you'll find a restored mill dating from 1778—one of 32 that once dotted the area. There's also a 19th-century Greek-revival farmhouse occupied by John Cabe McCown, the one-time owner of the mill. The park is the site of an annual three-day folk festival held each year near July 4; musicians, artists, and craftspeople come from around the region. ⊠ *5101 N. Roxboro Rd., U.S. 501N, North Metro* ☎ *919/471–1623* 🎫 *Free* ☉ *Park daily 8–sunset; buildings weekends 1–5.*

Sports & the Outdoors

BASEBALL   The **Durham Bulls** (⊠ Durham Bulls Athletic Park, 409 Blackwell St., North Metro ☎ 919/687–6500 ⊕ www.dbulls.com), a tradition since 1902, were immortalized in the hit 1988 movie *Bull Durham*. This AAA affiliate of the Tampa Bay Devil Rays plays in the $16 million 10,000-seat Durham Bulls Athletic Park.

BASKETBALL   Durham's Atlantic Coast Conference team is Duke's **Blue Devils** (☎ 919/681–2583 ⊕ www.goduke.com), which plays its home games at the 8,800-seater Cameron Indoor Stadium.

GOLF   **Duke University Golf Club.** Twice host of the NCAA men's championship, this course was designed in 1955 by the legendary Robert Trent Jones; his son, Rees Jones, completed a renovation of the links in 1994. The whopping 417-yard par 4 on hole 18 separates serious players from duffers. ⊠ *3001 Cameron Blvd. at Science Dr.* ☎ *919/490–0999 or 800/443–3853* ⊕ *www.washingtondukeinn.com/golfclub.html* ⚑ *18 holes. 6721 yds. Par 72. Green Fee: $25–$75* ⚐ *Facilities: Driving range, golf carts, rental clubs, pro shop, golf academy/lessons, restaurant, bar.*

Hillandale Golf Course. The oldest course in the area, Hillandale was designed by the incomparable architect Donald Ross, but was redesigned by George Cobb following the course's move in 1960. The pro shop is consistently named one of the best in the country. The course, with a couple of doglegs and a slew of water hazards, gives even experienced golfers a strategic workout. ⊠ *1600 Hillandale Rd.* ☎ *919/286–4211* ⊕ *www.hillandalegolf.com* ⚐ *Reservations essential* ⚑ *18 holes. 6339 yds. Par 71. Green Fee: $20–$29* ⚐ *Facilities: Driving range, golf carts, rental clubs, pro shop, golf academy/lessons, restaurant, bar.*

Where to Stay & Eat

$$$$ ✕ **Magnolia Grill.** This bistro is consistently one of the area's finest,
Fodor'sChoice   most innovative places to dine. The food created by chef-owners Ben
★   and Karen Barker is as eye-catching as the art on the walls. The daily menu, which maintains a Southern sensibility, may include spicy green-tomato soup with crab and country ham or striped bass with oyster stew. ⊠ *1002 9th St., Downtown* ☎ *919/286–3609* ▤ *AE, MC, V* ☉ *Closed Sun. and Mon. No lunch.*

$$$–$$$$ ✕ **Kemp's Seafood House.** Everything about Kemp's is big. The wooden interior was built to resemble a boat hull, and the platters of shrimp, stuffed crab, and flounder are as big as dinghies. The seafood is cooked in a variety of ways, but the specialty of the house is calabash style, meaning lightly battered and fried. Entrées are meant to be shared, assuming you haven't filled up on hush puppies and tea beforehand. Show up early on weekends or be prepared for a lengthy wait. ⊠ *115 Page Point Circle, Southeast Metro* ☎ *919/957–7155* ⚐ *Reservations not accepted* ▤ *AE, D, MC, V.*

$$–$$$$ ✕ **Restaurant Starlu.** This hip little eatery's menu combines ingredients in ways that make you wonder why nobody ever tried them before. Entrées might start with a simple item like roasted chicken breast, then serve it over something new like white truffle-corn pudding. A favorite is the refreshing fruits de mer—cold salmon, scallops, shrimp, clams, and mussels in chilled tomato broth. Choose between the lovely dining room decorated in black, red, and white and the roomier brick-edged terrace. ✉ *3211 Shannon Rd., South Square* ☎ *919/489–1500* ▭ *AE, D, MC, V.*

$–$$$ ✕ **George's Garage.** This restaurant defies pigeonholing. It's part nouvelle restaurant, part prepared-food market, part bar, and part bakery—all in a cavernous, pumped-up room. Fresh fish and Mediterranean fare are specialties, but you can also dine on grilled chicken, pork, lamb, and beef. Live entertainment and dancing make this a popular after-hours hangout. Don't miss brunch every Sunday. ✉ *737 9th St., Downtown* ☎ *919/286–1431* ▭ *AE, D, MC, V.*

★ $$$–$$$$ ✕▢ **Washington Duke Inn & Golf Club.** On the campus of Duke University, this luxurious hotel evokes the feeling of an English country inn. Guest rooms with floral bedspreads and creamy striped wall coverings overlooks a Robert Trent Jones and Rees Jones–designed golf course. On display in the public rooms are memorabilia belonging to the Duke family, for whom the hotel and university are named. At the quietly sophisticated Fairview restaurant ($$$$), you can dine on poached tiger shrimp and mango cocktail sauce followed by prosciutto-wrapped monkfish with goat-cheese grits. ✉ *3001 Cameron Blvd., Duke University, 27705* ☎ *919/490–0999 or 800/443–3853* 🖷 *919/688–0105* ⊕ *www.washingtondukeinn.com* ⛉ *164 rooms, 7 suites* ⌂ *Restaurant, room service, cable TV, in-room broadband, Wi-Fi, driving range, 18-hole golf course, putting green, indoor pool, health club, 12 tennis courts, bar, laundry service, concierge, business services, meeting rooms* ▭ *AE, D, MC, V.*

$–$$$ ▢ **Arrowhead Inn.** Brick chimneys and tall Doric columns distinguish this federal-revival plantation situated on 6 acres dotted with 200-year-old magnolias. Antiques and working fireplaces in every room create a cozy environment. ✉ *106 Mason Rd., North Metro, 27712* ☎ *919/477–8430 or 800/528–2207* 🖷 *919/471–9538* ⊕ *www.arrowheadinn.com* ⛉ *7 rooms, 1 cabin, 1 cottage* ⌂ *Picnic area, Wi-Fi, business services* ▭ *AE, D, MC, V* ⊠◎ *BP.*

$–$$ ▢ **Blooming Garden Inn.** With its yellow exterior, this B&B is literally and figuratively a bright spot in the Holloway Historic District. Inside, the inn explodes with color and warmth, thanks to exuberant hosts Dolly and Frank Pokrass. Your gourmet breakfast might be walnut crepes with ricotta cheese and warm raspberry sauce. A sister B&B across the street, the Holly House, accommodates extended stays. ✉ *513 Holloway St., Downtown, 27701* ☎ *919/687–0801 or 888/687–0801* 🖷 *919/688–1401* ⊕ *www.bloominggardeninn.com* ⛉ *3 rooms, 2 suites* ⌂ *Some in-room hot tubs, cable TV, in-room data ports* ▭ *AE, D, MC, V* ⊠◎ *BP.*

$–$$ ▢ **Durham Marriott at the Civic Center.** Given this nine-story hotel's excellent downtown location, the rates here are reasonable. Several fountains run through the lobby entrance, and the rooms are spacious and well appointed. Guests have access to the YMCA across the street. ⊠ *201 Foster St., Downtown, 27701* ☎ *919/768–6000* 🖶 *919/768– 6037* ⊕ *www.marriotthotels.com* ➪ *185 rooms, 2 suites* ♿ *Restaurant, room service, in-room safes, cable TV, in-room broadband, Wi-Fi, bar, laundry service, concierge, business services* ▭ *AE, D, MC, V* |⊚| *EP.*

Nightlife & the Arts

THE ARTS Performances that are part of the internationally known **American Dance Festival** (☎ 919/684–6402 ⊕ www.americandancefestival.org), held annually in June and July, take place at various locations around town.

The beaux arts **Carolina Theatre** (⊠ 309 W. Morgan St., Downtown ☎ 919/ 560–3030 ⊕ www.carolinatheatre.org), dating from 1926, hosts classical, jazz, and rock concerts, as well as April's Full Frames Film Festival and August's North Carolina Gay and Lesbian Film Festival. **ManBites Dog Theater** (⊠ 912 W. Main St., Downtown ☎ 919/682–3343 ⊕ www. manbitesdogtheater.org) performs edgy, socially conscious plays.

NIGHTLIFE The scene is red hot at **Club Montás** (⊠ 2223 E. Hwy. 54 ☎ 919/270– 7127). The Triangle's best salsa club, it offers salsa and mambo classes for those who want to join in the fun. With 18 beers on tap, the **James Joyce Irish Pub** (⊠ 912 W. Main St., Downtown ☎ 919/683–3022) is a popular meeting place. Traditional Irish music starts at 10 PM on Friday and Saturday.

Shopping

SHOPPING
CENTERS Durham's funky **9th Street** (⊠ 9th St., at Markham Ave. West Durham ☎ 919/572–8808) is lined with shops and restaurants. The **Streets of Southpoint Mall** (⊠ 6910 Fayetteville Rd., off I–40, Southeast Metro ☎ 919/ 572–8808) dominates Durham's shopping scene with its village look, restaurants, movie theaters, and upward of 150 stores, including Nordstrom and Restoration Hardware.

CRAFTS Now in larger digs, **One World Market** (⊠ 811 9th St., Duke University ☎ 919/286–2457) has more space for its unique, affordable arts and crafts collected around the world, from home accessories to children's toys.

FOOD A bit pricey, **Fowler's** (⊠ 112 S. Duke St., Downtown ☎ 919/683–2555) stocks pricey international spices, wines, chocolates, teas and coffees, and more. Gift baskets can be shipped all over the country.

Chapel Hill

⑲ *28 mi northwest of Raleigh; 12 mi southwest of Durham.*

Chapel Hill may be the smallest city in the Triangle but its reputation as a seat of learning looms large. This is the home of the nation's first state university, the University of North Carolina, which opened its doors in 1795. Despite the large number of students and retirees, Chapel Hill retains the feel of a quiet village. Franklin Street, with its interesting mix of trendy bars, tasty eateries, and oddball stores, has always been the heart of downtown Chapel Hill.

Piedmont Gardens

EXPLORING THE GORGEOUS GARDENS in North Carolina's Piedmont is a year-round pleasure. For starters, there are lots of them, and they are diverse in size, style, and plant life. Many offer the charm of surprise, as they can be found in little-known places as well as open but unlikely spaces. From April until the first frost in November, for example, wildflowers offer dazzling bursts of color along the roads. Here's a sample of the state's signature gardens, regional treasures, and smaller gardens of note:

Asheboro: In the Uwharries mountains are the city of Asheboro and the **North Carolina Zoological Park** (⊠ 4401 Zoo Pkwy. ☎ 336/879–7000 or 800/488–0444 ⊕ www.nczoo.org), home not just to creatures great and small, but also botanicals from the Arctic to the tropics.

Belmont: The **Daniel Stowe Botanical Garden** (⊠ 6500 S. New Hope Rd., 13 mi west of Charlotte ☎ 704/825–4490 ⊕ www.stowegarden.org) is known for its painterly display of colors in a vast perennial garden, wildflower meadow, Canal Garden, and other themed areas.

Charlotte: At the **Wing Haven Garden & Bird Sanctuary** (⊠ 248 Ridgewood Ave. ☎ 704/331–0664 ⊕ www.winghavengardens.com), 4 acres of formal gardens in one of the city's most exclusive neighborhoods create a serene environment for feathered visitors and others.

Fayetteville: Cape Fear Botanical Garden (⊠ 536 N. Eastern Blvd., 45 mi east of Aberdeen ☎ 910/486–0221 ⊕ www.capefearbg.org), at the confluence of the Cape Fear River and Cross Creek, consists of old-growth forest, a laboratory for ornamental horticulture, and a heritage garden with a re-created 19th-century farmstead.

Greensboro: Sandwiched between two busy roads, the **Bicentennial Gardens & Bog Garden** (⊠ Hobbs Rd. and Starmount Farms Dr. ☎ 336/373-2199 ⊕ www.greensborobeautiful.org) flourish almost despite themselves. The garden beds are carefully tended, especially compared to the nearby bog, whose natural setting includes wooden walkways over water and wetlands.

Hillsborough: In its annual paean to America's best private gardens, the Garden Conservancy has hailed historic Hillsborough's **Chatwood Garden** (⊠ 1900 Faucette Mill Rd., 12 mi north of Chapel Hill ☎ 919/644–0791), with its camellia collections, walled rose garden, woodland area, and heritage fruit-and-vegetable garden. Tours are by reservation only for groups of five or more.

Raleigh: JC Raulston Arboretum at North Carolina State University (⊠ 4415 Beryl Rd. ☎ 919/515–3132 ⊕ www.ncsu.edu/jcraulstonarboretum) is primarily a working, research, and teaching garden; it has the most diverse collection of hardy temperate-zone plants in the southeastern United States, a white garden, a 450-foot-long perennial border, and more.

Franklin Street runs along the northern edge of the **University of North Carolina** campus, which is filled with oak-shaded courtyards and stately old buildings. The **Ackland Art Museum** (⊠ Columbia and Franklin Sts., University ☎ 919/966–5736 ⊕ www.ackland.org) showcases one of the Southeast's strongest collections of art from India, plus a good selection of old-master paintings and sculptures. The **Louis Round Wilson Library** (⊠ Polk Pl., between E. Cameron Ave. and South Rd., University ☎ 919/962–0114 ⊕ www.lib.unc.edu/wilson) houses the largest single collection of state literature in the nation.

Morehead Planetarium and Science Center, where the original Apollo astronauts trained, is one of the largest in the country. You can learn about the constellations, take in laser-light shows, and tour otherworldly exhibits. ⊠ *250 E. Franklin St., University* ☎ *919/962–1236* ⊕ *www. moreheadplanetarium.org* ⊒*$5.25* ⊙ *Mon.–Wed. 10–5, Thurs.–Sat 10–5 and 6:30–9:30; Sun. 12:30–5.*

The **North Carolina Botanical Garden,** south of downtown, has the largest collection of native plants in the Southeast. Nature trails wind through a 300-acre piedmont forest. The herb garden and carnivorous-plant collection are impressive. ⊠ *Totten Center, Old Mason Farm Rd., South Metro* ☎ *919/962–0522* ⊕ *www.ncbg.unc.edu* ⊒ *Free* ⊙ *Weekdays 8–5, Sat. 9–6, Sun. 1–6.*

Sports & the Outdoors

BASKETBALL   The University of North Carolina's **Tarheels** (☎ 919/962–2296 or 800/ 722–4335 ⊕ tarheelblue.cstv.com) are Chapel Hill's Atlantic Coast Conference team. They play in the Dean E. Smith Student Activities Center, commonly known as the "Dean Dome."

GOLF   **UNC Finley Golf Course.** This public golf course was designed by golf legend Tom Fazio, who gave the links wide fairways and fast greens. ⊠ *Finley Golf Course Rd.* ☎ *919/962–2349* ⊠ *919/843–5974* ⊕ *www. uncfinley.com* ⚑ *18 holes. 6580 yds. Par 72. Green Fee: $33–$77* ☞ *Facilities: Driving range, putting green, golf carts, pro shop, golf academy/lessons, restaurant.*

Where to Stay & Eat

$$–$$$ ✕ **Weathervane Café.** This 30-year-old eatery, tucked into an expansive fine-foods shop, uses those top-notch ingredients for such dishes as mustard-glaze salmon and goat-cheese risotto. There's plenty of comfortable seating around the open kitchen, but the spacious courtyard, filled with plants and fountains, is why people stand in line. The all-day Sunday brunch is a big draw; French toast stuffed with mascarpone and strawberries is popular, as are poached eggs and crabmeat on a buttermilk biscuit. There's live jazz weekday evenings. ⊠ *Eastgate Shopping Center, 201 S. Estes Dr., North Metro* ☎ *919/929–9466* ▤ *AE, D, MC, V.*

★ $–$$$ ✕ **Crook's Corner.** In business since 1982, this small restaurant has been an exemplar of Southern chic. The menu, which changes nightly, highlights local produce and regional specialties such as green-pepper chicken with hoppin' john (black-eyed peas), crab gumbo, buttermilk pie, and honeysuckle sorbet. A wall of bamboo and a waterfall fountain make the patio a delightful alfresco experience (it's heated for wintertime dining). Look for the faded pink pig atop the building. ✉ *610 W. Franklin St., Downtown* ☎ *919/929–7643* ▤ *AE, D, MC, V* ☺ *Closed Mon. No lunch.*

★ **$–$$** ✗ **Mama Dip's Country Kitchen.** In Chapel Hill, Mildred Edna Cotton Council—better known as Mama Dip—is just about as famous as Michael Jordan. That's because she and her eponymous restaurant, which serves authentic home-style Southern meals in a roomy but simple setting, have been on the scene since the early '60s. Everything from chicken and dumplings, ribs, and country ham to fish, beef, salads, a mess of fresh vegetables, and melt-in-your-mouth buttermilk biscuits appear on the lengthy menu. ■ TIP→ **Mama Dip's two cookbooks explain her famed "dump cooking" method and offer up more than 450 recipes.** ✉ *408 W. Rosemary St., Downtown* ☎ *919/942–5837* ▤ *MC, V.*

$–$$ ✗ **The Rathskeller.** More than a restaurant, "The Rat" is a local institution. Students probably can't graduate unless they can produce a receipt for the excellent lasagna. Located since 1948 downstairs in an alley off Franklin Street, it has a grottolike interior. In addition to cheese-laden Italian fare, there's the onion-smothered Gambler steak, a full menu of burgers, and other favorites. It's kid-friendly, too. ✉ *157½ E. Franklin St., University* ☎ *919/942–5158* ▤ *AE, D, MC, V.*

★ **$$$$** ✗▣ **Fearrington House Country Inn.** A member of the prestigious Relais & Châteaux group, this inn sits on a 200-year-old farm that has been remade to resemble a country village. "Oreo" cows (belted Galways that are black on the ends, white in the middle) roam the pasture near the entrance. Carefully chosen antiques, English-pine furnishings, and oversize tubs fill the inn's modern guest rooms, which overlook a courtyard and the gardens. Some suites have a whirlpool or fireplace. The prix-fixe restaurant ($$$$) serves dressed-up regional food, such as collard-pecan-pesto-stuffed chicken breast with cheddar grits. Gourmet breakfasts might include shrimp and grits or homemade granola. The hotel is in Pittsboro, 8 mi south of Chapel Hill. ✉ *2000 Fearrington Village Center, Pittsboro 27312* ☎ *919/542–2121* 🖶 *919/542–4202* ⊕ *www. fearringtonhouse.com* ⇪ *33 rooms, 5 suites* ♿ *2 restaurants, cable TV, Wi-Fi, pool, 2 tennis courts, croquet, laundry service, business services, meeting rooms* ▤ *AE, MC, V* ⅋◯ℓ *BP.*

$$$ ✗▣ **Siena Hotel.** Sam and Susan Longiotti's love for Italy has carried over to their posh European-style hotel. The lobby and rooms have imported carved-wood furniture, along with fabrics and artwork that conjure up the Italian Renaissance. The public areas are filled with plush furniture grouped for conversation. Tuscan cuisine is the hallmark of Il Palio Ristorante ($$$–$$$$), open for breakfast, lunch, and dinner. You won't be hurried here, which is a good thing because it takes a while just to get through the antipasto while you anticipate entrées such as prosciutto-wrapped black grouper filled with greens and served in a saffron broth or coffee-crusted beef filet with parsnip puree and grilled portobello mushrooms. ✉ *1505 E. Franklin St., North Metro, 27514* ☎ *919/929–4000 or 800/223–7379* 🖶 *919/968–8527* ⊕ *www.sienahotel. com* ⇪ *67 rooms, 12 suites* ♿ *Restaurant, room service, cable TV, bar, laundry service, concierge, in-room data ports, Wi-Fi, business services, meeting room* ▤ *AE, MC, V* ⅋◯ℓ *BP.*

$$–$$$ ⊞ **Sheraton Chapel Hill.** The guest rooms here are done in a Scandinavian style, with sleek modern furnishings, including work desks. The marble lobby has a clean, spare look as well. Almost all of the rooms overlook pine-dotted grounds. It's on U.S. 15/501 at the far edge of the University of North Carolina campus; there's easy access to Durham and Raleigh. ⊠ *1 Europa Dr., University, 27517* ☎ *919/968–4900 or 800/ 325–3535* 🖷 *919/968–3520* ⊕ *www.sheratonchapelhill.com* ⛺ *168 rooms, 4 suites* ⚙ *Restaurant, room service, in-room broadband, Wi-Fi, exercise room, pool, bar, business services, meeting rooms* ▤ *AE, D, MC, V* ⦿ *EP.*

Nightlife & the Arts

THE ARTS The University of North Carolina's **Dean E. Smith Center** (⊠ Skipper Bowles Dr., University ☎ 919/962–2296 or 800/722–4335 ⊕ tarheelblue.cstv. com) hosts not only basketball games, but also concerts and other special events.

The **Playmakers Repertory Company** (⊠ Country Club Dr., University ☎ 919/962–7529 ⊕ www.playmakersrep.org), a professional theater company, performs in the Paul Green Theatre.

NIGHTLIFE The Chapel Hill area is the place to hear live rock and alternative bands. Smoky and dark, **Cat's Cradle** (⊠ 300 E. Main St., Carrboro ☎ 919/967– 9053) has nightly entertainment primarily from local and regional bands; a Sunday Showcase features new talent—eight bands for $2 admission. The **West End Wine Bar** (⊠ 450 W. Franklin St., Downtown ☎ 919/967–7599) attracts a more affluent crowd with its comprehensive wine list (more than 100 by the glass), dinner menu, and rooftop patio. The downstairs speakeasy-style Cellar has three pool tables, 10 draft beers, and a 1,200-song juke box.

Shopping

SHOPPING Minutes from downtown, the lively **Eastgate Shopping Center** (⊠ E. CENTERS Franklin St. at U.S. 15/501 bypass, North Metro ☎ No phone) sells everything from antiques to wine. **Fearrington Village,** (⊠ 2000 Fearrington Village Center, Pittsboro ☎ 919/542–2121) 8 mi south of Chapel Hill on U.S. 15/501 in Pittsboro, has upscale shops selling art, garden items, handmade jewelry, and more.

BOOKS At the independent **McIntyre's Bookstore** (⊠ Fearrington Village, 2000 Fearrington Village Center, Pittsboro ☎ 919/542–3030) you can read by the fire in one of the cozy rooms. McIntyre's has a big selection of mysteries, as well as gardening and cook books. The store also hosts some 125 readings throughout the year.

FOOD **A Southern Season** (⊠ Eastgate Shopping Center, 201 S. Estes Dr., North Metro ☎ 919/929–7133 or 800/253–3663) stocks a dazzling variety of items for the kitchen, from classic recipe books to the latest gadgets. Most of the foods, such as barbecue sauces, peanuts, and hams, are regional specialties. Custom gift baskets can be sent anywhere in the world.

THE TRIAD

Although they share geography and the major arteries of the region, and claim rich histories as well as institutions of higher learning, the Triad's leading cities have very distinct personalities. Greensboro, to the east, bustles as a center of commerce. Smaller Winston-Salem, to the west, may catch you by surprise with its eclectic arts scene. High Point, to the south, has managed to fuse the simplicity of Quaker forebearers with its role as a world-class furniture market.

Greensboro

20 *96 mi northeast of Charlotte; 26 mi east of Winston-Salem; 58 mi west of Durham.*

The Gate City earned its nickname when it became a railway hub in the 1840s, becoming so important in transporting textiles that many of the mills moved to town. Today the textile industry isn't what it used to be, and Greensboro, with the third largest population in the state, has diversified into insurance, banking, and other industries. Commerce aside, the complex history—of soldiers, and protestors, of writers and journalists—makes Greensboro an enriching place to visit.

The diversity of Greensboro's museums and historic sites range from hands-on children's exhibits to meticulously explained rare collections to open fields where your imagination has to create the scene. The city also has a thriving arts community, with college, community, or professional theater most weekends, as well as small galleries that showcase local and regional artists. With six colleges and universities, Greensboro also plays host to a diverse selection of seminars and lectures by both celebrities and educators.

Guilford Courthouse National Military Park, established in 1917, has more than 200 acres with wooded hiking trails. It memorializes one of the earliest events in the area's recorded history and a pivotal moment in the life of the colonies. On March 15, 1781, the Battle of Guilford Courthouse so weakened British troops that they surrendered seven months later at Yorktown. ⊠ *2332 New Garden Rd., Northwest Metro* ☎ *336/ 288–1776* ⊕ *www.nps.gov/guco* ☕ *Free* ⊙ *Daily 8:30–5.*

Tannenbaum Historic Park, near Guilford Courthouse National Military Park, draws you into the life of early settlers. Among the buildings you'll find here is the restored 19th-century Hoskins House. Exhibits in the Colonial Heritage Center provide a hands-on history lesson. The park has one of the country's most outstanding collections of original colonial settlement maps. ⊠ *2200 New Garden Rd., Northwest Metro* ☎*336/545–5315* ⊕*www.greensboro-nc.gov/departments/parks/facilities/ tannenbaum* ☕ *Free* ⊙ *Tues.–Sat. 9–5.*

You can roam through a room filled with dinosaurs, learn about gems and minerals, and see the lemurs and other creatures at the **Natural Science Center of Greensboro.** A planetarium, a petting zoo, and a herpetarium are on the premises. Animal Discovery, a 22-acre science museum-zoological garden is scheduled to open in April 2007. ⊠ *4301 Lawndale Dr., Northwest Metro* ☏ *336/288–3769* ⊕ *www.natsci. org* ☙ *Center $6, planetarium $2* ⊙ *Mon.–Sat. 9–5, Sun. 12:30–5.*

In a Romanesque-style church dating from 1892, the **Greensboro Historical Museum** has displays about the city's own O. Henry and Dolley Madison. There's also an exploration of the Woolworth sit-in, which launched the civil rights

OH, HENRY!

It's easy to overlook a three-piece sculpture celebrating writer O. Henry. Before adopting his pen name, William Sydney Porter spent his youth in Greensboro. The life-size sculpture, on the corner of North Elm and Bellemeade streets, depicts the writer, his faithful dog, and a huge bronze book revealing some of his most famous characters.

movement's struggle to desegregate eating establishments. Permanent exhibits include collections of Confederate weapons and Jugtown pottery. Behind the museum are the graves of several Revolutionary War soldiers. ⊠ *130 Summit Ave., Downtown* ☏ *336/373–2043* ⊕ *www. greensborohistory.org* ☙ *Free* ⊙ *Tues.–Sat. 10–5, Sun. 2–5.*

Home to the offices of 15 art, dance, music, and theater organizations, the **Greensboro Cultural Center at Festival Park** also has four small art galleries, a studio theater, an outdoor amphitheater, a sculpture garden, and a restaurant with outdoor seating. Green Hill's **ArtQuest** (☏ *336/333– 7460* ⊕ *www.greenhillcenter.org*) is North Carolina's first hands-on art gallery for children. ⊠ *200 N. Davie St., Downtown* ☏ *336/373–2712* ☙ *Free* ⊙ *Weekdays 8 AM–10 PM, Sat. 9–5, Sun. 2–5.*

Exhibits and activities at the **Greensboro Children's Museum** are designed for children under 12. They can tour an airplane cockpit with an interactive screen, conduct an orchestra in the music room, or learn about buildings in the construction zone. ■ TIP➔ **Admission is reduced to $2 Friday 5 to 8 and Sunday 1 to 5.** ⊠ *220 N. Church St., Downtown* ☏ *336/ 574–2898* ⊕ *www.gcmuseum.com* ☙ *$6* ⊙ *Early Sept.–late May, Tues.–Sat. 9–5, Sun. 1–5; late May–early Sept., Mon.–Sat. 9–5, Sun. 1–5.*

Elm Street, with its turn-of-the-20th-century architecture, is the heart of **Old Greensborough** (⊠ Elm St., between Market St. and Lee St., Downtown ⊕ www.downtowngreensboro.net). Listed on the National Register of Historic Places, it has become one of Greensboro's most vibrant areas, with lively galleries, trendy nightspots, and interesting boutiques and antique shops. "Friday After Five" brings weekly live music to the district in summer. ■ TIP➔ **If you need to get online, there's even wireless Internet access throughout the area.**

The elegant **Blandwood Mansion**, home of former governor John Motley Morehead, is considered the prototype of the Italian-villa architecture that swept the country during the mid-19th century. Noted architect Alexander Jackson Davis designed the house, which has a stucco exterior and towers and still contains many of its original furnishings.

A carriage house at this National Historic Landmark can be viewed by appointment. ⊠ *447 W. Washington St., Downtown* ☎ *336/272–5003* ⊕ *www.blandwood.org* ⊠ *$5* ⊙ *Tours Feb.–Dec., Tues.–Sat. 11–2, Sun. 2–5.*

On the campus of the University of North Carolina at Greensboro, the **Weatherspoon Art Museum** consists of six galleries and a sculpture gaden. It's known for its permanent collection, which includes lithographs and bronzes by Henri Matisse, and for its changing exhibitions of 20th-century American art. ⊠ *Tate and Spring Garden Sts., University* ☎ *336/334–5770* ⊕ *http://weatherspoon.uncg.edu* ⊠ *Free* ⊙ *Tues., Wed., and Fri. 10–5, Thurs. 10–9, weekends 1–5.*

> ## MAKING HISTORY
>
> On February 1, 1960, four young black men from North Carolina A&T State University walked into the Woolworth's on Elm Street and did the unthinkable—they sat down at the white section of the segregated lunch counter. Although refused service, they stayed. And when they left, others took their place. Within two months, the concept of sit-ins had spread to more than 50 other cities. Woolworth's will soon become the **International Civil Rights Center and Museum** (⊠ 301 N. Elm St., Downtown ☎ 336/274-9199 or 800/748-7116 ⊕ www.sitinmovement.org).

Sports & the Outdoors

GOLF **Bryan Park & Golf Club.** These two public courses, 6 mi north of Greensboro, have 36 holes of great golf. The Players Course, designed by Rees Jones in 1988, reopened after a major renovation in 2006; it features 79 bunkers and eight water hazards. Jones outdid himself on the lovely 1990 Champions Course, in which seven holes hug Lake Townsend. ⊠ *6275 Bryan Park Rd., Browns Summit* ☎ *336/375–2200* ⊠ *336/375–8557* ⊕ *www.bryanpark.com* ⚐ *2 18-hole courses. Players: 6499 yds. Champions: 6622 yds. Players: Par 72 Champions: Par 72. Green Fee: $42–$54* ⚐ *Facilities: Driving range, golf carts, pro shop, golf academy/lessons, restaurant.*

Grandover Resort & Conference Center. Greensboro's only resort hotel tempts you with 36 holes on the East and West courses, designed by golf architects David Graham and Gary Panks. Golf packages are available; the deluxe package includes dinner for two at the resort's Di Valletta Restaurant. The resort is parallel to Interstate 85, but it's set so deep into 1,500 acres, you'll never think about the traffic. ⊠ *1000 Club Rd.* ☎ *336/294–1800* ⊠ *336/856–9991* ⊕ *www.grandoverresort.com* ⚐ *2 18-hole courses. East: 6600 yds. West: 6300 yds. East: Par 72. West: Par 72. Green Fee: $75* ⚐ *Facilities: Driving range, putting green, golf carts, pull carts, caddies, rental clubs, pro shop, golf academy/lessons, restaurant, bar.*

Greensboro National Golf Club. The clubhouse is known for its hot dogs, so you know this course lacks the pretense of others in the area. Called "a golf course for guys who like golf courses," the Don and Mark Charles–designed semiprivate links features wide fairways, expansive greens, and layouts that are challenging without resorting to blind spots and other trickery. ⊠ *330 Niblick Dr., Summerfield* ☎ *336/342–1113*

🖷 336/349–8541 ⊕ *www.greensboronatl.com* ⚑ *18 holes. 6417 yds. Par 72. Green Fee: $35–$40* ☞ *Facilities: Driving range, golf carts, restaurant, bar.*

Where to Stay & Eat

$–$$$
Fodor's Choice
★
× **Revival Grill.** This is the type of place where you feel welcome whether you're in blue jeans or a tuxedo. The award-winning international wine list is impeccable, and the best local microbrew, Red Oak, is one of the eight beers on tap. The food is sublime and unusual, such as jerk shrimp cocktail, porcini-crusted chicken, or veal scallopini served with polenta. Don't forget to save room for dessert, even if it's just the lightly flavored housemade ginger ice cream. It's behind Quaker Village Shopping Center. ⊠ *604 Milner Dr., Guilford College* 🖀 *336/297–0950* ▤ *AE, D, MC, V.*

$–$$
× **Bianca's.** Four- and five-course meals offer a lot of bang for the buck at this Italian-style eatery. But you can still impress your date, as it has been consistently voted the city's most romantic restaurant. Paneled walls painted peach and blue, royal-blue window treatments, and twinkling white lights set the mood. Ample portions abound; the pork chops are as popular as some of the pastas. The wine list is extensive. ⊠ *1901 Spring Garden St., Coliseum* 🖀 *336/273–8114* ▤ *AE, D, MC, V* ☺ *No lunch Tues.–Sat.*

$–$$
× **Liberty Oak.** When it moved downtown several years ago, this restaurant's longtime customers grieved the loss. Now the upscale but reasonably priced food has found a new audience. Whether you try the flakey croissant sandwiches served at lunch or the grilled pork chops topped with a demiglace of dried pear, sherry vinegar, and bourbon that are offered at dinner, your taste buds—and your wallet—are going to thank you. ⊠ *100–D W. Washington St., Downtown* 🖀 *336/273–7057* ▤ *AE, D, MC, V.*

$–$$
× **Pho Hien Vuong.** Don't be fooled by the appearance of this storefront restaurant decorated with a few items that speak to the owners' Vietnamese and Thai ancestry. There's nothing unassuming about the food. The flavors and textures of the dishes are excellent, permeating everything from the hot-and-sour shrimp soup to the vegetable curry to the sliced grilled pork. If you want the food to have extra kick, request it "hot." ⊠ *4109-A Spring Garden St., Downtown* 🖀 *336/294–5551* ▤ *D, MC, V.*

★ **$$$**
×▦ **O. Henry Hotel.** This boutique hotel, named for the renowned author who grew up in Greensboro, evokes turn-of-the-20th-century luxury with lots of wood paneling, leather sofas, and mohair club chairs. Particularly nice are the oversize rooms, which have soaring ceilings ringed by crown molding. The equally large bathrooms have separate showers and tubs. A complimentary breakfast buffet is served in a sunny pavilion overlooking a small garden. For lunch or dinner, grab a table in the courtyard of the Green Valley Grill ($–$$), a European-style restaurant with a wood-fired oven. ⊠ *624 Green Valley Rd., Friendly, 27408* 🖀 *336/854–2000 or 800/965–8259* 🖷 *336/854–2223* ⊕ *www. o.henryhotel.com* ⬐ *121 rooms, 10 suites* ♨ *Restaurant, room service, in-room safes, microwaves, refrigerators, cable TV with movies, in-*

room broadband, Wi-Fi, exercise room, pool, laundry service, business services, meeting room, airport shuttle ⊟ AE, D, MC, V ⊺⊙⊺ BP.

$$–$$$ 🖼 **Sheraton Greensboro Hotel at Four Seasons.** It's no surprise that business travelers dominate this place because it's adjacent to the convention center. Accommodations are a notch above standard. It's convenient to major thoroughfares and to the Four Seasons Town Centre, an enormous three-story mall. ⊠ 3121 High Point Rd., West Metro, 27407 ☎ 336/292–9161 or 800/242–6556 🖷 336/292–1407 ⊕ www. sheratongreensboro.com ⟿ 910 rooms, 80 suites ⚭ 5 restaurants, room service, cable TV, in-room broadband, Wi-Fi, 2 pools, health club, racquetball, 4 bars, nightclub, laundry facilities, business services, meeting rooms, airport shuttle ⊟ AE, D, DC, MC, V ⊺⊙⊺ EP.

$ 🖼 **Biltmore Greensboro Hotel.** In the heart of the central business district, the Biltmore has an old-world, slightly faded feel, with 16-foot ceilings, a cage elevator, and a lobby with walnut-panel walls and a fireplace. Some guest rooms have Victorian-era or Victorian-reproduction furniture and electric candle sconces. ⊠ 111 W. Washington St., Downtown, 27401 ☎ 336/272–3474 or 800/332–0303 🖷 336/275–2523 ⟿ 25 rooms, 2 suites ⚭ Room service, minibars, in-room data ports, Wi-Fi, business services, meeting room ⊟ AE, D, MC, V ⊺⊙⊺ BP.

Nightlife & the Arts

THE ARTS The **Broach Theatre** (⊠ 520-C S. Elm St., Downtown ☎ 336/378–9300 ⊕ www.broachtheatre.org) stages six professional shows each year in the Old Greensborough historic district. It specializes in little-known comedy gems. **Triad Stage** (⊠ 232 S. Elm St., Downtown ☎ 336/274–0067 ⊕ www.triadstage.org) is a professional company that mixes classic and original plays.

The 1927 **Carolina Theatre** (⊠ 310 S. Greene St., Downtown ☎ 336/333–2605 ⊕ www.carolinatheatre.com) serves as one of the city's principal performing-arts centers, showcasing dance, music, films, and plays. The vast **Greensboro Coliseum Complex** (⊠ 1921 W. Lee St. ☎ 336/373–7474 ⊕ www.greensborocoliseum.com) hosts arts and entertainment events throughout the year. The Greensboro Symphony and the Greensboro Opera Company perform here.

The **Eastern Music Festival** (⊠ 200 N. Davie St., Downtown ☎ 336/333–7450 or 877/833–6753 ⊕ www.easternmusicfestival.com), whose guests have included Billy Joel, André Watts, and Wynton Marsalis, brings a month of more than four dozen classical-music concerts to Greensboro's Guilford College and music venues throughout the city beginning in late June.

NIGHTLIFE The **Blind Tiger** (⊠ 2115 Walker Ave., Coliseum ☎ 336/272–9888), a Greensboro institution, is one of the best places in the Triad to hear live music. The schedule includes mostly rock and blues, with a bit of alternative thrown in for good measure. **Natty Greene's Pub & Brewing Company** (⊠ 345 S. Elm St., Downtown ☎ 336/274–1373) has six of its own beers on tap, from a pale ale to a stout. The food isn't imaginative, but the potato chips are made on the premises. Upstairs is a noisy sports bar with pool tables and smallish TVs. There's patio seating in nice weather.

Shopping

Replacements, Ltd. (✉ I–85/I–40 at Mt. Hope Church Rd., Exit 132 ☎ 800/737–5223), between Greensboro and Burlington, is the world's largest retailer of discontinued and active china, crystal, flatware, and collectibles. It stocks more than 10 million pieces in 200,000 patterns. The cavernous showroom is open 9 to 7 daily, and free tours begin every half hour between 9:30 and 6:30.

Winston-Salem

㉑ *26 mi west of Greensboro; 81 mi north of Charlotte.*

Two historical areas—Old Salem and Bethabara—are welcome reminders of the hard-working Moravians who founded the area in the mid-18th century. With its Williamsburg-like period reconstruction (and tasty, tasty cookies), Old Salem in particular shouldn't be missed even if you have only an afternoon to spend in the Twin Cities.

With two world-class art museums, a symphony orchestra, a film festival, the internationally respected North Carolina School of the Arts, and the biannual National Black Theatre Festival, there's plenty for visitors to do within the city limits.

Fodor'sChoice ★ Founded in 1766 as a backcountry trading center, **Old Salem Museum & Gardens** is one of the nation's most well-documented colonial sites. This living-history museum, a few blocks from downtown Winston-Salem, is filled with dozens of original and reconstructed buildings. Costumed guides explain household activities common in the late-18th and early-19th century Moravian communities. Tours include a stop by the 1861 St. Philip's Church, the state's oldest-standing African-American church. Old Salem also has a toy museum, a children's museum, and a restaurant. ■ TIP→ **Don't miss the "world's largest coffeepot," a 12-foot-tall vessel built by Julius Mickey in 1858 to advertise his tinsmith shop. Having survived two car-coffeepot collisions, it was moved to its present location at the edge of Old Salem in 1959.** ✉ *600 S. Main St., Old Salem* ☎ *336/721–7300 or 888/653–7253* ⊕ *www.oldsalem.org* ✉ *$21, includes admission to Museum of Early Southern Decorative Arts* ☉ *Mon.–Sat. 8:30–5:30, Sun. 12:30–5:30.*

NEED A BREAK? No trip to the Old Salem Museum & Gardens is complete without a trip to the **Winkler Bakery** (✉ 525 S. Main St. ☎ 336/721–7302), where you can buy bread and other items baked in the traditional brick ovens. Moravian ginger cookies, paper thin and dense with spice, are the traditional treat, although they also come in lemon, sugar, black walnut, and other flavors.

★ The **Museum of Early Southern Decorative Arts,** on the southern edge of Old Salem, is the only museum dedicated to the decorative arts of the early South. Two dozen intricately detailed period rooms and seven galleries showcase the furniture, painting, ceramics, and metalware used through 1820. The bookstore carries hard-to-find books on Southern culture and history. ✉ *924 S. Main St., Old Salem* ☎ *336/721–7360 or 888/653–7253* ⊕ *www.mesda.org* ✉ *$21, includes admission to Old Salem Museum & Gardens* ☉ *Mon.–Sat. 9:30–5, Sun. 1:30–5.*

The **SciWorks** complex has 45,000 square feet of interactive and hands-on exhibits. There's also a 120-seat planetarium. ⊠ *400 W. Hanes Mill Rd., North Metro* ☎ *336/767–6730* ⊕ *www.sciworks.org* ✉ *$10* ⊙ *Weekdays 10–4, Sat. 11–5.*

In a wooded 180-acre wildlife preserve, **Historic Bethabara Park** was the site of the first Moravian settlement in North Carolina. The 1753 community—whose name means "house of passage"—was never intended to be permanent. It fell into decline after Salem's completion. You can tour restored buildings, such as the 1788 Gemeinhaus congregation house, or wander the colonial and medicinal gardens. God's Acre, the first colony cemetery, is a short walk away. Children love the reconstructed fort from the French and Indian War. Brochures for self-guided walking tours are available year-round at the visitor center. ⊠ *2147 Bethabara Rd., University* ☎ *336/924–8191* ⊕ *www.bethabarapark.org* ✉ *$2* ⊙ *Apr.–Dec., Tues.–Fri. 10–4:30, weekends 1:30–4:30.*

> **BARN TO BE WILD**
>
> As you're driving through the Piedmont, you'll notice two-story wood structures in various states of disrepair. The differences in architecture are subtle, but fascinating: a wide tin awning, a small overhang, a roof patched together as abstract art. These are tobacco barns, where tobacco was hung to be "cured." Although most have been left to fall apart, some have been transformed into workshops, studios, garages, or even small apartments.

The **Reynolda House Museum of American Art** was the home of Katharine Smith Reynolds and her husband Richard Joshua Reynolds, founder of the R. J. Reynolds Tobacco Company. Their 1917 home is filled with paintings, prints, and sculptures by such artists as Thomas Eakins, Frederic Church, and Georgia O'Keeffe. There's also a costume collection, as well as clothing and toys used by the Reynolds children. The museum is next to **Reynolda Village**, a collection of shops, restaurants, and gardens that fill the estate's original outer buildings. ⊠ *2250 Reynolda Rd., University* ☎ *336/758–5150 or 888/663–1149* ⊕ *www.reynoldahouse. org* ✉ *$10* ⊙ *Tues.–Sat. 9:30–4:30, Sun. 1:30–4:30.*

The ever-changing exhibits at the sleek **Southeastern Center for Contemporary Art,** near the Reynolda House Museum of American Art, showcase art works by nationally known artists. The shop sells many one-of-a-kind pieces. ■ TIP➡ A nice time to visit is the first Thursday of every month when the museum is open until 8 PM. ⊠ *750 Marguerite Dr., University* ☎ *336/725–1904* ⊕ *www.secca.org* ✉ *$5* ⊙ *Wed.–Sat. 10–5, Sun. 2–5.*

On land once claimed for Queen Elizabeth by Sir Walter Raleigh is **Tanglewood Park,** open to the public for golfing, boating, hiking, fishing, horseback riding, and swimming. The Tanglewood Festival of Lights, the largest holiday-lights festival in the Southeast, runs from mid-November to early January every year. ⊠ *U.S. 158 off I–40, Clemmons* ☎ *336/778–6300* ⊕ *www.forsyth.cc/tanglewood* ✉ *$2 per car* ⊙ *Daily dawn–dusk.*

Sports & the Outdoors

BASKETBALL Winston-Salem's Atlantic Coast Conference entry is the Wake Forest University **Demon Deacons** (☎ 336/758–3322 or 888/758–3322 ⊕ http://wake-forestsports.cstv.com). The team plays in Lawrence Joel Veterans Memorial Coliseum.

GOLF **Reynolds Park Golf Course.** This is the elder statesman of local links, a public course designed by Ellis Maples in 1930. The final hole tests any player's stamina with a 425-yard fairway that ends on an elevated green. ⊠ *2931 Reynolds Park Rd.* ☎ *336/650–7660* 🖷 *336/650–7664* ⚐ *18 holes. 6320 yds. Par 71. Green Fee: $20–$31* ⚲ *Facilities: Putting green, golf carts, pro shop.*

Tanglewood Park Golf Club. In addition to Tanglewood Park's Reynolds Course, there's the course that is home to the annual Vantage Championship. Both courses were designed by Robert Trent Jones in the mid-'50s, and both feature pine-lined fairways (narrower on the Reynolds course) and lakes that come into play several times. ⊠ *U.S. 158 off I–40, Clemmons* ☎ *336/778–6320* ⊕ *www.forsyth.cc/tanglewood* ⚐ *3 18-hole courses. Reynolds: 6068 yds. Championship: 6638 yds. Reynolds: Par 72. Championship: Par 72. Green Fee: $25–$46* ⚲ *Facilities: 2 driving ranges, golf carts, pro shop.*

Where to Stay & Eat

$$$$ ✕ **Noble's Grille.** French and Mediterranean flavors are key to the menu, which changes nightly. Typical entrées, grilled or roasted over the omnipresent oak-and-hickory fire, might include risotto–stuffed portobello mushrooms with roasted polenta or veal sweetbreads with garlic mashed potatoes. The dining room, with tall windows and track lighting, has a view of the grill. ⊠ *380 Knollwood St., Thruway* ☎ *336/777–8477* ▭ *AE, D, MC, V.*

$$$–$$$$ ✕ **The Vineyards.** Heart-healthy options such as poached-salmon salad are served in what was once the 1912 boiler room of the Reynolds family estate. An intimate setting, it seats only 47. The innovative seasonal menu might include pan-seared duck breast with sautéed mushrooms and a bordeaux-and-sun-dried-tomato sauce. The homemade bread pudding is considered the best in town. There's live classical guitar Thursday to Saturday. ⊠ *Reynolda Village, 120 Reynolda Village Rd., University* ☎ *336/748–0269* ▭ *AE, D, MC, V* ☺ *Closed Sun. No lunch.*

$$–$$$ ✕ **Old Salem Tavern Dining Room.** The costumed staff happily details the varied lunch and dinner menus, from which you might order traditional Moravian bratwurst or chicken pie. You can also opt for something more innovative, such as lobster-crab cakes or fillet of beef with brandied green peppercorns. In warmer months drinks are served under the arbor, and outdoor seating draws diners to the covered back porch. ⊠ *736 S. Main St., Old Salem* ☎ *336/748–8585* ▭ *AE, D, MC, V.*

$–$$ ✕ **Grecian Corner.** In a white building with blue trim, this Greek eatery has been dishing up gyros and chicken and pork souvlakia since 1970. Patrons, from workers at the nearby hospital to soccer moms, appreciate the friendly service and ample portions of moussaka, spanakopita, and salads, plus more familiar fare like hamburgers and pizza. The

North Carolina's Wineries

BET YOU DIDN'T KNOW that North Carolina was home to the nation's first cultivated grape. French explorer 1524 Giovanni de Verazano took note of the "big white grape" he found in the Cape Fear River valley in 1524. Two centuries later, settlers were cultivating these "scuppernongs." Most of North Carolina's 25 wineries were closed by Prohibition. But wineries are making a robust comeback. Today there are around 50 wineries in the state, many of them located in the Piedmont.

Benjamin Vineyards & Winery (✉ 283 Vineyard La., Graham ☎ 336/376-1080 ⊕ www.benjaminvineyards.com) uses an 1840 recipe to make scuppernong wine. **Black Wolf Vineyards** (✉ 283 Vineyard La., Dobson ☎ 336/374-2532 ⊕ www.blackwolfvineyards.com) is also home to the Wolf's Lair Restaurant. **Buck Shoals Vineyard** (✉ 6121 Vintner Way, Hamptonville ☎ 336/468-9274 ⊕ www.buckshoalsvineyard.com) produces Merlot, Pinot Grigio, Syrah, and other wines. An award-winning Riesling is a highlight of **Chatham Hill Winery** (✉ 3500 Gateway Centre Blvd., Morrisville ☎ 800/808-6768 ⊕ www.chathamhillwine.com).

At **Dennis Vineyards** (✉ 24043 Endy Rd., Albermarle ☎ 800/230-1743 ⊕ www.dennisvineyards.com), father and son turned a hobby into a profession. **GlenMarie Vineyard & Winery** (✉ 1838 Johnson Rd., Burlington ☎ 336/578-3938 ⊕ www.glenmariewinery.com) is planted with 23 varieties of French hybrids and American grapes. **Grove Winery** (✉ 7360 Brooks Bridge Rd.,

Gibsonville ☎ 336/584-4060 ⊕ www.grovewinery.com) grows grapes like Merlot and Cabernet Franc. After honeymooning in France, Michael and Amy Helton started **Hanover Park Vineyard** (✉ 1927 Courtney-Huntsville Rd., Yadkinville ☎ 336/463-2875 ⊕ www.hanoverparkwines.com). **Laurel Gray Vineyards** (✉ 5726 Old Hwy. 21, Hamptonville ☎ 336/468-8463 ⊕ www.laurelgray.com) plant grapes on land owned by the same family for 10 generations.

Raffaldini Vineyards (✉ 450 Groce Rd., Ronda ☎ 336/835-9463 ⊕ www.raffaldini.com) focuses on Italian varietals. The whimsical logo for **RagApple Lassie Vineyards & Winery** (✉ 3724 Rockford Rd., Boonville ☎ 336/367-6000 ⊕ www.ragapplelassie.com) shows a cow sipping a glass of wine. **Round Peak Vineyards** (✉ 765 Round Peak Church Rd., Mt. Airy ☎ 336/352-5595 ⊕ www.roundpeak.com) was established by two Davidson College buddies and their wives.

Weathervane Winery (✉ 765 Round Peak Church Rd., Mt. Airy ☎ 336/775-9717 ⊕ www.weathervanewinery.com) Produces Viognier and 11 other wines. The October Harvest Festival is popular at **Westbend Vineyards** (✉ 5394 Williams Rd., Lewisville ☎ 336/945-5032 ⊕ www.westbendvineyards.com). **The Winery at Iron Gate Farm** (✉ 2540 Lynch Store Rd., Mebane ☎ 919/304-9463 ⊕ www.irongatevineyards.com) makes Pack House Red, a blend of Sangiovese, Merlot, and Cabernet Sauvignon.

wine list includes Greek reds and whites. ⊠ *1st St. at Cloverdale Ave., Downtown* ☎ *336/722–6937* ▬ *No credit cards* ☉ *Closed Sun.*

★ **$$–$$$** ▣ **Brookstown Inn.** Handmade quilts, tubs big enough for two, and wine and cheese in the lobby are just a few of the amenities at this lovely lodging. The rooms, with their exposed rafters, high ceilings, and brick walls, retain the character of the original 1837 textile mill. The graffiti wall, where young female factory workers left their mark, has been carefully preserved. ⊠ *200 Brookstown Ave., Old Salem, 27101* ☎ *336/725–1120 or 800/845–4262* 🖷 *336/773–0147* ⊕ *www.brookstowninn.com* ↻ *40 rooms, 31 suites* ⚴ *Cable TV, fitness room, in-room data ports, Wi-Fi, business services, meeting room* ▬ *AE, MC, V* ﹖◎﹖ *BP.*

$$–$$$ ▣ **Marriott Winston-Salem.** This hotel is part of Twin Tower Quarters, a planned shopping and dining quarter in downtown Winston-Salem. There are plenty of restaurants nearby, as well as WS Prime, a steak house with a 150-bottle wine list, right in the hotel. The location, adjacent to the Benton Convention Center, makes this hotel an ideal destination for business travelers. The rooms are designed with luxury in mind, with down pillows and premium bedding. ⊠ *425 N. Cherry St., Downtown, 27101* ☎ *336/725–3500 or 800/444–2326* 🖷 *336/728–4025* ⊕ *www.marriott.com* ↻ *309 rooms, 6 suites* ⚴ *Restaurant, cable TV with movies, in-room broadband, Web TV, Wi-Fi, pool, fitness equipment, laundry services, concierge, business center* ▬ *AE, D, MC, V* ﹖◎﹖ *EP.*

$–$$ ▣ **Henry F. Shaffner House.** Accessible to downtown, this B&B is a favorite with business travelers and honeymooners. The rooms in the restored turn-of-the-20th-century house are meticulously furnished in Victorian elegance. Rates include evening wine and cheese. ⊠ *150 S. Marshall St., Old Salem, 27101* ☎ *336/777–0052 or 800/952–2256* 🖷 *336/777–1188* ⊕ *www.shaffnerhouse.com* ↻ *6 rooms, 3 suites* ⚴ *Restaurant, business services, meeting room* ▬ *AE, MC, V* ﹖◎﹖ *BP.*

Nightlife & the Arts

THE ARTS Many North Carolina School of the Arts musical and dramatic performances are held at the **Stevens Center** (⊠ 405 W. 4th St., Downtown ☎ 336/721–1945), a restored 1929 movie palace.

Every other August, the North Carolina Black Repertory Company hosts the **National Black Theatre Festival** (⊠ 610 Coliseum Dr., University ☎ 336/723–2266 ⊕ www.nbtf.org). This weeklong showcase of African-American arts attracts tens of thousands of people to venues all over the city. The next festival is scheduled for 2007.

NIGHTLIFE The **Garage** (⊠ 110 W. 7th St., Downtown ☎ 336/777–1127) offers up two or three performances a week from mostly regional talent. A country music bar for people who don't like country music, **Red Roosters** (⊠ 703 Jonestown Rd. ☎ 336/760–4499) plays plenty of college rock, too. The joint boasts a 40-foot-long bar and the requisite mechanical bull. In the heart of downtown, the **Speakeasy** (⊠ 410 W. 4th St., Downtown ☎ 336/722–6555) is the kind of place where live jazz spills out into the street. Performances begin at 5. Latin dance lessons are offered on Tuesday, with a martini-tasting beforehand to loosen you up.

Shopping

ANTIQUES **Farmstead Antiques** (⌧ 120 Farmstead La., Mocksville ☏ 336/998–3139) is housed in a former dairy barn about 15 mi southwest of Winston-Salem. It carries antiques, furniture, and decorative objects from the South as well as England and France.

CRAFTS Contemporary and traditional works from more than 350 craftspeople fill the **Piedmont Craftsmen's Shop & Gallery** (⌧ 601 N. Trade St., Downtown ☏ 336/725–1516 ⊕ www.piedmontcraftsmen.org). The organization has held an annual fair in November for more than 40 years.

OFF THE BEATEN PATH **BOB TIMBERLAKE GALLERY –** North Carolina's most successful artist is best known for his landscapes of the rural South, especially his native Lexington. Many of his original paintings, done in a highly detailed "American Realist" style, are exhibited in this gallery about 20 mi from Winston-Salem. You'll also find his personal collections: canoes, decoys, quilts. ⌧ 1714 E. Center St. Extension, Exit 94 off I–85, Lexington ☏ 800/244–0095 ☐ 336/249–0765 ⊕ www.bobtimberlake.com ⌧ Free ⊙ Mon.–Sat. 10–5.

High Point

㉒ 18 mi southeast of Winston-Salem; 76 mi northeast of Charlotte; 20 mi southwest of Greensboro.

High Point earned its name by simple geography: it was the highest point on the railroad line between Goldsboro and Charlotte. Nowadays the city's annual high point is hosting the International Home Furnishings Market, the largest wholesale furniture trade show in the world. Each spring and fall for a week or more, so many people flood the town that its population of 93,000 nearly doubles. The city is also the home of the North Carolina Shakespeare Festival.

The **High Point Museum & Historical Park,** focusing on Piedmont history and Quaker heritage, lets you wander through the 1786 Haley House and the 1801 Hoggatt House. Exhibits highlight furniture, pottery, communication, transportation, and military artifacts. Tours of the buildings, conducted by costumed staff, are available weekends. Ever wonder about candle-dipping and writing with a quill? You can try these and other activities here. ⌧ 1859 E. Lexington Ave. ☏ 336/885–1859 ⊕ www.highpointmuseum.org ⌧ Free ⊙ Museum: Tues.–Sat. 10–4:30, Sun. 1–4:30; Park: Sat. 10–4, Sun. 1–4.

The **Angela Peterson Doll & Miniature Museum** houses a collection of more than 2,500 dolls, costumes, miniatures, and dollhouses. Highlights include 125 Shirley Temple dolls and an extensive crèche with figures dating back to 1490. ⌧ 101 W. Green Dr. ☏ 336/885–3655 ⌧ $5 ⊙ Apr.–Nov., Tues.–Fri. 10–5, Sat. 9–5, Sun. 1–5.

In the 1920s, a building shaped like an 18th-century chest of drawers was constructed to call attention to the city's standing as the "furniture capital of the world." The **World's Largest Chest of Drawers** (⌧ 508 N. Hamilton St.) rises 40 feet high; dangling from one drawer are two 6-

2

foot-long socks meant to symbolize the city's hosiery industry. The building now houses the offices for the High Point Jaycees.

A few miles northwest of High Point is the **Mendenhall Plantation,** a well-preserved example of 19th-century domestic architecture. As Quakers, the Mendenhalls opposed slavery, and here you can find one of the few surviving false-bottom wagons, used to help slaves escape to freedom on the Underground Railroad. ■ TIP→ Come in July, when kids can learn how to make a cornhusk doll or design a quilt square during the Village Fair. ✉ *603 W. Main St., Jamestown* ☎ *336/454–3819* ⊕ *www. mendenhallplantation.org* ✍ *$2* ⊙ *Mid-Apr.–Nov., Tues.–Fri. 11–2, Sat. 1–4, Sun. 2–4.*

Sports & the Outdoors

GOLF **Oak Hollow.** The Pete Dye–designed public course makes use of its lakeside position by including peninsula greens and an island tee on the par 4 sixth hole. ✉ *3400 N. Centennial St.* ☎ *336/883–3260* 🖷 *336/883–3489* ⊕ *www.oakhollowgc.com* ⚑ *18 holes. 6564 yds. Par 72. Green Fee: $27–$35* ☞ *Facilities: Driving range, golf carts, pro shop, golf academy/lessons, restaurant.*

HIKING The 376-acre **Piedmont Environmental Center** (✉ 1220 Penny Rd. ☎ 336/883–8531 ⊕ www.piedmontenvironmental.com) has 11 mi of hiking trails adjacent to City Lake Park.

Where to Stay & Eat

★ $$$–$$$$ ✕ **J. Basul Noble's.** Locals hold this place in high esteem, and it's easy to see why. It's architecturally dramatic, with 10-foot-tall pillars, a pyramid-shape glass ceiling, and a river-rock wall. The menu includes creative dishes like roasted chicken with honeyed spaghetti squash or pan-seared halibut with truffles and pork belly. You could make a meal out of the fine breads (baked daily on the premises) and desserts. There's live jazz Thursday to Saturday. ✉ *101 S. Main St.* ☎ *336/889–3354* ⊙ *No lunch* ▤ *AE, MC, V.*

$–$$$ ✕ **Liberty Steakhouse & Brewery.** With a melting pot of a menu, Liberty's offers food ranging from New England to New Orleans and from the South to the Southwest. Steaks, seafood, salads, and soups are all amply represented. The on-site brewery offers up internationally influenced stouts, lagers, and ales. ✉ *Oak Hollow Mall, 914 Mall Loop Rd.* ☎ *336/882–4677* ▤ *AE, D, MC, V.*

$$ 🏨 **Radisson Hotel High Point.** The central location makes this chain hotel a favorite with people arriving for weekend shopping trips. Guest rooms are standard, but each suite is outfitted with furniture from the different manufacturers in the area. ✉ *135 S. Main St., 27260* ☎ *336/889–8888* 🖷 *336/885–2737* ⊕ *www.radisson.com* ⇆ *239 rooms, 13 suites* ♿ *Restaurant, microwaves, refrigerators, cable TV, in-room broadband, Wi-Fi, indoor*

PLANNING AHEAD

If your visit to High Point coincides with the International Home Furnishings Show, make dinner reservations as far ahead as possible. Well-regarded restaurants in town—and neighboring towns, too—book far in advance.

pool, fitness room, sauna, business services, meeting rooms, airport shuttle ⊟ *AE, D, MC, V* ◎ *EP.*

$–$$ ⊞ **Toad Alley Bed & Bagel.** A wraparound porch fronts this three-story Victorian house in a quiet neighborhood 1 mi north of downtown. Some of the frog-theme rooms have 9-foot ceilings. The "Lilly Pad" is a two-story suite that sleeps six. Relax while sipping wine by the fireplace or on the front-porch swing. ⊠ *1001 Johnson St., 27262* ☎ *336/886–4773 or 800/409–7946* ⊟ *336/886–6646* ⊕ *www.toadalley.com* ⇨ *6 rooms* ⚭ *Some refrigerators, in-room VCRs* ⊟ *MC, V* ◎ *BP.*

Nightlife & the Arts

Headquartered in the High Point Theatre is the **North Carolina Shakespeare Festival** (⊠ High Point Theatre, 220 E. Commerce Ave. ☎ 336/887–3001 ⊕ www.ncshakes.org). The professional troupe, founded in 1977, performs two of the Bard's plays in September and October and *A Christmas Carol* in December.

Shopping

There are more than 70 retail furniture stores in and around High Point. The more than 22 stores in the **Atrium Furniture Mall** (⊠ 430 S. Main St. ☎ 336/882–5599 ⊕ www.atriumfurniture.com) carry items by more than 700 manufacturers. It's closed Sunday.

Solo and group shows rotate through the three exhibition spaces of the **Theatre Art Galleries** (⊠ 220 E. Commerce Ave. ☎ 336/887–2137 ⊕ www.tagart.org), in the same building as the High Point Theatre.

CHARLOTTE

Although it dates from Revolutionary War times (it's named for King George III's wife), Charlotte is definitely part of the New South. Uptown Charlotte has broad streets and a skyline of gleaming skyscrapers. It also has some fashionable historic neighborhoods that are noted for their architecture and their winding, tree-shaded streets. Public art—such as the sculptures at the four corners of Trade and Tryon streets—is increasingly displayed in the city. Erected at Independence Square, the sculptures symbolize Charlotte's roots and aspirations: a gold miner (commerce), a mill worker (the city's textile heritage), a railroad builder (transportation), and a mother holding her baby aloft (the future).

Heavy development has created some typical urban problems. Outdated road systems in this metropolis make traffic a nightmare during rush hours, and virtually all the city's restaurants are packed on weekends. But the locals' Southern courtesy is contagious, and people still love the laid-back pleasures of jogging, picnicking, and sunning in Freedom Park.

You'll be able to walk around Uptown and the historic Fourth Ward, and buses are adequate for getting around within the city limits. Cars, however, remain the best bet for touring.

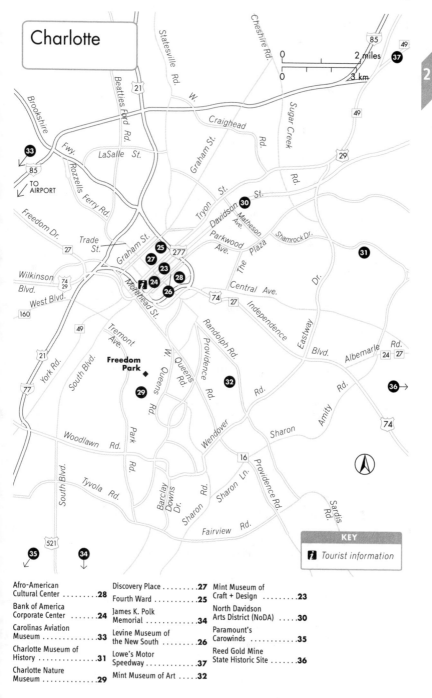

Charlotte

2

KEY

🛈 *Tourist information*

Uptown Charlotte

Uptown Charlotte is ideal for walking. The city was laid out in four wards around Independence Square, at Trade and Tryon streets. The Square, as it is known, is the center of the Uptown area.

What to See

㉔ Bank of America Corporate Center. Architecture fans should make time for a trip to see one of the city's most striking buildings. The Cesar Pelli–designed structure rises 60 stories to a crownlike top. The main attractions are three monumental lobby frescoes by world-renowned Ben Long, whose themes are making/building, chaos/creativity, and planning/knowledge. Also in the tower are the **North Carolina Blumenthal Performing Arts Center** and the restaurants, shops, and exhibition space of **Founders Hall.** ✉ *100 N. Tryon St., Uptown.*

★ ☾ **㉗ Discovery Place.** Allow at least two hours for the **aquariums,** the three-story **rain forest,** the **IMAX Dome Theater,** and the **Morphis MovieRide Simulator,** a motion ride in a space-age capsule. A ham-radio room, a puppet theater, and a 10-foot model of an eyeball that you can walk through are other highlights. Check the schedule for special exhibits. ✉ *301 N. Tryon St., Uptown* ☎ *704/372–6261 or 800/935–0553* ⊕ *www.discoveryplace.org* ✑ *$10* ☉ *Labor Day–May, weekdays 9–5, Sat. 10–6, Sun. 12:30–6; June–Labor Day, Mon.–Sat. 10–6, Sun. 12:30–6.*

㉕ Fourth Ward. Charlotte's popular old neighborhood began as a political subsection created for electoral purposes in the mid-1800s. The architecture and sensibility of this quiet, homespun neighborhood provide a glimpse of life in a less hectic time. A brochure includes 18 historic places of interest.

㉖ Levine Museum of the New South. With its 8,000-square-foot centerpiece exhibit "Cotton Fields to Skyscrapers: Charlotte and the Carolina Piedmont in the New South" as a jumping-off point, this museum offers a comprehensive interpretation of post–Civil War Southern history. Interactive exhibits and different "environments"—a tenant farmer's house, an African-American hospital, a bustling street scene—bring to life the history of the region. ✉ *200 E. 7th St., Uptown* ☎ *704/333–1887* ⊕ *www.museumofthenewsouth.org* ✑ *$6* ☉ *Tues.–Sat. 10–5, Sun. noon–5.*

㉓ Mint Museum of Craft + Design. This museum is a showplace for contemporary crafts. In addition to the 16,000-square-foot gallery, with its spectacular 40-foot-tall glass wall, the permanent collections of ceramics, glass, fiber, metal, and wood make this one of the country's major crafts museums. ■ TIP→ Use your ticket stub from the crafts museum for free same-day the Mint Museum of Art. ✉ *220 N. Tryon St., Uptown* ☎ *704/337–2000* ⊕ *www.mintmuseum.org* ✑ *$6* ☉ *Tues.–Sat. 10–5, Sun. noon–5.*

Fodor'sChoice
★

Greater Charlotte

Farther afield lie many of Charlotte's most interesting sights, from gardens to museums. You can reach the ones listed below by car or by city bus; for visits elsewhere a car is essential.

What to See

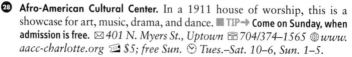

28 Afro-American Cultural Center. In a 1911 house of worship, this is a showcase for art, music, drama, and dance. ■ TIP→ **Come on Sunday, when admission is free.** ⊠ *401 N. Myers St., Uptown* ☎ *704/374–1565* ⊕ *www. aacc-charlotte.org* 🗐 *$5; free Sun.* ⊙ *Tues.–Sat. 10–6, Sun. 1–5.*

31 Charlotte Museum of History. Built in 1774, this stone building is the oldest dwelling in the county. Hezekiah Alexander and his wife, Mary, reared 10 children in this house and farmed the land. Seasonal events commemorate the early days. Permanent and rotating exhibits in the museum span 300 years of southern Piedmont history. ■ TIP→ **Admission is free on Sunday.** ⊠ *3500 Shamrock Dr., East Charlotte/Merchandise Mart* ☎ *704/568–1774* ⊕ *www.charlottemuseum.org* 🗐 *Tues.–Sat. $6; Sun. free* ⊙ *Tues.–Sat. 10–5, Sun. 1–5.*

29 Charlotte Nature Museum. You'll find a butterfly pavilion, bugs galore, live animals, nature trails, a puppet theater, and hands-on exhibits just for children at this museum affiliated with Discovery Place. ⊠ *1658 Sterling Ave., next to Freedom Park, Uptown* ☎ *704/372–0471* ⊕ *www. discoveryplace.org* 🗐 *$4* ⊙ *Weekdays 9–5, Sat. 10–5, Sun. 1–5.*

★ **32 Mint Museum of Art.** Built in 1836 as the first U.S. Mint, this building has been a home for art since 1936. Among the holdings in its impressive permanent collections are American and European paintings, furniture, and decorative arts; African, pre-Columbian, and Spanish-colonial art; porcelain and pottery; and regional crafts and historic costumes. ■ TIP→ **Your ticket stub gets you free admission to downtown's Mint Museum of Craft + Design.** ⊠ *2730 Randolph Rd., East Charlotte/Merchandise Mart* ☎ *704/337–2000* ⊕ *www.mintmuseum.org* 🗐 *$6* ⊙ *Tues. 10–10, Wed.–Sat. 10–5, Sun. noon–5.*

30 North Davidson Arts District. Charlotte's answer to SoHo or TriBeCa is NoDa, a neighborhood as funky as Uptown is elegant. Creative energy flows through the reclaimed textile mill and mill houses, cottages, and commercial spaces of this north Charlotte neighborhood where you'll find both the kooky and the conformist—artists, musicians, and dancers; street vendors; and restaurateurs—sharing space.

A 1945 movie palace called the Astor Theater has been given new life as the 700-seat **Neighborhood Theatre** (⊠ 511 E. 36th St. ☎ 704/358–9298 ⊕ www.neighborhoodtheatre.com), hosting concerts by the likes of Johnny Winter, Little Feat, and the Nitty Gritty Dirt Band.

On the first and third Friday of every month, an evening "gallery crawl" is held from 6 to 9:30 through the exhibition spaces of NoDa. The **Center of the Earth Gallery** (⊠ 3204 N. Davidson St. ☎ 704/375–5756 ⊕ www.centeroftheearth.com), displays contemporary art from 50 regional and national painters, sculptors, and craftspeople.

The **Smelly Cat Coffeehouse** (⊠ 514 E. 36th St. ☎ 704/374–9656) is a tiny place with a big choice of pastries. The **Dog Bar** (⊠ 3307 N. Davidson St. ☎ 704/370–3595) is a neighborhood tavern where pooches are welcome (and their birthdays are celebrated). Live music plays five

nights a week in the **Evening Muse** (✉ 3227 N. Davidson St. ☎ 704/
376–3737 ⊕ www.theeveningmuse.com).

Other Area Attractions

Historic sites, a speedway, and a theme park provide plenty to explore
beyond the city.

③④ James K. Polk Memorial. A state historic site 10 mi south of Charlotte
marks the humble birthplace and childhood home of the 11th U.S. president. Guided tours of the log cabins (replicas of the originals) show what
life was like for settlers back in 1795. ✉ *12031 Lancaster Hwy., Pineville*
☎ *704/889–7145* ⊕ *www.ah.dcr.state.nc.us* ✎ *Free* ☉ *Apr.–Oct.,*
Tues.–Sat. 9–5; Nov.–Mar., Tues.–Sat. 10–5.

③③ Carolinas Aviation Museum. At the Charlotte-Douglas International Airport, the museum has a collection of 45 major aircraft, including an A-
26C Invader and a F-14D Super TomCat. ✉ *4108 Airport Dr.* ☎ *704/*
359–8442 ⊕ *www.carolinasaviation.org* ✎ *$5* ☉ *Tues.–Fri. 10–4, Sat.*
10–5, Sun. 1–5.

③⑦ Lowe's Motor Speedway. This state-of-the-art facility, holding 167,000
fans, is considered the heart of NASCAR. An estimated 90% of driving teams live within 50 mi. Hosting more than 350 events each year,
this is one of the busiest sports venues in the United States. Racing season runs April to November. The Speedway Club, an upscale restaurant, is on the premises. ■ TIP➜ When there's a race, the population of Concord
can jump from 60,000 to more than 250,000. Make sure you book your lodging well in advance. ✉ *5555 Concord Pkwy. S, northeast of Charlotte,*
Concord ☎ *704/455–3200 or 800/455–3267* ⊕ *www.*
lowesmotorspeedway.com.

If you want to indulge the driver in you, you can take lessons through
the **Richard Petty Driving Experience** (☎ 704/455–9443
⊕ www.1800bepetty.com). Classes are available throughout the year,
though only when there's no event at Lowe's Motor Speedway. Prices
vary, but start at $400 for eight laps around the track.

☾ ③⑤ Paramount's Carowinds. This 100-acre amusement park, 15 mi from
Charlotte, has dozens of rides and attractions. Costumed movie and TV
characters greet visitors, and the Palladium stages musical concerts with
star entertainers. ✉ *14523 Carowinds Blvd., off I-77 at Carowinds Blvd.,*
South Charlotte/Pineville ☎ *704/588–2600 or 800/888–4386* ⊕ *www.*
carowinds.com ✎ *$50* ☉ *Late Mar.–May and mid-Aug.–early Oct., week-*
ends; June–mid-Aug., daily. Park opens at 9; closing hrs vary.

☾ ③⑥ Reed Gold Mine State Historic Site. This historic site, about 22 mi east of
Charlotte, is where America's first documented gold rush began, following Conrad Reed's discovery of a 17-pound nugget in 1799. Forty-minute
guided underground tours of the gold mine are available, as well as seasonal gold panning, walking trails, and a stamp mill. ✉ *9621 Reed Mine*
Rd., north of Rte. 24/27, Midland ☎ *704/721–4653* ⊕ *www.reedmine.*
com ✎ *Free* ☉ *Apr.–Oct., Tues.–Sat. 9–5; Nov.–Mar., Tues.–Sat. 10–4.*

Sports & the Outdoors

Auto Racing

NASCAR races, such as May's Coca-Cola 600, draw huge crowds at the **Lowe's Motor Speedway** (✉ 5555 Concord Pkwy. S, northeast of Charlotte, Concord ☎ 704/455–3200 or 800/455–3267 ⊕ www. lowesmotorspeedway.com).

Boating

Inlets on Lake Norman are ideal for canoeing. You can rent canoes, rowboats, and paddleboats for $3 to $5 an hour from the **North Carolina Division of Parks and Recreation** (☎ 704/528–6350 ⊕ www.ils.unc.edu/ parkproject/visit/lano/do.html).

Fishing

You can find good fishing in Charlotte's neighboring lakes and streams. A license can be bought at local bait-and-tackle shops or over the phone from the **North Carolina Wildlife Commission** (☎ 888/248–6834 ⊕ www. ncwildlife.org). A one-day, out-of-state license is $10, or $20 if you want to fish for mountain trout. Game fish in Lake Norman waters include crappie, bluegill, and yellow perch, as well as striped, largemouth, and white bass.

Football

The National Football League's **Carolina Panthers** (✉ 800 S. Mint St., Airport/Coliseum ☎ 704/358–7800 ⊕ www.panthers.com) play from August through December—and hopefully into the post-season playoffs as well—in the 73,000-seat Ericsson Stadium.

Golf

Larkhaven Golf Club. The oldest public course in Charlotte, Larkhaven opened in 1958. Mature trees have narrowed the fairways, and there's a 60-foot elevation drop on hole 9, a par 3. ✉ *4801 Camp Stewart Rd.* ☎ *704/545–4653* 🖷 *704/573–0030* ⊕ *www.larkhavengolf.com* ⅃. *18 holes. 6328 yds. Par 72. Green Fee: $30–$42* ☞ *Facilities: Golf carts, pro shop.*

Paradise Valley Golf Center. This short course is perfect for players without much time, as a round usually takes just an hour. But don't let that fool you: this course can challenge the best of them. Unique elements include two island tees. There's also a miniature golf course called the Lost Duffer set in a 19th-century mining town. ✉ *110 Barton Creek Dr.* ☎ *704/548–1808* 🖷 *704/548–9283* ⊕ *www.charlottepublicgolf.com/ paradisevalley.html* ⅃. *18 holes. 1264 yds. Par 54. Green Fee: $7–$16* ☞ *Facilities: Golf carts.*

Woodbridge Golf Links. This semiprivate course is lovely to look at and challenging to play. You have to be careful with the water hazards; there are water features on 13 holes. ✉ *7001 Highland Creek Pkwy.* ☎ *704/ 875–9000* 🖷 *704/882–8571* ⊕ *www.highlandcreekgolfclub.com* ⅃. *18 holes. 6520 yds. Par 72. Green Fee: $50–$65* ☞ *Facilities: Driving range, putting green, golf carts, pro shop, restaurant, bar.*

Where to Eat

$$$$ ✕ **Bentley's on 27th.** Where to look? To one side is the city skyline, viewed from the 27th floor. To the other is the impressive display at the *gueridon*, a French cooking cart. The food itself is elegant in its simplicity: a salad of baby greens, shallots, pearl tomatoes, and a champagne vinaigrette dressing, for instance, or a filet mignon with grilled asparagus, baby carrots, roasted pears, and blue-cheese risotto. You'd close your eyes to savor the taste, but then you'd miss the view. ⊠ *Charlotte Plaza, 201 S. College St., Uptown* ☎ *704/343–9201* ▤ *AE, MC, V.*

$$–$$$$ ✕ **Latorre's.** The emphasis at this downtown eatery is on the heat, color, and flavor of Latin America Art splashed with vibrant shades of mango, lemon, and papaya complement exposed-brick walls and hardwood floors. Live salsa and merengue is the perfect backdrop for the likes of orange-and-cumin-encrusted salmon over black-bean rice cakes, and tender grilled *chimichurri* (a piquant Argentinian herb sauce) flank steak served with tortillas and three salsas. On weekends the place is open for dancing until 2:30 AM. ⊠ *118 W. 5th St., Uptown* ☎ *704/377–4448* ▤ *AE, MC, V* ⊙ *Closed Sun.*

$–$$$$ ✕ **Providence Café.** The signature purple awnings lead you to this lively café. New dishes, many with subtle Asian influences, are introduced every spring and fall, but the menu always includes options for meat eaters as well as vegetarian. Delicious focaccia is baked daily on the premises. It's a great place for Sunday brunch, and on Wednesday and Thursday evening there's often live jazz. ⊠ *110 Perrin Pl., South Park* ☎ *704/ 376–2008* ⊕ *www.providencecafe.com* ▤ *AE, MC, V.*

$$–$$$ ✕ **Campania.** This Italian eatery is so authentic that you might be
Fodor'sChoice   tempted to take along your Italian–English dictionary to help with the
★   menu. The food is as good as it gets outside southern Italy. Try the excellent shrimp sautéed in garlic butter and herbs, smoked salmon with a cognac-tomato-cream sauce, or the veal chops. Golden textured walls, richly toned wood, and lots of candlelight define the dining room. ⊠ *6414 Rea Rd., South Park* ☎ *704/541–8505* ▤ *AE, D, MC, V* ⊙ *No dinner Sun.*

★ **$–$$$**   ✕ **300 East.** The gentrified neighborhood in which this casual spot resides doesn't lack for charming older houses. Even so, 300 East makes its mark, and not just because of its brightly hued signage. The bold contemporary menu—pork tenderloin with banana-mango salsa and saffron rice, for instance, or penne with duck and lobster—attracts a hip and eclectic bunch. Choose a table in one of the private dining nooks and crannies, or outside on the open-air patio. Here, people-watching is as much fun as eating. ⊠ *300 East Blvd., South Park* ☎ *704/332– 6507* ▤ *AE, D, MC, V.*

$–$$ ✕ **Landmark Diner.** This spacious and informal diner is a cut above most other inexpensive restaurants, and it's open until 3 AM on weeknights and 24 hours on weekends. The chef's salad with grilled chicken is a must, as is chicken sorrento made with sautéed artichokes, spinach, and sun-dried tomatoes. For dessert there's chocolate-cream pie. ⊠ *4429 Central Ave., East Charlotte/Merchandise Mart* ☎ *704/532–1153* ▤ *AE, MC, V.*

$–$$ ✕ **Mert's Heart and Soul.** Talk about the New South. Business executives

Fodor'sChoice and arts patrons make their way to Mert's—named for Myrtle, a fa-

★ vorite customer with a sunny disposition. Owners James and Renee
Bezzelle serve large portions of Low Country and Gullah staples, such
as fried chicken with greens, macaroni and cheese, and corn bread. Lowcountry specialties include shrimp-and-salmon omelets and red beans
and rice. ⊠ *214 N. College St., Uptown* ☎ *704/342–4222* ▤ *AE, MC,
V* ⊗ *No dinner Mon. and Tues.*

¢–$ ✕ **College Place.** Expect simple down-home cooking—and plenty of it—
at this cafeteria. At breakfast or lunch you'll have to work hard to spend
more than $5. The big breakfasts include any combination of eggs, pan-
cakes, grits, bacon, and sausage. Lunch has lots of vegetable dishes, homemade corn bread, and a soup-and-salad bar. ⊠ *300 S. College St., Uptown*
☎ *704/343–9268* ▤ *No credit cards* ⊗ *Closed weekends. No dinner.*

Where to Stay

$$$–$$$$ ⬚ **Ballantyne Resort Hotel.** Nestled on 2,000 acres, Ballantyne is a stately
structure, with towering two-story window in the lobby that make a
strong impression. Even if you check-in expecting a vacation filled with
golf and tennis, you might find you can barely budge from the spa. The
spacious guest rooms have classic furniture and color schemes of gold,
cream, and sage. You can choose a sunset view or golf view. The Lodge,
designed for corporate retreats, has a great room with a fireplace and
a porch with rocking chairs. ⊠ *10000 Ballantyne Commons Pkwy., South
Charlotte, 28277* ☎ *704/248–4000 or 866/248–4824* 🖶 *704/248–
4005* ⊕ *www.ballantyneresort.com* ⌖ *200 rooms, 2 restau-
rants, room service, in-room safes, minibars, cable TV with video games,
in-room broadband, in-room data ports, Wi-Fi, 18-hole golf course, pro
shop, pool, health club, spa, 3 tennis courts, basketball court, bar,
concierge, dry-cleaning, laundry services, business services, meeting
rooms* ▤ *AE, D, MC, V* ⦿ *EP.*

$$–$$$ ⬚ **Hyatt Charlotte at SouthPark.** The focal point of this hotel's four-story
atrium is a fountain surrounded by 25-foot-tall olive trees. The guest
rooms show a Mediterranean influence, with soothing earth tones and
lots of greenery. Scalini, the restaurant, serves northern Italian cuisine;
the Club piano bar is a favorite. The hotel lies within walking distance
of the upscale South Park Mall. ⊠ *5501 Carnegie Blvd., South Park,
28209* ☎ *704/554–1234 or 800/233–1234* 🖶 *704/554–8319* ⊕ *www.
hyatt.com* ⌖ *258 rooms, 4 suites* ⦿ *Restaurant, room service, refrig-
erators, cable TV, in-room broadband, Wi-Fi, indoor pool, health club,
hot tub, sauna, piano bar, business services* ▤ *AE, D, MC, V* ⦿ *EP.*

$$–$$$ ⬚ **Omni Charlotte Hotel.** This 16-story hotel is in the heart of downtown,
within walking distance of the convention center as well as many arts and
sports venues. An escalator whisks you to the OverStreet Mall, where you'll
find shops, restaurants, and a lounge. Many guest rooms have glass walls
overlooking the city skyline. Satin hangers and rainfall showers are among
the ways a guest feels pampered. You can also request a "Get Fit" room
with a portable treadmill. ⊠ *132 E. Trade St., Uptown, 28202* ☎ *704/
377–0400 or 800/843–6664* 🖶 *704/347–4835* ⊕ *www.omnicharlotte.com*

🖙 *374 rooms, 33 suites △ Restaurant, minibar, cable TV with movies, in-room broadband, Wi-Fi, pool, lounge, concierge, laundry services, business services, meeting rooms* ≡ *AE, D, MC, V* †◯| *BP.*

$–$$$ 🖭 **Hilton Charlotte Center City.** In the financial district, this hotel sits across the street from the Charlotte Convention Center. The wood-panel lobby, with marble floors and a sweeping staircase, is impressive. Guest rooms are large and comfortable, if unimaginatively decorated. Each has a nice view of the city. ⊠ *222 E. 3rd St., Uptown, 28202* ☎ *704/377–1500 or 800/445–8667* 🖷 *704/331–4319* ⊕ *www.charlottecentercity. hilton.com* 🖙 *407 rooms, 25 suites △ Room service, cable TV with movies and video games, in-room data ports, Wi-Fi, indoor pool, health club, dry cleaning, laundry service, bar, business services* ≡ *AE, D, MC, V* †◯| *BP.*

¢–$ 🖭 **Econo Lodge Lake Norman.** This motel for the budget-minded is north of Charlotte on Interstate 77, within 3 mi of Lake Norman and Davidson College. All rooms have refrigerators and coffeemakers, and a gym is right across the street. ⊠ *20740 Torrence Chapel Rd., Cornelius 28031* ☎ *704/892–3500 or 800/848–9751* 🖷 *704/892–6473* ⊕ *www. choicehotels.com* 🖙 *90 rooms △ Some microwaves, refrigerators, cable TV, Wi-Fi, pool, business services, meeting room* ≡ *AE, D, MC, V* †◯| *BP.*

¢ 🖭 **Sterling Inn.** This economy option has an upscale sensibility, with large and tasteful rooms with oversize beds and coffeemakers. The inn is near interstates 77 and 85. ⊠ *242 E. Woodlawn Rd., Airport/Coliseum, 28217* ☎ *704/525–5454* 🖷 *704/525–5637* 🖙 *100 rooms △ Refrigerators, health club, laundry service, meeting room, airport shuttle* ≡ *AE, D, MC, V* †◯| *BP.*

Bed-and-Breakfasts

$$–$$$ 🖭 **Morehead Inn.** Built in 1917, this grand colonial-revival home is in the Dilworth neighborhood. Wedding parties and family reunions frequently reserve the entire estate. Rooms are filled with period antiques, including several with impressive four-poster beds. ⊠ *1122 E. Morehead St., South Park, 28204* ☎ *704/376–3357 or 888/667–3432* 🖷 *704/ 335–1110* ⊕ *www.moreheadinn.com* 🖙 *12 rooms △ Room service, fans, cable TV, Wi-Fi, bicycles, meeting room* ≡ *AE, DC, MC, V* †◯| *BP.*

$$–$$$ 🖭 **The VanLandingham Estate Inn.** Built in 1913 as a private home in the historic Midwood neighborhood, this inn has earned a spot on the National Register of Historic Places. Period furnishings fill the rooms, which are spread among the main house—a California-style bungalow—and the nearby carriage house. Highlights of the estate include a solarium, library, and 4 acres of gardens. ⊠ *2010 The Plaza, South Park, 28205* ☎ *704/334–8909 or 888/524–2020* 🖷 *704/940–8830* ⊕ *www. vanlandinghamestate.com* 🖙 *9 rooms △ Room service, fans, some kitchenettes, cable TV, Wi-Fi, library, meeting room* ≡ *AE, D, MC, V* †◯| *BP.*

Camping

Lake Norman State Park (⊠ 159 Inland Sea La., Troutman ☎ 704/528–6350) is ideal for hiking and water sports. More than 30 sites have tent pads, picnic tables, and grills. Group camp sites for up to 25 people have picnic tables and a fire ring. Near Charlotte, 56 campsites for tents and RVs can be found at **McDowell Park and Nature Reserve** (⊠ 15222 York Rd., South Charlotte/Pineville ☎ 704/588–5224).

Nightlife & the Arts

The Arts

With the 2,100-seat Belk Theatre, the **North Carolina Blumenthal Performing Arts Center** (⊠ 130 N. Tryon St., Uptown ☎ 704/372–1000 ⊕ www.performingartsctr.org) houses several resident companies, such as the Charlotte Symphony Orchestra, North Carolina Dance Theatre, and Opera Carolina. At Paramount's Carowinds, the **Paladium Amphitheater** (⊠ 14523 Carowinds Blvd., South Charlotte/Pineville ☎ 704/588–2600 or 800/888–4386 ⊕ www.paramountparks.com) presents family-friendly acts spring to fall. The **Verizon Wireless Amphitheater** (⊠ 707 Pavilion Blvd., Speedway ☎ 704/549–5555 ⊕ www.verizonwirelessamphitheater.com) spotlights big-name concerts—Norah Jones, Tim McGraw, Melissa Etheridge—spring through fall.

Nightlife

The Big Chill (⊠ 911 E. Morehead St., Dilworth ☎ 704/347–4447) has a house band that plays music primarily from the '40s, '50s, and '60s every Friday and Saturday night. In business since 1973, the **Double Door Inn** (⊠ 218 E. Independence Blvd., Uptown ☎ 704/376–1446) is a staple of the national blues circuit. Eric Clapton, Junior Walker, and Stevie Ray Vaughn are among the legends who've played at this laid-back venue. **Ri Ra** (⊠ 208 N. Tryon St., Uptown ☎ 704/333–5554), Gaelic for "uproar," serves up traditional food, ale, and, on Thursday to Sunday night, live music.

Shopping

Charlotte is the largest retail center in the Carolinas. Most stores are in suburban malls; villages and towns in outlying areas have shops selling regional specialties.

Shopping Malls

Two-story **Carolina Place Mall** (⊠ 11025 Carolina Place Pkwy., off I–485, South Charlotte/Pineville ☎ 704/543–9300) is on the interstate. Destination shopping has been raised to an art form at **Concord Mills** (⊠ 8111 Concord Mills Blvd., off I–85, Concord ☎ 704/979–5000), which sells hundreds of brand names and discounted designer labels. Look for stores carrying Ralph Lauren, Louis Vitton, Burburry, and OshKosh B'Gosh. **SouthPark Mall** (⊠ 4400 Sharon Rd., South Park ☎ 704/364–4411) has such high-end stores as Tiffany & Co., Montblanc, Coach, and Godiva.

Specialty Stores

ANTIQUES The nearby towns of Waxhaw, Pineville, and Matthews are the best places to find antiques. Waxhaw sponsors an antiques fair each February. You can find a good selection of antiques and collectibles at the sprawling **Metrolina Expo** (⊠ 7100 N. Statesville Rd., off I–77, North Charlotte/Lake Norman ☎ 704/596–4643) on the first weekend of the month.

FOOD The **Charlotte Regional Farmers Market** (⊠ 1801 Yorkmount Rd., Airport/Coliseum ☎ 704/357–1269) sells produce, eggs, plants, and crafts.

THE SANDHILLS

Because of their sandy soil—they were once Atlantic beaches—the Sandhills weren't of much use to early farmers, most of whom switched to lumbering and making turpentine for a livelihood. Since the turn of the 20th century, however, this area, with its vast pine forests and lakes, has proved ideal for golf, tennis, and horse farms. A panel of experts assembled by *Golf Digest* magazine has named the region one of the top three golfing destinations in the world. First-class resorts are centered around the region's 40 championship golf courses, which have seen their share of PGA tournaments. Public and private tennis courts abound, and dozens of equestrian events are held each year, including professional steeplechase and harness racing.

The Highland Scots who settled the area left a rich heritage perpetuated through festivals and gatherings. In colonial times English potters were attracted to the rich clay deposits in the soil, and today their descendants and others turn out beautiful wares sold in more than 40 local shops.

Southern Pines

38 *104 mi east of Charlotte; 71 mi southwest of Raleigh.*

The center of the Sandhills, Southern Pines is a good place to begin exploring the region. The three-block Cameron Historical District, once the end of the line for the Raleigh-Augusta Railroad, is now a thriving antiques center. You'll find a dozen shops lining Carthage Street.

Sandhills Horticultural Gardens has a wetland area that can be observed from elevated boardwalks. It's part of a 32-acre series of gardens showcasing roses, fruits and vegetables, herbs, conifers, hollies, a formal English garden, pools, and a waterfall. ⊠ *Sandhills Community College, 2200 Airport Rd., Pinehurst* ☏ *910/695–3964 or 800/338–3944* ⊕ *www.sandhills.cc.nc.us/lsg/hort.html* ⊠ *Free* ☉ *Daily sunrise–sunset.*

OFF THE BEATEN PATH

HOUSE IN THE HORSESHOE – The two-story 1772 home 10 mi from Carthage earned its name because it was built in a bend of Deep River, the cotton plantation home of Gov. Benjamin Williams. It survived the Revolutionary War unscathed, but in 1781 David Fanning's Tories defeated Philip Alston's Whigs in the colonial era's equivalent of a hail of gunfire, and you can still view the bullet holes from the skirmish today. ⊠ *324 Alston House Rd., Sanford* ☏ *910/947–2051* ⊠ *Free* ☉ *Apr.–Oct., Tues.–Sat. 9–5, Sun. 1–5; Nov.–Mar., Tues.–Sat. 10–4, Sun. 1–4.*

The 1820 **Shaw House** is typical of the sturdy homes built by the Scottish families who settled the region. It serves as headquarters for the Moore County Historical Association. Two other restored cabins, both of which date to the 1700s, help illustrate the lives of early settlers. ⊠ *S. W. Broad St. and Morganton Rd.* ☏ *910/692–2051* ⊕ *www.moorehistory.com* ⊠ *Free* ☉ *Tues.–Fri. 1–4.*

Weymouth Woods Sandhills Nature Preserve, on the eastern outskirts of town, is a 900-acre wildlife preserve with 4 mi of hiking trails. A staff naturalist will answer your questions about the beaver pond and other interesting sights. ✉ *1024 N. Fort Bragg Rd., off U.S. 1* ☎ *910/692–2167* ⊕ *www.ncparks.net* ✉ *Free* ☉ *Apr.–Oct., daily 8–7; Nov.–Mar., daily 8–6.*

OFF THE
BEATEN
PATH

CAMERON – The town of Cameron, with a historic district on the National Register of Historic Places, has pockets that haven't changed all that much since the 19th century. This is the place to shop for antiques: approximately 60 antiques

> ### ANTS IN YOUR PANTS?
>
> In the past several years a type of fire ant from Brazil has moved into this part of North Carolina. These vicious insects swarm when disturbed, then bite their victims before stinging them repeatedly. The bites burn terribly, and can raise a small white blister within six hours. If you're sensitive to bee stings, be extra vigilant.

dealers operate out of several stores. Most shops are open Tuesday through Saturday 10 to 5, Sunday 1 to 5. Another draw is a collection of barns, farm equipment, and tractor-trailers whimsically painted by the Barnstormers, an artists' collective led by David Ellis, a native of Cameron now living in New York City. Most of the murals can be found along Route 24. ✉ *Off U.S. 1, 12 mi north of Southern Pines* ☎ *910/ 245–7001 for information on antiques shops.*

Where to Stay & Eat

$$$–$$$$ ✕ **Lob Steer Inn.** Salad and dessert bars complement generous broiled seafood and prime-rib dinners at this casual, dimly lighted steak house. As you'd expect from the name, the surf and turf is a good bet. ✉ *U.S. 1* ☎ *910/ 692–3503* ⚅ *Reservations essential* ▭ *AE, MC, V* ☉ *No lunch.*

¢–$ ✕ **Sweet Basil.** This cozy corner café is run by a family whose considerable expertise is plain to see: lots of homemade breads, hefty loaded sandwiches, and lush salads. Special treats are the soups—especially the flavorful ginger-carrot and red-pepper varieties—and decadent desserts. ■ TIP➜ Make sure to arrive early to avoid the lunch rush. ✉ *134 N.W. Broad St.* ☎ *910/693–1487* ▭ *MC, V* ☉ *Closed Sun. No dinner.*

$$$$ ▦ **Pine Needles Lodge & Golf Club.** One of the bonuses of staying at this resort is the chance to meet Peggy Kirk Bell, a champion golfer who built the place with her late husband. The club, known for its excellent golf course, has hosted the U.S. Women's Open. The rooms are done in a rustic chalet style; many have exposed beams, pine paneling, and fireplaces. Private lodges with four bedrooms are great for families. ✉ *1005 Midland Rd., 28387* ☎ *910/692–7111 or 800/747–7272* 🖷 *910/692– 5349* ⊕ *www.pineneedles-midpines.com* ➥ *78 rooms* ⚅ *Restaurant, cable TV, in-room data ports, driving range, 18-hole golf course, putting green, pool, gym, 2 tennis courts, bicycles, bar, business services, meeting room, airport shuttle* ▭ *AE, MC, V* ⦿ *FAP.*

$$ ▦ **Mid Pines Inn & Golf Club.** In a building dating from 1921, this resort is the sibling of Pine Needles Lodge. On the premises is a Georgian-style clubhouse and a golf course designed by Donald Ross that has hosted numerous tournaments. The spacious rooms are done up in Wedgwood blue and are filled with authentic antiques and good copies. Seven private villas with kitchenettes are also available. ✉ *1010 Midland Rd.,*

28387 ☎ *910/692–2114 or 800/323–2114* 🖶 *910/692–4615* ⊕ *www. pineneedles-midpines.com* 🛏 *112 rooms, 7 villas* ⚴ *Restaurants, cable TV, in-room data ports, 18-hole golf course, putting green, pool, gym, 4 tennis courts, bar, game room, business services, meeting room, airport shuttle* ▭ *AE, D, MC, V* 🍽 *FAP.*

Sports & the Outdoors

GOLF **Club at Longleaf.** Photos from 30 years ago reveal how this golf course was built on the site of a steeplechase. Some elements of the horse track still can be spotted on holes 1, 8, and 9. ✉ *19 N. Knoll Rd.* ☎ *910/ 692–6100* ⊕ *www.longleafgolf.com* 🏌 *18 holes. 6098 yds. Par 71. Green Fee: $39–$90* 🖙 *Facilities: Driving range, putting green, pitching area, golf carts, pro shop, restaurant.*

Mid Pines Golf Club. This course, designed in 1921 by Donald Ross, has been completely restored. This course is shorter than at the Pine Needles Golf Club, but its hillier terrain means it provides an ample challenge. ✉ *1010 Midland Rd.* ☎ *910/692–2114 or 800/323–2114* 🖶 *910/ 692–4615* ⊕ *www.pineneedles-midpines.com* 🏌 *18 holes. 6528 yds. Par 71. Green Fee: $105–$175* 🖙 *Facilities: Driving range, putting green, pitching area, golf carts, rental clubs, pro shop, golf academy/lessons, restaurant, bar.*

Pine Needles Golf Club. Following a recent renovation, the greens here have returned to their original long lines. The par-5 hole 10 presents a particular challenge, with a sand trap along the inside curve of a dogleg. ✉ *1005 Midland Rd.* ☎ *910/692–7111 or 800/747–7272* 🖶 *910/ 692–5349* ⊕ *www.pineneedles-midpines.com* 🏌 *18 holes. 3222 yds. Par 71. Green Fee: $65–$175* 🖙 *Facilities: Driving range, putting green, pitching area, golf carts, pull carts, pro shop, golf academy/lessons, restaurant, bar.*

Talamore at Pinehurst. Now you can answer that age-old question, "Do llamas make good caddies?" The answer, as even the lowliest duffer at this course knows, is yes. They won't cough when you're putting, either. Architect Rees Jones probably didn't predict the presense of llamas here, but since their feet don't harm the grass, he probably wishes someone had thought of it sooner. ✉ *1595 Midland Rd.* ☎ *910/692– 5884 or 800/552–6292* 🖶 *910/692–4421* ⊕ *www.pinehurstgolf.com* 🏌 *18 holes. 3534 yds. Par 71. Green Fee: $50–$100* 🖙 *Facilities: Driving range, rental clubs, rental carts, restaurant.*

Shopping

Regional authors read from their works at the **Country Bookshop** (✉ 140 N.W. Broad St. ☎ 910/692–3211). The store, in the historic downtown district, stocks a lot of everything, including children's books and classical and jazz CDs.

Pinehurst

❸❾ *6 mi west of Southern Pines.*

Pinehurst is a New England–style village with quiet, shaded streets and immaculately kept homes ranging from massive Victorians to tiny cot-

2

tages. It was laid out in the late 1800s in a wagon-wheel pattern by landscape genius Frederick Law Olmsted, who also designed New York City's Central Park. Annie Oakley lived here for a number of years, and while she was here headed the local gun club. Today Pinehurst is renowned for its golf courses.

The **Tufts Archives** recount the founding of Pinehurst in the letters, pictures, and news clippings, dating from 1895, of James Walker Tufts, who once served as president of the United States Golf Association. Pinehurst owes its origins to Tuft, who chose this area to build a health resort. ⊠ *Given Memorial Library, 150 Cherokee Rd.* ☎ *910/295–6022 or 910/ 295–3642* 🖃 *Free* ☉ *Weekdays 9:30–5, Sat. 9:30–12:30.*

Where to Stay & Eat

$$–$$$ ✕ **Theo's Taverna.** Behind some shops facing Chinquapin Road you'll find this authentic taverna. It's as sunny as the Greek countryside from which owner Elias Dalitsouris hails. Fresh flowers, brightly colored artwork, vaulted ceilings, lots of windows, and outdoor seating on a garden patio draw diners; the made-from-scratch food, including breads and desserts, keeps them coming back. The seafood and lamb are the specialties of the house. Wash it all down with strong Greek coffee served in traditional small cups. ⊠ *140 Chinquapin Rd.* ☎ *910/295–0780* 🖃 *MC, V* ☉ *Closed Sun.*

¢ ✕ **Players Café.** This casual spot is *the* place to meet for soups, sandwiches, and pizza. It's in the shop-filled Theater Building in the heart of the village. ⊠ *100 W. Village Green* ☎ *910/295–8873* 🚗 *Reservations not accepted* 🖃 *No credit cards* ☉ *Closed Sun. No dinner.*

$$$$ ✕🏨 **The Carolina.** In business since 1901, this stately hotel has never lost
Fodor'sChoice its turn-of-the-20th-century charm. Civilized pleasures await in the spa-
★ cious public rooms and elegantly traditional accommodations, on the rocker-lined wide verandas, and amid the gardens. You can tee off on one of eight golf courses or relax in the spa, with warm, dark wood accented by a moss-green-and-cream color scheme. The 45-room Manor Inn has the feel of a B&B; guests have access to all the resort facilities, including the formal Carolina Dining Room, with an eclectic menu. ⊠ *1 Carolina Vista Dr., 28374* ☎ *910/295–6811 or 800/487–4653* 🖷 *910/ 295–8503* ⊕ *www.pinehurst.com* 🛏 *222 rooms, 130 condos* 🔷 *2 restaurants, room service, cable TV, in-room braodband, Wi-Fi, 8 18-hole golf courses, 5 pools, health club, massage, spa, 24 tennis courts, windsurfing, boating, fishing, bicycles, croquet, bar, children's programs (ages 3–12), concierge, business services, meeting room* 🖃 *AE, D, MC, V.*

$$$$ ✕🏨 **The Holly Inn.** The first in the village, the Holly has crown molding, elegant lighting, and other architectural features that recall the 1890s. Luxuries include silk-covered hangers, embroidered robes, and afternoon sandwiches, cookies, and iced tea. The prix-fixe menu at the 1895 Grille, the bistro-style restaurant, changes seasonally. Inventive entrées include pinecone-smoked free-range chicken with truffles, tarragon-scented roast tenderloin of veal, and Carolina blue-crab hash. Jackets are required at the restaurant. The more casual Tavern has a pub atmosphere. ⊠ *Cherokee Rd., 28374* ☎ *910/295–6811 or 800/487–*

4653 🖨 *910/295–8503* ⊕ *www.pinehurst.com* 🛏 *78 rooms, 7 suites* ⚴ *Restaurants, room service, cable TV, Wi-Fi, 8 18-hole golf courses, pool, 24 tennis courts, croquet, bar, concierge, library, business services, meeting room* ▭ *AE, MC, V* ⵏⵓⵍ *MAP.*

$ 🏨 **Magnolia Inn.** This 110-year-old inn, once just a hangout for golfing buddies, now draws a more diverse crowd after being tastefully decorated with unusual antiques. Most guest rooms are Victorian style with wicker and brass beds; bathrooms have original fixtures such as clawfoot tubs. The inn's dining rooms, with their dusty-rose wallpaper and fireplaces, are cozy. The regional menu includes Magnolia duck breast and leg of duck with a pear, sweet-potato, and wild-cherry glaze. There's also an English-style pub. ⊠ *Magnolia and Chinquapin Rds., Box 818, 28370* ☎ *910/295–6900 or 800/526–5562* 🖨 *910/215–0858* ⊕ *www. themagnoliainn.com* 🛏 *11 rooms* ⚴ *Restaurant, pool, business services* ▭ *AE, MC, V* ⵏⵓⵍ *BP.*

¢–$ 🏨 **Pine Crest Inn.** Chintz and mahogany fill the rooms of this slightly faded gem. The chefs whip up meals reminiscent of Sunday supper: homemade soups, fresh fish dishes, and the house specialty, stuffed pork chops. Mr. B's Lounge is one of the liveliest nightspots in town. Guests have golf and tennis privileges at local clubs. ⊠ *50 Dogwood Rd., Box 879, 28370* ☎ *910/295–6121 or 800/371–2545* 🖨 *910/295–4880* ⊕ *www. pinecrestinnpinehurst.com* 🛏 *40 rooms* ⚴ *Dining room, cable TV, golf privileges, bar* ▭ *AE, D, MC, V* ⵏⵓⵍ *MAP.*

Sports & the Outdoors

GOLF **Pinehurst Resort.** Pinehurst has been the site of more championships than any other golf resort in the country. The eight courses—unfortunately known by their numbers—can bring a tear to a golfer's eye with their beauty. The courses range from the first, designed in 1898 by Donald Ross, to the most recent, designed in 1996 by Tom Fazio to mark the resort's centennial. The hilly terrain of Course Seven, completely renovated in 2003, makes it especially tough. ⊠ *1 Carolina Vista Dr.* ☎ *910/ 235–8125 or 800/487–4653* ⊕ *www.pinehurst.com* 🏌 *8 18-hole courses. Average of 6600 yds. Par 70–72. Green Fee: $78–$310* ⚲ *Facilities: Driving range, putting green, pitching area, golf carts, pull carts, caddies, rental clubs, pro shop, golf academy/lessons, restaurant, bar.*

Pit Golf Links. Designed by Pinehurst native Dan F. Maples, this course runs through 230 acres of an abandoned sand quarry. ⊠ *1 Carolina Vista Dr.* ☎ *910/944–1600 or 800/574–4653* 🖨 *910/944–7069* ⊕ *www. pitgolf.com* 🏌 *18 holes. 6600 yds. Par 71. Green Fee: $54–$109* ⚲ *Facilities: Driving range, putting green, pitching area, golf carts, pro shop, golf academy/lessons, restaurant, bar.*

HORSEBACK **McClendon Hills Equestrian Center** (⊠ Hwy. 211, West End ☎ 910/673–
RIDING 4971) offers horseback riding for those over eight years old. Riding lessons are available.

TENNIS The **Lawn and Tennis Club of North Carolina** (⊠ 1 Merrywood ☎ 910/ 692–7270) has seven courts and a swimming pool.

Aberdeen

40 *5 mi southeast of Pinehurst; 5 mi southwest of Southern Pines.*

Aberdeen, a small town of Scottish ancestry, has a beautifully restored early-20th-century train station and plenty of shops with antiques and collectibles.

East of town, the **Bethesda Presbyterian Church** was founded in 1790. The present wooden structure, often used for weddings and other festive events, was built in the 1860s. It has preserved its slave gallery as well as exterior bullet holes from a Civil War battle. The cemetery, where many early settlers are buried, is always open. ⊠ *1002 N. Sandhills Blvd.* ☎ *910/ 944–1319* ⊕ *bethesdapres.net.*

Malcolm Blue Farm, one of the few remaining examples of the 19th-century Scottish homes that once dotted the area, has farm buildings and an old gristmill. Things are especially festive in September, when an annual celebration recalls life here in the 1800s. The farm is part of the North Carolina Civil War Theme Trail. ⊠ *Bethesda Rd. at E. L. Ives Dr.* ☎ *910/944–7558* ⊕ *www.malcolmbluefarm.org* ⊠ *Free* ☉ *Wed.–Sat. 1–4.*

OFF THE BEATEN PATH

AIRBORNE AND SPECIAL OPERATIONS MUSEUM – The story of the fabled airborne and special-ops units is told through film and video, interactive displays, walk-through dioramas, and rare artifacts. ⊠ *100 Bragg Blvd., Fayetteville* ☎ *910/483–3003* ⊕ *www.asomf.org* ⊠ *Free* ☉ *Tues.–Sat. 10–5, Sun. noon–5.*

Where to Stay

$–$$ 🏠 **Inn at Bryant House.** One block east of U.S. 1, this charming B&B was originally built in 1913. All the guest rooms are individually decorated; some have romantic canopy beds. The inn has golf packages and can arrange tennis and horseback riding. ⊠ *214 N. Poplar St., 28315* ☎ *910/944–3300 or 800/453–4019* 🖶 *910/944–8898* ⊕ *www. innatbryanthouse.com* ⇨ *9 rooms, 7 with bath* ♿ *Picnic area, business services* ⊟ *AE, D, MC, V* ⊚| *BP.*

Sports & the Outdoors

GOLF **Legacy Golf Links.** Proving that the golf ball doesn't fall far from the tee, this public course was designed by Jack Nicklaus Jr. The last hole, nicknamed "The Bear," is 479-yard monster. ⊠ *Legacy Dr. at U.S. 15/501* ☎ *910/944–8825 or 800/344–8825* 🖶 *910/944–9416* ⊕ *www. legacypinehurst.com* 🏌 *18 holes. 6495 yds. Par 72. Green Fee: $49–$99* ☞ *Facilities: Driving range, 2 putting greens, pitching area, golf carts, rental clubs, pro shop, golf academy/lessons.*

Seagrove

★ **41** *40 mi northwest of Aberdeen; 35 mi northwest of Pinehurst.*

Potters, some of whom are carrying on traditions that have been in their families for generations and others who are newer to the art, handcraft mugs, bowls, pitchers, platters, vases, and clay "face jugs" in the Seagrove area. Some of the work of local artisans is exhibited in national museums, including the Smithsonian. More than 90 potteries are scattered along and off Route 705 and U.S. 220. The annual Seagrove Pottery Festival, held in November, is always a much anticipated event.

★ The **North Carolina Pottery Center** exhibits pottery from all around the state. You can pick up maps of the various studios around the area. ⊠ *250 East Ave.* ☎ *336/873–8430* ⊕ *www.ncpotterycenter.com* ☜ *$3* ⊘ *Tues.–Sat. 10–4.*

Asheboro

⓬ *13 mi north of Seagrove; 23 mi south of Greensboro.*

Asheboro, the seat of Randolph County, sits in the Uwharrie National Forest, which is popular with those who like hiking, biking, and horseback riding. At 500 million years old, the Uwharries are the oldest mountain range in North America. This part of the southern Piedmont is a lovely place to view scenery and visit crafts shops.

★ ⌾ The 1,500-acre **North Carolina Zoological Park,** home to more than 1,100 animals, was the first zoo in the country designed from the get-go as a natural-habitat facility. The park includes the 300-acre African pavilion, a Sonoran Desert habitat, a 200-acre North American habitat with polar bears and sea lions, and an Australian "walkabout." ■ TIP→ **This is a massive park, so take advantage of the tram that connects the various areas.** ⊠ *4401 Zoo Pkwy.* ☎ *336/879–7000 or 800/488–0444* ⊕ *www.nczoo. org* ☜ *$10* ⊘ *Apr.–Sept., daily 9–5; Oct.–Mar., daily 9–4.*

OFF THE BEATEN PATH

TOWN CREEK INDIAN MOUND HISTORIC SITE – About 30 mi south of Asheboro, this historic site is a glimpse into North Carolina's pre-Columbian past. A self-guided tour takes you through reconstructions of buildings that belonged to the Pee Dee people. Excavations of the site began in 1937 and are still in progress. ⊠ *509 Town Creek Mound Rd., Mt. Gilead* ☎ *910/439–6802* ⊕ *www.ah.dcr.state.nc.us* ☜ *Free* ⊘ *Tues.–Sat. 10–4, Sun. 1–4.*

THE PIEDMONT & THE SANDHILLS ESSENTIALS

Transportation

BY AIR

The Raleigh-Durham International Airport, off Interstate 40 between the two cities, is served by most major airlines. RDU Airport Taxi Service provides taxi service from the airport.

Charlotte-Douglas International Airport, served by most major airlines, is west of Charlotte off Interstate 85. From the airport, taxis charge a set fee to designated zones. From the airport to most destinations in Charlotte the cost is $15 to $20 (plus $2 for each additional passenger). Airport vans are approximately $8 per person.

Just west of Greensboro, the Piedmont Triad International Airport is off Route 68 north from Interstate 40; it's served by American Eagle,

Continental Express, Delta, Northwest, United, and US Airways. Taxi service to and from Piedmont Triad International Airport is provided by Prime Time Airport Shuttle.

Moore County Airport, based in the Southern Pines community of the Sandhills, serves only private aircraft.

🖪 Airport Information **Charlotte-Douglas International Airport** ✉ 5501 Josh Birmingham Blvd., Airport/Coliseum, Charlotte ☎ 704/359-4013 ⊕ www.charlotteairport. com. **Moore County Airport** ✉ Rte. 22, Southern Pines-Pinehurst. ☎ 910/692-3212 ⊕ www.airnav.com/airport/ksop. **Piedmont Triad International Airport** ✉ 6451 Bryan Blvd., Greensboro ☎ 336/665-5666 ⊕ http://www.flyfrompti.com. **Raleigh-Durham International Airport** ✉ 1600 Terminal Blvd., Morrisville ☎ 919/840-2123 ⊕ www. rdu.com.

🖪 Transfers **PTI Airport Transportation** ✉ Greensboro ☎ 336/668-9808. **RDU Airport Taxi Service** ✉ Raleigh-Durham ☎ 919/840-7277.

BY BUS

Greyhound–Carolina Trailways serves the Charlotte area; Burlington, Greensboro, High Point, Lexington, and Winston-Salem in the Piedmont; and Raleigh, Durham, and Chapel Hill in the Triangle.

Capital Area Transit is Raleigh's public transport system, Chapel Hill Transit serves Chapel Hill, and Durham Area Transit Authority is Durham's intracity bus system. The fare for each system is 75¢.

The Triangle Transit Authority, which links downtown Raleigh with Cary, Research Triangle Park, Durham, and Chapel Hill, runs weekdays except major holidays. Rates start at $2.

Chapel Hill Transit offers free bus transportation on a fixed route throughout the city and into Carrboro.

🖪 **Capital Area Transit** ☎ 919/833-5701 ⊕ www.raleighnc.gov/transit. **Chapel Hill Transit** ☎ 919/968-2769 ⊕ www.townofchapelhill.org. **Durham Area Transit Authority** ☎ 919/683-3282 ⊕ www.durhamnc.gov. **Greyhound/Carolina Trailways** ☎ 800/231-2222 ⊕ www.greyhound.com. **Triangle Transit Authority** ☎ 919/549-9999 ⊕ www. ridetta.org.

BY CAR

U.S. 1 runs north–south through the Sandhills and the Triangle and is the recommended route from the Raleigh-Durham area to Southern Pines.

Charlotte is a transportation hub; Interstate 77 comes in from Columbia, South Carolina, to the south, and then continues north to Virginia, intersecting Interstate 40 on the way. Interstate 85 arrives from Greenville, South Carolina, to the southwest, and then goes northeast to meet Interstate 40 in Greensboro. From the Triangle Interstate 85 continues northeast and merges with Interstate 95 in Petersburg, Virginia.

Greensboro and Winston-Salem are on Interstate 40, which runs east–west through North Carolina. From the east Interstate 40 and Interstate 85 combine coming into the Triad, but in Greensboro, Interstate 85 splits off to go southwest to Charlotte. High Point is off a business bypass of Interstate 85 southwest of Greensboro.

U.S. 1 runs north–south through the Triangle and links to Interstate 85 going northeast. U.S. 64, which makes an east–west traverse across the Triangle, continues eastward all the way to the Outer Banks. Interstate 95 runs northeast–southwest to the east of the Triangle and the Sandhills, crossing U.S. 64 and Interstate 40 from Virginia to South Carolina.

Like Washington, D.C., Raleigh has a highway that loops around the city. The terms "Inner Beltline" and "Outer Beltline refer to your direction: The Inner Beltline runs clockwise; the Outer Beltline runs counterclockwise. Don't confuse the Outer Beltline with the Outher Loop, which refers to Interstate 540.

BY TAXI & SHUTTLE

Taxis and airports vans service all the area towns and airports and are an alternative to renting a car if you don't plan on doing a lot of sightseeing. Reputable companies include Blue Bird Taxi in Greensboro, Central Piedmont Transportation in Winston-Salem, and Crown Cab and Yellow Cab in Charlotte.

🚖 Taxis & Shuttles **Blue Bird Taxi** ✉ Greensboro ☎ 336/272-5112. **Central Piedmont Transportation** ✉ Winston-Salem ☎ 336/668-9808. **Crown Cab** ✉ Charlotte ☎ 704/334-6666. **Yellow Cab** ✉ Charlotte ☎ 704/332-6161.

BY TRAIN

From Charlotte, there's daily service to Washington, D.C., Atlanta, and points beyond, as well as daily service to the Triangle cities of Raleigh, Durham, and Cary. In Greensboro, Amtrak's *Crescent* stops in before continuing from New York to New Orleans (or vice versa). And the *Carolinian* also stops in Greensboro as it goes from Charlotte to Raleigh and then north to Baltimore, Washington, and New York. The in-state *Piedmont* connects nine cities—including Greensboro—between Raleigh and Charlotte each day.

Both southbound and northbound Amtrak trains—one daily in each direction—stop in Southern Pines.

🚂 **Amtrak** ☎ 800/872-7245 ⊕ www.amtrak.com.

Contacts & Resources

BANKS & EXCHANGE SERVICES

As you might expect in one of the country's largest banking centers, there's no shortage of branches with ATMs in the Piedmont. Banks are usually open Monday to Thursday 9 to 5 and Friday 9 to 6. Most are closed on weekends, although some are open 9 to 1 on Saturday. Both Bank of America and Wachovia are headquartered in Charlotte and have a statewide presence. The corporate headquarters for BB&T is in Winston-Salem.

🏦 Contracts **Bank of America** ✉ 137 Franklin St., Chapel Hill ☎ 919/918-4200 ✉ 101 W. Friendly Ave., Greensboro ☎ 336/805-3669 ✉ 4325 Glenwood Ave., Raleigh ☎ 919/829-6657. **BB&T** ✉ 101 Queens Rd., Charlotte ☎ 704/954-2005 ✉ 2705 N. Main St., High Point ☎ 336/889-2090 ✉ 200 S.W. Broad St., Southern Pines ☎ 910/693-2000. **Wachovia** ✉ 2821 Chapel Hill Blvd., Durham ☎ 919/493-3580 ✉ 100 North Main St., Durham ☎ 336/732-5391.

EMERGENCIES

For minor emergencies go to one of the many urgent-care centers in any sizable Piedmont city.

🈂 Emergency Services**Ambulance, fire, police** ☎ 911.

🈂 Hospitals**Carolinas Medical Center** ⊠ 1001 Blythe Blvd., South Park, Charlotte ☎ 704/ 355-2000. **Duke University Medical Center** ⊠ 223 Medical Sciences Research, Durham ☎ 919/ 684-8111. **FirstHealth Moore Regional Hospital** ⊠ 155 Memorial Dr., Pinehurst ☎ 910/215-1000. **North Carolina Baptist Hospital** ⊠ 200 Hawthorne La., Downtown, Winston-Salem ☎ 336/716-4467. **Presbyterian Hospital** ⊠ 200 Hawthorne La., East Charlotte/Merchandise Mart, Charlotte ☎ 704/384-2273. **University Hospital** ⊠ 8800 N. Tryon St., University/Speedway, Charlotte ☎ 704/548-6000. **Wake Medical Center** ⊠ 3024 New Bern Ave., Raleigh ☎ 919/350-8228.

🈂 Late-Night Pharmacies**Eckerd Drug Store** ⊠ Lake Boone Shopping Center, 2462 Wycliff Rd., Raleigh ☎ 919/781-4070. **Eckerd Drugs** ⊠ Park Road Shopping Center, 4133 Park Rd., South Park, Charlotte ☎ 704/523-3031 ⊠ 3740 E. Independence Blvd., East Charlotte/Merchandise Mart, Charlotte ☎ 704/536-3600 ⊠ 3527 Hillsborough Rd., Durham ☎ 919/383-5591. **Walgreens** ⊠ 3529 N. Elm St., Greensboro ☎ 336/540-0359.

INTERNET, MAIL & SHIPPING

Wireless Internet is increasingly common in hotels in the Piedmont. Even some smaller hotels are offering it in guest rooms or common areas. The Piedmont also has a few cybercafés, usually in college neighborhoods.

You'll also find Internet access at FedEx Kinko's branches, enabling you to kill two birds with one stone. FedEx Kinko's locations in Cary, Chapel Hill, Charlotte, Durham, Greensboro, and Raleigh where you can check your e-mail and ship packages overnight.

🈂 **FedEx Kinko's** ⊠ 100 N. Tryon St., Charlotte ☎ 704/338-1770 ⊠ 4800 Express Dr., Charlotte ☎ 704/359-8638 ⊠ 65 T. W. Alexander Dr., Durham ☎ 919/541-9183 ⊠ 1 Bryan Center Durham ☎ 919/684-3207 ⊠ 610 Pembroke Rd., Greensboro ☎ 336/294-6385 ⊠ 150 Blake Blvd., Pinehurst ☎ 910/295-1231 ⊠ 4325 Glenwood Ave., Suite 2115, Raleigh ☎ 919/788-8272 ⊠ 1995 Pleasant St., Winston-Salem ☎ 336/784-9801.

MEDIA

There are many daily newspapers that cover the region. The best known is the *News & Observer,* a media powerhouse serving the Triangle. It also publishes five community papers. The *Charlotte Observer,* North Carolina's largest daily newspaper, has a weekday circulation of 220,000. The *News & Record* has the largest circulation in the Triad. The *Herald-Sun* focuses on Durham and Orange Counties. The *High Point Enterprise* covers the Sandhills region. The *Winston-Salem Journal* covers Forsyth County and the small communities in nine northwest counties.

There are other newspapers that publish less frequently. The *Chapel Hill News* is a twice-weekly newspaper that hits the streets on Sunday and Wednesday. Published on Thursday, the *Charlotte Post* has served the African-American community for more than a century. The *Pilot,* covering the Sandhills, publishes on Monday, Wednesday, and Friday.

Creative Loafing, a free arts tabloid published in Charlotte, publishes on Wednesday. *Go Triad,* a free weekly arts tabloid covering the Triad, is published on Thursday by the *News & Record*. The *Independent Weekly* is a free arts tabloid serving the Triangle. It's published on Wednesday.

🔳 *Chapel Hill News* ⊠ Chapel Hill ☎ 910/932-2000 ⊕ www.chapelhillnews.com. *Charlotte Observer* ⊠ Charlotte ☎ 704/358-5000 ⊕ www.charlotte.com. *Charlotte Post* ⊠ Charlotte ☎ 704/376-0496 ⊕ www.thecharlottepost.com. *Creative Loafing* ⊠ Charlotte ☎ 704/522-8334 ⊕ charlotte.creativeloafing.com. *Go Triad* ⊠ Greensboro ☎ 336/373-7000 ⊕ www.gotriad.com. *Herald-Sun* ⊠ Durham ☎ 919/419-6500 ⊕ www.heraldsun.com. *High Point Enterprise* ⊠ High Point ☎ 336/888-3500 ⊕ www.hpe.com. *Independent Weekly* ⊠ Durham ☎ 919/286-1972 ⊕ www.indyweek.com. *News & Observer* ⊠ Raleigh ☎ 919/829-4500 ⊕ www.newsobserver.com. *News & Record* ⊠ Greensboro ☎ 336/373-7000 ⊕ www.news-record.com. *The Pilot* ⊠ Southern Pines ☎ 910/692-7271 ⊕ www.thepilot.com. *Winston-Salem Journal* ⊠ Winston-Salem ☎ 336/727-7211 ⊕ www.journalnow.com.

TOUR OPTIONS

The *Catawba Belle* and the *Catawba Queen* paddle wheelers give dinner cruises and tours on Lake Norman, near Charlotte.

From mid-April to mid-November, the hour-long Historical Chapel Hill Trolley Tour is given on Wednesday at 2 PM. The tour, which costs $5 per person, departs from the Horace Williams House.

🔳 *Catawba Belle* and *Catawba Queen* ⊠ Rte. 150, Exit 36, Mooresville ☎ 704/663-2628 ⊕ www.queenslanding.com. **Historical Chapel Hill Trolley Tour** ⊠ Horace Williams House, 610 E. Rosemary St., Chapel Hill ☎ 919/942-7818 ⊕ http://ils.unc.edu/freenet/Tours.html.

VISITOR INFORMATION

🔳 Tourist Information **Capital Area Visitor Center** ⊠ 301 N. Blount St., Raleigh ☎ 919/733-3456 ⊕ ncmuseumofhistory.org/vs/index.html. **Chapel Hill/Orange County Visitors Bureau** ⊠ 501 W. Franklin St., Suite 104, Chapel Hill 27516 ☎ 919/968-2060 ⊕ www.chocvb.org. **Downtown Chapel Hill Welcome Center** ⊠ Old Post Office Bldg., 179 E. Franklin St. ☎ 919/929-9700. **Durham Convention and Visitors Bureau** ⊠ 101 E. Morgan St., 27701 ☎ 919/687-0288 or 800/446-8604 ⊕ www.dcvb.durham.nc.us. **Greater Raleigh Convention and Visitors Bureau** ⊠ Bank of America Bldg., 421 Fayetteville St. Mall, Suite 1505, 27601 ☎ 919/834-5900 ⊕ www.raleighcvb.org. **Greensboro Area Convention and Visitors Bureau** ⊠ 317 S. Greene St., 27401 ☎ 336/274-2282 ⊕ www.greensboronc.org. **High Point Convention and Visitors Bureau** ⊠ 300 S. Main St., 27260 ☎ 336/884-5255 ⊕ www.highpoint.org. **Pinehurst Area Convention and Visitors Bureau** ⊠ 1480 U.S. 15/501, Box 2270, Southern Pines 28388 ☎ 910/692-3330 ⊕ www.homeofgolf.com. **Visit Charlotte/Main Street Charlotte** ⊠ 330 S. Tryon St., Uptown, 28202 ☎ 704/331-2700 ⊕ www.charlottecvb.org. **Winston-Salem Convention and Visitors Bureau** ✉ Box 1409, 27102 ☎ 336/728-4200 ⊕ www.visitwinstonsalem.com.

The North Carolina Mountains

WORD OF MOUTH

"Asheville has a neat, vibrant downtown—great restaurants, a couple very good brew pubs and a great laid-back atmosphere. I also like the nearby town of Black Mountain—cute little town with good casual restaurants. While it enjoys visitors, it would be a stretch to call it touristy (though I haven't been in leaf season)."

–Brian_in_Charlotte

"Highlands is a good base if you like to hike or mountain bike. There are a few good places to eat, but you may want to pack a picnic hamper for the trail and enjoy your food by the river five miles east of town. If you want more nightlife or shopping, Asheville might be the place for you."

–palmettoprincess

By Lan Sluder

THE MAJESTIC PEAKS, meadows, balds, and valleys of the Appalachian, Blue Ridge, and Great Smoky Mountains epitomize the western corner of North Carolina. The Great Smoky Mountains National Park, national forests, handmade-crafts centers, Asheville's eclectic and sophisticated pleasures, the astonishing Biltmore Estate, and the Blue Ridge Parkway are the area's main draws, providing prime opportunities for shopping, skiing, hiking, bicycling, camping, fishing, canoeing, and just taking in the views.

The city of Asheville is one of the stops on the counterculture trail and a center of the New Age movement, as well as being a popular retirement area. Its restaurants regularly make the TV food show circuit. Thanks to their monied seasonal residents and long histories as resorts, even smaller towns like Highlands, Cashiers, Flat Rock, and Hendersonville are surprisingly sophisticated, boasting restaurants with daring chefs and professional summer theater. In the High Country, where summer temperatures are as much as 15 degrees cooler than in the flatlands, and where snow skiing is a major draw in winter, affluent retirees and hip young entrepreneurs bring a panache to even the most rural enclaves.

Some of the most important arts and culture movements of the 20th century, including abstract impressionist painting and the Beat movement, had roots just east of Asheville, at Black Mountain College, where in the 1930s and 1940s the notables included famed artists Josef Albers, Willem de Kooning, and Robert Motherwell, dancemeisters John Cage and Merce Cunningham, thinker Buckminster Fuller, architect Walter Gropius, and writers Charles Olson and Paul Goodman.

Exploring the North Carolina Mountains

For sightseeing purposes, western North Carolina can be divided into four areas: Asheville, for decades a retreat for the wealthy and famous and now home to a vibrant mix of artists, relocatees and retirees, hippies, and proud natives; the North Carolina portion of the Great Smoky Mountains National Park, together with the towns and areas that border the park; the northern mountains, known as the High Country (Blowing Rock, Boone, Banner Elk and other high-altitude towns); and, finally, the Southern Mountains, including areas to the south and west of Asheville, such as Hendersonville, Brevard, and the chic summer enclaves of Lake Toxaway, Cashiers, and Highlands.

Spanning much of western North Carolina is the Blue Ridge Parkway. The parkway, ranked as one of the most beautiful drives in North America, winds across parts of all these areas except the Great Smoky Mountains National Park itself; the parkway terminates near the entrance of the Great Smokies.

About the Restaurants

You can still get traditional mountain food, served family-style, at places like Dan'l Boone Inn in Boone and Pisgah View Ranch in Candler, near

TOP 5 REASONS TO GO

Biltmore Estate: The 250-room Biltmore House is the largest private home in America. It's modeled after the great Renaissance châteaux of the Loire Valley in France. The 8,000-acre estate, which includes a winery, extensive gardens, deluxe hotel, and restaurants, is the most-visited attraction in North Carolina.

Blue Ridge Parkway: This winding two-lane road, which ends at the edge of the Great Smokies and shows off the highest mountains in eastern America, is the most scenic drive in the South. It's perfect for an afternoon joyride, a weeklong exploration, or something in between.

Asheville: Hip, artsy, sometimes funky, with scores of restaurants and active nightlife, Asheville flouts its history as the preeminent Southern mountain resort city and its current status as one of America's coolest places to live. Stay in a classy B&B or historic inn and soak in the vibes of the "Santa Fe of the South."

Great Smoky Mountains National Park: Though it's the most-visited national park in America, the half-million acres of this park provide plenty of opportunities to commune quietly with nature. Ditch the car and hike into the backcountry. You're sure to see beautiful mountain scenery, and you may even spot an elk or black bear.

Mountain Arts and Crafts: The mountains are a center of handmade art and crafts, with more than 4,000 working craftspeople. Two nationally noted crafts schools—the Penland School of Crafts and John C. Campbell Folk School—are in the region. Pottery, quilting, and wood carving are particularly strong here.

Asheville. Increasingly, though, mountain cooks are offering more sophisticated fare. Chefs, trained at Asheville-Buncombe Technical College's culinary program, and in Charleston, New York, and even Paris, are creating innovative dishes. At many places, especially in Asheville, the emphasis is on "slow food"—locally grown ingredients, often organic. You can find nearly every world cuisine somewhere in the region, from Thai to Jamaican to northern Indian.

About the Hotels

Around the mountains, at least in the larger cities and towns such as Asheville, Hendersonville, and Boone, you can find the usual chain motels and hotels. For more of a local flavor, look at the many mountain lodges and country inns, some with just a few rooms with simple comforts, others with upmarket amenities like tennis courts, golf courses, and spas. The mountains also have a few large resorts, with all the offerings of a grand hotel, of which the Grove Park Inn in Asheville is the prime example.

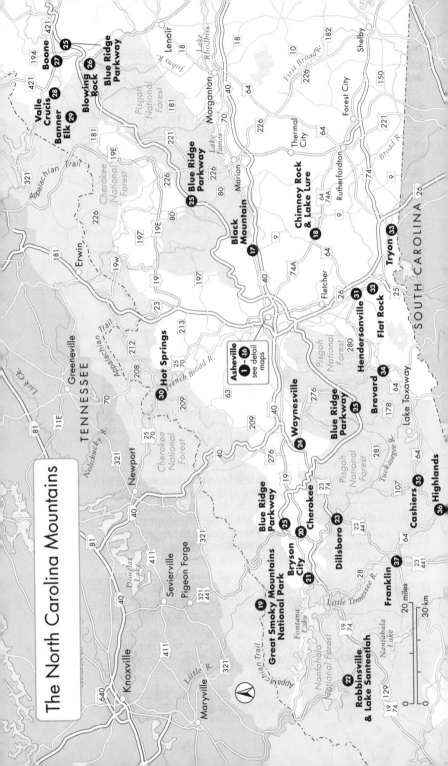

WHAT IT COSTS					
	$$$$	**$$$**	**$$**	**$**	**¢**
RESTAURANTS	over $22	$17–$22	$12–$16	$7–$11	under $7
HOTELS	over $220	$161–$220	$111–$160	$70–$110	under $70

Restaurant prices are for a main course at dinner. Hotel prices are for two people in a standard double room in high season.

Timing

Western North Carolina is a four-season destination. Dates for high season, when hotel demand is strongest and rates are highest, vary from hotel to hotel, but generally it's from Memorial Day in late May through early November, at the end of the fall color season. Mid-June to mid-August draws a lot of families, since kids are out of school. Around ski resorts, winter, especially January and February, is prime time; elsewhere, these winter months are dead, and some hotels are closed.

ASHEVILLE

Asheville is the hippest city in the South. At least that's the claim of Asheville's fans, who are legion. Visitors flock to Asheville to experience the arts and culture scene, which rivals that of Santa Fe, and to experience the city's blossoming downtown, with its myriad restaurants, coffeehouses, museums, galleries, bookstores, antiques shops, and boutiques.

Named "the best place to live" by many books and magazines, Asheville is also the destination for retirees escaping the cold North, or of "halfbacks," those who moved to Florida but who are now coming half the way back to the North. Old downtown buildings have been converted to upmarket condos for these affluent retirees, and new housing developments are springing up south, east, and west of town. As a result of this influx, Asheville has a much more cosmopolitan population than most cities of its size (70,000 people in the city, 385,000 in the metro area).

Asheville has a diversity you won't find in many cities in the South. There's a thriving gay community, many aging hippies, and young alternative-lifestyle seekers. In 2006, People for the Ethical Treatment of Animals (PETA) named Asheville the most vegetarian-friendly city in America.

The city really comes alive at night, with the restaurants, sidewalk cafés, and coffeehouses luring locals and visitors alike; so visit after dark to see the city at its best. Especially on warm summer weekends, Pack Square, Biltmore Avenue, Haywood Street, Wall Street, and Battery Park Avenue are busy until well after midnight.

Exploring Asheville

A city of neighborhoods, Asheville rewards careful exploration, especially on foot. You can break up your sightseeing with stops at the more than 50 restaurants in downtown alone, and at any of hundreds of unique shops.

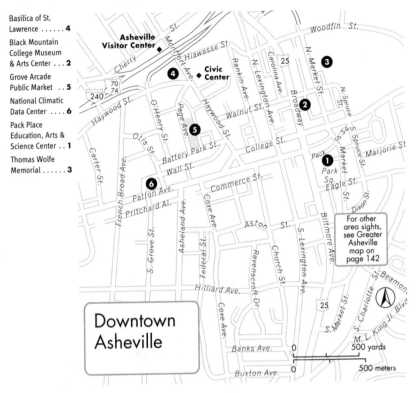

Downtown
Asheville

For other area sights, see Greater Asheville map on page 142

Downtown Asheville has the largest extant collection of art-deco buildings in the Southeast outside of Miami Beach, most notably the S&W Cafeteria (1929), Asheville City Hall (1928), First Baptist Church (1927), and Asheville High School (1929). It's also known for its architecture in other styles: Battery Park Hotel (1924) is neo-Georgian; the Flatiron Building (1924) is neoclassical; the Basilica of St. Lawrence (1912) is Spanish baroque; and Pack Place, formerly known as Old Pack Library (1925), is in the Italian-Renaissance style.

North Asheville, the historic Montford section (home to more than a dozen B&Bs), and the Grove Park neighborhood all have fine Victorian-era homes, including many remarkable Queen Anne houses. Biltmore Village, across from the entrance to the Biltmore Estate, was constructed at the time that Biltmore House was being built, and is now predominantly an area of retail boutiques and galleries. The River District, along the French Broad River, is an up-and-coming arts area, with many studios and lofts. Across the river, West Asheville has suddenly become the hottest part of the city, with its main artery, Haywood Road, sporting new restaurants, edgy stores, and popular clubs.

At a minimum, you need three full days to see Asheville. Downtown is most profitably explored on foot. To discover the outer reaches of the city and sights in the rural areas of Buncombe County you'll want to drive.■ TIP➔ A narrated trolley tour and the Urban Trail walking tour are good ways to orient yourself to Asheville's main sights and neighborhoods.

Main Attractions

❹ Basilica of St. Lawrence. A collaboration of Biltmore House–head architect Richard Sharp Smith and the Spanish engineer-architect Rafael Gustavin, this elaborate Catholic basilica was completed in 1908. It follows a Spanish-Renaissance design, rendered in brick and polychrome tile, and has a large, self-supporting dome with Catalan-style vaulting. ⊠ *97 Haywood St., Downtown* ☎ *828/252–6042* 🖭 *Free* ☉ *Weekdays 9–4.*

Fodor'sChoice
★

❿ Biltmore Estate. Built in the 1890s as the private home of George Vanderbilt, the astonishing 250-room French-Renaissance château is America's largest private residence. (Some of Vanderbilt's descendants still live here, but the bulk of the home and grounds are open to visitors.) Richard Morris Hunt designed it, and Frederick Law Olmsted landscaped the original 125,000-acre estate (now 8,000 acres), which faces Biltmore Village. It took 1,000 workers five years to complete the gargantuan project. On view are the priceless antiques and art collected by the Vanderbilts, along with 75 acres of gardens and formally landscaped grounds. You can also see the state-of-the-art winery and take candlelight tours of the house at Christmastime. The 4th floor, whose rooms are now open to the public, includes an observatory with sweeping views of the surrounding landscape, an architectural model room housing Hunt's 1889 model of the house, and servants' bedrooms and meeting hall, so you can see how the staff lived. Allow at least a full day to tour the house and grounds.■ TIP➔ If possible, avoid visiting on weekends during fall color season and the weeks between Thanksgiving and Christmas, when crowds are at their largest. Weekend admission prices are about 10% higher than weekday rates; the second visit in two days is only $10. ⊠ *Exit 50 off I–40, South Metro* ☎ *828/255–1700 or 800/624–1575* ⊕ *www.biltmore.com* 🖭 *$38 Mon.–Thurs., $42 Fri.–Sun.* ☉ *Admission gate and reception and ticket center: Jan.–Mar., daily 9–4; Apr.–Dec., daily 8:30–5.*

⓭ Biltmore Village. Across from the Biltmore Estate, Biltmore Village is a highly walkable collection of restored English village–style houses, now mostly shops and galleries. Badly flooded in 2004, with many buildings damaged and shops closed, the Village has come back to life, with nearly all shops now reopened. Of particular note is **All Souls Cathedral,** one of the most beautiful churches in America. It was designed by Richard Morris Hunt following the traditional Norman cross plan and opened in 1896. ⊠ *3 Angle St., South Metro* ☎ *828/274–2681* 🖭 *Free* ☉ *Daily, hrs vary.*

❷ Black Mountain College Museum & Arts Center. Famed Black Mountain College (1933–56), 16 mi east of Asheville, was important in the development of several groundbreaking 20th-century art, dance, and literary movements. A museum and gallery dedicated to the history of the radical college occupies a small space in downtown Asheville. It puts on occasional exhibits and publishes material about the college. Call ahead to find out what's currently happening. ✉ *54 Broadway, Downtown* ☎ *828/299–9306* ⊕ *www.blackmountaincollege.org* ☞ *Varies, depending on the exhibit; usually $5* ⊗ *Wed.–Sat. noon–4.*

❺ **Grove Arcade Public Market.** When it opened in 1929, the Grove Arcade was trumpeted as "the most elegant building in America" by its builder, W. E. Grove, the man also responsible for the Grove Park Inn. With the coming of the Great Depression and World War II, the Grove Arcade evolved into a dowdy government building. In late 2002 its polished limestone elegance was restored, and it reopened as a public market patterned in some ways after Pike Place Market in Seattle. The market covers a full city block and has about 50 locally owned stores and restaurants (though it has struggled to keep some of its tenants), along with apartments and office space. The building is an architectural wonder, with gargoyles galore, and well worth a visit even if you don't shop or dine here. ✉ *1 Page Ave., Downtown* ☎ *828/252–7799* ⊕ *www.grovearcade.com* ☞ *Free* ⊗ *Mon.–Sat. 10–6, some stores open Sun. noon–6; store hrs vary.*

⓰ **North Carolina Arboretum.** Part of the original Biltmore Estate, these 434

FodorsChoice ★ acres completed Frederick Law Olmsted's dream of creating a world-class arboretum in the western part of North Carolina. Highlights include southern Appalachian flora in stunning settings, such as the Blue Ridge Quilt Garden, with bedding plants arranged in patterns reminiscent of Appalachian quilts. An extensive network of trails is available for walking or mountain biking. A bonsai exhibit, featuring miniature versions of many native trees, opened in 2005. ■ TIP→ **For an unusual view of the arboretum, try the Segway tour, where you can glide through the forest for two hours on the gyroscopically controlled "Human Transporter" invented by Dean Kamen.** The $65 cost includes training on the Segway. Riders must be at least 18 years old and weigh between 80 and 250 pounds. ✉ *100 Frederick Law Olmsted Way, 10 mi southwest of downtown Asheville, at Blue Ridge Pkwy., near I–26 and I–40, South Metro* ☎ *828/665–2492* ⊕ *www.ncarboretum.org* ☞ *$6 per car parking fee; free Tues.* ⊗ *Visitor education center: Mon.–Sat. 9–5, Sun. noon–5. Gardens and grounds: Apr.–Oct., daily 8 AM–9 PM; Nov.–Mar., daily 8 AM–7 PM.*

🐾 ❶ **Pack Place Education, Arts & Science Center.** This 92,000-square-foot complex in downtown Asheville houses the **Asheville Art Museum, Colburn Earth Science Museum, Health Adventure,** and **Diana Wortham Theatre.** The **YMI Cultural Center,** also maintained by Pack Place, and focusing on the history of African-Americans in western North Carolina, is across the street. The Health Adventure has 11 galleries with hands-on exhibits, all of interest to children. The Asheville Art Museum stages major exhibits several times a year, with some highlighting regional artists. The Colburn Earth Science Museum displays local gems and minerals. ✉ *2 S. Pack Sq., Downtown* ☎ *828/257–4500* ⊕ *www.packplace.org* ☞ *Combined ticket $17, art museum $6, Health Adventure $6, earth science museum $4, YMI Cultural Center $5* ⊗ *Tues.–Sat. 10–5, Sun. 1–5.*

❸ **Thomas Wolfe Memorial.** Asheville's most famous son, novelist Thomas

FodorsChoice ★ Wolfe (1900–38), grew up in a 29-room Queen Anne–style home that his mother ran as a boardinghouse. The house, a state historic site, was badly damaged in a 1998 fire (a still-unsolved case of arson); it reopened in mid-2004 following a painstaking $2.4 million renovation. Though about one-fourth of the furniture and artifacts were lost in the fire, the house—memorialized as "Dixieland" in Wolfe's novel *Look Homeward, Angel*—has been restored to its original 1916 condition, including a light canary yellow paint on the exterior. You'll find a visitor center and many displays, and there are guided tours of the house and heirloom gardens. ☒ *52 Market St., Downtown* ☏ *828/253–8304* ⊕ *www.wolfememorial.com* ☞ *$1* ☉ *Apr.–Oct., Tues.–Sat. 9–5, Sun. 1–5; Nov.–Mar., Tues.–Sat. 10–4, Sun. 1–4.*

⓯ **WNC Farmers Market.** The highest-volume farmers market in North Carolina is a great place to buy local jams, jellies, honey, stone-ground grits and cornmeal, and, in season, local fruits and vegetables. In spring look for ramps, a wild cousin of the onion with a very strong odor. A wholesale section below the main retail section (both are open to all) offers produce in bulk. ☒ *570 Brevard Rd., 5 mi southwest of downtown Asheville, off I–40, South Metro* ☏ *828/253–1691* ☞ *Free* ☉ *Apr.–Oct., daily 8–6; Nov.–Mar., daily 8–5.*

Also Worth Seeing

Asheville Historic Trolley Tour. A motorized trolley bus takes you to the main points of interest around Asheville, including the Grove Park Inn, Biltmore Village, the Thomas Wolfe Memorial, the Montford area, and Pack Square and downtown. You can buy tickets and board the trolley at the Asheville Convention and Visitors Bureau and get on or off at any stop on this narrated tour. Reservations are available but usually aren't necessary. ☒ *Asheville Convention and Visitors Bureau, 36 Montford Ave.* ☏ *888/667–3600* ⊕ *www.ashevilletrolleytours.com* ☞ *$18.*

Asheville Urban Trail. This 1.7-mi walk developed by the City of Asheville has about 30 "stations," with plaques marking places of historical or architectural interest. The self-guided tour begins at Pack Place Education, Arts & Science Center. ■ TIP➔ **To enhance your walking experience, rent an audio guide at the Asheville Art Museum, which is part of the Pack Place complex.** From April to November, guided group tours are usually scheduled at 10 and 3 on Saturday, weather permitting. Construction, which began in mid-2006 around Pack Square and City-County Plaza may result in temporary changes in the Urban Trail route; the construction is expected to be completed by 2008. ☒ *2 S. Pack Sq., at Pack Place, Asheville Art Museum* ☏ *828/258–0710* ⊕ *www.urbantrails.net* ☞ *Audio guide $5, tour $5.*

⑧ **Botanical Gardens at Asheville.** Adjoining the University of North Carolina at Asheville campus, this 10-acre site has walking trails and displays of native plants, including a bog with carnivorous plants such as Venus's-flytraps, pitcher plants, and sundew. ■ TIP➔ **It's a fine place for a picnic, and not far from the busy downtown.** ☒ *151 Weaver Blvd., at Broadway, 2 mi north of downtown Asheville, North Metro* ☏ *828/252–5190* ⊕ *www.ashevillebotanicalgardens.org* ☞ *Free* ☉ *Daily dawn–dusk.*

★ ⑨ **Grove Park Inn.** This large resort overlooking Asheville is well worth a visit even if you don't stay here. The oldest section was built in 1913

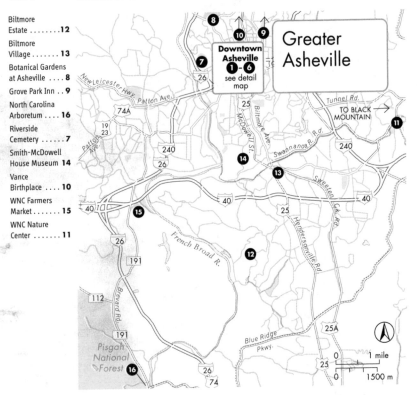

using huge, locally mined granite stones, some weighing 10,000 pounds. Inside there's the largest collection of Arts and Crafts furniture in the world. On the grounds are two small but interesting museums. The **North Carolina Homespun Museum** tells the story of a training school established by the Vanderbilt family (of Biltmore Estate fame) to revive interest in native crafts. A collection of antique cars assembled by a local car dealer is the main feature of the **Estes-Winn Memorial Automobile Museum.** ■ TIP→ **If you visit in the cooler months, be sure to warm yourself in front of the two enormous stone fireplaces in the lobby.** ⊠ *290 Macon Ave., North Metro* ☎ *800/438–5800 or 828/252–2711* ⊕ *www.groveparkinn. com* ⊡ *Free* ☉ *Hotel daily 24 hrs; Homespun Museum and Estes-Winn Automobile Museum Apr.–Dec., Mon.–Sat 10–5, Sun. 1–5.*

❻ **National Climatic Data Center.** The world's largest active archive of global weather data, the National Climatic Data Center provides weather data to researchers all over the world. Users range from large engineering firms planning energy-efficient development to individuals planning a retirement move. ■ TIP→ **At present, only group tours of the center are available, and must be arranged in advance.** ⊠ *Federal Plaza, 151 Patton Ave., Downtown* ☎ *828/271–4237* ⊕ *www.ncdc.noaa.gov* ⊡ *Free* ☉ *Weekdays 8–4:30.*

7 **Riverside Cemetery.** Authors Thomas Wolfe and O. Henry are buried here, along with about 13,000 others, including some of Asheville's most prominent citizens. The 87-acre cemetery, overlooking the French Broad River in the historic Montford area, has flower gardens and ancient oaks and poplars. ■ TIP→ **Take the drive through the cemetery, where signs direct you to the graves of noted people.** ⊠ *Birch St. off Pearson Dr., North Metro* ☎ *828/258–8480.*

14 **Smith-McDowell House Museum.** This is the oldest surviving house in Asheville, dating from 1840. The grounds were designed by Frederick Law Olmsted in 1900. The interior has much of the house's original Greek-revival woodwork, and restored rooms date from 1840 to 1900. Exhibits in the gallery focus on Asheville's early history. From mid-November to early January, the house has Victorian Christmas displays, and some years it hosts the campy Aluminum Christmas Tree Museum, a large collection of aluminum trees, mostly from the 1950s and '60s. ⊠ *283 Victoria Rd., East Metro* ☎ *828/253–9231* ⊕ *www.wnchistory.org* ⊠ *Jan.–Nov. $5, Dec. $7* ☉ *Tues.–Sat. 10–4, Sun. 1–4.*

10 **Vance Birthplace.** A reconstructed pioneer cabin and outbuildings mark the childhood home of Zebulon Vance, three-time governor of North Carolina and United States senator from 1879 to 1894. You can tour the site, which is representative of more prosperous mountain homesteads during the early 19th century. ⊠ *911 Reems Creek Rd., 13 mi north of downtown Asheville, North Metro* ☎ *828/645–6706* ⊠ *Free* ☉ *Apr.–Oct., Tues.–Sat. 9–5; Nov.–Mar., Tues.–Sat. 9–4.*

Ⓒ **11** **WNC Nature Center.** On a 42-acre Natural Heritage site, the WNC Nature Center is one of the region's most popular attractions for kids. It's basically a zoo focusing on animals native to the region, with cougars, bobcats, black bears, white-tailed deer, gray and red wolves, and gray and red foxes in natural-like settings. The center also has an excellent area on native reptiles and amphibians, plus a petting zoo. ⊠ *75 Gashes Creek Rd., East Metro* ☎ *828/298–5600* ⊕ *www.wildwnc.org* ⊠ *$7* ☉ *Daily 10–5.*

Sports & the Outdoors

Baseball

A Class A farm team of the Colorado Rockies, the **Asheville Tourists** (⊠ McCormick Pl., off Biltmore Ave. ☎ 828/258–0428) play April to early September at historic McCormick Field, which opened in 1924. McCormick Field appears briefly in the 1987 movie *Bull Durham,* starring Kevin Costner and Susan Sarandon. Many well-traveled baseball fans consider McCormick Field one of the most appealing minor league stadiums in the country.

Golf

Asheville Municipal Golf Course (⊠ 226 Fairway Dr. ☎ 828/298–1867), is a par-72, 18-hole public municipal course designed by Donald Ross. Fees start at $20. **Broadmoor** (⊠ 101 French Broad La., Fletcher ☎ 828/687–1500), 15 mi south of Asheville, is a public Scottish-style links course, playing to 7,111 yards, par 72. **Colony Lake Lure Golf Resort** (⊠ 201 Blvd.

of the Mountains, Lake Lure ☎ 828/625–2888 or 800/260–1040), 25 mi from Asheville, has two 18-hole, par-72 courses known for their beauty.

Grove Park Inn Resort (✉ 290 Macon Ave. ☎ 828/252–2711 Ext. 1012, 800/438–5800) has a par-70 course that's more than 100 years old. You can play the course ($85 if you start after 2 PM) even if you're not a guest at the hotel. **Southern Tee** (✉ 111 Howard Gap Rd., Fletcher ☎ 828/687–7273) is an 18-hole course with attractive rates—$20 with cart even on weekends in peak season.

Horseback Riding

Cataloochee Ranch (✉ 119 Ranch Rd., Maggie Valley ☎ 828/926–1401 or 800/868–1401) allows riders to explore the property's mile-high vistas on horseback. Trail rides are offered by stables throughout the region between April and November, including **Pisgah View Ranch** (✉ Pisgah View Ranch Rd., Candler ☎ 828/667–9100), where you can gallop through the wooded mountainside.

Llama Treks

Avalon Llama Trek (✉ 310 Wilson Cove Rd., Swannanoa ☎ 828/298–5637) leads llama trips on the lush trails of the Pisgah National Forest. One-day and overnight hikes with llamas carrying your pack through local forests are arranged by **Windsong Llama Treks, Ltd.** (✉ 120 Ferguson Ridge Rd., Clyde ☎ 828/627–6111).

Skiing

In addition to having outstanding skiing, **Cataloochee Resort** (✉ Rte. 1, Maggie Valley ☎ 828/926–0285 or 800/768–0285) hosts lots of different activities for the whole family. **Fairfield-Sapphire Valley** (✉ 4000 U.S. 64W, Sapphire Valley ☎ 828/743–3441 or 800/533–8268) offers basic skiing despite minimal snowfall. **Wolf Laurel** (✉ Rte. 3, Mars Hill ☎ 828/689–4111) has night skiing and excellent snowmaking capabilities.

Where to Eat

Because of the large number of visitors to Asheville and the many upscale retirees who've moved here, the city has a dining scene that's much more vibrant and varied than its size would suggest. You'll find everything from Greek to Vietnamese, Moroccan to Southern soul food, and barbecue to sushi. Asheville has more vegetarian restaurants per capita than any other city, and there are coffee houses on many corners.

$$$$
FodorsChoice
★

✕ **Gabrielle's.** From the moment you're met at the door, offered an ice-cold martini, and invited to stroll the lovely Victorian gardens while your table is readied, you suspect that dinner at Gabrielle's is going to be your best dining experience in the mountains—and chances are it will be. The best does come at a price, however. The five-course "grande menu," which changes frequently, is $90, or $110 with paired wines. The somewhat less expensive ($60) prix-fixe menu has items such as rosemary-rubbed rack of lamb and ginger-soy glazed yellowfin tuna. The near-perfect service and the setting in an elegant, art-filled 19th-century cherry-panel space, with piano music in the background, make for a memorable splurge. ✉ *87 Richmond Hill Dr., at Richmond Hill Inn, North Metro* ☎ *828/*

3

252–7313 or 800/545–9238 ⌖ *Reservations essential* ▭ *AE, MC, V* ☉ *No lunch.*

$$$–$$$$ ✕ **The Market Place.** Clean lines, neutral colors, and brushed-steel mobiles create a sophisticated style at one of Asheville's longest-lived fine-dining establishments. (It opened in 1979.) The food offers refreshing twists on ingredients indigenous to the mountains, such as game and trout, and the South in general. Possible entrées are roasted trout with portobello mushrooms ($19), and venison with a sweet-potato custard ($21). Iron gates open onto an exterior courtyard and dining patio. ⌧ *20 Wall St., Downtown* ☏ *828/252–4162* ⌖ *Reservations suggested* ▭ *AE, MC, V* ☉ *Closed Sun. No lunch.*

★ $$$–$$$$ ✕ **Zambras.** Sophisticated tapas selections, such as several varieties of paella, Kobe beef, and steamed mussels, many influenced by the cuisine of Mediterranean Spain and North Africa, and a wine list featuring unusual Spanish wines and sherries, make this one of the most interesting restaurants in the mountains. Voluptuous Moorish colors and live gypsy music (and belly dancers on weekends) lend an exotic air. ⌧ *85 Walnut St., Downtown* ☏ *828/232–1060* ⌖ *Reservations essential* ▭ *AE, D, MC, V* ☉ *No lunch.*

★ $$–$$$$ ✕ **Bistro 1896.** Bistro 1896 (in a building on Pack Square dating from that year) focuses on seafood but also offers other dishes. Start with oysters on the half shell, so fresh you can smell the salt air, or fried calamari, then jump to herbed salmon or ahi tuna with black-and-white sesame seeds. The bistro look comes from the period photos on the walls and glass-top tables with fresh flowers. On Sunday there's a brunch with a build-it-yourself Bloody Mary bar. ⌧ *7 Pack Sq., Downtown* ☏ *828/251–1300* ▭ *AE, MC, V.*

$–$$$$ ✕ **Laurey's Catering and Gourmet-to-Go.** This is a terrific place to pick up a ready-to-eat picnic lunch or complete gourmet dinner to take back to your room. Owner Laurey Masterton uses fresh, locally grown foods where possible. For a picnic, try the Tuscan lunch, with caesar salad, grilled salmon with roasted peppers and dilled Yukon Gold potatoes, herbed foccacia, seasonal fruit, a meringue pastry, and iced tea. ⌧ *67 Biltmore Ave., Downtown* ☏ *828/252–1500* ▭ *MC, V* ☉ *Closed Sun. Closes at 6 PM weekdays and at 4 PM Sat.*

$$$ ✕ **Rezaz.** With abstract art displayed on the cinnamon and apricot-color walls and waiters dressed in black rushing around pouring wine, you'd never know this sophisticated Mediterranean restaurant is in the site of a former hardware store. Try the veal osso bucco milanese or the aborio-crusted sea scallops. There are daily specials, such as goat cheese ravioli on Monday and seared ahi tuna on Friday. You enter the restaurant through Enoteca, Rezaz's wine bar, which serves panini sandwiches and other less expensive fare in a casual setting. ⌧ *28 Hendersonville Rd., Biltmore Village* ☏ *828/277–1510* ⌖ *Reservations essential* ▭ *AE, MC, V* ☉ *Closed Sun.*

$–$$$ ✕ **Tupelo Honey.** Hello, darlin'! This is the place for down-home Southern cooking with an uptown twist. Owner Sharon Schott delivers a lot more than grits, with dishes like seared salmon with corn bread, and hormone-free pork chop with mashed sweet potatoes. Breakfast is served anytime. The atmosphere is loud and a little funky. There's a jar of tupelo honey on every table. ⊠ *12 College St., Downtown* ☎ *828/ 255–4863* ⌂ *Reservations not accepted* ☰ *AE, MC, V* ☺ *Closed Mon. No lunch Fri. and Sat.*

¢–$$$ ✕ **Asheville Pizza and Brewing Company.** Locally known as the "Brew 'n View," this funky brewery-cum-eatery-cum-movie theater is extremely popular. Grab a microbrew beer and a pizza with portobello mushrooms and fresh spinach, and watch *Pink Floyd The Wall* from the comfort of an old sofa. ⊠ *675 Merrimon Ave., North Metro* ☎ *828/254–1281* ☰ *MC, V.*

$–$$ ✕ **Early Girl Eatery.** Named after an early-maturing tomato variety, Early Girl Eatery is casually Southern, with a cheerfully chic twist. A wall of south-facing windows provides wonderful light most of the day. No white tablecloths here: you eat on brown butcher paper. The dinner menu runs to items like grilled duck with collard greens. At breakfast, choose huge stacks of buttermilk pancakes or Creole catfish and stone-ground grits. ⊠ *8 Wall St. Ave., Downtown* ☎ *828/259–9592* ☰ *MC, V.*

$–$$ ✕ **Mela Indian Restaurant.** Mela opened in 2005 and quickly established itself as the best Indian restaurant in the city. Rather than specialize in one type of Indian cuisine, it offers dishes from across the country. The tandoori dishes (chicken, salmon, or lamb) are especially delicious. En-trées are served with basmati rice, lentil stew, and *papadum* (lentil wafers). Portions are large, making this one of the best values down-town. The space is unexpectedly modern, with rough tile walls and a high ceiling, though accented with woodwork, doors, and furnishings from India. ⊠ *70 N. Lexington, Downtown* ☎ *828/225–8880* ☰ *AE, D, MC, V.*

$–$$ ✕ **Salsa's.** In an expanded space with a slightly retro-hippy look, you'll find spicy and highly creative Mexican and Caribbean fare in huge por-tions. Pan-fried fish tacos, roast pumpkin empanadas, and organic chicken enchiladas are among the recommended entrées, each under $10. ⊠ *6 Patton Ave., Downtown* ☎ *828/252–9805* ☰ *AE, D, MC, V* ☺ *Closed Sun.*

¢–$$ ✕ **Laughing Seed Café.** You'll get more than brown rice and beans at this vegetarian eatery, with a bold mural on one wall and a bar. The exten-sive menu ranges from fruit drinks to sandwiches and pizzas to dinner specialties influenced by the flavors of India, Thailand, and Morocco. Fruits and vegetables come from local organic farms during the grow-ing season. Breads are baked daily on premises. There's outdoor dining on charming Wall Street. ⊠ *40 Wall St., Downtown* ☎ *828/252–3445* ☰ *AE, D, MC, V* ☺ *Closed Tues.*

¢–$$ ✕ **Sunny Point Café and Bakery.** In a restored storefront in up-and-com-ing West Asheville, Sunny Point lives up to its name with bright, cheer-ful decor. It's a good spot for breakfast, where free-range pork sausage shares the menu with granola, herbed potatoes, and some of the biggest biscuits in town. Now open for dinner, it experiments a little at this meal, with dishes like chicken-fried tofu. In good weather the best tables are outside on the patio. ⊠ *626 Haywood Rd., West Metro* ☎ *828/252– 0055* ☰ *MC, V* ☺ *Closed Sun. and Mon.*

¢–$$ ✕ **12 Bones Smokehouse.** You'll recognize this spot by the long line of customers snaking out the door. Open only weekdays 11 to 4, the wait

CAFFEINATED ASHEVILLE

Given Asheville's artsy sensibilities, it shouldn't come as a surprise that the city has a flourishing café scene.

City Bakery Café (⊠ 60 Biltmore Ave. ☎ 828/254–4426) has so-so coffee but great European-style breads, in about 20 varieties, made from organic flours. **Clingman Ave. Coffee and Catering Co.** (⊠ 242 Clingman Ave. ☎ 828/253–2177) is in the River District, near many pottery and other art-and-crafts studios. **Dripolator** (⊠ 144 Biltmore Ave. ☎ 828/252–0021) serves "Fair Trade" coffees and attracts a mixed crowd of alternative younger folks and businesspeople. **Malaprop's Café** (⊠ 55 Haywood St. ☎ 828/254–6734) is associated with a first-rate downtown independent bookstore. **Port City Java** (⊠ 870 Merrimon Ave. ☎ 828/255–3881) is a branch of a small Wilmington, NC, specialty coffee roaster.

to place your order often is a half hour. True to the barbecue joint ethos, with concrete floors and old Formica-top tables, 12 Bones has no atmosphere. What it does have is the smokiest baby back ribs you've ever tasted, and delicious sides including collard greens, corn pudding, and "mashed sweet taters." The crowd ranges from hippie potters from the River District art-studio types to downtown suits—the staff will call you "Sweetie." ⊠ *5 Riverside Dr., River District* ☎ *828/253–4499* ▤ *MC, V* ⊘ *Closed weekends. No dinner.*

¢–$ ✕ **Doc Chey's.** "Peace, love, and noodles" is the theme at this outpost of an Atlanta noodle house, with Vietnamese, Thai, Japanese, and Chinese noodle bowls and rice plates served fast, cheap, and tasty. It's always packed. ⊠ *37 Biltmore Ave., Downtown* ☎ *828/252–8220* ▤ *AE, MC, V.*

¢–$ ✕ **Old Europe.** The Hungarian owners, Zoltan and Melinda Vetro, bring a European sensibility to this immensely popular pastry shop and coffee house, which moved to a larger downtown location in mid-2006. It's usually jammed; the crowd spills over to the courtyard, slurping coffee—served with a piece of chocolate—and liqueurs and downing delicious tortes, cakes, and other European pastries. There's live entertainment on weekends, in a nightclub upstairs. ⊠ *41 N. Lexington Ave., Downtown* ☎ *828/252–0001* ▤ *MC, V.*

Where to Stay

Asheville has a nice mix of B&Bs, motels, and small owner-operated inns. There are at least two dozen B&Bs, one of the largest concentrations in the South. Most are in the Montford area near downtown and the Grove Park area north in the city. About 100 chain motel properties are dotted around the metropolitan area, with large clusters on Tunnel Road near the Asheville Mall, on U.S. Highway 25 near the Biltmore Estate, and southwest near Biltmore Square Mall. Also, you'll find inns and boutique hotels, both downtown and around the city. In rural areas around the city are a few lodges and cabin colonies.

★ **$$$$** ⊡ **Grove Park Inn Resort & Spa.** Asheville's premier large resort has an imposing granite edifice that dates from 1913 and panoramic views of the Blue Ridge Mountains. Henry Ford, F. Scott Fitzgerald (who stayed in room 441), and Michael Jordan have stayed here. It's furnished with oak antiques in the Arts and Crafts style, and the lobby fireplaces are as big as cars. Four restaurants offer plenty of choices. The spa is one of the finest in the country. As the hotel's main focus is on group meetings, alas, sometimes individual guests get short shrift. Rooms in the original section are mostly smaller but have more character than those in the newer additions. ⊠ *290 Macon Ave., North Metro, 28804* ☎ *828/252–2711 or 800/438–5800* ⊟ *828/252–6102* ⊕ *www.groveparkinn.com* ⇨ *498 rooms, 12 suites* ⟁ *4 restaurants, cable TV, in-room broadband, Wi-Fi, 18-hole golf course, putting green, 9 tennis courts, 2 pools (1 indoor), health club, hot tub, spa, 3 bars, nightclub, shops, playground, laundry service, concierge, business services, meeting rooms, no-smoking rooms* ▤ *AE, D, DC, MC, V* ⎸○⎸ *EP.*

$$$$
Fodor'sChoice
★
⊡ **Inn on Biltmore Estate.** Many people who visit the Biltmore mansion long to stay overnight; if you're one of them, your wish is granted in the form of this posh hill-top property. The hotel mimics the look of Biltmore House with natural stone and copper. French manor houses inspired the interior. Nice touches include afternoon tea in the library. The dining room is bookended by large windows with mountain views and a massive fireplace. Menus deftly blend local and international ingredients. ⊠ *Biltmore Estate, Exit 50 off I–40, South Metro, 28803* ☎ *800/922–0084* ⊟ *828/225–1629* ⊕ *www.biltmore.com/inn* ⇨ *207 rooms, 9 suites* ⟁ *Restaurant, room service, cable TV, in-room broadband, golf privileges, pool, health club, hot tub, mountain bikes, hiking, horseback riding, bar, library, shops, concierge, meeting rooms, no-smoking rooms* ▤ *AE, D, DC, MC, V* ⎸○⎸ *EP.*

$$$–$$$$ ⊡ **Black Walnut Inn.** The Biltmore House supervising architect Richard Sharp Smith built this 1899 home in Asheville's Monford section. Today it's a B&B on the National Register of Historic Places. Most of the rooms—all redone in 2004 by owners Peter and Lori White—have working fireplaces. Parts of the 2000 movie *28 Days* were filmed here. (The star, Sandra Bullock, stayed in the Dogwood Room.) ⊠ *288 Montford Ave., North Metro, 28801* ☎ *828/254–3878 or 800/381–3878* ⊕ *www.blackwalnut.com* ⇨ *6 rooms, 1 cottage* ⟁ *Fans, cable TV, VCRs; no smoking* ▤ *D, MC, V* ⎸○⎸ *BP.*

$$$–$$$$ ✕⊡ **Haywood Park Hotel.** The lobby of this all-suites downtown hotel, once a department store, has golden oak woodwork accented with gleaming brass. The suites are spacious, with baths done in Spanish marble. A continental breakfast is delivered to your room. The long-popular Flying Frog Café, with an astonishingly eclectic menu—mixing French, Indian, and German cuisine—is in the hotel. There's a small shopping galleria in the atrium, and a sidewalk café. ⊠ *1 Battery Park Ave., Downtown, 28801* ☎ *828/252–2522 or 800/228–2522* ⊟ *828/253–0481* ⊕ *www.haywoodpark.com* ⇨ *33 suites* ⟁ *Restaurant, room service, some in-room safes, cable TV, in-room broadband, some in-room VCRs, gym, sauna, bar, shops, laundry service, concierge, business services, meeting rooms, no-smoking rooms* ▤ *AE, D, DC, MC, V* ⎸○⎸ *BP.*

★ **$$$–$$$$** 🖼 **1900 Inn on Montford.** Guests are pampered at this Arts and Crafts–style B&B, where most rooms have whirlpool baths, some have big-screen plasma TVs, and all have fireplaces. There are lots of nooks and corners in the expansive public spaces for snuggling up with a book. The inn has a social hour every evening and live mountain music on some nights. Innkeepers Ron and Lynn Carlson say that the Cloisters—a 1,300-square-foot suite in their newly built carriage house out back—is the largest suite in Asheville. Younger children are discouraged in the main house. ⊠ *296 Montford Ave., North Metro, 28801* ☎ *828/254–9569 or 800/254–9569* ⊕ *www.innonmontford.com* 🛏 *5 rooms, 3 suites* ⚐ *Fans, cable TV, in-room DVDs, some refrigerators, in-room broadband, Wi-Fi; no smoking* ⊟ *AE, D, MC, V* ¶⚭ *BP.*

$$$–$$$$ 🖼 **Richmond Hill Inn.** Once a private residence, this elegant Victorian mansion is on the National Register of Historic Places. Many rooms in the mansion are furnished with canopy beds, Victorian sofas, and other antiques, while the more modern cottages have contemporary pine poster beds. Although Richmond Hill does not enjoy the panoramic views of Asheville's other top hotels, and the immediate neighborhood is not exactly upscale, the 46-acre grounds are stunning, with ever-changing gardens. Its dinner restaurant, Gabrielle's, is one of the best in the region. ⊠ *87 Richmond Hill Dr., North Metro, 28806* ☎ *828/252–7313 or 888/742–4536* 🖷 *828/252–8726* ⊕ *www.richmondhillinn.com* 🛏 *24 rooms, 3 suites, 9 cottages* ⚐ *2 restaurants, cable TV, in-room broadband, croquet, library, business services, meeting rooms; no smoking* ⊟ *AE, MC, V* ¶⚭ *BP* ⊘ *Closed Jan.*

Fodor'sChoice
★

★ **$$–$$$$** 🖼 **Albemarle Inn.** Famed Hungarian composer Béla Bartók lived here in the early 1940s, creating his third piano concerto, the "Asheville Concerto." You can stay in his room on the third floor, although Juliet's Chamber, with its private balcony overlooking lovely gardens, may appeal more to modern Romeos. Owners Cathy and Larry Sklar left their jobs as lawyers in Connecticut in order to turn this 1907 Greek-revival mansion in a quiet North Asheville residential area into one of the top B&Bs in the region. Some rooms have working fireplaces and canopied beds. Gourmet breakfasts are prepared by the inn's chef. ⊠ *86 Edgemont Rd., 1 mi north of I–240, North Metro, 28804* ☎ *828/255–0027 or 800/621–7435* 🖷 *828/236–3397* ⊕ *www.albemarleinn.com* 🛏 *10 rooms, 1 suite* ⚐ *Fans, cable TV, some hot tubs; no kids under 12, no smoking* ⊟ *D, MC, V* ¶⚭ *BP.*

$$–$$$$ 🖼 **Cedar Crest Victorian Inn.** Biltmore craftspeople constructed this beautiful Queen Anne house, with its lead-glass front door and corbeled brick fireplaces, as a private residence in 1891. The lovingly restored guest rooms are furnished with period antiques. You are treated to afternoon tea; evening coffee or chocolate; and a hot breakfast with fruit, pastries, and coffee. Some rooms have fireplaces and whirlpools. ■ TIP➜ **It's better suited to older children than younger ones.** ⊠ *674 Biltmore Ave., South Metro, 28803* ☎ *828/252–1389 or 800/252–0310* 🖷 *828/252–7667* ⊕ *www.cedarcrestvictorianinn.com* 🛏 *9 rooms, 3 cottage suites* ⚐ *Croquet, cable TV, some whirlpools, some refrigerators, gift shop, business services, travel services; no smoking* ⊟ *AE, D, DC, MC, V* ¶⚭ *BP.*

$$–$$$ ⊡ **The Lion and the Rose.** One of the characters in Thomas Wolfe's *Look Homeward, Angel* lived in this house, an 1898 Queen Anne–Georgian in the historic Montford Park area near downtown. It couldn't have looked any better then than it does now. A special detail is a 6-foot Palladian-style stained-glass window at the top of oaks stairs. Innkeepers Jim and Linda Palmer keep the heirloom gardens and five guest rooms looking gorgeous. For the most privacy, choose the Craig-Toms suite, which occupies the entire 3rd floor. ⊠ *276 Montford Ave., North Metro, 28801* ☎ *828/255–6546 or 800/546–6988* 🖷 *828/285–9810* ⊕ *www.lion-rose.com* ⟿ *4 rooms, 1 suite* ♨ *Cable TV, in-room DVDs; no kids under 12, no smoking* ⊟ *D, MC, V* ⊓◎⊺ *BP.*

★ $$–$$$ ⊡ **Sourwood Inn.** Two miles from the Blue Ridge Parkway, down a narrow winding road, sits one of the most stunning small inns in the mountains. The inn is constructed of stone and cedar. Twelve large rooms each have a real wood-burning fireplace, a bathtub with a view (there's also a separate shower), and French doors that open onto a private balcony. ■ TIP→ **Unfortunately, the inn doesn't have air-conditioning. Even at 3,000 feet it can be a little warm at times in summer.** Sassafras Cabin is a private retreat about 100 yards from the inn. ⊠ *810 Elk Mountain Scenic Hwy., 28804* ☎ *828/255–0690* 🖷 *828/255–0480* ⊕ *www.sourwoodinn. com* ⟿ *12 rooms, 1 cabin* ♨ *Dining room, fans, billiards, hiking, library; no a/c, no TVs in rooms, no room phones, no smoking* ⊟ *AE, MC, V* ☉ *Closed Jan. and weekdays in Feb.* ⊓◎⊺ *BP.*

¢–$ ⊡ **Red Roof Inn Asheville West.** This is the most affordable of the chain motels in Asheville, with rates regularly under $60 for a double. For that you get clean, standard-issue Red Roof rooms. ⊠ *16 Crowell Rd., West Metro, 28806* ☎ *828/667–9803 or 800/733–7663* 🖷 *828/667–9810* ⟿ *109 rooms* ⊟ *AE, D, MC, V* ⊓◎⊺ *BP.*

Nightlife & the Arts

The Arts

The Asheville area has about 40 theaters and theater companies. Asheville also has a vibrant art and crafts gallery scene, with about two dozen galleries. Most of the galleries are within a block or two of Pack Square, while some, especially working studios, are in the River District. Biltmore Village also has several galleries.

One of the oldest community theater groups in the country, **Asheville Community Theatre** (⊠ 35 E. Walnut St., Downtown ☎ 828/254–1320) stages professional plays year-round in its own theater building. The biggest art gallery in town, with 14,000 square feet of exhibit space, **Blue Sprial 1** (⊠ 38 Biltmore Ave., Downtown ☎ 800/291–2513) has about 30 exhibits of sculpture, paintings, and photographs each year.

In the Pack Place complex, the 500-seat **Diana Wortham Theatre** (⊠ 2 S. Pack Sq., Downtown ☎ 828/257–4530) is home to more than 100 musical and theatrical events each year. As the headquarters of the prestigious craft group, the Southern Highland Craft Guild, as well as a Blue Ridge Parkway visitor center, the **Folk Art Center** (⊠ Blue Ridge Pkwy., MM 382 ☎ 828/298–7298), regularly puts on exceptional quilt, woodworking, pottery, and other crafts shows and demonstrations.

Owned by arts entrepreneur John Cram, **New Morning Gallery** (⊠ 7 Boston Way., Biltmore Village ☎ 828/274–2831 or 800/933–4438) has 12,000 square feet of exhibit space, focusing on more popular ceramics, garden art, jewelry, furniture, and art glass. In a tiny, 99-seat theater, **North Carolina Stage Company** (⊠ 33 Haywood St., Downtown ☎ 828/350–9090) is a professional company that puts on edgy, contemporary plays. With professional summer theater that often celebrates mountain culture, **Southern Appalachian Repertory Theatre (SART)** (⊠ Owen Hall, Mars Hill College ☎ 828/689–1239), produces plays such as William Gregg and Perry Deane Young's *Mountain of Hope,* about the 1835 controversy over whether or not Mt. Mitchell is the highest peak east of the Rockies.

The 2,400-seat **Thomas Wolfe Auditorium** (⊠ 87 Haywood St., Downtown ☎ 828/259–5736), in the Asheville Civic Center, hosts larger events including traveling Broadway shows and performances of the Asheville Symphony. The Civic Center, which is showing its age, is planning a $140 million expansion to include a new performing-arts theater.

Nightlife

More than a restaurant, more than a movie theater, **Asheville Pizza and Brewing Company** (⊠ 675 Merrimon Ave. ☎ 828/254–1281), also called Brew 'n' View, is a wildly popular place to catch a flick while lounging on a sofa, drinking a microbrew, and scarfing a veggie pizza. In a renovated downtown appliance store, the ever-popular **Barley's Taproom** (⊠ 42 Biltmore Ave. ☎ 828/255–0504) has live bluegrass and Americana music three or four nights a week. The bar downstairs has about two dozen microbrew beers on draft, and you can play pool and darts upstairs in the Billiard Room.

The camp decor at **Club Hairspray** (⊠ 38 N. French Broad Ave. ☎ 828/258–2027) will make you feel like you're back in 1961, though the music is contemporary. The crowd is diverse but predominately gay and lesbian. **The Orange Peel Social Aid and Pleasure Club** (⊠ 101 Biltmore Ave. ☎ 828/225–5851) is far and away the number one nightspot in downtown Asheville. Bob Dylan, Hootie and the Blowfish, and Steve Winwood have played here in an intimate, smoke-free setting for audiences of up to 950. For smaller events, it also has a great dance floor, with springy wood slats.

Asheville's best-known gay and lesbian club, **Scandals** (⊠ 11 Grove St. ☎ 828/252–2838), has a lively dance floor and drag shows on weekends. In a 1913 downtown building, the jazz and blues club **Tressa's** (⊠ 28 Broadway ☎ 828/254–7072) is nominally private, but lets nonmembers in for a small cover charge. There's a quieter, no-smoking room upstairs. In happening West Asheville, the smoke-free **Westville Pub** (⊠ 777 Haywood Rd. ☎ 828/225–9782) has about 50 different beers on the menu, and a different band plays nearly every night.

Shopping

Biltmore Village (⊠ Hendersonville Rd. ☎ 828/274–5570), across from the Biltmore Estate, is a cluster of specialty shops, restaurants, galleries, and hotels in an early-20th-century-English-hamlet style. You'll find everything from children's books to music, antiques, and wearable art. **New Morning Gallery,** a jewelry, crafts, and art gallery at 7 Boston Way attracts customers from all over the Southeast.

Shopping is excellent all over **Downtown Asheville,** with at least 200 stores, including about 30 art galleries and over a dozen antiques shops. Several streets, notably **Biltmore Avenue, Lexington Avenue,** and **Wall Street** are lined with small, independently owned stores.

The **Grove Arcade Public Market** (⊠ 1 Page Ave., Downtown ☎ 828/252–7799), one of America's first indoor shopping centers, originally opened in 1929. The remarkable building, which covers an entire city block, was totally redone and reopened in 2002 as a collection of some 50 local specialty shops and restaurants.

Grovewood Gallery at the Homespun Shops (⊠ 111 Grovewood Rd. ☎ 828/253–7651), adjacent to the Grove Park Inn and established by Mrs. George Vanderbilt, sells furniture and contemporary and traditionally crafted woven goods made on the premises.

SIDE TRIPS FROM ASHEVILLE

Black Mountain

⑰ *16 mi east of Asheville via I–40.*

Black Mountain is a small town that has played a disproportionately large role in American cultural history, because it's the site of Black Mountain College. For 20 years in the middle of the 20th century, from its founding in 1933 to its closing in 1953, Black Mountain College was one of the world's leading centers for experimental art, literature, architecture, and dance, with a list of faculty and students that reads like a *Who's Who* of American arts and letters.

On a different front, Black Mountain is also the home of evangelist Billy Graham. The Graham organization maintains a training center near Black Mountain, and there are several large church-related conference centers in the area, including Ridgecrest, Montreat, and Blue Ridge Assembly. Downtown Black Mountain is small and quaint, with a collection of little shops and several B&Bs.

Fodor'sChoice
★

Originally housed in rented quarters at nearby Blue Ridge Assembly, in 1941 **Black Mountain College** moved across the valley to its own campus at Lake Eden, where it remained until it closed in 1953. The school's buildings were originally designed by the Bauhaus architects Walter Gropius and Marcel Breuer, but at the start of World War II the college turned to an American architect, Lawrence Kocher, and several intriguing buildings resulted, including one known as "The Ship," which still stands, with murals by Breuer. Among the students who enrolled at Black Mountain College in the 1940s were Arthur Penn, Kenneth Noland, Robert Rauschenberg, and James Leo Herlihy. Today, the site is a privately owned 550-acre summer camp for boys. ■ TIP→ **Although the site of Black**

Mountain College usually is closed to the public, during the Lake Eden Festival, a music and arts festival in mid-May and mid-October, you can visit the grounds, either on a one-day pass or for weekend camping. Other times of the year, you can rent a cabin on the grounds for overnight stays. The Ship building and other campus buildings are viewable from Lake Eden Road. There's a small museum devoted to Black Mountain College in Asheville. ⊠ *375 Lake Eden Rd., 5 mi west of Black Mountain* ☎ *828/686–3885.*

Sports & the Outdoors

GOLF Black Mountain doesn't have the plethora of golf courses that some other mountain towns do, but **Black Mountain Golf Course** (⊠ Black Mountain ☎ 828/669–2710), a par-72, 6,215-yard public course, boasts the longest par 6 in the country, the 747-yard 17th hole.

Where to Stay & Eat

$–$$$ ✕⌂ **Red Rocker Inn.** A dozen red rocking chairs line the front porch of this inn in a quiet residential area two blocks from downtown. Your room may have a golf theme (the Pinehurst Room) or skylights, a fireplace, and a claw-foot tub (the Garrett Room). The restaurant ($$$–$$$$) is open to the public for breakfast and dinner by reservation. At dinner, you'll enjoy heaping portions of Southern food, served by candlelight. ⊠ *136 N. Dougherty St., 28711* ☎ *888/669–5991 or 828/669–5991* ⊕ *www.redrockerinn.com* ↝ *17 rooms* ⌂ *Fans, restaurant; in-room safes; no smoking* ➡ *MC, V* ⊙❘ *BP.*

Shopping

Part authentic small-town hardware store and part gift shop, **Town Hardware & General Store** (⊠ 103 W. State St. ☎ 828/669–7723) sells hard-to-find tools like scythes and push plows, along with cast-iron cookware, Case knives, and Radio Flyer red wagons.

Chimney Rock & Lake Lure

18 *24 mi southeast of Asheville on U.S. 64/74A; 20 mi southeast of Black Mountain.*

Chimney Rock and neighboring Lake Lure—both popular day trips from Asheville—were the dream projects of a single man, Dr. Lucius Morse. In the early 1900s he bought and began developing Chimney Rock, and in the 1926 he dammed the Rocky Broad River to create Lake Lure. The Depression interrupted his plans, but his descendants still own much of this area. In mid-2006, however, the family announced its intention to sell the 1,000-acre park. Although the scenery, particularly when viewed from atop Chimney Rock, is spectacular—several movies have been filmed here—the commercial development along parts of Hickory Nut Gorge is not so appealing. Lake Lure, with 27 mi of shoreline, is one of the most beautiful lakes in the mountains.

☾ At privately owned **Chimney Rock Park** an elevator travels through a 26-story shaft of rock for a staggering view of Hickory Nut Gorge and the surrounding mountains. Trails, open year-round, lead to 400-foot Hickory Nut Falls, where the 1992 movie *The Last of the Mohicans* was filmed. The Old Rock Café can prepare picnics to go. ⊠ *U.S. 64/74A* ☎ *828/*

625–9611 or 800/277–9611 ⊕ *www.chimneyrockpark.com* ⊠ *$14*
⊘ *May–Oct., daily 8:30–5:30; Nov.–Apr., daily 8:30–4:30.*

Sports & the Outdoors

WATER SPORTS   The 720-acre **Lake Lure** (⊠ U.S. 64/74A ☎ 877/386–4255 or 828/625–
1373 ⊕ www.lakelure.com) draws the region's water-sports enthusiasts.
You can rent boats (from kayaks and water bikes to pontoon boats) at
the marina, water ski, swim, and fish. ■ TIP➔**A small sandy beach on Lake
Lure is open Memorial Day to Labor Day. Admission is $5.**

Where to Stay

★ **$$–$$$$**   ▦ **The Lodge on Lake Lure.** Originally built in the 1930s as a retreat for
the North Carolina Highway Patrol, this lodge is a place to slow down
and enjoy life at the lakeside. All but three of the inn's 17 rooms have
lake views, and the others have views of the well-tended gardens, with
azaleas, rhododendrons, and other flowers and shrubs. The "gathering
room" in the main lodge has soaring ceilings, with rare chestnut pan-
eling, and a rock fireplace whose centerpiece is a huge millstone. Rooms
are beautifully furnished with antiques. Rates include a full breakfast,
afternoon tea and pastries, and evening hors d'oeuvres and wine. ⊠ *361
Charlotte Dr., Lake Lure, 28746* ☎ *828/625–2789 or 800/733–2785*
🖷 *828/625–2421* ⊕ *www.lodgeonlakelure.com* ⇆ *12 rooms in main
lodge, 5 rooms in cottage* ⚹ *Restaurant, fans, cable TV, lake, boating,
fishing, marina; no smoking* ⊟ *AE, D, MC, V* ⫶⊙⫶ *BP.*

THE GREAT SMOKY MOUNTAINS NATIONAL PARK & ENVIRONS

At 521,495 acres, the Great Smoky Mountains National Park is one of
the great wild areas in the eastern United States. The most visited of all
national parks, the Great Smokies gets some 10 million visitors each year.
Even so, if you get out of your car, you can soon be in a remote cove
where your only neighbors are deer and black bears. About half of the
park is in North Carolina, with the remainder in Tennessee. (Only the
North Carolina section is included in this guide.)

Due to a fortuitous combination of moderate climate and diverse geog-
raphy, the Great Smoky Mountains National Park is one of the most
biologically rich spots on earth. Naturalists think the park contains at
least 100,000 different species of plants and animals, although to date
only about 10,000 have been identified. More than 1,600 types of wild-
flowers and more than 140 species of trees flourish in this wildlife sanc-
tuary. Bears are the most famous life form in the park; biologists estimate
that about 1,500 black bears live in the Smokies, a density of about two
per square mile. For the first time in 150 years, elk now roam the Great
Smokies; more than 50 elk were brought to the park in 2001–'02, and
elk cows have given birth to calves in the late spring of each year since.

Weather in the park is highly changeable, especially in the spring. On
one day it can be a balmy 70°F, and on the next bitterly cold and snowy.
By mid-June, haze, heat, and high humidity have arrived. Of course, tem-
peratures vary with elevation. In July, highs at the lower elevations av-

erage 88°F, but at Clingsmans Dome (elevation 6,643 feet) the average high is 65. In September a pattern of warm, sunny days and cool nights is established. Winters in the park see some snow, especially at the higher elevations. Newfound Gap gets an average of almost 6 feet of snow a year. Highway 441 and other park roads are sometimes closed due to snow.

Alas, air pollution is taking a toll on the park. Fifty years ago, from Clingman's Dome on an average day you could see 113 mi. Today, you can see only about 25 mi. The whitish haze you see in the Smokies, especially in summer, is not in fact what the park was named for. It consists of airborne particles, mostly sulfates from coal-burning power plants as far away as the Ohio Valley, the Gulf Coast, and the Northeast.

> ## THE BEAR FACTS
>
> Black-bear attacks in the Great Smokies or elsewhere in the mountains are extremely rare, but they do happen occasionally. If you see a bear—there are about 1,600 black bears in the Great Smokies—don't approach too closely. Never feed bears or leave food out, as most human–bear conflicts result from bears becoming used to eating human food. If a bear comes toward you making loud noises or swatting the ground, it's likely demanding more space. Don't run, but back away slowly. If the bear follows, especially if it is not vocalizing or swatting, stand your ground, shout, and try to intimidate it by throwing rocks.

Other than camping, the North Carolina side of the park has no accommodations or commercial operations of any kind—no shops, gas stations, or other services. You can take care of such needs at the park's main gateway towns—Cherokee, Bryson City, and Waynesville. Cherokee and Bryson City, along with Gatlinburg on the Tennessee side, have the easiest access to the park. Waynesville is the most charming, and Cherokee (along with Gatlinburg) the most tacky.

Great Smoky Mountains National Park

19 *Major gateway: Cherokee, 51 mi west of Asheville.*

Fodor'sChoice
★

U.S. Highway 441, also called Newfound Gap Road, is the main road through the park. On the North Carolina side, it runs from Cherokee to Newfound Gap, then continues on down into Tennessee near Gatlinburg. Branching off U.S. 441, and throughout the park, are secondary roads, most of them unpaved. Also throughout the park are hiking trails, with the level of difficulty ranging from short easy walks to backcountry trips that test veteran mountain hikers. The quality of your experience in the park likely will be in direct relation to how far you are from paved roads and automobiles. The biggest crowds in the park arrive mid-June to mid-August, and all of the month of October, peak fall color season. There are six times as many visitors in the park in July as in January.

Except at **Le Conte Lodge** (☎ 865/429–5704) on the Tennessee side, which is accessible by trail only, the only accommodations in the park are at 10 developed campsites, but these have no showers or RV hookups. Some campsites can be reserved in advance, by contacting the **National Park Service** (☎ 865/365–2267, 865/436–1231 for permit ⊕ http://reservations.nps.gov). Backcountry camping is also available, but such camping requires a (free) **permit.** Admission to the park is free.

A car will only take you so far in the Great Smokies. You can drive the main road, U.S. 441, which traverses the park, and you can also reach several key sights by car, including the Mountain Farm Museum, Mingus Mill, Clingman's Dome, and the "ghost towns" of the

> ### THE AT
>
> Each spring about 1,500 hikers set out to conquer the Appalachian Trail (AT), the 2,175-mi granddaddy of all hikes. Most hike north from Springer Mountain, Georgia, to Mt. Katahdin, Maine. By the time they get to the Great Smokies, where the AT reachs its highest elevation (6,625 feet) near Clingman's Dome, 160 mi from the trailhead in Georgia, about one-half of the hikers will already have dropped out. Typically, only about 400 hikers per year complete the entire AT.

Smokies, Cataloochee on the North Carolina side and Cades Cove on the Tennessee side. However, the best of the park is inaccessible by motorized vehicle. **The Appalachian Trail** runs along the crest of the rugged mountains through the park. Within the park's 800 square mi are 800 mi of trails and more than 600 mi of trout streams. Among the most interesting hikes are seven waterfalls, including an easy two-miler to three falls at Deep Creek, near Bryson City. Another rewarding walk is the 3.4 mi round-trip hike from Clingmans Dome along Forney Ridge Trail. You can see a mountaintop meadow, Andrews Bald, with high-elevation plants including flame azalea and Catawba rhododendron.

Fodor'sChoice ★ One of the most memorable, and eeriest, sites in all of the Smokies is **Cataloochee Cove.** At one time Cataloochee was a community of more than 1,200 people, in some 200 buildings. After the land was taken over in 1934 for the national park, the community dispersed. Although many of the original buildings are now gone, about a dozen houses, cabins, and barns, two churches, and other structures have been kept up. You can visit the Palmer Methodist Chapel, a one-room schoolhouse, Beach Grove School, and the Woody and Messer homesteads. It's much like Cades Cove on the Tennessee side, but much less visited. On a quiet day, you can almost hear the ghosts of the former Cataloochee settlers. Elk have been reintroduced around Cataloochee, and despite some losses the population now is approaching 60. This is the first time in 150 years that the Smokies have had an elk population. You can often see them from the road in the evening and early morning. Cataloochee is the most remote part of the Smokies reachable by car, via a narrow, winding, gravel road. ⊠ *Cataloochee Community, via U.S. 276 near Maggie Valley, off Exit 20 of I–40, to Cove Creek Rd.* ☎ *865/436–1200 for general park information.*

At an elevation of more than 6,600 feet, **Clingmans Dome** is one of the highest peaks east of the Rockies, only a few feet shorter than Mt.

Literary Mountain Lions

THEY MAY NOT BE ABLE to go home again, but many famous writers have made their homes in the North Carolina Mountains. The one most closely associated with the terrain is Thomas Wolfe (1900–38), author of *Look Homeward, Angel*, who was born and buried in Asheville. His contemporary F. Scott Fitzgerald visited Asheville and environs frequently in the 1930s, staying for long periods at the Grove Park Inn and at other hotels in the area. Fitzgerald's wife, Zelda, an author and artist in her own right, died in a 1948 fire at Highland Hospital, then a psychiatric facility in North Asheville.

William Sydney Porter, who under the pen name O. Henry, wrote "The Ransom of Red Chief," "The Gift of the Magi," and many other stories, married into an Asheville-area family and is buried in Asheville at Riverside Cemetery. Carl Sandburg, Pulitzer Prize–winning poet and biographer of Lincoln, spent the last 22 years of his life on a farm in Flat Rock. A younger generation of poets, including Jonathan Williams, Robert Creeley, Joel Oppenheimer, Robert Duncan, and Charles Olson, made names for themselves at Black Mountain College, an avant-garde hotbed during the 1940s and early 1950s.

More recently, Jan Karon and Sharyn McCrumb have set popular mystery series in the area. Novelist Charles Frazier, born in Asheville in 1950, made Cold Mountain, in the Shining Rock Wilderness of the Pisgah National Forest, the setting (and the title) for his million-selling Civil War drama. The mountain can be viewed from the Blue Ridge Parkway at mile marker 412. The movie, however, was filmed in Romania.

Mitchell. Walk up a paved, but steep, ½-mi trail to an observation tower offering 360-degree views of the Smokies. ⊠ *At end of Clingmans Dome Rd., 7 mi from U.S. 441* ☎ *865/436–1200 for general park information.*

For the effort of a 2-mi hike, **Deep Creek Waterfalls** will reward you with three pretty waterfalls, Tom Branch, Indian Creek, and Juney Whank. Deep Creek also has a picnic area and campground. ⊠ *Trailhead at end of Deep Creek Rd., near Bryson City entrance to park* ☎ *865/436–1200 for general park information.*

The **Mingus Mill** is a working, water-powered gristmill. In its time, the late 19th century, this was the state-of-the-art in grist mills, the two large grist stones powered by a store-bought turbine rather than a hand-built wheel. You can watch the miller make cornmeal, and even buy a pound of it. ⊠ *U.S. 441, 2 mi north of Cherokee* ☎ *828/497–1904* ☉ *Mid-Mar–late Nov.*

★ The **Mountain Farm Museum** at the Oconaluftee Visitors Center is perhaps the best re-creation anywhere of a mountain farmstead. The nine farm buildings, all dating from around 1900, were moved here from locations within the park. Besides a furnished two-story log cabin, you'll see a barn, apple house, corn crib, smokehouse, chicken coop, and other outbuildings. In season, corn, tomatoes, pole beans, squash, and other mountain crops are grown in the garden. The museum celebrated its 50th year of operation in 2004. ⊠ *U.S. 441 at Oconaluftee Visitors Center* ☎ *828/497–1904.*

Cherokee

⓴ *178 mi east of Charlotte; 51 mi west of Asheville; 2 mi from entrance to Great Smoky Mountains National Park.*

The 56,000-acre Cherokee reservation is known as the Qualla Boundary, and the town of Cherokee is its capital. Truth be told, there are two Cherokees. There's the Cherokee with the sometimes tacky pop culture, designed to appeal to the masses of tourists, many of whom are visiting the nearby Great Smoky Mountains National Park or have come to gamble at the massive Harrah's casino (the largest private employer in the region). But there's another Cherokee that's a window onto the rich heritage of the tribe's Eastern Band. Although now relatively small in number—tribal enrollment is 12,500—these Cherokee and their ancestors have been responsible for keeping alive the Cherokee culture. They are the descendants of those who hid in the Great Smoky Mountains to avoid the Trail of Tears, the forced removal of the Cherokee Nation to Oklahoma in the 19th century. They are survivors, extremely attached to the hiking, swimming, trout fishing, and natural beauty of their ancestral homeland.

The **Museum of the Cherokee Indian,** with displays and artifacts that cover 12,000 years, is one of the best Native American museums in the United States. Computer-generated images, lasers, specialty lighting, and sound effects help re-create events in the history of the Cherokee: for example, you'll see children stop to play a butter bean game while adults shiver along the snowy Trail of Tears. The museum has an art gallery, a gift shop, and an outdoor living exhibit of Cherokee life in the 15th century. ⊠ *U.S. 441 at Drama Rd.* ☎ *828/497–3481* ⊕ *www. cherokeemuseum.org* ⊡ *$9* ⊙ *June–Aug., Mon.–Sat. 9–8, Sun. 9–5; Sept.–May, daily 9–5.*

☺ At the historically accurate, re-created **Oconaluftee Indian Village,** guides in native costumes will lead you through a village of 225 years ago while others demonstrate traditional skills such as weaving, pottery, canoe construction, and hunting techniques. ⊠ *U.S. 441 at Drama Rd.* ☎ *828/ 497–2315* ⊕ *www.oconalufteevillage.com* ⊡ *$13* ⊙ *May 15–Oct. 25, daily 9:30–5.*

☺ Every mountain county has significant deposits of gems and minerals, and at the **Smoky Mountain Gold and Ruby Mine,** on the Qualla Boundary, you can search for gems such as aquamarines. Children love panning precisely because it can be wet and messy. Here they're guaranteed a find. Gem ore can be purchased, too: gold ore costs $11 per bag. ⊠ *U.S. 441N* ☎ *828/497–6574* ⊡ *$4–$11, depending on gems* ⊙ *Mar.–Nov., daily 10–6.*

Sports & the Outdoors

FISHING There are 30 mi of regularly stocked trout streams on the **Cherokee Indian Reservation** (☎ 828/497–5201 or 800/438–1601). To fish in tribal water, you need a tribal fishing permit, available at nearly two dozen reservation businesses. The $7 permit is valid for one day and has a creel limit of 10. A five-day permit is $28. Fishing is permitted from late March to October.

HIKING A five-minute hike from the **Mingo Falls Campground** (⊠ Big Cove Rd., about 4 mi north of Acquoni Rd.) will reward you with a view of the 200-foot-high Mingo Falls. In the downtown area you can cross the Oconaluftee River on a footbridge to **Oconaluftee Islands Park & Trail** (⊠ Off U.S. 441, across from Cherokee Elementary School) and walk a trail around the perimeter of the Island Park, which also has picnic facilities. The flat 1½-mi **Oconaluftee River Trail** begins at the Great Smoky Mountains National Park entrance sign on U.S. 441 (near the entrance to the Blue Ridge Parkway) and ends at the Mountain Farm Museum–Park Visitor Center.

HORSEBACK Privately operated **Smokemont Stables** (⊠ U.S. 441 in Great Smoky RIDING Mountains National Park ☎ 828/497–2373) offers riding trips in the Smokies from one hour to all day, including a waterfall trip.

Where to Stay & Eat

$$–$$$$ ✕📶**Harrah's Cherokee Casino Hotel.** The 15-story hotel, which opened in 2002 and doubled in size with an addition in 2005, towers over the mom 'n' pop motels nearby and the casino next door, to which it is umbilically attached via a series of escalators and walkways. The lobby and other public areas incorporate Cherokee traditional art themes. Rooms are large, about 500 square feet, and have 32-inch TVs. For high-rollers, there are suites on the top floor. The Selu Garden Café ($–$$$$) in the hotel and the Seven Sisters restaurant in the casino ($$$–$$$$) are handy after a day of playing the slots. ⊠ *U.S. 19 at U.S. 441 Business, 28719* ☎ *800/427–7247 or 828/497–7777* ⊕ *www.harrahs.com* ⤳ *576 rooms* ⟋ *5 restaurants, cable TV, gym, casino, indoor pool, recreation room* ⊟ *AE, D, DC, MC, V* ⏀⊙ *EP.*

$–$$ 📶**Fairfield Inn & Suites.** Opened in 2003, this three-story chain motel is directly across from Harrah's Casino, so you can walk to the casino without worrying about parking. Rooms here are typical of the Fairfield Inn chain—comfortable and clean but not deluxe. ⊠*568 Painttown Rd., 28719* ☎ *828/497–0400* 🖷 *828/497–4242* ⊕ *www.marriott.com* ⤳ *96 rooms, 4 suites* ⟋ *Cable TV, Wi-Fi, pool, refrigerators, exercise equipment, recreation room, laundry facilities, laundry service, business services, meeting room, free parking, no-smoking rooms* ⊟ *AE, D, DC, MC, V* ⏀⊙ *CP.*

Nightlife & the Arts

THE ARTS ***Unto These Hills*** (⊠ Mountainside Theater on Drama Rd., off U.S. 441N ☎ 828/497–2111 or 866/554–4557) is a colorful and well-staged history of the Cherokee from the time of Spanish explorer Hernando de Soto's visit in 1540 to the infamous Trail of Tears. The show runs from mid-June to late August and tickets start at $16. The drama was updated in 2006 with a new script and new costumes.

NIGHTLIFE Owned by the Eastern Bank of the Cherokee, **Harrah's Casino** (✉ 777 Casino Dr., U.S. 19 at U.S. 441 Business ☎ 828/497–7777 or 800/ 427–7247) has more than 3,600 video-gaming machines in a casino the size of more than three football fields. Digital blackjack and digital baccarat combine live dealers with digital cards. Big-name stars such as Wayne Newton, Jay Leno, and Willie Nelson, provide entertainment at the casino, which has a theater seating 1,500.

Shopping

The **Qualla Arts and Crafts Mutual** (✉ U.S. 441 at Drama Rd. ☎ 828/ 497–3103), across the street from the Museum of the Cherokee Indian, is a cooperative that displays and sells items created by 300 Cherokee craftspeople. The store has a large selection of high-quality baskets, masks, and wood carvings, which can cost hundreds of dollars.

Bryson City

㉑ *65 mi east of Asheville; 11 mi southwest of Cherokee.*

Bryson City is a little mountain town on the Nantahala River, one of the lesser-known gateways to the Great Smokies. The town's most striking feature is a city hall with a four-sided clock. Since becoming a tourist stop on the Great Smoky Mountains Railroad, the downtown shopping area has been rejuvenated, mostly with T-shirt shops and ice-cream stands.

The most popular river in western North Carolina for rafting and kayaking is **Nantahala River,** which races through the scenic Nantahala Gorge, a 1,600-foot-deep gorge that begins about 13 mi west of Bryson City on U.S. 19. Class III and Class IV rapids (Class V are the most dangerous) make for a thrilling ride. Several outfitters run river trips or rent equipment. ■ TIP➔ **At several points along the river you can park your car and watch rafters run the rapids—on a summer day you'll see hundreds of rafts and kayaks going by.** ✉ *U.S. 19, beginning 13 mi west of Bryson City.*

Overly commercial and overpriced, the **Smoky Mountain Model Railroad Museum** nevertheless appeals to kids or anyone with a fond memory of model trains. More than 2,500 model trains are displayed, around two model railroad operating layouts. ✉ *100 Greenlee St., near Great Smoky Mountains Railroad Depot* ☎ *828/488–5200 or 866/914–5200* ⊕ *www.smokymtntrains.com* ✉ *$9* ☾ *Mon.–Sat. 8:30–5:30.*

WET OR DRY?

The mountains sometimes seem to have a schizophrenic attitude toward alcohol. Making moonshine was once a major industry here, and it's still made and sold illegally in some remote areas. At the same time, many communities refuse to authorize the legal sale of alcohol. Four counties in western North Carolina—Clay, Graham, Mitchell, and Yancey—are completely dry; no alcohol can be sold, although it's not illegal to drink. Others operate on a spectrum, with a range of different rules and prohibitons. For all the details, visit the Web site of the **North Carolina Alcoholic Beverage Control Commission** (⊕ www. ncabc.com).

Sports & the Outdoors

GOLF The par-71, 5,987-yard course at semiprivate **Smoky Mountain Country Club** (⊠ Conley Creek Valley, Box 937, Whittier ☎ 828/4497–4653 or 800/474–0070), has 400 feet of elevation change over the 18 holes, not to mention stunning views of the mountains.

HORSEBACK RIDING Privately owned **Deep Creek Stables** (⊠ Deep Creek Picnic Area, near Bryson City entrance to Great Smokies National Park ☎ 828/488–8504) offers trail riding in the Smokies.

RIVER RAFTING & KAYAKING **Nantahala Outdoor Center (NOC)** (⊠U.S. 19/74 ☎800/232–7238 ⊕www.noc.com), guides more than 30,000 rafters every year on the Nantahala and six other rivers: the Chattooga, Cheoah, French Borad, Nolichucky, Ocoee, and Pigeon. ■ TIP➡ **In 2005 and 2006, the Cheoah River was reopened for rafting and kayaking, after being dammed and closed for years. Serious rafters and kayakers looking for a challenge on Class IV/IV+ river should consider the Cheoah.** NOC also rents kayaks, ducks, and other equipment. The NOC complex on the Nantahala River is virtually a tourist attraction itself, especially for young people, with three restaurants, cabin and campground rentals, an inn, and a depot for the Great Smokies Railroad, and an outdoor store.

Where to Stay & Eat

¢–$ ✕ **River's End at Nantahala Outdoor Center.** The casual riverbank setting and high-energy atmosphere at NOC's eatery draws lots of hungry people just returned from an invigorating day of rafting. There are salads, soups, and sandwiches during the day and fancier fixins' in the evening. The chili's a winner—there's black- and white-bean versions. For more upscale fare at NOC, try Relia's Garden, which specializes in steak and trout. ⊠ *U.S. 19/74 W* ☎ *828/488–2176* ▭ *MC, V* ☉ *Closed Nov.–Mar.*

$$$ ✕▣ **Hemlock Inn.** This folksy, friendly mountain inn on 50 acres above Bryson City is the kind of place where you can rock, doze, and play Scrabble. Even if you're not a guest at the inn, you can make a reservation for dinner Monday through Saturday and for lunch on Sunday. The all-you-can-eat meals ($$; breakfast and dinner are included in the rates) are prepared with regional foods and served family-style on lazy susans at big round tables. Fly-fishing and river rafting–kayaking and other packages are available. ⊠ *Galbraith Creek Rd., 1 mi north of U.S. 19, 28713* ☎ *828/488–2885* 🖷 *828/488–8985* ⊕ *www.hemlockinn.com* ⇨ *22 rooms, 3 cottages* ⌂ *Restaurant, fans, recreation room, gift shop; no a/c, no room phones, no room TVs* ▭*D, MC, V* ☉ *Closed Nov.–mid-Apr.* ⍾❁ *MAP.*

$$ ✕▣ **Fryemont Inn.** An institution in Bryson City for eight decades, the Fryemont Inn is on the National Register of Historic Places. The lodge exterior is bark, rooms in the main lodge are paneled in real chestnut, and the lobby has a fireplace big enough for 8-foot logs. If you need more luxury, choose one of the suites with fireplaces and air-conditioning. The restaurant ($–$$$), serving Southern fare, is open to the public for breakfast and dinner. ⊠ *Freymont St., Box 459, 28713* ☎ *828/488–2159 or 800/845–4879* ⊕ *www.fryemontinn.com* ⇨ *37 rooms, 3 suites, 1 cabin* ⌂ *Restaurant, pool; no a/c in some rooms, no room*

phones, no TV in some rooms ▭ *D, MC, V* ⊙ *Main lodge and restaurant closed late Nov.–mid-Apr. No lunch* 🍽 *MAP.*

Robbinsville & Lake Santeetlah

22 *98 mi southwest of Asheville; 35 mi southwest of Bryson City.*

If you truly want to get away from everything, head to the area around Robbinsville in the far southwest corner of North Carolina, a little south of the southern edge of the Great Smokies. The town of Robbinsville offers little, but the Snowbird Mountains, Lake Santeetlah, Fontana Lake, the rugged Joyce Kilmer–Slickrock Wilderness, and the Joyce Kilmer Memorial Forest, with its giant virgin poplars and sycamores, definitely are highlights of this part of North Carolina.

More than 29 mi long, **Fontana Lake & Dam** borders the southern edge of the Great Smokies. Unlike most other lakes in the mountains, Fontana has a shoreline that is almost completely undeveloped, since about 90% of its 240 mi are owned by the federal government. Fishing here is excellent, especially for small-mouth bass, muskie, and walleye. On the downside, the Tennessee Valley Authority (TVA) manages the lake for power generation, and at peak visitor period in the fall the lake is drawn down, leaving large areas of mudflats. Fontana Dam, completed in 1944, at 480 feet is the highest dam east of the Rockies. The Appalachian Trail crosses the top of the dam. ✉ *Fontana Dam Visitor Center, off Rte. 28, 3 mi from Fontana Village* ☎ *865/632–2101 TVA* 🎫 *Free* ⊙ *Visitor center May–Nov., daily 9–7.*

Fodor'sChoice ★

One of the few remaining sections of the original Appalachian forests, **Joyce Kilmer Memorial Forest,** a part of the 17,000-acre Joyce Kilmer–Slickrock Wilderness, has 400-year-old yellow poplars that are as much as 20 feet in circumference, along with huge hemlocks, oaks, sycamores, and other trees. ■ TIP→ **If you haven't seen a true virgin forest, you can't imagine what America must have looked like in the early days of settlement.** A 2-mi trail takes you through wildflower- and moss-carpeted areas of incredible beauty. The forest is named for the early-20th-century poet, killed in World War I, who is famous for the lines "I think I shall never see / A poem lovely as a tree." ✉ *15 mi west of Robbinsville, off Cherohala Skyway via Hwy. 143 and Kilmer Rd.* ☎ *828/479–6431 Cheoah Ranger District* 🎫 *Free.*

Formed in 1928 with the construction of the Santeetlah Dam, **Lake Santeetlah,** meaning "blue waters" in the Cherokee language, has 76 mi of shoreline, with good fishing for crappie, bream, and lake trout. The lake is managed by Alcoa as a hydro-electric project, but most of the land is owned by the federal government, a part of the Nantahala National Forest. ✉ *Cheoah Point Recreation Area, Rte. 1145 off U.S. 129, about 7 mi north of Robinsville* ☎ *828/479–6431 Nantahala National Forest/ Cheoah Ranger District* 🎫 *Free.*

Sports & the Outdoors

BOATING Boat rentals, including a 65-foot houseboat, are available at **Fontana Marina** (✉ Fontana Village, Fontana Dam ☎ 800/849–2258 or 828/498–

2211), open late May–early September. For a fast boating experience, try **Smoky Mountain Jet Boats** (✉ U.S. 74 at Needmore Rd. ☎ 828/488–0522 or 888/900–9091), offering half-hour rides on Fontana Lake for $25 a person.

Where to Stay & Eat

★ **$$$–$$$$** ✕🏠 **Snowbird Mountain Lodge.** When it's 95°F and the paperwork is piling up, Snowbird is the kind of mountain lodge you daydream about. The main lodge, built in 1941 and now in the National Register of Historic Places, has two massive stone fireplaces, solid chestnut beams across the ceiling, and beautiful views across the valley. If you run out of things to do, there are 10,000 books in the library. The restaurant serves "rustic" meals like fresh trout with grilled vegetable salsa. For more luxury than the main lodge rooms offer, choose a room in the Chestnut Lodge or a king suite in a separate cottage. Some rooms have whirlpool baths and fireplaces. ✉ *4633 Santeetlah Rd., Robbinsville 28771* ☎ *828/479–3433 or 800/941–9290* 🖨 *828/479–3473* ⊕ *www.snowbirdlodge.com* � *21 rooms, 2 suites in separate cottage* ⚭ *Restaurant, some refrigerators, Wi-Fi, some hot tubs, library, gift shop; no a/c in some rooms, no room phones, no room TVs, no children under 12, no smoking* ⊟ *MC, V* ⊙ *Closed late Nov.–early Apr.* ⦿| *FAP.*

$–$$ 🏠 **Blue Boar Inn.** On the outside, it looks like a mountain inn for bear and wild boar hunters. Inside, it has been totally redone, with upscale modern furnishings, including air-conditioning and TVs. Each room has a porch. You can kayak or canoe on nearby Lake Santeetlah. A full breakfast is included, and dinner is available at an extra charge. Originally built in 1950 by a Cincinnati beer magnate, today—because the county is legally dry—no alcohol is sold at the lodge. ✉ *1283 Blue Boar Rd., Robbinsville 28771* ☎ *828/479–8126 or 866/479–8126* 🖨 *828/479–2415* ⊕ *www.blueboarinn.com* � *8 rooms* ⚭ *Dining room, refrigerators, pond, boating; no smoking* ⊟ *AE, D, MC, V* ⊙ *Closed late Nov.–late Mar.* ⦿| *BP.*

Dillsboro

㉓ *51 mi southwest of Asheville; 13 mi southeast of Cherokee on U.S. 441.*

The tiny town of Dillsboro, in Jackson County, has developed a big reputation for shopping, especially if you like crafts and gift shops. The Great Smoky Mountains Railroad arrivals and departures add to the hustle and bustle of the two-block "downtown," especially in season. Crowds line up to eat country ham at the Jarrett House, an institution in Dillsboro since 1884, across the street from the railway depot.

The popular train rides of the **Great Smoky Mountains Railroad** include four regular excursions from Dillsboro, along with four originating in Bryson City, and several special trips. Diesel-electric or steam locomotives go through Nantahala Gorge or along the Tuckasegee River. Open-sided cars or standard coaches are ideal for picture taking as the mountain scenery glides by. Some rides include a meal: on Friday evenings there's a mystery theater train with dinner, and on Saturday a gourmet dinner train. ✉ *119 Front St., Dillsboro* ☎ *828/586–8811 or 800/872–4681* ⊕ *www.gsmr.com* ✉ *$15–$82 plus $3 parking fee.*

Sports & the Outdoors

RIVER TUBING & KAYAKING On the Tuckaseegee River, much gentler than the Nantahala River, **Tuck-aseegee Outfitters** (⊠ U.S. 74/441 ☎ 800/539–5683) offers nonguided trips by tube, raft, and inflatable kayak.

Where to Stay & Eat

$ ✕ Jarrett House. The food ($$) here may not win any awards for creative cooking, but folks love the mountain trout, country ham with redeye gravy, and fried chicken at the Jarrett House, in continuous operation since 1884 and now on the National Register of Historic Places. Rooms in this three-story country inn, with porches on all three levels, are small and unpretentious, but you can't beat the location right across from Dillsboro's shops and the train depot. ⊠ Box 219, U.S. 441, 28725 ☎ 828/ 586–0265 or 800/972–5623 ⊕ www.jarretthouse.com ➷ 44 rooms ♨ Restaurant; no room phones, no room TVs ⊟ No credit cards ☺ BP ☺ Closed Jan.–Apr.

Shopping

Dillsboro has a cluster of mostly tourist-oriented shops, in the several blocks adjoining the Great Smokies Railroad depot. A co-op of more than 80 area artisans owns and runs **Dogwood Crafters** (⊠ 90 Webster St. ☎ 828/586–2248), where you can purchase pottery, rugs, baskets, and other crafts. You can see potters throwing pots at **Mountain Pottery** (⊠ 152 Front St. ☎ 828/586–9183), where pottery, including ceramics made in the Japanese raku style, by about 75 different local potters are for sale.

Waynesville

㉔ *17 mi east of Cherokee on U.S. 19.*

This is where the Blue Ridge Parkway meets the Great Smokies. Pretty, arty Waynesville is the seat of Haywood County. About 40% of the county is occupied by the Great Smoky Mountains National Park, Pisgah National Forest, and the Harmon Den Wildlife Refuge. The town of Waynesville is a rival of Blowing Rock and Highlands as an upmarket summer and vacation home retreat for the well-to-do, though the atmosphere here is a bit more countryfied. A Ramp Festival, celebrating the smelly local cousin of the onion, is held in Waynesville annually in early May. New B&Bs are springing up around Wayneville like wildflowers after a heavy rain.

The **Museum of North Carolina Handicrafts,** in the Shelton House (circa 1875), has a comprehensive exhibit of 19th-century heritage crafts. ⊠ 307 Shelton St. ☎ 828/452–1551 ☺ $5 ☺ May–Oct., Tues.–Fri. 10–4.

Cold Mountain, the vivid best-selling novel by Charles Frazier, has made a destination out of the real **Cold Mountain.** About 15 mi from Waynesville in the Shining Rock Wilderness Area of Pisgah National Forest, the 6,030-foot rise had long stood in relative anonymity. But with the success of Frazier's book, people want to see the region that Inman and Ada, the book's Civil War–era protagonists, called home.

For a view of the splendid mass—or at least of the surrounding area—stop at any of a number of overlooks off the Blue Ridge Parkway. Try the Cold Mountain Parking Overlook, just past mile marker 411.9; the Wagon Road Gap parking area, at mile marker 412.2; or the Waterrock Knob Interpretive Station, at mile marker 451.2. You can climb the mountain, but beware, as the hike to the summit is strenuous. No campfires are allowed in Shining Rock, so you'll need a stove if you wish to cook. Inform the **ranger station** (☎ 828/877–3350) if you plan to hike or camp.

Sports & the Outdoors

FISHING If you want to fly fish for rainbow, brown, or native brook trout, try **Lowe Fly Shop** (✉ 15 Woodland Dr. ☎ 828/452–0039), which runs wading and floating trips on area streams and lakes. A full-day wade trip for two with guide costs around $300.

GOLF A public course at the Methodist conference center, **Lake Junaluska Golf Course** (✉ 19 Golf Course Rd. ☎ 828/456–5777) is short but surprisingly tricky, due to all the trees. At **Waynesville Country Club Inn** (✉ 300 Country Club Dr. ☎ 828/452–4617), you can play three 9-hole courses in any combination.

Where to Stay & Eat

$$$–$$$$ ✗ **Lomo Grill.** Waynesville's best restaurant combines Mediterranean-style ingredients with the chef-owner's Argentine background. The grilled steaks are perfectly prepared and served with delicately cooked, fresh local vegetables. Many of the fruits and vegetables are grown in the chef's garden. In a 1920s downtown space with a high, crimson-red ceiling, Lomo Grill has superlative servers, efficient and friendly without being obsequious. Try the key lime pie—it's the best in the mountains. The restaurant serves beer and wine, but no hard alcohol. ✉ 44 Church St. ☎ 828/452–5222 ▭ AE, D, DC, MC, V ⊘ Closed Sun. and Mon. No lunch.

★ $$$$ ▥ **The Swag Country Inn.** This exquisite, rustic inn sits 5,000 feet, high atop the Cataloochee Divide overlooking a swag—a deep depression in otherwise high ground. Its 250 wooded acres share a border with Great Smoky Mountains National Park and have access to the park's hiking trails. Guest rooms and cabins were assembled from six authentic log structures and transported here. All have exposed beams and wood floors and are furnished with early American crafts. Dinners here are social events, with hors d'oeuvres, conversation, and an option of family-style or individual seating. There's a two-night minimum stay; bring your own beverages, as the inn is in a dry county. ✉ 2300 Swag Rd., 28786 ☎ 828/926–0430 or 800/789–7672 ▤ 828/926–2036 ⊕ www.theswag. com ⇆ 16 rooms, 3 cabins ⚲ Dining room, pond, massage, sauna, badminton, croquet, racquetball, library, business services; no room TVs ▭ AE, D, MC, V ⊘ Closed Nov.–Mar. ⏐◉⏐ FAP.

$$$–$$$$ ▥ **The Yellow House on Plott Creek Road.** Just outside town, this lovely two-story Victorian sits on a knoll, with gorgeous, colorful surrounding gardens. The hotel strives for an impressionist feel, with light, dappling pastoral colors. The rooms and suites are named for and decorated to evoke other destinations, from Savannah to the Caribbean island of

Saba to E'staing, France. Part of the house was renovated in 2006. Most rooms have fireplaces, and some suites have whirlpool baths. ⊠ *89 Oak View Dr., at Plott Creek Rd., 1 mi west of Waynesville, 28786* ☎ *828/452–0991 or 800/563–1236* 🖷 *828/452–1140* ⊕ *www.theyellowhouse. com* 🖵 *4 rooms, 6 suites* ♿ *Fans, some refrigerators, some in-room whirlpools; no room TVs, no children under 13* ▤ *MC, V* ⦿⃝ *BP.*

Shopping
The **Downtown Waynesville** (⊠ Main St.) shopping area stretches three blocks from the city hall to the Haywood County courthouse, with a number of small boutiques, bookstores, and antique shops.

THE HIGH COUNTRY

Here you'll find the highest, steepest, coldest, snowiest, windiest, and, some say, friendliest parts of the mountains. The High Country has not only the tallest mountains east of the Rockies, but the highest average elevation in all of eastern America. With temperatures 10 to 15 degrees cooler than in the foothills and flatlands, even folks from Asheville come to the High Country in the summer to cool down.

Unlike the rest of the mountains, winter is the peak season in much of the High Country. The reason? The white stuff. Towns like Boone, Blowing Rock, and Banner Elk have boomed in the 40 years since the introduction of snowmaking equipment, and the ski resorts of Beach Mountain, Sugar Mountain, and Appalachian Ski Mountain attract skiers, snowboarders, and snowtubers from all over the Southeast. The fiery colors of autumn against the green backdrop of firs also bring carloads of visitors to the High Country, and many come for the cool summers, too. Luxury resorts dot the valleys and mountaintops, and there are many crafts shops, music festivals, and theater offerings.

The Blue Ridge Parkway is highlighted in this section, as this magnificent road enters the High Country from Virginia, but the parkway actually transverses much of western North Carolina, including Asheville and parts of the Southern Mountains, until it terminates at the entrance of the Great Smoky Mountains National Park. ▪ TIP➡ **Take special care when driving at higher elevations (4,000 to 6,000 feet and higher) of the Blue Ridge Parkway and in the High Country.** In the spring, summer, and fall, thick fog and clouds can cover the mountain tops, especially during and after rains. In winter, snow and ice are common. Four-wheel drive is necessary at times; few steep, high areas, especially near ski resorts, may require snow chains.

Blue Ridge Parkway

㉕ *Entrance 2 mi east of Asheville, off I–40 and at many other points.*

The Blue Ridge Parkway's 252 mi within North Carolina wind down the High Country through Asheville, ending near the entrance of the Great Smoky Mountains National Park. Highlights on and near the parkway include Mt. Mitchell, the highest mountain peak east of the Rockies, Grandfather Mountain, and Mt. Pisgah. Although in this section we list sights, lodging, and restaurants that are close to the park, nearly all the towns and cities along the parkway route offer accommodations, dining, and sightseeing. In particular, look at the listings for Boone, Blowing Rock, Burnsville, Asheville, Waynesville, Brevard, and Cherokee, all of which are near popular entrances to the parkway.

Fodor'sChoice ★ The beautiful **Blue Ridge Parkway** gently winds through mountains and meadows and crosses mountain streams for more than 469 mi on its way from Cherokee, North Carolina, to Waynesboro, Virginia, connecting the Great Smoky Mountains and Shenandoah national parks. With elevations ranging from 649 to 6,047 feet, and with more than 250 scenic lookout points, it is truly one of the most beautiful drives in North America. No commercial vehicles are allowed, and the entire parkway is free of billboards, although in a few places residential or commercial development encroaches close to the road. The parkway, which has a maximum speed limit of 45 mph, is generally open year-round but often closes during inclement weather. In winter, sections can be closed for weeks at a time due to snow, and even in good weather fog and clouds occasionally make driving difficult. Maps and information are available at visitor centers along the highway. Mile markers (MMs) identify points of interest and indicate the distance from the parkway's starting point in Virginia. ■ TIP➔ **Gas up before you get on the parkway. Although there are no gas stations on the parkway itself, you'll find stations at intersecting highways near parkway exits.** ⊠ *Superintendent, Blue Ridge Pkwy., 199 Hemphill Knob Rd., Asheville 28803* ☎ *828/298–0398* ⊕ *www. nps.gov/blri* ⊠ *Free.*

Craggy Gardens at mile marker 364.6, at 5,500 to 6,000 feet, has some of the parkway's most colorful displays of rhododendrons, usually in June. You can also hike trails and picnic here. ⊠ *MM 364.6* ☎ *828/ 298–0398* ⊠ *Free.*

☺ At **Emerald Village** you can tour an underground mine or dig for gems of your own. ⊠ *McKinney Mine Rd. at Blue Ridge Pkwy., MM 334, Little Switzerland* ☎ *828/765–6463 or 877/389–4653* ⊕ *www. emeraldvillage.com* ⊠ *Mine $5, gem bucket $3–$100* ☉ *May–Oct., weekdays 9–5, weekends 9–6; Apr., daily 10–4.*

The **Folk Art Center** displays and sells authentic mountain crafts made by members of the Southern Highland Craft Guild. Demonstrations are held frequently. ■ TIP➔ **This is one of the best places in the region to buy high-quality crafts.** ⊠ *Blue Ridge Pkwy., MM 382 at Asheville* ☎ *828/ 298–7928* ☉ *Jan.–Mar., daily 9–5; Apr.–Dec., daily 9–6.*

Just off the parkway at mile marker 305, **Grandfather Mountain** soars to 6,000 feet and is famous for its Mile-High Swinging Bridge, a 228-foot-long bridge that sways over a 1,000-foot drop into the Linville Valley. The **Natural History Museum** has exhibits on native minerals, flora and fauna, and pioneer life. The annual **Singing on the Mountain,** in June, is an opportunity to hear old-time gospel music and preaching, and the **Highland Games** in July bring together Scottish clans from all over North America for athletic events and Highland dancing. The owner of Grandfather Mountain, Hugh Morton, was a noted nature photographer; he died in 2006 at age 86. ☒ *Blue Ridge Pkwy. and U.S. 221, Linville* ☏ *828/733–4337 or 800/468–7325* ⊕ *www.grandfather.com* ✉ *$14* ☾ *Apr.–mid-Nov., daily 8–dusk; mid-Nov.–Mar., daily 8–5.*

Green spaces along the parkway include **Julian Price Park,** which has hiking, canoeing on a mountain lake, trout fishing, and camping. ☒ *MM 295–MM 298.1.*

Linville Caverns are the only caverns in the Carolinas. They go 2,000 feet beneath Humpback Mountain and have a year-round temperature of 51°F. North of Asheville, exit the parkway at mile marker 317.4 and turn left onto U.S. 221. ☒ *U.S. 221, between Linville and Marion* ☏ *828/756–4171* ⊕ *www.linvillecaverns.com* ✉ *$6* ☾ *June–early Sept., daily 9–6; Apr., May, and mid-Sept.–Oct., daily 9–5; Nov. and Mar., daily 9–4:30; Dec.–Feb., weekends 9–4:30.*

From the **Linville Falls Visitor Center,** ½-mi hike leads to one of North Carolina's most photographed waterfalls. The easy trail winds through evergreens and rhododendrons to overlooks with views of the series of cascades tumbling into Linville Gorge. There are also a campground and a picnic area. ☒ *Rte. 1, MM 316.3, Spruce Pine* ☏ *828/765–1045.*

The **Moses H. Cone Park** has a turn-of-the-20th-century manor house that's now the **Parkway Craft Center.** The center sells fine work by area craftspeople. ☒ *MM 292.7–MM 295* ☏ *828/295–7938* ☾ *Mar. 15–Nov. 30, daily 9–5.*

Mt. Mitchell State Park includes the highest mountain peak east of the Rockies, Mt. Mitchell at 6,684 feet. The summit was named after Elisha Mitchell, who died from a fall while trying to prove the mountain's true height. At the 1,855-acre park, you can climb an observation tower and get food at a restaurant. Keep an eye on the weather here, as high winds and snow can occur at almost any time, occasionally even in summer. The lowest temperature ever recorded in North Carolina was at Mt. Mitchell on Jan. 21, 1985: -34°F. Clouds obscure the views here for at least parts of 8 days out of 10. ☒ *2388 NC Hwy. 128, MM 355, Burnsville* ☏ *828/675–4611* ✉ *Free.*

Mt. Pisgah, at 5,721 feet one of the most easily recognized peaks due to the television tower installed there in the 1950s, has walking trails, an amphitheater where nature programs are given most evenings June through October, a campground, inn, picnic area, and small grocery. The nearby area called **Graveyard Fields** is popular for blueberry picking in July. In 1992 a snowstorm in *May* dropped more than 5 feet of snow here. ☒ *Blue Ridge Pkwy., MM 408.6* ☏ *campground 828/648–2664.*

Museum of North Carolina Minerals at mile marker 331 has hands-on displays about gold, copper, kaolin, and other minerals found nearby. The museum was recently renovated. ☒ *MM 331 at U.S. 226* ☏ *828/765–2761* ✉ *Free* ☾ *May–Oct., daily 9–5; Nov.–Apr., daily 9–noon and 1–5.*

Sports & the Outdoors

HIKING More than 100 trails lead off the Blue Ridge Parkway, from easy strolls to strenuous hikes. For more information on parkway trails, contact the

National Park Service Blue Ridge Parkway office (☎ 828/298–0398 ⊕ www. nps.gov/blri). Another good source is *Walking the Blue Ridge: A Guide to the Trails of the Blue Ridge Parkway*, by Leonard Adkins, available at most parkway visitor center gift shops. The **Bluff Mountain Trail**, at Doughton Park (MM 238.5), is a moderately strenuous 7½-mi trail winding through forests, pastures, and valleys, and along the mountainside. Moses H. Cone Park's (MM 292.7) **Figure 8 Trail** is an easy and beautiful trail that the Cone family designed for their morning walks. The ½-mi loop winds through a tunnel of rhododendrons and a hardwood forest. Those who tackle the strenuous, ½-mi **Waterrock Knob Trail** (MM 451.2), near the south end of the parkway, will be rewarded with spectacular views from the 6,400-foot-high Waterrock Knob summit.

ROCK CLIMBING   One of the most challenging climbs in the country is the **Linville Gorge** (⊠ MM 317 ☎ 828/652–2144), often called "the Grand Canyon of North Carolina." Permits are available from the district forest ranger's office in Nebo or from the Linville Falls Texaco station on U.S. 221.

SKIING   **Moses H. Cone Park** (☎ 828/295–7591) is known for its cross-country skiing trails. On the Blue Ridge Parkway, **Roan Mountain** (☎ 615/772–3303), open daily during the winter, is famous for its deep powder. Tours and equipment are available from **High Country Ski Shop** (☎ 828/733–2008), in Pineola on U.S. 221.

Where to Stay & Eat

★ $$$$ ✗☷ **Eseeola Lodge and Restaurant.** Rebuilt in 1936 after a fire, this lakeside lodge, best described as dressed-up rustic, sits 3,800 feet above sea level and is one sure way to beat summer's heat. Golf is a passion here, but the diversions are many. All rooms overlook the manicured grounds and gardens. Rich chestnut paneling and stonework grace the public areas. Entrées at the restaurant ($$$$) may include free-range chicken and rainbow trout; jacket and tie are required at dinner. ⊠ *175 Linville Ave., off U.S. 221, Linville 28646* ☎ *828/733–4311 or 800/742–6717* 🖷 *828/733–3227* ⊕ *www.eseeola.com* ⇨ *19 rooms, 5 suites, 1 cottage* ♨ *Restaurant, 18-hole golf course, putting green, 8 tennis courts, cable TV, pool, exercise equipment, boating, fishing, croquet, hiking, bar, playground, business services; no-smoking rooms* ▤ *AE, MC, V* ⊗ *Closed late Oct.–mid-May* ⦿ *MAP.*

¢–$$$ ✗☷ **Little Switzerland Inn.** Families cozy up in the lobby of this old mountain inn, which dates to 1910, to play Monopoly or just doze over a book. The staff is cheerful, and you have a choice of comfy lodge rooms (without a/c) or bigger, brighter rooms in newer buildings. The Swiss theme is carried through to the Chalet restaurant ($–$$) and there are ice-cream and sweet shops on the grounds. ⊠ *MM 334 at Hwy. 226A, Little Switzerland 28749* ☎ *828/765–2153 or 800/654–4026* 🖷 *828/765–0049* ⊕ *www.switzerlandinn.com* ⇨ *59 rooms, 5 cottages* ♨ *Restaurant, cable TV, 2 tennis courts, pool, shuffleboard, shops, no-smoking rooms; no a/c in some rooms* ▤ *MC, V* ⊗ *Closed Nov.–mid-Apr.* ⦿ *BP.*

$–$$ ✗☷ **Pisgah Inn.** This inn, run by a park-service concessionaire, has motel-like rooms of no distinction, but the setting, at almost 1 mi high right on the parkway, is spectacular. Rooms have small porches or balconies with rocking chairs. Although an inn has been on this site since 1919, the present structure was built in 1964. The restaurant ($–$$$) has great views to the west and offers mountain trout, along with burgers and other standard fare. ⊠ *MM 408, Waynesville 28786* ☎ *828/ 235–8228* ⊕ *www.pisgahinn.com* ⟲ *Restaurant, some refrigerators, shops; no a/c* ⊟ *MC, V* ⊘ *Closed Nov.–late Mar.* ❢◯❨ *EP.*

Blowing Rock

㉖ *86 mi northeast of Asheville; 93 mi west of Winston-Salem.*

Blowing Rock, a draw for mountain visitors since the 1880s, has retained the flavor of a quiet New England village, with stone walls and buildings with wood shakes or bark siding. About 1,000 people are permanent residents of this town at a 4,000-foot elevation, but the population swells each summer. To ensure that the town would remain rural, the community banded together to prohibit large hotels and motels. Blowing Rock is the inspiration for the small town in resident Jan Karon's novels about country life in the fictional town of Mitford. To get here from the Blue Ridge Parkway, take U.S. 221/321 to just north of the entrance to Moses H. Cone Park.

The **Blowing Rock** looms over the Johns River Gorge. If you throw your hat over the sheer precipice, it may blow back to you, should the wind gods be playful. The story goes that a Cherokee man and a Chickasaw maiden fell in love. Torn between his tribe and his love, he jumped from the cliff, but she prayed to the Great Spirit, and he was blown safely back to her. ⊠ *Off U.S. 321* ☎ *828/295–7111* ⊕ *www.blowingrock. org* ▧ *$6* ⊘ *June–Oct., daily 8–8; Jan.–Mar., daily 8:30–5; Apr., daily 8:30–6; May, daily 8:30–7; Nov. and Dec., daily 9–5.*

㋡ The **Tweetsie Railroad** is a popular Wild West theme park built into the side of a mountain and centered on a steam locomotive beset by robbers. A petting zoo, carnival amusements, gem panning, shows, and concessions, all mostly of interest to young children, are also here. Several of the attractions are at the top of the mountain and can be reached by foot or ski lift. ⊠ *U.S. 321/221, off Blue Ridge Pkwy. at MM 291* ☎ *828/264– 9061 or 800/526–5740* ⊕ *www.tweetsie-railroad.com* ▧ *$27* ⊘ *Early May and mid-Aug.–Oct., Fri.–Sun. 9–6; mid-May–late Aug., daily 9–6.*

Sports & the Outdoors

RAFTING You can go white-water rafting on Wilson Creek or the Nolichucky or Wautaga rivers with **High Mountain Expeditions** (⊠ 1380 Hwy. 105 S, Boone ☎ 828/264–7368 or 800/262–9036).

SKIING There's downhill skiing and snowboarding at **Appalachian Ski Mountain** (⊠ 940 Ski Mountain Rd. ☎ 828/295–7828 or 800/322–2373).

Where to Stay & Eat

¢–$$ ✕ **Canyons.** The long-range view from the deck of Canyons is so dramatic that owner Bart Conway put a live minicam on the restaurant's Web site. While oohing over the mountain scenery, or eyeing the funky artwork on the walls inside, you can munch on fresh-made tortilla chips, chimichangas, veggie burritos, or a classic drive-in burger slathered with chili and slaw. On most days, the restaurant is the busiest one in town. There's live entertainment Thursday to Sunday nights and a Sunday brunch. ⊠ *Off U.S. 321 bypass* ☎ *828/295–7661* ▤ *AE, D, MC, V.*

$$$$ ▦ **Westglow Spa.** If you want to get buff, lose weight, and be pampered at a beautiful mountain estate, and if money is no object, Westglow Spa may be your cup of herbal tea. Housed in an elegant 1916 mansion on 20 acres, once the home of 19th-century impressionist painter Elliott Daingerfield, the health resort spares nothing for its few, select guests. The fitness center is packed with the latest workout machines, health gizmos, spa facilities, and an indoor pool with a stunning view of the mountains. Meals, emphasizing low-fat and high-fiber items, are served in the Elliott restaurant in the manor house. The owner leads guests on hikes every morning promptly at 9. ⊠ *2845 U.S. 221S, 28605* ☎ *828/ 295–4463 or 800/562–0807* ⊕ *www.westglow.com* ⇨ *8 rooms, 2 cottages* ⌂ *Restaurant, tennis court, indoor pool, fitness classes, hair salon, hot tubs, massage, saunas, spa; no kids under 16, no smoking* ▤ *AE, MC, V* ▯◯▯ *FAP.*

$$$–$$$$ ▦ **Inn at Ragged Gardens.** With a grand stone staircase in the entry hall, colorful gardens, richly toned chestnut paneling, and the chestnut-bark siding found on many older homes in the High Country, it's no wonder that this manor-style house in the heart of Blowing Rock gets rave reviews. You're likely to appreciate the attention to detail: the European and American antiques blended with contemporary art and the all-hours butler's pantry. All rooms have fireplaces, and some have private balconies. A two-night minimum is required on weekends. ⊠ *203 Sunset Dr., 28605* ☎ *828/295–9703* ⊕ *www.ragged-gardens.com* ⇨ *6 rooms, 5 suites* ⌂ *Dining room, some in-room hot tubs, meeting room; no kids under 13, no smoking* ▤ *MC, V* ▯◯▯ *BP.*

$$–$$$ ▦ **Chetola Resort.** This inn and condo resort, named for the Cherokee word meaning "haven of rest," grew out of an early-20th-century stone-and-wood lodge. The original building now houses the resort's restaurant and meeting rooms and is adjacent to the 1988 lodge. Many guest rooms in the lodge have private balconies facing either the mountains, a small lake, or both. In late 2004 the resort opened a new section, the Bob Timberlake Inn. Condominiums are spread among the hills, and the 87-acre property adjoins Moses H. Cone Park, with hiking trails and riding facilities. ⊠ *N. Main St., Box 17, ½ mi north of Blue Ridge Pkwy. via U.S. 321, 28605* ☎ *828/295–5500 or 800/243–8652* ▤ *828/295– 5529* ⊕ *www.chetola.com* ⇨ *45 rooms, 5 suites, 62 condominiums* ⌂ *2 restaurants, minibars, cable TV, some in-room DVDs, some in-room safes, some hot tubs, 3 tennis courts, indoor pool, health club, massage, sauna, lake, boating, fishing, bicycles, Ping-Pong, racquetball, piano bar, playground, business services, meeting rooms, laundry facilities, gift shop, no-smoking rooms* ▤ *AE, D, MC, V* ▯◯▯ *EP.*

¢–$$$ ▦ **Alpine Village Inn.** This motel in the heart of Blowing Rock harks back to a simpler time. Rooms are neat and attractive in a homey way. Owners Rudy and Lynn Cutrera have decorated them with antiques, quilts, even flowers on holidays. They were renovated in 2005. Room refrigerators are available, and morning coffee is served. ⊠ *297 Sunset Dr., 28605* ☎ *828/295–7206* ⊕ *www.alpine-village-inn.com* ⇨ *17 rooms*

⚘ *Cable TV, some refrigerators; no smoking* ▤ *D, MC, V* ⭐ *EP*
⊘ *Closed Jan.–mid-Apr.*

Shopping

Classic, high-quality women's clothing goes at outlet sale prices at **Tanner Factory Store** (⊠ U.S. 321 bypass ☎ 828/295–7031).

Bolick Pottery (⊠ Rte. 8 off U.S. 321, Lenoir ☎ 828/295–3862), 3 mi southeast of Blowing Rock, sells mountain crafts and pottery handcrafted by Glenn and Lula Bolick, fifth-generation potters.

Boone

27 *8 mi north of Blowing Rock.*

Boone, at the convergence of three major highways—U.S. 321, U.S. 421, and Route 105—is a fast-growing college town, home to Appalachian State University (ASU) and its 14,000 students. Suburban sprawl has arrived, especially along U.S. 321 with its clusters of fast-food restaurants, chain motels, and a small mall, the only enclosed mall in the High Country. Closer to ASU, however, you get more of the college-town vibe, with organic-food stores and boutiques. The town was named for frontiersman Daniel Boone, whose family moved to the area when Daniel was 15. Restaurants here serve only wine and beer, not mixed drinks.

On 6 acres adjacent to the Horn in the West amphitheater, **Daniel Boone Native Gardens** highlights local plants and trees in a setting of quiet beauty. The wrought-iron gate to the gardens was a gift of Daniel Boone VI, a direct descendant of the pioneer. ⊠ *651 Horn in the West Dr., ¼ mi off U.S. 321* ☎ *828/264–6390* 🎟 *$2* ⊘ *May–mid-June and mid-Aug.-Oct., daily 10–6; mid-June–mid-Aug., Tues.–Sun. 10–8.*

★ The **Appalachian Cultural Museum** at Appalachian State University examines the lives of Native Americans and African-Americans in the High Country, showcases the successes of such mountain residents as stock-car racer Junior Johnson and country singers Lula Belle and Scotty Wiseman, and exhibits a vast collection of antique quilts, fiddles, and handcrafted furniture. ⊠ *University Hall Dr. off U.S. 321* ☎ *828/262–3117* ⊕ *www.museum.appstate.edu* 🎟 *$4, free on Tues.* ⊘ *Tues.–Sat. 10–5, Sun. 1–5.*

Sports & the Outdoors

CANOEING & RAFTING Near Boone and Blowing Rock, the New River, a federally designated Wild and Scenic River (Class I and II rapids) provides excitement for canoeists and rafters, as do the Watauga River, Wilson Creek, and the Toe River. One outfitter is **Wahoo's Adventures** (☎ 828/262–5774 or 800/444–7238).

GOLF The High Country has many challenging courses. **Boone Golf Club** (⊠ Fairway Dr. ☎ 828/264–8760) is a good par-71 course for the whole family. **Hound Ears Club** (⊠ Rte. 105 ☎ 828/963–4312) has a par-72 18-hole course with great mountain views. **Linville Golf Club** (⊠ 83 Roseboro Rd., Linville ☎ 828/733–4363), 17 mi from Boone, has a par-72 Donald Ross–designed course.

MOUNTAIN FOOD

Traditional mountain cooking is rib-sticking fare, intended for people who work hard on the farm all day. It dates to a time when the biggest meal of the day was dinner, taken at noon, and the food was heavy: country ham with red-eye gravy, pan-fried chicken, and vegetables from the garden such as half-runner beans seasoned with fatback, creamed sweet corn, and new potatoes. With it came cat-head biscuits (so called because of their size), fresh-churned butter, sourwood honey (light-color honey from sourwood trees that bloom in late spring), and tall glasses of springwater and buttermilk. Some of the more unusual mountain dishes, only rarely available at local restaurants, include ramps (a smelly cousin of the onion) with eggs; baked groundhog; bear meat (prepared as a roast or stew); creases or creasie greens (a salad of wild wintercress); leather-britches (beans dried in the pod and boiled with salt pork); and dried-apple pie.

Where to Stay & Eat

$$–$$$$ ✕ **Wildflower Casually Eclectic.** Wildflower lives up to its name, with a frequently changing and varied menu featuring unusual combinations of flavors and colors, such as peanut-encrusted salmon with soba noodles and crab cakes with roasted red peppers. Sometimes, though, the chefs' reach exceeds their grasp—an otherwise well-prepared tenderloin steak was overwhelmed by globs of black-eye pea relish, crabmeat, and fried green tomatoes. The restaurant is in a light, airy but minimalist space inside a small office and retail building. ⊠ *Market Place at King, 783 West King St.* ☎ *828/264–3463* ▭ *AE, D, MC, V* ☉ *No lunch Mon. and Tues.*

★ **$$** ✕ **Dan'l Boone Inn Restaurant.** Near Appalachian State University, in a former hospital surrounded by a picket fence and flowers, Dan'l Boone offers old-fashioned food served family style. Warning: the portions of fried chicken, country-style steak, ham, mashed potatoes, scrambled eggs, bacon, and breads (to name a few) are extremely generous. Lunch or dinner, including beverage and dessert, is a bargain at $13.95, and breakfast is $7.95. (You can't get breakfast on weekdays.) There's usually a line waiting to get in. The kitchen and part of the restaurant were renovated in mid-2006. ⊠ *130 Hardin St.* ☎ *828/264–8657* ▭ *No credit cards* ☉ *No lunch weekdays, Nov.–late May.*

$$$$ ▦ **Hound Ears Lodge and Club.** This alpine inn and golf resort, overlooking Grandfather Mountain and a lush golf course designed by George Cobb (greens fees are $80, plus $20 cart fee), offers amenities such as a swimming pool secluded in a natural grotto and comfortable, well-kept rooms dressed in Waverly print fabrics. From April through October the room rate for special packages includes breakfast and dinner. The dining area is open only to guests and members; reservations are required, as are a jacket and tie for dinner. ⊠ *328 Shulls Mill Rd., off*

Rte. 105, 6 mi from Boone, 28605 ☎ *828/963–4321* 🖷 *828/963–8030* ⊕ *www.houndears.com* 📞 *29 rooms* ♿ *Dining room, cable TV, 18-hole golf course, 8 tennis courts, pool, fishing, business services, meeting rooms, no-smoking rooms* 🚫 *AE, MC, V* ⦿⦿ *BP.*

★ **$$–$$$** 🖳 **Lovill House Inn.** This restored two-story country farmhouse once housed the law offices of Captain Edward Francis Lovill, a decorated Confederate officer and a founding trustee of what became Appalachian State University. Built in 1875 and featuring unusual details such as wormy chestnut woodwork, the inn occupies 11 wooded acres in a quiet area just west of downtown. On the grounds are a picnic area, gardens, and a stream with a waterfall. Some rooms have antique iron bedsteads or sleigh beds and fireplaces. Every evening owners Scott and Anne Peecook host a social hour. ⊠ *404 Old Bristol Rd., 28607* ☎ *828/264–4204 or 800/849–9466* ⊕ *www.lovillhouseinn.com* 📞 *6 rooms* ♿ *Dining room; no a/c in some rooms, no kids under 12, no smoking* 🚫 *MC, V* ⊗ *Closed Mar.* ⦿⦿ *BP.*

Nightlife & the Arts

Horn in the West, a project of the Southern Appalachian Historical Association, is an outdoor drama that traces the story of the lives of Daniel Boone and other pioneers, as well as the Cherokee, during the American Revolution. ⊠ *Amphitheater off U.S. 321* ☎ *828/264–2120* 💲 *$15* ⊗ *Performances mid-June–mid-Aug., Tues.–Sun. at 8 PM.*

A part of Appalachian State University, and expanded in 2004 with new gallery space and a 135-seat lecture hall, the **Turchin Center for the Visual Arts** (⊠ 423 W. King St. ☎ 828/262–3017) is the largest visual-arts center in the High Country, with regular exhibitions of regional as well as national and international art.

Valle Crucis

28 *5 mi south of Boone.*

This tiny mountain town has the state's first rural historic district; vintage stores line the downtown streets.

Everything from ribbons and overalls to yard art and cookware is sold in the original **Mast General Store** (⊠ Rte. 194 ☎ 828/963–6511). Built in 1882, the store has plank floors worn to a soft sheen and an active old-timey post office. You can take a shopping break by sipping bottled soda pop while sitting in a rocking chair on the store's back porch. For more shopping, an annex is just down the road.

Sports & the Outdoors

GOLF The par-72 **Gauntlet at St. James Plantation** (⊠ Rte. 211 ☎ 910/253–3008 or 800/247–4806) lives up to its reputation as a challenging course.

Where to Stay & Eat

$$$–$$$$ ✕🖳 **Mast Farm Inn.** You can turn back the clock and still enjoy modern amenities at this charming pastoral inn, built in the 1800s and now on the National Register of Historic Places. Rooms are in the farmhouse or in log cottages. The restaurant ($$–$$$$) uses locally and organically grown vegetables to enhance its innovative uptown menu. Organic gardening demonstrations are held in the inn's gardens. ⊠ *2543 Broad-stone Rd., Box 704, 28691* ☎ *828/963–5857 or 888/963–5857* ☒ *828/963–6404* ⊕ *www.mastfarminn.com* ↪ *7 rooms, 7 cottages* ♿ *Restaurant, pond* ═ *AE, D, MC, V* ⦿⊚⦿ *BP.*

Shopping

If you're looking for a mountain painting, stop by **Gallery Alta Vista** (⊠ 2839 Broadstone Rd. ☎ 828/963–5247), which features the work of some 200 artists, many from western North Carolina. If shopping wears you out, you can overnight here, because the gallery is also a B&B.

Banner Elk

㉙ *6 mi southwest of Valle Crucis; 11 mi southwest of Boone.*

Banner Elk is a ski-resort town, which bills itself as the "highest town in the East," surrounded by the lofty peaks of Grandfather, Hanging Rock, Beech, and Sugar mountains. The massively ugly condo tower you'll see on top of Little Sugar Mountain (not a part of the Sugar Mountain ski resort) is the only scar on the scenic beauty of the area. At least something good came of the monstrosity—it so outraged local residents that it prompted the passing of a ridge line law preventing such mountain-top development.

Sports & the Outdoors

CANOEING & RAFTING **Edge of the World Outfitters** (⊠ Rte. 184 ☎ 828/898–9550 or 800/789–3343) offers white-water rafting, rappelling, canoeing, and snowboarding lessons in the Banner Elk area.

SKIING At 5,506 feet above sea level, **Ski Beech** (⊠ Rte. 184, Beech Mountain ☎ 828/387–2011 or 800/438–2093) is the highest resort in the eastern United States. One of the larger resorts in the area, **Sugar Mountain** (⊠ Off Rte. 184, Banner Elk ☎ 828/898–4521 or 800/784–2768) has an equipment shop and lessons and tubing for the kids. A higher-end resort, **Hawksnest Golf and Ski Resort** (⊠ 1800 Skyland Dr., Seven Devils ☎ 828/963–6561 or 800/822–4295) has full snowmaking capability and challenging slopes. Call for **ski conditions** (☎ 800/962–2322).

Where to Stay

$-$$$$ 🏨 **Banner Elk Inn Bed & Breakfast and Cottages.** Here, less than ½ mi from Banner Elk's only stoplight, you have the choice of either traditional B&B rooms in a restored 1912 farmhouse or spacious cottages with kitchens. Even if you opt for one of pewter-gray, newly constructed cottages at the back of the main house, you can get a full B&B breakfast on weekends, or a continental breakfast weekdays. Owner Beverly Lait also offers several vacation rental houses nearby. ⊠ *407 Main St. E, 28604* ☎ *828/898–6223 or 800/295–7851* ⊕ *www.bannerelkinn.com* ↪ *6 rooms, 3 cottages* ♿ *Dining room, some kitchens; no a/c in some rooms, no TV in some rooms* ═ *MC, V* ⦿⊚⦿ *CP, BP.*

Shopping

For hardware, firewood, a half gallon of milk, locally grown vegetables, pumpkins for Halloween, snowboard and ski rentals, gourmet bird seed, today's *Wall Street Journal,* and just about anything else you need, **Fred's General Mercantile** (✉ 501 Beech Mountain Pkwy. ☎ 828/387–4838), half general store and half boutique, is the place to go in Banner Elk, and has been for more than 25 years.

Hot Springs

30 *30 mi northwest of Asheville via U.S. 23/19 and U.S. 25/70 past Marshall.*

This little village is a way station for hikers on the Appalachian Trail. Since the early 1800s, Hot Springs, not far from the Tennessee border in Madison County, has attracted visitors seeking relief from real or imagined ailments in its 104°F mineral water. In the mid-1800s, the town boasted a 350-room hotel, one of the largest in the South, with a dining room seating 600. By the early 20th century, however, fewer people "took the waters," and the town's only remaining hotel burned to the ground. Since around the 1980s, thanks to its location beside the French Broad River, Hot Springs has attracted rafters and other visitors seeking a quiet, unpretentious vacation. Don't leave town without meeting the delightful Helen Gosnell, who staffs the visitor information center, in a red caboose on Bridge Street. Helen, a Madison County native who has lived in Hot Springs since 1962, knows everything and everybody in Hot Springs.

The mineral springs at **Hot Springs Resort & Spa** maintain a natural 104°F temperature year-round and for many decades have provided relief for those suffering from various ailments, including rheumatism and pelvic troubles. Today, however, the atmosphere is more like a trailer park than a spa. The water still flows naturally hot, but to experience it you sit in a hot tub like the ones sold at your local building-supply store, in a wood shack. It can still be fun, but upscale it's not. Massage therapy is also available. ✉ 315 Bridge St. ☎ 828/622–7676 or 800/462–0933 ⊕ www.nchotsprings.com ✉ $12–$40 per hr, depending on time of day and number of people in tub ☉ Feb.–Nov., daily 9 AM–11 PM; Dec. and Jan., hrs vary, call in advance.

| OFF THE BEATEN PATH | **MAX PATCH BALD** – A bald is a big grassy area at the top of a mountain where no trees grow. How balds come to be is not clearly understood, but it has something to do with the combination of wind, weather, and soil conditions. Max Patch Bald, right on the Appalachian Trail, is one of the best examples, and it has been called one of the crown jewels of the trail. At 4,629 feet, on a clear day you can see both Mt. Mitchell and into the Great Smokies. To get here from Hot Springs, go south on NC 209 6.4 mi to Meadow Fork Road. Continue south for 3.5 mi, mostly on a gravel road. At the top of the mountain, turn right on SR 1182 and go 1.5 mi to Max Patch parking area. From there you go by foot on a pleasant trail; the total walk is less than 1½ mi. ✉ NC SR 1182. |

Where to Stay & Eat

$$–$$$$ ✕🏠 **Mountain Magnolia Inn and Retreat.** This restored 1868 inn is about all that remains of the grandeur that was once Hot Springs. On a shady

and hidden back road beside the French Broad River, the inn sits among well-tended perennial gardens. If you want the best digs, ask for the Walnut Room, with a king bed, small whirlpool bathtub, and balcony overlooking the gardens and the river. The dining room ($$–$$$$) is open to the public for dinner, offering mountain trout, steaks, and other dishes. ⊠ *204 Lawson St., Hot Springs 28743* ☎ *828/622–3543* 🖷 *828/622–9953* ⊕ *www.mountainmagnoliainn.com* 🛏 *5 rooms, 1 cottage* ⚮ *Restaurant; no room TVs, no smoking* ☱ *AE, MC, V* ⦿⧈ *BP.*

¢–$ ✕🖬 **Bridge Street Café & Inn.** This renovated storefront, circa 1922, is right on the Appalachian Trail and overlooks Spring Creek. Upstairs are four simply decorated rooms and two shared baths filled with antiques. One bathroom has a claw-foot tub. The café ($–$$$) downstairs has a wood-fired oven and grill, from which emerge delicious pizzas and grilled fish and meats. There's live music most Saturdays on the outdoor dining deck. ⊠ *Bridge St., Box 502, 28743* ☎ *828/622–0002* 🖷 *828/622–7282* ⊕ *www.bridgestreetcafe.com* 🛏 *4 rooms with shared bath* ⚮ *Restaurant; no room TVs, no room phones, no smoking* ☱ *AE, D, MC, V* ⊘ *Inn and restaurant closed Nov.–mid-Mar.; restaurant closed Mon.–Wed.* ⦿⧈ *BP.*

THE SOUTHERN MOUNTAINS

The Southern Mountains encompass a diverse area in 10 North Carolina counties south and west of Asheville. They include the towns of Hendersonville and Flat Rock in Henderson County, and Brevard in Transylvania County. The Southern Mountains also include Cashiers, Highlands, and Lake Toxaway, chic summer enclaves where some lakefront building lots now cost a million dollars.

Hendersonville

③① *23 mi south of Asheville via I–26.*

Hendersonville, with about 11,000 residents, has one of the most engaging and vibrant downtowns of any small city in the South. Historic Main Street, as it's called, extends 10 serpentine blocks, lined with flower boxes and about 40 shops, including many antiques stores. Each year from April through October Main Street has displays of public art. Within walking distance of downtown are several B&Bs and many restaurants.

The Hendersonville area is North Carolina's main apple-growing area, and some 200 apple orchards dot the rolling hills around town. An Apple Festival attracting some 200,000 people is held each year in August.

🄲 The **Holmes Educational State Forest,** a 235-acre state forest, has "talking trees," a fun way for kids to learn about the forests of western North Carolina—just punch a button on a hickory or poplar, and a recording tells you about the tree. ⊠ *Crabtree Rd., 9 mi from downtown Hendersonville* ☎ *828/692–0100* 🎟 *Free* ⊙ *Mid-Mar.–mid-Nov., Tues.–Fri. 9–5, weekends 11–8.*

🕐 The **Historic Johnson Farm,** a 19th-century tobacco farm that is now operated by Henderson County Public Schools, has the original farmhouse, barn, outbuildings, and a museum with about 1,000 artifacts typical of farm life of the time. ✉ *3346 Haywood Rd., 4 mi north of downtown Hendersonville* ☎ *828/697–4733* 🖼 *Guided tours $3* 🕐 *Tues.–Fri. 9–2:30; closed on school holidays.*

OFF THE
BEATEN
PATH

THOMAS WOLFE'S ANGEL – In his novel *Look Homeward, Angel,* Asheville-born Thomas Wolfe makes many references to an angel statue. The famous angel, in real life carved from Italian marble by Wolfe's father, W. O. Wolfe, stands in Hendersonville's Oakdale Cemetery, marking the graves of a family named Johnson, to whom the senior Wolfe sold the statue. The statue is protected by an iron fence. ✉ *U.S. 64, just west of downtown Hendersonville.*

Sports & the Outdoors

GOLF   Among the five golf courses in Hendersonville, the 6,719-yard, par-71, private **Champion Hills Golf Club** (✉ 1 Hagen Dr. ☎ 828/693–3600) is the home course of famed golf-course designer Tom Fazio. An enjoyable public course is **Crooked Tree Golf Club** (✉ 764 Crooked Tree Rd. ☎ 828/692–2011), where the clubhouse was once a corporate retreat owned by Warner Bros., the movie company.

Where to Stay & Eat

$$–$$$$ ✕ **Expressions.** Opened in 1982 by Chef Tom Young, Expressions is one of the region's most consistently dependable places for interesting meals. Right on Main Street, the interior is understated, with brick walls and wood accents (it can be a bit noisy). At lunch, you can choose a sidewalk table under a green umbrella. The menu changes daily but features items such as smoked mountain trout, lamb with dijon herb sauce, and roast duck breast. ✉ *114 N. Main St.* ☎ *828/693–8516* ▬ *AE, MC, V* 🕐 *Closed Sun.*

$$–$$$$ 🏨 **Waverly Inn.** On a warm afternoon, you'll love to "sit a spell" in a rocking chair on the front porch of Hendersonville's oldest inn. All 14 rooms in the 1898 three-story Victorian, two blocks from downtown, are named after native flowers and shrubs and outfitted with antique furnishings. The Mountain Magnolia suite has a king canopy bed, and the Silverbell room, painted an airy yellow and white, has a four-poster bed and a claw-foot bathtub. ✉ *783 N. Main St., 28792* ☎ *828/698–9193 or 800/537–8195* ⊕ *www.waverlyinn.com* ⇥ *13 rooms, 1 suite* ⚭ *Cable TV, some in-room DVDs; no smoking* ▬ *AE, D, DC, MC, V* 🍽 *BP.*

Nightlife & the Arts

THE ARTS   The Skyland Hotel is one of the places where Jazz Age novelist F. Scott Fitzgerald stayed when he visited his wife in a mental institution in Asheville, and the building is now the **Arts Center** (✉ 538 N. Main St. ☎ 828/693–8504), a nonprofit organization that puts on art exhibits and other cultural programs.

NIGHTLIFE   While local nightlife is limited, you can hear live music on weekend nights and enjoy one of about 125 types of beer at **Hannah Flanagan's Pub** (✉ 300 N. Main St. ☎ 828/696–1665).

Shopping

If you like to shop, you'll enjoy browsing the 40 shops on **Historic Main Street,** including several antiques stores, a branch of Mast General Store, and local boutiques.

Flat Rock

32 *3 mi south of Hendersonville; 26 mi south of Asheville via I–26.*

Flat Rock has been a summer resort since the early 19th century. It was a favorite of wealthy planters from Charleston, eager to escape the Lowcountry heat. The trip from Charleston to Flat Rock by horse and carriage took as long as two weeks, so you know there must be something here that made the long trek worthwhile.

★ ☼ The **Carl Sandburg Home National Historic Site** is the spot to which the poet and Lincoln biographer Carl Sandburg moved with his wife, Lillian, in 1945. Guided tours of their house, Connemara, where Sandburg's papers still lie scattered on his desk, are given by the National Park Service. In summer the productions *The World of Carl Sandburg* and *Rootabaga Stories* are presented at the amphitheater. Kids enjoy a walk around the grounds of the farm, which still maintains descendants of the Sandburg family goats. ⊠ *1928 Little River Rd.* ☎ *828/693–4178* ⊕ *www.nps.gov/carl* ☜ *$5* ☉ *Daily 9–5.*

The **Flat Rock Playhouse** has a high reputation for summer stock theater. The season runs from May to mid-December. ⊠ *2661 Greenville Hwy.* ☎ *828/693–0731* ⊕ *www.flatrockplayhouse.org.*

Tryon

33 *30 mi southeast of Asheville; 19 mi southeast of Flat Rock.*

Tryon is western North Carolina's horse country—not as in trail horse rides, but as in riding to the hounds. The annual mid-April running of the **Blockhouse Steeplechase Races** attracts big crowds to this little town, which is ½ mi from the South Carolina state line. For information about the race, contact the **Tryon Riding & Hunt Club** (⊠ 1 Depot St. ☎ 828/ 859–6109 or 800/438–3681 ⊕ www.trhcevents.com). The equally tiny nearby town of Saluda is famous for its steep railroad grade up Saluda mountain.

Where to Stay & Eat

$$–$$$$ ✕⬚ **Pine Crest Inn.** A former hunt club, this is *the* place to stay and dine in Tryon. Built in 1906 and first used as a lodging in 1917, the inn was visited by Hemingway and Fitzgerald and is now on the National Register of Historic Places. The Fox and Hounds bar will put you in mind of a weekend at an English country home. The restaurant ($$–$$$$) is noted for its flawless service. It has won *Wine Spectator* magazine's Excellence award for many years, and the local wine society meets here weekly. ⊠ *895 Pine Crest La., 28782* ☎ *828/859–9135* 🖷 *828/859–9135* ⊕ *www.pinecrestinn.com* ☜ *23 rooms, 7 suites, 3 cottages* ⚷ *Restaurant, some in-room hot tubs, cable TV, some in-room DVDs,* *business services, meeting rooms, gift shop; no smoking* ▭ *AE, D, MC, V* ⦿| *BP.*

Brevard

34 *40 mi southwest of Asheville on Rte. 280.*

With its friendly, highly walkable downtown, Brevard is Mayberry RFD transported to the Pisgah National Forest. In fact, a popular toy store in town is called O. P. Taylor's—get it?

Brevard residents go nuts over the white squirrels, which dart around the town's parks. These aren't albinos, but a variation of the eastern gray squirrel. About one-fourth of the squirrels in town are white. The white squirrels are thought to have come originally from Hawaii by way of Florida; they possibly were released in Brevard by a visitor in the 1950s. Whatever the truth, today Brevard capitalizes on it by holding a White Squirrel Festival in late May. One of the best places to see the little devils is on the **Brevard College** (✉ 400 N. Broad St.) campus.

The oldest frame house in western North Carolina, the **Allison-Deaver House** was built in the early 1800s, and has been renovated and expanded several times. ✉ *N.C. Hwy. 280, Pisgah Forest, near Forest Gate Shopping Center* ☎ *828/884–5137* ✉ *Donations accepted* ☉ *Apr.–Oct., Fri. and Sat. 10–4, Sun. 1–4.*

★ ♺ Nearby Pisgah National Forest has the **Cradle of Forestry in America National Historic Site,** the home of the first forestry school in the United States, with a 1-mi interpretive trail, the school's original log buildings, and a visitor center with many hands-on exhibits of interest to kids. The road from Brevard to the Cradle of Foresty, a scenic byway, continues on to connect with the Blue Ridge Parkway near Mt. Pisgah. ✉ *1001 Pisgah Hwy., U.S. 276* ☎ *828/884–5823* ⊕ *www.cradleofforestry.com* ✉ *$5* ☉ *Mid-Apr.–early Nov., daily 9–5.*

The newest addition to nature sites near Brevard is **DuPont State Forest,** which was established in 1996 and expanded in 2000. You'll find 10,400 acres with four waterfalls and 80 mi of old dirt roads to explore, with ideal conditions for biking or horseback riding. ✉ *U.S. 64 and Little River Rd.* ☎ *828/877–6527* ⊕ *www.dupontforest.com* ✉ *Free.*

Near the road and easy to get to, **Looking Glass Falls** is a classic, with water cascading 60 feet into a clear pool. ✉ *Pisgah National Forest, north of Brevard, off U.S. 276* ✉ *Free.*

♺ At the **Pisgah Center for Wildlife Education** the fish hatchery produces more than 400,000 brown, rainbow, and native brook trout each year for release in local streams. You can see the fish up close in tanks called raceways and even feed them (approved trout feed is sold for a quarter). There's also a small visitor center with information about the life cycle of trout and an educational nature trail. ✉ *Rte. 475 off U.S. 276 in Pisgah National Forest* ☎ *828/877–4423* ☉ *Daily 8–5* ✉ *Free.*

♺ At **Sliding Rock** in summer you can skid 60 feet on a natural waterslide. Wear old jeans and tennis shoes and bring a towel. ✉ *Pisgah National*

Forest, north of Brevard, off U.S. 276 ☎ *828/877–3265* ☞ *$3 per car* ☉ *Late May–early Sept., daily 10–5:30.*

Sports & the Outdoors

FISHING Catch rainbow, brown, or brook trout on the Davidson River, named one of the top 100 trout streams in the United States by Trout Unlimited. **Davidson River Outfitters** (✉ 26 Pisgah Forest Hwy. ☎ 828/877–4181) arranges trips and also has a fly-fishing school and a fly shop.

GOLF **Etowah Valley Country Club and Golf Lodge** (✉ U.S. 64, Etowah ☎ 828/891–7141 or 800/451–8174), has three very different (one par-72, two par-73) 18-hole courses and offers good package deals.

SKATEBOARDING Western North Carolina's largest indoor skateboard, skating, and BMX biking facility is **Zero Gravity Skatepark** (✉ 1800 Old Hendersonville Hwy. ☎ 828/862–6700), with fun boxes, ramps, launch boxes, ledges, roll-ins, and a pyramid and bowl.

MOUNTAIN BIKING

The North Carolina Mountains offer some of the best mountain biking in the East. Among the favorite places for mountain biking are **Tsali**, a peninsula sticking out into Lake Fontana near Bruston City, in the Nantahala National Forest; **Dupont State Forest**, just south of Brevard; and the **Bent Creek, Davidson River**, and **Mills River** sections of the Pisgah Ranger District of the Pisgah National Forest.

Where to Stay & Eat

$$–$$$$ ✕ **Hobnob.** You can hobnob with old and new friends at this casual spot in a colorfully painted house near downtown. The co-owners, who formerly ran a restaurant in Charleston, have brought a Lowcountry edge to dining in Brevard, with dishes like Carolina crab cake on sweet corn salad. Other dishes have a French influence. ✉ *226 Main St.* ☎ *828/966–4662* ▤ *AE, MC, V.*

¢ ✕ **Cardinal Drive-In.** The cheeseburgers are just fair and the onion rings are like fried cardboard, but this is an authentic piece of Americana—a real drive-in, with car hops and everything. ✉ *7328 S. Broad St.* ☎ *828/884–7085* ▤ *No credit cards.*

$$–$$$$ ▥ **The Inn at Brevard.** Built in 1885 as a private home, this white, two-story inn with stately entrance columns sits on a shady corner three blocks from downtown Brevard. With old photos and art on the walls, some by the Irish portrait painter Eileen Fabian, and mix-and-match antique furniture, it may remind you of your grandmom's house, but the overall effect is homey and comfortable. The inn is on the National Register of Historic Places. A motel-like annex next door has 10 rooms with knotty pine paneling. Guests staying here have access to the privately owned Slatton waterfalls adjoining Pisgah National Forest. ✉ *410 E. Main St., 28712* ☎ *828/884–2105* 🖷 *828/885–7996* ⊕ *www.innatbrevard.8m.com* ➾ *14 rooms, 2 with shared bath, 3 suites* ⚘ *Restaurant* ▤ *AE, DC, MC, V* ☉ *Closed Dec.–early Apr.* ⦿ *BP.*

$–$$ ▥ **The Red House Inn.** One of the oldest houses in Brevard, the Red House Inn was built in 1851 as a trading post and later served as a courthouse, tavern, post office, and school. Now it's an unpretentious but pleasant

B&B four blocks from the center of town. There are four rooms in the main house and an efficiency cottage. The common area has a working fireplace. ⊠ *412 W. Probart St., 28712* ☎ *828/884–9349* ⤳ *4 rooms, 2 with shared bath, 1 cottage* ⚬ *Some refrigerators; no TV in some rooms, no children under 12, no smoking* ▤ *MC, V* ⦿ *BP.*

Nightlife & the Arts

THE ARTS The nationally known **Brevard Music Center** (☎ 828/884–2011 ⊕ www. brevardmusic.org) has a seven-week music festival each summer, with about 80 concerts from mid-June to early August.

As unlikely as it may be, Brevard is home to a cowboy museum, the **Jim Bob Tinsley Museum and Research Center** (⊠ 20 W. Jordan St. ☎ 828/884–2347), dedicated to the life and interests of this Brevard native, a musicologist and author of 10 books who played with Gene Autry. There are displays of art by Frederick Remington, Western memorabilia, and much more.

Lake Toxaway

40 mi southwest of Asheville.

A century ago a group called the Lake Toxaway Company created a 640-acre lake in the high mountains between Brevard and Cashiers. Nearby, a grand 500-room hotel built with the finest materials, providing the most modern conveniences and serving European cuisine, attracted many of the country's elite. That hotel is long gone, but the scenic area, which some still call "America's Switzerland," has a number of fine resorts and some of the priciest real estate in the North Carolina Mountains.

Where to Stay

★ $$$$ ▦ **Earthshine Mountain Lodge.** You can have as much solitude or adventure as you want at this spacious cedar log cabin with stone fireplaces. The lodge, which sits on 70 acres midway between Brevard and Cashiers on a ridge that adjoins the Pisgah National Forest, offers horseback riding, hiking, fishing, and even an opportunity to gather berries, feed the goats, pan for gems, take guided trail rides, and try the 30-foot climbing wall or zip line. In the evening families gather around an open fire to sing songs, square dance, and exchange stories. ■ TIP➔ **Rates include all meals. On a week's stay, the seventh day is free.** ⊠ *Golden Rd., 28747* ☎ *828/862–4207* ⊕ *www.earthshinemtnlodge.com* ⤳ *10 rooms* ⚬ *Dining room, fishing, hiking, horseback riding, babysitting, children's programs (ages 6 and up), meeting rooms; no room TVs, no smoking* ▤ *D, MC, V* ⦿ *FAP.*

$$$$ ▦ **Greystone Inn.** In 1915 Savannah resident Lucy Molz built a second home on Lake Toxaway. Today the six-level Swiss-style mansion is an inn listed on the National Register of Historic Places and is known for its pampering of its guests. Rooms have antiques or period reproductions, and suites that border the lake of this mountain resort are modern. Rates include breakfast and dinner, afternoon tea and cake, and cocktails. The inn is open weekends only January through March. ⊠ *Greystone La., 28747* ☎ *828/966–4700 or 800/824–5766* 🖶 *828/*

862–5689 ⊕ *www.greystoneinn.com* ↩ *31 rooms, 2 suites* ⚲ *Dining room, cable TV, in-room VCRs, golf privileges, putting green, 6 tennis courts, pool, lake, massage, spa, dock, waterskiing, fishing, business services; no smoking* 🖃 *AE, MC, V* ⚎ *MAP.*

Cashiers

㉟ *74 mi southwest of Asheville via U.S. 74 and NC 107; 14 mi west of Lake Toxaway.*

Cashiers is not a quite a town. Until recently, it was just a crossroads, with a store or two, a summer getaway for wealthy South Carolinians escaping the heat. But with the building of many exclusive gated developments, the Cashiers area, at a cool 3,500 foot elevation, is seeing new restaurants, lodges, and golf courses open seemingly every month.

Whiteside Mountain is one of the highest continuous cliffs in the East. The sheer cliffs of white granite rise up to 750 feet, overlooking the Chattooga River in the Nantahala National Forest. The cliffs are popular with climbers. ⊠ *Whiteside Mountain Rd., 4.6 mi from Cashiers on U.S. 64* ☎ *828/586–2155* ☯ *Closed to climbers Jan.–July.*

Sports & the Outdoors

GOLF At the golf course at the **High Hampton Inn & Country Club** (⊠ 1525 NC 107S ☎ 828/743–2411) is a par-71, 6,012-yard George Cobb design, with a famous 8th hole. The newest course in the Cashiers area, a par-71, 6,699-yard semiprivate course designed by Tom Jackson, **Highlands Cove** (⊠ U.S. 64 ☎ 828/526–4185) has an elevated Highlands side and a flatter Cove side. Perched at 4,500 feet, **Trillium Links** (⊠ 975 New Trillium Way ☎ 828/743–4251), a public course built in 1998, plays to 6,505 yards at par 71.

Where to Stay & Eat

$$–$$$$ ✕ **The Orchard.** Widely considered the best restaurant in the Cashiers area, the Orchard, in a cozy house with brown wood shakes, puts a Southern twist on traditional American dishes. Try the trout served three ways—pan-fried, baked, or grilled. ⊠ *NC 107S* ☎ *828/743–7614* ☯ *Closed Mon. No lunch.*

¢–$$ ✕ **Cornucopia.** In the second-oldest building in Cashiers, built in 1892, you can sit on the huge, airy, covered back porch and eat some of the best sandwiches in the region. Specialties include the "Arabian Club," with turkey, bacon, sprouts, and black olives on pita bread. The Black Angus burgers are excellent, and for a Southern treat try the Coca-Cola Ribs. ⊠ *Hwy. 107 S* ☎ *828/743–3750* 🖃 *MC, V.*

$$$–$$$$ ⊞ **High Hampton Inn & Country Club.** On the front lawn of this old inn are some of the most ancient trees in the region, including a giant Fraser fir that is a national champion. Many of the buildings are bark-covered, and inside the main building, you'll find rare wormy chestnut. With rustic rooms—30 in the main lodge and 90 in small cottages around the 1,400-acre property—the atmosphere is more down-home than country club. Meals are served buffet-style in a huge hunting lodge-style dining room. On the National Register of Historic Places, and family-owned

for three generations, High Hampton Inn stubbornly sticks to traditions such as requiring coats and ties for dinner and declining to install televisions or telephones in guest rooms. A new 5,000-square-foot fitness center opened in 2006. ⊠ *1525 NC 107S, Cashiers 28717* ☎ *828/ 743–2411 or 800/334–2551* 🖷 *828/743–5991* ⊕ *www.highhamptoninn. com* ⟳ *120 rooms in main lodge, 18 cottages; 40 rental houses* ⟲ *Restaurant, some kitchens, 18-hole golf course, 6 tennis courts, 35-acre lake, fitness center, boating, fishing, hiking, shops, laundry service, meeting rooms; no a/c in some rooms, no room phones, no room TVs, no smoking* ▤ *AE, D, DC, MC, V* ☽ *Closed mid-Nov.–mid-Apr.* ❢◧ *FAP.*

\$\$–\$\$\$\$ ⊡ **Innisfree Victorian Inn.** On a hill above Lake Glenville, you can indulge your literary, or romantic, fantasies in the Bronte Suite or one of the other garden-house rooms named after writers. And a fine fantasy it would be, with a four-poster bed and a glassed-in fireplace so you can see the fire from either the comfy bed or the two-person tub. The main inn has a wraparound veranda, an observatory, and an octagonal dining room. ⊠ *NC 107N, Glenville 28736* ☎ *828/743–2946* ⊕ *www.innisfreeinn. com* ⟳ *9 rooms, 1 suite* ⟲ *Some refrigerators, pond; no TV in some rooms, no kids, no smoking* ▤ *AE, D, MC, V* ❢◧ *BP.*

Highlands

③⑥   *85 mi southwest of Asheville; 11 mi south of Cashiers on U.S. 64.*

Highlands is a tony small town of around 900 people, but the surrounding area swells to 10,000 or more in summer and fall, when those with summer homes here flock back, like wealthy sparrows of Capistrano. Once Highlands billed itself as the highest town in the East, but it relinquished the title when Banner Elk and other tiny communities a little higher up in the High Country were incorporated as towns. Still, at 4,118 feet it is usually cool and pleasant when even Asheville gets hot. The town's five-block downtown is, not surprisingly given the local demographics, lined with upscale shops, antiques stores, and coffeehouses.

West of Highlands via U.S. 64 toward Franklin, the **Cullasaja Gorge** (Cullah-SAY-jah) is an 8-mi gorge passing Lake Sequoyah and several waterfalls, including **Bridal Veil Falls** and the 200-foot **Cullasaja Falls.** ⊠ *U.S. 64.*

In the center of downtown Highlands, the **Highlands Botanical Garden and Biological Station,** run by Western Carolina University, is a 30-acre biological reserve of native plants. There's also a small nature center, open seasonally. ⊠ *265 6th St.* ☎ *828/526–2602* ☽ *Garden: daily sunrise–sunset. Nature center: June–Sept., Mon.–Sat. 10–5* 🕮 *Free.*

Where to Stay & Eat

\$\$\$–\$\$\$\$ ✕ **On the Verandah.** You'll enjoy views of Lake Sequoyah from the big windows of this former speakeasy. The owner has a collection of more than 1,300 hot sauces, any of which you can sample. The menu is long and varied, and many dishes are infused with Asian or Caribbean flavors. There's live piano music nightly. ⊠ *1536 Franklin Rd.* ☎ *828/526– 2338* ▤ *D, MC, V* ☽ *Closed Dec.–mid-Mar. No lunch Mon.–Sat.*

$$–$$$$ ✕ **Ristorante Paoletti.** At this storefront restaurant on Main Street you are taken care of in a style that's more Italian-provincial than nouveau riche. The menu includes a lengthy section of fresh-made pastas, along with veal and seafood. The wine list includes more than 800 selections. ✉ *440 Main St.* ☎ *828/526–4906* ▭ *AE, MC, V* ☉ *Closed Jan. and Feb. No lunch.*

★ **$$$$** ✕▢ **Old Edwards Inn and Spa.** A two-year-long, $40-million renovation turned this 115-year-old inn into the smartest hotel in Highlands. Guest rooms have plasma TVs, DVDs, and a central digital-control screen for lights, music, and media. Bath amenities are by Bulgari. The hotel could be on Manhattan's Upper East Side, as could the prices, with two-night spa packages as much as $4,000 per couple. Madison ($$$$), the inn's new restaurant, is light and sunny, but luxuriously appointed, with Oriental rugs on the stone floors and Christoffe silverware on the tables. It takes High Country cooking to new heights of service and style, with dishes such as Brown Butter Glazed Citrus Trout with jasmine rice and melted leeks. Due to local liquor laws, the bar is for guests only. ✉ *445 Main St., 28741* ☎ *828/526–8008 or 866/526–8008* 🖨 *828/526–8301* ⊕ *www.oldedwardsinn.com* ➥ *25 rooms, 5 suites* ♲ *Restaurant, room service, in-room safes, minibars, cable TV, in-room DVDs, in-room broadband, Wi-Fi, gym, spa, bar, concierge, meeting rooms, convention center, laundry service, no-smoking rooms* ❝◯❞ *BP* ▭ *AE, D, MC, V.*

The Arts

The well-respected **Highlands Playhouse** (✉ Oak St. ☎ 828/526–2695), an equity theater, puts on four or five productions each summer.

Shopping

The nightly antiques auctions from June through October at **Scudder's Gallery** (✉ 352 Main St. ☎ 828/526–4111), a high-end antiques dealer and estate liquidator established in 1925, are a form of local entertainment.

Since 1963, **Elephants Foot Antiques** (✉ U.S. 64 at Foreman Rd. ☎ 828/526–5451) has sold decorative furniture, antique lamps and other antiques.

Franklin

㊲ *32 mi south of Cherokee on U.S. 441; 19 mi northwest of Highlands via Rte. 28.*

Franklin, the Macon County seat, lies at the convergence of U.S. 441, U.S. 64, and Route 28, and although only around 2,200 feet high, it's a gateway to the higher reaches of the Nantahala National Forest. In the 1500s Hernando de Soto came in search of gold and overlooked the wealth of gemstones for which this area is so famous. A dozen gem mines and nearly as many gem stores are nearby. Many large rubies and sapphires have been found in the area. ■ TIP➜ **For a more authentic gem-mining experience, choose a mine that offers "native" buckets of earth, preferably ones you can dig yourself, not "salted" buckets containing stones that the mine owners have buried in the dirt.** Suffering from rural-suburban sprawl and an invasion of fast-food chains, Franklin does not have a quaint downtown filled with B&Bs, though the courthouse square is pleasant.

The **Scottish Tartans Museum** has the official registry of all publicly known tartans and is the only American extension of the Scottish Tartans Society. Scottish heritage can be traced in the research library. There are more people of Scottish descent in North Carolina than anywhere else except Scotland. ⊠ *86 E. Main St.* ☎ *828/524–7472* ⊕ *www.scottishtartans.org* ▨ *$1* ⊙ *Mon.–Sat. 10–5.*

☾ Founded in 1974 and in a former Macon County Jail, the **Franklin Gem and Mineral Museum** is the place to go before you go mining. Volunteer staff will help you learn about gems native to the area. In the jail cells are displays of hundreds of minerals, fossils, Native American artifacts, and some rare Wedgewood porcelain made from Franklin clay. ⊠ *25 Philips St.* ☎ *828/369–7831* ⊕ *www.fgmm.org* ▨ *Free* ⊙ *Weekdays noon–4, Sat. 11–3.*

☾ **Old Cardinal Gem Mine** is among the Franklin area's commercial mines that does not "salt" its dirt with gemstones for you to find—or when it does, it clearly labels buckets that are salted rather than "native." ⊠ *71 Rockhaven Dr.* ☎ *828/369–7534* ▨ *$6, additional buckets $3* ⊙ *Apr.–Oct., daily 9–5.*

OFF THE BEATEN PATH	**WAYAH BALD –** This is one of the best areas to see flame azaleas, with brilliant, fire-color blossoms, along with other native rhododendrons and laurels when they bloom in May and June. At 5,350 feet, Wayah Bald (pronounced Why-Yah) has a stone watchtower you can climb for panoramic views of the nearby mountains. To get here, go 5 mi southwest on U.S. 64 from Franklin, then 10 mi west on Wayah Bald Road, and 6 mi north on FR 69 (follow the signs). ⊠ *Wayah Rd.*

THE NORTH CAROLINA MOUNTAINS ESSENTIALS

Transportation

BY AIR

Asheville Regional Airport (AVL), one of the most pleasant and modern airports in the South, is served by ASA/Delta Connection, Continental Express, Northwest, and US Airways. In 2005 the airport completed a $20-million expansion and improvement project. There are nonstop flights to and from Atlanta, Charlotte, Cincinnati, Detroit, Houston, Minneapolis, Newark, Philadelphia, Raleigh-Durham, and Washington (Ronald Reagan). US Airways Express serves the Hickory Airport (HKY), about 40 mi from Blowing Rock.

🛂 *Airport Information* **Asheville Regional Airport** ⊠ 708 Airport Rd., Fletcher ☎ 828/684-2226 ⊕ www.flyavl.com. **Hickory Airport** ⊠ U.S. 321 ☎ 828/323-7408 ⊕ www.flyavl.com.

🛂 *Carriers* **ASA/Delta Connection** ☎ 800/221-1212 ⊕ www.delta.com. **Continental Express** ☎ 800/523-3273 ⊕ www.continental.com. **Northwest** ☎ 800/225-2525 ⊕ www.nwa.com. **US Airways** ☎ 800/428-4322 ⊕ www.usair.com.

BY CAR

Interstate 40 runs east–west through Asheville. Interstate 26 runs from Charleston, South Carolina, to Asheville and, partly on a temporary route, continues northwest into Tennessee. Interstate 240 forms a perimeter around the city. U.S. 19/23 is a major north and west route. The Blue Ridge Parkway runs northeast from Great Smoky Mountains National Park to Shenandoah National Park in Virginia, passing Cherokee, Asheville, and the High Country. U.S. 221 runs north to the Virginia border through Blowing Rock and Boone and intersects Interstate 40 at Marion. U.S. 321 intersects Interstate 40 at Hickory and heads to Blowing Rock and Boone.

Contacts & Resources

BANKS & EXCHANGE SERVICES

Wachovia, Bank of America, Branch Banking & Trust, and RBC Centura are the major national and regional banks that have offices in western North Carolina. In addition, there are dozens of local independent banks. Wachovia and Bank of America in particular have branches in most major towns in the region. Most bank offices are open weekdays 9 to 5, often until 6 PM on Friday. Saturday hours are uncommon. Nearly all of the bank offices have 24-hour ATMs.

Bank of America ⊠ 68 Patton Ave., Asheville ☎ 828/251-8243 ⊕ www.bankofamerica. com. **BB&T** ⊠ 1 West Pack Sq., Asheville ☎ 828/225-2000 ⊕ www.bbt.com. **RBC Centura** ⊠ 8 O. Henry Ave., Asheville ☎ 828/236-8700 ⊕ www.rbccentura.com. **Wachovia** ⊠ 1 Haywood St., Asheville ☎ 828/232-3838 ⊕ www.wachovia.com.

EMERGENCIES

Dial 911 for police and ambulance service everywhere but the Cherokee Reservation, where the police and the EMS can be reached at the numbers listed *below*.

Mission Hospitals in Asheville is the largest medical center in the North Carolina Mountains and the regional medical referral center for the mountain region.

Emergency Services Ambulance, police ☎ 911. **Cherokee Reservation Police and EMS** ☎ 828/497-4131 for police, 828/497-6402 for EMS.

Hospitals Blowing Rock Hospital ⊠ 416 Chestnut Dr., Blowing Rock ☎ 828/295-3136. **Cannon Memorial Hospital** ⊠ 805 Shawneehaw Ave., Banner Elk ☎ 828/898-5111. **Haywood Medical Center** ⊠ 262 Leroy George Dr., Clyde ☎ 828/456-7311. **Mission Hospitals** ⊠ 509 Biltmore Ave., Asheville ☎ 828/213-1111. **Pardee Hospital** ⊠ 800 N. Justice St., Hendersonville ☎ 828/696-1000. **Wautauga Medical Center** ⊠ 336 Deerfield Rd., Boone ☎ 828/262-4100.

INTERNET, MAIL & SHIPPING

There are post offices in most mountain towns of any size, including all the towns listed in this guide. Asheville has seven post offices, along with a dozen or more post offices in suburban areas and towns around the city. FedEx, UPS, and DHL also are ubiquitous.

Most chain motels and larger hotels and inns in the region now have broadband Internet, either wired or wireless. Increasingly, broadband connections are included in the room rate, but some properties charge a fee, typically $5 to $10 a day. Some B&Bs and small mountain resorts don't offer Internet in guest rooms but usually can provide a connection on request. Most coffeehouses in the region, which total close to 50, are wireless hot spots where customers can use their laptops to check e-mail and surf the Web at no cost.

🗎 **Asheville Downtown Post Office** ✉ 33 Coxe Ave., Asheville ☎ 828/271-6428 ⊕ www.usps.com. **DHL Worldwide Express** ✉ 1 Haywood St., Asheville ☎ 800/225-5345 ⊕ www.dhl.com. **FedEx Kinko's** ✉ 17 State Rd. 81, Asheville ☎ 828/254-0021 ⊕ www.fedex.com. **UPS Store** ✉ 1854 Hendersonville Rd., Asheville ☎ 828/277-7445 ⊕ www.ups.com.

MEDIA

The region's major newspaper is the daily *Asheville Citizen-Times*. In the eastern end of the mountains, many people also get the *Charlotte Observer* or other newspapers from the Piedmont. Most mountain towns have a small weekly newspaper, and Waynesville has a newspaper, the *Mountaineer,* that is published three times a week.

The dominant television station in the mountains is WLOS-TV, an ABC affiliate. The area is also served by TV stations in Greenville and Spartanburg, SC. WCQS Radio in Asheville (it plays classical music) and WNCW in Rutherford-Spindale (eclectic mix of country and popular music) are the region's two public radio stations.

Asheville, as the mountain region's cultural center, has a number of local and chain bookstores, but there are good independent bookshops in many mountain towns. The largest chain bookstore in the region is Barnes & Noble in Asheville. If you love bookstores, don't miss Malaprop's, the largest and best indepedent bookstore in the mountains, and one of the best in the entire South.

🗎 *Asheville Citizen-Times* ✉ 14 O. Henry Ave., Asheville ☎ 828/252-5611 ⊕ www.citizen-times.com. **Barnes & Noble** ✉ 89 S. Tunnel Rd., Asheville ☎ 828/296-9330. **Malaprop's Bookstore/Café** ✉ 55 Haywood St., Asheville ☎ 828/254-6734 ⊕ www.malaprops.com. *Mountaineer* ✉ Main St., Waynesville ☎ 828/452-0661 ⊕ www.themountaineer.com. *Smoky Mountain News* ✉ 629 W. Main St., Sylva ☎ 828/452-4251 ⊕ www.smokymountainnews.com. **WCQS Radio** ✉ 73 Broadway, Asheville ☎ 828/253-6875 or 800/768-6698 ⊕ www.wcqs.org. **WNCW Radio** ☏ Box 804 ✉, Spindale ☎ 828/287-8080 ⊕ www.wncw.org. **WLOS-TV** ✉ 110 Technology Dr., Asheville ☎ 828/684-1340 ⊕ www.wlos.com.

TOUR OPTIONS

If you don't care to walk or drive around downtown Asheville, an alternative way to hit high spots is the Asheville Historic Trolley Tour, which costs $18. Call to make arrangements.

🗎 **Asheville Historic Trolley Tours** ☎ 888/667-3600.

VISITOR INFORMATION

In Asheville, a new visitor center operated by the Asheville Convention and Visitors Bureau, in association with the Asheville Chamber of Commerce and the Buncombe County Tourism Development Authority, opened downtown in 2006. It's one of the best visitor centers in the South, with interactive displays on hotels, a bank of computers for visitor use, tons of brochures, helpful and friendly staff, and plenty of free parking. The Cherokee Visitors Center provides information on the reservation. North Carolina High Country Host is a complete information center for the High Country counties of Watauga, Ashe, and Avery. Smoky Mountain Host of North Carolina has information about the state's seven westernmost counties.

🚹 **Asheville Convention and Visitors Bureau** ✉ 36 Montford Ave., Box 1010, 28802 ☎ 828/258-6101 or 888/247-9811 ⊕ www.exploreasheville.com. **Cherokee Visitors Center** ✉ U.S. 441 Business ☎ 828/497-9195 or 800/438-1601 ⊕ www.cherokee-nc. com. **North Carolina High Country Host** ✉ 1701 Blowing Rock Rd., Boone 28607 ☎ 828/264-1299 or 800/438-7500 ⊕ www.visitboonenc.com. **Smoky Mountain Host of NC** ✉ 4437 Georgia Rd., Franklin 28734 ☎ 828/369-9606 or 800/432-4678 ⊕ www. visitsmokies.org.

Myrtle Beach & the Grand Strand

WORD OF MOUTH

"There is so much to do [in Myrtle Beach]. The one must-do, though, in my opinion, is to hit the beach at low tide, preferably morning or early evening. We have wide, flat beaches here, great for walking (the shelling is hit or miss, but can be really good). Take a picnic basket to Huntington Beach State Park or Myrtle Beach State Park."

—beach_dweller

"If you like history and antiques, you will love [Hopsewee]. Never restored, but actually lived in by only a few families over the past 200 some years; the black cypress original house and period furnishings are highlights. Grounds are pleasant and tree covered."

—birgator

By Katie
McElveen

THE LIVELY, FAMILY-ORIENTED GRAND STRAND, a booming resort area along the South Carolina coast, is one of the eastern seaboard's megavacation centers. The main attraction, of course, is the broad, beckoning beach—60 mi of white sand, stretching from the North Carolina border south to Georgetown, with Myrtle Beach at the hub. People come to the Strand for all of the traditional beach-going pleasures: shell hunting, fishing, swimming, sunbathing, sailing, surfing, jogging, and strolling. Most of the sand is packed hard, so that at low tide you can explore for miles on a bicycle. Away from the water, golfers have more than 120 courses to choose from, designed by the likes of Arnold Palmer, Robert Trent Jones, Jack Nicklaus, and Tom and George Fazio. There are also excellent seafood restaurants; giant shopping malls and factory outlets; amusement parks, waterslides, and arcades; a dozen shipwrecks for divers to explore; campgrounds, most of them on the beach; plus antique-car and wax museums, an aquarium, the world's largest outdoor sculpture garden, an antique German band organ and merry-go-round, and a museum dedicated entirely to rice. The Strand has also emerged as a major center for country music, with an expanding number of theaters. When it comes to diversions, you could hardly be better served.

Myrtle Beach is the center of activity on the Grand Strand; its year-round population of 23,000 explodes to about 450,000 in summer, and as a result it alone accounts for about 40% of South Carolina's tourism revenue. Here you'll find the amusement parks and other children's activities that make the area so popular with families, as well as most of the nightlife that keeps parents and teenagers alike entertained. As Myrtle Beach's reputation as a family-friendly destination has grown, so have the size, sophistication, and number of activities available. Water and amusement parks are huge, well maintained, and offer name-brand attractions such as a NASCAR SpeedPark and an IMAX Discovery Theater. Immense live-performance theaters offer everything from Vegas-style reviews to a reenactment of the Civil War (on horseback no less).

The communities to the north of Myrtle Beach—Little River and North Myrtle Beach among others—are more residential and lack the glitz of their neighbor. On the South Strand the family retreats of Surfside Beach and Garden City offer more summer homes and condominiums, as well as small boardwalks and old-timey arcades, miniature golf, and snow-cone stands. Farther south, Murrells Inlet was once a pirates' haven (Blackbeard is said to have landed here) and is now a center for seafood restaurants, boat, jet-ski, and kayak rentals, and fishing and sightseeing charters. A boardwalk lets you wander along the marsh from one of Murrells' famed seafood restaurants and outdoor bars to another.

Exploring Myrtle Beach & the Grand Strand

The Grand Strand's main drag is north–south U.S. Highway 17, which has the Atlantic Ocean to one side and the Intracoastal Waterway to the other. Between Murrells Inlet and the north end of Myrtle Beach, the road splits into U.S. 17 Bypass and U.S. 17 Business.

TOP 5 REASONS TO GO

Bike the beach: From North Myrtle Beach all the way down to Pawleys Island, Grand Strand sand is hard packed and smooth, making it perfect for biking next to the crashing waves. Zoom for miles past surfers, fishermen, and kids playing with Frisbees. If you're lucky, you'll see dolphins, who often come in close in the early morning or just before sunset.

Golf, golf, and more golf: 120 golf courses at all skill levels meander through pine forests, dunes, and marshes. It's all about tradition at Pine Lakes in Myrtle Beach, where golfers are greeted by white-gloved caddymasters in full Scottish attire. The Tom Fazio–designed Tournament Players Club course weaves through both pine forest and wetlands.

Southern culture: Explore Southern history on a plantation tour; taste it in the form of barbecue, boiled peanuts, and other local foods; bring it home with folk art or a hammock woven right in Pawleys Island.

Brookgreen Gardens: More than 500 works from American artists are set amid 250-year-old oaks, palm trees, and flowers in America's oldest sculpture garden. A restored plantation, nature trail, and animal sanctuary where fox, otters, and deer live in their natural environment are also part of the 9,200-acre property.

Tours from the water: Paddle a kayak or ride a pontoon boat past the ruins of the rice plantations that line the shores around Georgetown. Look closely and you can often see the ancient wooden irrigation gates that were raised by hand to allow water into the paddies.

U.S. 17 takes you through most of the cultures that exist on the Grand Strand, from the quiet homes of North Myrtle Beach to the hopping family resorts of Myrtle Beach to the pristine marshes of Murrells Inlet and beyond. Traffic, particularly in summer, can be quite heavy on U.S. 17 (both the business and bypass routes). It's wise to hit the road as early in the day as possible during high season, which is roughly May through mid-September.

About the Restaurants

Not surprisingly, the Grand Strand specializes in seafood. For many years the restaurant scene was dominated by uninspired fried-fish buffets, where the emphasis was decidedly on quantity over quality. Today such establishments remain, but thanks to the Strand's increasing number of year-round residents and visitors, there are a surprising number of excellent restaurants (seafood and otherwise) in all price ranges.

In summer, waits at some of the moderately priced restaurants—even for breakfast—can be an hour or more. A hotel room or condo with kitchen facilities can be a blessing, allowing you to save time and money by preparing some of your own meals. ■ TIP→ Another good bet is to take advantage of the early-bird dinner specials offered at many restaurants.

About the Hotels

Although high-rise condominiums have replaced many of the smaller, locally owned motels along Myrtle Beach's Ocean Boulevard, there's still a wide variety of accommodations on the Strand, including beachside camping, motels, luxury hotels, resort communities, and rental houses (mostly available by the week). Generally, smaller properties won't have restaurants (except for the occasional coffee shop), but just about every option, with the exception of houses, has a pool. Many hotel rooms, particularly in Myrtle Beach, come with kitchenettes. Since many people return again and again to the same property, some options, particularly beach houses, need to be reserved months in advance for summer stays.

WHAT IT COSTS				
$$$$	**$$$**	**$$**	**$**	**¢**
RESTAURANTS over $22	$17–$22	$12–$16	$7–$11	under $7
HOTELS over $220	$161–$220	$111–$160	$70–$110	under $70

Restaurant prices are for a main course at dinner. Hotel prices are for two people in a standard double room in high season.

Timing

The Grand Strand was developed as a summer resort, and with its gorgeous beaches, flowering tropical plants, and generally good—if warm—weather, it continues to shine during the height of the season. That said, the fall and spring shoulder seasons may be even more pleasant. Warm temperatures allow for beach activities, but the humidity drops and the heat of summer has passed.

Winter—November through February—isn't usually thought of as a time to visit the beach, but the region can be quite pleasant. Although there are certainly cold days here and there, for the most part golfers, tennis players, and other outdoor enthusiasts can enjoy their pursuits during these months—at rock-bottom prices.

THE MYRTLE BEACH AREA

Myrtle Beach was a late bloomer. Until 1901 it didn't have an official name; that year the first hotel went up, and oceanfront lots were selling for $25. Today, more than 13 million people a year visit the region, and no wonder: lodging, restaurants, shopping, and entertainment choices are varied and plentiful. The 120 golf courses in the area add to the appeal. ■ TIP→ **Be sure to take note of whether an establishment is on Business 17 or the bypass when getting directions—confusing the two could lead to hours of frustration.**

Myrtle Beach has a reputation as a frenzied strip of all-you-can-eat buffets, T-shirt shops, and bars. That reputation isn't completely unwarranted, but this side of Myrtle Beach's character is generally limited to parts of Ocean Boulevard (the "strip"), Kings Highway, and Restaurant Row (sometimes called the Galleria area). Some blocks may be a bit seedy, but the pedestrian-friendly strip is generally safe and clean (though at

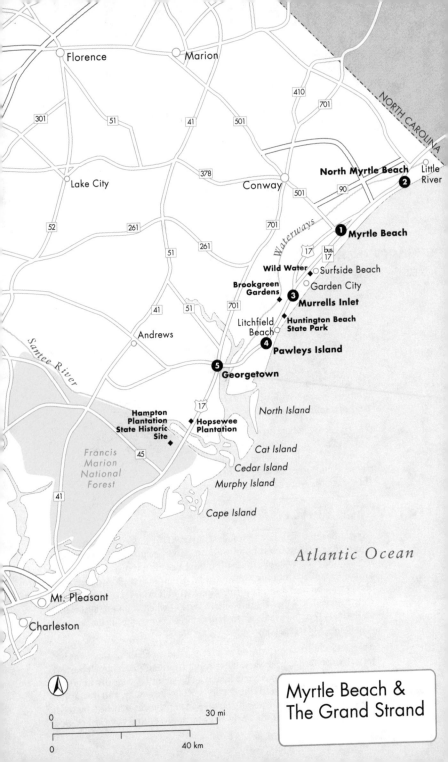

Myrtle Beach &
The Grand Strand

night the sidewalks can be crowded with the young bar crowd). Attractions such as Family Kingdom Amusement Park and Ripley's Haunted Adventure can add a dose of fun to your afternoon.

What may come as a surprise is that it's also not terribly difficult to spend a quiet vacation here, dining in sophisticated spots after spending the day on relatively uncrowded beaches. Myrtle Beach State Park, for instance, is a bastion of peace and quiet, as are the beaches adjacent to the residential areas of Myrtle Beach at either end of the strip. ■ TIP→ **Those looking for a quieter time take note: Biker Week, an annual gathering of thousands of motorcycle afficianados, usually falls somewhere around the third week of May and can cause noise, congestion, and a spike in prices.**

Myrtle Beach

4

❶ *94 mi northeast of Charleston via U.S. 17; 138 mi east of Columbia via U.S. 76 to U.S. 378 to U.S. 501.*

Myrtle Beach, with its high-rises and hyperdevelopment, is the nerve center of the Grand Strand and one of the major seaside destinations on the East Coast. Visitors are drawn here for the swirl of classic vacation activity, from beaches to arcades to live music shows.

To capture the flavor of the place, take a stroll along Ocean Boulevard. Here's where you'll find an eclectic assortment of gift and novelty shops, a wax museum, and a museum of oddities. When you've had your fill, turn east and make your way back onto the beach amid the sunbathers, kite-fliers, and kids building sand castles.

On **Carolina Safari Jeep Tours** you'll visit everything from a plantation house to an alligator-laden salt marsh to an 18th-century church. Along the way you'll learn fun facts and scary ghost stories, told from a script that keeps even history-phobes entertained. The 3 ½-hour tour, which includes some walking, provides a surprisingly complete overview of the region and beautiful views of the Grand Strand's varied ecosystem. Call to make a reservation; you'll be picked up at your hotel in a Jeep that seats about a dozen people. ⊠ *725 Seaboard Ave. Unit E* ☎ *843/497–5330* ⊕ *www.carolinasafari.com* 🖃 *$33* ☉ *Arrange tour times when making reservation.*

The medieval-theme **Dragon's Lair Fantasy Golf** miniature-golf course is well maintained and well lighted—and it has a 30-foot-tall fire-breathing dragon. The course has no steps, making it perfect for strollers and wheelchairs. ⊠ *Broadway at the Beach, U.S. 17 Bypass between 21st Ave. N and 29th Ave. N* ☎ *843/444–3215* 🖃 *$7* ☉ *Daily 10–10.*

Dominated by a gigantic white wooden roller coaster called the Swamp Fox, **Family Kingdom Amusement Park** is set right on the ocean. There are thrill and children's rides, a log flume, go-cart track, old-fashioned carousel, and the Slingshot Drop Zone, which rockets riders straight down a 110-foot tower. It's a bit like going to a state fair that runs all summer long. Operating hours can vary, so it's worthwhile to call before visiting, especially on Saturday when the park is often rented by groups. ■ TIP→ **Money-saving bundled tickets and multiday passes for water parks** and other recreational venues are readily available, check out Web sites for more information. ⊠ *300 S. Ocean Blvd., The Strip* ☎ *843/626–3447* ⊕ *www.family-kingdom.com* ☎ *Fees vary for individual attractions; 1-day unlimited access to most rides $19.50* ☉ *June–mid-Aug., daily 4 PM–midnight; mid-Apr.–May and late Aug.–Sept., weekdays 6 PM–10 PM, Sat. 1–10, Sun. 1–8.*

☺ **Myrtle Waves** is South Carolina's largest water park. You can shoot through twisty chutes, swim in the Ocean in Motion Wave Pool, float the day away on an inner tube on the LayZee River, or ride a boogie board on the Racer River. There's beach volleyball, too, for when you've had enough water. ■ TIP→ **Invest in a waterproof pouch to keep money and valuables safe.** ⊠ *U.S. 17 Bypass and 10th Ave. N, South End* ☎ *843/913–9301* ⊕ *www.myrtlewaves.com* ☎ *$23.95 for full day, $15.95 after 3* ☉ *Early May–early Sept., daily 10–6.*

☺ At **NASCAR SpeedPark** you can drive on seven different NASCAR-replica tracks. The cars vary in their sophistication and speed; to use the most advanced track you need to be a licensed driver. The 26-acre facility also has racing memorabilia, an arcade, and miniature golf. ■ TIP→ **Lines at attractions are shortest on Monday.** ⊠ *U.S. 17 Bypass and 21st Ave. N, at Broadway at the Beach, Central Myrtle Beach* ☎ *843/918–8725* ⊕ *www.nascarspeedpark.com* ☎ *$24.95 unlimited day pass or $6 each ride* ☉ *Mar.–Oct., weekdays 5 PM–midnight, weekends noon–midnight; hrs vary, call to confirm.*

☺ **Ripley's Aquarium** has an underwater tunnel exhibit longer than a football field and exotic marine creatures on display, from poisonous lionfish to moray eels to an octopus. Children can examine horseshoe crabs and eels in touch tanks. ⊠ *Broadway at the Beach, U.S. 17 Bypass between 21st Ave. N and 29th Ave. N, Central Myrtle Beach* ☎ *843/916–0888 or 800/734–8888* ⊕ *www.ripleysaquarium.com* ☎ *$16.95* ☉ *Sun.–Thurs. 9 AM–10 PM, Fri. and Sat. 9 AM–11 PM.*

Convincing vampires and other costumed characters will taunt and entice you to come inside **Ripley's Haunted Adventure**, a fun, creepy haunted house. Once you're inside, high-tech animation and other special effects keep the scream factor high. ⊠ *915 N. Ocean Blvd., The Strip* ☎ *843/448–2331* ☎ *$11.95* ☉ *Mid-Apr.–Oct., Mon.–Thurs. 4 PM–7 PM; Fri.–Sun. noon–8 PM.*

☺ About 9 mi south of Myrtle Beach, **Wild Water** has 25 water-oriented rides and activities, along with go-carts and minigolf. If your children are old enough to navigate the park on their own, spend a few minutes at the adults-only lounge pool, where you can sit immersed in Jacuzzi-like bubbles. ⊠ *910 U.S. 17S, Surfside Beach* ☎ *843/238–3787* ⊕ *www.wild-water.com* ☎ *$24.98, $16.98 after 3* ☉ *Late May–early Sept., daily 10–7.*

Sports & the Outdoors

BEACHES Regardless of whether you're staying on the beach, you shouldn't have too much trouble getting to a spot of sand. There are nearly 150 public beach-access points in the city, all marked with signs. Most have ample parking and "shower towers" for cleaning up; few have rest-room facilities.

Since much of Myrtle Beach's coastline is dominated by high-rise hotels, there are plenty of places to get lunch or a cool drink without having to get back in your car. Many of these hotels also rent beach chairs and boogie boards. Some also have nets set up for games of beach volleyball. ■ TIP➔ Myrtle Beach's cabana district, located on North Ocean Boulevard between Beach Place and Seaside Place, has some of the quietest beaches around.

Dogs, kayaks, and surfboards are limited on many beaches from May through September. Be sure to read the ordinances posted at each access point for details. ■ TIP➔ Summer heat can be brutal so don't leave pets or food in the car during the hot summer months.

For a more out-of-the-way experience, head south of Myrtle Beach to **Myrtle Beach State Park.** There you can swim in the ocean, hike on a nature trail, and fish in the surf or from a pier. You can also camp, but you need to book in advance. ⊠ *U.S. 17, 3 mi south of Myrtle Beach* ☎ *843/238–5325* ⊑ *$4, $4.50 to fish off pier, no license required.*

FISHING The Gulf Stream makes for good fishing from early spring through December. Anglers can fish from 10 piers and jetties for amberjack, sea trout, and king mackerel. Surfcasters may snare bluefish, whiting, flounder, pompano, and channel bass. In the South Strand, salt marshes, inlets, and tidal creeks yield flounder, blues, croakers, spots, shrimp, clams, oysters, and blue crabs.

Held each year from April through October, the **Grand Strand Fishing Rodeo** (☎ 843/626–7444) holds a fish-of-the-month contest, with prizes for the largest catch of a designated species. There's no registration fee; entrants must take their catch to designated weigh stations for consideration.

GOLF Many of the Grand Strand's more than 100 courses are championship layouts; most are public. **Tee Times Central** (☎ 843/347–4653 or 800/344–5590) makes it easy to book tee times at nearly all the Strand's courses. ■ TIP➔ Alligators have taken up residence in many of the Strand's golf courses. If you see one, don't investigate: they're faster than they look.

Two of Myrtle Beach's courses are particularly notable. Built in the 1920s, **Pine Lakes** (⊠ 5603 Woodside Ave. ☎ 843/315–7700 ⊕ www.pinelakes. com) is considered the granddaddy of Strand courses. In spring, you can get mimosas on the 10th tee; in winter they serve clam chowder. Pine Lakes is a terrific walking course. Former home to the Senior PGA Tour, the Tom Fazio–designed **Tournament Players Club at Myrtle Beach** (⊠ 1189 TPC Blvd., Murrells Inlet ☎ 888/742–8721 ⊕ www.tpc.com) is a challenging journey through the salt marshes.

A bit less demanding, but still interesting, thanks to surprising changes in elevation, **The Witch** (⊠ 1900 Hwy. 44, East Conway ☎ 843/448–1300 ⊕ www.mysticalgolf.com) is built on wetlands and contains nearly 4,000 feet of bridges. Known for its top-notch condition, regardless of the season, **Arrowhead** (⊠ 1201 Burcale Rd. ☎ 800/236–3243 ⊕ www.

arrowheadcc.com) is the only Raymond Floyd–designed course in the region. Several of the 27 holes run along the Intracoastal Waterway and you might spot dolphins cavorting in the smooth water.

There are a few bargains on the Myrtle Beach golfing scene. One is **Indigo Creek** (⊠ 9480 Indigo Creek Dr., Murrells Inlet ☎ 800/718–1830 ⊕ www.indigocreekgolfclub.com), which is cut through forests of huge oaks and pines. Built on the site of an old airbase, **Whispering Pines** (⊠ U.S. 17 Business and 22nd Ave. S ☎ 843/918–2305 ⊕ www.mbteetime. com) is recognized as an Audubon Cooperative Sanctuary.

SCUBA DIVING In summer, many warm-water tropical fish travel to the area from the Gulf Stream. Off the coast of Little River, near the North Carolina border, rock and coral ledges teem with coral, sea fans, sponges, reef fish, anemones, urchins, and crabs. Several outlying shipwrecks are flush with schools of spadefish, amberjack, grouper, barracuda, and even the occasional octopus and loggerhead turtle. ■ TIP→ Most dive shops can have you PADI-certified in a weekend.

Instruction and equipment rentals, as well as an indoor dive tank, are available in the Sports Corner shopping center from **New Horizons Dive and Travel** (⊠ 515 U.S. 501, Suite A ☎ 843/839–1932).

TENNIS There are more than 200 courts on the Grand Strand. Facilities include hotel and resort courts, as well as free municipal courts in Myrtle Beach, North Myrtle Beach, and Surfside Beach. ■ TIP→ Many tennis clubs offer weekly round robin tournaments that are open to players of all levels.

Prestwick Tennis and Swim Club (⊠ 1375 McMaster Dr. ☎ 843/828–1000) offers court time, rental equipment, and instruction; courts are lighted for nighttime play. **Grande Dunes Tennis** (⊠ U.S. 17 Bypass at Grande Dunes Blvd. ☎ 843/449–4486) is a full fitness facility with 10 Har-Tru courts, 5 of which are lighted; the club also offers private and group lessons.

WATER SPORTS Hobie Cats, Jet Skis, Windsurfers, and sailboats are available for rent at **Downwind Sails** (⊠ Ocean Blvd. at 29th Ave. S, South End ☎ 843/ 448–7245); they also have banana-boat rides (where you're towed in a long, yellow inflatable raft) and parasailing. ■ TIP→ Don't forget to bring your own towels and sunscreen when you head out. **Ocean Watersports** (⊠ 4th Ave. S and beach, next to Family Kingdom amusement park, The Strip ☎ 843/445–7777) rents water-sports equipment.

Where to Stay & Eat

★ $$$$ ✕ **Collectors Café.** A successful restaurant, art gallery, and coffeehouse rolled into one, this unpretentiously arty spot has bright, funky paintings and tile work covering its walls and tabletops. The cuisine is among the most inventive in the area. Try the grilled tuna with Indian spices, served with Cuban black-bean sauce and mango salsa—it's a far cry from standard Myrtle Beach fish-house fare. ⊠ 7726 N. Kings Hwy., North End ☎ 843/449–9370 ☐ AE, D, MC, V ☉ Closed Sun. No lunch.

$$$–$$$$ ✕ **Thoroughbreds.** For a special night out, or to fulfill a red-meat craving, Thoroughbreds, with its dark wood, leather banquettes, and top-notch meat, is a romantic escape from the whirlwind of Myrtle Beach.

Fish selections are fresh and well prepared, but steaks, pork chops, and rack of lamb steal the show. There's a great wine list, too. ⊠ *9706 N. Kings Hwy.* ☎ *843/497–2636* ⚲ *Reservations essential* ▭ *AE, D, MC, V* ⊙ *No lunch.*

$$–$$$$ ✗ **Key West Grill.** Known for its Caribbean flair and daily fish specials, such as cashew-crusted red snapper, Key West Grill has a fun, beachy vibe, but the food is well-crafted and well-presented. There are large entrées such as the mojito grilled pork chop, as well as less substantial choices such as burgers and salads with grilled fish. ■ **TIP→ Call about early-bird and bar specials: you'll get a good deal, and arriving early lessens the likelihood of having to wait for a table.** ⊠ *Broadway at the Beach, U.S. 17 Bypass between 21st Ave. N and 29th Ave. N* ☎ *843/444–3663* ⚲ *Reservations not accepted* ▭ *AE, D, MC, V.*

$$–$$$$ ✗ **Sea Captain's House.** At this picturesque restaurant with a nautical theme, the best seats are in the windowed porch room, which overlooks the ocean. The fireplace in the wood-panel dining room inside is warmly welcoming on cool off-season evenings. Menu highlights include Lowcountry crab casserole and avocado-seafood salad. The breads and desserts are baked on the premises. ⊠ *3000 N. Ocean Blvd., The Strip* ☎ *843/448–8082* ▭ *AE, D, MC, V.*

★ $–$$$ ✗ **Villa Romana.** It's all about family at Villa Romana, where owners Rinaldo and Franca come in early to make the gnocchi and stick around to greet customers. It's hard to resist filling up on the stracciatella soup, bruschetta, salad, and rolls (perhaps the best on the Strand) that accompany every meal, but try. The gnocchi is a perfect foil for any of the homemade sauces, and the veal Absolut (sautéed veal in a sauce of cream, mushrooms, and vodka) is a specialty. ■ **TIP→ Michael the accordian player can entertain diners with songs that range from "Mack the Knife" to "Stairway to Heaven."** ⊠ *707 S. Kings Hwy.* ☎ *843/448–4990* ⚲ *Reservations essential* ▭ *AE, D, MC, V* ⊙ *No lunch.*

$–$$ ✗ **E. Noodles & Co.** The dramatic lighting, sleek furnishings, and topnotch Asian specialties transport diners out of the beach and straight to the city. The menu pulls from Chinese, Thai, and Japanese flavors. Double panfried noodles promise to foil all but the most die-hard Atkins follower. Grouper tempura is a terrific local take on the classic. ⊠ *400 20th. Ave. S* ☎ *843/916–8808* ⚲ *Reservations not accepted* ▭ *MC, V* ⊙ *Closed Sun.*

¢–$ ✗ **Croissants Bakery & Café.** The lunch crowd loves this spot, which has an on-site bakery. Black-and-white tile floors, café tables, checked tablecloths, and glass pastry cases filled with sweets create an appetizing feel to the place. Try the chicken or broccoli salads, a Reuben or Monte Cristo sandwich, or one of the pasta specials, and save room for the peanutbutter cheesecake. ⊠ *504A 27th Ave. N, The Strip* ☎ *843/448–2253* ▭ *D, MC, V* ⊙ *Closed Sun. No dinner.*

¢–$ ✗ **Dagwood's Deli.** Dagwood and Blondie could split one of the masterful sandwiches at Dagwood's Deli. There are the usual suspects—ham, turkey, and the like—but you won't regret trying one of the more distinctive creations, such as blackened mahimahi with homemade pineapple salsa, or the grilled chicken breast with bacon, provolone, and ranch dressing. Salads and burgers round out the menu, and they deliver (for

$1) to most of Myrtle Beach. Dagwood's is open until 6 on Friday and Saturday, so you can duck in on those days for an early dinner. (On other days they close at 4.) ✉ *400 11th Ave. N* ☎ *843/448–0100* ✍ *Reservations not accepted* 💳 *MC, V* ⏲ *Closed Sun. No dinner.*

¢–$ ✕ **Southern Market.** Part restaurant, part food emporium, Southern Market features seven food stations that serve everything from pancakes in the morning to salmon with brandied peppercorn gravy at dinner. Everything is available to go, or take your tray and eat in the dining room or the outdoor courtyard. The market's butcher case is packed with prime meat, free-range poultry, and fresh seafood for cooking at home. The wine selection is extensive, and the cakes, pies, and brownies are made on-site. ✉ *959 Lake Arrowhead Rd.* ☎ *843/497–4901* ✍ *Reservations not accepted* 💳 *AE, D, MC, V.*

★ $$$–$$$$ **Hampton Inn and Suites Oceanfront.** This property combines the reliability of an established hotel chain with the joys of a beach resort. Rooms have balconies and a cheerful style; all have ocean views. There's a lazy river—a pool with a moving current—that carries swimmers along its course. ✉ *1803 S. Ocean Blvd., South End, 29577* ☎ *843/946–6400 or 877/946–6400* 📠 *843/946–0031* 🌐 *www.hamptoninnoceanfront.com* *80 rooms, 36 suites* *Microwaves, refrigerators, cable TV, 3 pools (1 indoor), gym, hot tub, business services, meeting rooms* 💳 *AE, D, DC, MC, V* 🍽 *BP.*

★ $$$–$$$$ **Myrtle Beach Marriott Resort at Grande Dunes.** Entering this plantation-chic high-rise resort, with its airy wicker furniture, giant palms, and mahogany details, will take you away from the hubbub of Myrtle Beach and straight to a tropical locale. Green-and-gold guest rooms have plush carpet that makes them quiet and serene, perfect for watching the waves break on the beach. The spa, which offers a full range of treatments, is top notch, and the health club has well-maintained, state-of-the-art machines. The golf and tennis clubs are both on-site, as is a marina with charters and jet-ski, boat, and kayak rentals. ✉ *8400 Costa Verde Dr., 29572* ☎ *843/449–8880* 📠 *843/449–8669* 🌐 *www.myrtlebeachmarriott.com* *400 rooms* *Restaurant, snack bar, room service, refrigerator, cable TV, tennis court, 3 pools (1 indoor), marina, business services* 💳 *AE, D, MC, V* 🍽 *EP.*

$$–$$$$ **Kingston Plantation.** This complex includes two hotels, as well as restaurants, shops, and one- to three-bedroom condominiums and villas, on 145 acres of ocean-side woodlands. One hotel, an Embassy Suites, has guest rooms with bleached-wood furnishings and kitchenettes. The other, a Hilton, has a more classic decor and no kitchen facilities. The villas and condos are privately owned, but you can reserve one through the central booking number and Web site. Although these options are decorated to the taste of their owners, they all have the same standard amenities such as sheets and towels, and kitchen equipment. Beachgoing is enhanced by a beach club with bathrooms, water fountains, and parking. ✉ *9800 Lake Dr., North End, 29572* ☎ *843/449–0006 or 800/876–0010* 📠 *843/497–1110* 🌐 *www.kingstonplantation.com* *385 rooms, 255 suites, 414 villas, 414 condos* *3 restaurants, golf privileges, tennis courts, 8 pools, fitness classes, health club, sauna, racquetball* 💳 *AE, D, MC, V* 🍽 *BP.*

$$$ ▦ **Carolina Grande.** Soothing tones of russet and taupe along with dark tropical wood give these one-bedroom condo units a British-colonial feel. Full kitchens outfitted with black countertops and new appliances—the hotel was totally refurbished in March 2006—are sleek and modern. Although the hotel is across the street from the ocean, there's a breeze-way that makes the walk easy. Every unit has a pull-out couch, balcony, and a washer and dryer. ⊠ *2503 N. Ocean Blvd., 29577* ☎ *800/456–0009* ↵ *118 units* ⚐ *Kitchens, cable TV, pool, hot tub, concierge* ⊟ *AE, D, DC, MC, V* ⊧ *EP.*

$$–$$$ ▦ **Breakers Resort Hotel.** The rooms in this four-tower oceanfront hotel are airy and spacious, with contemporary furnishings. Most have kitchenettes and Murphy beds; the Paradise Tower has one-, two- and three-bedroom suites. There are several pools, a lazy river, and a pirate-ship facade that kids can swim in and around. The hotel is right in the middle of the Myrtle Beach Strip. ■ TIP→ **There's a Starbucks coffee shop across the street.** ⊠ *2006 N. Ocean Blvd., Box 485, 29578* ☎ *843/444–4444 or 800/952–4507* 🖷 *843/626–5001* ⊕ *www.breakers.com* ↵ *204 rooms, 186 suites* ⚐ *2 restaurants, room service, refrigerators, 3 pools, gym, outdoor hot tubs, saunas, lounge, video game room, children's programs (ages 4–10), laundry service* ⊟ *AE, D, DC, MC, V* ⊧ *EP.*

$$–$$$ ▦ **Grande Shores.** Like many of the newer properties in Myrtle Beach—this one was built in 2001—Grande Shores is a combination of rentable condos with full kitchens and standard hotel rooms outfitted with refrigerators, coffeemakers and, in a few cases, kitchenettes. Whichever you choose, all of the airy rooms at Grande Shores have balconies with a view of the ocean and free high-speed Internet. Pools abound: there's an indoor pool, an outdoor pool with a meandering stream that gently propels swimmers, and a rooftop garden with a pool and four hot tubs. ⊠ *201 77th Ave. N, 29572* ☎ *843/692–2397 or 877/798–4074* 🖷 *843/449–7438* ⊕ *www.grandeshores.com* ↵ *236 rooms* ⚐ *Restaurant, 4 pools (1 indoor), gym, lounge, playground, business services, free parking* ⊟ *AE, D, DC, MC, V* ⊧ *EP.*

$$–$$$ ▦ **Sheraton Myrtle Beach Convention Center Hotel.** With its round, glass-encased tower, cantilevered lobby windows, sweeping staircases and curved balconies, the Sheraton is a stylish addition to the landscape. Although the blond-wood-appointed rooms have an airy feel, the atmosphere is more that of an urban hotel than a beach one: amenities include in-room coffee service and super-luxe bedding rather than microwaves or a children's program. The hotel is connected to the Myrtle Beach Convention Center. ⊠ *2101 N. Oak St., 29578* ☎ *843/918–5000* 🖷 *843/918–5011* ⊕ *www.sheraton.com/myrtlebeach* ↵ *392 rooms, 10 suites* ⚐ *Indoor pool, beach, airport shuttle* ⊟ *AE, D, MC, V* ⊧ *EP.*

$–$$ ▦ **Cabana Shores Hotel.** Although the Cabana Shores is across Ocean Boulevard from the beach, thanks to the area's designation as a "cabana district" there are no buildings across the street and the beach is blissfully quiet and uncrowded. The spacious rooms have dark-wood furniture, balconies, and full kitchens; larger rooms have two balconies. Behind the hotel is a lovely old residential neighborhood that's great for strolling. ⊠ *5701 N. Ocean Blvd., 29577* ☎ *843/449–6441 or 800/277–7562* 🖷 *843/449–6441* ⊕ *www.cabanashores.com* ↵ *72 rooms* ⚐ *Cable TV, pool* ⊟ *AE, D, MC, V* ⊧ *EP.*

$–$$ ⊞ **Driftwood on the Oceanfront.** After 66 years, the Driftwood came under new ownership in 2005, but it remains one of the few small, independent hotels in Myrtle Beach. Its well-maintained facilities and reasonable rates are especially popular with families. Some rooms are on the oceanfront, and all are decorated in sea, sky, or earth tones. ⊠ *1600 N. Ocean Blvd., Box 275, 29578* ☎ *843/448–1544 or 800/942–3456* 🖷 *843/448–2917* ⊕ *www.driftwoodlodge.com* 🛏 *90 rooms* ♨ *Microwaves, refrigerators, cable TV, 2 pools, shuffleboard, laundry facilities* ☰ *AE, D, MC, V* ⊠ *EP.*

$–$$ ⊞ **Seashore Hotel.** With its funky aqua-and-white-stripe awnings and pale stucco exterior, the Seashore Motel looks more Miami than Myrtle Beach. Inside, the clean rooms are decorated in blue tones and with cheerful cottage furniture. Oceanfront rooms have balconies, and larger rooms have kitchenettes. ■ **TIP→** One of the nicest things about this hotel is its location a block away from an amusement park and the Strand's only oceanfront water park. ⊠ *107 S. Ocean Blvd., 29577* ☎ *843/448–3700 or 800/ 826–5810* ⊕ *www.myrtlebeachinns.com* 🛏 *51 rooms* ♨ *Pool, laundry facilities* ☰ *AE, D, MC, V* ⊠ *EP.*

$ ⊞ **Serendipity Inn.** This cozy Spanish-villa-style inn is about 300 yards from the beach. Though the layout is much like a hotel, each guest room is decorated in a different way, most with four-poster beds and antique chests in pine or mahogany. There's also a colorful pool area dotted with hanging flowers and a trickling fountain. A breakfast of homemade coffee cake, hardboiled eggs, yogurt, cereal, and fruit is served in the wicker-appointed garden room. ⊠ *407 71st Ave. N, North End, 29572* ☎ *843/449–5268 or 800/762–3229* ⊕ *www.serendipityinn.com* 🛏 *12 rooms, 2 suites* ♨ *Some kitchenettes, refrigerators, Wi-Fi, pool, outdoor hot tub, Ping-Pong, shuffleboard; no room phones* ☰ *MC, V* ⊠ *BP.*

Nightlife & the Arts

CLUBS & LOUNGES Clubs offer varying fare, including beach music, the Grand Strand's unique '50s-style sound. Some clubs and resorts have sophisticated live entertainment in summer. Some hotels and resorts also have piano bars or lounges.

South Carolina's only Hard Rock Cafe, Planet Hollywood, and NASCAR Cafe are just a few of the hot spots in **Broadway at the Beach** (⊠ U.S. 17 Bypass between 21st and 29th Aves. N, The Strip ☎ 843/444–3200), which also has shopping. In the evenings, dueling piano players compete to perform the most outlandish versions of audience requests at **Crocodile Rocks** (⊠ Broadway at the Beach, U.S. 17 Bypass between 21st and 29th Aves. N, The Strip ☎ 843/444–2096); singing along is part of the fun. The shag (South Carolina's state dance) is popular at **Studebaker's** (⊠ 2000 N. Kings Hwy., The Strip ☎ 843/448–9747 or 843/626– 3855).

FILM The **IMAX Discovery Theater** (⊠ Broadway at the Beach, U.S. 17 Bypass between 21st and 29th Aves. N, The Strip ☎ 843/448–4629) shows educational films on a six-story-high screen.

MUSIC & LIVE SHOWS Live acts, and country-and-western shows in particular, are a big draw in Myrtle Beach. There are many family-oriented shows to choose from.

Carolina Opry (✉ 82nd Ave. N, North End ☎ 843/238–8888 or 800/843–6779) is a family-oriented variety show featuring country, light rock, show tunes, and gospel. At **Dolly Parton's Dixie Stampede** (✉ 8901B U.S. 17 Business, North End ☎ 843/497–9700 or 800/843–6779) dinner theater, dozens of actors on horseback recreate Civil War cavalry battles. **Legends in Concert** (✉ 301 U.S. 17 Business, Surfside Beach ☎ 843/238–7827 or 800/843–6779) has high-energy shows by impersonators of Little Richard, Elvis, Cher, and the Blues Brothers.

The elegant **Palace Theater** (✉ Broadway at the Beach, U.S. 17 Bypass between 21st and 29th Aves. N, The Strip ☎ 843/448–0588 or 800/905–4228) hosts Broadway shows such as *Les Miserables* and *Stomp* and headliner performances by the likes of Jerry Seinfeld and the Marshall Tucker Band. Watch knights on horseback battle for their kingdom, followed by a real jousting tournament, at **Medieval Times Dinner & Tournament** (✉ 2904 Fantasy Way ☎ 888/935–6878).

Shopping

For recreational shopping, Myrtle Beach's main attraction is **Broadway at the Beach** (✉ U.S. 17 Bypass between 21st Ave. N and 29th Ave. N). More than 100 shops include everything from high-end apparel to Harley Davidson–theme gifts.

DISCOUNT OUTLETS The **Tanger 501 Outlet Center** (✉ U.S. 501, Waccamaw Pottery Area ☎ 843/236–5100) is a large outlet center with Gap, Nike, Polo, Brooks Brothers, and J. Crew. **Tanger 17 Outlet Center** (✉ 10785 Kings Rd., at U.S. 17, North End ☎ 843/449–0491) has 75 factory outlet stores, including Polo, Banana Republic, and Old Navy.

North Myrtle Beach

❷ *5 mi north of Myrtle Beach via U.S. 17.*

North Myrtle Beach, best known as the site where the shag, South Carolina's state dance, originated, is made up of the beach towns Cherry Grove, Crescent Beach, Windy Hill, and Ocean Drive. Entering North Myrtle Beach from the south on U.S. 17, you'll see Barefoot Landing, a huge shopping and entertainment complex that sits on the Intracoastal Waterway. As you make your way east toward the ocean, then north on Ocean Boulevard South, high-rises give way to small motels, then to single beach houses, many of which are available for rent. This end of the strand marks the tip of a large peninsula, and there are lots of little islands, creeks, and marshes between the ocean and the Intracoastal to explore by kayak or canoe. ■ TIP→ **Mosquitos can be a problem on the marsh, especially in the early evening. Be sure to pack repellent.**

★ ☾ **Alligator Adventure** has interactive reptile shows, including an alligator-feeding demonstration. Boardwalks lead through marshes and swamps on the 15-acre property, where you'll see wildlife of the wetlands, including a pair of rare white albino alligators; Utan, the largest known crocodile in captivity; giant Galápagos tortoises; and all manner of reptiles, including boas, pythons, and anacondas. Unusual plants and exotic birds also thrive here. ⊠ *U.S. 17 at Barefoot Landing* ☎ *843/361–0789* 🖶 *843/361–0742* ⊕ *www.alligatoradventure.com* 🖃 *$14.95* ☼ *Daily 10–9.*

⛳ **Hawaiian Rumble** is the crown jewel of Myrtle Beach miniature golf. The course hosts championship tournaments, and is best known for its smoking volcano, which rumbles and belches fire at timed intervals. ⊠ *3210 33rd Ave. S, at U.S. 17* ☎ *843/272–7812* 🖃 *$9 all day (9–5), $7 per round after 5 PM* ☼ *Mar.–Dec., daily 9 AM–11 PM.*

⛳ **Myrtle Beach Grand Prix Family Thrill Park** is a hot spot for would-be auto racers. You can navigate courses in ¾-scale Formula 1 race cars, go-carts, and bumper boats, and there's a kids' park with mini-go-carts and self-guided kids' cars. To drive the Formula 1 cars you need to have a driver's license. ⊠ *3201 U.S. 17* ☎ *843/272–7770* ⊠ *3900 U.S. 17S* ☎ *843/272–7770* ⊕ *www.mbgrandprix.com* 🖃 *$29.98 unlimited rides, individual rides $3–$6* ☼ *Mar.–Oct., daily 1–11.*

Sports & the Outdoors

FISHING   The **Cherry Grove Fishing Pier** (⊠ 3500 N. Ocean Blvd. ☎ 843/249–1625) has a two-story observation deck and reaches 985 feet into the ocean, making it the place to catch pompano, bluefish, and mackerel. You can rent tackle and buy bait at the pier. ■ TIP→ **Early morning and late afternoon are the best time to catch fish.** For full- and half-day deep-sea fishing excursions, contact the **Hurricane Fishing Fleet** (⊠ River Rd., Calabash waterfront ☎ 843/249–3571). They also conduct a dolphin adventure cruise using a working shrimp boat.

GOLF   In Cherry Grove Beach you'll find the much-touted 18-hole, par-72 **Tidewater Golf Club** (⊠ 1400 Tidewater Dr. ☎ 866/639–6962 ⊕ www. myrtlebeachgolftrips.com), one of only two courses in the area with ocean views. A 2002 renovation restored the greens to tournament condition and speed; the high bluffs are reminiscent of Pebble Beach.

The four 18-hole championship courses at **Barefoot Resort and Golf** (⊠ 4980 Barefoot Resort Bridge Rd. ☎ 843/390–7999) were designed by Tom Fazio, Davis Love III, Pete Dye, and Greg Norman and have proven to be new favorites of Grand Strand golfers. Notable details include a replica of plantation ruins on the Love course and only 60 acres of mowable grass on the Norman course.

WATER SPORTS   You can rent your own pontoon boats or jet skis at **Myrtle Beach Water Sports, Inc.** (⊠ 4495 Mineola Ave. ☎ 843/280–7777), or let them take you parasailing. Learn to scuba dive, take a dive trip, or just rent equipment at **Coastal Scuba** (⊠ 1501 U.S. 17S ☎ 800/249–9388 or 843/361–3323 ⊕ www.coastalscuba.com), which is PADI-certified.

Where to Stay & Eat

★ $$$–$$$$ ✕ **Greg Norman's Australian Grille.** Overlooking the Intracoastal Waterway, this large restaurant in Barefoot Landing has leather booths, Australian aboriginal art on the walls, an extensive wine list, and a classy bar area. The menu features grilled meats, and many of the selections have an Asian flair. (The Australian theme comes through more strongly

CLOSE UP

Lights Out for Sea Turtles!

YOU'LL NOTICE THAT MANY OF THE STRAND'S BEACHFRONT RESORTS keep the lights turned down low on the ocean side. This may add to the romance of a night-time stroll along the sand, but the primary beneficiaries of the darkness aren't humans . . . they're turtles.

Loggerhead sea turtles have been nesting on the beaches of the Grand Strand for thousands of years. (Seeing one of these often-giant reptiles come ashore to lay eggs in the sand is a rare thrill.) Today, loggerheads are a

threatened species, so it's important to cut down on obstacles to their breeding.

That's where the darkness comes in. After a 60-day incubation period, the baby turtles hatch and begin to crawl toward the ocean. But bright lights confuse their navigation systems, causing them to head toward the light instead of the water, and making them easy prey for sand crabs and sea birds. Keeping lights to a minimum allows the baby turtles to heed their instincts and make it to the ocean.

in the decor, and the Greg Norman merchandise for sale, than in the food.) Highlights are the lobster dumplings, miso-marinated sea bass, and habanero-rubbed tenderloin. ⊠ *4930 U.S. 17S* ☎ *843/361–0000* ⚑ *Reservations essential* ▤ *AE, D, MC, V* ☉ *No lunch.*

$$–$$$$ ✗ **Rockefellers Raw Bar.** Yes it's a raw bar—and a good one, with a bounty of fresh seafood—but don't sell the cooked items short at this small, casual locals' joint. The oysters Rockefeller, with their splash of Pernod and fresh spinach, are the real deal, and the iron pot of steamed mussels, clams, scallops, and other goodies is a terrific version of a Lowcountry staple. ⊠ *3613 U.S. 17S* ☎ *843/361–9677* ⚑ *Reservations not accepted* ▤ *AE, D, MC, V.*

$–$$$ ✗ **White Point Seafood.** Get your fried-fish fix without the guilt: White Point's signature flounder (there are other fish available every day) is nearly grease-free, and comes from local waters to boot. Homemade coleslaw and hushpuppies round out the meal. You can also get fish grilled or broiled, salads, and sandwiches. ⊠ *3303A U.S. 17S* ☎ *843/272–6732* ⚑ *Reservations not accepted* ▤ *AE, D, MC, V* ☉ *Closed Jan. and Feb. No lunch.*

¢–$ ✗ **Rick's Cafe.** Join Rick and his wife at this coffee shop on the ground floor of the Blockade Runner Motor Inn for tasty eggs, burgers, and salads. If you're really hungry, consider tackling Ernie's Breakfast in a Bowl, filled with the South's four food groups (grits, cheese, eggs, and bacon). At lunch, the Redneck Burger—topped with chili and slaw—is another deliciously daunting meal that will have you reaching for the napkins. ⊠ *1910 N. Ocean Blvd.* ☎ *843/249–3561* ⚑ *Reservations not accepted* ▤ *No credit cards* ☉ *Closed Sun. No dinner.*

$–$$ ▨ **Barefoot Resort.** This luxury golf resort includes more than 325 one- to- four-bedroom condominium units along fairways as well as in the 62-unit, 14-story North Tower, which overlooks the Intracoastal Waterway. Furnishings in each unit vary, but all have been tastefully decorated and have all the amenities of a hotel, including daily maid service. The waterfront pool covers an acre of land and is said to be one of the largest on the east coast. The Barefoot Landing shopping and entertainment center is just across the inlet. ⊠ *4980 Barefoot Resort Bridge Rd., North Myrtle Beach 29582* ☎ *877/237–3767* ⊕ *www.barefootgolfresort.com* ⇆ *387 condos* ⚓ *3 restaurants, 4 18-hole golf courses, 10 pools, marina, lounge* ⊟ *AE, D, MC, V.*

$–$$ 🏨 **Best Western Ocean Sands.** One of the few fairly small, family-owned properties left in North Myrtle Beach, the Ocean Sands has some nice touches that make it a good choice for families, including full kitchens in every room and large suites with true separate bedrooms. Although it's not luxurious, it's clean and breezy, and all rooms have balconies. ■ TIP→ **The exercise room is very small, with just a treadmill and stair climber.** ⊠ *1525 S. Ocean Blvd., 29582* ☎ *843/272–6101 or 800/588–3570* ⊟ *843/272–7908* ⊕ *www.oceansands.com* ⇆ *80 rooms, 36 suites* ⚓ *Kitchens, 3 pools (1 indoor), no-smoking rooms* ⊟ *AE, D, MC, V* ⊜ *BP.*

Nightlife & the Arts

CLUBS & LOUNGES Sassy and saucy, but with live music that ranges from R&B to classic rock to beach favorites, **Dick's Last Resort** (⊠ Barefoot Landing, 4700 U.S. 17S ☎ 843/272–7794) is big and loud, and the beer is cold.

You can dance the shag at **Duck's** (⊠ 229 Main St. ☎ 843/249–3858). **Sandals** (⊠ 500 Shore Dr. ☎ 843/449–6461) is an intimate lounge with live entertainment.

MUSIC & LIVE SHOWS Live acts, and country-and-western shows in particular, are a big draw on the Grand Strand. Music lovers have many family-oriented shows to choose from. The 2,250-seat **Alabama Theater** (⊠ Barefoot Landing, 4750 U.S. 17S ☎ 843/272–1111) has a regular variety show with a wonderful patriotic closing; the theater also hosts different guest music and comedy artists during the year. The **House of Blues** (⊠ Barefoot Landing, 4640 U.S. 17S ☎ 843/272–3000 for tickets) showcases big names and up-and-coming talent in blues, rock, jazz, country, and R&B on stages in its Southern-style restaurant and patio as well as in its 2,000-seat concert hall. The gospel brunch is a great deal. Shows at the **Tribute Theater** (⊠ 701 Main St., North Myrtle Beach ☎ 800/313–6685 for tickets) feature talented impersonators re-creating performances of pop music's biggest stars. Featured "stars" have included Cher, Frank Sinatra, and Shania Twain.

Shopping

MALLS **Barefoot Landing** (⊠ 4898 S. Kings Hwy. ☎ 843/272–8349) has more than 100 specialty shops, along with numerous entertainment activities. Shops include many mall standards, gift shops, jewelry stores, and even a bakery for dogs. Among the 13 outlets within the complex are Birkenstock and Izod.

SPECIALTY STORES Beach-music lovers have been finding their long-lost favorites at **Judy's House of Oldies** (⊠ 300 Main St. ☎ 843/249–8649), for years. Find classics on cassette and CD at this small but packed-to-the-gills music emporium.

THE SOUTHERN GRAND STRAND

Unlike the more developed area to the north, the southern end of the Grand Strand—Murrells Inlet, Litchfield, Pawleys Island, and Georgetown—has a barefoot, laid-back vibe that suits its small restaurants, shops, galleries, and outdoor outfitters. And what this part of the Strand lacks in glitz, it more than makes up for in natural beauty. The beaches are wide and empty enough for bike riding, bocci ball, and surf fishing. Spanish moss hangs gracefully from tree branches overlooking salt marshes alive with herons, egrets, and shrimp. Several large preserves, parks, and nature centers make it easy to observe the alligators, wild boar, deer, otter, and rare plants that inhabit the wild land between the ocean and the rivers, and there are a number of 18th- and 19th-century plantation houses and churches to explore.

Murrells Inlet

❸ *15 mi south of Myrtle Beach on U.S. 17.*

Murrells Inlet, a fishing village with some popular seafood restaurants, is a perfect place to rent a fishing boat or join an excursion. A notable garden and state park provide other diversions from the beach.

What to See

Fodor's Choice ⭐ Just beyond *The Fighting Stallions,* the Anna Hyatt Huntington sculpture alongside U.S. 17, lies **Brookgreen Gardens**, one of the Grand Strand's most magnificent hidden treasures. Here, in the oldest and largest sculpture garden in the United States, are more than 550 examples of figurative American sculpture by such artists as Frederic Remington and Daniel Chester French. Each is carefully set within garden rooms and outdoor galleries graced by sprawling live oak trees, colorful flowers, and peaceful ponds. The gardens are lush and full in spring and summer, and in winter splashes of color from winter-blooming shrubs are set off against the stark surroundings.

The 9,000-acre property was originally a winter home for industrialist Archer Huntington and his wife Anna Hyatt Huntington, but they quickly decided to open it to the public as a sculpture garden and wildlife sanctuary. Today, more than 70 years later, their legacy endures as a center for not only American art but Lowcountry culture and nature preservation. You'll find a wildlife park, an aviary, a cypress swamp, nature trails, and an education center. Several tours, including a boat tour of tidal creeks and a Jeep excursion into the preserve, leave from Brookgreen. ▪ TIP➔ **Outdoor concerts under the stars are a tradition, check the Web site for dates.** ✉ *West of U.S. 17, 3 mi south of Murrells Inlet* ☎ *843/237–4218 or 800/849–1931* ⊕ *www.brookgreen.com* ✑ *$12, good for 7 days* ☉ *June–Sept., Wed.–Fri. 9:30–9, Sat.–Tues. 9:30–5; Oct.–May, daily 9:30–5.*

Huntington Beach State Park, the 2,500-acre former estate of Archer and Anna Huntington, lies east of U.S. 17, across from the couple's Brookgreen Gardens. The park's focal point is **Atalaya** (circa 1933), their Moorish-style 30-room home. There are nature trails, fishing, an education

The Ghosts of the Grand Strand

SPEND ANY TIME on the Grand Strand and you'll likely hear about two of the area's eeriest residents: Alice Flagg and the Gray Man.

Alice Flagg was the teenage sister of the wealthy owner of the Hermitage, a rice plantation near Murrells Inlet. She was sent by her family to boarding school in Charleston to keep her away from a boy who'd captured her heart. The young lovers managed to see each other on the sly and soon became secretly engaged. Alice wore her engagement ring around her neck, hidden next to her heart. She came down with a high fever and returned to the Hermitage, where she died with the name of her fiancé on her lips. Her brother discovered the ring and, in a rage, threw it in the marsh.

Although she was buried at the Hermitage, her body was later moved to the cemetery at All Saints Church near Pawleys Island, where it now

rests under a marble slab bearing only the name "Alice." For many years, her ghost was seen wandering the marsh near the house, looking for the ring. Her spirit, it is said, can be summoned by walking around the grave backward 13 times.

The Gray Man, according to most renditions of his story, was a young man who, while rushing to see his sweetheart, was thrown from his horse and died. After his funeral, his love took to walking along the beach each night. One evening, she was approached by a ghostly version of her lover. "Leave the island at once," he warned. "You are in great danger." She heeded the warning, and later that day a hurricane struck. Ever since, the Gray Man has delivered storm warnings to island residents, most famously before Hurricane Hugo hit in September 1989.

center with aquariums and a loggerhead sea turtle nesting habitat, picnic areas, a playground, concessions, and a campground. ⊠ *East of U.S. 17, 3 mi south of Murrells Inlet* ☎ *843/237-4440* ⊕ *www. southcarolinaparks.com* ⬚ *$5* ☉ *Mid-Mar.–Oct., daily 6 AM–10 PM; Nov.–mid-Mar., daily 6–6.*

Sports & the Outdoors

BOATING **Capt. Dick's** (⊠ U.S. 17 Business ☎ 843/651–3676) runs half- and full-day fishing and sightseeing trips. You can also rent boats and kayaks and go parasailing. The evening ghost story cruise is scary fun.

Where to Eat

★ $$$–$$$$ ✕ **Lee's Inlet Kitchen.** They're closed at lunchtime, on Sunday, and in winter; they don't take reservations or have a view, but nobody fries up a mess of seafood like Lee's. Even the biggest eaters will get their fill when they order the Shore Dinner: fried or broiled flounder, shrimp, oysters, scallops, deviled crab, and lobster, along with a shrimp cocktail, clam chowder, hush puppies, fries, and coleslaw. Sure, you can get your fish broiled or grilled, but why mess with deep-fried perfection? ⊠ *4660 U.S. 17 Business* ☎ *843/651–2881* ⌔ *Reservations not accepted* ▭ *AE, MC, V* ☉ *Closed Sun., Dec., and Jan. No lunch.*

★ **$–$$$$** ✕ **Bovine's Wood-Fired Specialties.** What started as a meat-lovers-only restaurant has quietly morphed into a local favorite not just for delicious mesquite-grilled beef, lamb, pork, and fish, but also for superb crisp-crusted pizzas, baked in an imported brick oven and topped with a creative assortment of toppings. Add to that a terrific view of Murrells Inlet and Surfside Beach in the distance, and a sleek, modern decor, and Bovine's is a nice change from the usual waterfront establishment. ⊠ *3979 U.S. 17 Business* ☎ *843/651–2888* ⩘ *Reservations essential* ▭ *AE, D, MC, V* ⊗ *No lunch.*

★ **$–$$$$** ✕ **Nance's Creekfront Restaurant.** You can smell the brine and Old Bay seasoning the minute you leave your car and head toward the front door of Nance's. There's not much atmosphere, but that's okay. Oysters, the small local ones that taste of saltwater and seaweed, are the specialty, available raw or steamed in an iron pot and served with butter. There are other selections on the menu, but it's really all about the oysters— and the 10-layer chocolate cake, made specially for Nance's by a local baker. ⊠ *4883 U.S. 17 Business* ☎ *843/651–2696* ⩘ *Reservations not accepted* ▭ *D, MC, V* ⊗ *No lunch.*

¢–$$ ✕ **Inlet Crab House.** Locals love this weathered pink crab shack for its attitude-free atmosphere as well as its unfussy food. Oyster stew and fish chowder are specialties, simple and good, and the odd crab pizza dip is surprisingly tasty. Fresh fish, burgers, salads, and spicy boiled shrimp round out the menu. ⊠ *3572 U.S. 17 Business* ☎ *843/651–8452* ⩘ *Reservations not accepted* ▭ *AE, D, MC, V* ⊗ *Closed Sun.; Nov.–Mar., call ahead to confirm hrs.*

Nightlife

You can have a drink, watch boats come back from a day of fishing, and enjoy the evening breeze on the deck at **Captain Dave's Dockside** (⊠ 4037 U.S. 17 Business ☎ 843/651–5850), where there's live music most nights in summer. Strewn with party lights and offering live bands every night, the **Gazebo at the Hot Fish Club** (⊠ 4911 U.S. 17 Business ☎ 843/357–9175) is a happening spot with a great view.

Pawleys Island

❹ *10 mi south of Murrells Inlet via U.S. 17.*

About 4 mi long and ½ mi wide, this island, sometimes referred to as "arrogantly shabby," began as a resort before the Civil War, when wealthy planters and their families summered here. It's mostly made up of weathered old summer cottages nestled in groves of oleander and oak trees. You can watch the famous Pawleys Island hammocks being made and bicycle around admiring the beach houses, many dating to the early 1800s. Golf and tennis are nearby. ■ TIP→ **Parking is limited on Pawleys and facilities are nil, so arrive early and bring what you need.**

Sports & the Outdoors

GOLF The live-oak alley and wonderful greens help make the **Heritage Club** (⊠ 478 Heritage Dr. ☎ 800/530–1875 ⊕ www.legendsgolf.com) one of the South Strand's top courses, and its fees are lower than courses of similar difficulty and condition. The **Litchfield Beach and Golf Resort**

(⊠ U.S. 17S, Litchfield Beach ☎ 843/237–3000 or 800/845–1897) is a popular 18-hole course. **Litchfield Country Club** (⊠ U.S. 17S ☎ 843/237–3411) is a mature, old-style course with tight fairways and moss-laden oaks.

Pawleys Plantation Golf & Country Club (⊠ U.S. 17S ☎ 843/237–8497 or 800/367–9959) is a Jack Nicklaus–designed course; several holes play along saltwater marshes. **Willbrook** (⊠ U.S. 17S ☎ 843/247–4900) is on a former rice plantation and winds past historical markers, a slave cemetery, and a tobacco shack.

TENNIS   You can get court time, rental equipment, and instruction at **Litchfield Country Club** (⊠ U.S. 17S ☎ 843/237–3411).

Where to Stay & Eat

★ **$$$–$$$$**   ✕ **Frank's.** This local favorite serves dishes that give traditional cooking methods and ingredients a new twist. In a former 1930s grocery store with wood floors, framed French posters, and cozy fireside seating, diners indulge in large portions of fish, seafood, beef, and lamb cooked over an oak-burning grill. The local grouper with mustard-bacon butter, served with a side of stone-ground grits, is a star. Behind Frank's is the casual (but still pricey) Outback, a lush candlelit garden with a huge stone fireplace. ■ TIP→ **Enjoy a before- or after-dinner drink at Outback's bar. Heaters will keep you warm in winter.** ⊠ *10434 U.S. 17* ☎ *843/237–3030* ⚐ *Reservations essential* ▱ *D, MC, V* ☉ *Closed Sun. No lunch.*

$$$–$$$$ ✕ **Louis's at Pawleys.** A perfectionist to the core, Chef Louis Osteen creates delicious renditions of traditional dishes such as crab cakes, barbecued shrimp, and lobster bisque, and he's not afraid to try his hand at more inventive dishes, such as crab-and-bacon-stuffed trout. Whatever you order, the food sings. For a casual night, have dinner outside on the deck at the Fish Camp. On Sunday stop by for a lunch of fried chicken with all the fixings. ⊠ *10880 U.S. 17* ☎ *843/237–8757* ⚐ *Reservations essential* ▱ *AE, D, MC, V.*

Fodor'sChoice ★

$–$$$ ✕ **Pawleys Island Tavern.** This little eatery has terrific crab cakes, hickory-smoked barbecue, roasted chicken, and pizza. Summer weekend nights tiki torches outside blaze and live music rocks the place. They also deliver. ⊠ *The Island Shops, U.S. 17* ☎ *843/237–8465* ▱ *AE, MC, V* ☉ *Closed Mon.*

¢–$$$ ✕ **Hog Heaven.** Part barbecue joint, part raw bar (after 5), Hog Heaven's wonderful smoky aroma perfumes U.S. 17 for miles. Pulled-pork barbecue has the tang of vine-

Fodor'sChoice ★

HANGIN' AROUND

Created nearly 100 years ago by a riverboat captain tired of sleeping on his grain-filled mattress, the original Pawleys Island rope hammock is handcrafted in Pawleys Island exactly as it was by Captain Ward. More than 1,000 feet of rope are knitted by hand, pulled between oak stretcher bars, and tied with bowline knots to the body. In the 1930s, Captain Ward's brother-in-law began selling the hammocks at a general store called the Hammock Shop. Still standing at the same location on U.S. Highway 17, the shop's weaving room is open to visitors most Saturdays.

gar and the taste of long hours in the pit. Although sandwiches are available, the buffet, which includes fried chicken, greens, and sweet-potato casserole, is the main event. In the evening, try the seafood tray, an assortment of shellfish steamed to order and served piping hot. ☒ *7147 U.S. 17* ☎ *843/237–7444* ⌃ *Reservations not accepted* ▤ *MC, V* ⊘ *Closed Sun.–Tues.*

¢–$ ✕ **Landolphi's.** This Italian pastry shop and restaurant, fourth-generation-owned, has excellent coffee, hearty hoagies, pizzas, homemade sorbet, and delicious and authentic pastries, including cannoli and *pasticciotti* (a rich cookielike pastry filled with jam). Both counter and table service is available. ☒ *9305 Ocean Hwy.* ☎ *843/237–7900* ▤ *AE, MC, V* ⊘ *Closed Sun. No dinner Mon.–Wed.*

¢ ✕ **Sam's Corner.** Some people call Sam's Corner a dive, but most folks think of it as the best place on the Strand for a hot dog. Deep fried and covered in the traditional South Carolina style with chili and coleslaw, these dogs are legendary. Try them with a side of onion rings and sweet tea or a super-cold beer. ☒ *12036 U.S. 17* ☎ *843/235–3741* ⌃ *Reservations not accepted* ▤ *No credit cards* ☒ *101 Atlantic Ave., Garden City;* ☒ *7718 N. Kings Hwy., Myrtle Beach.*

★ $$–$$$$ ✕▢ **Litchfield Plantation.** Period furnishings adorn four spacious suites of this impeccably restored 1750 rice-plantation manor house–turned–country inn. All of the rooms are lovely, with rich fabrics and views of lakes, woods, or creeks. Use of a beach-house club a short drive away is part of the package, as is a full breakfast at the elegant Carriage House Club; guests also have golf privileges at eight nearby courses. The resort is approximately 2 mi south of Brookgreen Gardens on U.S. 17 (turn right at the Litchfield Country Club entrance and follow signs). ☒ *Kings River Rd., Box 290, 29585* ☎ *843/237–9121 or 800/869–1410* ▤ *843/237–8558* ⊕ *www.litchfieldplantation.com* ⇆ *35 rooms, 4 suites, 9 2- and 3-bedroom cottages* ⌂ *Restaurant, 2 tennis courts, pool, library, concierge* ▤ *AE, D, DC, MC, V* ⦿ *BP.*

$$$–$$$$ ▢ **Sea View Inn.** A "barefoot paradise," Sea View is a no-frills beachside boardinghouse (there are no TVs or in-room phones) with long porches. Rooms in the main inn, with views of the ocean or marsh, have half baths; showers are down the hall and outside. Cottage rooms are marshside and have air-conditioning. Three meals, served family style—with grits, gumbo, crab salad, pecan pie, and oyster pie—make this an unbeatable deal. There's a two-night minimum stay during May and September and a one-week minimum from June through August. ■ TIP→ **If you can't stay over but the menu sounds too good to pass up, give the owners a call. They may let you join them for lunch.** ☒ *414 Myrtle Ave., 29585* ☎ *843/237–4253* ▤ *843/237–7909* ⊕ *www.seaviewinn.com* ⇆ *20 rooms, 1 cottage* ⌂ *Dining room; no a/c in some rooms, no room phones, no room TVs* ▤ *No credit cards* ⊘ *Closed Nov.–Mar.* ⦿ *FAP.*

$$$ ▢ **Pawleys Island Hampton Inn.** Ongoing upgrades keep this hotel in tiptop condition. Like most Hampton Inns, the property offers a wide array of amenities and is clean and well maintained. The beach at Pawleys is a 10-minute drive away. ☒ *150 Willbrook Blvd., 29585* ☎ *843/235–3000* ▤ *843/235–2099* ⊕ *www.pawleysislandhamptoninn.com* ⇆ *66 rooms* ⌂ *Cable TV, pool, health club* ▤ *AE, D, MC, V* ⦿ *BP.*

$-$$$ ▣ **Litchfield Beach and Golf Resort.** This beautifully landscaped 4,500-
Fodor'sChoice acre resort runs along both sides of U.S. 17. The almost 2-mi stretch of
★ oceanfront accommodations ranges from condos to the 160-room Litch-
field Inn, which has motel rooms; other options, such as high-rise con-
dos, duplexes, and even Charleston-style beach houses, overlook fairways,
lakes, or the marsh. All accommodations are grouped into miniresorts,
each with its own pool and tennis courts. A bike trail connects them all
to the large lake, which has a small fishing dock and a couple resident
alligators. There's a one-week minimum for oceanfront rentals during
June, July, and August, except at the Inn, where the minimum is three
nights. ■ TIP➔ Resort guests have access to Litchfield's oceanfront cabana,
where there's parking, bathrooms, and a water fountain. ✉ *U.S. 17, 2 mi
north of Pawleys Island, Litchfield Beach, 29585* ☎ *843/237–3000 or
800/845–1897* 🖷 *843/237–4282* ⊕ *www.litchfieldbeach.com* ⇆ *140
rooms, 216 suites, 200 condominiums, cottages, and villas* ♻ *2 restau-
rants, 3 18-hole golf courses, 26 tennis courts, 18 pools (2 indoor), health
club, bicycles, business services* 🖃 *AE, D, MC, V* ¹⊚¹ *EP.*

The Arts

Pawleys Island comes alive each September during the **Pawleys Island Fes-
tival of Music & Art** (⌀ Box 1975, 29585 ☎ 843/237–4774 ⊕ www.
pawleysmusic.org), which brings national and local artists together for
a month of concerts, exhibitions, and readings. Past performers have
included David Sanborn and Delbert McClinton.

Shopping

The **Hammock Shops at Pawleys Island** (✉ 10880 Ocean Hwy. ☎ 843/
237–8448) is a complex of two dozen boutiques, gift shops, and restau-
rants built with old beams, timber, and ballast brick. Outside the Orig-
inal Hammock Shop, in the Hammock Weavers' Pavilion, craftspeople
demonstrate the 19th-century art of weaving the famous cotton-rope
Pawleys Island hammocks. Also look for jewelry, toys, antiques, and de-
signer fashions.

Georgetown

❺ *13 mi south of Pawleys Island via U.S. 17.*

Founded on Winyah Bay in 1729, Georgetown became the center of Amer-
ica's colonial rice empire. A rich plantation culture developed on a scale
comparable to Charleston's, and the historic district is among the pret-
tiest in the state. Today oceangoing vessels still come to Georgetown's
busy port, and the **Harborwalk,** the restored waterfront, hums with ac-
tivity. ■ TIP➔ Many of the restaurants along the riverside of Front Street have
back decks overlooking the water that come alive in the early evening for
happy hour.

What to See

Hampton Plantation State Historic Site preserves the home of Archibald
Rutledge, poet laureate of South Carolina for 39 years until his death
in 1973. The 18th-century plantation house is a fine example of a Low-
country mansion. The exterior has been restored; cutaway sections in
the finely crafted interior show the changes made through the centuries.

The grounds are landscaped, and there are picnic areas. ⊠ *Off U.S. 17, at edge of Francis Marion National Forest, 16 mi south of Georgetown* ☎ *843/546–9361* ✉ *Mansion $4, grounds free* ☼ *Mansion June–Aug., daily 11–4; Sept.–May, Thurs.–Mon. 1–4. Grounds Thurs.–Mon. 9–6.*

☪ **Hobcaw Barony Visitors Center** is at the entrance of Hobcaw Barony, on the vast estate of the late Wall Street financier Bernard M. Baruch; Franklin D. Roosevelt and Winston Churchill came here to confer with him. A small interpretive center has exhibits on coastal ecology and history, with special emphasis on the Baruch family. There are aquariums, touch tanks, and video presentations; there are guided three-hour tours of the 17,500-acre wildlife refuge Tuesday, Wednesday, and Friday morning and Thursday afternoon. ⊠ *On U.S. 17, 2 mi north of Georgetown* ☎ *843/546–4623* ⊕ *www.hobcawbarony.com* ✉ *Visitors center free, tours $15* ☼ *Weekdays 10–5; reservations necessary for tour.*

Hopsewee Plantation, surrounded by moss-draped live oaks, magnolias, and tree-size camellias, overlooks the North Santee River. The circa-1740 mansion has a fine Georgian staircase and hand-carved lighted-candle moldings. ⊠ *U.S. 17, 12 mi south of Georgetown* ☎ *843/546–7891 or 800/648–0478* ⊕ *www.hopsewee.com* ✉ *Mansion $10; grounds $5 per car; parking fees apply toward tour* ☼ *Mansion: Mar.–Nov., weekdays 10–4:30; Dec.–Feb., Thurs. and Fri 10–4:30, or by appointment. Grounds, including nature trail: daily dawn–dusk.*

Overlooking the Sampit River from a bluff is the **Kaminsky House Museum** (circa 1769). It's especially notable for its collections of regional antiques and furnishings, its Chippendale and Duncan Phyfe furniture, Royal Doulton vases, and silver. ⊠ *1003 Front St.* ☎ *843/546–7706* ✉ *$5* ☼ *Mon.–Sat. 10–4, Sun. 1–5.*

Prince George Winyah Episcopal Church (named after King George II) still serves the parish established in 1721. It was built in 1737 with bricks brought from England. ⊠ *Broad and Highmarket Sts., Georgetown* ☎ *843/546–4358* ✉ *Donation suggested* ☼ *Mar.–Oct., weekdays 11:30–4:30.*

☪ The graceful market and meeting building in the heart of Georgetown, topped by an 1842 clock and tower, has been converted into the **Rice Museum,** with maps, tools, and dioramas. At the museum's Prevost Gallery next door is the Brown's Ferry river freighter, the oldest American-built water-going vessel in existence. The museum gift shop has local pine needle baskets, African dolls, and art (including baskets made from whole cloves), and carries South Carolina rice and honey. ⊠ *Front and Screven Sts.* ☎ *843/546–7423* ✉ *$7* ☼ *Mon.–Sat. 10–4:30.*

Sports & the Outdoors

BOATING Cruise past abandoned rice plantations and hear stories about the belles who lived there with Captain Rod of **Lowcountry Plantation Tours** (⊠ Front St. Harborwalk ☎ 843/477–0287); other tours include a lighthouse expedition and a ghost-stories cruise. Feel the spray on your face as you explore Winyah Bay aboard a 40-foot yacht with Captain Dave of **Wallace Sailing Charters** (⊠ 607 Front St. ☎ 843/902–6999). Each trip is limited to six passengers, so it feels like you're touring on a private yacht.

CANOEING &
KAYAKING
★

Black River Outdoor Center and Expeditions (✉ 21 Garden Ave., U.S. 701 ☎ 843/546–4840 ⊕ www.blackriveroutdoors.com) offers naturalist-guided canoe and kayak day and evening tours (including moonlight tours) of the tidelands of Georgetown. Guides are well versed not just in the wildlife, but in local lore. Tours take kayakers past settings such as Drunken Jack's (the island that supposedly holds Blackbeard's booty), and Chicora Wood plantation, where dikes and trunk gates mark canals dug by slaves to facilitate rice growing in the area. It's said that digging the canals required as much manual labor as Egypt's pyramids. Black River also rents and sells equipment. ■ TIP→ **Wildlife tends to be more active during the early mornings or late afternoons; there's a good chance you'll hear owls hooting on the evening tours, especially during the fall.**

GOLF

The premier course in the Georgetown area is the 18-hole, par-73 **Wedgefield Plantation** (✉ 129 Club House La., off U.S. 701 ☎ 843/448–2124 or 843/546–8587). The 18-hole, par-70 **Winyah Bay Golf Club** (✉ 336 Golf Dr. ☎ 877/527–7765) is a popular option with some challenging water holes.

Where to Stay & Eat

★ $$$-$$$$

✕ **Rice Paddy.** At lunch, locals flock to this Lowcountry restaurant for the shrimp and bacon quesadilla and the creative salads and sandwiches. Dinner in the Victorian building, with windows overlooking Front Street, is more relaxed. Grilled local tuna with a ginger-soy glaze is a winner, as are the crab cakes, which you can get uncooked to go. ✉ 732 *Front St.* ☎ *843/546–2021* ⌂ *Reservations essential* ▭ *AE, MC, V* ☽ *Closed Sun.*

★ $-$$$

✕ **Dogwood Cafe.** The menu is large and varied at this casual eatery housed in one of Georgetown's old riverfront buildings. Share appetizers like bacon-wrapped shrimp and fried green tomatoes—they're the real thing—or, on Thursday, Frogmore Stew, a Lowcountry dish composed of layers of shrimp, corn, smoked sausage, and potatoes that have been boiled together in a big pot. ■ TIP→ **The best seats are on the rustic back deck that overlooks the river.** ✉ 713 *Front St.* ☎ *843/545–7777* ▭ *AE, D, MC, V* ☽ *Closed Sun.*

$-$$$

✕ **River Room.** This restaurant on the Sampit River specializes in char-grilled fish, Cajun fried oysters, seafood pastas, and steaks. For lunch you can have shrimp and grits or your choice of sandwiches and salads. The dining room has river views from most tables. It's especially romantic at night, when the oil lamps and brass fixtures cast a warm glow on the dark wood and brick interior of the early-20th-century building. ✉ 801 *Front St.* ☎ *843/527–4110* ⌂ *Reservations not accepted* ▭ *AE, MC, V* ☽ *Closed Sun.*

¢-$$

FodorsChoice
★

✕ **Kudzu Bakery.** Come here for the justifiably famous key lime pie and red velvet cake, both of which are available whole or by the slice, and can be eaten in the garden. Kudzu is also a great source for ready-to-cook specialties such as cheese biscuits, macaroni and cheese, and quiche. In addition you'll find fresh bread, deli items, and a terrific selection of wines. ✉ 714 *Front St.* ☎ *843/546–1847* ▭ *MC, V* ☽ *Closed Sun. No dinner.*

¢-$

✕ **Thomas Café.** There's great fried chicken, homemade biscuits, and pie at this lunch counter, not to mention grits, eggs, country ham, and other breakfast favorites served every day but Sunday (when the café opens at 11 AM instead of 7). Join the regulars at the counter, or sit in one of the booths or café tables in the 1920s storefront building. ✉ *714 Front St.* ☎ *843/546–7776* ▬ *MC, V* ☺ *No dinner.*

$$–$$$ 🏨 **Hampton Inn Georgetown Marina.** Watch boats cruise up and down the river at this riverside resort; spectacular sunsets are an easy trade for being a little farther from the beach. An upgraded Hampton Inn, the Georgetown property offers a hot breakfast, signature Cloud 9 bedding, and a choice of pillows. Suites have pull-out sofas, all rooms have a microwave, refrigerator, and coffeemaker. ✉ *420 Marina Dr., 29440* ☎ *843/545–5000 or 800/426–7866* 🖷 *843/545–5099* ⊕ *www.georgetownhamptoninn.com* ⇆ *98 rooms* ⛆ *Pool, cable TV, Wi-Fi, exercise room, business center* ▬ *AE, D, MC, V* ⑪ *BP.*

$$–$$$ 🏨 **Harbor House Bed and Breakfast.** Watch the shrimp boats come into the harbor from the front porch of Georgetown's only waterfront B&B; if you're lucky, innkeeper Meg Tarbox will turn some of the catch into shrimp and grits for breakfast. All four rooms (named for ships that have docked at Georgetown) have water views, as well as decades-old heart-pine floors and family antiques. Refreshments in the afternoon include more of those shrimp, this time in the family's locally famous dip. ✉ *15 Cannon St., 29440* ☎ *843/546–6532 or 877/511–0101* 🖷 *843/546–0014* ⊕ *www.harborhousebb.com* ⇆ *4 rooms* ⛆ *Bicycles* ▬ *MC, V* ☺ *Closed mid-Dec.–mid-Feb.* ⑪ *BP.*

Shopping
You'll find hand-carved wooden bowls and trays as well as an assortment of dishes and kitchen tools at **Kudzu Mercantile** (✉ 932 Front St. ☎ 843/546–0040). The cookbook selection is also good.

MYRTLE BEACH & THE GRAND STRAND ESSENTIALS

Transportation

BY AIR

The Myrtle Beach International Airport is served by AirTran, Continental, COMAIR, Delta's regional carrier Atlantic Southeast, Northwest, PanAm, Spirit, Vanguard, US Airways, and Vacation Express.
🛈 **Myrtle Beach International Airport** ✉ 1100 Jetport Rd. ☎ 843/448-1580.

BY BOAT & FERRY

Boaters traveling the Intracoastal Waterway may dock at Hague Marina, Harbor Gate, and Marlin Quay.
🛈 **Hague Marina** ✉ Myrtle Beach ☎ 843/293-2141. **Harbor Gate** ✉ North Myrtle Beach ☎ 843/249-8888. **Marlin Quay** ✉ Murrells Inlet ☎ 843/651-4444.

BY BUS

Greyhound Bus Lines serves Myrtle Beach, Georgetown, and McClellanville.
🛈 **Greyhound Bus Lines** ☎ 800/231-2222.

BY CAR

Midway between New York and Miami, the Grand Strand isn't connected directly by any interstate highways but is within an hour drive of Interstate 95, Interstate 20, Interstate 26, and Interstate 40. U.S. 17 is the major north–south coastal route through the Strand.

BY TAXI

Taxi service in Myrtle Beach is provided by Coastal Cab Service.
🚹 **Coastal Cab Service** ☎ 843/448-4444.

Contacts & Resources

EMERGENCIES

Both the Grand Strand Regional Medical Center and Georgetown Memorial Hospital have emergency rooms open 24 hours a day. The Grand Strand Regional Medical Center has the only pharmacy in the area open all night.

🚹 Emergency Services **Ambulance, fire, police** ☎ 911.

🚹 Hospitals **Georgetown Memorial Hospital** ✉ 606 Black River Rd., Georgetown ☎ 843/527-7000. **Grand Strand Regional Medical Center** ✉ 809 82nd Pkwy., off U.S. 17, Myrtle Beach ☎ 843/692-1000.

🚹 24-Hour Pharmacies **Grand Strand Regional Medical Center Pharmacy** ✉ 809 82nd Pkwy., off U.S. 17, Myrtle Beach ☎ 843/692-1000.

INTERNET, MAIL & SHIPPING

Most Grand Strand hotels and resorts offer high-speed or Wi-Fi access. Many provide it at no charge. Rates at coffee shops and bookstores vary widely. Free wireless Internet is available at the Living Room, a used-book store and coffee shop in Myrtle Beach, and at Latte Litchfield in Pawleys Island.

Ship your treasures home at FedEx Kinko's, through UPS at Mail Boxes, Etc., or via the U.S. Postal Service at the U.S. Post Office in Myrtle Beach or Pawleys Island, where there's rarely a line.

🚹 **Barnes & Noble** ✉ 1145 Seaboard St., Myrtle Beach ☎ 843/444-4046. **FedEx Kinko's** ✉ 1170 Seaboard St., Myrtle Beach ☎ 843/626-5592. **Latte Litchfield** ✉ 13088 Ocean Blvd., Pawleys Island ☎ 843/235-7575. **The Living Room** ✉ Hwy. 17 Bypass at 38th Ave., Myrtle Beach ☎ 843/626-8363. **Mail Boxes, Etc.** ✉ 1818 Hwy. 17, Myrtle Beach ☎ 843/238-1064. **U.S. Post Office** ✉ 505 N. Kings Hwy., Myrtle Beach ✉ 10993 Ocean Hwy., Pawleys Island ☎ 800/275-8777.

MEDIA

The *Myrtle Beach Sun News* publishes seven days a week and covers national, local, and regional news and events. Pick up beach reading at Litchfield Books, an independent bookseller in Pawleys Island, or at Barnes & Noble.

🚹 **Barnes & Noble** ✉ 1145 Seaboard St., Myrtle Beach ☎ 843/444-4046. **Litchfield Books** ✉ 14427 Ocean Hwy., Pawleys Island ☎ 843/237-8138. **Myrtle Beach Sun News** ✉ 914 Frontage Rd. E, Myrtle Beach ☎ 843/626-8555.

TOUR OPTIONS

Palmetto Tour & Travel and Leisure Time Unlimited/Gray Line, both in Myrtle Beach, offer tour packages and guide services.

🔳 **Georgetown County Chamber of Commerce and Information Center** ☎ 843/546-8436 or 800/777-7705. **Leisure Time Unlimited/Gray Line** ☎ 843/448-9483. **Palmetto Tour & Travel** ☎ 843/626-2660.

VISITOR INFORMATION

Local chambers of commerce are bursting with information—and discount coupons—from local attractions.

🔳 **Georgetown County Chamber of Commerce and Information Center** ✉ 1001 Front St., Box 1776, Georgetown 29442 ☎ 843/546-8436 ⊕ www.georgetownchamber.com ⊘ Closed evenings and weekends. Call for hrs. **Murrells Inlet 2007** ⎘ Box 1357, Murrells Inlet 29576 ☎ 843/357-2007 ⊕ www.murrellsinletsc.com. **Myrtle Beach Area Chamber of Commerce and Information Center** ✉ 1200 N. Oak St., Box 2115, Myrtle Beach 29578 ☎ 843/626-7444 or 800/356-3016 ⊕ www.myrtlebeachinfo.com ⊘ Closed evenings. Closed Sun. at 2 PM. **Pawleys Island Chamber of Commerce** ✉ U.S. 17, Box 569, Pawleys Island 29585 ☎ 843/237-1921.

Charleston

WORD OF MOUTH

"I hope you plan to stay in the historic district. A walking map is all you need. Go to the [Old City Market] for fun flea market shopping. Slip into an old church for a rest. Be cheesy . . . take a carriage ride. Eat shrimp and grits. Read some Pat Conroy before you go."

–twigsbuddy

"You're in for a real treat visiting Charleston. Definitely take your walking shoes with you, because you can walk fairly easily all over downtown and the surrounding residential areas. That way you can check out all of the little sunlit alleys and quaint gardens that catch your eye, but may not halt a carriage."

–allanbot25

Updated by
Eileen
Robinson Smith

WANDERING THROUGH THE CITY'S HISTORIC DISTRICT, you would swear it was a movie set. The spires and steeples of more than 180 churches punctuate the low skyline, and the horse-drawn carriages pass centuries-old mansions and carefully tended gardens overflowing with heirloom plants. It's known for its quiet charm, and has been called the most mannerly city in the country.

Immigrants settled here in 1670. They flocked here initially for religious freedom and later for prosperity (compliments of the rice, indigo, and cotton plantations). Preserved through the poverty following the Civil War, and natural disasters like fires, earthquakes, and hurricanes, many of Charleston's earliest public and private buildings still stand. And thanks to a rigorous preservation movement and strict Board of Architectural Review, the city's new structures blend with the old ones. In many cases, recycling is the name of the game—antique handmade bricks literally lay the foundation for new homes. But although locals do live—on some literal levels—in the past, the city is very much a town of today.

Take the internationally heralded Spoleto Festival, for instance. For two weeks every summer, arts patrons from around the world come to enjoy local and international concerts, dance performances, operas, improv shows, and plays at venues citywide. Day in and out, diners can feast at upscale Southern restaurants, shoppers can look for museum-quality paintings and antiques, and outdoor adventurers can explore all Charleston's outlying beaches, parks, and marshes. But as cosmopolitan as the city has become, it's still the south, and just outside the city limits are farm stands cooking up boiled peanuts, recently named the state's official snack.

EXPLORING CHARLESTON

The heart of the city is on a peninsula, sometimes just called "downtown" by the nearly 100,000 residents who populate the area. Walking Charleston's peninsula is the best way to get to know the city. The main downtown historic district is roughly bounded by Lockwood Boulevard to the west, Calhoun Street to the north, the Cooper River to the east, and the Battery to the south. More than 2,000 historic homes and buildings occupy this fairly compact area divided into South of Broad (Street) and North of Broad. King Street, the main shopping street in town, cuts through Broad Street, and the most trafficked tourist area ends a few blocks south of the Crosstown, where U.S. 17 cuts across Upper King. Downtown is best explored by foot. Otherwise, there are bikes, pedicabs, and trolleys. Street parking is irksome, as meter readers are among the city's most efficient public servants. Parking garages, both privately and publicly owned, charge around $1.50 an hour.

Beyond downtown, the Ashley River hugs the west side of the peninsula, and the region on the far shore is called West Ashley. The Cooper River runs along the east side of the peninsula, with Mount Pleasant on the opposite side and the Charleston Harbor in between. Last, there are outlying sea islands (James, Folly Beach, Johns, Kiawah, Isle of Palms,

TOP 5 REASONS TO GO

Dining Out: Charleston has become a culinary destination, with talented chefs who offer innovative twists on the city's traditional cuisine. Bob Waggoner at the Charleston Grill is one outstanding example.

Seeing Art: The city is home to more than 133 galleries, so you'll never run out of places to see world-class art. The Charleston Museum and dozens of others add to the mix.

Spoleto Festival USA: If you're lucky enough to visit in May, you'll find a city under siege: Spoleto's flood of indoor and outdoor perfomances (opera, music, dance, and theater) is impossible to miss and almost as difficult not to enjoy.

The Battery: The views from the point—both natural and man-made—are the loveliest in the city. Look west to see the harbor; to the east you'll find elegant Charleston mansions.

Historic Homes: Charleston's preserved 19th-century houses, including the Nathaniel Russell House, are highlights; outside the city, plantations like Boone Hall, with its extensive garden and grounds, make scenic excursions.

Sullivan's), with their own appealing attractions. Everything that entails crossing the bridges is best explored by car or bus.

North of Broad

Large tracts of available land made the area North of Broad ideal for suburban plantations during the early 1800s. A century later, the peninsula had been built out, and today the area is a vibrant mix of residential neighborhoods and commercial clusters, with verdant parks scattered throughout. Though there are a number of majestic homes and prerevolutionary buildings in this area (including the oldest public building in the city, the Old Powder Magazine), the main draw is the area's collection of stores, museums, restaurants, and historic churches.

As you explore, note that the farther north you travel (up King Street in particular), the newer and more commercial development becomes. Although pretty much anywhere on the peninsula is considered prime real estate these days, the farther south you go, the more expensive the homes become. In times past, Broad Street was considered the cutoff point for the most coveted addresses. Those living in the area Slightly North of Broad were called mere "SNOBs," and their neighbors South of Broad were nicknamed "SOBs."

Numbers in the text correspond to numbers in the margin and on the Charleston map.

Main Attractions

★ ☺ ❷ **Charleston Museum.** Founded in 1773, the country's oldest museum is housed in a contemporary complex. The museum's decorative-arts holdings and its permanent Civil War exhibit are extraordinary. There are

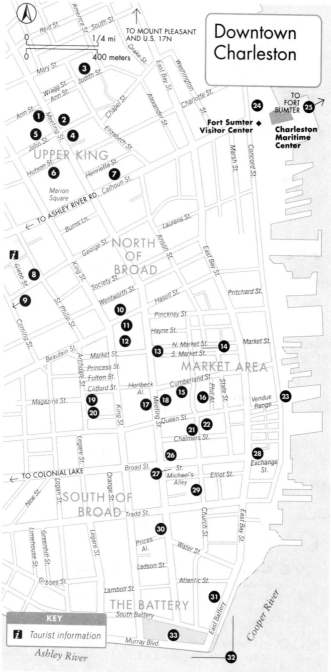

Downtown Charleston

TO MOUNT PLEASANT
AND U.S. 17N

0   1/4 mi

0   400 meters

TO
FORT
SUMTER

Fort Sumter ◆
Visitor Center

Charleston
Maritime
Center

UPPER KING

Marion
Square

← TO ASHLEY RIVER RD.

NORTH
OF
BROAD

MARKET AREA

← TO COLONIAL LAKE

SOUTH OF
BROAD

THE BATTERY

KEY

ℹ *Tourist information*

Ashley River

Cooper River

Reid St.
America St.
South St.
Drake St.
Mary St.
Wragg St.
Ann St.
Judith St.
Chapel St.
Alexander St.
East Bay St.
Washington St.
Charlotte St.
Ann St.
Meeting St.
John St.
Elizabeth St.
Hutson St.
Henrietta St.
Calhoun St.
Marsh St.
Concord St.
Burns Ln.
Laurens St.
George St.
Anson St.
East Bay St.
Glebb St.
King St.
Society St.
Wentworth St.
Hasell St.
Pritchard St.
Pinckney St.
Hayne St.
N. Market St.
Market St.
S. Market St.
Coming St.
St. Philip St.
Beaufain St.
Archdale St.
Market St.
Princess St.
Fulton St.
Clifford St.
Horlbeck Al.
Cumberland St.
State St.
Phil Al.
Vendue
Range
Magazine St.
King St.
Meeting St.
Queen St.
Chalmers St.
Legare St.
Broad St.
St.
Michael's
Alley
Elliot St.
Exchange
St.
New St.
Logan St.
Orange St.
Tradd St.
Church St.
East Bay St.
Limehouse St.
Greenhill St.
Legare St.
Prices
Al.
Water St.
Ladson St.
Atlantic St.
Gibbes St.
Lamboll St.
South Battery
East Battery
Murray Blvd.

more than 500,000 items in the collection, including silver, toys, and snuffboxes. There are also fascinating exhibits on natural history, archaeology, and ornithology. ■ TIP→ **Combination tickets that also give you admission to the Joseph Manigault House and the Heyward-Washington House are a bargain at $18.** ⊠ *360 Meeting St., Upper King* ☎ *843/722–2996* ⊕ *www.charlestonmuseum.org* ⊠ *$9* ☉ *Mon.–Sat. 9–5, Sun. 1–5.*

★ ⑫ **Charleston Place.** The city's most historic hotel is flanked by upscale boutiques and specialty shops. Wander into the luxe lobby and have cocktails at the classy Thoroughbred Club. The finest public restrooms are downstairs by the shoe-shine station. Entrances for the garage and reception area are on Hasell Street between Meeting and King streets. ⊠ *130 Market St., Market area* ☎ *843/722–4900.*

❶ **Charleston Visitors Center.** The center's 20-minute film *Forever Charleston* is a fine introduction to the city. ■ TIP→ **Bargain alert: garage parking here is just $1 per hour.** ⊠ *375 Meeting St., Upper King* ☎ *843/853–8000 or 800/868–8118* ⊕ *www.charlestoncvb.com* ⊠ *Free* ☉ *Mar.–Oct., daily 8:30–5:30; Nov.–Feb., daily 8:30–5.*

★ ☾ ❺ **Children's Museum of the Lowcountry.** Hands-on exhibits at this top-notch museum keep kids up to 12 occupied for hours. They can climb on a replica of a local shrimp boat, play in exhibits that show how water evaporates, and wander the inner workings of a medieval castle. ⊠ *25 Ann St., Upper King* ☎ *843/853–8962* ⊕ *www.explorecml.org* ⊠ *$5* ☉ *Tues.–Sat. 10–5, Sun. 1–5.*

NEED A BREAK? | Take a break with an icy treat at **Paolo's Gelato Italiano** (⊠ 41 John St., Upper King ☎ 843/577–0099). Flavors include various fruits and florals, as well as traditional flavors like pistachio. It also serves crepes covered with delicious sauces.

⑱ **Circular Congregational Church.** The first church building erected on this site in the 1680s gave bustling Meeting Street its name. The present-day Romanesque structure, dating from 1890, is configured on a Greek-cross plan and has a breathtaking vaulted ceiling. Explore the graveyard, the oldest in the city, with records dating to 1696. ⊠ *150 Meeting St., Market area* ☎ *843/577–6400* ⊕ *www.circularchurch.org.*

❽ **College of Charleston.** Randolph Hall—an 1828 building designed by Philadelphia architect William Strickland—anchors the central Cistern area of the college. Majestic oaks envelop the Cistern's lush green quad, where graduation ceremonies and concerts take place. The college was founded in 1770. Scenes from *Cold Mountain* were filmed here. ⊠ *St. Philip and George Sts., College of Charleston Campus* ⊕ *www.cofc.edu.*

㉑ **Dock Street Theatre.** Incorporating the remains of the Old Planter's Hotel (circa 1809), this theater is draped in red-velvet curtains and has wonderful woodwork. It's slated to close in 2007 for two years of much-needed renovations. ⊠ *135 Church St., Market area* ☎ *843/720–3968* ⊕ *www.charlestonstage.com.*

★ ☾ ㉕ **Fort Sumter National Monument.** The first shot of the Civil War was fired at Fort Sumter on April 12, 1861. After a 34-hour bombardment,

Union forces surrendered the fort, which became a symbol of Southern resistance. The Confederacy held it, despite almost continual bombardment, for nearly four years; when it was finally evacuated, the fort was a heap of rubble. Today, the National Park Service oversees it. The **Fort Sumter Liberty Square Visitor Center,** next to the South Carolina Aquarium, contains exhibits on the Civil War. This is a departure point for ferries

> ### HISTORY LESSON
>
> A ferry ride to Fort Sumter is a great way to sneak in a history lesson for the kids. For about the same price as a standard harbor cruise you get a narrated journey that points out the historic sites and explains how the Civil War began.

headed to the island where you'll find Fort Sumter itself. ✉ *340 Concord St., Upper King* ☎ *843/883–3123* ✉ *Free* ⊗ *Daily 8:30–5.*

Rangers conduct guided tours of the restored **Fort Sumter.** Tours begin at 9:30, noon, and 2:30 March to November and at 11 and 2:30 December to February. ■ TIP➜ **To reach the fort, you have to take a ferry; boats depart from Liberty Square Visitor Center and from across Cooper's River Bridges at Patriot's Point in Mount Pleasant.** ✉ *Charleston Harbor* ☎ *843/577–0242* ⊕ *www.nps.gov/fosu* ✉ *Fort free; ferry ride $14* ⊗ *Apr.–early Sept., daily 10–5:30; early Sept.–Mar., daily 10–4.*

❷ **French Protestant (Huguenot) Church.** The tiny Gothic-style church is the only one in the country still using the original Huguenot liturgy. English-language services are held Sunday at 10:30. ✉ *136 Church St., Market area* ☎ *843/722–4385* ⊕ *www.frenchhuguenotchurch.org* ⊗ *Mid-Mar.–mid-June and mid-Sept.–mid-Nov., Mon.–Thurs. 10–4, Fri. 10–1.*

❿ **Gibbes Museum of Art.** Housed in a beautiful Beaux-Arts building, this museum's collection of American works includes notable 18th- and 19th-century portraits of Carolinians. Don't miss the miniatures— shadow boxes set in dark-panel walls decorated with tiny fabrics and furnishing. ✉ *135 Meeting St., Market area* ☎ *843/722–2706* ⊕ *www.gibbesmuseum.org* ✉ *$9* ⊗ *Tues.–Sat. 10–5, Sun. 1–5.*

❹ **Joseph Manigault House.** An outstanding example of federal architecture, this home was designed by Charleston architect Gabriel Manigault in 1803. It's noted for its carved-wood mantels, elaborate plasterwork, and garden "folly." The pieces of rare tricolor Wedgwood are noteworthy. ✉ *350 Meeting St., Upper King* ☎ *843/722–2996* ⊕ *www.charlestonmuseum.org* ✉ *$8* ⊗ *Mon.–Sat. 10–5, Sun. 1–5.*

❻ **Old Citadel Building.** A fortresslike building on Marion Square was the first home of the Carolina Military College and once housed troops and arms. The present-day Citadel is in Hampton Park on the Ashley River. ✉ *341 Meeting St., Upper King* ☎ *843/723–6900.*

❁ ❿ **Old City Market.** This area is often called the Slave Market because it's where house slaves once shopped for produce and fish. Today stalls are lined with restaurants and shops selling children's toys, leather goods, and regional souvenirs. Local "basket ladies" weave and sell sweetgrass, pine-straw, and palmetto-leaf baskets—a craft passed down through generations from their West African ancestors. ⊠ *North and South Market Sts. between Meeting and E. Bay Sts., Market area* ⊙ *Daily 9–dusk.*

16 **St. Philip's (Episcopal) Church.** The namesake of Church Street, this graceful late-Georgian building is the second on its site: the congregation's first building burned down in 1835 and was rebuilt in 1838. During the Civil War, the steeple was a target for shelling; one Sunday a shell exploded in the church yard. The minister bravely continued his sermon. Afterward, the congregation gathered elsewhere for the duration of the war. Notable Charlestonians like John C. Calhoun are buried in the graveyard. ⊠ *146 Church St., Market area* ☎ *843/722–7734* ⊕ *www.stphilipschurchsc.org* ⊙ *Church weekdays 9–11 and 1–4; cemetery daily 9–4.*

> **ON THE CHEAP**
>
> A $34.95 Charleston Heritage Passport, sold at the Charleston Visitors Center, gets you into the Gibbes Museum of Art, the Nathaniel Russell House, the Edmondston-Alston House, the Aiken-Rhett House, Drayton Hall, and Middleton Place. It's good for two days.

★ ☾ **24** **South Carolina Aquarium.** The 380,000-gallon Great Ocean Tank has the tallest aquarium window in North America. Exhibits display more than 10,000 creatures, representing more than 500 species. You travel through the five major regions of the Southeast Appalachian Watershed: the Blue Ridge Mountains, the Piedmont, the coastal plain, the coast, and the ocean. Little ones can pet stingrays at one touch tank and horseshoe crabs and conchs at another. ⊠ *100 Aquarium Wharf, Upper King* ☎ *843/720–1990 or 800/722–6455* ⊕ *www.scaquarium.org* ⊠ *$15* ⊙ *Mid-Apr.–mid-Aug., Mon.–Sat. 9–5, Sun. noon–5; mid-Aug.–mid-Apr., Mon.–Sat. 9–4, Sun. noon–4.*

20 **Unitarian Church.** Completed in 1787, this church was remodeled in the mid-19th century using plans inspired by the Chapel of Henry VII in Westminster Abbey. The Gothic fan-tracery ceiling was added during that renovation. An entrance to the church grounds is at 161½–163 King Street and leads to a secluded, overgrown Victorian-style graveyard that invites contemplation. Sunday service is at 11 AM. ⊠ *8 Archdale St., Market area* ☎ *843/723–4617* ⊠ *Free* ⊙ *Church Fri. and Sat. 10–1, graveyard daily 9–5.*

★ **23** **Waterfront Park.** Enjoy the fishing pier's porch-style swings, stroll along the waterside path, or relax in the gardens overlooking Charleston Harbor. You can even jump into the fountain nicknamed "the pineapple" to get refreshed on hot summer days. The park is at the foot of Vendue Range, along the east side of Charleston Harbor and Cooper River. ⊠ *Prioleau St., Market area* ☎ *843/724–7321* ⊠ *Free* ⊙ *Daily 6 AM–midnight.*

Also Worth Seeing

3 **Aiken-Rhett House.** This stately 1819 mansion still has its original wallpaper, paint schemes, and even some of its furnishings. The kitchen, slave quarters, and work yard are much as they were when the original occupants lived here, making this one of the most complete examples of urban slave life. Confederate general P. G. T. Beauregard made his headquarters here in 1864. ⊠ *48 Elizabeth St., Upper King* ☎ *843/723–1159* ⊕ *www.historiccharleston.org* ⊠ *$8; $14 with admission to Nathaniel Russell House* ⊙ *Mon.–Sat. 10–5, Sun. 2–5.*

❾ **Avery Research Center for African-American History and Culture.** This center, part museum and part archive, was once a school for freed slaves. Collections include slavery artifacts like badges, manacles, and bills of sale. A riveting mural chronicles the Middle Passage—the journey slaves made from Africa to Charleston's shores. The free tours include a brief film. ⊠ *125 Bull St., College of Charleston Campus* ☎ *843/953–7609* ⊕ *www.cofc.edu* ⊠ *Free* ⊙ *Weekdays noon–5, mornings by appointment.*

❼ **Emanuel African Methodist Episcopal Church.** Home of the South's oldest African Methodist Episcopal congregation, the church had its beginnings in 1818. Authorities closed it in 1822 when they suspected freedman Denmark Vesey used the sanctuary to plan a massive slave uprising. The church reopened on the present site after the Civil War ended. ⊠ *110 Calhoun St., Upper King* ☎ *843/722–2561* ⊠ *Donations accepted* ⊙ *Daily 9–4.*

❿ **Kahal Kadosh Beth Elohim Reform Temple.** Considered one of the nation's finest examples of Greek-revival architecture, this temple was built in 1840 to replace an earlier one. The original was the birthplace of American Reform Judaism in 1824. Tours are conducted Sunday to Friday. ⊠ *90 Hasell St., Market area* ☎ *843/723–1090* ⊕ *www.kkbe.org* ⊠ *Free* ⊙ *Weekdays 10–noon, Sun. 12:30–3:45.*

⓭ **Market Hall.** Built in 1841, this imposing landmark was modeled after the Temple of Nike in Athens. The hall contains the **Confederate Museum**, in which the United Daughters of the Confederacy displays flags, uniforms, swords, and other Civil War memorabilia. ⊠*188 Meeting St., Market area* ☎ *843/723–1541* ⊠*$5* ⊙ *Tues.–Sat. 11–3:30.*

⓯ **Old Powder Magazine.** Built in 1713, the oldest public building in South Carolina is the only one that remains from the time of the Lords Proprietors. The city's volatile—and precious—gun powder was kept here during the Revolutionary War. The building was designed to implode if detonated (and thus save Charleston). ⊠ *79 Cumberland St., Market area* ⊠ *$2* ⊙ *Tues.–Sat. 11–3:30.*

> ### BUILDING BOOM
>
> Charleston boomed with the plantation economy in the years before the Civil War. South Carolina's rice, indigo, and cotton crops produced an extraordinary concentration of wealth. Seeking a social and cultural lifestyle to match its financial success, the plantocracy entertained itself in style. The city was also renowned for its talented goldsmiths, silversmiths, gunsmiths, tobacconists, brewers, and cabinetmakers. More than 200 private residences were built during this period, and the city was one of the top shopping places in North America.

⑲ St. John's Lutheran Church. This Greek-revival church with delicate wrought-iron gates was completed in 1817 for a congregation that was established in 1742. Its most noteworthy leader, Dr. John Bachman, served as preacher 1815–74 and was known for ministering to local African-Americans and for collaborating on two books with his friend, naturalist John James Audubon. ⊠ *5 Clifford St., Market area* ☎ *843/723–2426* ⊕ *www.stjohnscharleston.org.*

⑪ St. Mary's Catholic Church. Beautiful stained glass, wall paintings, and an interesting cemetery tucked between stone walls are highlights of the earliest Roman Catholic church in the Carolinas and Georgia. The white-pillar structure was constructed in 1839. ⊠ *95 Hasell St., Market area* ☎ *843/722–7696* ☉ *By appointment.*

The Battery & South of Broad

Locals have long joked that just off the Battery (at Battery Street and Murray Boulevard), the Ashley and Cooper rivers join to form the Atlantic Ocean. Such a lofty proclamation speaks volumes about the area's rakish flair. To take in their pride and joy, head to the point of the downtown peninsula. Here, handsome mansions surrounded by elaborate gardens greet incoming boats and passersby. The look is reminiscent of the West Indies with good reason: before coming to the Carolinas in the late 17th century, many early British colonists had first settled on Barbados and other Caribbean isles where homes with high ceilings and broad porches caught the sea breezes.

The heavily residential area south of Broad Street and west of the Battery brims with beautiful private homes, most of which bear plaques with a short written description of the property's history. Mind your manners, but feel free to peek through iron gates and fences at the verdant displays in elaborate gardens. Although an open gate once signified that guests were welcome to venture inside, that time has mostly passed—residents tell stories of how they came home to find tourists sitting in their front porch rockers. But you never know when an invitation to look around from a friendly owner-gardener might come your way. Several of the city's lavish house museums call this famously affluent neighborhood home.

> ### OLD-FASHIONED WALK
>
> In spring and summer, Charleston's gardens are in full glory. In fall and winter the homes are dressed in their holiday finest. Twilight strolls are a Dickensian experience, with homes lit from within showing off one cozy scene after another.

Numbers in the text correspond to numbers in the margin and on the Charleston map.

Main Attractions

㉜ Battery. From the intersection of Water Street and East Battery you can look east toward the city's most photographed mansions; look west for views of Charleston Harbor and Fort Sumter. Walk south along East

FodorsChoice
★

Battery to White Point Gardens, where the street curves and becomes Murray Boulevard. ⊠ *East Bay St. and Murray Blvd., South of Broad.*

29 Heyward-Washington House. The area where rice planter Daniel Heyward built his home in 1772 is believed to have been the inspiration for the folk opera *Porgy and Bess.* President George Washington stayed in the house during his 1791 visit. The period furnishings include the Holmes Bookcase, one of the finest remaining American furniture pieces of the late 18th century. Pay attention to the restored kitchen, the only one like it in Charleston open to the public. ⊠ *87 Church St., South of Broad* ☎ *843/722–2996* ⊕ *www.charlestonmuseum.org* ☞ *$8* ☉ *Mon.–Sat. 10–5, Sun. 1–5.*

> **IF THE SHOE FITS**
>
> Wear good walking shoes, because the sidewalks, brick streets, and even Battery Promenade are very uneven. Take a bottle of water, or take a break to sip from the fountains in White Point Gardens, as there are practically no shops south of Broad Street.

★ **30 Nathaniel Russell House.** One of the nation's finest examples of Adam-style architecture, the Nathaniel Russell House was built in 1808. The interior is distinguished by its ornate detailing, its lavish period furnishings, and the "free flying" staircase that spirals three stories with no visible support. The garden is well worth a stroll. ⊠ *51 Meeting St., South of Broad* ☎ *843/724–8481* ⊕ *www.historiccharleston.org* ☞ *$8; $14 with admission to Aiken-Rhett House* ☉ *Mon.–Sat. 10–5, Sun. 2–5.*

27 St. Michael's Episcopal Church. The first cornerstone of St. Michael's was set in place in 1752, making it Charleston's oldest surviving church. Through the years other elements were added: the steeple clock and bells (1764); the organ (1768); the font (1771); and the altar (1892). The pulpit—original to the church—was designed to maximize natural acoustics. ⊠ *14 St. Michael's Alley, South of Broad* ☎ *843/723–0603* ⊕ *www. stmichaelschurch.net* ☉ *Weekdays 9–4:30, Sat. 9–noon.*

★ ☺ **33 White Point Gardens.** Pirates once hung from gallows here; now it's a serene park with Charleston benches—small wood-slat benches with cast-iron sides—and views of the harbor and Fort Sumter. Children love to climb on the replica cannon and pile of cannonballs. ⊠ *Murray Blvd. and E. Battery, South of Broad* ☎ *843/724–7327* ☉ *Weekdays 9–5, Sat. 9–noon.*

Also Worth Seeing

26 City Hall. The intersection of Meeting and Broad streets is known as the Four Corners of Law, representing the laws of nation, state, city, and church. On the northeast corner is the graceful, pale pink City Hall, dating from 1801. The second-floor council chambers double as a museum where you'll find John Trumbull's 1791 satirical portrait of George Washington and Samuel F. B. Morse's likeness of James Monroe. ⊠ *80 Broad St., South of Broad* ☎ *843/577–6970 or 843/724–3799* ☞ *Free* ☉ *Weekdays 8:30–5.*

31 Edmondston-Alston House. First built in 1825 in late-federal style, the Edmondston-Alston House was transformed into the imposing Greek-revival structure you see today during the 1840s. Tours of the home—furnished with antiques, portraits, silver, and fine china—are informative. ⊠ *21 E. Battery, South of Broad* ☎ *843/722–7171* ⊕ *www.middletonplace.org* ⊠ *$10* ⊙ *Tues.–Sat. 10–4:30, Sun. and Mon. 1:30–4:30.*

🕓 **㉘ Old Exchange Building & Provost Dungeon.** Originally a customs house with a waterside entrance, this building was used by the British to house prisoners during the Revolutionary War. Today costumed guides bring the revolutionary era to life. ⊠ *122 E. Bay St., South of Broad* ☎ *843/727–2165* ⊕ *www.oldexchange.com* ⊠ *$8* ⊙ *Daily 9–5.*

Mount Pleasant & Vicinity

East of Charleston across the Cooper River Bridge, via U.S. 17N, is the town of Mount Pleasant, named not for a mountain or a hill but for a plantation in England from which some of the area's settlers hailed. In its Old Village neighborhood are antebellum homes and a sleepy, old-time town center with a drugstore where patrons sidle up to the soda fountain and lunch counter for egg-salad sandwiches and floats. Along Shem Creek, where the local fishing fleet brings in the daily catch, several seafood restaurants serve the area's freshest (and most deftly fried) seafood. Other attractions in the area include military and maritime museums, plantations, and, farther north, the Cape Romain National Wildlife Refuge.

Main Attractions

★ **Boone Hall Plantation and Garden.** A ½-mi drive through a live-oak alley draped in Spanish moss introduces you to the still-operating plantation, the oldest of its kind. Tours take you through the 1935 mansion, the butterfly pavilion, the heirloom rose garden, and nine antebellum-era brick slave cabins. Stroll along the winding river, tackle the fields to pick your own strawberries or pumpkins, or dine in Serena's Kitchen, which serves Southern fare. *North and South, Queen,* and Nicholas Sparks's *The Notebook* were filmed here. ■ TIP→ Plan your visit to coincide with annual events like June's Blue Grass Festival and January's Oyster Festival. ⊠ *1235 Long Point Rd., off U.S. 17N, Mount Pleasant* ☎ *843/884–4371* ⊕ *www.boonehallplantation. com* ⊠ *$14.50* ⊙ *Apr.–early Sept., Mon.–Sat. 8:30–6:30, Sun. 1–5; early Sept.–Mar., Mon.–Sat. 9–5, Sun. 1–4.*

🕓 **Fort Moultrie National Monument.** Here Colonel William Moultrie's South Carolinians repelled a British assault in one of the first Patriot victories of the Revolutionary War. Completed in 1809, this is the third fort on this site at **Sullivan's Island,** reached on Route 703 off U.S. 17N (10 mi southeast of Charleston). A 20-minute film tells the history of

BASKET LADIES

Drive along U.S. 17N, through and beyond Mount Pleasant, to find the basket ladies set up at rickety roadside stands, weaving sweetgrass, pine-straw, and palmetto-leaf baskets. Baskets typically cost less on this stretch than in downtown Charleston. Each purchase supports the artisans, who are becoming fewer and fewer each year.

the fort. ■ TIP➡ Plan to spend the day relaxing bicycling through Sullivan's Island, a cluster of early-20th-century beach houses. ⊠ *1214 Middle St., Sullivan's Island* ☎ *843/883–3123* ⊕ *www.nps.gov* ⊡ *$3* ⊙ *Daily 9–5.*

★ ⑅ **Patriots Point Naval & Maritime Museum.** Ships berthed here include the aircraft carrier USS *Yorktown,* the World War II submarine USS *Clamagore,* the destroyer USS *Laffey,* and the Coast Guard cutter *Ingham,* responsible for sinking a U-boat during World War II. A Vietnam exhibit showcases naval air and watercraft used in the military action. ⊠ *Foot of Ravenel Bridge, Mount Pleasant* ☎ *843/884–2727* ⊕ *www. patriotspoint.org* ⊡ *$15* ⊙ *Daily 9–6:30.*

Also Worth Seeing

Cape Romain National Wildlife Refuge. A grouping of barrier islands and salt marshes, this 60,000-acre refuge is one of the most outstanding in the country. The **Sewee Visitor & Environmental Education Center** has information and exhibits on the refuge, trails, and rescued or breeding live birds of prey and red wolves. ■ TIP➡ From Cape Romain National Wildlife Refuge you can take a $30 ferry ride to Bull Island. The island is a nearly untouched wilderness; the beach here, strewn with bleached driftwood, is nicknamed Boneyard Beach. ⊠ *5821 U.S. 17N, Awendaw* ☎ *843/928–3368* ⊕ *http://caperomain.fws.gov* ⊡ *Free* ⊙ *Tues.–Sun. 9–5.*

Charles Pinckney National Historic Site. Across the street from Boone Hall Plantation, this is a remnant of the country estate of Charles Pinckney, drafter and signer of the Constitution. A self-guided tour focuses on African-American farm life, including the plantation owner–slave relationship. You can also tour an 1820s tidewater cottage. ⊠ *1254 Long Point Rd., off U.S. 17N, Mount Pleasant* ☎ *843/881–5516* ⊟ *843/881– 7070* ⊕ *www.nps.gov* ⊡ *Free* ⊙ *Daily 9–5.*

Old Village. This neighborhood is distinguished by white-picket-fenced colonial cottages, antebellum manses, tiny neighborhood churches, and restored (or new) waterfront homes with pricetags in the millions. It's a lovely area to stroll or bike. The Blessing of the Fleet seafood festival takes place each April. ⊠ *South of Alhambra Park.*

⑅ **Palmetto Islands County Park.** This 943-acre park has a playground, paved trails, an observation tower, and boardwalks extending over the marshes. You can rent bicycles and paddleboats, or pay an extra fee for a small water park. ⊠ *Long Point Rd., ½ mi past Boone Hall Plantation, Mount Pleasant* ☎ *843/884–0832* ⊕ *www.ccprc.com* ⊡ *$2* ⊙ *Apr., Sept., and Oct., daily 9–6; May–Aug., daily 9–7; Nov.–Feb., daily 10–5; Mar., daily 10–6.*

West of the Ashley River

Ashley River Road, Route 61, begins a few miles northwest of downtown Charleston, over the Ashley River Bridge. Sights are spread out along the way and those who love history, old homes, and gardens may need several days to explore places like Drayton Hall, Middleton Place, and Magnolia Plantation and Gardens. Spring is a peak time for the flowers, although the gardens are in bloom throughout the year.

Main Attractions

Magnolia Plantation and Gardens. The extensive informal garden, begun in 1685, has evolved into an overflowing collection of plants that bloom year-round, including a vast array of azaleas and camellias. You can take a tram or boat to tour the grounds. Rent a canoe to paddle through the 125-acre Waterfowl Refuge, or explore the 30-acre Audubon Swamp Garden along boardwalks and bridges. You can walk or rent bikes to traverse the more than 500 acres of trails. There are also a petting zoo and a miniature-horse ranch. You can tour the 19th-century plantation house, which originally stood in Summerville. The home was taken apart, floated down the Ashley River, and reassembled here. ⊠ *3550 Ashley River Rd., West Ashley* ☎ *843/571–1266 or 800/367–3517* ⊕ *www.magnoliaplantation.com* ⊠ *Grounds $14; tram $7; boat $7* ☉ *Daily 8–5:30.*

FodorsChoice
★

Middleton Place. Blooms of all seasons form floral *allées* (alleys) along terraced lawns, and around ornamental lakes shaped like butterfly wings. Much of the year, the landscaped gardens, begun in 1741, are ablaze with camellia, magnolia, azalea, and rose blossoms. A large part of the mansion was destroyed during the Civil War, but the gentlemen's wing has been restored and houses impressive collections of silver, furniture, paintings, and historic documents. In the stable yard craftspeople use authentic tools to demonstrate spinning, weaving, and other skills from the plantation era. Farm animals, peacocks, and other creatures roam freely. The Middleton Place restaurant serves Lowcountry specialties for lunch and dinner. There are also a delightful gift shop that carries local arts, crafts, and souvenirs, and a garden shop that sells rare seedlings. You can sign up for kayak, bike, wagon, or horseback tours, and you can stay overnight at the inn, where floor-to-ceiling windows splendidly frame the Ashley River. ⊠ *4300 Ashley River Rd., West Ashley* ☎ *843/556–6020 or 800/782–3608* ⊕ *www.middletonplace.org* ⊠ *Grounds $25; house tour $10* ☉ *Grounds daily 9–5; house tours Tues.–Sun. 10–4:30, Mon. noon–4:30.*

Also Worth Seeing

★
Charles Towne Landing State Historic Site. Commemorating the site of the original 1670 Charleston settlement, this park has a reconstructed village and fortifications, English park gardens with bicycle trails and walkways, and a replica 17th-century vessel moored in the creek. In the animal park native species roam freely—among them alligators, bison, pumas, bears, and wolves. Bicycle rentals are available. ⊠ *1500 Old Towne Rd., Rte. 171, West Ashley* ☎ *843/852–4200* ⊕ *www.southcarolinaparks.com* ⊠ *$5* ☉ *Daily 8:30–5.*

Drayton Hall. Considered the nation's finest example of unspoiled Georgian–Palladian architecture, this mansion is the only plantation house on the Ashley River to have survived the Civil War. A National Trust historic site, built between 1738 and 1742, it's an invaluable lesson in history as well as in architecture. Drayton Hall has been left unfurnished to highlight the original plaster moldings, opulent hand-carved woodwork, and other ornamental details. Watch *Connections*, which details the conditions under which slaves were brought from Africa. You can also see copies of documents that recorded the buying and selling of local

Charleston Preserved

IT'S EASY TO THINK CHARLESTON is a neverland, sweetly arrested in pastel perfection. But look at Civil War–era images of the Battery mansions on East Bay Street, one of the most photographed areas in town today, and you see the surrounding homes disfigured with crippling battle scars. Because of the poverty that followed the Civil War, on the whole locals simply couldn't afford to build anew from the late 1860s through the latter part of the 20th century, so they put the homes they had back together.

In the 1920s it was community activism that rescued the old homes from being destroyed. According to Jonathan Poston, author of *Buildings of Charleston*, the preservation movement began when an Esso gas station was slated to take the place of the Joseph Manigault House. Citizens formed the Society for the Preservation of Old Dwellings (the first such group in the nation) and saved what's now a popular house museum. By 1931 Charleston's City Council had created the Board of Architectural Review (BAR), and designated the historic district protected from unrestrained development—two more national firsts. The Historic Charleston Foundation was established in 1947, and preservation is now second nature (by law).

As you explore, look for Charleston single houses: just one room wide, these houses were built with the narrow end streetside and multistory south or southwestern porches (often called piazzas) to catch prevailing breezes. Cool air drifts across these shaded porches, entering houses through open windows. Look at the northern wall of a single house (the wall that faces a neighbor's garden and piazza), and you see few windows original to the structure. That's a tipping of the hat to privacy, a little urban built-in gentility.

You'll see numerous architectural vestiges along Charleston's preserved streets. Many houses have plaques detailing their history, and others have Carolopolis Awards given for fine restoration work. Old fire-insurance plaques are more rare; they denote the company that insured the home and that would extinguish the flames if a fire broke out. Notice the bolt heads and washers that dot house facades along the Battery; some are in the shape of circles or stars, and others are capped with lion heads. These could straighten sagging houses when tightened via a crank under the floorboards.

The streetside slabs of marble or stone are horse mounts, and boot scrapes are set in the sidewalk beside the front doors of many homes. Note the iron spikes that line the tops of some residential gates, doors, walls, and windows. Serving the same purpose as razor wire atop prison fences, most of these *cheveux de frise* (French for frizzy hair) were added after a thwarted 1822 slave rebellion, to deter break-in–or escape.

5

slaves. Tours depart on the hour; guides are known for their in-depth knowledge of the era. ⊠ *3380 Ashley River Rd., West Ashley* ☎ *843/ 769–2600* ⊕ *www.draytonhall.org* ⊠ *$14* ☉ *Mar.–Oct., daily 9:30–4; Nov.–Feb., daily 9:30–3.*

SPORTS & THE OUTDOORS

Baseball

The **Charleston Riverdogs** (⊠ Joseph P. Riley, Jr. Stadium, 360-Fishburne St. ☎ 843/577–3647 ⊕ www.riverdogs.com) play at "The Joe," on the banks of the Ashley River near to the Citadel. Kids love their mascot, Charlie T. Riverdog. The season runs April to October.

Beaches

The Charleston area's mild climate means you can swim March to October. Public beaches, run by the Charleston County Parks & Recreation Commission, generally have lifeguards in season, snack bars, restrooms and dressing areas, outdoor showers, umbrella and chair rental, and large parking lots.

The public **Kiawah Beachwalker Park,** about 28 mi southwest of Charleston, has 500 feet of deep beach. ⊠ *Beachwalker Dr., Kiawah Island* ☎ *843/ 768–2395* ⊠ *$5 per car* ☉ *Mar., weekends 10–5; Apr. and Oct., weekends 10–6; May–Aug., daily 10–7; Sept., daily 10–6.*

Trees, palmettos, and other natural foliage cover the interior, and there's a river that winds through **Folly Beach County Park.** The beach, 12 mi southwest of Charleston, is more than six football fields long. ⊠ *1100 W. Ashley Ave., off U.S. 17, Folly Island* ☎ *843/588–2426* ⊠ *$5 per car* ☉ *Apr., Sept., and Oct., daily 10–6; May–Aug., daily 9–7; Nov.–Mar., daily 10–5.*

Play beach volleyball or rent a raft at the 600-foot-long beach in the **Isle of Palms County Park.** ⊠ *1 14th Ave., Isle of Palms, Mount Pleasant* ☎ *843/ 886–3863 or 843/768–4386* ⊠ *$5 per car* ☉ *May–Aug., daily 9–7; Apr., Sept., and Oct., daily 10–6; Nov.–Mar., daily 10–5.*

Biking

The historic district is ideal for bicycling as long as you stay off the busier roads. Many of the city's green spaces, including Colonial Lake and Palmetto Islands County Park, have biking trails.

You can rent bikes at the **Bicycle Shoppe** (⊠ 280 Meeting St., Market area ☎ 843/722–8168 ⊠ 1539 Johnnie Dodds Blvd., Mount Pleasant ☎ 843/884–7433). **Bike the Bridge Rentals** (⊠ 360 Concord St., Upper King ☎ 843/853–2453) can set you up with a seven-speed bike to ride the paths on the spectacular Ravenel Bridge. You'll get a map, a self-guided tour booklet, and free water-taxi ride back. **Carolina Beach Cruisers** (⊠ 4053 Rhett Ave., North Charleston ☎ 843/747–245 ⊕ www. carolinabeachcruisers.com) rents all kinds of bikes, including those with special seats for youngsters. It delivers to all area islands.

Boating

Kayak through marsh rivers and to outlying islands with **Coastal Expeditions** (⊠ 514B Mill St., Mount Pleasant ☎ 843/884–7684). You can rent kayaks from **Middleton Place Plantation** (✉ 4300 Ashley River Rd., West Ashley ☎ 843/556–6020 ⊕ www.theinnatmiddletonplace.com) and glide along the Ashley River.

To hire a sailing charter, contact **AquaSafaris** (✉ Patriots Point Marina, Mount Pleasant ☎ 843/886–8133 ⊕ www.aqua-safaris.com). To learn how to command your own sailboat, enlist with **Ocean Sailing Academy** (✉ 24 Patriots Point Rd., Mount Pleasant ☎ 843/971–0700 ⊕ www. oceansail.com).

Fishing

Anglers can rent gear ($8 to $10) and cast a line at the 1,000-foot fishing pier at **Folly Beach County Park** (✉ 101 E. Arctic Ave., Folly Beach ☎ 843/795–3474). Baby sharks are commonly on the end of your line.

Fly-fishing guides generally charge between $300 and $400 for two people for a half-day. Fly-fishers looking for a native guide do best by calling **Captain Richard Stuhr** (✉ 547 Sanders Farm La., North Charleston ☎ 843/881–3179 ⊕ www.captstuhr.com); he'll haul his boat to you.

Deep-sea fishing charters cost about $1,400 for 12 hours for a boatload of anglers. March through October is the time to go for yellowfin tuna aboard the 54-foot boat run by **Aut-top-Sea Charters** (✉ Shem Creek docks, Mount Pleasant ☎ 843/454–0312). **Palmetto Charters** (✉ 224 Patriots Point Rd., Mount Pleasant ☎ 843/849–6004 ⊕ www. palmettocharters.com) has guided trips that take you out in the ocean or stay close to shore. **Bohicket Yacht Charters** (✉ 1880 Andell Bluff Blvd., Seabrook Island ☎ 843/768–7294 ⊕ www.bohicketboat.com) has half- and full-day charters on 24- to 48-foot boats. It also offers dolphin-watching and dinner cruises.

Golf

With fewer golfers than in Hilton Head, the courses around Charleston have more choice starting times available. Nonguests can play at private island resorts, such as Kiawah Island, Seabrook Island, and Wild Dunes. To find out about golf vacation packages in the area, contact the **Charleston Area Gold Guide** (☎ 800/774–4444 ⊕ www.charlestongolfinc.com).

Tom Fazio designed the Links and the Harbor courses at **Wild Dunes Resort** (✉ 10001 Back Bay Dr., Isle of Palms ☎ 843/886–2180 ✉ 5881 Palmetto Dr., Isle of Palms ☎ 843/886–2301). **Seabrook Island Resort** (✉ Seabrook Island Rd., Seabrook Island ☎ 843/768–2529) has two championship courses: Crooked Oaks, by Robert Trent Jones Sr., and Ocean Winds, by Willard Byrd. The prestigious **Ocean Course** (✉ 1000 Ocean Course Dr., Kiawah Island ☎ 843/768–7272), designed by Pete Dye, was the site of the 1991 Ryder Cup. Of the three championship courses at **Kiawah Island Resort** (✉ 12 Kiawah Beach Dr., Kiawah Island), Gary Player designed Marsh Point; Tom Fazio designed Osprey Point; and Jack Nicklaus designed Turtle Point.

The public **Charleston Municipal Golf Course** (✉ 2110 Maybank Hwy., James Island ☎ 843/795–6517) is a walker-friendly course. **Patriots Point** (✉ 1 Patriots Point Rd., Mount Pleasant ☎ 843/881–0042) has a partly covered driving range and spectacular harbor views. **Shadowmoss Golf Club**

(✉ 20 Dunvegan Dr., West Ashley ☎ 843/556–8251) is a well-marked, forgiving course with one of the best finishing holes in the area.

Charleston National Country Club (✉ 1360 National Dr., Mount Pleasant ☎ 843/884–7799) is well maintained and tends to be quiet on weekdays. The **Dunes West Golf Club** (✉ 3535 Wando Plantation Way, Mount Pleasant ☎ 843/856–9000) has great marshland views and lots of modulation on the greens. **Links at Stono Ferry** (✉ 4812 Stono Links Dr., Hollywood ☎ 843/763–1817) is a popular public course with reasonable rates.

Horseback Riding

About 7 mi south of Charleston, **Stono River Stables & Farms** (✉ 3000 River Rd., John's Island ☎ 843/559–0773 ⊕ www.stonoriverstable.com) offers trail rides through maritime forests. **Seabrook Island Equestrian Center** (✉ Seabrook Island Rd., Seabrook Island ☎ 843/768–7541) is open to the public. The center, 24 mi southwest of Charleston, has trail rides on the beach and through maritime forests. There are also pony rides for kids.

Scuba Diving

Experienced divers can explore the Cooper River Underwater Heritage Diving Trail, upriver from Charleston. The 2-mi-long trail has six submerged sites, including ships that date to the Revolutionary War. Charters will run you out to the starting point.

Charleston Scuba (✉ 335 Savannah Hwy., West Ashley ☎ 843/763–3483 ⊕ www.charlestonscuba.com) has maps, equipment rentals, and charters trips to the Cooper River Trail.

Soccer

Charleston Battery (✉ Blackbaud Stadium, 1990 Daniel Island Dr., Daniel Island ☎ 843/971–4627 ⊕ www.charlestonbattery.com) plays from April to September. After the games, fans retreat to the clubby English pub.

Spas

Charleston Place Spa (✉ 130 Market St., Market Area ☎ 843/722–4900 ⊕ www.charlestonplacespa.com), a truly deluxe day spa, has nine treatment rooms and a wet room where seaweed body wraps and other treatments are administered. Four-handed massages for couples are a popular option. Locker rooms for men and women have showers and saunas; men also have a steam room. Adjacent is a fitness room, an indoor pool with skylights, and a spacious hot tub.

In a historic home, **Stella Nova** (✉ 78 Society St., Ansonborogh ☎ 843/723–0909 ⊕ www.stella-nova.com) lets you enjoy refreshments on the breezy verandas. This boutique spa is serious about all of its treatments, from waxings to salt-scrubs. For couples there are aromatherapy massages.

Tennis

You can play for free at neighborhood courts, including several near Colonial Lake and at the Isle of Palms Recreation Center. **Charleston Tennis**

Center (✉ 19 Farmfield Ave., West Ashley ☎ 843/724–7402) is a city facility with lots of courts and locker rooms. **Maybank Tennis Center** (✉ 1880 Houghton Dr., James Island ☎ 843/406–8814) has lights on its six courts. The women's tennis Family Circle Cup is hosted each April at the **Family Circle Tennis Center** (✉ 161 Seven Farms Dr., Daniel Island ☎ 843/534–2400 ⊕ www.familycirclecup.com). The 17 lighted courts (13 clay, 4 hard) are open to the public.

Water Sports

The pros at **McKevlin's Surf Shop** (✉ 8 Center St., Folly Beach ☎ 843/588–2247) can teach you what you need to know about surfing at Folly Beach County Park.

WHERE TO EAT

Eating is a serious pastime in Charleston. You can dine at nationally renowned restaurants serving the best of Southern nouveau, or if you prefer, a waterfront shack with some of the best fried seafood south of the Mason-Dixon line. Big-name chefs, including Bob Waggoner of the Charleston Grill, Robert Carter of the Peninsula Grill, Ken Vedrinski of Sienna, Frank Lee of Slightly North of Broad, Mike Lata of FIG, and Craig Deihl of Cypress, have earned reputations for preparing Lowcountry cuisine with a contemporary flair. Incredible young talents, including Tarver King of the Woodlands, Jason Scholz of High Cotton, Ciaran Duffy of Tristan's, and Sean Brock of McCrady's are also putting a new spin on things.

Reservations are a good idea for dinner year-round, especially on weekends, as there is almost no off-season for tourism. Tables are especially hard to come by during the Southeastern Wildlife Expo (President's Day weekend in February) and the Spoleto Festival (late May to mid-June). The overall dress code is relaxed: unless noted below, casual khakis and an oxford or polo shirt for men, casual slacks (or a skirt), top, and sandals for women work for any place you might pull up a chair.

Prices

A gastro-tour here can get expensive. You might try several of the small plates that many establishments now serve as an option to keep costs down. In general, prices downtown are higher than those in restaurants over the bridges and on the islands.

	WHAT IT COSTS				
	$$$$	$$$	$$	$	¢
AT DINNER	over $22	$17–$22	$12–$16	$7–$11	under $7

Restaurant prices are for a main course at dinner.

American–Casual

¢ ✕ **Jack's.** There *is* a Jack, and he personally greets regulars and newcomers alike. Juicy burgers and just-right fries attract locals to this no-frills

Where to Stay & Eat in Charleston

0 ⊢——————⊣ 1/4 mile

0 ⊢——————⊣ 400 meters

(25)

KEY

① *Hotels*

❶ *Restaurants*

diner. Try the cheese-steak subs or the fat Reubens for lunch, or the made-from-scratch biscuits for breakfast. The restaurant is one block off King Street's busiest shopping area. ⊠ *41 George St., College of Charleston Campus* ☎ *843/723–5237* ▭ *MC, V* ☽ *Closed weekends. No dinner.*

Contemporary

★ **$$$$** ✕ **Circa 1886.** If you're celebrating, come to this formal, conducive-to-conversation dining room in a carriage house behind the Wentworth Mansion. There is a formality here, and the waitstaff has both skill and decorum. Chef Marc Collins has created dishes that are real originals; don't resist the Vidalia onion cream soup or the foie gras with crushed almonds. Crabmeat is the central ingredient in his signature soufflé. The coffee-rubbed strip loin with corn pudding, asparagus, and truffles is remarkable. After all that beef, you may experience a chemical need for dessert—try the chocolate tasting with wonders like chocolate-chunk-brownie gelato. ⊠ *149 Wentworth St., Market area* ☎ *843/853–7828* ⌨ *Reservations essential* ▭ *AE, D, DC, MC, V* ☽ *No lunch.*

★ **$$$$** ✕ **Robert's of Charleston.** Owner Robert Dickson is both a classically trained chef and an effusive baritone who belts out show tunes in the intimate dining room. The set menu changes, but might include scallop mousse with lobster sauce, duck with Asian barbecue sauce, and chateaubriand with a red wine sauce. Manager Joseph Raya picks the best wines to pair with each course. The restaurant is a family-run affair, which puts a warm spin on the experience. Robert's daughter, Maria-Elena, now reigns in the kitchen. ⊠ *182 E. Bay St., Market area* ☎ *843/577–7565* ⌨ *Reservations essential* ▭ *D, MC, V* ☽ *Closed Sun.–Wed. No lunch.*

$$$–$$$$ ✕ **Cypress.** From the owners of Magnolias and Blossom comes a renovated 1834 brick-wall building with an urbane contemporary decor. Rust-color leather booths, a ceiling with light sculptures that change color, and a "wine wall" of 5,000 bottles keep it interesting. The cuisine is classic American, with fresh local ingredients accented with exotic flavors, notably from the Pacific Rim. Try fabulous salads like the arugula with Gorgonzola, pecans, and apples. The green-tea–smoked duck is a good entrée choice. The fillet, cooked over hickory, comes with a Madeira wine sauce and a house-made soft cheese with herbs. Executive Chef Craig Deihl consistently creates simple yet elegant fare. ⊠ *167 E. Bay St., Market area* ☎ *843/727–0111* ⌨ *Reservations essential* ▭ *AE, DC, MC, V* ☽ *No lunch.*

$$$–$$$$ ✕ **McCrady's.** This restaurant finally found someone to fill the shoes of its acclaimed former chef, Michael Kramer. Sean Brock is passionate about his profession, and spends his nights coming up with innovative pairings, most of which work. Try the butter-poached lobster with parsnips and tonka beans or the seared Hawaiian tuna with pistachios, carrots, and bay laurel jus. Although Brock is gradually making the menu his own, the desserts continue to dazzle: like the tangerine-pistachio Napoléan and the famous lava cake. The encyclopedia-size wine list gave rise to the adjoining McCrady's Wine Bar, a more casual establishment. ⊠ *2 Unity Alley, Market area* ☎ *843/577–0025* ⌨ *Reservations essential* ▭ *AE, MC, V* ☽ *No lunch.*

★ **$$$-$$$$** ✕ **Peninsula Grill.** Eighteenth century–style portraits hang on walls covered in olive-green velvet in this dining room. You sit beneath black-iron chandeliers feasting on longtime executive chef Robert Carter's imaginative entrées, including rack of lamb with a sesame-seed crust and a coconut-mint pesto. The bourbon-grilled jumbo shrimp with lobster-basil hush puppies is scrumptious. The signature dessert is the three-way chocolate that comes with a shot of ice-cold milk. The servers, who work in tandem, are pros; the personable sommelier makes wine selections that truly complement your meal. The atmosphere is animated and convivial. ✉ *Planters Inn, 112 N. Market St., Market area* ☎ *843/723–0700* ⌂ *Reservations essential* 🏛 *Jacket required* 🖃 *AE, D, DC, MC, V* ◷ *No lunch.*

★ **$$$-$$$$** ✕ **Tristan.** Within the French Quarter Inn, this fine dining room has a sleek, contemporary style with lots of metal, glass, and fresh flowers. Chef Ciaran Duffy purposely tailored the menu to complement the decor; it's ultra-chic, innovative, and always evolving. The prix-fixe lunch, consisting of three courses from the dinner menu, is an astounding $15—less expensive than the chicken wings place down the block. Imagine sitting down to a lunch of a salad of baby greens in a honey vinaigrette, then poached oysters with gingered caviar, then profiteroles. After dark, the prices escalate—it's a status place—except Wednesday, when a five-course wine dinner is $50. Locals love the complimentary amuse bouche and digestif. On Sunday there's a fab brunch with a jazz trio. ✉ *55 S. Market St., Market area* ☎ *843/534–2155* 🖃 *AE, D, MC, V.*

$$-$$$$ ✕ **Wentworth Grill.** A continental flair prevails in this dining room with ceiling-to-floor windows, a handsome fireplace, and a mesmerizing pattern in the mosaic-tile floor. The cuisine begins in France with dishes like escargot and leeks sautéed in Pernod and stuffed in a puff pastry, then travels around the Mediterranean with offerings such as grouper with pancetta, arugula, and white beans. It returns to the Lowcountry with the bourbon–mustard barbecued scallops and pecan-dressed mustard greens. On Sunday there's a popular jazz brunch. ✉ *Renaissance Charleston Hotel, 68 Wentworth St., Ansonborough* ☎ *843/534–0300* 🖃 *AE, DC, MC, V.*

$$$ ✕ **FIG.** Acronyms are popular here; the name, for instance, stands for Food Is Good. Chef Michael Lata's mantra is KIS, a reminder for him to Keep It Simple. Spend an evening here for fresh-off-the-farm ingredients cooked with unfussy, flavorful finesse. The menu changes frequently, but the family-style vegetables might be young beets in sherry vinegar placed in a plain, white bowl. But his dishes do get more complex: there's the pureed cauliflower soup with pancetta, incredible veal sweetbreads with crusty morels, and black grouper with a perfect golden crust. The servers are pros, well informed, and make eating here fun. The bar scene is lively. ✉ *232 Meeting St., Market area* ☎ *843/805–5900* 🖃 *AE, D, DC, MC, V* ◷ *No lunch.*

$$-$$$ ✕ **Cru Café.** The laid-back dining room is one reason to come to this cheery yellow house, but another is the inventive menu. Fried chicken breasts are topped with poblano peppers and mozzarella, and the duck confit is served with carmelized pecans and goat cheese, topped with fried shoestring onions, and dressed with port-wine vingagrette. Chef

John Zucker likes to go heavy on the starches, and his flavorful whipped potates are made with heavy cream. Meat dishes come with sauces made with green peppercorns, port wine, pear sherry, chipotle peppers, and horseradish. ⊠ *18 Pinckney St., Market area* ☎ *843/534–2434* ▭ *AE, D, DC, MC, V* ☾ *Closed Sun. and Mon.*

$$–$$$ ✕ **Old Village Post House.** If you've been on the road too long, this circa-1888 inn will provide warmth and sustenance. Many residents of this tree-lined village consider this their neighborhood tavern. The second, smaller dining room is cozy, and the outdoor space under the market umbrellas is open and airy. Expect contemporary takes on Southern favorites. Frank Sinatra serenades as you sample the fried eggplant Napoléon and the sautéed sea bass with fried green tomatoes and the city's best succotash. In season, plump soft-shell crabs are deftly fried. And you'll love thyme ice cream! ⊠ *101 Pitt St., Mount Pleasant* ☎ *843/388–8935* ▭ *AE, MC, V.*

$$ ✕ **Five Loaves Cafe.** At this café tucked in the back of Millennium Music, the food is as fresh as that sold at the farmers' market in nearby Marion Square. Each day there are five new soups—if you're lucky, one of them will be pureed eggplant. A favorite is the spinach salad with grilled polenta croutons, fresh mozzerella, and toasted almonds. The mix-and-match lunch options are ideal, particularly for small appetites. For $7.50 you can choose a cup of soup or a small salad and half a sandwich. Everything is super healthful (if you can forgo the sinful desserts). ⊠ *372 King St., Upper King* ☎ *843/805–7977* ⊠ *Blvd., Mount Pleasant* ☎ *843/937–1043* ▭ *AE, DC, MC, V.*

$–$$ ✕ **Sermet's Corner.** Bold artwork by Chef Sermet Aslan decorates the walls of this lively eatery. The dining room's plate-glass windows look out onto the King Street shopping district. Sermet gets artistic in the kitchen, which means the Mediterranean menu is speckled with innovations. The poached pear and salmon salad and lavender pork are favorites, as is the calamari with fennel. ⊠ *276 King St., Market area* ☎ *843/853–7775* ▭ *AE, MC, V.*

French

★ $$–$$$ ✕ **La Fourchette.** French owner Perig Goulet moves agilely through the crowded dining room of this bistro, one of the newest on the scene. With back-to-back chairs making it, well, cozy, this place could be in Paris. Kevin Kelly, formerly of Vintage, chooses the wines—predominately French and esoteric, but befitting the authentic fare. Perig boasts of his country pâté, from a recipe handed down from his *grand-mère*. Other favorites include duck salad, scallops sautéed in cognac, and shrimp in a leek sauce. Dieters may be shocked by the golden *frites* fried in duck fat and served with aioli, but they keep putting their hungry hands in the basket. Check the blackboard for fish straight off the boats. ⊠ *432 King St., Upper King* ☎ *843/722–6261* ▭ *AE, DC, MC, V* ☾ *Closed Sun. No lunch mid-June–Sept.*

$$–$$$ ✕ **39 Rue de Jean.** In classic French-bistro style—gleaming wood, cozy booths, and white-papered tables—Charleston's trendy set wines and dines until late on such favorites as steamed mussels in a half-dozen preparations. Order them with *pomme frites*, as the French do. Each night of

the week there is a special, such as the bouillabaisse on Sunday. Rabbit with a whole-grain mustard sauce was so popular it jumped to the nightly menu. Those seeking quiet should ask for a table in the dining room on the right. It's noisy—but so much fun—at the bar, especially since it has the city's best bartenders. ⊠ *39 John St., Upper King* ☎ *843/ 722–8881* ⌀ *Reservations essential* ▭ *AE, D, DC, MC, V.*

$$ ✕ **Coco's Cafe.** A nondescript strip mall hosts this gem of a bistro. Make the trip over the bridge to Mount Pleasant for freshly made duck pâté, escargot in garlic butter, rabbit in a red wine and mushroom sauce, and panfried flounder in brown butter. Prices are less inflated here than downtown. The $10.95 prix-fixe lunch includes soup or salad, a main course, *and* a glass of wine. ⊠ *863 Houston Northcutt Blvd., Mount Pleasant* ☎ *843/881–4949* ▭ *AE, MC, V* ☺ *Closed Sun.*

$–$$ ✕ **Gaulart and Maliclet Café.** Sharing high, family-style tables for breakfast, lunch, or dinner leads to camraderie at this bistro. Thursday brings crowd for fondue. The cheese fondue is disappointing, but the seafood, which you cook yourself in broth, is better. Nightly specials, such as bouillabaisse and couscous, are reasonably priced and come with a petite glass of wine. The subtly sweet chocolate mousse cake is the best. ⊠ *98 Broad St., South of Broad* ☎ *843/577–9797* ▭ *AE, D, MC, V* ☺ *Closed Sun. No dinner Mon.*

Italian

$$$–$$$$ ✕ **Fulton Five.** In the antique district, this romantic restaurant has chartreuse walls and antique brass accents. In warm weather you can opt for a seat on the second-floor terrace. Either way, the northern Italian specialties are worth savoring. Mushroom risotto with sweet corn accompanies the beef with porcini mushrooms. There's pappardelle with rabbit, and crabmeat and tarragon-laced butter flavor the spinach gnocchi. ⊠ *5 Fulton St., Lower King St.* ☎ *843/853–5555* ⌀ *Reservations essential* ▭ *AE, DC, MC, V* ☺ *Closed Sun. and late Aug.–early Sept. No lunch.*

★ **$$–$$$$** ✕ **Sienna.** Sumptuous meals here have all the flavor and flair befitting a celebrity chef—but without the pomp. Ken Vedrinski, who earned the Woodlands rave reviews, opened this laid-back eatery in 2004. You may taste things you have never heard of before, such as his "deconstructed" tiramisu that separates the cake, the gelato, and the panacotta. Four- and seven-course tasting menus are the way to dine. Well worth the drive over the bridges, it's the best of downtown dining, minus the crowding and price markups. ⊠ *901 Island Park Dr., Daniel Island* ☎ *843/881–9211* ▭ *AE, MC, V* ☺ *Closed Sun. No lunch weekends.*

$$–$$$ ✕ **Il Cortile del Re.** Hearty soups and pastas, fresh cheeses and breads, and great wines make this a slice of Tuscany. This trattoria has an Italian-born chef whose dishes couldn't be more authentic: braised lamb shank, porcini-mushroom ravioli, baby arugula salad. An expansion to this charming old building, which has lots of character, added streetfront views. The animated bar is popular with locals. ⊠ *193A King St., Lower King St.* ☎ *843/853–1888* ▭ *MC, V* ☺ *Closed Sun. No lunch Sun.–Wed.*

Kosher

$–$$$$ ✕ **Pita King.** The renderings of typical Middle Eastern dishes—falafel, hummus, and *shawarma* (a type of gyro)—are uncommonly good at the city's only fully glatt kosher establishment. The baba ghanoush is excellent, as is the Israeli salad. ⊠ *437 King St., Upper King* ☎ *843/722–1977 or 843/224–5100* ▭ *AE, D, MC, V* ☉ *Closed Sat. and Jewish holidays. No dinner Fri.*

Lowcountry & Southern

$$$$ ✕ **Charleston Grill.** Club chairs, dark paneling, and live jazz create a so-
Fodor'sChoice   phisticated home for Bob Waggoner's ground-breaking New South cui-
★   sine. This affable and highly talented chef raised the culinary bar in this town, and continues to provide what many think of as its highest gastronomic experience. He accepts only the best possible product, like the organic ingredients in the golden beet salad. His love of the Lowcountry means that there will always be dishes like the "uptown" Frogmore Stew. Desserts are divine creations like praline parfait. The sommelier, Rick Rubel, is stellar. ⊠ *Charleston Place Hotel, 224 King St., Market area* ☎ *843/577–4522* ⌕ *Reservations essential* ▭ *AE, D, DC, MC, V* ☉ *No lunch.*

$$$–$$$$ ✕ **Anson.** Nearly a dozen windows afford views of passing horse-drawn carriages from this restaurant. The softly lighted, gilt-trim dining room is extremely romantic. Southern specialties are favored, like shrimp and grits (served as an appetizer) and oysters fried in cornmeal (on the bar menu). The she-crab soup is some of the best around. The chef takes liberty with Lowcountry classics, like the crispy flounder in apricot sauce and the roasted red snapper with succotash and shrimp. ⊠*12 Anson St., Market area* ☎ *843/577–0551* ▭ *AE, D, DC, MC, V* ☉ *No lunch.*

$$$–$$$$ ✕ **Carolina's.** On a quiet side street between East Bay Street and Waterfront Park, this longtime favorite occupies a former wharf building. The smartened-up decor includes banquettes and some walls done in red velvet. The evolving menu by Chef Tin Dizdarevic has a strong emphasis on things natural and healthful. Well-known Lowcountry flavors still reign: avocado salsa with black-eyed pea cakes; shrimp-paste and green-tomato grits next to fried quail; and sweet potato–covered flounder spiced up with green apples. ⊠ *10 Exchange St., South of Broad* ☎ *843/724–3800* ⌕ *Reservations essential* ▭ *D, MC, V* ☉ *No lunch.*

★ **$$$–$$$$**   ✕ **High Cotton.** Lazily spinning paddle fans, palm trees, and brick walls make you feel like you're on a plantation. Chef Jason Scholz combines wonderful flavors and flawless presentation for memorable meals. His take on foie gras, for example, is a terrine with port-wine cherry chutney. You can feast on bourbon-glazed pork and white-cheddar grits. The chocolate soufflé with blackberry sauce and the praline soufflé are fabulous; live jazz further sweetens the scene. ⊠ *199 E. Bay St., Market area* ☎ *843/724–3815* ⌕ *Reservations essential* ▭ *AE, D, DC, MC, V* ☉ *No lunch weekdays.*

$$$–$$$$ ✕ **Magnolias.** The theme here is evident in the vivid paintings of creamy white blossoms that adorn the walls. A visit from Oprah Winfrey revived this culinary landmark, but many locals, particularly the younger

CLOSE UP

Lowcountry Cuisine

COLONIAL SETTLERS TO CHARLES TOWNE found maritime forests, winding rivers, and vast marshes along a flat coastal plain, which came to be called the Lowcountry. This expansive backyard provided a cornucopia of sustenance—seafood, game, and produce—and the recipes French and English settlers brought from their homeland were altered to match the ingredients found here. After slaves were brought in from the West Indies and West Africa to work the rice fields, the Gullah language—a rollicking creole of English with African words and accents—and culture developed. Because blacks and whites were in such close proximity (slaves outnumbered whites for generations), the two groups' languages, accents, and cuisines melded. The mix of continental recipes and African flavors, made by using the harvest of the region, became known as Lowcountry cooking.

Rice, rice, and more rice is ever-present in Lowcountry dishes, including *pilau*, also spelled *purlieu* (both pronounced pur-*low*), which is a pilaf—rice cooked in meat or vegetable broth. Salty-sweet shrimp and grits is on menus of every price category in Charleston. You can buy creamy she-crab soup in restaurants and stores. Other essential dishes are Hoppin' John (rice and beans), and Frogmore Stew (with shrimp, sausage, and corn). Okra, eggplant, *hominy* (cooked grits), tomatoes, butterbeans, benne seeds, ham, shrimp, fish, and game are all part of the regional cuisine. Southern favorites like fried green tomatoes, fried fish and oysters, bacon-wrapped shad roe, and stuffed quail are popular here, too. But Charleston cuisine is not all about things past; true to the spirit of Lowcountry cooking, town chefs continue to innovate and create using the local harvest of farm-fresh heirloom vegetables and seafood caught daily just offshore.

---

ones, prefer its younger sibling, Cypress. Executive Chef Don Drake refreshes classic dishes like fried green tomatoes (adding a dash of jalapeño) and cheddar grits with country ham (serving it with tomato chutney). As for the mains, his grilled filet is topped with pimento cheese, fried potato cake, and a madeira sauce. Brunch is served Sunday. ✉ *185 E. Bay St., Market area* ☎ *843/577–7771* ⚱ *Reservations essential* ▤ *AE, DC, MC, V.*

★ **$$$–$$$$** ✕ **Slightly North of Broad.** This former warehouse with brick-and-stucco walls has a chef's table that looks directly into the open kitchen. It's a great place to perch, as Chef Frank Lee, who wears a baseball cap while at work, is one of the city's culinary characters. Known for his talent in preparing game, his venison is exceptional. One of his signature dishes is maverick grits with scallops, shrimp, ham, and smoked sausage. Many of the items come as small plates, which make them perfect for sharing. Lunch is a great value: imagine braised lamb shanks with a ragout of white beans for an unbelievable $9.95. ✉ *192 E. Bay St., Market area* ☎ *843/723–3424* ▤ *AE, D, DC, MC, V* ☾ *No lunch weekends.*

$$–$$$ ✕ **Blossom.** Exposed white rafters and linenless tables make this place casual and yet upscale. The terrace, with a view of St. Philip's majestic spire, the dining room, and the bar are heavily populated with young professionals. The open kitchen adds to the high-energy atmosphere. The pastas are made on the premises, with the crab ravioli with porcini mushroom cream being particularly popular. Lowcountry seafood is a specialty, too, but with a contemporary spin. ⊠ *171 E. Bay St., Market area* ☎ *843/772–9200* ☰ *AE, DC, MC, V.*

★ **$$–$$$** ✕ **Gullah Cuisine.** Charlotte Jenkins cooks up a mean lunch buffet stocked with fried chicken, collard greens with ham, crispy okra, and macaroni pie. But it's the Gullah dishes—with roots in African cuisines—that make her place unique. The Gullah rice—with chicken, sausage, shrimp, and vegetables—and the fried alligator tails are both delightful lessons in regional flavors. Dinner options have expanded to include lobster. ⊠ *1717 U.S. 17N, Mount Pleasant* ☎ *843/881–9076* ☰ *AE, MC, V* ⊘ *Closed Sun.*

$–$$$ ✕ **Hominy Grill.** The wooden barber poles from the last century still frame the door of this small, homespun café. Chalkboard specials are often the way to go here, be it breakfast, lunch, or dinner. Chef Robert Stehling is a Carolina boy who lived in New York; that dichotomy shows in his "uptown" comfort food. Have the perfect soft-shell crab sandwich with homemade fries, but leave room for the tangy buttermilk pie or the chocolate peanut butter pie. The young servers are sometimes frantic. ⊠ *207 Rutledge Ave., Canonboro* ☎ *843/937–0930* ☰ *AE, MC, V* ⊘ *No dinner Sun.*

$–$$$ ✕ **J. Bistro.** Funky steel cutouts liven up outside and inside walls, and quirky lights hang low over tables. A varied list of appetizers and small plates makes this a great place to graze. Main dishes include pistachio-encrusted duck breast with a cassis glaze or loin of lamb with lingonberry port-wine sauce. Sunday Brunch has heavenly choices like crab cakes Benedict. ⊠ *819 Coleman Blvd., Mount Pleasant* ☎ *843/971–7778* ⌸ *Reservations essential* ☰ *AE, MC, V* ⊘ *Closed Mon. No lunch Tues.–Sat.*

$–$$$ ✕ **Sticky Fingers.** The sound of blues and the aroma of ribs reaches the street—where you may have to wait to get seated at this family-oriented chain restaurant. The barbecued pulled pork is popular, but the ribs are *it*. You have your choice of five different sauces, including some made with honey or bourbon. ⊠ *235 Meeting St., Market area* ☎ *843/853–7427* ⊠ *341 Johnnie Dodds Blvd., Mount Pleasant* ☎ *843/856–9840* ⊠ *1200 N. Main St., Summerville* ☎ *843/875–7969* ☰ *AE, DC, MC, V.*

¢–$$ ✕ **Boulevard Diner.** This former Dairy Queen is now a no-frills counter-and-booth diner. The service is attentive, but the waitresses don't call you hon. The food, soulfully prepared, includes a fried eggplant-and-blue-cheese sandwich, Cajun-style meat loaf, and chili served in a sundae glass with sour cream and a cherry tomato on top. ⊠ *409 W. Coleman Blvd., Mount Pleasant* ☎ *843/216–2611* ☰ *MC, V* ⊘ *Closed Sun.*

¢–$$ ✕ **Jestine's Kitchen.** Enjoy dishes made from passed-down family recipes—like sweet chicken with limas—at the last of the true down-home, blue-plate Southern restaurants in the historic district. This casual eatery is known for its fried everything: chicken, okra, shrimp, pork chops, and green tomatoes. The cola cake and coconut-cream pie are divine. ✉ *251 Meeting St., Upper King* ☎ *843/722–7224* ▤ *MC, V* ◷ *Closed Mon.*

Pizza

$ ✕ **Andolini's Pizza.** A cheap-date spot, Andolini's caters to college students who hide out in tall booths or on the rear patio. The dough and sauce are made daily, and the cheese is freshly grated. Toppings include the expected, plus banana peppers, feta, jalapeños, and extra-tasty Italian sausage. Call in advance for take-out. ✉ *82 Wentworth St., College of Charleston Campus* ☎ *843/722–7437* ▤ *AE, D, MC, V.*

Seafood

$$–$$$$ ✕ **Boathouse Restaurant.** Large portions of fresh seafood at reasonable prices make both Charleston-area locations wildly popular. The shrimp hush puppies with spicy mayonnaise, grilled fish with specialty sauces, and lightly battered fried shrimp and oysters are irresistible. Entrées come with mashed potatoes, grits, collard greens, or blue-cheese coleslaw. The original Isle of Palms location is right on the water, so seating is hard to come by. Brunch is served Sunday. ✉ *101 Palm Blvd., Isle of Palms* ☎ *843/886–8000* ✉ *549 E. Bay St., Upper King* ☎ *843/577–7171* ⌕ *Reservations essential* ▤ *AE, DC, MC, V* ◷ *No lunch Mon.–Sat.*

$$–$$$$ ✕ **Coast Bar & Grill.** Tucked off a little alley in a restored warehouse, Coast has pared-down trappings like exposed brick-and-wood floors. Fried fare and heavy sauces are on the menu, but lighter dishes such as the fish tacos and ceviche make it a standout. The best choices include oak-grilled fish and lobster served with pineapple-chili salsa, white-wine-and-lemon sauce, or garlic butter. ✉ *39D John St., Upper King* ☎ *843/722–8838* ▤ *AE, D, DC, MC, V* ◷ *No lunch.*

$$–$$$$ ✕ **Hank's Seafood.** A lively spot with a popular bar and community dining area flanked by paper-topped private tables, Hank's is an upscale fish house. Seafood platters come with sweet-potato fries and coleslaw. Fishes include grouper, snapper, and tuna. That location off the Old Market, and the fact it's sister restaurant to the fancy-pants Peninsula Grill, makes the place noteworthy. ✉ *Church and Hayne Sts., Market area* ☎ *843/723–3474* ▤ *AE, D, DC, MC, V* ◷ *Closed Mon. No lunch.*

$$–$$$ ✕ **Charleston Crab House.** When you cross over the Wapoo Creek Bridge to James Island, you catch a glimpse of this tiered restaurant. Its decks are splashed by the waters of the Intracoastal Waterway. Boaters tie up and mingle with the fun crowd. Crab is the specialty, of course, with she-crab soup a perennial award winner. There's also good crab cakes and baked oysters. ✉ *125A Wapoo Creek Dr., James Island* ☎ *843/795–1963* ✉ *1101 Stockade La., Mount Pleasant* ☎ *843/884–1617* ✉ *41 S. Market St., Market area* ☎ *843/853–2900* ▤ *AE, DC, MC, V.*

★ $$–$$$ ✕ **The Wreck of the Richard and Charlene.** At first glance you think the name refers to the waterfront restaurant—a shabby, screened-in porch and small dining area. In actuality, the *Richard and Charlene* was a trawler that slammed into the building during a hurricane in 1989. The kitchen serves up Southern tradition on a plate: boiled peanuts, fried shrimp, and stone crab claws. The best deal is the most expensive, the $18 platter with fried flounder, shrimp, oysters and scallops. ⊠ *106 Haddrell St., Mount Pleasant* ☎ *843/884–0052* ⚐ *Reservations not accepted* ▭ *No credit cards* ⊘ *No lunch.*

$–$$$ ✕ **Bubba Gump.** If you loved Forrest, Jenny, Lieutenant Dan, and the others from *Forrest Gump,* then head to this chain restaurant. The food, particularly the shrimp with mango-pineapple salsa, is surprisingly good. The shrimp New Orleans will satisfy you, as will the charbroiled mahimahi with shrimp in a lemon-butter sauce. You won't be able to resist the chocolate-chip-cookie sundae. Children who weren't even born when the movie came out in 1994 adore the Gumpisms scrawled on the dining room tables. ⊠ *96 S. Market St., Market area* ☎ *843/ 723–5665* ▭ *AE, DC, MC, V.*

Steak

$$$$ ✕ **Grill 225.** Expect hefty portions and upscale renderings of steakhouse favorites, accompanied by silver pitchers of special barbecue sauces. Blue-crab chowder and the seared tuna tower are superior starters. The veal chop stuffed with prosciutto and provolone is a revered house specialty. The pastry chef shines; the banana-bread pudding with caramel ice cream and the molten chocolate cake with raspberry couli are the best sweet flings. Wood floors, white linens, and red-velvet upholstery add to the elegance. ⊠ *Market Pavilion Hotel, 225 E. Bay St., Market area* ☎ *843/266–4222* ▭ *AE, D, DC, MC, V.*

$$$–$$$$ ✕ **Oak Steakhouse.** In a 150-year-old bank building, this dining room juxtaposes old crystal chandeliers with contemporary art. It's pricey, but the filet mignon with a foie-gras-black-truffle butter is excellent and the side dishes, such as creamed spinach, are perfectly executed. Favorite appetizers include beef carpaccio and gorgonzola fondue. The bar is definitely a place to see and be seen. A Cuban band electrifies Friday night. ⊠ *17 Broad St., Market area* ☎ *843/722–4220* ▭ *AE, MC, V* ⊘ *Closed Sun. No lunch.*

Tex-Mex

¢   ✕ **Juanita Greenberg's Nacho Royale.** Fast and fresh are the priorities here. Order a brick-size burrito, or try the tasty quesadillas. Wash down the Royale Nachos (steak, salsa, black beans, black olives, jalapeños, and cheese) with a Mexican soda or a foamy draft. ⊠ *439 King St., Upper King* ☎ *843/723–6224* ▭ *AE, D, MC, V.*

WHERE TO STAY

In a city known for its old mansions, atmospheric bed-and-breakfasts are found in the residential blocks of the historic district. Upscale hotels are in the heart of downtown. Unique, boutique hotels provide a one-of-a-kind experience. Chain hotels line the busy, car-trafficked areas (like Meeting Street). In addition, there are chain properties in the nearby areas of West Ashley, Mount Pleasant, and North Charleston.

Prices

Charleston's downtown lodgings have three seasons: high season (spring, March to May and fall, September to November); mid-season (summer,

June to August); and low season (late November to February). Prices drop significantly during the short low season, except during holidays and special events; high season is summer at the island resorts; rates drop for weekly stays and during off-season. ■ TIP→ **If you're on a budget, lodgings outside the city limits tend to be less expensive. Also try booking online, where you can often find good deals.**

	WHAT IT COSTS				
	$$$$	$$$	$$	$	¢
FOR 2 PEOPLE	over $220	$161–$220	$111–$160	$70–$110	under $70

Prices are for two people in a standard double room in high season.

Hotels & Motels

★ **$$$$** 🏨 **Charleston Place.** Even casual passersby enjoy gazing up at the hand-blown Moreno glass chandelier in the hotel's open lobby, clicking across the Italian marble floors, and admiring the antiques from Sotheby's. A gallery of upscale shops complete the ground floor. Rooms are furnished with period reproductions. The impeccable service is what you would expect from an Orient-Express property. A truly deluxe day spa, with an adjacent fitness room, has an inviting indoor pool illuminated by skylights. ■ TIP→ **Even if you aren't staying here, stop by for high tea at the equestrian-theme Thoroughbred Club.** ✉ *130 Market St., Market area, 29401* ☎ *843/722–4900 or 800/611–5545* 🖷 *843/724–7215* ⊕ *www.charlestonplacehotel.com* ⇆ *400 rooms, 42 suites* ⚐ *2 restaurants, room service, minibars, cable TV with movies, in-room broadband, indoor pool, health club, hot tub, spa, bar, lobby lounge, dry cleaning, concierge, concierge floor, business services, convention center, parking (fee), no-smoking rooms* ▭ *AE, D, DC, MC, V* ⍥ *EP.*

★ **$$$$** 🏨 **French Quarter Inn.** The first architectural detail you'll notice is a circular staircase with a wrought-iron bannister embellished with iron leaves. This award-winning property is known for its chic French style. Guests appreciate the lavish breakfasts, the afternoon wine and cheese, and evening cookies and milk. The pillow menu is a luxury; you can order whatever kind you desire, including big body pillows. Some rooms have fireplaces, others balconies. Among the best are No. 220, a business suite with a corner office niche overlooking the courtyard, and No. 104, with a spacious L-shape design. ✉ *166 Church St., Market area, 29401* ☎ *843/722–1900 or 866/812–1900* 🖷 *843/722–5682* ⊕ *www.fqicharleston.com* ⇆ *46 rooms, 4 suites* ⚐ *Restaurant, room service, cable TV with movies, in-room broadband, Wi-Fi, bar, dry cleaning, concierge, business services, meeting rooms, parking (fee), no-smoking* ▭ *AE, MC, V* ⍥ *BP.*

★ **$$$$** 🏨 **Market Pavilion Hotel.** The melee of one of the busiest corners in the city vanishes as soon as the uniformed bellman opens the lobby door to dark, wood-panel walls, antique furniture, and chandeliers hung from high ceilings. It resembles a grand hotel from the 19th century—there are even 3 mi of plaster moldings. Get used to being pampered—smartly attired bellmen and butlers are quick at hand. Room amenities

5

include French-style chaises and magnificent marble baths. One of Charleston's most prestigious fine-dining spots, Grill 225, is here. ■ TIP→ Join sophisticated Charlestonians who *do* cocktails at the rooftop **Pavilion Bar.** ⊠ *225 E. Bay St., Market area, 29401* ☎ *843/723–0500 or 877/440–2250* 🖷 *843/723–4320* ⊕ *www.marketpavilion.com* ⤶ *61 rooms, 9 suites* ♨ *Restaurant, café, room service, in-room fax, cable TV, in-room broadband, pool, bar, babysitting, dry cleaning, concierge, concierge floor, Internet room, travel services, parking (fee); no smoking* ▭ *AE, D, DC, MC, V* ⋈ *EP.*

$$$$ ▥ **Renaissance Charleston Hotel Historic District.** A sense of history prevails in this hotel, one of Charleston's newest upscale properties. Legend has it that British Admiral George Anson won this neighborhood, dubbed Ansonborough, in a card game in 1726. (Which is probably why his image is one the playing cards in the library lounge.) This upscale Marriott property has a warm, caring staff, a pool, and gentile characteristics such as guest rooms, which are smallish but have nice touches like period-style bonnet beds. The Wentworth Grill serves a mix of French and Lowcountry specialties. ⊠ *68 Wentworth St., Ansonborough, 29401* ☎ *843/534–0300* 🖷 *843/534–0700* ⊕ *www. renaissancecharlestonhotel.com* ⤶ *163 rooms, 3 suites* ♨ *Restaurant, room service, cable TV with movies, in-room data ports, Web TV, Wi-Fi, pool, health club, bar, concierge, business center, meeting rooms, parking (fee), no smoking rooms* ▭ *AE, D, DC, MC, V* ⋈ *EP.*

$$$–$$$$ ▥ **Charleston Harbor Resort & Marina.** Mount Pleasant's finest hotel sits on Charleston Harbor, so you can gaze at the city's skyline. If you'd rather be there, a water taxi will get you across in 10 minutes. A lot goes on here, from splashy boat shows at the marina to wedding celebrations on the white sand. Ask for one of the renovated rooms with fireplaces and plasma TVs. Children can jump into the mini-mariners' program, while parents are navigating a sailboat. ⊠ *20 Patriots Point Rd., Mount Pleasant, 29464* ☎ *843/856–0028 or 888/856–0028* 🖷 *843/856–8333* ⊕ *www. charlestonharborresort.com* ⤶ *160 rooms, 6 suites* ♨ *Restaurant, cable TV, Wi-Fi, pool, hot tub, marina, boating, bar, children's programs (ages 7–12), free parking, some pets allowed (fee)* ▭ *AE, DC, MC, V* ⋈ *BP.*

$$$–$$$$ ▥ **Doubletree Guest Suites Historic Charleston.** This one-time bank wears a restored entrance portico from 1874. Fountains bubble in the three interior garden courtyards. This is not a glamorous property, but it has clean, spacious suites with nice touches like antique reproductions and canopy beds. The efficient and friendly staff dotes on families and dispense chocolate-chip cookies. ⊠ *181 Church St., Market area, 29401* ☎ *843/577–2644 or 877/408–8733* 🖷 *843/577–2697* ⊕ *www.doubletree. com* ⤶ *47 rooms, 165 suites* ♨ *Some microwaves, some refrigerators, cable TV with movies, in-room broadband, Wi-Fi, gym, lounge, shop, laundry facilities, business services, meeting room, parking (fee), no-smoking rooms* ▭ *AE, D, DC, MC, V* ⋈ *EP.*

$$$–$$$$ ▥ **Embassy Suites Historic Charleston.** A courtyard where cadets once marched is now an atrium with skylights, palm trees, and a fountain. The restored brick walls of the breakfast room and some guest rooms in this contemporary hotel contain original gun ports, reminders that the 1822 building was the Old Citadel. Handsome teak and mahogany furniture and sisal rugs in the common areas recall the British-colonial era. Guest rooms are not nearly as chic, but are clean and serviceable. *⊠ 337 Meeting St., Upper King, 29403 ☎ 843/723–6900 or 800/ 362–2779 ⊟ 843/723–6938 ⊕www.embassysuites.com ↩153 suites ⌂ Restaurant, room service, some in-room hot tubs, kitchenettes, cable TV with movies and video games, Wi-Fi, pool, gym, outdoor hot tub, lounge, shop, babysitting, laundry facilities, business services, meeting rooms, parking (fee), no-smoking rooms ☰ AE, D, DC, MC, V ⎮O⎮ BP.*

> **DOGGIE DAY CARE**
>
> If you have brought your dog along, but don't want to leave him in your room all day, call Charlie Freeman at **Dog Daze** (⊠ 307 Mill St., Mount Pleasant ☎ 843/844–7387). His services are $20 a day. With advance notice he'll even pick up Rover at your hotel for an additional $10.

$$$–$$$$ 🏨 **HarbourView Inn.** Ask for a room facing the harbor and you can gaze down at the landmark pineapple fountain of Waterfront Park. Calming earth tones and rattan soothe and relax; four-poster beds and sea-grass rugs complete the Lowcountry look. Some of the rooms are in a former 19th-century shipping warehouse with exposed brick walls, plantation shutters, and whirlpool tubs. Afternoon wine and cheese and evening milk and cookies are included. *⊠ 2 Vendue Range, Market area, 29401 ☎ 843/853–8439 or 888/853–8439 ⊟ 843/853–4034 ⊕ www. harbourviewcharleston.com ↩52 rooms ⌂ Some in-room hot tubs, some minibars, cable TV, Wi-Fi, concierge, Internet room, business services, parking (fee), no-smoking rooms ☰ AE, D, DC, MC, V ⎮O⎮ BP.*

$$$–$$$$ 🏨 **Mills House.** A favorite local landmark, the Mills House is reconstruction of an 1853 hotel where Robert E. Lee waved from the wrought-iron balcony. All of the guest rooms have been completely refurbished and have nice touches like antique reproductions. There are some additions to the original design, such as a fitness center and a delightful pool deck. Lowcountry specialties are served in the Barbados Room, which opens onto the terrace courtyard. *⊠ 115 Meeting St., Market area, 29401 ☎ 843/577–2400 or 800/874–9600 ⊟ 843/722–0623 ⊕ www. millshouse.com ↩199 rooms, 16 suites ⌂ Restaurant, room service, cable TV, Wi-Fi, pool, health club, bar, lounge, laundry service, concierge, concierge floor, Internet room, business services, meeting rooms, parking (fee), no-smoking rooms ☰ AE, D, DC, MC, V ⎮O⎮ EP.*

$$$ 🏨 **Francis Marion Hotel.** Wrought-iron railings, crown moldings, and decorative plasterwork speak of the elegance of 1924, when the Francis Marion was the largest hotel in the Carolinas. Bountiful throw pillows and billowy curtains add flair to the guest rooms, many of which have views of Marion Square. Some are small, however. Flavorful Lowcountry cuisine is served at the Swamp Fox. *⊠ 387 King St., Upper King, 29403 ☎ 843/722–0600 or 877/756–2121 ⊟ 843/723–4633 ⊕ www. francismarioncharleston.com ↩193 rooms, 34 suites ⌂ Restaurant, coffee shop, room service, cable TV, in-room data ports, Wi-Fi, gym, spa, lounge, shop, concierge, Internet room, business services, meeting rooms, parking (fee), no-smoking rooms ☰ AE, D, DC, MC, V ⎮O⎮ EP.*

$$$ ⊞ **Hampton Inn–Historic District.** Hardwood floors and a fireplace in the lobby of what was once an 1800s warehouse help elevate this chain hotel a bit above the rest. Spindle posts on the headboards give guest rooms a little personality. Rooms are not large but have little perks like coffeemakers. The location is perfect for exploring downtown. ⊠ *373 Meeting St., Upper King, 29403* ☎ *843/723–4000 or 800/426–7866* 🖷 *843/722–3725* ⊕ *www.hamptoninn.com* 🛏 *166 rooms, 5 suites* ⚒ *Some microwaves, some refrigerators, cable TV with movies, in-room data ports, pool, babysitting, laundry facilities, concierge, Internet room, business services, meeting rooms, travel services, parking (fee), no-smoking rooms* ⊟ *AE, D, DC, MC, V* ⦿ *BP.*

★ **$$$** ⊞ **Holiday Inn Historic District.** Thanks to its staff, this hotel has an outstanding track record for guest satisfaction. And then there's the great location—across from Marion Square and a block from Gaillard Auditorium. Rooms are traditional with wood armoires, headboards, and side tables. ⊠ *125 Calhoun St., Upper King, 29401* ☎ *843/805–7900 or 877/805–7900* 🖷 *843/805–7700* ⊕ *www.charlestonhotel.com* 🛏 *122 rooms, 4 suites* ⚒ *Restaurant, cable TV, in-room data ports, pool, bar, concierge, concierge floor, Internet room, business services, meeting rooms, parking (fee), no-smoking rooms* ⊟ *AE, D, DC, MC, V* ⦿ *BP.*

Inns, B&Bs & Guesthouses

To find rooms in homes, cottages, and carriage houses, contact **Historic Charleston Bed and Breakfast** (⊠ 60 Broad St., South of Broad ☎ 843/722–6606 ⊕ wwwhistoriccharlestonbedandbreakfast.com).

★ **$$$$** ⊞ **Governors House Inn.** This quintessential Charleston lodging radiates 18th-century elegance. Its stately architecture typifies the grandeur, romance, and civility of the city's bountiful colonial era. A National Historic Landmark, it is filled with family antiques and period reproductions in the public rooms and the high-ceiling guest rooms. The best room is the Rutledge Suite, a legacy to the original owner, Governor Edward Rutledge. Nice touches include a proper afternoon tea. ⊠ *117 Broad S., South of Broad, 29401* ☎ *843/720–2070 or 800/720–9812* 🖷 *843/805–6549* ⊕ *www.governorshouse.com* 🛏 *7 rooms, 4 suites* ⚒ *Dining room, Wi-Fi, cable TV, concierge, free parking, no-smoking rooms* ⊟ *AE, MC, V* ⦿ *BP.*

$$$$ ⊞ **Hayne House.** Vintage furnishings combine with a fresh, light spirit at Hayne House. Colonial brickwork, working fireplaces, and a narrow cypress stairway are characteristic of the mid-1700s, when the original wings were built. Ceilings in the guest rooms are low, and the bathrooms are small and need some work. A full Southern breakfast is served on English porcelain. The price is a bit high for what you get. ⊠ *30 King St., South of Broad, 29401* ☎ *843/577–2633* 🖷 *843/577–5906* ⊕ *www.haynehouse.com* 🛏 *4 rooms* ⚒ *Dining room, microwaves, minbars; no room phones, no room TVs, no smoking* ⊟ *MC, V* ⦿ *BP.*

★ **$$$$** ⊞ **John Rutledge House Inn.** In 1791 George Washington visited this elegant mansion, residence of one of South Carolina's most influential politicians, John Rutledge. This National Historic Landmark has spacious accommodations within the lovingly restored main house (Nos. 6, 8, and 11 are the most appealing). Solid painted walls—in forest green and buttercream yellow—complement the billowy fabrics on the four-poster beds. Parquet floors sit beneath 14-foot ceilings adorned with plaster moldings. Families gravitate to the privacy of the two carriage houses overlooking the shaded brick courtyard. Afternoon tea or port are served in the lounge. ⊠ *116 Broad St., South of Broad, 29401* ☏ *843/723–7999 or 800/476–9741* ⊟ *843/720–2615* ⊕ *www.charminginns. com* ↩ *16 rooms, 3 suites* ⟡ *Some in-room hot tubs, refrigerators, cable TV, Wi-Fi, concierge, business services, meeting room, parking (fee), no-smoking rooms* ⊟ *AE, D, DC, MC, V* ⦿*⊦ BP.*

★ **$$$$** ▦ **Planters Inn.** Part of the Relais & Châteaux group, this boutique property is a stately sanctuary amid the bustle of Charleston's Market. Light streams into a front parlor with its velvets and Oriental antiques. It serves as the lobby for this exclusive inn that has both an historic side and a new building wrapped around a two-story piazza and overlooking a tranquil garden courtyard. Yet the rooms all look similar, and are beautifully maintained. Service is gentile and unobtrusive, and the hospitality is genuine. Best choice rooms are those with fireplaces, or verandas, four-poster canopy beds, and the newer "piazza" suites with whirlpool baths. ⊠ *112 N. Market St., Market area, 29401* ☏ *843/722–2345 or 800/845–7082* ⊟ *843/577–2125* ⊕ *www.plantersinn.com* ↩ *56 rooms, 6 suites* ⟡ *Restaurant, room service, in-room safes, some in-room hot tubs, Wi-Fi, concierge, business services, meeting room, parking (fee), no-smoking floors* ⊟ *AE, D, DC, MC, V* ⦿*⊦ EP.*

$$$$ ▦ **Vendue Inn.** This lodging's rooftop restaurant and bar have sweeping views of the nearby waterfront (but rooms look out on a condo). Two 19th-century warehouses have been transformed into an inn with a variety of nooks and crannies filled with antiques. Bathrobes hang in the closet, and full buffet breakfast, afternoon wine and hors d' oeuvres, and evening milk and cookies are complimentary. ⊠ *19 Vendue Range, Market area, 29401* ☏ *843/577–7970 or 800/845–7900* ⊕*www. vendueinn.com* ↩ *31 rooms, 35 suites* ⟡ *Restaurant, some in-room safes, some in-room hot tubs, cable TV, Wi-Fi, bicycles, bar, business services, meeting room; no smoking* ⊟ *AE, D, DC, MC, V* ⦿*⊦ BP.*

$$$$ ▦ **Wentworth Mansion.** Charlestonian Francis Silas Rodgers made his
Fodor's Choice money in cotton, and in 1886 had built this four-story mansion with
★ such luxuries as Austrian crystal chandeliers and hand-carved marble mantles. Guests admire the Second Empire antiques and reproductions, the rich fabrics, and inset wood paneling. In the colder months, the baronial, high-ceiling guest rooms have the velvet drapes drawn and the gas fireplaces lighted. The breakfast buffet and evening wine and cheese are complimentary. Circa 1886, the restaurant shares the former carriage house with a spa. ⊠ *149 Wentworth St., College of Charleston Campus, 29403* ☏ *843/853–1886 or 888/466–1886* ⊟ *843/720–5290* ⊕ *www.wentworthmansion.com* ↩ *21 rooms* ⟡ *Restaurant, in-room hot tubs, spa, cable TV, in-room data ports, lounge, concierge, meeting rooms, free parking; no smoking* ⊟ *AE, D, DC, MC, V* ⦿*⊦ BP.*

$$$–$$$$ ▦ **Ansonborough Inn.** A shipping warehouse dating from the early 1900s, this building's architectural details have been emphasized by leaving brick walls exposed and designing around the grand, heart-pine beams and wood ceilings. Oil paintings of hunting dogs hang above clubby leather chairs and sofas. Guests enjoy evening wine and cheese on a rooftop terrace while they watch the ships sail past. ⊠ *21 Hasell St., Market area, 29401* ☎ *843/723–1655 or 800/522–2073* 🖷 *843/577–6888* ⊕ *www.ansonboroughinn.com* 🛏 *37 suites* 🕭 *In-room safes, microwaves, refrigerators, cable TV, in-room data ports, Wi-Fi, bar, business services, meeting room, parking (fee); no smoking* ⊟ *AE, MC, V* ⦿I *BP.*

$$$–$$$$ 🏨 **Cannonboro Inn and Ashley Inn.** These sister B&Bs on the edge of the historic district have a lot in common. At both inns expect a full breakfast served on a wide porch overlooking a garden, tea in the afternoon, and free use of bicycles. Rooms have antiques from the 19th century, when they were built. The pinkish Ashley Inn has a two-bedroom carriage house with kitchen, while the gray Cannonboro has one suite with a kitchen. ⊠ *Cannonboro Inn, 184 Ashley Ave., Medical University of South Carolina, 29403* ☎ *843/723–8572 or 800/235–8039* 🖷 *843/723–8007* ⊕ *www.charleston-sc-inns.com* 🛏 *7 rooms, 1 suite* 🕭 *Dining room, cable TV, bicycles, business services, free parking; no kids under 10, no smoking* ⊟ *AE, D, DC, MC, V* ⦿I *BP* ⊠ *Ashley Inn, 201 Ashley Ave., Medical University of South Carolina, 29403* ☎ *843/723–1848 or 800/581–6658* 🖷 *843/579–9080* ⊕ *www.charleston-sc-inns.com* 🛏 *6 rooms, 1 suite, 1 house* 🕭 *Dining room, some kitchenettes, cable TV, bicycles, business services, free parking; no room phones, no kids under 10, no smoking* ⊟ *AE, D, DC, MC, V* ⦿I *BP.*

$$$–$$$$ 🏨 **Phoebe Pember House.** The 1807 property is split between a carriage house with two guest rooms and a coach house with three guest rooms. The decor is tastefully done, and each room has nice touches like lace-covered canopy beds. The vibrant artwork is by Charleston artists. Enjoy breakfast in the walled garden shaded by an arbor. ⊠ *26 Society St., Ansonborough, 29401* ☎ *843/722–4186* 🖷 *843/722–0557* ⊕ *www.phoebepemberhouse.com* 🛏 *5 rooms* 🕭 *Cable TV, in-room data ports, hot tub, massage, free parking; no smoking* ⊟ *MC, V* ⦿I *BP.*

★ $$$–$$$$ 🏨 **Two Meeting Street.** As pretty as a wedding cake, this Queen Anne mansion has overhanging bays, colonnades, balustrades, and a turret. While rocking on the front porch you can look through soaring arches to White Point Gardens and the Ashley River. Tiffany windows, carved-oak paneling, and a crystal chandelier dress up the public spaces. Two guest rooms have balconies and working fireplaces. Expect to be treated to afternoon high tea. ⊠ *2 Meeting St., South of Broad, 29401* ☎ *843/723–7322* ⊕ *www.twomeetingstreet.com* 🛏 *9 rooms* 🕭 *Dining room; no room phones, no room TVs, no kids under 12, no smoking* ⊟ *No credit cards* ⦿I *BP.*

$$–$$$ 🏨 **Andrew Pinckney Inn.** The lobby of this boutique inn has a homey ambience that blends South Carolina and the West Indies. The two-story town-house suites, which sleep four, are ideal for longer stays. A heavenly breakfast with fresh-baked pastries and biscuits with sausage gravy is taken on its rooftop, which overlooks the church spires. It's in the bustling market area, so ask for an interior room. ☒ *40 Pinckney St., Market area, 29401* ☎ *843/937–8800 or 800/505–8983* 🖷 *843/937–8810* ⊕ *www.andrewpinckneyinn.com* ➷ *41 rooms, 3 town houses, 1 suite* ⟁ *Dining room, some in-room hot tubs, some kitchenettes, some refrigerators, cable TV, Wi-Fi, in-room data ports, laundry service, concierge, babysitting, Internet room, business services, parking (fee); no smoking* ▤ *AE, MC, V* ⦿❘ *BP.*

$$–$$$ ▣ **Broad Street Guesthouse.** Hadassah Rothenberg, an accomplished cook and baker, has realized her dream of opening the city's first kosher B&B. She completely transformed this 1880s frame house, artfully decorating it with a mix of Victorian furnishings, religious art, and vintage family photos. Friday evening guests can join in traditional prayers and partake in a multicourse Shabbat dinner. Rothenberg's glatt kosher dishes are lovely and fresh, the baked goods delectable. The wholesome breakfast is wonderful on the veranda. ☒ *133 Broad St., South of Broad, 29401* ☎ *843/577–5965* 🖷 *843/202–8601* ⊕ *www.charlestonkosherbedandbreakfast.com* ➷ *2 suites, 1 cottage* ⟁ *Dining room, kitchenettes, Wi-Fi, free parking; no room phones, no smoking* ▤ *AE, D, MC, V* ⦿❘ *BP.*

$$–$$$ ▣ **1837 Bed and Breakfast and Tea Room.** A hospitable staff helps you get a sense of what it would be like to live in one of Charleston's grand old homes. Antique lace-canopy beds fill much of the guest rooms, which are in the main house and in the carriage house. A delicious breakfast includes homemade breads and hot entrées such as sausage pie or ham frittatas. ☒ *126 Wentworth St., Market area, 29401* ☎ *843/723–7166 or 877/723–1837* 🖷 *843/722–7179* ⊕ *www.1837bb.com* ➷ *8 rooms, 1 suite* ⟁ *Refrigerators, cable TV; no room phones* ▤ *AE, DC, MC, V* ⦿❘ *BP.*

$$–$$$ ▣ **Elliott House Inn.** Listen to the chimes of St. Michael's Episcopal Church as you sip wine in the courtyard of this lovely inn in the heart of the historic district. You can then retreat to a cozy room with period furniture, including canopied four-posters and Oriental carpets. Some previous loyal guests complain that it has lost some of its personal, homey ambience since it was taken over by a corporate management company; others seem quite pleased with the change. ☒ *78 Queen St., Market area, 29401* ☎ *843/723–1855 or 800/729–1855* 🖷 *843/722–1567* ⊕ *www.elliotthouseinn.com* ➷ *24 rooms* ⟁ *Hot tub, bicycles; no kids, no smoking* ▤ *AE, D, MC, V* ⦿❘ *BP.*

$$–$$$ ▣ **Meeting Street Inn.** This 1874 house with second- and third-story porches originally had a tavern on the ground floor. Rooms overlook a lovely courtyard with fountains and a garden; many have hardwood floors and handwoven rugs. Four-poster or canopy beds, chair rails, and patterned wallpaper create a period feel. Despite its good downtown location, the inn has managed to keeps its prices affordable. ☒ *173 Meeting St., Market area, 29401* ☎ *843/723–1882 or 800/842–8022* 🖷 *843/577–0851* ⊕ *www.meetingstreetinn.com* ➷ *56 rooms* ⟁ *Some refrigerators, cable TV, Wi-Fi, outdoor hot tub, bar* ▤ *AE, D, DC, MC, V* ⦿❘ *BP.*

$$–$$$ 🏠 **Old Village Post House.** This white wooden building anchoring Mount Pleasant's historic district is a cozy inn, an excellent restaurant, and a neighborly tavern. Up the high staircase, rooms have hardwood floors and reproduction furnishings that will remind you of Cape Cod. The dark-wood furnishings feel right at home in a building with roots in the 1880s. The food is wonderful, from the pastries at breakfast to the entrées at dinner. Staying on this charming tree-lined village, you're within walking distance to Charleston Harbor. ✉ *101 Pitt St., Mount Pleasant 29464* ☎ *843/388–8935* 📠 *843/388–8937* ⊕ *www. oldvillageposthouse.com* 🛏 *6 rooms* ⚬ *Restaurant, dining room, fans, some in-room hot tubs, cable TV, bar, free parking; no smoking* ⊟ *AE, D, DC, MC, V* 🍽 *BP.*

¢   🏠 **Not So Hostel.** Several 1840s-era buildings were combined to make this hostel. Pancakes and waffles for breakfast, a garden where you can pick vegetables, and prices that put the rest of the city's lodgings to shame make this a great place to stay. Of course, you need to be able to handle a little peeling paint, a bit of clutter, and a less gentile neighborhood. Linens, a locker, and Internet access are free. ✉ *156 Spring St., Medical University of South Carolina, 29403* ☎ *843/722–8383* ⊕ *www.notsohostel.com* 🛏 *14 dorm beds, 7 rooms with communal baths* ⚬ *Dining room, bicycles, recreation room, laundry facilities, Internet room, free parking; no room phones, no room TVs, no smoking* ⊟ *AE, D, DC, MC, V* 🍽 *BP.*

Resorts

For condo and house rentals on Kiawah Island, Seabrook Island, Sullivan's Island, the Isle of Palms, and Wild Dunes, call **Resort Quest** (✉ *1517 Palm Blvd., Isle of Palms 29451* ☎ *800/344–5105* ⊕ *www. resortquest.com*).

★ $$$$ 🏠 **Wild Dunes Resort.** This 1,600-acre island resort has as its focal point the plantation-style Boardwalk Inn. It sits among a cluster of villas that have been painted in pastels to resemble Charleston's Rainbow Row. The guest rooms and suites on the fourth and fifth floors have balconies that overlook the ocean. You can also choose one- to six-bedroom villas that sit near the sea or the marshes. You have a long list of recreational options here including Tom Fazio golf courses and nationally ranked tennis programs; packages are available. Nearby is a yacht harbor on the Intracoastal Waterway. Chef Enzo Steffenelli reigns over the highly-rated Sea Island Grill. ✉ *Palm Blvd. at 41st Ave., Isle of Palms* ☊ *Box 20575, Charleston 29413* ☎ *843/886–6000 or 888/845–8926* 📠 *843/886–2916* ⊕ *www.wilddunes.com* 🛏 *430 units, 93 rooms* ⚬ *3 restaurants, ice-cream parlor, pizzeria, snack bar, fans, some in-room hot tubs, some minibars, cable TV, Wi-Fi, 2 18-hole golf courses, 17 tennis courts, 4 pools, health club, hair salon, massage, boating, fishing, bicycles, volleyball, lounge, video game room, children's programs (ages 3–12), concierge, Internet room, meeting rooms, airport shuttle, no-smoking rooms* ⊟ *AE, D, DC, MC, V* 🍽 *EP.*

$$–$$$$ 🏠 **Kiawah Island Golf Resort.** Choose from one- to four-bedroom villas and three- to seven-bedroom private homes in two upscale resort villages on 10,000 wooded and oceanfront acres. Or opt to stay at the Sanc-

FodorsChoice ★

tuary at Kiawah Island, an amazing 255-room luxury waterfront hotel and spa. The vast lobby is stunning, with walnut floors covered with handwoven rugs and a wonderful collection of artworks. The West-Indies theme is evident in the guest rooms; bedposts are carved with impressionistic pineapple patterns, and plantation-style ceilings with exposed planks are painted white. Along with the 10 mi of island beaches, recreational options include kayak and surfboard rental, nature tours, and arts-and-crafts classes. ⊠ *12 Kiawah Beach Dr., Kiawah Island 29455* ☎ *843/768–2121 or 800/654–2924* 🖷 *843/768–6099* ⊕ *www.kiawahresort.com* ⇥ *255 rooms, 600 villas and homes* ♨ *10 restaurants, room service, some in-room safes, some kitchens, some minibars, cable TV, some in-room VCRs, Wi-Fi, 5 18-hole golf courses, 28 tennis courts, pro shop, 4 pools, wading pool, health club, spa, beach, boating, fishing, bicycles, lounge, shops, children's programs (ages 3–12), concierge, concierge floor, Internet room, business services, convention center, parking (fee), no-smoking rooms* ☰ *AE, D, DC, MC, V* ⑩ *EP.*

$–$$$$ 🏨 **Seabrook Island.** The most private of the area's island resorts, Seabrook is endowed with true Lowcountry beauty. Wildlife sightings are common: look for white-tailed deer and even bobcats. Going to the beach is as popular as playing golf or tennis, but erosion has whisked away a lot of the sand. About 200 fully equipped one- to six-bedroom homes are available. The Beach Club and Island House are centers for dining and leisure activities. ⊠ *3772 Seabrook Island Rd., Seabrook Island 29455* ☎ *843/768–1000 or 800/845–2233* 🖷 *843/768–2361* ⊕ *www.seabrook. com* ⇥ *200 units* ♨ *3 restaurants, café, kitchens, cable TV, some in-room VCRs, 2 18-hole golf courses, 15 tennis courts, 2 pools, wading pool, fitness classes, gym, massage, beach, boating, fishing, bicycles, basketball, billiards, horseback riding, volleyball, 3 bars, video game room, shops, babysitting, children's programs (ages 4–17), playground, no-smoking rooms* ☰ *AE, D, DC, MC, V* ⑩ *EP.*

NIGHTLIFE & THE ARTS

The Arts

Concerts

The **Charleston Symphony Orchestra** (☎ 843/723–7528 ⊕ www.charlestonsymphony.com) season runs from October through April, with pops series, chamber series, family-oriented series, and holiday concerts.

Dance

Anonymity Dance Company (☎ 843/886–6104), a modern-dance troupe, performs throughout the city. The **Charleston Ballet Theatre** (⊠ 477 King St., Upper King ☎ 843/723–7334 ⊕ www.charlestonballet.com) performs everything from classical to contemporary dance. The **Robert Ivey Ballet Company** (☎ 843/556–1343 ⊕ www.cofc.edu), a semiprofessional company that includes College of Charleston students, puts on a fall and spring program of jazz, classical, and modern dance at the Sottile Theater.

CLOSE UP

Celebrating Charleston

SPOLETO USA IS ONLY THE BEGINNING—there are dozens of festivals held throughout the city each year. Some focus on food and wine, whereas others are concerned with gardens and architecture. The **Charleston Visitor Center** (✉ 375 Meeting St., Upper King 🚗 423 King St., 29403 ☎ 843/853-8000 or 800/868-8118 ⊕ www.charlestoncvb.com) can give you a complete list of annual events.

Charleston is one of the few American cities that can claim a distinctive regional cuisine. The **Distinctively Charleston Food & Wine Festival** (☎ 843/763-0280 or 866/369-3378 ⊕ www.charlestonfoodandwine.com) allows this important culinary city to "strut its stuff" at an annual festival. Some of the most sought-after events, such as the Restaurant Dine-Around with celebrity chefs, the Charleston Gospel Breakfast with entertainment by local gospel choirs, and the Celebration of Charleston with two-dozen top local restaurants serving their finest cuisine, sell out early. Reserve well in advance.

The **Fall Candlelight Tours of Homes and Gardens** (☎ 843/722-4630 ⊕ www.preservationsociety.org), sponsored by the Preservation Society of Charleston in September and October, provides an inside look at Charleston's private buildings and gardens.

More than 100 private homes, gardens, and historic churches are open to the public for tours during the **Festival of Houses and Gardens** (☎ 843/722-3405 ⊕ www.historiccharleston.org), held during March and April each year. There are also symphony galas in stately drawing rooms, plantation oyster roasts, and candlelight tours.

The **MOJA Arts Festival** (☎ 843/724-7305 ⊕ www.mojafestival.com), which takes place during the last week of September and first week of October, celebrates African heritage and Caribbean influences on African-American culture. It includes theater, dance, and music performances, art shows, films, lectures, and tours of the historic district.

Piccolo Spoleto (☎ 843/724-7305 ⊕ www.piccolospoleto.org) is the spirited companion festival of Spoleto Festival USA, showcasing the best in local and regional talent from every artistic discipline. There are hundreds of events—from jazz performances to puppet shows and expansive art shows in Marion Square—from mid-May through early June, and many of the best performances are free.

The **Southeastern Wildlife Exposition** (☎ 843/723-1748 or 800/221-5273 ⊕ www.sewe.com) in mid-February is one of Charleston's biggest annual events, with fine art by renowned wildlife artists, live animals, an oyster roast, and a gala.

Spoleto USA (☎ 843/722-2764 ⊕ www.spoletousa.org), founded by the composer Gian Carlo Menotti in 1977, is a world-famous celebration of the arts and Charleston's premiere cultural event. From late May to early June, the city teems with events from sunup to well past sundown. Concert halls, theaters, parks, churches, streets, and gardens become the stage for opera, dance, theater, symphonic and chamber music, jazz, and the visual arts.

Film

The **IMAX Theater** (✉ 360 Concord St., Upper King ☎ 843/725–4629) is next to the South Carolina Aquarium.

Theater

Charleston Stage Company (✉ 135 Church St., Market area ☎ 843/965–4032 ⊕ www.charlestonstage.com) performs at the Dock Street Theatre. The **Footlight Players** (✉ 20 Queen St., Market area ☎ 843/722–4487 ⊕ www.footlightplayers.net) regularly perform fun plays and musicals.

Venues

Bluegrass, blues, and country musicians grace the stage at **Charleston Music Hall** (✉ 37 John St., Upper King ☎ 843/853–2252 ⊕ www.charlestonmusichall.com).

Gaillard Municipal Auditorium (✉ 77 Calhoun St., Upper King ☎ 843/577–7400) hosts symphony and ballet companies, as well as numerous festival events. The box office is open weekdays from 10 to 6.

Dance, symphony, and theater productions are among those staged at the **North Charleston Performing Art Center** (✉ 5001 Coliseum Dr., North Charleston ☎ 843/529–5050 ⊕ www.coliseumpac.com).

Performances by the College of Charleston's theater department and musical recitals are presented during the school year at the **Simons Center for the Arts** (✉ 54 St. Phillips St., College of Charleston Campus ☎ 843/953–5604).

The chamber series by the Charleston Symphony takes place at the **Sottile Theater** (✉ 44 George St., Market area ☎ 843/953–6340), as do performances by area ballet companies and Spoleto Festival events.

Nightlife

Bars & Breweries

More than 20 on-tap beers make **Charleston Beer Works** (✉ 468 King St., Upper King ☎ 843/577–5885) a student hangout. **Club Habana** (✉ 177 Meeting St., Market area ☎ 843/853–5900) is a chic martini bar (open late), with a cigar shop downstairs. Adjacent rooms of dark hardwood are dimly lighted, furnished with couches and have an intimate ambience. Cheap "mystery beers" make **Cumberland's** (✉ 301 King St., Market area ☎ 843/577–9469) the favorite of laid-back locals.

A list of 100 bottled brews make **King Street Grille** (✉ 304 King St., Upper King ☎ 843/723–5464) a hard-core sports bar for those who like the game loud and the beer cold. **Mad River Bar & Grille** (✉ 2–B N. Market St., Market area ☎ 843/723–0032) attracts a young, high-energy crowd. It's in the atmospheric Old Seamen's Chapel. **Southend Brewery** (✉ 161 E. Bay St., Market area ☎ 843/853–4677) has a lively bar serving beer brewed on the premises; try the wood-oven pizzas and the smokehouse barbecue. Thursday is salsa night, Friday showcases a bluegrass band, and Saturday features a guitarist.

Drinks and appetizers draw young professionals to the covered rooftop at the **Terrace on Marion Square** (✉ 145 Calhoun St., Market area ☎ 843/

Spoleto Festival USA

FOR 17 GLORIOUS DAYS in late May and early June, Charleston gets a dose of culture from the Spoleto Festival USA (☎ 843/722-2764 ⊕ www.spoletousa.org). This internationally acclaimed performing-arts festival features a mix of distinguished artists and emerging talent from around the world. Performances take place in magical settings, such as beneath a canopy of ancient oaks or inside a centuries-old cathedral. Everywhere you turn, the city's music halls, auditoriums, theaters, and outdoor spaces (including the Cistern at the College of Charleston) are filled with the world's best in opera, music, dance, and theater.

The 140 events include everything from improv to Shakespeare, from rap to chamber music, from ballet to salsa. A mix of formal concerts and casual performances is what Pulitzer Prize-winning composer Gian Carlo Minotti had in mind when, in 1977, he initiated the festival as a complement to his opera-heavy Italian festival. He chose Charleston because of its European looks, and because its residents love the arts—and any cause for celebration. Most events are between $25 and $50.

The finale is a must, particularly for the younger crowd. Staged outdoors at Middleton Place, the plantation house and lush landscaped gardens provide a dramatic backdrop. The inexpensive seating is unreserved and unlimited. The lawn is covered with blankets and chairs, and many cooks prepare lavish spreads. After the Spoleto Festival Orchestra plays a spirited concert of contemporary and classic pieces, spectacular fireworks explode over the Ashley River.

Because events sell out quickly, insiders say you should buy your tickets several months in advance. (Tickets to midweek performances are a bit easier to secure.) Hotels fill up quickly, so book a room at the same time. While you're at it, reserve a table at that trendy downtown restaurant. You won't be able to get in the door if you wait until the last minute.

The Italian word *piccolo* means "little," but this hardly applies to **Piccolo Spoleto** (☎ 843/724-7305 ⊕ www.piccolospoleto.com). The only thing small about this younger sibling of the Spoleto Festival USA is the ticket prices. Most are inexpensive, and some are even free, making this a popular attraction for everyone from young children to senior citizens.

Each year this cultural celebration—which runs concurrently with Spoleto—becomes richer, with visual-arts exhibits, poetry readings, film, theater, music, dance, and a wealth of children's activities. Not to be missed is the Reggae Block Dance, a free party that takes place in front of the U.S. Customs House at the corner of Concord and Market streets.

The events at Piccolo Spoleto are more casual, and more spontaneous, than Spoleto. Most of the 700 events focus on local and regional artists, most of whom are innovative and offbeat. Performances can be hilarious, even ribald.

937–0314). Downstairs is the Dark Room, which offers a mix of live bands and DJs playing techno and hip-hop. **Vickery's Bar & Grill** (⊠ 139 Calhoun St., Market area ☎ 843/577–5300) is a festive nightspot with an outdoor patio and good late-night food.

Dance Clubs

The throbbing dance beat of DJ Amos draws the crowds at **213 Top of the Bay** (⊠ 213C E. Bay St., Market area ☎ 843/722–1311), a lively and lighthearted part of downtown's single scene. There's a see-and-be-seen crowd at the **City Bar** (⊠ 5 Faber St., Market area ☎ 843/577–7383). Dance to the music Wednesday through Saturday at **Trio Club** (⊠ 139 Calhoun St., Upper King ☎ 843/965–5333), where funky '70s sounds are perennially popular. Thursday means live Latin tunes.

Dinner Cruises

Cruise the harbor on the *Charleston Belle* (☎ 843/344–4483 ⊕ www. charlestonharbortours.com). Dine and dance the night away aboard the luxury yacht *Spirit of Carolina* (☎ 843/881–7337 ⊕ www. spiritlinecruises.com). ■ TIP→ Remember that reservations for all evening cruises are essential.

Jazz Clubs

The elegant **Charleston Grill** (⊠ Charleston Pl., 224 King St., Market area ☎ 843/577–4522) has live jazz and dinner nightly. Make a reservation. ★ There are 40 types of martinis at **Cintra** (⊠ 16 N. Market St., Market area ☎ 843/377–1090), where you can hear live jazz on Thursday, Friday, and Sunday. At **Mistral** (⊠ 99 S. Market St., Market area ☎ 843/722–5709) there's a great Dixieland jazz band Monday through Saturday and a four-piece jazz combo on Sunday.

Live Music

Best Friend Lounge (⊠ Mills House Hotel, 115 Meeting St., Market area ☎ 843/577–2400) has a guitarist playing on weekends. The cavernous **Music Farm** (⊠ 32 Ann St., Upper King ☎ 843/853–3276), in a renovated train station, showcases live local and national rock and alternative bands. Listen to authentic Irish music at **Tommy Condon's** (⊠ 15 Beaufain St., Market area ☎ 843/577–5300).

JB Pivot's Beach Club (⊠ 1662 Savannah Hwy., West Ashley ☎ 843/571–3668) is a no-frills place, with live beach music and shag or swing dancing lessons Tuesday to Thursday. **Bert's Bar** (⊠ 2209 Middle St., Sullivan's Island ☎ 843/883–3924), a true beach-bum hangout, has live music on weekends. The **Windjammer** (⊠ 1000 Ocean Blvd., Isle of Palms ☎ 843/886–8596) is an oceanfront bar with local and national rock bands playing Thursday through Sunday.

SHOPPING

Shopping Districts

The Market area is a cluster of shops and restaurants centered around the **Old City Market** (⊠ E. Bay and Market Sts., Market area). Sweetgrass basket weavers work here, and you can buy the resulting wares.

King Street is the major shopping street in town. Lower King (from Broad to Market streets) is lined with high-end antiques dealers. Middle King (from Market to Calhoun streets) is a mix of national chains like Banana Republic and Pottery Barn. Upper King (from Calhoun Street to Cannon street) is the up-and-coming area where fashionistas like the alternative shops like Putumayo.

Antiques

Birlant & Co. (⊠ 191 King St., Lower King ☎ 843/722–3842) mostly carries 18th- and 19th-century English antiques, but keep your eye out for a Charleston Battery bench. **Livingstons' Antiques** (⊠ 163 King St., Lower King ☎ 843/723–9697) deals in 18th- and 19th-century English and continental furnishings, clocks, and bric-a-brac. **Period Antiques** (⊠ 194 King St., Lower King ☎ 843/723–2724) carries 18th- and 19th-century pieces. **Petterson Antiques** (⊠ 201 King St., Lower King ☎ 843/723–5714) sells objets d'art, porcelain, and glass.

English Rose Antiques (⊠ 436 King St., Upper King ☎ 843/722–7939) has country-style accessories at some of the best prices on the Peninsula. The **King Street Antique Mall** (⊠ 495 King St., Upper King ☎ 843/723–2211) is part flea market, part antiques store.

On James Island, **Carolopolis Antiques** (⊠ 2000 Wappoo Dr., James Island ☎ 843/795–7724) has good bargains on country antiques. In Mount Pleasant, **Hungryneck Mall** (⊠ 401 Johnnie Dodds Blvd., Mount Pleasant ☎ 843/849–1744) has more than 60 antiques dealers hawking sterling silver, oak and mahogany furnishings, and Civil War memorabilia. **Page's Thieves Market** (⊠ 1460 Ben Sawyer Blvd., Mount Pleasant ☎ 843/884–9672) has furniture, glassware, and occasional auctions.

Art Galleries

The downtown neighborhood known as the French Quarter, named after the founding French Huguenots, has become a destination for art lovers. The French Quarter Gallery Association consists of roughly 30 art galleries within the original walled city. Galleries here host an art walk from 5 to 8 PM on the first Friday in March, May, October, and December.

Serious art collectors head to **Ann Long Fine Art** (⊠ 12 State St., Market area ☎ 843/577–0447) for neoclassical and modern works. The **Charleston Renaissance Gallery** (⊠ 103 Church St., South of Broad ☎ 843/723–0025) carries museum-quality Southern art. The **Corrigan Gallery** (⊠ 62 Queen St., Market area ☎ 843/722–9868) displays the paintings of owner Lese Corrigan, as well as rotating shows from other painters and photographers.

The **Eva Carter Gallery** (⊠ 132 E. Bay St., Market area ☎ 843/722–0506) displays the paintings of owner Eva Carter and abstract works by the late William Halsey. **Horton Hayes Fine Art** (⊠ 30 State St., Market area ☎ 843/958–0014) displays sought-after Lowcountry paintings by brothers Bernie Horton and Mark Kelvin Horton. These atmospheric origi-nals depict coastal life. The **John Carroll Doyle Art Gallery** (⊠ 54½ Broad

St., South of Broad 📞 843/577–7344) displays works by this native Charlestonian, who earned national acclaim with his impressionistic oils of wildlife and fishing scenes.

★ The **Martin Gallery** (✉ 18 Broad St., South of Broad 📞 843/723–7378) hangs art by nationally and internationally acclaimed artists. **Nina Liu and Friends** (✉ 24 State St., Market area 📞 843/722–2724) sells contemporary art, including pottery, handblown glass, jewelry, and photographs. **Smith-Killian Fine Art** (✉ 9 Queen St., Market area 📞 843/853–0708) exhibits the paintings of Betty Smith and her talented triplets, Jennifer, Shannon, and Tripp. Her son is a nature photographer specializing in black-and-white images.

Books

The **Preservation Society of Charleston** (✉ King and Queen Sts., Market area 📞 843/722–4630) carries books and tapes of historic and local interest, as well as sweetgrass baskets, prints, and posters. Look for out-of-print and rare books at **Boomer's Books & Collectibles** (✉ 420 King St., Upper King 📞 843/722–2666).

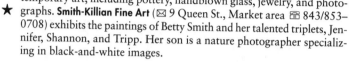

Clothing

Charleston's own **Ben Silver** (✉ 149 King St., Market area 📞 843/577–4556), premier purveyor of blazer buttons, has more than 800 designs, including college and British regimental motifs. He also sells British neckties, embroidered polo shirts, and blazers. **Bob Ellis** (✉ 332 King St., Market area 📞 843/722–2515) sells shoes from Dolce & Gabbana, Prada, and Manolo Blahnik. **Christian Michi** (✉ 220 King St., Market area 📞 843/723–0575) carries chi-chi women's clothing and accessories.

Shop **Copper Penny** (✉ 311 King St., Market area 📞 843/723–2999) for trendy dresses. **Moo Roo** (✉ 316 King St., Market area 📞 843/724–1081) carries handbags that are popular with Hollywood's A-Listers. **Nula** (✉ 320 King St., Market area 📞 843/853–6566) sells hipster wear.

Need a ballgown? **Berlins** (✉ 114 King St., South of Broad 📞 843/723–5591) is your place for designer outfits. **Magar Hatworks** (✉ 557 ½ King St., Upper King 📞 843/577–7740) sells hand-crafted hats. **The Trunk Show** (✉ 281 Meeting St., Market area 📞 843/722–0442) is an upscale women's consignment store with designer dresses and vintage apparel among the racks.

Gifts

ESD (✉ 314 King St., Market area 📞 843/577–6272) is a top local interior-design firm; its King Street shop sells coffee-table books, jewelry, and pillows. Look for cool kitchen gear at **Fred** (✉ 237 King St., Market area 📞 843/723–5699). **Indigo** (✉ 4 Vendue Range, Market area 📞 843/723–2983) stocks funky home and garden accessories.

Magnets, cards, and books are at **Metropolitan Deluxe** (✉ 164 Market St., Market area 📞 843/722–0436). Artsy and hip baby gear, house-warming gifts, jewelry, books, and even office supplies make the mundane fun at **Worthwhile** (⊠ 268 King St., Market area ☎ 843/723–4418).

Foodstuffs

Bull Street Gourmet (⊠ 60 Bull St., College of Charleston Campus ☎ 843/720–8992) sells upscale picnic fare made fresh daily. It has great deals on wine and sponsors friendly tastings. **Charleston Candy Kitchen** (⊠ 32A N. Market St., Market area ☎ 843/723–4626) sells freshly made fudge, Charleston chews, and sesame-seed wafers. The downtown, 24-hour **Harris Teeter** (⊠ 290 E. Bay St., Market area ☎ 843/722–6821) has Charleston foodstuffs.

Kennedy's Bakery and Market (⊠ 60 Calhoun St., Upper King ☎ 843/723–2026) sells wine and cheeses, as well as freshly baked breads, muffins, and scones. Make time to stop at **Market Street Sweets** (⊠ 100 N. Market St., Market area ☎ 843/722–1397) for the melt-in-your-mouth pralines and fudge.

Furniture

Historic Charleston Reproductions (⊠ 105 Broad St., South of Broad ☎ 843/723–8292) has superb replicas of Charleston furniture and accessories, all authorized by the Historic Charleston Foundation. Royalties from sales contribute to restoration projects. At the **Old Charleston Joggling Board Co.** (⊠ 652 King St., Upper King ☎ 843/723–4331) these Lowcountry oddities (on which people bounce) can be purchased. **Carolina Lanterns** (⊠ 917 Houston Northcutt Blvd., Mount Pleasant ☎ 843/881–4170 ⊕ www.carolinalanterns.com) sells gas lanterns based on designs from downtown's historic district.

SIDE TRIPS FROM CHARLESTON

Gardens, parks, and the charming town of Summerville are good reasons to travel a bit farther afield for day trips.

Moncks Corner

30 mi northwest of Charleston on U.S. 52.

This town is a gateway to a number of attractions in Santee Cooper Country. Named for the two rivers that form a 171,000-acre basin, the area brims with outdoor pleasures centered on the basin and nearby Lakes Marion and Moultrie.

Explore the inky swamp waters of **Cypress Gardens** in a complimentary flat-bottom boat; walk along paths lined with moss-draped cypress trees, azaleas, camellias, daffodils, wisteria, and dogwood; and marvel at the clouds of butterflies in the butterfly house. The swamp garden was created from what was once the freshwater reserve of the vast Dean Hall rice plantation. It's about 24 mi north of Charleston via U.S. 52, between Goose Creek and Moncks Corner. ⊠ *3030 Cypress Gardens Rd.* ☎ *843/553–0515* 🔊 *$10* ☉ *Daily 9–5; last admission at 4.*

Mepkin Abbey is an active Trappist monastery overlooking the Cooper River. The site was the former plantation home of Henry Laurens and, later, of publisher Henry Luce and wife Clare Boothe Luce. You can tour the gardens and abbey or even stay here for a spiritual retreat—one- to six-night stays are open to anyone, including married couples, willing to observe the rules of the abbey and who don't mind spartan accommodations. (Reservations are required, and donations are greatly appreciated). The gift shop carries items the monks have produced—soaps, honey, and sweets—and eggs farmed on the premises. Tours depart at 11:30 and 3. ☒ *1098 Mepkin Abbey Rd., off Dr. Evans Rd.* ☏ *843/761–8509* ⊕ *www.mepkinabbey.org* ☒ *Grounds free; tours $5* ☉ *Tues.–Fri. and Sun. 9–4:30, Sat. 9–4.*

On the banks of the Old Santee Canal is the **Old Santee Canal Park,** which you can explore on foot or by canoe. The park includes a 19th-century plantation house. The on-site Berkeley Museum focuses on cultural and natural history. ☒ *900 Stony Landing Rd., off Rembert C. Dennis Blvd.* ☏ *843/899–5200* ⊕ *www.oldsanteecanalpark.org* ☒ *$3* ☉ *Daily 9–5.*

Francis Marion National Forest consists of 250,000 acres of swamps, vast oaks and pines, and little lakes thought to have been formed by falling meteors. It's a good place for picnicking, hiking, camping, horseback riding, boating, and swimming. ☒ *U.S. 52* ☏ *843/336–3248* ☒ *Free* ☉ *Daily 9–4:30.*

For more information about area lakes and facilities, contact **Santee Cooper Counties Promotion Commission & Visitors Center** ☒ *9302 Old Hwy. 6, Drawer 40, Santee 29142* ☏ *803/854–2131* ⊕ *www. santeecoopercountry.org.*

Where to Stay

$–$$$ 🏨 **Rice Hope Plantation.** On a former rice plantation outside of Moncks Corner, this inn overlooks the Cooper River. The grounds, studded with live oaks, were designed by landscape architect Loutrell Briggs. Antiques and reproductions fill the big, sprawling house with five working fireplaces. Guest rooms have wood floors and four-poster beds. This is not a white-pillared mansion, though; it's a more modest farmhouse. ☒ *206 Rice Hope Dr., Moncks Corner 29461* ☏ *843/849–9000 or 800/569–4038* ⊕ *www.ricehope.com* ⇆ *4 rooms, 1 suite* ♿ *Tennis court, boating, fishing, basketball; no smoking* ☰ *AE, MC, V* ⊙ *BP.*

Summerville

25 mi northwest of Charleston via I–26 and Rte. 165.

Victorian homes, many of which are listed on the National Register of Historic Places, line the public park. Colorful gardens brimming with camellias, azaleas, and wisteria abound. Downtown and residential streets curve around tall pines, as a local ordinance prohibits cutting them down. Visit for a stroll in the park, or to go antiquing on the downtown shopping square. Summerville was originally built by wealthy planters.

For more information about Summerville, stop by the **Greater Summerville/ Dorchester County Chamber of Commerce and Visitor Center** (⊠ 402 N. Main St., 29484 ☎ 843/873–2931 ⊕ www.summervilletourism.com).

Where to Stay & Eat

$$$$

Fodor's Choice

★

✕⊞ **Woodlands Resort & Inn.** With the distinct feel of an English country estate, this Relais & Châteaux property has individually decorated rooms with nice touches like Frette linens. The service and quality of the accommodations are exceptional. In the kitchen, Chef Tarver King is proving himself with every challenging, multicourse menu. Wine pairings by longterm sommelier Stéphane Peltier are perfect. Get here soon, as this little gem is about to grow. An expansion plan includes a destination spa, an indoor pool, and many, many more rooms. ⊠ *125 Parsons Rd., 29483* ☎ *843/875–2600 or 800/774–9999* ☎ *843/875–2603* ⊕ *www. woodlandsinn.com* ➘ *10 rooms, 9 suites* ⚭ *Restaurant, room service, in-room safes, some in-room hot tubs, cable TV, in-room VCR, in-room data ports, 2 tennis courts, pool, bicycles, croquet, lounge, meeting rooms, some pets allowed, no-smoking rooms* ▭ *AE, D, DC, MC, V* ⏐⃝ *EP.*

CHARLESTON ESSENTIALS

Transportation

BY AIR

Charleston International Airport, about 12 mi west of downtown, is served by American Eagle, Continental, Delta, United Express, Northwest, and US Airways.

Wings Air, a commuter airline that flies to and from Atlanta, operates out of Mount Pleasant Regional Airport and the Charleston Executive Airport. Private planes can also use Charleston Executive Airport.

Several cab companies serve the airport, including the Charleston Black Cab Company, which has London-style taxis with uniformed drivers that cost about $25 to downtown. Airport Ground Transportation arranges shuttles, which cost $14 per person to downtown.

If you want to add a little excitement to your life, you can arrange for an executive sedan, a stretch limo, or even a super-stretch limo to pick you up at the airport. A Star Limousine has the largest and most varied fleet in town.

🛈 Airport Contacts **Charleston Executive Airport** ⊠ 2700 Fort Trenholm Rd., John's Island ☎ 877/754–7285. **Charleston International Airport** ⊠ 5500 International Blvd., North Charleston ☎ 843/767–1100. **Mt.Pleasant Regional Airport** ⊠ 700 Airport Rd., Mount Pleasant ☎ 843/884–8837.

🛈 Airport Transfers **Airport Ground Transportation** ☎ 843/767–1100. **A Star Limousine** ☎ 843/745–6279. **Charleston Black Cab Company** ☎ 843/216–2627.

BY BOAT & FERRY

Boaters—many traveling the Intracoastal Waterway—dock at Ashley Marina and City Marina, in Charleston Harbor, or at Wild Dunes Yacht Harbor, on the Isle of Palms. The Charleston Water Taxi is a delightful way to travel between Charleston and Mount Pleasant. Some people take the $8 round-trip journey for fun. It departs from the Charleston Maritime Center, half a block south of Adger's Wharf.

🚩 **Ashley Marina** ⊠ Lockwood Blvd., Medical University of South Carolina ☎ 843/722-1996. **Charleston Water Taxi** ⊠ Charleston Maritime Center, 10 Wharfside St., Upper King ☎ 843/330-2989. **City Marina** ⊠ Lockwood Blvd., Medical University of South Carolina ☎ 843/723-5098.

BY BUS

Greyhound connects Charleston with other destinations. The Charleston Area Regional Transportation Authority, the city's public bus system, takes passengers around the city and to the suburbs. Bus 11, which goes to the airport, is convenient for travelers. CARTA operates DASH, which runs buses that look like trolleys along three downtown routes. A single ride is $1.25, and a daylong pass is $4. You should have exact change.

🚩 **CARTA** ⊠ 3664 Leeds Ave., North Charleston ☎ 843/747-0922 ⊕ www.ridecarta.com. **Charleston Bus Station** ⊠ 3610 Dorcester Rd., North Charleston ☎ 843/744-4247. **Greyhound** ☎ 843/744-4247 or 800/231-2222 ⊕ www.greyhound.com.

BY CAR

Interstate 26 traverses the state from northwest to southeast and terminates at Charleston. U.S. 17, the coastal road, also passes through Charleston. Interstate 526, also called the Mark Clark Expressway, runs primarily east–west, connecting the West Ashley area, North Charleston, Daniel Island, and Mount Pleasant.

🚩 **Alamo** ☎ 843/767-4417 ⊕ www.alamo.com. **Avis** ☎ 843/767-7030 ⊕ www.avis.com. **Budget** ☎ 843/577-5195 ⊕ www.budget.com. **Hertz** ☎ 843/767-4552 ⊕ www.hertz.com. **National** ☎ 843/767-3078 ⊕ www.nationalcar.com.

BY TAXI

Fares within the city average about $5 per trip. Reputable companies include Safety Cab and Yellow Cab, which are available 24 hours a day. Taxis, particularly the Charleston Black Cabs, line up near Charleston Place.

Charleston Rickshaw Company will take you anywhere in the historic district for $7 to $12.

🚩 **Charleston Rickshaw Company** ⊠ 21 George St., Market area ☎ 843/723-5685. **Safety Cab** ☎ 843/722-4066. **Yellow Cab** ☎ 843/577-6565.

BY TRAIN

Amtrak has service from such major cities as New York, Philadelphia, Washington, Richmond, Savannah, and Miami. The Amtrak station is somewhat isolated, but a visible police presence means there are few reports of crime in the area. Taxis meet every train; a ride to downtown averages between $20 and $25.

🚩 **Amtrak** ⊠ 4565 Gaynor Ave., North Charleston ☎ 843/744-8264 or 800/872-7245 ⊕ www.amtrak.com.

Contacts & Resources

BANKS & EXCHANGE SERVICES

As in most cities, banks are open weekdays 9 to 5. There are countless branches in the downtown area, all with ATMs.

⛶ **BB&T** ✉ 151 Meeting St., Ansonborough ☏ 843/720–5100. **Bank of America** ✉ 544 King St., Upper King ☏ 843/720–4913. **Bank of South Carolina** ✉ 256 Meeting St., Ansonborough ☏ 843/724–1500.

EMERGENCIES

Medical University of South Carolina Hospital and Roper Hospital have 24-hour emergency rooms.

⛶ Emergency Services **Ambulance, police** ☏ 911.

⛶ Hospitals **Medical University of South Carolina Hospital** ✉ 169 Ashley Ave., Medical University of South Carolina ☏ 843/792–2300. **Roper Hospital** ✉ 316 Calhoun St., Upper King ☏ 843/724–2000.

⛶ Late-Night Pharmacy **Eckerds** ✉ 261 Calhoun St., Upper King ☏ 843/805–6022.

INTERNET, MAIL & SHIPPING

The main post office is downtown on Broad Street, while a major branch is at West Ashley. To ship packages, FedEx Kinkos has a downtown branch and another at West Ashley. The UPS Store has locations in Mount Pleasant and West Ashley.

Most area lodgings have in-room data ports or in-room broadband, and some have wireless connections in the rooms or public areas. Internet cafés are rare, but many coffee shops, including Starbucks, will let you use their wireless connection for a fee. The FedEx Kinko's branch on Orleans Road has computers you can use for 25¢ a minute.

⛶ Post Offices **Downtown Station** ✉ 83 Broad St., South of Broad ☏ 843/577–0690. **West Ashley Station** ✉ 78 Sycamore St., West Ashley ☏ 843/766–4031.

⛶ **FedEx Kinkos** ✉ 73 St. Philip St., Upper King ☏ 843/723–5130 ✉ 873 Orleans Rd., West Ashley ☏ 843/571–4746. **UPS Store** ✉ 1000 Johnnie Dodds Blvd., Mount Pleasant ☏ 843/856–9099 ✉ 1836 Ashley River Rd., West Ashley ☏ 843/763–6894.

MEDIA

The major daily newspaper is the *Post and Courier*. The Preview section in Thursday editions lists weekend events. *Charleston City Paper* is a free weekly that has gained a large, mostly young, following. It gives a rundown of local nightspots and has good restaurant listings.

⛶ **The Post and Courier** ☏ 843/577–7111 ⊕ www.charleston.net. **Charleston CityPaper** ☏ 843/577–5304 ⊕ www.charlestoncitypaper.com.

TOUR OPTIONS

AIR TOURS   Flying High Over Charleston provides aerial tours of the city and surrounding areas. Trips begin at $60 per person.

⛶ **Flying High Over Charleston** ✉ Mercury Air Center, W. Aviation Ave., North Charleston ☏ 843/569–6148 ⊕ www.flyinghighovercharleston.com.

BOAT TOURS   Charleston Harbor Tours offers tours that give the history of the harbor. Spiritline Cruises, which runs the ferry to Fort Sumter, also offers harbor tours and dinner cruises. The latter leave from Patriots Point Marina in Mount Pleasant and include a three-course dinner and dancing to a live band. Sandlapper Tours has tours focused on regional history, coastal wildlife, and ghostly lore.

⛶ **Charleston Harbor Tours** ✉ Charleston Maritime Center, 10 Wharfside St., Upper King ☏ 843/722–1691 ⊕ www.charlestonharbortours.com. **Sandlapper Tours**

✉ Charleston Maritime Center, 10 Wharfside St., Upper King ☎ 843/849-8687 ⊕ www. sandlappertours.com. **Spiritline Cruises** ✉ 360 Concord St, Market area ☎ 843/881- 7337 or 800/789-3678 ⊕ www.spiritlinecruises.com.

BUS TOURS Adventure Sightseeing leads bus tours of the historic district. Associated Guides of Historic Charleston pairs local guides with visiting tour groups. Doin' the Charleston, a van tour, makes a stop at the Battery. Sites and Insights is a van tour that covers downtown and nearby is- lands. Gullah Tours focuses on sights significant to African-American culture. Chai Y'All shares stories and sights of Jewish interest.

🚩 **Adventure Sightseeing** ☎ 843/762-0088 or 800/722-5394 ⊕ www.touringcharleston. com. **Associated Guides of Historic Charleston** ☎ 843/724-6419 ⊕ www. historiccharleston.org. **Chai Y'All** ☎ 843/556-0664. **Doin' the Charleston** ☎ 843/ 763-1233 or 800/647-4487 ⊕ www.dointhecharlestontours.com. **Gullah Tours** ☎ 843/ 763-7551 ⊕ www.gullahtours.com. **Sites and Insights** ☎ 843/762-0051 ⊕ www. sitesandinsightstours.com.

CARRIAGE TOURS Carriage tours are a great way to see Charleston. Carolina Polo & Car- riage Company, Old South Carriage Company, and Palmetto Carriage Tours run horse- and mule-drawn carriage tours of the historic district. Each tour, which follows one of four routes, last about one hour. Most carriages queue up at North Market and Anson streets. Charleston Carriage and Polo, which picks up passengers at the Doubletree Guest Suites Historic Charleston on Church Street, has a historically authen- tic carriage that is sought after for private tours and wedding parties.

🚩 **Charleston Carriage & Polo Company** ☎ 843/577-6767 ⊕ www.cpcc.com. **Old South Carriage Company** ☎ 843/723-9712 ⊕ www.oldsouthcarriagetours.com. **Palmetto Carriage Tours** ☎ 843/723-8145.

ECOTOURS Barrier Island Ecotours, at the Isle of Palms Marina, runs three-hour pontoon-boat tours to a barrier island. Coastal Expeditions has half- day and full-day naturalist-led kayak tours on local rivers. Charleston Explorers leads educational boat tours that are great for kids.

🚩 **Barrier Island Ecotours** ✉ Isle of Palms Marina, off U.S. 17, Isle of Palms ☎ 843/ 886-5000 ⊕ www.nature-tours.com. **Coastal Expeditions** ✉ 514-B Mill St., Mount Pleas- ant ☎ 843/884-7684 ⊕ www.coastalexpeditions.com. **Charleston Explorers** ✉ 40 Pa- triots Point Rd., Mount Pleasant ☎ 843/723-5656 ⊕ www.charlestonexplorers.org.

PRIVATE GUIDES To hire a private guide to lead you around the city and outlying plan- tations, contact Charleston's Finest Historic Tours. Janice Kahn has been leading customized tours for more than 30 years. Christine Waggoner, of Promenade with Christine, offers tours in French and English.

🚩 **Charleston's Finest Historic Tours** ☎ 843/577-3311. **Janice Kahn** ☎ 843/556- 0664. **Promenade with Christine** ☎ 843/971-9364 or 843/200-1766.

WALKING TOURS Walking tours on various topics—horticulture, slavery, or women's his- tory—are given by Charleston Strolls and the Original Charleston Walks. Bulldog Tours has walks that explore the city's supernatural side. Listen to the infamous tales of lost souls with Ghosts of Charleston, which travel to historic graveyards.

Military history buffs should consider Jack Thompson's Civil War Walk- ing Tour. The food-oriented tours by Carolina Food Pros explore culinary strongholds—gourmet grocers, butcher shops, and restaurants, sampling all along the way.

🚶 **Bulldog Tours** ⊠ 40 N. Market St., Market area ☎ 843/568-3315 ⊕ www. cobblestonewalkingtours.com. **Carolina Food Pros** ⊠ 701 East Bay St., Market area ☎ 843/ 723-3366 ⊕ www.carolinafoodpros.com. **Charleston Strolls** ⊠ Charleston Pl., 130 Market St., Market area ☎ 843/766-2080 ⊕ www.charlestonstrolls.com. **Ghosts of Charleston** ⊠ 184 E. Bay St., French Quarter ☎ 843/723-1670 or 800/723-1670. **Jack Thompson's Civil War Walking Tour** ⊠ Mills House Hotel, 115 Meeting St., Market area ☎ 843/722-7033. **Original Charleston Walks** ⊠ 58½ Broad St., South of Broad ☎ 843/577-3800 or 800/729-3420.

VISITOR INFORMATION

The Charleston Area Convention & Visitors Bureau runs the Charleston Visitor Center, which has information about the city as well as Kiawah Island, Seabrook Island, Mount Pleasant, North Charleston, Edisto Island, Summerville, and the Isle of Palms. The Historic Charleston Foundation and the Preservation Society of Charleston have information on house tours.

🚶 Tourist Information **Charleston Visitor Center** ⊠ 375 Meeting St., Upper King ☎ 423 King St., 29403 ☎ 843/853-8000 or 800/868-8118 ⊕ www.charlestoncvb.com. **Historic Charleston Foundation** ☎ Box 1120, 29402 ☎ 843/723-1623 ⊕ www.historiccharleston. org. **Preservation Society of Charleston** ☎ Box 521, 29402 ☎ 843/722-4630 ⊕ www. preservationsociety.org.

Hilton Head &
the Lowcountry

WORD OF MOUTH

"Fripp, especially at south end, has a wide beach. During high tide north beach disappears. Fripp can be traversed on foot in about 30 minutes, if the marsh deer get out of your way. They're everywhere. Enjoy."

—Lex1

"Edisto Beach is a much less commercialized, laid-back beach with rental homes and a golf course about an hour out of Charleston. It's not fancy, i.e., Hilton Head or Isle of Palms, but much less crowded. It has several miles of walking beach available and very nice houses."

—JimF

Updated by
Eileen
Robinson Smith

THE ACTION-PACKED ISLAND of Hilton Head anchors the southern tip of South Carolina's coastline and attracts 2.5 million visitors each year. Although it historically has drawn an upscale clientele, and it still does, you'll find that the crowd here is much more diverse than you might think. Although it has more than its fair share of millionaires (you might run into director Ron Howard at the Starbucks, for instance), it also attracts families in search of a good beach.

This half-tame, half-wild island is home to more than 25 world-class golf courses and even more resorts, hotels, and top restaurants. Still, it's managed development thanks to building restrictions that aim to marry progress with environmental protection. North of Hilton Head, the coastal landscape is peppered with quiet small towns and flanked by rural sea islands. Beaufort is a cultural treasure, a graceful antebellum town with a compact historic district and waterfront promenade. Many of the 18th- and 19th-century mansions have been converted to bed-and-breakfasts. Continuing north, midway between Beaufort and Charleston is Edisto Island, where you can comb the beach for shells and camp out on the mostly barren Edisto Beach State Park, or rent the modest waterfront cottages that have been in the same families for generations.

Exploring Hilton Head & the Lowcountry

Hilton Head is just north of the South Carolina–Georgia border. It's so close to Savannah that they share an airport. This part of the state is best explored by car, as its points of interest spread over a flat coastal plain that is a mix of wooded areas, marshes, and sea islands, the latter of which are sometimes accessible only by boat or ferry. Take U.S. 170 and 17 to get from one key spot (Hilton Head, Beaufort, and Edisto) to another. It's a pretty drive that winds through small towns and over old bridges. Charleston, the Queen Belle of the South, is at the northern end of the region.

About the Restaurants

Given the proximity to the Atlantic and small farms on the mainland, most locally owned restaurant menus are still heavily influenced by the catch of the day and seasonal field harvests. But things are changing. There are numerous national chain restaurants and high-end spots in addition to the down-home holes-in-the-wall. Many restaurants open at 11 and don't close until 9 or 10, but some take a break between 2:30 and 6. During the height of the summer season, book ahead on weekends.

About the Hotels

Hilton Head is known as one of the best vacation spots on the East Coast, and its hotels are a testimony to the reputation. The island is covered in resorts and hotels, or you can rent beachfront or golf-course-view villas, cottages, and mansions. Here, and on private islands, expect the most modern conveniences and world-class service at the priciest places. Clean, updated rooms and friendly staff are everywhere—even at lower-rate establishments—this is the South, after all. Staying in cooler months, for extended periods of time, or commuting from nearby Bluffton,

TOP 5 REASONS TO GO

Lowcountry Beauty: Despite all of the man-made amenities, this is one gorgeous sea island. To truly appreciate it, try kayaking, turtle-watching, horseback riding, or simply witnessing the ocean sunsets.

Beach Combing: This island has 12 mi of ocean beaches. You can swim, soak up the sun, or walk along the sand. The differential between the tides leaves a multitude of shells, sand dollars, and starfish.

Challenging Golf: Hilton Head's nickname is "Golf Island," and its

many challenging courses have an international reputation.

Serving up Tennis: One of the nation's top tennis destinations, with academies run by legends like Stan Smith, former Wimbleton champion.

Staying Put: This semitropical island has been a resort destination for decades and it has all of the desired amenities for visitors: a vast array of lodgings, an endless supply of restaurants, and excellent shopping.

where there are some new limited-service properties, chains like Hampton Inn, can mean better deals.

The region's high season lasts from spring through summer (June through August), plus holiday and festival weekends. Hilton Head is the most demanding in which to score a good deal, or even a room—unless you plan ahead. The choicest locations are booked a year to six months in advance, almost year-round, but booking agencies can help you make room reservations, and in winter the crowds thin, rates drop.

	WHAT IT COSTS				
	$$$$	**$$$**	**$$**	**$**	**¢**
RESTAURANTS	over $22	$17–$22	$12–$16	$7–$11	under $7
HOTELS	over $220	$161–$220	$111–$160	$70–$110	under $70

Restaurant prices are for a main course at dinner. Hotel prices are for two people in a standard double room in high season.

Timing

The high season follows typical beach-town cycles, with May through August and holidays year-round being the busiest and most costly. However, as local guides will tell you, thanks to the Lowcountry's mostly moderate temperatures year-round, tourists are ever-present. Spring is the most glorious time to visit, especially in Beaufort, as the historic district is awash in blooming azaleas, wisteria, and jasmine.

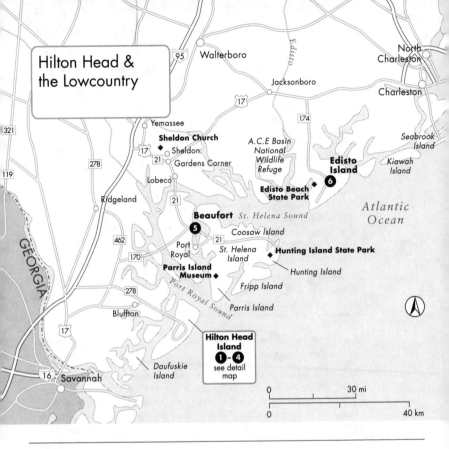

HILTON HEAD ISLAND

No matter how many golf courses pepper its landscape, Hilton Head will always be a semitropical barrier island. That means the 12 mi of beaches are lined with towering pines, palmetto trees, and wind-sculpted live oaks; the interior is a blend of oak and pine woodlands and meandering lagoons. Rental villas, lavish private houses, and luxury hotels line the coast as well.

Since the 1950s, resorts like Sea Pines, Palmetto Dunes, and Port Royal have sprung up all over. Although the gated resorts are private residential communities, all have public restaurants, marinas, shopping areas, and recreational facilities. All are secured, and cannot be toured unless arrangements are made at the visitor office near the main gate of each plantation. Hilton Head prides itself on strict laws that keep light pollution to a minimum. ■ TIP→ **The lack of street lights makes it difficult to find your way at night, so be sure to get good directions.**

Exploring Hilton Head

Driving Hilton Head by car or tour bus is the only way to get around. Off Interstate 95, take Exit 8 onto U.S. 278, which leads you through

Bluffton and then onto Hilton Head proper. A 5¾-mi Cross Island Parkway toll bridge ($1) is just off 278, and makes it easy to bypass traffic and reach the south end of the island, where most of the resort areas and hotels are. Know that U.S. 278 can slow to a standstill at rush hour and during holiday weekends, and the signs are so discreet that it's easy to get lost without explicit di-

AROUND IN CIRCLES

Locals call the island's many traffic circles the "tourist's nemesis." So they won't be your undoing, get very precise directions. And if you miss a turn, don't brake violently, just go around again.

rections. ■ TIP➔ Be careful of putting the-pedal-to-the-metal, particularly on the Cross Island Parkway. The speed limits change dramatically.

What to See

❷ **Audubon-Newhall Preserve,** in the south, is 50 acres of pristine forest, where native plant life is tagged and identified. There are trails, a self-guided tour, and seasonal walks. ⊠ *Palmetto Bay Rd., near southern base of Cross Island Pkwy., South End* ☎ *843/842–9246* ⊕ *www.hiltonheadaudubon.org* 🎟 *Free* ☉ *Daily dawn–dusk.*

❹ **Bluffton.** Tucked away from the resorts, charming Bluffton has several
Fodor'sChoice old homes and churches, a growing artists' colony, and oak-lined streets
★ dripping with moss. You could grab Southern-style picnic food and head to the boat dock at the end of Pritchard Street for great views. There are interesting little shops around, too. ⊠ *Route 46, 8 mi northwest on U.S. 278.*

❶ **Coastal Discovery Museum.** Here you find two types of permanent exhibits—depicting Native American island life and sea island biodiversity—along with various temporary displays. The museum also sponsors historical and natural history tours of Native American sites, forts, and plantations as well as kayak trips, turtle watches, birding treks, and visits to wildlife preserves. ⊠ *100 William Hilton Pkwy., North End* ☎ *843/689–6767* ⊕ *www.coastaldiscovery.org* 🎟 *Free* ☉ *Mon.–Sat. 9–5, Sun. 10–3.*

Palmetto Dunes Resort. This complex is home to the renowned Rod Laver Tennis Center, a good stretch of beach, three golf courses, and several oceanfront rental villa complexes. The oceanfront Hilton Head Marriott Beach & Golf Resort and the Hilton Resort are also on this property. ⊠ *Queens Folly Rd. at U.S. 278, Mid-Island* ☎ *800/845–8160* ⊕ *www.palmettodunesresort.com.*

Port Royal Plantation. The main draws here are the posh Westin Resort, which is on the beach, three PGA-championship golf courses, and Port Royal racquet club, with 16 tennis courts. ⊠ *2 Grasslawn Ave., Mid-Island* ☎ *843/681–4000* ⊕ *www.westinhiltonhead.com.*

❸ **Sea Pines Forest Preserve.** At this 605-acre public wilderness tract, walking trails take you past a stocked fishing pond, waterfowl pond, and a

6

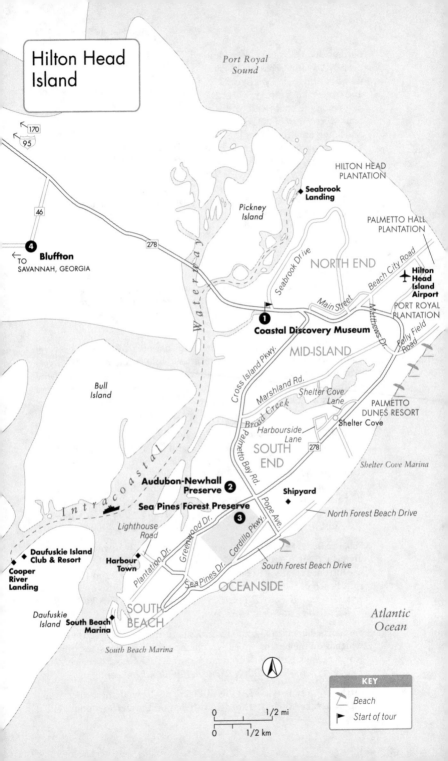

Hilton Head Island

Port Royal Sound

HILTON HEAD PLANTATION

◆ **Seabrook Landing**

Pickney Island

PALMETTO HALL PLANTATION

← 170
← 95

46

4 **Bluffton**
← TO
SAVANNAH, GEORGIA

278

Seabrook Drive

NORTH END

Beach City Road

Polly Field Road

✈ **Hilton Head Island Airport**

PORT ROYAL PLANTATION

Main Street

Matthews Dr.

1
Coastal Discovery Museum

MID-ISLAND

Cross Island Pkwy.

Marshland Rd.

Shelter Cove Lane

PALMETTO DUNES RESORT

Bull Island

Broad Creek

Harbourside Lane

Shelter Cove

SOUTH END

278

Shelter Cove Marina

Palmetto Bay Rd.

Audubon-Newhall Preserve **2**

Sea Pines Forest Preserve

◆ **Shipyard**

3

North Forest Beach Drive

Lighthouse Road

Pope Ave.

Greenwood Dr.

Cordillo Pkwy.

South Forest Beach Drive

Intracoastal

Waterway

◆ **Daufuskie Island Club & Resort**

Cooper River Landing

Harbour Town

Plantation Dr.

Sea Pines Dr.

OCEANSIDE

Daufuskie Island

South Beach Marina

SOUTH BEACH

South Beach Marina

Atlantic Ocean

⊛

0   1/2 mi
0   1/2 km

KEY
⌐ Beach
► Start of tour

3,400-year-old Indian shell ring. Pick up the extensive activity guide at the Sea Pines Welcome Center to take advantage of goings-on—moonlight hayrides, storytelling around campfires, and alligator- and bird-watching boat tours. The preserve is part of the grounds at Sea Pines Resort. ⊠ *Off U.S. 278, Sea Pines Resort, South End* ☎ *843/ 363–4530* ⊕ *www.seapines.com* ☏ *$5 per car* ☉ *Daily dawn–dusk.*

Fodor'sChoice **Sea Pines Resort.** The oldest and
★ best known of Hilton Head's developments, this resort occupies 4,500 thickly wooded acres with three golf courses, tennis clubs, stables, a fine beach, and shopping plazas. The focus of Sea Pines is **Harbour Town,** a charming marina with a luxury boutique hotel, shops, restaurants, some condominiums, and the landmark Hilton Head Lighthouse. A free trolley takes visitors around the resort. ⊠ *Off U.S. 278, South End* ☎ *843/363–4530* ⊕ *www.seapines.com* ☏ *$5 per car.*

PAMPER YOURSELF

Don't forget to treat yourself to a little R&R. The low-key **Faces** (⊠ The Village at Wexford, 1000 William Hilton Pkwy., North End ☎ 843/785-3075 ⊕ www. facesdayspa.com) has been pampering loyal clients for some 20 years. The **Spa at Palmetto Bluffs** (⊠ 476 Mount Pelia Rd., Bluffton ☎ 843/706-6500 ⊕ www. palmettobluffresort.com) has been dubbed the "celebrity spa" by locals.

**OFF THE
BEATEN
PATH**

DAUFUSKIE ISLAND – From Hilton Head you can take a 45-minute ferry ride to nearby Daufuskie Island, the setting for Pat Conroy's novel *The Water Is Wide,* which was made into the movie *Conrack.* A few descendants of former slaves live on small farms here, among remnants of churches, homes, and schools—all reminders of antebellum times. Once on the island, you can rent a golf cart or take guided tours that include sights such as a 200-year-old cemetery, former slave quarters, a local winery, and the Haig Point Lighthouse. The scenic boat ride and the physically beautiful island itself will become etched in your memory bank.

Staying at the **Daufuskie Island Club & Resort** (⊠ Embarkation Center, 421 Squire Pope Rd., North End ☎ 843/341–4820 or 800/648–6778 ⊕ www. daufuskieresort.com)—with an oceanfront inn, cottages, golf courses, tennis, spa, pools, water sports, and several restaurants—is a wonderful getaway. **Calibogue Cruises** (⊠ Broad Creek Marina, 164B Palmetto Bay Rd., Mid-Island ☎ 843/342–8687 ⊕ www.freeport-marina.com) has several Daufuskie tour options, including guided tours with lunch and gospel-music performances starting at $40. **Vagabond Cruises** (⊠ Harbour Town Marina, South End ☎ 843/785–2662 ⊕ www.vagabondcruise. com) conducts daytime boat rides, from dolphin tours to runs to Savannah, sails on the Stars & Stripes, of America's Cup fame, and dinner cruises.

Sports & the Outdoors

Beaches

Although resort beach access is reserved for guests and residents, there are four public entrances to Hilton Head's 12 mi of ocean beach. The two main parking spots are off U.S. 278 at Coligny Circle in the South End, near the Holiday Inn, and on Folly Field Road, Mid-Island. Both have changing facilities. South of Folly Field Road, Mid-Island along U.S. 278, Bradley Beach Road and Singleton Road lead to beaches where parking space is limited. ■ TIP➡ A delightful stroll on the beach can end with an unpleasant surprise if you don't put your towels, shoes, and other earthly possessions way up on the sand. Tides here can fluctuate as much as 7 feet. Check the tide chart at your hotel.

Biking

There are more than 40 mi of public paths that crisscross Hilton Head island, and pedaling is popular along the firmly packed beach. ■ TIP➡ Bikes with wide tires are a must if you want to ride on the beach. They can save you a spill should you hit loose sand on the trails.

Bicycles can be rented at most hotels and resorts. You can also rent bicycles from the **Hilton Head Bicycle Company** (⊠ 112 Arrow Rd., South End ☎ 843/686–6888 ⊕ www.hiltonheadbicycle.com). **South Beach Cycles** (⊠ Sea Pines Resort, off U.S. 278, South End ☎ 843/671–2453 ⊕ www.southbeachracquetclub.com) rents bikes, helmets, tandems, and adult tricycles. **Pedals Bicycles.** ⊠ 71 Pope Ave., South End ☎ 843/842–5522.

> **HOT WHEELS**
>
> An amazing array of bicycles can be hired, from beach cruisers to mountain bikes to bicycles built for two. Many can be delivered to your hotel, along with helmets, baskets, locks, child carriers, and whatever else you might need. There are 40 mi of trails, as well as 12 mi of hard-packed beach, so the possibilities are endless.

Canoeing & Kayaking

Outside Hilton Head (⊠ Sea Pines Resort, off U.S. 278, South End ⊠ Shelter Cove La. at U.S. 278, Mid-Island ☎ 843/686–6996 or 800/686–6996 ⊕ www.outsidehiltonhead.com) is an ecologically sensitive company that rents canoes and kayaks; it also runs nature tours and dolphin-watching excursions.

Golf

Hilton Head is nicknamed "Golf Island" for good reason: the island itself has 24 championship courses (most semiprivate), and the outlying area has 16 more. Each offers its own packages, some of which are great deals. Almost all charge the most in the morning and lower the rates as the day goes on. Some offer lower rates in the hot summer months. ■ TIP➡ The dress code on island golf courses does not permit blue jeans, gym shorts, or jogging shorts. Men's shirts must have collars.

Arthur Hills at Palmetto Hall. A player favorite from the renowned designer Arthur Hills, this course has his trademark: undulating fairways. The course, punctuated with lakes, gently flows across the island's rolling hills, winding around moss-draped oaks and towering pines. The clubhouse is a replica of an antebellum greathouse. ☒ *108 Fort Howell Dr., Mid-Island* ☎ *843/689–5891 or 800/827–3006* 🖷 *843/689–9205* ⊕ *www.golfisland.com* ⚓ *Reservations essential* 🏌 *18 holes. 6918 yds. Par 72. Green Fee: $99–$75–$65* ☞ *Facilities: Driving range, putting green, pitching area, golf carts, rental clubs, pro-shop, golf academy/lessons, restaurant, bar.*

Country Club of Hilton Head. Although it's part of a country club, the course is open for public play. A well-kept secret, it's never overcrowded. In 2005 it was a U.S. Open–qualifying site. ☒ *70 Skull Creek Dr. N, North End* ☎ *843/681–4653 or 888/465–3475* 🖷 *843/689–9976* ⊕ *www.golfisland.com* ⚓ *Reservations essential* 🏌 *18 holes. 6919 yds. Par 72. Green Fee: $89–$69–$49* ☞ *Facilities: Driving range, putting green, pitching area, golf carts, pull carts, rental clubs, pro-shop, golf academy/lessons, restaurant, bar.*

Fodor'sChoice ★ **Harbour Town Golf Links.** Many golfers say this is one of those must-play-before-you die courses. It's extremely well known because it has hosted the Verizon Heritage Classic every spring for the last three decades. Designed by Pete Dye, the layout is reminiscent of Scottish courses of old. The Golf Academy is ranked among the top 10 in the country. ☒ *Sea Pines Resort, 11 Lighthouse La., South End* ☎ *843/842–8484 or 800/955–8337* 🖷 *843/363–8372* ⊕ *www.golfisland.com* ⚓ *Reservations essential* 🏌 *18 holes. 6973 yds. Par 71. Green Fee: $270–$230* ☞ *Facilities: Driving range, putting green, pitching area, golf carts, pull carts, caddies, rental clubs, pro-shop, golf academy/lessons, restaurant, bar.*

Old South Golf Links. This course has scenic holes with marshland and views of the Intracoastal Waterway. ☒ *50 Buckingham Plant Dr., North End* ☎ *843/785–5353* 🖷 *843/837–7375* ⊕ *www.golfisland.com* ⚓ *Reservations essential* 🏌 *18 holes. 6772 yds. Par 72. Green Fee: $50–$90* ☞ *Facilities: Driving range, putting green, pitching area, golf carts, rental clubs, pro-shop, golf academy/lessons, restaurant, bar.*

Robert Trent Jones at Palmetto Dunes. This course is one of the island's most popular layouts. Its beauty and character are accentuated by the par-5, 10th hole, which offers a panoramic view of the ocean. It's one of only two oceanfront holes on Hilton Head. ☒ *7 Robert Trent Jones Way, North End* ☎ *843/785–1138* 🖷 *843/785–3220* ⊕ *www.golfisland.com* ⚓ *Reservations essential* 🏌 *18 holes. 7005 yds. Par 72. Green Fee: $59–$105* ☞ *Facilities: Driving range, putting green, pitching area, golf carts, rental clubs, pro-shop, golf academy/lessons, restaurant, bar.*

Horseback Riding

★ ⏲ **Lawton Stables** (☒ Sea Pines Resort, Plantation, off U.S. 278, South End ☎ 843/671–2586) gives riding lessons and pony rides, in addition to having horseback tours through the Sea Pines Forest Preserve.

Tennis

There are more than 300 courts on Hilton Head. **Port Royal** (☒ 15 Wimbledon Ct., North End ☎ 843/686–8803 ⊕ www.heritagegolfgroup.

com) has 16 courts, including two grass. **Sea Pines Racquet Club** (⊠ Sea Pines Resort, off U.S. 278, 32 Greenwood Dr., South End ☎ 843/363–4495) has 23 courts, instructional programs, and a pro-shop. **Palmetto Dunes Tennis Center** (⊠ 6 Trent Jones La., Mid-Island ☎ 843/785–1152 ⊕ www.palmettodunes.com) welcomes nonguests. Highly rated **Van der Meer Tennis Center/Shipyard Racquet Club** (⊠ Shipyard Plantation, 19 de Allyon Rd., Mid-Island ☎ 843/686–8804 ⊕ www.vandermeer.com) is recognized for tennis instruction. Four of its 28 courts are covered.

Where to Eat

$$$$ ✕ **Aqua.** A good bit was spent on creating the ambiance here—the waterfall on the first level, the fireplace lounge adjacent to the second-story dining room. The food—particularly the shellfish—and portions are commendable, the wine list up with the trends, the servers savvy. Grazing is the way to go: the oysters with champagne mignonette or chile lime remoulade; the delicious sashami; the bibb and red-leaf salad with macadamias dressed with orange-miso vinaigrette. (Forget the spring rolls.) A late-night menu is served from 10 to midnight. ⊠ *10 Forest Beach Dr., South End* ☎ *843/341–3331* ▭ *AE, MC, V* ☽ *No lunch.*

★ $$$–$$$$ ✕ **Old Fort Pub.** Overlooking the sweeping marshlands of Skull Creek, this romantic restaurant has almost panoramic views. It just may be the island's best overall dining experience, for the building is old enough to have personality, as are the professional waiters. The kitchen serves flavorful food, like the appetizer of roasted calamari with sun-dried tomatoes and olives. Entrées like duck confit in rhubarb sauce, and fillet with shitake mushrooms hit the spot. The wine list is extensive, and there's outdoor seating plus a 3rd-floor porch for toasting the sunset. Sunday brunch includes a mimosa. ⊠ *65 Skull Creek Dr., North End* ☎ *843/ 681–2386* ▭ *AE, D, DC, MC, V* ☽ *No lunch.*

$$$–$$$$ ✕ **Redfish.** The "naked" catch of the day—seafood grilled with olive oil, lime, and garlic—stands out here; it's a welcome change from the fried fare at many other local spots. Caribbean and Cuban flavors pervade the rest of the menu in dishes such as red trout with Boursin-cheese grits; *tasso* (a spicy cured ham) in a cream sauce spiked with amaretto, Tabasco, and Worcestershire; and Dominican braised pork, roasted with bananas, chilis, and coconut. Its wine cellar is full with some 1,000 bottles and there's a retail wineshop. Although its commercial strip location isn't inspired, the lively crowd sitting amid candlelight, subdued artwork, dark furniture, and white linens more than makes up for this typical island shortcoming. However, some locals have signed off this place, saying the food and service is not worth the elevated prices. ⊠ *8 Archer Rd., corner Palmetto Bay Rd., South End* ☎*843/686–3388* ▭*AE, D, MC, V* ☽ *No lunch on Sun.*

$$–$$$$ ✕ **Brick Oven Café.** Velvet drapes, dramatic chandeliers, and '40s lounge-style entertainment—on top of good, reasonably priced food served late—make this an *in* place. It's a refreshingly quirky joint on an island that is more luxe than funky and the menu is equally eclectic: appetizers include sweet-potato and lobster cakes or shrimp and pork spring rolls; entrées are wood-fired pizzas, roasted veggie sandwiches, and veal meat loaf. The wine list has a good range and pricing. ⊠ *Park Plaza, Green-*

wood Dr., South End ☎ 843/686–2233 ⚱ *Reservations essential* ▤ *AE, D, DC, MC, V* ⊙ *No lunch.*

$–$$$$ ✕ **Truffles Cafe.** When a restaurant survives here for more than 20 years, there's a reason. This place has personable, hands-on owners; prices low enough to keep the islanders coming all year, and food that is fresh and flavorful. There's none of the namesake truffles, but there's grilled salmon with a mango-barbecue glaze and—if you're gonna be bad—barbecued baby back ribs. ⊠ *Sea Pines Center, 71 Lighthouse Rd.* ☎ *843/ 671–6138* ▤ *AE, MC, V.*

¢–$$ ✕ **Mi Tierra.** At this friendly Mexican restaurant, freshness is the key to tasty fare like fried-fish tacos. Next door, Baja Tacos—run by the same people—is a simple taco stand with counter service, café tables, and a condiments bar with fresh salsas and relishes. Down a *cerveza* (beer) as you watch Mexican *telenovelas* (soap operas). ⊠ *160 Fairfield Sq., North End* ☎ *843/342–3409* ▤ *MC, V.*

¢–$ ✕ **Kenny B's French Quarter Café.** Surrounded by Mardi Gras memorabilia, Kenny himself cooks up jambalaya, gumbo, and muffaletta sandwiches. His wife runs the dining room, serving hungry working folks golden fried oyster po' boys topped with real remoulade sauce. Go for the Sunday buffet brunch; there's chicory coffee, perfect beignets, spicy omelets, and various Benedicts. A local haunt for nearly 10 years, this place in a shopping center is open from morning until 9 PM. ⊠ *Bi-Lo Circle, 70 Pope Ave., Mid-Island* ☎ *843/785–3315* ▤ *AE, D, MC, V* ⊙ *No dinner Sun.*

★ ¢ ✕ **Signe's Heaven Bound Bakery & Café.** Mornings find locals rolling in for the deep-dish French toast, crispy polenta, and whole-wheat waffles. For 34 years, European-born Signe has been feeding islanders soups (the chilled cucumber has pureed watermelon, green apples, and mint), curried chicken salad, and loaded hot and cold sandwiches. The beach bag ($10 for a cold sandwich, pasta or fresh fruit, chips, a beverage, and cookie) is a great deal. The key-lime bread pudding is amazing, as are the melt-in-your mouth cakes and the rave-worthy breads, especially the Italian ciabatta. Dine in the new room, with original art by—who else?—Signe. ⊠ *93 Arrow Rd., South End* ☎ *843/785–9118* ▤ *AE, D, MC, V* ⊙ *Closed Sun. No dinner.*

Where to Stay

$$$$ ⊞ **Crowne Plaza Hilton Head Island Beach Resort.** Decorated in a nautical theme and set in a luxuriant garden, the Crowne Plaza is appropriately resplendent. It's the centerpiece of Shipyard Plantation, which means guests have access to all its amenities. However, this resort has the fewest oceanfront rooms of the majors and is the farthest from the water. Its latticed bridge and beach pavilion have seen many an island wedding. ⊠ *130 Shipyard Dr., Shipyard Plantation, Mid-Island, 29928* ☎ *843/842–2400 or 800/334–1881* ⊟ *843/785–8463* ⊕ *www. crowneplazaresort.com* ⇥ *331 rooms, 9 suites* ⚷ *2 restaurants, snack bar, room service, minibars, cable TV, Wi-Fi, 3 18-hole golf courses, 3 pools (1 indoor), health club, hot tub, bicycles, lounge, children's programs (ages 3–12), business services, meeting room, no-smoking rooms* ▤ *AE, D, DC, MC, V* ⏀ *EP.*

★ ♻ $$$$ 🖼 **Disney's Hilton Head Island Resort.** Disney's typical cheery colors and whimsical designs create a look that's part Southern beach resort, part Adirondack hideaway. The villas here have fully furnished dining, living, and sleeping areas, as well as porches with rocking chairs and picnic tables. It's on a little islet in Broad Creek; many units have marsh or marina views. The smallest villa is a studio, the largest has three bedrooms, four baths, and space to sleep a dozen. The resort has a fishing pier and a lively beach club a mile from the accommodations (shuttle service provided). Kids are kept happy and busy, be it crabbing or roasting marshmallows. Surprisingly, it's popular with couples unaccompanied by children. ⊠ *22 Harbourside La., Mid-Island, 29928* ☎ *843/341–4100 or 407/939–7540* 🖨 *843/341–4130* ⊕ *www.dvcmagic.com* ☞ *102 units* ♻ *2 snack bars, fans, some in-room hot tubs, kitchens, cable TV, in-room data ports, golf privileges, miniature golf, 2 pools, gym, outdoor hot tub, dock, boating, marina, fishing, bicycles, billiards, horseshoes, Ping-Pong, shuffleboard, recreation room, video game room, children's programs (ages 3–16), playground, laundry service, no-smoking rooms* ⊟ *AE, MC, V* ⦿ *EP.*

♻ $$$$ 🖼 **Hilton Head Marriott Beach & Golf Resort.** Marriott's standard rooms get a tropical twist at this palm-enveloped resort: sunny yellow-and-green floral fabrics and cherry furnishings are part of the peppy decor. All guest rooms have private balconies, writing desks, and down comforters. The grandaddy of the island's resorts, it's looking good after a $27 million renovation that includes revamped pool areas and restaurants. Kids love the real sand castle in the lobby. To take in the sea views, you can lounge by the pool or lunch at the exceptional outdoor snack bar. ⊠ *1 Hotel Circle, Palmetto Dunes, Mid-Island, 29928* ☎ *843/686–8400 or 800/228–9292* 🖨 *843/686–8450* ⊕ *www.hiltonheadmarriott.com* ☞ *476 rooms, 36 suites* ♻ *Restaurant, café, pizzeria, room service, some kitchens, some minibars, cable TV, Wi-Fi, driving range, 3 18-hole golf courses, putting green, 26 tennis courts, 2 pools (1 indoor), gym, 2 hot tubs (1 indoor), beach, bicycles, bar, piano bar, shop, babysitting, children's programs (ages 3–12), concierge, business services, meeting rooms, no-smoking rooms* ⊟ *AE, D, DC, MC, V* ⦿ *EP.*

$$$$ 🖼 **Hilton Oceanfront Resort.** There's a Caribbean sensibility to this five-story chain hotel; the grounds are beautifully landscaped with deciduous and evergreen bushes, and palms run along the beach. All the rooms face the ocean and are decorated with elegant wood furnishings, such as hand-carved armoires. Warm reds accent neutral beiges and creams in the linens and upholstery. Its lounge, called Regatta, is a happening nightspot. ⊠ *23 Ocean La., Mid-Island* ⓓ *Box 6165, 29938* ☎ *843/842–8000 or 800/845–8001* 🖨 *843/842–4988* ⊕ *www.hiltonheadhilton. com* ☞ *303 studios, 20 suites* ♻ *2 restaurants, kitchenettes, cable TV, in-room data ports, Wi-Fi, 3 18-hole golf courses, 2 pools, health club, hot tub, sauna, boating, fishing, bicycles, Ping-Pong, volleyball, lounge, children's programs (ages 5–12), no-smoking rooms* ⊟ *AE, D, DC, MC, V* ⦿ *EP.*

★ $$$$ 🖼 **The Inn at Harbour Town.** The most buzzworthy of Hilton Head's properties is this European-style boutique hotel. A proper staff, clad in kilts, pampers you with British service and a dose of Southern charm. Butlers are on hand any time of the day or night, and the kitchen delivers around the clock. The spacious guest rooms, decorated with neutral palettes, have luxurious touches like Frette bed linens, which are turned down for you each night. Harbour Town Grill serves some of the best steaks on the island. ⊠ *Lighthouse La., off U.S. 278, Sea Pines South End, 29926* ☎ *843/363–8100 or 888/807–6873* ⊕ *www.seapines.com* ⮧ *60 rooms* ♨ *Restaurant, room service, refrigerators, cable TV, in-room data ports, Wi-Fi, 3 18-hole golf courses, 4 tennis courts, bicycles, laundry service, concierge, no-smoking rooms* ☰ *AE, D, DC, MC, V* ⊺◎⊺ *EP.*

$$$$ 🏨 **The Inn at Palmetto Bluff.** Fifteen minutes from Hilton Head is the Low-
Fodor's Choice country's most luxurious new resort. This 22,000-acre property has been
★ transformed into a perfect replica of a small island town, complete with its own clapboard church. As a chauffered golf cart takes you to your cottages, you'll pass the clubhouse, which resembles a mighty antebellum greathouse. All of the cottages are generously sized—even the one-bedroom cottages have more than 1,100 square feet of space. The decor is coastal chic, with sumptuous bedding, gas fireplaces, surround-sound home theaters, and marvelous bathroom suites with steam showers. Your screened-in porch puts you immediately in touch with nature. ⊠ *476 Mount Pelia Rd., Bluffton 29910* ☎ *843/706–6500 or 866/706–6565* ☐ *843/706–6550* ⊕ *www.palmettobluffresort.com* ⮧ *50 cottages* ♨ *3 restaurants, room service, refrigerators, cable TV, in-room DVDs, in-room data ports, Wi-Fi, 18-hole golf course, pool, spa, dock, boating, fishing, bicycles, bar, shops, dry cleaning, concierge, business services, meeting rooms, free parking; no smoking* ☰ *AE, MC, V* ⊺◎⊺ *EP.*

★ **$$$$** 🏨 **Westin Resort, Hilton Head Island.** A circular drive winds around a metal sculpture of long-legged marsh birds as you approach this luxury resort. The lush landscape lies on the island's quietest, least inhabited stretch of sand. Guest rooms, most with ocean views from the balconies, have homey touches, crown molding, and contemporary furnishings. If you need space to spread out, there are two- and three-bedroom villas. The service is efficient and caring. Expect additional pampering touches when a spa opens in mid-2007. ⊠ *2 Grass Lawn Ave., North End, 29928* ☎ *843/681–4000 or 800/228–3000* ☐ *843/681–1087* ⊕ *www.westin. com* ⮧ *412 rooms, 29 suites* ♨ *3 restaurants, in-room data ports, driving range, 3 18-hole golf courses, 16 tennis courts, pro shop, 2 pools (1 indoor), wading pool, health club, outdoor hot tub, massage, beach, bicycles, children's programs (ages 4–12), concierge, concierge floor, Internet, business services, meeting rooms, no-smoking rooms* ☰ *AE, D, DC, MC, V* ⊺◎⊺ *EP.*

$$$–$$$$ 🏨 **Holiday Inn Oceanfront Resort.** This high-rise, on one of the island's busiest beaches, is within walking distance of shops and restaurants. Standard rooms are spacious and furnished in a contemporary style; golf and tennis packages are available. The outdoor Tiki Hut lounge, a poolside bar, is hugely popular. ⊠ *S. Forest Beach Dr., South End* ☐ *Box 5728, 29938* ☎ *843/785–5126 or 800/423–9897* ☐ *843/785–6678* ⊕ *www. hihiltonhead.com* ⮧ *201 rooms* ♨ *Restaurant, snack bar, microwaves, minibars, cable TV, in-room data ports, Wi-Fi, pool, wading pool, gym, bicycles, volleyball, lounge, bar, children's programs (ages 3–12), meeting rooms, no-smoking rooms* ☰ *AE, D, DC, MC, V* ⊺◎⊺ *EP.*

6

$$$–$$$$ Fodor's Choice ★ **Main Street Inn.** This Italianate villa has stucco facades ornamented with lions' heads, elaborate ironwork, and shuttered doors—there's even a formal garden. Staying here is like being a guest at a rich friend's estate. Guest rooms have velvet and silk brocade linens, feather duvets, and porcelain and brass sinks. The ample breakfast buffet is served in a petite, sunny dining room. ✉ *2200 Main St., North End, 29926* ☎ *843/681–3001 or 800/471–3001* 🖷 *843/681–5541* 🌐 *www.mainstreetinn.com* *33 rooms* *Dining room, some in-room hot tubs, pool, hot tub, bar; no smoking* 💳 *AE, MC, V* 🍽 *BP.*

$$ **Hampton Inn.** This hotel, sheltered from the noise and traffic, is a good choice if you have kids. The two-bedroom family suites are surprisingly upscale; the parents' rooms are tastefully appointed, and the kids' room are *cool* enough to have foosball tables. King-size studios with sleeper sofas are another alternative for families. Breakfast is as Southern as country gravy and biscuits or as European as Belgian waffles. ✉ *1 Dillon Rd., Mid-Island, 29926* ☎ *843/681–7900* 🖷 *843/681–4330* 🌐 *www.hampton-inn.com* *115 rooms, 7 suites* *Cable TV, in-room data ports, Wi-Fi, microwaves, refrigerators, pool, shop, no-smoking rooms* 💳 *AE, D, DC, MC, V* 🍽 *BP.*

$$ **Residence Inn by Marriott.** The island's only all-suites property, the Residence Inn has a homey feel. Each suite has a full kitchen, so there's no need to eat out for every meal. You can cool in the pool after heating up on the tennis courts. The public beach is 2 mi away. ✉ *12 Park La., South End, 29928* ☎ *843/686–5700* 🖷 *843/686–3952* 🌐 *www.residenceinnhhi.com* *156 suites* *Kitchens, cable TV, in-room data ports, Wi-Fi, tennis court, pool, hot tub, bicycling, basketball, shop, meeting room, some pets allowed, no-smoking rooms* 💳 *AE, D, MC, V* 🍽 *BP.*

Nightlife & the Arts

The Arts

In warm weather free outdoor concerts are held at Harbour Town and Shelter Cove Harbour; at the latter fireworks light up the night Tuesday from June to August. Guitarist Gregg Russell has been playing for children under Harbour Town's mighty Liberty Oak tree for decades. He begins strumming nightly at 8 PM, except on Saturday.

The **Native Islander Gullah Celebration** (☎ 843/689–9314 🌐 www.gullahcelebration.com) takes place in February and showcases Gullah life through arts, music, and theater.

The **Arts Center of Coastal Carolina** (✉ Shelter Cove La., Mid-Island ☎ 843/686–3945 🌐 www.artscenter-hhi.org) has a gallery and a theater with programs for young people. The Hallelujah Singers, Gullah performers, appear regularly.

Nightlife

Hilton Head has always been a party place, and now more than ever. Bars, like everything else in Hilton Head, are often in strip malls.

Reggae bands play at **Big Bamboo** (✉ Coligny Plaza, N. Forest Beach Dr., South End ☎ 843/686–3443), a bar with a South Pacific theme.

The **Hilton Head Brewing Co.** (⊠ Hilton Head Plaza, Greenwood Dr., South End ☎ 843/785–2739) lets you shake your groove thing to '70s-era disco on Wednesday. There's live music on Friday and karaoke on Saturday. **Monkey Business** (⊠ Park Plaza, Greenwood Dr., South End ☎ 843/686–3545) is a dance club popular with young professionals. On Friday there's live beach music.

The latest hot spot, **Santa Fe Cafe** (⊠ Plantation Center in Palmetto Dunes, 700 Plantation Center, North End ☎ 843/785–3838) is where you can lounge about in front of the fireplace or sip top-shelf margaritas on the rooftop. **Turtle's** (⊠ 2 Grass Lawn Ave., North End ☎ 843/681–7009), the oceanfront bar at the Westin Resort, has a laid-back Caribbean vibe. **Turtle's** (⊠ 2 Grass Lawn Ave. ☎ 843/681–4000) appeals to anyone who still likes to hold their partner when they dance.

Shopping

Art Galleries
Linda Hartough Gallery (⊠ Harbour Town, 140 Lighthouse Rd., South End ☎ 843/671–6500) is all about golf. There's everything from landscapes of courses to gold balls to pillows embroidered with sayings like "Queen of the Green." The **Red Piano Art Gallery** (⊠ 220 Cordillo Pkwy., Mid-Island ☎ 843/785–2318) showcases 19th- and 20th-century works by regional and national artists.

Jewelry
The **Bird's Nest** (⊠ Coligny Plaza, Coligny Circle and N. Forest Beach Dr., South End ☎ 843/785–3737) sells locally made shell and sand-dollar jewelry, as well as island-theme charms. The **Goldsmith Shop** (⊠ 3 Lagoon Rd., Mid-Island ☎ 843/785–2538) carries classic jewelry and island charms. **Forsythe Jewelers** (⊠ 71 Lighthouse Rd., South End ☎ 843/342–3663) is the island's leading jewelry store.

Nature
The **Audubon Nature Store** (⊠ The Village at Wexford, U.S 278, Mid-Island ☎ 843/785–4311) has gifts with a wildlife theme. **Outside Hilton Head** (⊠ The Plaza at Shelter Cove, U.S. 278, Mid-Island ☎ 843/686–6996 or 800/686–6996) sells Pawleys Island hammocks (first made in the late 1800s) and other items that let you enjoy the great outdoors.

THE LOWCOUNTRY

The stretch of coastline between Hilton Head and Charleston is one of the most scenic parts of the state, and is still a mostly rural blend of small towns, winding country roads, and semitropical wilderness that turns into pristine beachfront before ending at the Atlantic. Here, especially along U.S. 17, look for roadside stands that sell boiled peanuts and homemade jams, and small-time shrimpers selling their catch out of coolers. Listen, too, for Gullah-tinged accents among the African-American natives—the sound is musical.

Beaufort

❺ *38 mi north of Hilton Head via U.S. 278 and Rte. 170; 70 mi southwest of Charleston via U.S. 17 and U.S. 21.*

Charming homes and churches grace this old town on Port Royal Island. Come here on a day trip from Hilton Head, Savannah, or Charleston, or to spend a quiet weekend at a B&B, shopping and strolling the historic district. A truly Southern town, its charms have lured moviemakers here to film favorites such as *The Big Chill* and *The Prince of Tides*. Author Pat Conroy calls the place home and has waxed poetic about the area in some of his best-selling books, including *The Water Is Wide*.

Built in 1795 and remodeled in 1852, the Gothic-style building that was the home of the Beaufort Volunteer Artillery now houses the **Beaufort Museum & Arsenal.** Prehistoric relics, Native American pottery, and Revolutionary War and Civil War exhibits are on display. ⊠ *713 Craven St.* ☎ *843/379–3331* 🎟 *$3* ☉ *Mon.–Sat. 11–4.*

John Mark Verdier House Museum, built in the federal style, has been restored and furnished as it would have been between its construction in 1805 and the visit of Lafayette in 1825. It was the headquarters for Union forces during the Civil War. ■ TIP➡ **A ticket that gets you into the Beaufort Museum & Arsenal and the John Mark Verdier House Museum saves you $1.** ⊠ *801 Bay St.* ☎ *843/379–6335* 🎟 *$6* ☉ *Mon.–Sat. 10–3:30.*

The 1724 **St. Helena's Episcopal Church** was turned into a hospital during the Civil War, and gravestones were brought inside to serve as operating tables. ⊠ *505 Church St.* ☎ *843/522–1712* ☉ *Tues.–Fri. 10–4, Sat. 10–1.*

Henry C. Chambers Waterfront Park, off Bay Street, is a great place to survey the scene. Trendy restaurants and bars overlook these 7 landscaped acres along the Beaufort River. There's a farmers' market here on Saturday, April through August, 8 to noon.

St. Helena Island, 9 mi southeast of Beaufort via U.S. 21, is the site of the Penn Center Historic District. Established in the middle of the Civil War, Penn Center was the South's first school for freed slaves; today it provides community services and has cottages for rent.

The **York W. Bailey Museum** has displays on the Penn Center and on the heritage of Sea Island blacks. These islands are where Gullah, a musical language that combines English and African languages, developed. ⊠ *Martin Luther King Jr. Blvd., St. Helena Island* ☎ *843/838–2432* ⊕ *www.penncenter.com* 🎟 *$4* ☉ *Mon.–Sat. 11–4.*

★ Secluded **Hunting Island State Park** has nature trails and about 3 mi of public beaches—some dramatically and beautifully eroding. The 1,120-foot-long fishing pier is among the longest on the East Coast. You can climb the 181 steps of the **Hunting Island Lighthouse** (built in 1859 and abandoned in 1933) for sweeping views. The nature center has exhibits, an aquarium, and lots of turtles. A stroll along the marsh boardwalk is to be at one with nature. The park is 18 mi southeast of Beaufort via

CLOSE UP

The World of Gullah

IN THE LOWCOUNTRY, Gullah refers to several things: language, people, and a culture. Gullah (the word itself is believed to be a version of Angola), an English-based dialect rooted in African languages, is the unique language of the African-Americans of the Sea Islands of South Carolina and Georgia. More than 300 years old, this rhythmic language has survived, in part, because of the geographic isolation of the people who speak it; most locally born African-Americans of the area can understand, if not speak, Gullah.

Descended from thousands of slaves who were imported by planters in the Carolinas during the 18th century, the Gullah people have maintained not only their dialect but also their heritage. Much of Gullah culture traces back to the African rice-coast culture and survives today in the art forms and skills, including sweetgrass basket-making, of Sea Islanders. During the colonial period, when rice was king, Africans from the West African rice kingdoms drew high premiums as slaves. Those with basket-making skills were extremely valuable because baskets were needed for agricultural and household use. Made by hand, sweet-grass baskets are intricate coils of a marsh grass with a sweet, haylike aroma.

Nowhere is Gullah culture more evident than in the foods of the region. Rice appears at nearly every meal—Africans taught planters how to grow rice and how to cook and serve it as well. Lowcountry dishes use okra,

peanuts, *benne* (the African word for sesame seeds), field peas, and hot peppers. Gullah food reflects the bounty of the islands: shrimp, crabs, oysters, fish, and such vegetables as greens, tomatoes, and corn. Many dishes are prepared in one pot, a method similar to the stew-pot cooking of West Africa. Frogmore Stew combines shrimp, potatoes, sausage, and corn. Hoppin' John—a mixture of rice and field peas traditionally served on New Year's Day—is similar to rice and pigeon peas, a mainstay in West Africa.

On St. Helena Island, near Beaufort, Penn Center is the unofficial Gullah headquarters, preserving the culture and developing opportunities for Gullahs. In 1852 the first school for freed slaves was established at Penn Center, and later Dr. Martin Luther King Jr. and the Southern Christian Leadership Council regularly met here to organize civil rights activities. You can delve into the culture further at the York W. Bailey Museum.

On St. Helena, many Gullahs still go shrimping with hand-tied nets, harvest oysters, and grow their own vegetables. Nearby on Daufuskie Island, as well as on Edisto, Wadmalaw, and Johns islands near Charleston, you can find Gullah communities as well. A famous Gullah proverb says: *If oonuh ent kno weh oonuh dah gwine, oonuh should kno weh oonuh come f'um.* Translation: if you don't know where you're going, you should know where you come from.

U.S. 21; call for cabin and camping reservations. ✉ *1775 Sea Island Pkwy., off St. Helena Island, Hunting Island* ☎ *843/838–2011* ⊕ *www. southcarolinaparks.com* ⊠ *$4* ☉ *Park Apr.–Oct., daily 6 AM–9 PM; Nov.–Mar., daily 6–6. Lighthouse daily 11–4.*

Sports & the Outdoors

BIKING Beaufort is great for biking. Some inns rent them to guests; otherwise, call **Lowcountry Bicycles** (✉ 102 Sea Island Pkwy. ☎ 843/524–9585).

CANOE & BOAT TOURS Beaufort is where the Ashepoo, Combahee, and Edisto rivers form the A.C.E. Basin, a vast wilderness of marshes and tidal estuaries loaded with history. For sea kayaking, try **Beaufort Kayak Tours** (✉ 2709 Oaklawn St. ☎ 843/525–0810 ⊕ www.beaufortkayaktours.com).

A.C.E. Basin Tours (✉ 1 Coosaw River Dr., Coosaw Island ☎ 843/521–3099 ⊕www.acebasintours.com) might be the best bet for the very young, or anyone with limited mobility, as it operates a 38-foot pontoon boat tour. **A.C.E. Basin Adventures** (✉ U.S. 17, Jacksonboro ☎ 843/844–2514) leads kayak, powerboat, and driving tours.

GOLF Most golf courses are about a 10- to 20-minute scenic drive from Beaufort.

Dataw Island. In a gated community, Dataw Island has Tom Fazio's Cotton Dike Course, with spectacular marsh views, and Arthur Hill's Morgan River Course, with ponds, marshes, and wide-open fairways. The lovely 14th hole overlooks the river. You must be accompanied by a member or belong to another private club. ✉ *Dataw Club Rd., off U.S. 21, Dataw Island, 6 mi east of Beaufort* ☎ *843/838–8250* 🖶 *843/838–8211* ⊕ *www.dataw.org* ⌖ *Reservations essential* ⚑ *Cotton Dike: 18 holes. 6799 yds. Par 72. Morgan River: 18 holes. 6646 yds. Par 72. Green Fee: $69 with a member; $120 unaccompanied* ⌨ *Facilities: Driving range, putting green, pitching area, golf carts, rental clubs, pro-shop, lessons, restaurant, bar.*

Fripp Island Golf & Beach Resort. This resort has a pair of championship courses. Ocean Creek Golf Course, designed by Davis Love, has sweeping views of saltwater marshes. Designed by George Cobb, Ocean Point Golf Links runs along the ocean the entire way. This is a wildlife refuge, so you'll see plenty of it. ✉ *201 Tarpon Blvd., Fripp Island* ☎ *843/838–2131* 🖶 *843/838–9251* ⊕ *www.frippislandresort.com* ⌖ *Reservations essential* ⚑ *Ocean Creek: 18 holes. 6643 yds. Par 71. Ocean Point: 18 holes. 6556 yds. Par 72. Green Fee: $89–$99* ⌨ *Facilities: Driving range, putting green, pitching area, golf carts, pull carts, rental clubs, pro-shop, PGA instruction, restaurant, bar.*

South Carolina National Golf Course. This is a semiprivate club, so members get priority. Its scenic course is considered tight with plenty of water hazards. ✉ *8 Waveland Ave., Port Royal* ☎ *843/524–0300* 🖶 *843/524–4722* ⊕ *www.scnational.com* ⌖ *Reservations essential* ⚑ *18 holes. 6625 yds. Par 71. Green Fee: $50–$65* ⌨ *Facilities: Driving range, putting green, pitching area, golf carts, rental clubs, pro-shop, lessons, restaurant, bar.*

Where to Stay & Eat

$$$$
Fodor'sChoice
★
✕ **Bateaux.** This contemporary restaurant has poetic views of the Beaufort River. Chef Charles Ulbrich has made imaginative Southern cuisine his mission. His food is fresh, elegant, and artistically presented. Foodies love that they can get foie gras in crepes and other dishes. Seafood is the obvious specialty; try the shrimp and scallops over red-pepper risotto with fried prosciutto and spinach. The staff is well-trained and knowledgeable. ⊠ *27 Whitehall Landing, Lady's Island* ☎ *843/379–0777* ⊟ *AE, MC, V* ☾ *Closed Sun. No lunch Sat.*

$$$–$$$$
✕ **Emily's.** Long, narrow, and wood-paneled, Emily's is a lively restaurant. Crowds linger over the tapas, including spring rolls, garlic beef, and even baby lamb chops. This is a great place to come early or late, as the kitchen serves from 4 PM to 11 PM. The piano bar is a hot ticket, but definitely *not* a no-smoking haven. ⊠ *906 Port Republic St.* ☎ *843/ 522–1866* ⊟ *AE, MC, V* ☾ *Closed Sun. No lunch.*

$$$–$$$$
Fodor'sChoice
★
✕ **Saltus River Grill.** The hippest eatery in Beaufort wins over epicureans with its cool design (subdued lighting, mod booths, dark-wood bar), waterfront patio, and nouveau Southern menu. A flawless meal might start off with the velvety crab bisque, then segue to the flounder stuffed with local shrimp and blue crab and topped with fried capers and crumbled bacon. The wine list is admirable, and the staff is adept at pairings. Desserts change nightly; the pineapple upside-down cake can be the perfect end to your meal. ⊠ *802 Bay St.* ☎ *843/379–3474* ⊟ *AE, D, MC, V.*

$$–$$$$
✕ **11th Street Dockside.** The succulent fried oysters, shrimp, and fish are some of the best around. Other specialties are the steamed seafood pot filled with crab legs, oysters, shrimp, and lobster and—by request only— Frogmore stew (with shrimp, potatoes, sausage, and corn). Everything is served in a classic wharf-side environment, where you can eat on a screened porch. There are water views from nearly every table. ⊠ *1699 11th St. W, Port Royal, 6 mi southwest of Beaufort* ☎ *843/524–7433* ⊟ *AE, D, DC, MC, V* ☾ *No lunch.*

$–$$
✕ **Plums.** Down the alley behind Shipman's Gallery is this homey frame house with plum-color awnings shading the front porch. Plums still uses old family recipes for its crab-cake sandwiches and curried chicken salad, but now it also offers a blue cheese and portobello mushroom sandwich. Dinner has creative and affordable pasta and seafood dishes. There's live music on weekends. ⊠ *904½ Bay St.* ☎ *843/525–1946* ⊟ *AE, MC, V.*

$
✕ **Shrimp Shack.** On the way to Hunting Island, follow the cue of locals and stop at this endearing little place. The menu includes shrimp burgers, sweet-potato fries, and sweet tea. Dinner is served only until 8 PM. ⊠ *1929 Sea Island Pkwy., St. Helena, 18 mi southeast of Beaufort* ☎ *843/838–2962* ⊟ *No credit cards* ☾ *Closed Sun.*

$$–$$$$
✕▦ **Beaufort Inn and Veranda Restaurant.** This peach-color 1890s Victorian inn, dating from the 1890s, charms you with its gables and wraparound porches. Inside there's an acclaimed restaurant ($$$–$$$$) with dining on a screened porch or in two mahogany-panel dining rooms. The cuisine is a successful *ménage à trois* of Southern, continental, and contemporary fare. Pine-floor guest rooms have period reproductions, striped wallpaper, and comfy chairs. Several have fireplaces and four-

poster beds. ⊠ *809 Port Republic St., 29901* ☎ *843/521–9000* 🖶 *843/521–9500* ⊕ *www.beaufortinn.com* 🛏 *28 rooms* ⚘ *Restaurant, cable TV, in-room DVDs, bicycles; no kids under 8, no smoking* 🖃 *AE, D, MC, V* 🍴 *BP.*

$$$–$$$$ 🏨 **Cuthbert House Inn.** The owners have filled this 1790 home with 18th- and 19th-century heirlooms; it retains the original federal fireplaces and crown and rope mold-

NO ROOM AT THE INN

The military has a commanding presence in Beaufort, and throughout the year there are various graduation ceremonies on Wednesday and Thursday. Lodgings can fill up fast, so make sure to call ahead.

ing. Guest rooms and oversize suites are elegant but a bit busy, comfortable with hand-knotted rugs on the pine floors and commanding beds piled high with quilts. Its looks out on the waters of the bay. Beautifully lighted at night, this antebellum house, with white pillars and dual verandas, typifies the Old South. ⊠ *1203 Bay St., 29902* ☎ *843/521–1315 or 800/327–9275* 🖶 *843/521–1314* ⊕ *www.cuthberthouseinn.com* 🛏 *5 rooms, 2 suites* ⚘ *Some in-room hot tubs, some refrigerators, cable TV, in-room DVDs, in-room data ports, bicycles; no kids under 12, no smoking* 🖃 *AE, D, MC, V* 🍴 *BP.*

★ $$$–$$$$ 🏨 **Fripp Island Resort.** This resort sits on the island made famous in *Prince of Tides,* so expect miles of broad beaches and unspoiled scenery. It has long been known as one of the more affordable, casual island resorts. Here you can play a little golf or tennis, and then chill out on the beach. The more than 200 villas and two- and three-bedroom cottages have contemporary style. There's a pavilion with shops, restaurants with live entertainment, and a marina. ⊠ *1 Tarpon Blvd., Fripp Island 29920, 19 mi south of Beaufort* ☎ *843/838–3535 or 877/374–7748* 🖶 *843/838–9079* ⊕ *www.frippislandresort.com* 🛏 *210 units* ⚘ *5 restaurants, cable TV, 2 18-hole golf courses, 10 tennis courts, 4 pools, boating, bicycles, children's programs (ages 3–12), meeting rooms; no smoking* 🖃 *AE, D, DC, MC, V* 🍴 *EP.*

★ $$$–$$$$ 🏨 **Rhett House Inn.** Art and antiques abound in a circa 1820 home turned storybook inn. Look for the little luxuries—down pillows and duvets, a CD player in each room, and fresh flowers. The best rooms open out onto the veranda (No. 2) or the courtyard garden (No. 7). Breakfast, afternoon tea, evening hors d'oeuvres, and dessert are included in the rate. Visiting celebrities have included Barbra Streisand, Jeff Bridges, and Dennis Quaid. The remodeled house across the street has eight more rooms, each of which has a gas fireplace, a whirlpool bath, a private entrance, and a porch. ⊠ *1009 Craven St., 29902* ☎ *843/524–9030* 🖶 *843/524–1310* ⊕ *www.rhetthouseinn.com* 🛏 *16 rooms, 1 suite* ⚘ *Dining room, some in-room hot tubs, bicycles; no kids under, no smoking* 🖃 *AE, D, MC, V* 🍴 *BP.*

$$ 🏨 **Best Western Sea Island Inn.** At this well-maintained motel in the downtown historic district, you are within walking distance of shops and restaurants. You can see the bay from the front terrace. Ample rooms have two queen or king beds. Cookies and coffee are always available in the lobby. ⊠ *1015 Bay St., 29901* ☎ *843/522–2090 or 800/528–1234*

🖷 843/521–4858 ⊕ *www.sea-island-inn.com* ⏏ *43 rooms* ⚬ *Refrigerators, microwaves, cable TV, in-room data ports, pool, gym, nosmoking rooms, meeting rooms* ▱ *AE, D, DC, MC, V* ⏹ *BP.*

Nightlife & the Arts

The **Hallelujah Singers** (⊠ 806 Elizabeth St. ☎ 843/379–3594), Gullah performers, perform at Lowcountry venues.

The late-night hangout **Luther's** (⊠ 910 Bay St. ☎ 843/521–1888) rocks on weekends.

Shopping

ART GALLERIES At **Bay Street Gallery** (⊠ 719 Bay St. ☎ 843/525–1024 or 843/522–9210), Laura Hefner's oils of coastal wetlands magically convey the mood of the Lowcountry. The colorful designs of Suzanne and Eric Longo decorate the **Longo Gallery** (⊠ 103 Charles St. ☎ 843/522–8933). The **Rhett Gallery** (⊠ 901 Bay St. ☎ 843/524–3339) sells Lowcountry art by four generations of the Rhett family, as well as antique maps and Audubon prints.

Edisto Island

6 *62 mi northeast of Beaufort via U.S. 17 and Rte. 174; 44 mi southwest of Charleston via U.S. 17 and Rte. 174.*

On rural Edisto (pronounced *ed*-is-toh) Island, magnificent stands of age-old oaks festooned with Spanish-moss border, quiet streams, and side roads; wild turkeys may still be spotted on open grasslands and amid palmetto palms. The small "downtown" beachfront is a mix of public beach-access spots, restaurants, and old, shabby-chic beach homes that are a far cry from the palatial villas rented out on the resort islands. The outlying Edisto Beach State Park is a pristine wilderness and camper's delight.

FodorsChoice ★ **Edisto Beach State Park** covers 1,255 acres and includes marshland and tidal rivers, a 1½-mi-long beachfront, towering palmettos, and a lush maritime forest with a 3½-mi trail running through it. The one-time CCC project park has the best shelling on public property in the Lowcountry. Overnight options include rustic furnished cabins by the marsh and campsites by the ocean (although severe erosion is limiting availability). Luxury resort development has begun to encroach around the edges of the park. ⊠ *Route 174, off U.S. 17* ☎ 843/869–2156 ⊕ *www.discoversouthcarolina.com* ☞ *$3* ◷ *Early Apr.–late Oct., daily 8 AM–10 PM; Late Oct.–early Apr., daily 8–6.*

The ruins of **Sheldon Church**, built in 1753, make an interesting stop if you're driving from Beaufort to Edisto Island. The church burned down in 1779 and again in 1865. Only the brick walls and columns remain. ⊠ *18 mi northwest of Beaufort.*

Where to Stay & Eat

★ **$$$–$$$$** ✕ **Old Post Office.** On par with Charleston and Savannah kitchens—but with none of their big-city pretense—the Old Post Office is the best restaurant in this sleepy part of the state. The house specialties are shrimp and grits and, well, *anything* else with grits. Try signature dishes like "fussed-over" pork chops served with locally grown greens and fresh-baked bread. The green tomatoes come fried or in a soup garnished with crab. ⊠ *1442 Rte. 174* ☎ *843/869–2339* ▭ *MC, V* ⊗ *Closed Sun. Oct.–May. No lunch Mon.*

★ ¢–$ ✕ **Po' Pigs Bo-B-Q.** Step inside the super-casual restaurant for pork barbecue that has South Carolinians raving. Sample the different sauces (sweet mustard, tomato, or vinegar) and wash it all down with a tall glass of sweet tea. Don't miss down-home sides like squash casserole, pork skins, lima beans and ham, and red rice. The blink-and-you-miss-it location is on the tail end of an undeveloped road. ⊠ *2410 Rte. 174* ☎ *843/ 869–9003* ▭ *No credit cards* ⊗ *Closed Sun.–Tues.*

$–$$ ⊞ **Fairfield Ocean Ridge Resort.** Looking for resort amenities in a get-away-from-it-all escape? You've found it here. Although few of the accommodations (one- to five-bedroom villas and houses) are on the beach, most are just a short walk away from it. (Be sure to ask.) They're all attractive and tastefully furnished. A trolley transports guests to the resort's beach cabana. ⊠ *1 King Cotton Rd., Box 27, 29438* ☎ *843/ 869–2561 or 800/845–8500* ☐ *843/869–2384* ⊕ *www.fairfieldvacations. com* ⌫ *100 units* ⌂ *Restaurant, 18-hole golf course, miniature golf, 4 tennis courts, pool, wading pool, beach, boating, fishing, bicycles, hiking, lounge, no-smoking rooms* ▭ *D, MC, V* ⟋⊙⟍ *EP.*

$ ⊞ **Atwood Vacations.** For complete privacy, rent out a family-owned cottage on Edisto. The list of properties include everything from one-bedroom condos to six-bedroom homes. All kitchens are stocked with appliances and dishes, but you need to bring your own bed linens. Two-day minimum stays are required. ⊠ *495 Rte. 174, 29438* ☎ *843/869– 2151* ⊕ *www.atwoodvacations.com* ⌂ *BBQs, kitchens, cable TV* ▭ *AE, MC, V* ⟋⊙⟍ *EP.*

HILTON HEAD & THE LOWCOUNTRY ESSENTIALS

Transportation

BY AIR

Hilton Head Island Airport is served by US Airways Express. Most travelers use the Savannah/Hilton Head International Airport, about an hour from Hilton Head, which is served by AirTran, American Eagle, Continental Express, Delta, Northwest, United Express, and US Airways.

🛪 **Hilton Head Island Airport** ☎ 843/689–5400. **Savannah/Hilton Head International Airport** ⊠ 400 Airways Ave., Savannah, GA ☎ 912/964–0514.

BY BOAT & FERRY

Hilton Head is accessible via the Intracoastal Waterway, with docking available at Harbour Town Yacht Basin, Hilton Head Boathouse, and Shelter Cove Harbour.

🛪 **Harbour Yacht Basin** ☎ 843/671–2704. **Hilton Head Boathouse** ☎ 843/681–2628. **Shelter Cove Harbor** ☎ 843/842–7001.

BY BUS

Greyhound Bus connects Beaufort with other destinations in the area. The Lowcountry Regional Transportation Authority has a bus that leaves Beaufort in the morning for Hilton Head that costs $2.50. Exact change is required. This same company has a van that, with 24-hour notice, will pick you up at your hotel and drop you off at your destination for $3. You can request a ride weekdays 7 AM to 10 AM or 12:30 PM to 3 PM.

Greyhound ⊠ 3659 Trask Pkwy.,, Beaufort ☎ 843/524-4646 or 800/231-2222 ⊕ www.greyhound.com. **The Lowcountry Regional Transportation Authority** ☎ 843/757-5782 ⊕ www.gotohhi.com/bus.

BY CAR

Hilton Head Island is 40 mi east of Interstate 95 (Exit 28 off Interstate 95S, Exit 5 off Interstate 95N). If you're heading to the southern end of the island, your best bet to save time and avoid traffic is to take the Toll Expressway. The cost is $1 each way. Beaufort is 25 mi east of Interstate 95, on U.S. 21.

BY TAXI

At Your Service, Greyline Lowcountry Adventures, and Yellow Cab are good options in Hilton Head. In Beaufort, try Point Tours and Yellow Cab.

At Your Service ☎ 843/837-3783. **Greyline Lowcountry Adventures** ☎ 843/681-8212. **Point Tours** ☎ 843/522-3576. **Yellow Cab** ☎ 843/686-6666 in Hilton Head, 843/522-1121 in Beaufort.

BY TRAIN

Amtrak gets you as close as Savannah. Greyline Lowcountry Adventures will send a limo to pick you up at a cost of $66 per hour.

Savannah Amtrak Station ⊠ 2611 Seaboard Coastline Dr., Savannah ☎ 912/234-2611 or 800/872-7245 ⊕ www.amtrak.com. **Greyline Lowcountry Adventures** ☎ 843/681-8212.

Contacts & Resources

BANKS & EXCHANGE SERVICES

Banks have slightly different hours, but most are open on weekdays. Bank of America in the North End and Harbourside Community Bank in Mid-Island also have limited Saturday hours.

Bank of America ⊠ 59 Pope Ave., South End ☎ 843/342-1073. **Harbourside Community Bank** ⊠ 852 William Hilton Pkwy., Mid-Island ☎ 843/341-1200. **SunTrust Bank** ⊠ 2 Greenwood Dr., South End ☎ 843/341-2100. **Wachovia Bank** ⊠ 200 Merchant St., North End ☎ 843/686-9601.

EMERGENCIES

Emergency medical service is available at the Hilton Head Medical Center and Clinics. There are no 24-hour pharmacies, but CVS is open until 10 PM.

Emergency Services **Ambulance, fire, police** ☎ 911. **Hospitals** **Hilton Head Regional Medical Center** ⊠ Hospital Center Blvd., Mid-Island, Hilton Head Island ☎ 843/681-6122. **Late-Night Pharmacies** **CVS** ⊠ 10 Pope Ave., South End, Hilton Head Island ☎ 843/785-7786.

INTERNET, MAIL & SHIPPING

There are several Internet cafés, including Internet Café & Sundries in the South End, as well as numerous coffee shops and restaurants with free wireless connections. Nearly all hotels also have some way to get you wired.

There are two major post offices on Hilton Head, one in the South End and one on the North End. FedEx and UPS have locations on the island.

Internet Cafés **Internet Café & Sundries** ⊠ 1 N. Forest Dr., South End, Hilton Head Island 🕾 843/785-6600.

Overnight Services **FedEx** ⊠ 20 Hunter Rd., North End, Hilton Head Island 🕾 800/463-3339. **UPS Store** ⊠ 33 Office Park Rd., North End, Hilton Head Island 🕾 843/842-3171.

Post Offices **Fairfield Station Post Office** ⊠ 213 WIlliam Hilton Pkwy., North End, Hilton Head Island 🕾 843/682-3002. **Hilton Head Island Main Post Office** ⊠ Bow Circle, South End, Hilton Head Island 🕾 843/785-7002.

MEDIA

The Island Packet is Hilton Head's daily newspaper. The complimentary *Island Events* lists local and regional events.

Island Events 🕾 843/785-5924 ⊕ www.hiltonhead.com/events. **The Island Packet** 🕾 843/785-4293 ⊕ www.islandpacket.com.

TOUR OPTIONS

Hilton Head's Adventure Cruises hosts dinner, sightseeing, and murder-mystery cruises. Several companies, including H20 Sports and Lowcountry Nature Tours in Hilton Head, run dolphin sightseeing, shark fishing, and delightful environmental trips. Carolina Buggy Tours show you Beaufort's historic district by horse-drawn carriage.

Gullah Heritage Trail Tours give a wealth of history about slavery and the Union takeover of the island during the Civil War. Gullah 'n' Geechie Mahn Tours lead tours throughout Beaufort with a focus on African-American culture. Costumed guides sing and act out history during walking tours by the Spirit of Old Beaufort tour group.

Beaufort City Tours **Carolina Buggy Tours** ⊠ 901 Port Republic St., Beaufort 🕾 843/525-1300. **Gullah 'n' Geechie Mahn Tours** ⊠ 671 Sea Island Pkwy., Beaufort 🕾 843/838-7516 ⊕ www.gullahngeechietours.net. **Spirit of Old Beaufort** ⊠ 103 West St., Beaufort 🕾 843/525-0459 ⊕ www.thespiritofoldbeaufort.com.

Boat Tours **Adventure Cruises** ⊠ Shelter Cove Marina, 9 Shelter Cove La., Mid-Island, Hilton Head Island 🕾 843/785-4558 ⊕ www.hiltonheadisland.com. **H20 Sports** ⊠ Harbour Town Marina, 149 Lighthouse Rd., South End, Hilton Head Island 🕾 843/363-2628 ⊕ www.h2osportsonline.com. **Low Country Nature Tours** ⊠ Shelter Cover Harbour, Shelter Cove La., Mid-Island, Hilton Head Island 🕾 843/683-0187 ⊕ www.lowcountrynaturetours.com.

City Tours **Gullah Heritage Trail Tours** ⊠ 100 William Hilton Pkwy., North End, Hilton Head 🕾 843/681-7066 ⊕ www.gullaheritage.com.

VISITOR INFORMATION

For information on Edisto, call the Edisto Island Chamber of Commerce. The Regional Beaufort Chamber of Commerce has information about

Beaufort and the surrounding area. In Hilton Head your best bet for local information is to stop by the Welcome Center, on the island side of the bridge that connects Hilton Head to Bluffton.

🚩 Tourist Information **Edisto Island Chamber of Commerce** ⊠ 430 Rte. 174, Box 206, Edisto Island 29438 ☎ 843/869-3867 or 888/333-2781 ⊕ www.edistochamber.com. **Regional Beaufort Chamber of Commerce** ⊠ 1106 Carteret St., Box 910, Beaufort 29901 ☎ 843/986-5400 ⊕ www.beaufortsc.org. **Welcome Center of Hilton Head** ⊠ 100 William Hilton Pkwy., 29938 ☎ 800/523-3373 ⊕ www.hiltonheadisland.org.

The Midlands & Upstate

WORD OF MOUTH

"While you are in Columbia, visit the Vista and have dinner there and shop one evening. [It's] a revitalized downtown area with wonderful upscale shops and dining in 150-year-old buildings."
—GoTravel

"[Five Points in Columbia] has shops, bars and restaurants that cater mainly to a younger crowd but the older, professional crowd is welcomed and finds many opportunities for shopping or eating there also. Five Points has extended down Devine Street and there are many wonderful shops with everything from consignment shops to high-end antiques."
—SherrieA

By Katie
McElveen

SOUTH CAROLINA'S MIDLANDS, between the coastal Lowcountry and the mountains, is a varied region of swamps and flowing rivers, fertile farmland—perfect for horse raising—and hardwood and pine forests. Lakes have wonderful fishing, and the many state parks are popular for hiking, swimming, and camping. Small old towns with mansions turned bed-and-breakfasts are common, and the many public gardens provide islands of color during most of the year. At the center of the region is the state capital, Columbia, an engaging contemporary city enveloping cherished historic elements. Just outside of town, Congaree Swamp National Park has the largest intact tract of old-growth floodplain forest in North America. Aiken, the center of South Carolina's thoroughbred country, is where champions Sea Hero and Pleasant Colony were trained. Towns such as Abbeville and Camden preserve and interpret the past, with old house museums, history re-creations, and museum exhibits.

The Upstate of South Carolina is a land of waterfalls and wide vistas, cool pine forests and fast rapids. Camping, hiking, white-water rafting and kayaking are less than an hour from downtown Greenville and a paddle's-throw from the small hamlets that are scattered about. Greenville itself, artsy and refined, is a modern southern city with a thriving downtown full of trendy restaurants, boutiques, and galleries. Cinderella-cousin Spartanburg is also up and coming, thanks to an influx of high-level manufacturers such as BMW and Michelin and the rising popularity of area colleges.

7

Exploring the Midlands & Upstate

South Carolina's Midlands and Upstate regions are well endowed with highways: from Columbia, Interstate 26 heads toward the mountains, northwest, to Spartanburg. Greenville, just west of Spartanburg, is the gateway to dozens of tidy mountain towns. Interstate 20 will take you from Columbia east to Camden or southwest through Aiken and on to Atlanta. Interstate 77 runs north toward Charlotte, and is an easy connector to Interstate 85 in North Carolina, but it also cuts through Interstate 26 and Interstate 20, giving fairly direct cross-region access. Less direct, but providing pretty views, which range from peach orchards to mountain outcroppings (along with plenty of stops for local fruits and vegetables), is the two-lane Cherokee Foothills Scenic Highway (Route 11), which follows an old Cherokee Indian path in the northwestern corner of the state.

To get a true sense of the geographic diversity of this huge area—there are sand hills, rich farmland, and mountains within a two-hour drive—you'll need a car and a full tank of gas. But bring good walking shoes, or hiking boots, so you can take advantage of the many trails, paths, and parks—some quite wild—that wind through the region.

About the Restaurants

Most of the smaller towns have at least one dining choice that might surprise you with its take on sophisticated fare (filet mignon with pi-

TOP 5 REASONS TO GO

Small Town Charms: Small towns—most complete with shady town squares, jewel-box shops, a café or two, and historic churches—dot this region. Abbeville and Aiken are a couple of the nicest.

Rafting the Chattooga: The fact that the movie *Deliverance* was filmed here doesn't scare away rafting enthusiasts, who have discovered that some of the best white-water rafting in the country comes courtesy of the Chattooga River.

Antiquing in Camden: Camden's Art & Antique District, which comprises most of the downtown area, is a treasure trove of well-priced furniture: chests, sideboards, and dining tables from England, France, and the Southeast;

ironwork, mantles, and doors from plantations and estates; and high-quality paintings.

Congaree Swamp National Park: Massive hardwoods and towering pines form a tall canopy through which hazy light filters, transforming the woods into a hauntingly beautiful scene. Wander through 20 mi of trails or the 2½-mi boardwalk that meander over lazy creeks.

Waterfalls: More than 25 waterfalls tumble from the rocks and cliffs of South Carolina's Upstate; some, like 75-foot Twin Falls, are an easy walk from the road. Others, such as the over 400-foot Raven Falls, reward more serious hikers with jaw-dropping views.

mento cheese, anyone?). Larger cities such as Columbia, Greenville, and Spartanburg have both upscale foodie haunts and ultracasual grits-and-greens joints. Many local restaurants serve "meat and three," which is your choice of a meat main and three side dishes. Macaroni and cheese, rice and gravy, mashed potatoes, and Jell-o are popular sides. Barbecue and other down-home Southern specialties are sometimes served buffet-style. Thanks to the rich farmland in the area, fresh fruits and vegetables are easy to come by in restaurants and at roadside stands. Mexican food is usually a good bet because many of the farm workers have emigrated to South Carolina from Mexico, bringing their cooking skills with them. Plan ahead: many places close on Sunday.

About the Hotels

Your best bet is to stay in an area inn or B&B. These establishments tend to be owned and occupied by engaging locals who want to raise their families in the area where they grew up, or by couples from the North who have retired. Either way, count on just a handful of rooms, family favorites for breakfast and, if you're lucky, a garden for wandering and a restored town square just steps away. What you gain in charm, however, you may have to give up in convenience. If you want to be close to lots of dining options, and have an on-site workout room and cable television, you might opt for one of the chain motels that flourish in this part of South Carolina.

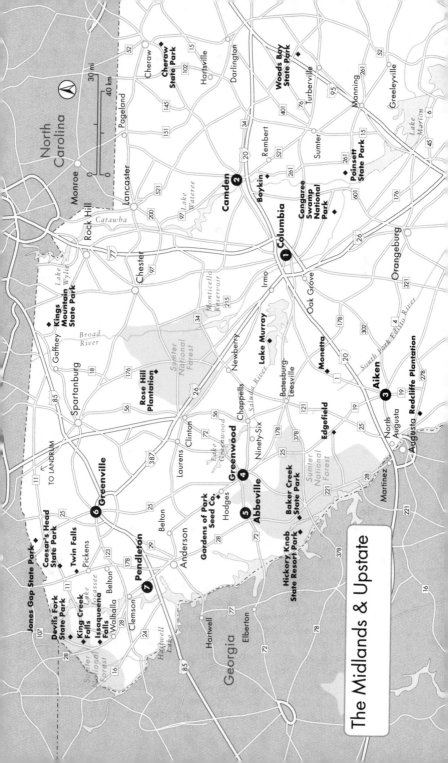

The Midlands & Upstate

	WHAT IT COSTS				
	$$$$	$$$	$$	$	¢
RESTAURANTS	over $22	$17–$22	$12–$16	$7–$11	under $7
HOTELS	over $220	$161–$220	$111–$160	$70–$110	under $70

Restaurant prices are for a main course at dinner. Hotel prices are for two people in a standard double room in high season.

Timing

Central South Carolina comes alive in spring, beginning in early March, when the azaleas, dogwoods, wisteria, and jasmine turn normal landscapes into fairylands of pink, white, and purple shaded by a canopy of pines. Days are bright and sunny, humidity is remarkable in its absence and cool night breezes blow heady floral scents. Late May through September can be oppressive, particularly in the Midlands; people do spend a lot of time outside and, as a result, parks, lakes and trails are usually busy—although not uncomfortably crowded. Festivals celebrating everything from peaches to okra are held in summer. Fall will bring the state fair in Columbia, SEC and ACC football to the University of South Carolina and Clemson University, rich yellows and reds of the changing trees in the mountains and a number of art and music festivals.

COLUMBIA & THE MIDLANDS

The wide swath of land that comprises the Midlands may have only one large city—the state capital, Columbia—but its profusion of small and medium-size towns makes this area a patchwork quilt of history and activity. The local museums and historic homes that line the shady streets often house surprisingly deep collections on everything from Civil or Revolutionary War battles to the lifestyle on 1850's plantations. Well informed and friendly docents are happy to share stories, not to mention some tips on who's got the best peach pie that day.

Columbia

❶ *112 mi northwest of Charleston via I–26; 101 mi southeast of Greenville via I–385 and I–26.*

Old as Columbia may be, trendy and collegiate neighborhoods have given the city an edge. The symphony, two professional ballet companies, several theaters that stage live—and often locally written—productions, and a number of engaging museums keep culture alive. The city is a sprawling blend of modern office blocks, suburban neighborhoods, and the occasional antebellum home. Here, too, is the expansive main campus of the University of South Carolina. Out of town, 550-acre Lake Murray is full of pontoon boats and jet skis, and Congaree Swamp National Park is waiting to be explored.

In 1786 South Carolina's capital was moved from Charleston to Columbia, along the banks of the Congaree River. One of the nation's first planned cities, Columbia has streets that are among the widest in America because it was then thought that stagnant air in narrow streets fostered the spread of malaria. The city soon grew into a center of political, commercial, and cultural activity, but in early 1865 General William Tecumseh Sherman invaded South Carolina and incinerated two-thirds of Columbia. A few homes, public buildings, and historic sights were spared. The First Baptist Church, where secession was declared, still stands because a janitor directed Sherman's troops to a Presbyterian church instead.

Columbia Museum of Art contains art from the Kress Foundation collection of Renaissance and baroque treasures, sculpture, decorative arts, including art glass, and European and American paintings, including a Monet and a Botticelli; there are also changing exhibitions. ⊠ *Main and Hampton Sts., Main Street area* ☎ *803/799–2810* ⊕ *www. columbiamuseum.org* ✉ *$5; free on Sat.* ☉ *Wed., Thurs., and Sat. 10–5, Fri. 10–9, Sun. 1–5.*

★ The alluvial floodplain, bordered by high bluffs, at the 22,200-acre **Congaree Swamp National Park** contains many old-growth bottomland hardwoods (the oldest and largest trees east of the Mississippi River). The water and trees are beautifully eerie. Hiking and canoe trails line the park, which is full of wildlife, such as otters, deer, and woodpeckers, as well as the occasional wild boar. Guided nature walks are held the first and second Saturday of each month at 9:30 AM. When darkness falls, join park naturalists for a hike deep into the forest in search of owls and other nighttime wildlife Friday nights in September and October. Call for reservations. ⊠ *Off Rte. 48, Old Bluff Rd., Hopkins, 20 mi southeast of Columbia* ☎ *803/776–4396* ⊕ *www.nps.gov* ✉ *Free* ☉ *Visitor center: daily 8:30–5.*

With more than 67,000 square feet for climbing, exploring, painting, playing, building—oh, and learning, too, **EdVenture Children's Museum** is a full day of hands-on fun. Eddie, a 40-foot-tall statue of a boy that can be climbed on and in by children and adults, stands as the museum centerpiece. Each of eight galleries has a theme, such as Body Works, World of Work, and Mission Imagination. Older children might like to anchor a newscast and take home a tape for their efforts, and participate in science experiments; the younger set might want go to the Bone Zone to meet a talking skeleton or climb aboard a real fire truck. ⊠ *211 Gervais St., Vista* ☎ *803/779–3100* ⊕ *www.edventure.org* ✉ *$8.95* ☉ *Tues.–Sat. 9–5, Sun. noon–5.*

The **Fort Jackson Museum,** on the grounds of a U.S. army–training center, displays heavy equipment from the two world wars and has exhibits on the history of the fort from 1917 to the present. ■ TIP➧ **You'll need photo identification to enter Fort Jackson.** ⊠ *Bldg. 4442, Jackson Blvd., East Columbia* ☎ *803/751–7419* ✉ *Free* ☉ *Thurs. 9–6.*

The **Hampton-Preston Mansion,** dating from 1818, is filled with lavish furnishings collected by three generations of two influential families. Buy a ticket for a tour at the Historic Columbia Foundation in the Robert Mills House. ⊠ *1615 Blanding St., Main Street area* ☎ *803/252–1770* ✉ *$5* ☉ *Tues.–Sat. 10–3, Sun. 1–4.*

FodorśChoice

Stop by the museum shop of the **Historic Columbia Foundation** to get maps of walking and driving tours of historic districts. You must buy tickets here to tour four old Columbia houses ($5 each): the Robert Mills House (on-site), the Hampton-Preston Mansion and Gardens, the Mann-Simons Cottage, and the Woodrow Wilson Family Home. ■ TIP→ **For $18 you can visit all four homes.** ⊠ *Robert Mills House, 1616 Blanding St., Main Street area* ☎ *803/252–1770* ⊕ *www.historiccolumbia.org* 🖾 *Free* ☉ *Tues.–Sat. 10–3, Sun. 1–4.*

The 41-mi-long **Lake Murray** has swimming, boating, picnicking, and superb fishing. There are many marinas and campgrounds in the area. The lake is off Interstate 26, 15 mi west of Columbia. ■ TIP→ **In summer a massive flock of purple martins turn the sky nearly black at sunset when they return to their roost on Bomb Island.** ⊠ *Capital City–Lake Murray Country Visitors Center, 2184 N. Lake Dr., Lake Murray* ☎ *803/781–5940 or 866/725–3935* ⊕ *www.scjewel.com.*

The **Mann-Simons Cottage** was the home of Celia Mann, one of only 200 free African-Americans in Columbia in the mid-1800s. Buy a ticket for a tour at the Historic Columbia Foundation in the Robert Mills House. ⊠ *1403 Richland St., Main Street area* ☎ *803/252–1770* 🖾 *$5* ☉ *Tues.–Sat. 10–3, Sun. 1–4.*

★ ⌘ **Riverbanks Zoological Park and Botanical Garden** contains more than 2,000 animals and birds, some endangered, in natural habitats. Walk along pathways and through landscaped gardens to see sea lions, polar bears, Siberian tigers, koalas, black rhinos, and penguins. The South American primate collection has won international acclaim, and the park is noted for its success in breeding endangered and fragile species. The Aquarium–Reptile Complex has South Carolina, desert, tropical, and marine specimens. At the Bird Pavilion you can view birds and wildlife under a safarilike tent. You can ride the carousel and also take a tram over the Saluda River to the 70-acre botanical gardens on the west bank. A forested section with walking trails has spectacular views of the river and passes Civil War ruins. ■ TIP→ **Stop by the Saluda Factory Interpretive Center for more information about the site's history and its connection to the Civil War.** ⊠ *I–126 and U.S. 76, at Greystone Riverbanks exit, West Columbia* ☎ *803/779–8717* ⊕ *www.riverbanks.org* 🖾 *$8.75* ☉ *Daily 9–5.*

⌘ **Riverfront Park and Historic Columbia Canal,** where the Broad and Saluda rivers form the Congaree River, was created around the city's original waterworks and hydroelectric plant. Interpretive markers describe the area's plant and animal life and tell the history of the buildings. ■ TIP→ **A 2.5-mi paved trail weaves between the river and the canal and is filled with runners and walkers enjoying one of the region's only flat paths.** ⊠ *312 Laurel St., Vista* ☎ *803/733–8613* 🖾 *Free* ☉ *Daily dawn–dusk.*

The classic, columned 1823 **Robert Mills House** was named for its architect, who later designed the Washington Monument. It has opulent Regency furniture, marble mantels, and spacious grounds. ⊠ *1616 Blanding St., Main Street area* ☎ *803/252–1770* 🖾 *$5* ☉ *Tues.–Sat. 10–3, Sun. 1–4.*

☾ Exhibits in the refurbished textile mill that is the **South Carolina State Museum** explore the state's natural history, archaeology, historical development, as well as technological and artistic accomplishments. An iron gate made for the museum by Phillip Simmons, the "dean of Charleston blacksmiths," is on display, as is the surfboard that biochemist Kary Mullis was riding when he heard he'd won the Nobel prize. A display on African-American astronauts is dedicated to native son Dr. Ronald McNair, who died aboard the space shuttle *Challenger.* In the Stringer Discovery Center children can check out microorganisms under a microscope and climb trees to observe the animals that live in the branches. Other subjects include a reproduction of the Confederate submarine the *Hunley,* and the state's cotton industry and slavery. ⊠ *301 Gervais St., Vista* ☎ *803/898–4921* ⊕ *www.museum.state.sc. us* ⊠ *$5* ☾ *Tues.–Sat. 10–5, Sun. 1–5.*

★ Six bronze stars on the western wall of the **State House** mark where direct hits were made by General Sherman's cannons. The Capitol building, started in 1851 and completed in 1907, is made of native blue granite in the Italian-Renaissance style. The interior is richly appointed with brass, marble, mahogany, and artwork. Guided tours are available by reservations. ⊠ *Main and Gervais Sts., Main Street area* ☎ *803/734–2430* ⊠ *Free* ☾ *Weekdays 9–5, Sat. 10–5, 1st Sun. of month 1–5.*

☾ Make sure it's dark out when you drive by **Tunnelvision,** a glowing optical illusion painted on the wall of the Federal Land Bank Building by local artist Blue Sky. Next to it is Sky's bigger-than-life silver "busted" Fire Hydrant, a working fountain. ⊠ *Taylor and Marion Sts., Main Street area.*

A highlight of the sprawling **University of South Carolina** is its original campus—the scenic, tree-lined **Horseshoe** (⊠ Bull St. at Pendleton St., USC Campus ☎800/922–9755)—dating to 1801. Two-hour guided walking tours leave from the visitor center. Although the tours are geared to prospective students, the public is welcome. Reservations are essential. Explore the special collections on state history and genealogy at the **South Caroliniana Library** (⊠ Sumter St., USC Campus ☎ 803/777–3131 ☾ Mon., Wed., and Fri. 8:30–5, Tues. and Thurs. 8:30–8, Sat. 9–1), established in 1840. The **McKissick Museum** (⊠ Sumter St., USC Campus ☎ 803/777–7251 ⊠ Free ☾ Weekdays 8:30–5, Sat. 11–3) has geology, gemstone, and folklife exhibits, as well as a fine display of silver. ⊠ *Sumter St., USC Campus* ☎ *803/777–0169* ⊕ *www.sc.edu.*

The **Woodrow Wilson Family Home** displays the gaslights, arched doorways, and ornate furnishings of the Victorian period. Buy a ticket for a tour at the Historic Columbia Foundation in the Robert Mills House. ⊠ *1705 Hampton St., Main Street area* ☎ *803/252–1770* ⊠ *$5* ☾ *Tues.–Sat. 10–3, Sun. 1–4.*

Sports & the Outdoors

CANOEING & KAYAKING   The Saluda River near Columbia has challenging Class III and IV rapids. Saluda access is out of town in Gardendale and Saluda Shoals Park as well as at the Riverbanks Zoo. The Broad and the Saluda rivers meet in the center of town to become the calmer Congaree River. There's public access for the Congaree behind EdVenture on Senate Street at the Senate Street Landing.

Guided Saluda and Congaree river (Saluda has rapids, Congaree is calm) trips and swamp canoeing excursions can be arranged, as can canoe rentals, at **Adventure Carolina** (⌂ 1107 State St., Cayce, 1 mi southwest of Columbia ☎ 803/796–4505). You can rent canoes or sign up for guided river or swamp expeditions at the **River Runner Outdoor Center** (⌂ 905 Gervais St., Vista ☎ 803/771–0353). Canoe and kayak rentals are available at **Saluda Shoals Park** (⌂ 5605 Bush River Rd., Columbia, 12 mi northwest of downtown Columbia ☎ 803/772–1228).

> ### SPORTS MANIA!
>
> With both ACC (Clemson) and SEC (University of South Carolina) schools within the region, college-sports fans can cheer their teams on from August, when football takes center stage, through baseball season in May. For tickets and schedules, visit **Clemson** (⊕ www.clemson.edu) or the **University of South Carolina** (⊕ www.sc.edu).

Self-guided canoe trails traverse **Congaree Swamp National Park** (⌂ Off Rte. 48, Old Bluff Rd., Hopkins ☎ 803/776–4396), 20 mi southeast of Columbia.

HIKING **Congaree Swamp National Park** (⌂ Off Rte. 48, Old Bluff Rd., Hopkins, 20 mi southeast of Columbia ☎ 803/776–4396) has 22 mi of trails and a ¾-mi boardwalk for people with disabilities. Guided nature walks leave Saturday at 9:30 AM.

Where to Stay & Eat

$$$–$$$$ ✕ **Hampton Street Vineyard.** Tucked into one of the first buildings constructed in the city after Sherman's infamous march, Hampton Street Vineyard is a cozy spot. Exposed brick walls, arched windows, and original wide-plank floors set the tone. Dinners, such as crab cakes drizzled with a Champagne-basil vinagrette, are creative but never over the top and change with the season. The 700-bottle wine list was the first in the state to receive *Wine Spectator*'s Best Award of Excellence. ⌂ *1201 Hampton St., Downtown* ☎ *803/252–0850* ⊟ *AE, D, MC, V* ☉ *Closed Sun. No lunch Sat.*

★ **$$–$$$$** ✕ **Mr. Friendly's New Southern Cafe.** Who knew that barbecue sauce could be the base for such tasty salad dressing or that lowly pimiento cheese could elevate a fillet to near perfection? That kind of creative thinking is what makes Mr. Friendly's such a treasure; the ever-changing wine-by-the-glass menu that's pulled from an eclectic list is another. ⌂ *2001 A Greene St., Five Points* ☎ *803/254–7828* ⌁ *Reservations not accepted* ⊟ *AE, D, MC, V* ☉ *No lunch weekends.*

$–$$$$ ✕ **Garibaldi's.** Although the name is Italian, locals flock here for the cre-
Fodor'sChoice ative fish dishes that might include grouper with a brandy- and pepper-
★ corn-cream sauce, or tilapia atop a hash of bacon, corn, and potatoes. The house specialty (quite delicious) is a whole flounder served with a tangy apricot glaze. Creative dinner salads make interesting starters and the ice cream in an almond basket makes a crunchy-smooth finale to a meal. ■ TIP➔ **Don't miss the chocolate martini for a very grown-up dessert.**

✉ *2013 Greene St., Five Points* ☏ *803/771–8888* ⌖ *Reservations essential* ▭ *AE, D, MC, V* ☾ *No lunch.*

$ ✕ **Little Pigs Barbecue.** Grab a plate, get in the buffet line and load up on barbecue, fried chicken, ribs, and fried fish, along with fixings such as collards, coleslaw, and macaroni and cheese. Since Little Pigs uses mustard-, tomato-, and vinegar-base barbecue sauces, you can sample all three and pick your favorite. ✉ *4927 Alpine Rd., Northeast Columbia* ☏ *803/788–8238* ⌖ *Reservations not accepted* ▭ *No credit cards* ☾ *Closed Mon. No dinner Wed.*

¢–$ ✕ **The Gourmet Shop.** Sit in a black-and-white French-inspired café where mirrors and art prints decorate the walls. The Gourmet Shop has long been serving wonderful coffee and sandwiches. The chicken salad, potato salad, and the tomato, feta, and basil salad are all super. Next door, the shop sells food to go, wine, kitchen gadgets, French table linens, and fancy food items. ✉ *724 Saluda Ave., Five Points* ☏ *803/799–9463* ⌖ *Reservations not accepted* ▭ *AE, MC, V* ☾ *No dinner Sun.*

¢–$ ✕ **Mediterranean Tea Room.** The tabbouleh, Greek salad, and kebabs are fresh and flavorful, served in a small and friendly restaurant. Specialties such as eggplant pita pizza and broiled shrimp with feta cheese are a nice change of pace. ✉ *2601 Devine St., Shandon* ☏ *803/799–3118* ⌖ *Reservations not accepted* ▭ *AE, D, MC, V* ☾ *Closed Sun.*

$$–$$$ ▣ **Claussen's Inn.** A bakery warehouse has been converted into a small hotel with generally traditional rooms, but each has its own personality: bright red or blue walls, for instance. Some have antique brass or iron beds, others have wooden four-posters. Eight loft suites have downstairs sitting rooms furnished in period reproductions, spiral staircases, and four-poster beds upstairs. Some travelers have complained about poor maintenance of rooms and common areas. ✉ *2003 Greene St., Five Points, 29205* ☏ *803/765–0440 or 800/622–3382* ⎙ *803/799–7924* ⊕ *www.claussensinn.com* ⬐ *21 rooms, 8 suites* ⚇ *Wi-Fi, meeting room; no smoking* ▭ *AE, D, MC, V* ⑩ *BP.*

$$–$$$ ▣ **Columbia Marriott.** Sweeping views of the Columbia skyline from upper-story rooms give this hotel urban appeal. A $10 million renovation in 2005 means that the hotel features some of Marriott's newest perks. Fluffy duvets, granite bathrooms, and an ingenious sectional desk are available in each room. ■ TIP➔ **Wireless Internet is available throughout the hotel.** ✉ *1200 Hampton St., 292021* ☏ *803/771–7000* ⎙ *803/254–2911* ⊕ *www.marriottcolumbia.com* ⬐ *303 rooms* ⚇ *2 restau-*

CELEBRATING FOOD

Summer kicks off the festival season in the Midlands, and there's plenty to celebrate. In July, indulge in fresh peach ice cream, or just bite into a sun-warmed peach at the **Lexington County Peach Festival** (☏ 803/892–5207 ⊕ www.midnet.sc.edu/peach) in Gilbert. In August, the peanut is king at Pelion's annual **South Carolina Peanut Party** (⊕ www.scpeanutparty.com). September's **Okra Strut** (☏ 803/781–6122 ⊕ www.irmookrastrut.com) in Irmo is slimy fun. In October, barbecue chefs from around the state show their stuff in Columbia at the **Carolina Q-Cup** (⊕ www.carolinaqcup.com).

MIDLANDS BARBECUE

Barbecue in the Midlands, like elsewhere in the Carolinas and Georgia, means pork (or on rare occasion, chicken), roasted all day over an open fire and basted with sauce, not cooked on a grill. What makes Midlands barbecue distinctive is the sauce, which has a mustard base, rather than the vinegar or tomato commonly used elsewhere. The result is a flavor that's pungent but not spicy, and meat that lacks the red tint often associated with Southern barbecue. (Some places serve a variety of sauces, so you can do a taste test and see what you think of the native style.)

rants, cable TV, some in-room broadband, Wi-Fi, pool, health club, lounge, business center ▤ AE, D, DC, MC, V ¶⊙¶ EP.

$$–$$$ 🏨 **Hampton Inn Downtown Historic District.** This classy chain is within walking distance of restaurants and nightlife in the Vista neighborhood. Blond-color wood furnishings are comfortable, though standard. The hotel's staff provides attentive service. ⊠ *822 Gervais St., Vista, 29201* ☎ *803/231–2000* 🖷 *803/231–2868* ⊕ *www.hamptoninncolumbia. com* ⏎ *122 rooms* ⏥ *Dining room, some in-room hot tubs, some microwaves, some refrigerators, cable TV, Wi-Fi, pool, gym, no-smoking rooms ▤ AE, D, DC, MC, V ¶⊙¶ BP.*

$$–$$$ 🏨 **The Whitney Hotel.** Because they were originally built as condos, the large rooms in the Whitney have full kitchens, dining rooms, bedrooms with doors and, in the two- and three-bedroom models, two full baths. Traditional wood and upholstered furnishings include formal desks and wingback chairs. Set among the trees in residential Shandon, from the hotel you can stroll to dinner and window-shop for trendy clothes, housewares, and shoes; there are even two grocery stores around the corner. ■ TIP➡ **Access to an off-site health club is provided.** ⊠ *700 Woodrow St., Shandon, 29205* ☎ *803/252–0845* 🖷 *803/771–0495* ⊕ *www. whitneyhotel.com* ⏎ *74 suites* ⏥ *Dining room, kitchens, cable TV, in-room broadband, pool, business services, meeting room, airport shuttle, no-smoking rooms ▤ AE, D, DC, MC, V ¶⊙¶ BP.*

$$ 🏨 **Embassy Suites Hotel Columbia–Greystone.** In the spacious seven-story atrium lobby—with skylights, fountains, pool, and live plants—you can enjoy your complimentary breakfast and evening cocktails. All rooms are suites that come with sleeper sofas in the living room. The staff, which caters mainly to a business clientele, works hard to please. ⊠ *200 Stoneridge Dr., St. Andrews, 29210* ☎ *803/252–8700 or 800/362–2779* 🖷 *803/256–8749* ⊕ *www.embassysuites.com* ⏎ *214 suites* ⏥ *Restaurant, microwaves, refrigerators, cable TV, in-room broadband, indoor pool, gym, hot tub, lounge, recreation room, business services, meeting rooms, no-smoking rooms ▤ AE, D, DC, MC, V ¶⊙¶ BP.*

$ 🏨 **Comfort Suites.** A short drive down the access road from a mall, shopping center, and cinema complex, the Comfort Suites is off Interstate 26 just west of downtown Columbia. Rooms are clean and as you'd expect from this chain. The exercise room and indoor pool are nice added benefits. ⊠ *750 Saturn Pkwy., Exit 103, Harbison, 29212* ☎ *803/407–4444 or 800/426–6423* 🖷 *803/407–4500* ⊕ *www.comfortinn.com* ➫ *82 suites* ⚲ *Dining room, microwaves, refrigerators, cable TV, in-room broadband, Wi-Fi, pool, gym, no-smoking rooms* ⊟ *AE, D, MC, V* ⦿I *BP.*

Nightlife & the Arts

THE ARTS   The **Colonial Center** (⊠ 801 Lincoln St., Vista ☎ 803/576–9200 ⊕ www. thecolonialcenter.com) is the largest arena in the state and hosts major entertainment events as well as University of South Carolina basketball games. The **Cultural Council of Richland and Lexington Counties** (☎ 803/ 799–3115 ⊕ www.getcultured.org) provides information by phone or on their Web site about local cultural events including the ballet and symphony. **Koger Center for the Arts** (⊠ Assembly St., USC Campus ☎ 803/777–7500 ⊕ http://koger.sc.edu) presents national and international theater, ballet, and musical groups, as well as individual performers. ■ **TIP**➔ **On nights where performances are being held at several venues, parking can be difficult. Check the newspaper and plan ahead.**

The **Town Theatre** (⊠ 1012 Sumter St., USC Campus ☎ 803/799–2510 ⊕ www.towntheatre.com), founded in 1919, stages six plays a year from September to late May, plus a special summer show. **Trustus** (⊠ 520 Lady St., Vista ☎ 803/254–9732 ⊕ www.trustus.org) is a local professional theater group. The **Workshop Theatre of South Carolina** (⊠ 1136 Bull St., USC Campus ☎ 803/799–4876 ⊕ www.workshoptheatre.com) produces a number of plays.

NIGHTLIFE   In the hopping Vista neighborhood, the **Art Bar** (⊠ 1211 Park St., Vista ☎ 803/254–4792) is funky, with splash-painted walls, lighted lunch boxes, and world music for dancing. **Goatfeathers** (⊠ 2017 Devine St., Five Points ☎ 803/256–3325 or 803/256–8133) is a bohemian bar–café that's popular with university and law-school students, and it also appeals to late-night coffee and dessert seekers.

If you're more into rock, **Hunter-Gatherer Brewery & Alehouse** (⊠ 900 Main St., USC Campus ☎ 803/748–0540), has it on tap most nights, along with an excellent selection of beers, some made in-house. Jazz is ★ king at **Mac's on Main** (⊠ 1710 Main St., Main Street area ☎ 803/929–0037), where local groups often jam into the night. **Willy's Restaurant & Grill** (⊠ 1200B Lincoln St., Vista ☎ 803/799–3111), in a former train station waiting room, has live music (bluegrass, rock, country) and an outdoor patio.

Shopping

Many of Columbia's antiques outlets, boutique shops, and restaurants are in the ever-growing Vista neighborhood around Huger and Gervais streets, between the State House and the river. A number of intriguing shops and cafés are in Five Points, around Blossom at Harden streets, as well as along Devine Street in the Shandon neighborhood to the east. There are also antiques shops across the river on Meeting and State streets in West Columbia.

Old Mill Antique Mall (✉ 310 State St., West Columbia ☎ 803/796–4229) has items from many dealers, including furniture, glassware, jewelry, and books.

The **State Farmers' Market** (✉ Bluff Rd., USC Campus ☎ 803/737–4664) is one of the 10 largest in the country. Fresh vegetables, along with flowers, plants, seafood, and more, are sold weekdays 6 AM to 9 PM and Sunday 1 to 6.

Camden

❷ *35 mi northeast of Columbia via I–20.*

A town with a horsey history and grand colonial homes, charming Camden has never paved some of its roads for the sake of the hooves that regularly trot over them. The Carolina Cup and Colonial Cup are run here.

Camden is South Carolina's oldest inland town, dating from 1732. British General Lord Cornwallis established a garrison here during the Revolutionary War and burned most of Camden before evacuating it. A center of textile trade from the late 19th century through the 1940s, Camden blossomed when it became a refuge for Northerners escaping the cold winters. Because General Sherman spared the town during the Civil War, most of its antebellum homes still stand.

When you stop in the **Kershaw County Chamber of Commerce** for brochures and information, take note of the Chamber's building: it was designed by Robert Mills, the architect of the Washington Monument. ✉ *607 S. Broad St.* ☎ *803/432–2525 or 800/968–4037* ⊕ *www.camden-sc.org* ⊘ *Weekdays 9–5.*

Bonds Conway House was built by the first black man in Camden to buy his freedom. The circa-1812 home has the fine details of a skilled craftsman, including wonderful woodwork and heart-pine floors. ✉ *811 Fair St.* ☎ *803/425–1123* ▣ *Free* ⊘ *Thurs. 1–5 or by appointment.*

National Steeplechase Museum contains the largest collection of racing memorabilia in the United States. (A steeplechase is a horse race over open land that has been set up with obstacles.) The Equisizer, a training machine used by jockeys for practice, let's you experience the race from the jockey's perspective; don't stay on too long, unless you want to feel the race all day. ✉ *200 Knights Hill Rd.* ☎ *800/780–8117* ⊕ *www.carolina-cup.org* ▣ *Free* ⊘ *Sept.–May, daily 10–5, other months by appointment.*

ↂ The **Historic Camden Revolutionary War Site** puts emphasis on the period surrounding the British occupation of 1780. Several structures dot the site, including the 1789 **Craven House** and the **Blacksmith Shed.** The **Kershaw House,** a reconstruction of the circa-1770 home of Camden's founder, Joseph Kershaw, also served as Cornwallis's headquarters; it's furnished with period pieces. A nature trail, fortifications, powder magazine, picnic area, and crafts shop are also here. Guided tours are available by prearrangement. ⊠ *U.S. 521, 1½ mi north of I–20* ☎ *803/432–9841* 🖼 *$5 grounds free* ☉ *Tues.–Sat. 10–5, Sun. 1–5.*

Sports & the Outdoors

EQUESTRIAN EVENTS You're likely to see Thoroughbreds working out most mornings October through April at the **Springdale Race Course** (⊠ 200 Knights Hill Rd. ☎ 803/432–6513 ⊕ www.carolina-cup.org). Camden puts on two steeplechase events here: the Carolina Cup, in late March or early April; and the Colonial Cup, in November.

Where to Stay & Eat

★ **$$–$$$$** ✕ **Mill Pond Steak House.** It's all about steak here, and what steaks they are: aged for at least 35 days before they're cut, the fillets, rib eyes, and strips are juicy, tender, and packed with flavor. You can dine alfresco overlooking the sprawling millpond or inside a trio of old buildings. The wood paneling was reclaimed from the Boykin Tractor Shed after it was destroyed by Hurricane Hugo. The more casual side of the restaurant has a vintage saloon-style bar, which, in its first life, was the soda fountain at Zemps, a drug store in Camden. Area farmers provide most of the produce; grits for the shrimp and grits are ground at the mill next door. ■ TIP➜ Save room for homemade fruit cobbler with ice cream. ⊠ *84 Boykin Mill Rd., Boykin, 10 mi south of Camden* ☎ *803/425–8825* ▤ *AE, MC, V* ☉ *Closed Sun. and Mon. No lunch.*

$–$$$$ ✕ **The Crescent Grille.** Named for the crescent moon that decorates the South Carolina state flag, this restaurant is all about Southern food with a twist. Red snapper arrives atop a hash of sweet potatoes, crawfish and corn, and the chicken breast comes stuffed with crab and spinach. Choose your space: the funky interior—think gold and red abstract murals painted by a local artist and faux-leather walls—is utterly cool—and the walled garden out back is charming. ⊠ *1035 Broad St.* ☎ *803/713–0631* ▤ *AE, D, MC, V* ☉ *Closed Sun.*

$$–$$$ 🏠 **Bloomsbury Inn.** Noted Civil War diarist Mary Boykin Chestnut wrote much of her famous account in this home that was built in 1849 by her husband's family. Bedrooms retain their antebellum feel with carved wood or wrought-iron beds and fireplaces with antique mantels. The bathrooms are decorated with original Italian tiles from the 1930s. Breakfast is a divine extravagance that begins with a fruit course, includes homemade bread, and ends with an entrée such as freshly baked quiche with ham and asparagus. ■ TIP➜ Innkeeper Bruce Brown's history tour of the home is fascinating. ⊠ *1707 Lyttleton St., 29020* ☎ *803/432–5858* ⊕ *www.bloomsburyinn.com* 🛏 *3 rooms* ⚬ *Dining room, cable TV, Wi-Fi; no room phones* ▤ *AE, D, MC, V* ◎ *BP.*

★ **$–$$** 🏠 **Greenleaf Inn of Camden.** The 1890 McLean house serves as the main inn, with four rooms on the second floor above the dining room; the nearby Joshua Reynolds (circa 1805) house has six more rooms. Furnishings are classic Victorian, with some four-poster beds, and all bathrooms are modern. Rooms in the main inn are more spacious, those in the separate house more private. In the dining room, high ceilings and elaborate tiled fireplaces make for an elegant breakfast. There's patio dining outside. ■ TIP➜ Cheese eggs–scrambled eggs with melted cheddar–are the comfort food you've always dreamed about. ⊠ *1308 Broad St.,*

29020 ☎ 803/425–1806 or 800/437–5874 📠 803/425–5853 🌐 www.greenleafinnofcamden.com 10 rooms ♁ Dining room; no smoking ▭ AE, D, MC, V 🍽 BP.

$ **Fairfield Inn.** Sometimes you need the conveniences of a chain hotel like this one: coffeemakers, hair dryers, free high-speed Internet access, and large workspaces. Suites have refrigerators and microwaves. There's also an exercise room and a pool. ✉ *220 Wall St., 29020* ☎ *803/425–1010* 📠 *803/425–4006* 🌐 *www.marriott.com 48 rooms, 18 suites* ♁ *Dining room, some microwaves, some refrigerators, cable TV, in-room data ports, pool, gym, no-smoking rooms* ▭ *AE, D, MC, V* 🍽 *BP.*

Shopping

Camden is known for its antiques shopping, with the heart of the antiques and arts district along Broad Street, as well as on the neighboring Rutledge, DeKalb and Market streets.

Shop for Dutch impressionist paintings at **Andries Van Dam** (✉ 845 Broad St. ☎ 803/432–0850)—it's as much a gallery as an antiques shop. **Charles Dixon Antiques & Auction Co.** (✉ 818 Broad St. ☎ 803/432–3676) has distinctive architectural pieces. The **Granary** (✉ 830 Broad St. ☎ 803/432–8811), which specializes in English, French, and American antiques, also has whimsical garden furniture.

If modern pieces are more your style, stroll over to **Rutledge Street Gallery** (✉ 508 Rutledge St. ☎ 803/425–0071) for sophisticated paintings, textiles, and sculpture. At **Springdale Antiques** (✉ 951 Broad St. ☎ 803/432–0312) the proprietor always provides great history on his items. Browse through the antiques mall, bookstore, and other shops that comprise the **TenEleven Galleria** (✉ 1011 Broad St. ☎ 803/424–1011), housed in a restored warehouse.

Sample almond Danish pastries, lemon bars, and macaroons at the delightful **Mulberry Market Bake Shop** (✉ 536 E. DeKalb St. ☎ 803/424–8401). European-style butter is key to the divine cheese sticks.

Aiken

❸ *56 mi southwest of Columbia via I–20 and U.S. 1.*

This is Thoroughbred Country, and Aiken first earned its fame in the 1890s, when wealthy Northerners wintering here built stately mansions and entertained one another with horse shows, hunts, and lavish parties. Many up-to-60-room homes stand as a testament to this era of opulence. The town is still a center for all kinds of outdoor activity, including the equestrian events of the Triple Crown, as well as tennis and golf.

The area's horse farms have produced many national champions, which are commemorated at the **Aiken Thoroughbred Racing Hall of Fame and Museum.** Exhibitions include horse-related decorations, paintings, and sculptures, plus racing silks and trophies. The Hall of Fame is on the grounds of the 14-acre **Hopelands Gardens,** where you can wind along paths, past quiet terraces and reflecting pools. There's a Touch and Scent Trail with Braille plaques. Open-air free concerts and plays are presented on Monday evening May through August. ⊠ *Dupree Pl. and Whiskey Rd.* ☎ *803/642–7630* ☜ *Free* ☉ *Museum: Tues.–Sun. 2–5; grounds: daily dawn–dusk.*

The **Aiken County Historical Museum,** in one wing of an 1860 estate, is devoted to early regional culture. It has Native American artifacts, firearms, an authentically furnished 1808 log cabin, a schoolhouse, and a miniature circus display. ⊠ *433 Newberry St. SW* ☎ *803/642–2015* ☜ *Donations suggested* ☉ *Tues.–Fri. 9:30–4:30, weekends 2–5.*

Aiken surrounds **Hitchcock Woods,** 2,000 acres of Southern forest with hiking trails and bridal paths. Three times the size of New York's Central Park, it's the largest urban forest in the country and is listed on the National Register of Historic Places. ■ TIP→ **Make use of the maps available at the entrances. The park's size makes it easy to get lost.** ⊠ *Enter from junction of Clark Rd. and Whitney Dr., Berrie Rd., and Dibble Rd.*

Home to James Hammond, who is credited with being first to declare that "Cotton is King," **Redcliffe Plantation** remained in the family until 1975 when it was willed to the state. The 10,000-square-foot mansion (which sits on 400 acres) remains just as it was, down to the 19th-century books on the carved shelves. Slave quarters still contain bedding pallets and other coarse furnishings. Once you've toured the house (starting at 1, 2, or 3 PM), be sure to explore the grounds on the 2-mi-long trail. ■ TIP→ **Be warned: the house has no central heat or air-conditioning.** ⊠ *181 Redcliffe Rd., Beech Island, 15 mi southwest of Aiken* ☜ *$2* ☉ *Thurs.–Mon. 9–5.*

Stephen Ferrell has an extensive collection of Edgefield pottery on display at his shop, **Old Edgefield Pottery.** Ferrell, like his father, is an accomplished potter in his own right. ■ TIP→ **Ask to see original pieces crafted by Dave, a literate slave who created some of the first "face vessels" that have made Edgefield stoneware so collectible.** ⊠ *230 Simpkins St., Edgefield, 20 mi northwest of Aiken* ☎ *803/637–2060* ☉ *Tues.–Sat. 10–5.*

Sports & the Outdoors

EQUESTRIAN
EVENTS
In Aiken, polo matches are played at **Whitney Field** (⊠ 200 Mead Dr., off Whiskey Rd., U.S. 19 ☎ 803/648–7874) Sunday at 3, September through November and March through July.

Three weekends in late March and early April are set aside for the famed **Triple Crown** (⊠ Horse district, off Whiskey Rd., U.S. 19 ☎ 803/641–1111), which includes thoroughbred trials of promising yearlings, a steeplechase, and harness races by young horses making their debut.

Where to Stay & Eat

$$-$$$$ ✕ **Linda's Bistro.** Chef Linda Rooney elevates traditional European favorites, turning out excellent mushroom-Gruyère tarts, risotto with roasted mushrooms and Asiago cheese, and steak and frites. Main courses come with a salad, a vegetable, and potatoes. Rum-coconut-cream bread pudding is a favorite for dessert. It's all served in an open, café-like environment. ⊠ *210 The Alley* ☎ *803/648–4853* ▭ *AE, D, DC, MC, V* ☉ *Closed Sun. and Mon. No lunch.*

$–$$$ ✕ **Malia's.** Locals love this busy contemporary restaurant, with dim lighting and dark fabrics that convey a cool class. Grilled chicken salad might be a menu staple, but here, thanks to the addition of seasonal fruit and greens, it seems new again. At dinner, creative international-influence cuisine includes lamb soup with curry, veal with shiitake mushrooms and a brandy sauce—and the lighter baked ham, Brie, and portobello mushroom sandwich. ☒ *120 Laurens St.* ☎ *803/643–3086* ▭ *D, MC, V* ⊙ *No lunch Mon. or weekends. No dinner Sun.–Wed.*

¢–$ ✕ **New Moon Cafe.** The coffee beans are roasted right next door. Here you can pair Aiken's best coffee with freshly baked muffins and sweet rolls, wraps and salads, and homemade soups. ◼ **TIP→ The black-bean and crab bisque are particularly good.** ☒ *116 Laurens St.* ☎ *803/643–7088* ⌂ *Reservations not accepted* ▭ *No credit cards* ⊙ *No dinner.*

¢–$ ✕ **Track Kitchen.** The who's who of Aiken's horsey set eat here most mornings, feasting on the heavy and hearty cooking of Carol and Pockets Curtis. The small dining room is unpretentious, with walls of mint-green cinder block and simple Formica counters. ☒ *420 Mead Ave.* ☎ *803/641–9628* ▭ *No credit cards* ⊙ *Closed May–Sept. No dinner.*

$$$–$$$$ ▥ **The Willcox.** Winston Churchill, Franklin D. Roosevelt, and the Astors have slept at this grand, 19th-century inn. Massive stone fireplaces, rosewood trim, heart-pine floors, and antiques grace the lobby. Guest rooms and suites contain upscale furniture with classic lines, like the sleek, dark-stain, four-poster beds. Choose to soak in the extra-deep tub, or relax beside your fireplace. Here you can pretend, at least for one night, that you're a Vanderbilt. ☒ *100 Colleton Ave., 29801* ☎ *803/648–1898 or 877/648–2200* ⌨ *803/643–0971* ⊕ *www.thewillcox.com* ⇨ *7 rooms, 15 suites* ⌂ *Dining room, spa, lobby lounge, some pets allowed; no smoking* ▭ *AE, D, DC, MC, V* ⦿ *BP.*

FodorsChoice ★

$ ▥ **Briar Patch.** You can learn plenty about both the Old and New South from the knowledgeable innkeepers of this terrific B&B, which was formerly tack rooms in Aiken's stable district. You get two choices—either the frilly room with French-provincial furniture or the less dramatic one with pine antiques and a weather vane. ☒ *544 Magnolia La. SE, 29801* ☎ *803/649–2010* ⊕ *www.bbonline.com/sc/briar* ⇨ *2 rooms* ⌂ *Dining room, tennis court; no room phones, no smoking* ▭ *No credit cards* ⦿ *BP.*

Greenwood

❹   *10 mi east of Abbeville on Rte. 248; 75 mi west of Columbia via U.S. 378 and U.S. 178.*

Founded by Irish settlers in 1802, Greenwood received its name from the site's gently rolling landscape and dense forests. Andrew Johnson, the 17th U.S. president, operated a tailor shop at Courthouse Square before migrating to East Tennessee. Anglers, swimmers, and boaters head for nearby Lake Greenwood's 200-mi shore. Two sections of Sumter National Forest are nearby.

★   **Gardens of Park Seed Co.,** one of the nation's largest seed supply houses, maintains colorful experimental gardens and greenhouses 6 mi north of Greenwood. The flower beds are especially vivid mid-June through July. Seeds and bulbs are for sale in the company store. The **South Car-**

olina Festival of Flowers—with a performing-artist contest, a beauty pageant, private house and garden tours, and live entertainment—is held at Park's headquarters annually at the end of June. ⊠ *Rte. 25, off U.S. 178, Hodges* ☎ *864/941–4213 or 800/845–3369* ⊕ *www.parkseed. com* ✉ *Free* ☉ *Gardens daily dawn–dusk; store Mon.–Sat. 9–5.*

Where to Stay & Eat

$–$$$ ✕ **T. W. Boons.** When Tony and Anna Wideman decided to open a restaurant, they wanted to make it a family venture. They've been very successful: their 10-year-old daughter helps wait tables, Anna works the front of the house, and Tony runs the kitchen. Although the restaurant resembles a diner, the food is a few steps above. Steaks are all hand cut, the shrimp po' boy is packed with wild-caught shrimp, and the shrimp and grits are a creamy delight. ⊠ *405 Main St.* ☎ *864/227–3338* ⊟ *MC, V* ☉ *Closed Sun.*

$ ▦ **Inn on the Square.** This inn was fashioned out of a warehouse in the heart of town. Simple, solid-color carpets and linens brighten spacious guest rooms furnished with 18th-century reproductions, four-poster beds, and writing desks. Also note thoughtful touches such as turndown service and complimentary continental breakfast, although the omelets available on the regular breakfast menu are hard to beat. ⊠ *104 Court St., 29648* ☎ *864/330–1010 or 866/373–2917* ⊟ *864/223–7067* ⊕ *www.innonthesquaresc.com* ⬎ *48 rooms* ⚲ *2 restaurants, room service, in-room broadband, cable TV, pool, lounge, business services, meeting rooms, no-smoking rooms* ⊟ *AE, D, DC, MC, V* ⦿ *BP.*

Abbeville

★ ❺ *14 mi west of Greenwood on Rte. 72; 102 mi west of Columbia.*

Abbeville may well be one of inland South Carolina's most satisfying lesser-known towns. An appealing historic district includes the old business areas, early churches, and residential areas. What was called the "Southern cause" by supporters of the Confederacy was born and died here: it's where the first organized secession meeting was held and where, on May 2, 1865, Confederate president Jefferson Davis officially disbanded the defeated armies of the South in the last meeting of his war council.

The **Abbeville Welcome Center** (⊠ 107 Court Sq. ☎ 864/366–4600) has on display a series of paintings by Wilbur Kurtz, a respected authority on pre–Civil War life in the early to mid-20th century. Kurtz, a consultant on the movies *Gone With the Wind* and *Song of the South,* also painted the Battle of Atlanta murals on the Atlanta Cyclorama. The oversize Abbeville paintings depict Civil War scenes including the first secession meeting and Jefferson Davis's final Council of War meeting. They have been completely restored and are quite mesmerizing because of their size and detail.

In 1865 the Confederate council met at the **Burt-Stark Mansion** (1820) and Jefferson Davis disbanded the Confederate armies, effectively ending the Civil War. The house was a private residence until 1971 when

Mary Stark Davis died. She willed the house to the city, with a provision that states nothing can be added or removed from the house. It's filled with lovely antiques, carved-wood surfaces, and old family photos. Her clothing is still in the dresser drawers. ⊠ *306 N. Main St.* ☎ *864/ 366–0166* ⊕ *www.burt-stark.com* ☜ *$3* ☼ *Sept.–May, Fri. and Sat. 1–5 and by appointment; June–Aug., Tues.–Sat. 1–5 and by appointment.*

The **Abbeville Opera House** faces the old town square. Built in 1908, it has been renovated to reflect the grandeur of the days when lavish road shows and stellar entertainers took center stage. Current productions range from contemporary light comedies to local renderings of Broadway musicals. Call for tours. ⊠ *Town Sq.* ☎ *864/366–2157.*

Where to Stay & Eat

★ **$–$$$** ✕ **Village Grille.** Many locals frequent the Village Grille because of the herb rotisserie chicken, but the ribs, the fillet with blue cheese and portobello mushrooms, and the cordial-laced desserts are just as good a reason to come. Antique mirrors hang on pomegranate-color walls below high ceilings. The feeling here is trendy yet easygoing; the staff bend over backward to please. ⊠ *114 Trinity St.* ☎ *864/366–2500* ▤ *AE, D, MC, V* ☼ *Closed Sun. and Mon.*

¢–$ ✕ **Yoder's Dutch Kitchen.** Try some authentic Pennsylvania-Dutch home cooking in this unassuming South Carolina redbrick building. There's a lunch buffet and evening smorgasbord with fried chicken, stuffed cabbage, Dutch meat loaf, breaded veal Parmesan, and plenty of vegetables. ■ TIP→ **Shoofly pie, Dutch bread, and apple butter can be purchased to go.** ⊠ *Rte. 72, east of downtown* ☎ *864/366–5556* ▤ *No credit cards* ☼ *Closed Sun.–Tues. No dinner Wed. and Thurs.*

$ 🏨 **Belmont Inn.** Because of the theater-dining-and-lodging packages, the Belmont Inn is a popular overnight stop for opera-house goers. The red-brick building with colonnade was built in the 1900s in a Spanish style. Guest rooms are spacious, with high ceilings, pine floors, and colonial-look furniture. The restaurant is open only on weekends when a show is playing at the opera house. ⊠ *104 E. Pickens St., 29620* ☎ *864/459– 9625 or 877/459–8118* ⊕ *www.belmontinn.net* ⇆ *25 rooms* ㊉ *Restaurant, cable TV, in-room data ports, Wi-Fi, business services, meeting rooms, no-smoking rooms* ▤ *AE, D, DC, MC, V* ⥾ *BP.*

THE UPSTATE

The Upstate, also known as the Upcountry, in the northwest corner of the state, has long been a favorite for family vacations because of its temperate climate and natural beauty. The abundant lakes and waterfalls and several state parks (including Caesar's Head, Keowee-Toxaway, Oconee, Table Rock, and the Chattooga National Wild and Scenic River) provide all manner of recreational activities. Beautiful anytime, the 130-mi Cherokee Foothills Scenic Highway (Route 11), which goes through the Blue Ridge Mountains, is especially delightful in spring (when the peach trees are in bloom) and autumn.

Greenville is growing fast and attracting lots of industry, much of it textile-related, in keeping with the area's history. Clemson, home of Clemson University and the "Orange Wave," is pretty much a university town. Pendleton, a few miles away, has one of the nation's largest historic districts. With its village green, surrounded by shops and restaurants, it's a lovely step back in time.

Greenville

6 *100 mi northwest of Columbia via I–26 and I–385.*

Once known for its textile and other manufacturing plants, Greenville has reinvented itself as a trendy and sophisticated city able to support a surprising number of restaurants, galleries, and boutiques along a tree-lined Main Street that passes a stunning natural waterfall. Anchored by two performance centers, the city's business district is alive well into most evenings with couples and families enjoying the energy of this revitalized southern city. Downtown development has been so successful that many young professionals are moving here and creating interesting living spaces from old warehouses and retail establishments.

★ The renowned international collection of religious art at **Bob Jones University Museum & Gallery** includes works by Botticelli, Rembrandt, Rubens, and van Dyck. Note that children younger than six are not permitted. ⊠ *Bob Jones University, 1700 Wade Hampton Blvd.* ☎ *864/242–5100* ⊕ *www.bjumg.org* ☛ *$5; free Sun.* ☉ *Tues.–Sun. 2–5.*

The **Greenville County Museum of Art** displays American works dating from the colonial era. Works by Paul Jenkins, Jamie Wyeth, Jasper Johns, and noted Southern artists are on exhibit. ⊠ *420 College St.* ☎ *864/271–7570* ⊕ *www.greenvillemuseum.org* ☛ *Free* ☉ *Tues.–Sat. 10–5, Sun. 1–5.*

There are more than 50 mi of hiking trails within **Mountain Bridge**
FodorsChoice **Wilderness Area**, 30 mi north of Greenville, which encompasses two state
★ parks. The trail leading to 420-foot-tall Raven Cliff Falls can be accessed 1 mi north of the main entrance to **Caesar's Head State Park** (⊠ *8155 U.S. 276, Cleveland* ☎ *864/836–6115*); along the way there are spectacular views of river gorges and pine-covered mountains. Cross Matthews Creek on a suspension bridge; the view of the falls is worth the terror of knowing you're held in the air by nothing but wire. Register at Park Headquarters before you head out on the trail. Near the headquarters are Table Rock and Devil's Kitchen, a geological phenomenon that stays cool even in the heat of summer.

Famous for the Rim of the Gap trail, which has views of Rainbow Falls, **Jones Gap State Park** (⊠ *Jones Gap Rd., 6 mi east off U.S. 276, Marionetta* ☎ *864/836–3647*) is 6 mi east of U.S. 276. Access several trails from the Park Headquarters, or pick up a map and drive to one of the well-marked trailheads. ■ TIP➔ **Be sure to pick up your trail map and register before venturing into the wilderness; some of the trails are long and strenuous.** ⊕ *www.discoversouthcarolina.com* ☛ *$2* ☉ *Daily 9–9 during daylight savings time; daily 9–6 rest of yr.*

Devils Fork State Park, on Lake Jocassee, has luxurious villas and camping facilities, hiking, boating, and fishing. Lower Whitewater Falls plunges more than 200 feet over huge boulders to splash into the lake waters. The falls can be viewed from an overlook or from a boat on the lake. ■ TIP→ **An underwater basketball court—boulders are used for balls—is a fun diversion for scuba divers.** ⊠ *Jocassee Lake Rd., off Rte. 11, north of Salem, 45 mi northwest of Greenville* ☎ *864/944–2639* ⊕ *www. discoversouthcarolina.com* ⊠ *$2* ⊙ *Daily 7–9 during daylight savings time; daily 7–7 rest of yr.*

Sports & the Outdoors

South Carolinians sometimes prefer Upstate golf courses to those on the coast, as they're less crowded and enjoy a slightly cooler climate. The area's rolling hills provide an added challenge.

Links O'Tryon (⊠ 11250 New Cut Rd., Campobello ☎ 864/472–6723) is an 18-hole course with stunning views of the Blue Ridge Mountains and fieldstone bridges and walls in the Tom Jackson–design layout. **Rock at Jocassee** (⊠ 171 Sliding Rock Rd., Pickens ☎ 864/878–2030) is a mountain course with many water hazards; its signature hole has a waterfall view.

Where to Stay & Eat

$$$–$$$$ ✕ **Soby's New South Cuisine.** The decorator palette of plums and golds is a stunning contrast to the original brick and wood that was uncovered during the renovation of this 19th-century cotton exchange building. Although the menu changes seasonally, perennial favorites—a layered appetizer of fried green tomatoes and jalapeño pimiento cheese, shrimp and locally ground grits, and the famous mind-numbing white-chocolate banana-cream pie—are always available. ⊠ *207 S. Main St.* ☎ *864/232–7007* ⊕ *www.sobys.com* ⊟ *AE, MC, V* ⊙ *No dinner Sun. No lunch.*

$$–$$$$ ✕ **Augusta Grill.** Depending on what's in season, and on the whims of the chef, menu selections change daily. Seafood such as triggerfish with creamy crabmeat beurre blanc and beef with one of chef Bob Hackell's made-from-scratch sauces are typical. You can also order dinner as a series of small plates. The crab-cake special on Wednesday night packs the house. ■ TIP→ **To be sure the kitchen hasn't run out of their signature blackberry cobbler by the time you have dessert, be sure to order yours at the beginning of the meal.** ⊠ *1818 Augusta St.* ☎ *864/242–0316* ⊕ *www.augustagrill.com* ⊟ *AE, D, MC, V* ⊙ *Closed Sun. No lunch Sat.*

¢–$$ ✕ **Stax's Omega Diner.** This contemporary diner has both booths and a half-circle counter with stools. The menu lists a little of everything:

BOILED WHAT?

Wondering about the hand-lettered signs advertising HOT BOILED PEANUTS on display in nearly every gas station, convenience store, and roadside stand? Hot boiled peanuts are exactly that: raw peanuts simmered in brine—often in a crock pot—for long periods. The result is a slightly slippery, but never slimy, treat. Boiled peanuts are eaten just like roasted peanuts, but the texture is more akin to a canned bean than a nut, and napkins are an absolute necessity. Route 11, in the Upstate area, has many roadside stands, and most sell boiled peanuts in addition to farm products. Go ahead, give 'em a try; you might just find these salty morsels addictive.

bacon and eggs, burgers, souvlaki, Greek-style chicken, shrimp, and grits. It's all good, and it's open almost around-the-clock (closed 2 AM to 6:30 AM weekdays, 3 AM to 6:30 AM weekends). ⊠ *72 Orchard Park Dr.* ☎ *864/297–6639* ▤ *AE, DC, MC, V.*

¢–$ ✗ **Two Chefs Delicatessen.** Mix and match from the deli's selection of delicious homemade sandwiches and salads. Try the roasted-potato salad, dried-cranberry-and-grilled-chicken salad, or pepper-crusted turkey on rosemary sourdough. There are a lot of tempting desserts, too, including apple-brandy cake, flourless chocolate cake, and fruit tarts. There's a second, to-go location on the east side. ⊠ *104 S. Main St., Suite 105* ☎ *864/370–9336* ✉ *Two Chefs To Go,* ⊠ *29 Pelham Rd.* ☎ *864/284–9970* ▤ *MC, V* ☺ *Closed Sun. No dinner Sat.*

¢ ✗ **Meador's Sandwich Shop.** Join generations of Greenville families who've been raised on Meador's "Vardry" burgers, big fat hamburgers named for Greenville founding father Vardry McBee. Try one topped with blue cheese made up the road at Clemson University. The pimiento cheese and BLT sandwiches are popular, too. ⊠ *15 Conestee Ave.* ☎ *864/233–6854* ✉ *123 S. Main St.* ☎ *864/235–9993* ▤ *AE, MC, V* ☺ *No dinner.*

★ $$$$ ✗▦ **La Bastide.** About 19 mi northwest (30 minutes) of Greenville in the sloping Piedmont hills, a French provincial–style inn—with surrounding vineyard—emulates a French-countryside experience. Rooms have European linens, French antiques and reproductions, elaborate wrought-iron chandeliers, gas fireplaces, and hillside views. French-country cuisine, such as duck with blood-orange sauce, and fine wine are served at the restaurant ($$$–$$$$). Guests have access to golf at a nearby country club. ⊠ *10 Road of Vines, Travelers Rest 29690* ☎ *864/836–8463 or 877/836–8463* 🖷 *864/836–4820* ⊕ *www.labastide. com* ✎ *12 rooms, 2 suites* ♨ *Restaurant, some in-room hot tubs, golf privileges, croquet, no-smoking rooms* ▤ *AE, D, DC, MC, V* ▥ *BP.*

$ ✗▦ **Phoenix–Greenville's Inn.** Ask for a room overlooking the courtyard gardens and pool at this accommodating Southern inn. The graceful spindles of the four-poster beds are painted or stained according to the room's decor (white, mahogany, cherry). Chef Tim Sprague cooks at the Palms Restaurant ($$–$$$$), one of Greenville's best. Sophisticated fare includes the signature hot smoked Atlantic salmon with ginger and soy, and roast rack of lamb with wild mushrooms, lentils, and fennel. Although there's no health club on-site, guests have free access to the Greenville Sports Club, a full service facility that's a five-minute drive away. ⊠ *246 N. Pleasantburg Dr., 29607* ☎ *800/257–3529* 🖷 *864/233–4651* ⊕ *www.phoenixgreenvillesinn.com* ✎ *181 rooms, 3 suites* ♨ *Restaurant, in-room data ports, Wi-Fi, pool, lounge, pub, business services, meeting rooms, airport shuttle, no-smoking rooms* ▤ *AE, D, DC, MC, V* ▥ *BP.*

$–$$$ ▦ **Hyatt Regency Hotel.** This upscale chain offering's best asset is its location in the midst of the revitalized downtown of shops and restaurants. Rooms come with one king or queen bed or two doubles. Make sure you ask for a room overlooking the palm-filled atrium, which are far better than those without views. ⊠ *220 N. Main St., 29601* ☎ *864/235–1234 or 800/633–7313* 🖷 *864/232–7584* ⊕ *www.hyatt.com* ✎ *330 rooms*

⚲ *Restaurant, room service, cable TV, pool, health club, lounge, airport shuttle, no-smoking rooms* ≣ *AE, D, DC, MC, V* 🍱 *EP.*

$–$$ ⌸ **Westin Poinsett Hotel.** A 1925, 12-story hotel has been brought back to life by Westin. In the public spaces, intricate moldings adorn the many columns, ironwork rails and chandeliers are apparent throughout, and decorative plasterwork has been restored. The large guest rooms have down comforters, marble baths, and high ceilings. ✉ *120 S. Main St., 29601* ☎ *864/421–9700* 📠 *864/421–9719* ⊕ *www.westin.com* ↱ *181 rooms, 9 suites* ⚲ *Restaurant, coffee shop, room service, in-room safes, cable TV, Wi-Fi, health club, lounge, concierge, business services, meeting rooms, no-smoking rooms* ≣ *AE, D, DC, MC, V* 🍱 *EP.*

Nightlife & the Arts

The **Handlebar** (✉ 304 E. Stone Ave. ☎ 864/233–6173) has been bringing small-stage live music to Greenville since 1994. Monday is known for no cover and lots of jazz, Tuesday brings a bluegrass jam to the bar and a swing dance to the concert hall. The 16,000-seat **Bi-Lo Center** (✉ 650 N. Academy St. ☎ 864/233–2525) hosts major concerts and sporting events. The **Peace Center for the Arts** (✉ 101 W. Broad St. ☎ 864/467–3030), which sits along the Reedy River, presents star performers, touring Broadway shows, dance companies, chamber music, and local groups.

Shopping

The shopping area along Greenville's Main Street and adjoining West End may be just a mile or so long, but it's chockablock full of interesting shops.

O. P. Taylors (✉ 117 N. Main St. ☎ 864/467–1984) is a super-cool toy emporium that even adults can love. Filling two floors with French linens, furniture, and home accessories **Postcard from Paris** (✉ 631 S. Main St. ☎ 864/233–6622) is a slice of the left bank in the deep South. The shop is hip, but the service is so friendly at **Augustatwenty** (✉ 20 Augusta St., at S. Main ☎ 864/233–2600) that you won't feel uncomfortable browsing the racks of designer duds. Open from mid-June until the first of November, **Perdue's Mountain Fruit Farm** (✉ Rte. 11 and Tigerville Rd. ☎ 864/244–5809) sells an always-changing selection of locally grown fruits such as peaches, blackberries, pears, apples, and raspberries. Owner Dick Perdue also makes the jams, jellies, and ciders that fill the shelves.

Pendleton

❷ *30 mi southwest of Greenville via U.S. 123.*

Walk among the interesting architecture of Pendleton's historic district, a few miles from Clemson University. The Farmers Hall (1826) was originally built to be a courthouse. The Square, a district of restaurants and shops, faces the Village Green. ■ TIP➔ **Keep your eyes peeled for Richard Burnside, a self-taught folk artist whose paintings decorate several House of Blues locations.** Burnside, who has lived in Pendleton since the 1980s, paints at various locations around the square.

Ⓒ The **South Carolina State Botanical Garden,** on the Clemson University campus, holds more than 2,000 varieties of plants on more than 295 acres, including wildflower, fern, and bog gardens. Niche gardens, and there are 20 of them, include a winter (February) blooming camellia garden, and a wildflower meadow buzzing with bees and hummingbirds. Some garden sculptures are buildings made totally from living trees. ■ TIP→ **Dogs, on leashes, are welcome.** The **Fran Hanson Discovery Center** has information on regional history and cultural heritage and a hands-on learning station on natural history. ✉ *102 Garden Trail, Clemson, 4 mi northwest of Pendleton* ☎ *864/656–3405* ⊕ *www.clemson.edu/scbg* ▣ *Free* ◷ *Daily dawn–dusk.*

Issaqueena Falls is said to be named for Issaqueena, an Indian princess in love with an Englishman. Rather than face the wrath of her angry tribe, she's said to have leaped off the edge of the 100-foot falls. There the legend takes a twist: it is said Issaqueena actually jumped to a hidden ledge, reunited with her lover and the two escaped to live happily ever after. One of the most popular of the state's waterfalls, Issaqueena can be reached via a trail that, although only ¼ mi long, is fairly steep. ✉ *Stumphouse Tunnel Park, off Rte. 28, 7 mi outside Wahalla, 28 mi northwest of Pendleton* ☎ *864/638–4343* ▣ *Free* ◷ *Daily 10–5.*

OFF THE BEATEN PATH

CHATTOOGA NATIONAL WILD AND SCENIC RIVER – Designated as a Wild and Scenic River by Congress in 1974, the Chattooga River can test the skills of even the most experienced rafters with Class V–plus runs that have names like "Crack-in-the-Rock," "Corkscrew," and "Sock-Em Dog" (which includes a stomach-sinking 7-foot drop). Commercial rafting outfitters, including **Nantahala Outdoor Center** (☎ 888/905–7238 ⊕ www.noc.com), **Southeastern Expeditions** (☎ 800/ 868–7238 ⊕ www.southeasternexpeditions.com), and **Wildwater Ltd.** (☎ 864/647–9587 or 800/451–9972 ⊕ www.wildwaterrafting.com), also run shorter, more gentle rides (Class II and below) that are appropriate for senior citizens and children as young as eight years old. The river is on the border of South Carolina and Georgia, about 38 mi northeast of Pendleton via U.S. 76 or Rte. 28, and is part of Sumter National Forest.

Where to Stay & Eat

$–$$$ ✕ **Sullivan's Metropolitan Grill.** Housed in a 19th-century building that was most recently a hardware store, Sullivan's interior is almost as interesting as its Mediterranean-influenced food. Massive plaster columns stand above heart-pine floors. Foodwise, duck is the star here. ■ TIP→ **Save room for owner Sabra Nickas's decidedly non-Med desserts that include huge wedges of peanut-butter pie, slabs of homemade cake, and even homemade cookies.** ✉ *208 S. Main St., Anderson, 8 mi south of Pendleton* ☎ *864/ 226–8945* ⌦ *Reservations essential* ▤ *AE, D, MC, V* ◷ *Closed Sun. No lunch Sat.*

$$–$$$ ✕▥ **Liberty Hall Inn.** A country inn in the middle of town: on-site owners have decorated the 1840s building with family heirlooms and antiques such as tall, carved, darkwood-headboards set dramatically against red walls. Breakfast specialties include eggs Benedict and homemade French toast with a brandied-apple compote. The restaurant, the Café at Liberty Hall ($$–$$$), displays intensely colorful art on red walls

and serves dishes such as crab cakes, chicken picatta with capers, and filet mignon with tomato-infused béarnaise sauce. ⊠ *621 S. Mechanic St., 29670* ☎ *800/643–7944* 🖶 *864/646–7500* ⊕ *www.bbonline. com/sc/liberty* ⌨ *7 rooms* ⌂ *Restaurant; no smoking* ⊟ *AE, D, MC, V* ⍾ *BP.*

$ 🖭 **Rocky Retreat.** A red tin roof tops the 1849 Boone-Douthit house that was once a summer home of the family that owned Charleston's Boone Hall Plantation. The B&B that has taken up residence was named for the large granite boulders that jut out of the nearby mountains. Rooms have original heart-pine floors, antiques, claw-foot tubs, and working fireplaces. Breakfast, prepared by innkeeper Jim Ligon, is hearty and delicious. ⊠ *1000 Milwee Creek Rd., 29670* ☎ *864/225–3494* ⊕ *www. bbonline.com/sc/rockyretreat* ⌨ *3 rooms* ⌂ *No room phones, no room TVs, no kids under 10, no smoking* ⊟ *MC, V* ⍾ *BP.*

THE MIDLANDS & UPSTATE ESSENTIALS

Transportation

BY AIR

Columbia Metropolitan Airport, 10 mi west of downtown Columbia, is served by American Eagle, ASA/DeltaConnection, Continental, Delta, Northwest, United Express, and US Airways/Express. Greenville-Spartanburg Airport, off Interstate 85 between the two cities, is served by American Eagle, Continental, Delta, Independence, Northwest, United Express, and US Airways/Express.

🖪 **Columbia Metropolitan Airport** ⊠ 3000 Aviation Way, Airport ☎ 803/822–5000 ⊕ www.columbiaairport.com. **Greenville-Spartanburg Airport** ⊠ 2000 G.S.P. Dr. ☎ 864/877–7426 ⊕ www.gspairport.com.

BY BUS

Greyhound serves Aiken, Camden, Columbia, Greenville, Greenwood, Spartanburg, and Sumter.

🖪 **Greyhound** ☎ 800/231–2222.

BY CAR

Interstate 77 leads into Columbia from the north, Interstate 26 runs through north–south, and Interstate 20 east–west. Interstate 85 provides access to Greenville, Spartanburg, Pendleton, and Anderson. Interstate 26 runs from Charleston through Columbia to the Upstate, connecting with Interstate 385 into Greenville. Car rental by all the national chains is available at the airports in Columbia and Greenville.

BY TAXI

Companies providing service in Columbia include Blue Ribbon and Checker-Yellow. Gamecock Cab Co. provides citywide service as well as service to other cities statewide. It's about $15 to $17 from the airport to downtown Columbia.

🖪 **Blue Ribbon** ☎ 803/754–8163. **Checker-Yellow** ☎ 803/799–3311. **Gamecock Cab Co.** ☎ 803/796–7700.

BY TRAIN

Amtrak makes stops at Camden, Columbia, Denmark, Florence, Greenville, Kingstree, and Spartanburg.

🚆 **Amtrak** ☎ 800/872-7245 ⊕ www.amtrak.com.

Contacts & Resources

BANKS & EXCHANGE SERVICES

Banks in larger cities such as Columbia, Greenville, and Spartanburg generally stay open until 5 PM, in smaller towns they'll usually close at 2 PM. In addition to BB&T, Wachovia, and Bank of America, you'll find local banks such as First Citizens, Palmetto First, and RegionsBank. Note that drive-throughs are only open to bank customers.

EMERGENCIES

Emergency-room services are available at Palmetto Health Richland. Kroger Sav-on has a pharmacy open 24 hours; other regional locations are open until 9.

🚨 Emergency Services **Ambulance, fire, police** ☎ 911.

🚨 Hospitals **Palmetto Health Richland** ⊠ 5 Richland Medical Park, Columbia ☎ 803/434-7000.

🚨 24-Hour Pharmacies **Kroger Sav-On** ⊠ 7467 Woodrow St., Irmo ☎ 803/732-0426.

INTERNET, MAIL & SHIPPING

Most hotels offer high-speed or wireless Internet access, many provide it at no charge. Coffee shops such as Jammin' Java in Columbia and Coffee Underground provide it free to customers.

Ship packages home at the UPS Store or the post office in Columbia and Greenville.

🌐 **Coffee Underground** ⊠ 1 Coffee St., Greenville ☎ 864/298-0494. **Jammin' Java** ⊠ 1530 Main St., Columbia ☎ 803/254-5282. **The UPS Store** ⊠ 701 Gervais St., Columbia ☎ 803/254-1601 ⊠ 209 N. Main St., Greenville ☎ 864/467-9678. **U.S. Post Office** ⊠ 1601 Assembly St., Columbia ⊠ 300 E. Washington St., Greenville ☎ 800/275-8777.

MEDIA

The State is Columbia's largest paper. It publishes daily and Sunday editions and covers local and national news. In Greenville, the daily *Greenville News* is the major paper.

There are two independent bookstores of note in the area. The Happy Bookseller has been a local fixture in Columbia since 1974. The Open Book in Greenville is the state's largest independent bookstore.

📰 **Greenville News** ⊠ 305 S. Main St., Greenville ☎ 800/800-5116. **The Happy Bookseller** ⊠ 4525 Forest Dr., Columbia ☎ 803/782-2665. **The Open Book** ⊠ 110 S. Pleasantburg Dr., Greenville ☎ 864/235-9651. **The State** 🖰 Box 1333 Columbia ☎ 800/888-5353.

TOUR OPTIONS

The City of Aiken runs a nearly two-hour tour of the historic district ($12) and will customize tours to suit individual interests. In Sumter the charismatic former mayor "Bubba" McElveen gives informal walking, bus, and auto tours of the area. In Camden, Camden Carriage Company takes you on a tour on a horse-drawn carriage through Camden's loveliest neighborhood and down unpaved roads. Historic Columbia runs guided tours of Columbia and rents out old properties.

🎫 **"Bubba" McElveen** ☎ 803/775-2851. **Camden Carriage Company** ☎ 803/425-5737 ⊕ www.camdencarriage.com. **City of Aiken** ☎ 888/245-3672 ⊕ www.aikenprt.net. **Historic Columbia** ☎ 803/252-7742 ⊕ www.historiccolumbia.org.

VISITOR INFORMATION

🎫 **Capital City/Lake Murray Country Visitors Center** ⊠ 2184 N. Lake Dr., Irmo 29063 ☎ 803/781-5940 or 866/725-3935 ⊕ www.scjewel.com. **Columbia Metropolitan Convention and Visitors Bureau** ⊠ 1101 Lincoln St., Columbia 29201 ☎ 803/545-0000 or 800/264-4884 ⊕ www.columbiacvb.com. **Discover Upcountry Carolina Association** ◌ Box 3116, Greenville 29602 ☎ 864/233-2690 or 800/849-4766 ⊕ www.theupcountry. com. **Greater Abbeville Chamber of Commerce** ⊠ 107 Court Sq., Abbeville 29620 ☎ 864/ 366-4600 ⊕ www.abbevillescchamber.com. **Greater Aiken Chamber of Commerce** ⊠ 121 Richland Ave. E, Box 892, Aiken 29802 ☎ 803/641-1111 ⊕ www.aikenchamber.net. **Greater Cheraw Chamber of Commerce** ⊠ 221 Market St., 29520 ☎ 843/537-8425 or 888/537-0014 ⊕ www.cheraw.com. **Greater Greenville Convention and Visitors Bureau** ⊠ 206 S. Main St., Box 10527, 29603 ☎ 864/233-0461 or 800/717-0023 ⊕ www. greatergreenville.com. **Greater Sumter Convention & Visitors Bureau** ⊠ 822 W. Liberty St., Sumter 29150 ☎ 803/436-2640 or 800/688-4748 ⊕ www.sumtertourism.com. **Kershaw County Chamber of Commerce** ⊠ 607 S. Broad St., Box 605, Camden 29021 ☎ 803/432-2525 or 800/968-4037 ⊕ www.camden-sc.org. **Ninety Six Chamber of Commerce** ⊠ 120 NW Main St., Box 8, 29666 ☎ 864/543-2900. **Spartanburg Convention and Visitors Bureau** ⊠ 298 Magnolia St., 29306 ☎ 864/594-5050 or 800/374-8326 ⊕ www.visitspartanburg.com.

Savannah

WORD OF MOUTH

"Stroll, stroll, stroll the squares. Spend very little time on River Street. It's become too commercial. Do step in one of the candy shops for a sample of a praline. You'll probably buy some to take home. Here's your homework assignment: Read 'The Book' or watch the movie. Everywhere you turn in Savannah you will hear a reference to 'The Book.' "

—starrville

"Outside the city, I recommend a visit to Fort Pulaski on Tybee Island. There's plenty of history to soak in and you can wander through the tunnels. We really enjoyed it. You can also visit the Tybee lighthouse but you do have to climb over 170 steps to get up to the top!"

—atlswan

Updated by
Chris McBeath

GENERAL JAMES OGLETHORPE, Savannah's founder, set sail for England in 1743, never to return. His last instructions, it's said, were, "Don't change a thing until I get back." That local joke holds more than a bit of truth. Savannah's elegant mansions, dripping Spanish moss, and sticky summer heat can make the city seem sleepy and stubbornly resistant to change. Which is exactly why many folks like the place.

Savannah, Georgia's oldest city, began its modern history on February 12, 1733, when Oglethorpe and 120 colonists arrived at Yamacraw Bluff on the Savannah River to found the 13th and last of the British colonies. As the port city grew, more settlers from England and Ireland arrived, joined by Scottish Highlanders, French Huguenots, Germans, Austrian Salzburgers, Sephardic and Ashkenazic Jews, Moravians, Italians, Swiss, Welsh, and Greeks.

In 1793 Eli Whitney of Connecticut, who was tutoring on a plantation near Savannah, invented a mechanized means of "ginning" seeds from cotton bolls. Cotton soon became king, and Savannah, already a busy seaport, flourished under its reign. Waterfront warehouses were filled with "white gold," and brokers trading in the Savannah Cotton Exchange set world prices. The white gold brought in hard currency; the city prospered.

General William Tecumseh Sherman's army rampaged across Georgia in 1864, setting fire to railroads, munitions factories, bridges, and just about anything else between them and the sea. Rather than see the city torched, Savannahians surrendered to the approaching Yankees.

As the cotton market declined in the early 20th century, the city's economy collapsed. For decades, Savannah's historic buildings languished; many were razed or allowed to decay. Cobwebs replaced cotton in the dilapidated riverfront warehouses. The tide turned in the 1950s, when residents began a concerted effort—which continues to this day—to restore and preserve the city's architectural heritage.

That link to the past is Savannah's main draw for travelers: the 2½-square-mi Historic District is the nation's largest. But Savannah's attraction also lies in its people, who give Southern charm their own special twist. As John Berendt's wildly popular book *Midnight in the Garden of Good and Evil* amply demonstrates, eccentricities can flourish in this hothouse environment.

EXPLORING SAVANNAH

The Historic District

Georgia's founder, General James Oglethorpe, laid out the city on a perfect grid. The Historic District is neatly hemmed in by the Savannah River, Gaston Street, East Street, and Martin Luther King Jr. Boulevard. Streets are arrow-straight, public squares of varying sizes are tucked into the grid at precise intervals, and each block is sliced in half by narrow, sometimes unpaved streets. Bull Street, anchored on the north by City Hall and the south by Forsyth Park, charges down the center of the grid and

TOP 5 REASONS TO GO

Intriguing Architecture: Close to half of the 2,500 buildings in Savannah have architectural or historical significance. The many building styles make exploring the tree-lined neighborhoods a delight. The 19th-century Telfair's Owens-Thomas house is a particular highlight. Like some other historic homes, it's open to the public.

Strolling the Squares: In the historic district, the city's famous squares are distinctive and thoroughly charming. Fountains, statues, and trees give each a different character, and all have stories to tell about different eras. To appreciate Savannah's unique appeal, take time to explore a few.

Gail Thurmond: Described as the female counterpart to Tony Bennett, Gail is a melodic fixture at Savannah's cozy Planters Tavern.

Expect to hear many schmoozing favorites from a repetoire that rivals her mentor, the late, great Emma Kelly who earned the moniker "lady of 6,000 songs." Gail's CD "Savannah Moon" is a great keepsake.

Midnight in the Garden of Good and Evil: John Berendt's famous 1994 book about a local murder and the city's eccentric characters attracted many travelers eager to visit the places mentioned. It's a good read, and you can still enjoy retracing some of the scenes.

Melon Bluff: If you want to see the coast with nary a hint of development, this is one of the few remaining places to do so. Explore it by kayak, by canoe, or simply by walking beneath the canopies of live oaks and soaking up the pristine landscape.

8

maneuvers around the five public squares that stand in its way. The layout means the area is easy to explore, and is best appreciated on foot. All the squares have some historical significance; many have fountains and shady resting areas; and all are bordered by beautiful houses and mansions that speak to another era.

Numbers in the margin correspond to numbers on the Savannah Historic District map.

Main Attractions

19 **Andrew Low House.** This residence was built in 1848 for Andrew Low, a native of Scotland and one of Savannah's merchant princes. The home later belonged to his son William, who married Juliette Gordon. After her husband's death, she founded the Girl Scouts in this house on March 12, 1912. The house has 19th-century antiques, stunning silver, and some of the finest ornamental ironwork in Savannah. ⊠ *329 Abercorn St., Historic District* ☎ *912/233–6854* ✉ *$7.50* ☉ *Mon.–Wed., Fri., and Sat. 10–4:30, Sun. noon–4.*

14 **Chippewa Square.** Daniel Chester French's imposing bronze statue of General James Edward Oglethorpe, founder of Savannah and Georgia, anchors the square. The bus-stop scenes of *Forrest Gump* were filmed on the north end of the square. Also note the **Savannah Theatre,** on

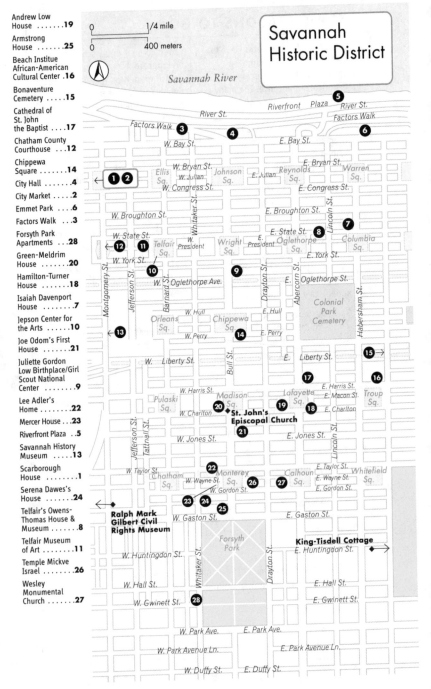

Savannah Historic District

Bull Street, which claims to be the oldest continuously operated theater site in North America. ⊠ *Bull St. between Hull and Perry Sts., Historic District.*

② City Market. Although the 1870s City Market was razed years ago, city fathers are enacting a three-year plan to capture the authentic atmosphere and character of its bustling origins. Already a lively destination for art studios, open-air cafés, theme shops, and jazz clubs, this popular pedestrian-only area will become the ever more vibrant, youthful heart of Savannah's Historic District. ⊠ *Between Franklin Sq. and Johnson Sq. on W. St. Julian St., Historic District* ☏ *912/525–2489 for current events.*

★ Colonial Park Cemetery. The park is the final resting place for Savannahians who died between 1750 and 1853. You may want to stroll the shaded pathways and read some of the old tombstone inscriptions. There are several historical plaques, one of which marks the grave of Button Gwinnett, a signer of the Declaration of Independence. ⊠ *Oglethorpe and Abercorn Sts., Historic District.*

Columbia Square. When Savannah was a walled city (1757–90), Bethesda Gate (one of six) was at this location. The square, which was laid out in 1799, was named "Columbia," the female personification of the U.S. Liberty Square, now lost to urban sprawl, was the only other square named in honor of the United States and the concept of freedom that stoked the fires of the American Revolution. Davenport House and Kehoe House are on Columbia Square. ⊠ *Habersham St. between E. State and E. York Sts., Historic District.*

③ Factors Walk. A network of iron crosswalks connects Bay Street with the multistory buildings that rise up from the river level, and iron stairways descend from Bay Street to Factors Walk. The area was originally the center of commerce for cotton brokers, who walked between and above the lower cotton warehouses. Cobblestone ramps lead pedestrians down to River Street. ■ TIP→ These are serious cobblestones, so wear comfortable shoes. ⊠ *Bay St. to Factors Walk, Historic District.*

> **GUNS OF PEACE**
>
> George and Martha are the affectionate names of the two bronze cannons that stand at the corner of Bay and Drayton streets. The guns were taken at the battle of Yorktown and presented to the Chatham Artillery as a dramatic "bread-and-butter" peace offering by General George Washington when he visited Savannah in May 1791.

NEED A BREAK?   The best place for an ice-cream soda is at **Leopold's** (⊠ 212 E. Broughton St., Historic District ☏ 912/234–4442), a Savannah institution since 1919. It's currently owned by Stratton Leopold, grandson of the original owner and a Hollywood producer whose films include *Mission Impossible 3, The General's Daughter,* and *The Sum of All Fears.* Movie paraphernalia makes for an entertaining sideline to the selection of ice creams and sorbets. Famed lyricist Johnny Mercer grew up a block away from Leopold's and was a faithful customer.

Forsyth Park. The park forms the southern border of Bull Street. On its 30 acres are a glorious white fountain dating to 1858, Confederate and Spanish–American War memorials, and the Fragrant Garden for the Blind, a project of Savannah garden clubs. There are tennis courts and a tree-shaded jogging path. Outdoor plays and concerts often take place here. At the northwest corner of the park, in **Hodgson Hall**, a 19th-century Italianate Greek–revival building, you'll find the **Georgia Historical Society**, which shows selections from its collection of artifacts and manuscripts. The park's 1-mi perimeter is among the prettiest walks in the city, and takes you past many beautifully restored and historic homes. ☒ *501 Whitaker St., Historic District* ☏ *912/651–2128* ⊕ *www.georgiahistory.com* ☺ *Tues.–Sat. 10–5.*

★ ⓴ **Green-Meldrim House.** Designed by New York architect John Norris and built in 1850 for cotton merchant Charles Green, this Gothic-revival mansion cost $90,000 to build—a princely sum back then. The house was bought in 1892 by Judge Peter Meldrim, whose heirs sold it to **St. John's Episcopal Church** to use as a parish house. General Sherman lived here after taking the city in 1864. Sitting on **Madison Square**, the house has Gothic features such as a crenellated roof, oriels, and an external gallery with filigree ironwork. Inside are mantels of Carrara marble, carved black-walnut woodwork, and doorknobs and hinges of either silver plate or porcelain. ☒ *1 W. Macon St., Historic District* ☏ *912/233–3845* ☏ *$7* ☺ *Tues., Thurs., and Fri. 10–4, Sat. 10–1. Closed last 2 wks of Jan. and 2 wks before Easter.*

★ ❼ **Isaiah Davenport House.** The proposed demolition of this historic Savannah structure galvanized the city's residents into action to save their treasured buildings. Semicircular stairs with wrought-iron trim lead to the recessed doorway of the redbrick federal mansion that master builder Isaiah Davenport built for himself between 1815 and 1820. Three dormered windows poke through the sloping roof of the stately house, and the interior has polished hardwood floors, fine woodwork and plasterwork, and a soaring elliptical staircase. Furnishings, from the 1820s, are Hepplewhite, Chippendale, and Sheraton. ☒ *324 E. State St., Historic District* ☏ *912/236–8097* ⊕ *www.davenporthousemuseum.org* ☏ *$8* ☺ *Mon.–Sat. 10–4, Sun. 1–4.*

❿ **Jepson Center for the Arts.** In **Telfair Square** is Telfair's newest gallery, an unexpectedly modern building amid so many 18th- and 19th-century structures that are the city's hallmark. Inside you'll find permanent hangings of Southern art, African-American art, and photography. There's a sculpture gallery and an outdoor sculpture terrace in addition to interactive, kid-friendly exhibits. ☒ *207 W. York St., Historic District* ☏ *912/232–1177* ⊕ *www.telfair.org* ☏ *$9* ☺ *Mon. noon–5, Tues.–Sat. 10–5, Sun. 1–5.*

Johnson Square. The oldest of James Oglethorpe's original 24 squares was laid out in 1733 and named for South Carolina governor Robert Johnson. A monument marks the grave of Nathanael Greene, a hero of the Revolutionary War. The square was once a popular gathering place: Savannahians came here to welcome President Monroe in 1819, to greet

MOSS MYSTIQUE

Spanish moss—the silky, snakelike garlands that drape over the branches of live oaks—has come to symbolize the languorous sensibilities of the Deep South. A relative of the pineapple, the moisture-loving plant requires an average year-round humidity of 70%, and thus thrives in subtropical climates—including Georgia's coastal regions.

Contrary to popular belief, Spanish moss is not a parasite; it's an epiphyte, or "air plant," taking water and nutrients from the air and photosynthesizing in the same manner as soil-bound plants. It reproduces using tiny flowers. When water is scarce, it turns gray, and when the rains come it takes on a greenish hue. The old saying "Good night, sleep tight, don't let the bed bugs bite," is thought to come from the past practice of stuffing mattresses with Spanish moss, which often harbored the biting menaces commonly known as chiggers.

the Marquis de Lafayette in 1825, and to cheer for Georgia's secession in 1861. ⊠ *Bull St. between Bryan and Congress Sts., Historic District.*

❾ Juliette Gordon Low Birthplace/Girl Scout National Center. This majestic Regency town house, attributed to William Jay (built 1818–21), was designated in 1965 as Savannah's first National Historic Landmark. "Daisy" Low, founder of the Girl Scouts, was born here in 1860, and the house is now owned and operated by the Girl Scouts of America. Mrs. Low's paintings and other artwork are on display in the house, restored to the style of 1886, the year of Mrs. Low's marriage. ⊠ *142 Bull St., Historic District* ☎ *912/233–4501* ⊕ *www.girlscouts.org/birthplace* ➲ *$8* ☺ *Mon.–Sat. 10–4, Sun. 11–4.*

Madison Square. A statue on the square, laid out in 1839 and named for President James Madison, depicts Sergeant William Jasper hoisting a flag and is a tribute to his bravery during the Siege of Savannah. Though mortally wounded, Jasper rescued the colors of his regiment in the assault on the British lines. A granite marker denotes the southern line of the British defense during the 1779 battle. The Green-Meldrim House is here. ⊠ *Bull St. between W. Harris and W. Charlton Sts., Historic District.*

❽ Telfair's Owens-Thomas House and Museum. English architect William Jay's first Regency mansion in Savannah is widely considered the country's finest example of that architectural style. Built in 1816–19, the English house was constructed mostly with local materials. Of particular note are the curving walls of the house, Greek-inspired ornamental molding, half-moon arches, stained-glass panels, and Duncan Phyfe furniture. The carriage house includes a gift shop and rare urban slave quarters, which have retained the original furnishings and "haint-blue" paint made by the slave occupants. ⊠ *124 Abercorn St., Historic District* ☎ *912/233–9743* ⊕ *www.telfair.org* ➲ *$9* ☺ *Mon. noon–5, Tues.–Sat. 10–5, Sun. 1–5; last tour at 4:30.*

Fodor'sChoice ★

8

Reynolds Square. John Wesley, who preached in Savannah and wrote the first English hymnal in the city in 1736, is remembered here. A monument to the founder of the Methodist Church is shaded by greenery and surrounded by park benches. The **Olde Pink House** (⊠ 23 Abercorn St.), built in 1771, is one of the oldest buildings in town. Now a restaurant, the portico pink-stucco Georgian mansion has been a private home, a bank, and headquarters for a Yankee general during the Civil War. ⊠ *Abercorn St. between E. Bryant and E. Congress Sts., Historic District.*

❺ Riverfront Plaza. Amid this nine-block brick concourse, you can watch a parade of freighters and pug-nose tugs. Youngsters can play in the tugboat-shape sandboxes. There are a plethora of outlets for shopping and eating. River Street is the main venue for many of the city's celebrations, including the First Saturday festivals, when flea marketers, artists, and artisans display their wares and musicians entertain the crowds. ⊠ *River St. between Abercorn and Barnard St., Historic District.*

> ## THE WAVING GIRL
>
> This charming statue at River Street and East Board Ramp is a symbol of Savannah's Southern hospitality, and commemorates Florence Martus, the lighthouse keeper's sister who waved to ships in Savannah's port for more than 44 years.

❸ Savannah History Museum. This museum in a restored railway station is an excellent introduction to the city. Exhibits range from old locomotives to a tribute to Savannah-born songwriter Johnny Mercer. Built on the **site of the Siege of Savannah,** it marks the spot where in 1779 the colonial forces, led by Polish count Casimir Pulaski, laid siege to Savannah in an attempt to retake the city from the redcoats. They were beaten back, and Pulaski was killed while leading a cavalry charge against the British. The dead lie underneath the building. ⊠ *303 Martin Luther King Jr. Blvd., Historic District* ☎ *912/238–1779* ⊕ *www.chsgeorgia.org/shm/home.htm* ⊠ *$4.25* ⊙ *Weekdays 8:30–5, weekends 9–5.*

★ ❶ Scarborough House. This exuberant Greek-revival mansion, built during the 1819 cotton boom for Savannah merchant prince William Scarborough, was designed by English architect William Jay. Scarborough was a major investor in the steamship *Savannah*. The house has a Doric portico capped by one of Jay's characteristic half-moon windows. Four massive Doric columns form a peristyle in the atrium entrance hall. Inside is the **Ships of the Sea Museum,** with displays of ship models, including steamships, and a nuclear-power ship. ⊠ *41 Martin Luther King Jr. Blvd., Historic District* ☎ *912/232–1511* ⊕ *www.shipsofthesea.org* ⊠ *$7* ⊙ *Tues.–Sun. 10–5.*

❶ Telfair Museum of Art. The oldest public art museum in the Southeast was designed by William Jay in 1819 for Alexander Telfair and sits across the street from **Telfair Square.** Within its marble rooms are American, French, and Dutch impressionist paintings; German tonalist paintings; a large collection of works by Kahlil Gibran; plaster casts of the Elgin

SPA SAVANNAH

As with the rest of the world, spa-ing is catching on in the city of Spanish Moss. **Vanilla Day Spa** (⌧ 1 E. Broughton St., Downtown ☎ 912/232–0040) is inside the Downtown Athletic Club—with access to steamrooms, sauna, and whirlpools—and offers a full menu of professional services for men and women such as manicures, pedicures, facials, and body treatments. In addition to traditional spa services, **Savannah**

Day Spa (⌧ 18 E. Oglethorpe St., Downtown ☎ 912/234–9100) also offers hydrotherpay and a complete line of skin-care products, accessories for your home spa, and a new line of vegan body products. The very chic **Poseidon Spa** (⌧ 700 Drayton St., Historic District ☎ 912/721–5004) at the Mansion on Forsyth Park is another first-class European-style spa, with a number of rejuvenating treatments and refinement services.

Marbles, the Venus de Milo, and the Laocoön, among other classical sculptures; and some of the Telfair family furnishings, including a Duncan Phyfe sideboard and Savannah-made silver. ⌧ *121 Barnard St., Historic District* ☎ *912/232–1177* ⊕ *www.telfair.org* ⌧ *$9* ☾ *Mon. noon–5, Tues.–Sat. 10–5, Sun. 1–5.*

Also Worth Seeing

🔟 **Beach Institute African-American Cultural Center.** Works by African-American artists from the Savannah area and around the country are on display in this building, which once housed the first school for African-American children in Savannah, established in 1867. On permanent exhibit are more than 230 wood carvings by folk artist Ulysses Davis. ⌧ *502 E. Harris St., Historic District* ☎ *912/234–8000* ⊕ *www.kingtisdell.org* ⌧ *$4* ☾ *Tues.–Sat. noon–5.*

🔟 **Cathedral of St. John the Baptist.** Soaring over the city, this French Gothic–style cathedral, with pointed arches and free-flowing traceries, is the seat of the diocese of Savannah. It was founded in 1799 by the first French colonists to arrive in Savannah. Fire destroyed the early structures; the present cathedral dates from 1874. ⌧ *222 E. Harris St., Historic District* ☎ *912/233–4709* ☾ *Weekdays 9–5.*

④ **City Hall.** Built in 1905 on the site of the Old City Exchange (1799–1904), this imposing structure anchors Bay Street. Notice the bench commemorating Oglethorpe's landing on February 12, 1733. ⌧ *1 Bay St., Historic District* ☎ *912/651–6410* ☾ *Weekdays 8:30–5.*

⑥ **Emmet Park.** Once an Indian burial ground, the lovely tree-shaded park is named for Robert Emmet, a late-18th-century Irish patriot and orator. The park contains monuments to German Salzburgers, Vietnam's fallen soldiers, and the Celtic Cross, among others. ⌧ *Borders E. Bay St., Historic District.*

Lafayette Square. Named for the Marquis de Lafayette who aided the Americans during the Revolutionary War, the square contains a grace-

Famous Faces in Savannah

LONG BEFORE the notoriety described in *Midnight in the Garden of Good and Evil*, interesting people were doing interesting things in this city. Here's a sampling of the figures who have etched themselves into Savannah's collective memory.

Actor Robert Mitchum (1917–97) gave one of his finest performances as a psychotic ex-convict in 1961's *Cape Fear*, which was filmed in and around Savannah. The shooting wasn't Mitchum's first visit to the city. In 1934, as a wayward 17-year-old, he roamed across America and was arrested on charges of vagrancy and begging while panhandling in Savannah. Six days after he was jailed, he escaped. When he returned to Savannah, his earlier transgressions were never mentioned.

James L. Pierpont (1822–93) wrote the Christmas classic "Jingle Bells" in Savannah—at least that's what locals will tell you. A native of Medford, Massachusetts, Pierpont became music director of Savannah's Unitarian church in the 1850s. In 1857 he obtained a copyright for "The One Horse Open Sleigh" (commonly known as "Jingle Bells"). In the 1980s tempers boiled when Medford claimed that Pierpont had written the song in their city, not in Savannah. The dispute has never been resolved.

John Wesley (1703–91), the founder of Methodism, had some rough times in Savannah. He arrived in 1735, and fell in love with Sophia Hopkey. But Wesley wasn't prepared to marry and Sophia found another suitor, William Williamson. The jealous Wesley charged Sophia with neglect of public church services and refused to let her participate in communion. Sophia's uncle, Thomas Causton, Savannah's chief magistrate, charged Wesley with defamation, claiming he was unfit to be a minister. Wesley, found guilty on some of the counts, fled to England. By the time he died, at 88, he had become one of the towering figures in religious history.

Names of note also include Johnny Mercer (1909–76), a fourth generation Savannah native and one of America's most popular and successful songwriters of the 20th century. Between 1929 and 1976 he composed lyrics to more than 1,000 songs, received 19 Academy Award nominations, and co-founded Capitol Records. He is buried in Bonaventure Cemetery. Fiction writer Flannery O'Connor (1925–64) spent the first 13 years of her life in Savannah. A devout Catholic, she was a regular presence at the Cathedral of St. John the Baptist. Her novels *Wise Blood* and *The Violent Bear It Away* amply convey her unique take on the Southern-Gothic style, but her greatest achievement is found in her short stories, published in the collections *A Good Man Is Hard to Find* and *Everything That Rises Must Converge*.

Savannah is also the proud hometown of Supreme Court Justice Clarence Thomas, America's second African-American Supreme Court Justice.

ful three-tier fountain donated by the Georgia chapter of the Colonial Dames of America. The Cathedral of St. John the Baptist and the childhood home of author Flannery O'Conner are on the square. ⊠ *Abercorn St. between E. Harris and E. Charlton Sts., Historic District.*

Monterey Square. Commemorating the victory of General Zachary Taylor's forces in Monterrey, Mexico, in 1846, this is the fifth and southernmost of Bull Street's squares. A monument honors General Casimir Pulaski, the Polish nobleman who lost his life in the Siege of Savannah during the Revolutionary War. Also on the square is Temple Mickve Israel. ⊠ *Bull St. between Taylor and Gordon Sts., Historic District.*

OFF THE
BEATEN
PATH

RALPH MARK GILBERT CIVIL RIGHTS MUSEUM – In Savannah's Historic District, this history museum has a series of 15 exhibits on segregation, from emancipation through the civil rights movement. The role of black and white Savannahians in ending segregation in their city is detailed in these exhibits, largely derived from archival photographs. The museum also has touring exhibits. ⊠ *460 Martin Luther King Jr. Blvd., Historic District* ☎ *912/231–8900* 🖷 *912/234–2577* 🖘 *$4* ⊙ *Mon.–Sat. 9–5.*

㉖ Temple Mickve Israel. A Gothic-revival synagogue on Monterey Square houses the third-oldest Jewish congregation in the United States; its founding members settled in town five months after the establishment of Savannah in 1733. The synagogue's collection includes documents and letters (some from George Washington, James Madison, and Thomas Jefferson) pertaining to early Jewish life in Savannah and Georgia. ⊠ *20 E. Gordon St., Historic District* ☎ *912/233–1547* ⊕ *www.mickveisrael. org* 🖘 *Free; tour $3* ⊙ *Weekdays 10–noon and 2–4.*

⓯ Wesley Monumental Church. This Gothic-revival style church memorializing the founders of Methodism is patterned after Queen's Kerk in Amsterdam. It dates from 1868 and is particularly noted for its magnificent stained-glass windows. ⊠ *429 Abercorn St., Historic District* ☎ *912/232–0191* ⊙ *By appointment only.*

Wright Square. Named for James Wright, Georgia's last colonial governor, this square has an elaborate monument in its center that honors William Washington Gordon, founder of the Central of Georgia Railroad. A slab of granite from Stone Mountain adorns the grave of Tomo-Chi-Chi, the Yamacraw chief who befriended General Oglethorpe and the colonists. ⊠ *Bull St. between W. State and W. York Sts., Historic District.*

Other Area Attractions

Ebenezer. When the Salzburgers arrived in Savannah in 1734, Oglethorpe sent them up the Savannah River to establish a settlement. The first effort was assailed by disease, and they sought his permission to move to better ground. Denied, they moved anyway and established Ebenezer. Here, they engaged in silkworm production and, in 1769, built the Jerusalem Church, which still stands. After the revolution, the silkworm operation never resumed, and the town faded into history. Descendants of these Protestant religious refugees have preserved the church and assembled a few of the remaining buildings, moving them

Spending Another Midnight in the Garden

TOWN GOSSIPS can provide the best introduction to a city, and as author John Berendt discovered, Savannah's not short on them. In his 1994 best-seller, *Midnight in the Garden of Good and Evil*, Berendt shares the juiciest of tales imparted to him during the eight years he spent here wining and dining Savannah's high society and dancing with Her Grand Empress, drag queen the Lady Chablis. By the time he left, there had been a scandalous homicide and several trials.

To fully appreciate the eccentric world of cutthroat killers, society backstabbers, voodoo witches, and garden-club ladies, you need to find a copy of the book, or at the very least, **"The Book" Gift Shop** (⊠ 127 E. Gordon St. ☎ 912/233–3867) on Calhoun Square. This quirky outlet heralds itself as the official *Midnight in the Garden of Good and Evil* headquarters and you'll find all manner of book-related souvenirs. Call for daily walking tour times and prices.

Most of the sights and historical homes in the book aren't open to the public, but the walk between them still makes a good stroll. Allow a leisurely two hours to walk the main points, plus another hour to visit the cemetery.

Begin at the southwest corner of Monterey Square, site of the **Mercer House** ㉓ (⊠ 429 Bull St.). The construction was begun by songwriter Johnny Mercer's great-grandfather just before the Civil War. This redbrick Italianate mansion became Jim Williams's Taj Mahal. He's the main character in the book and here, he ran a world-class antiques dealership and held *the* Christmas party of the

season. Williams himself died here of a heart attack in 1990, near the very spot where his sometime house partner, Danny Hansford, succumbed to gunshot wounds. This house is now open to the public for tours.

Two blocks south on Bull Street is **Armstrong House** ㉕ (⊠ 447 Bull St.), an earlier residence of Jim Williams. On a late-afternoon walk past the mansion, author John Berendt met Simon Glover, an 86-year-old singer and porter for the law firm of Bouhan, Williams, and Levy, occupants of the building. Glover confided that he earned a weekly $10 for walking the deceased dogs of a former partner of the firm up and down Bull Street. Baffled? So was the author. Behind the house's cast-iron gates are the offices of Frank Siler, Jim Williams's attorney, who doubles as keeper of Uga, the Georgia Bulldog mascot.

The **Forsyth Park Apartments** ㉖ (⊠ Whitaker and Gwinnett Sts.), where Berendt lived, are on the southwest corner of Forsyth Park. From his fourth-floor rooms Berendt pieced together the majority of the book. While parking his newly acquired 1973 Pontiac Grand Prix outside these apartments, he met the Lady Chablis coming out of her nearby doctor's office, freshly feminine from a new round of hormone shots.

Return through Forsyth Park to **Serena Dawes's House** ㉔ (⊠ 17 W. Gordon St.). Near the intersection of West Gordon and Bull streets, this house was owned by Helen Driscoll, also known as Serena Dawes. A high-profile beauty in the 1930s and '40s, she married into a Pennsylvania steel family. After her husband accidentally and fatally shot himself in the head, she retired here. Dawes, Berendt writes, "spent most of her day in bed, holding court, drinking martinis and pink ladies, playing with her white toy poodle, Lulu." Chief among Serena's gentlemen callers was Luther Driggers, rumored to possess a poison strong enough to wipe out the entire city.

Walk north on Bull Street where **Lee Adler's Home** ❷ (✉ 425 Bull St.) sits at Monterey Square. Just north of Mercer House, in half of the double town house facing West Wayne Street, Lee Adler, the adversary of Jim Williams, runs his business of restoring historic Savannah properties. Adler's howling dogs drove Williams to his pipe organ, where he churned out a deafening version of César Franck's *Pièce Heroïque*. Later, Adler stuck reelection signs in his front lawn, showing his support for the district attorney who prosecuted Williams three times before he was finally found not guilty.

Continue walking north on Bull Street to **Joe Odom's first house** ❷ (✉ 16 E. Jones St.), where Joe Odom, a combination tax lawyer, real-estate broker, and piano player, hosted a 24-hour stream of visitors. The author met Odom through Mandy Nichols, a former Miss Big Beautiful Woman, who stopped by to borrow ice after the power had been cut off.

Then head for **Hamilton-Turner House** ❸ (✉ 330 Abercorn St.), now a B&B. After one too many of Odom's deals went sour, Mandy Nichols, his fourth fiancée-in-waiting, left him and took over his third residence, a 2nd Empire–style mansion dating from 1873. Mandy filled it with 17th- and 18th-century antiques and transformed

it into a successful museum.

The remaining two sights are both about a 20-minute walk away. Head north, and then west along West York Street and you'll find the **Chatham County Courthouse** ❶ (✉ 133 Montgomery St.), the scene of three of Williams's murder trials that took place over the course of about eight years.

Head south on Abercorn Street to Victory Drive and turn left, going through Thunderbolt to Whatley Avenue, which leads directly to Bonaventure Road. Bear left, and on your right about a quarter mile up the road is **Bonaventure Cemetery** ❶ (✉ 330 Bonaventure Rd. ☎ 912/651–6843), the final resting place of Danny Hansford. The haunting female tombstone figure from the book's cover has been removed to protect surrounding graves from sightseers. The figure is now on display at the Telfair Museum of Art.

8

to this site from other locations. Be sure to follow Route 275 to its end and see Ebenezer Landing, where the Salzburgers came ashore. ⊠ *Ebenezer Rd., Rte. 21–Rte. 275, 25 mi north of Savannah, Rincon.*

Old Fort Jackson. About 2 mi east of Broad Street via President Street, you'll see a sign for the fort, which is 3 mi from the city. Purchased in 1808 by the federal government, this is the oldest standing fort in Georgia. It was garrisoned in the War of 1812 and was the Confederate headquarters of the river batteries. The fort guards Five Fathom Hole, the 18th century deep-water port in the Savannah River. The brick edifice is surrounded by a tidal moat, and there are 14 exhibit areas. Battle reenactments, blacksmithing demonstrations, and programs of 19th-century music are among the fort's activities for tour groups. ⊠ *1 Fort Jackson Rd., Fort Jackson* ☎ *912/232–3945* ⊕ *www.chsgeorgia.org/jackson/home.htm* ▣ *$4.25* ⊘ *Daily 9–5.*

★ ☉ **Fort Pulaski National Monument.** Named for Casimir Pulaski, a Polish count and Revolutionary War hero, this must-see sight for Civil War buffs was designed by Napoléon's military engineer and built on Cockspur Island between 1829 and 1847. Robert E. Lee's first assignment after graduating from West Point was as an engineer here. During the Civil War the fort fell, on April 11, 1862, after a mere 30 hours of bombardment by newfangled rifled cannons. The restored fortification, operated by the National Park Service, has moats, drawbridges, massive ramparts, and towering walls. The park has trails and picnic areas. It's 14 mi east of downtown Savannah; you'll see the entrance on your left just before U.S. 80 reaches Tybee Island. ⊠ *U.S. 80, Fort Pulaski* ☎ *912/786–5787* ⊕ *www.nps.gov/fopu* ▣ *$3* ⊘ *Daily 9–7.*

Melon Bluff. On land obtained with a Kings Grant in 1745, this 9,500 acre plantation has been in the same family ever since, and is one of the few remaining stretches of pristine Georiga coastline. ■ TIP→ Archaeological finds and historical records indicate that Melon Bluff is 37 years older than St. Augustine (long considered the oldest community in the United States). You'll find a nature center here and facilities for canoeing, kayaking, birdwatching, hiking, and other outdoor activities. You can camp here or stay at one of three B&Bs ($$–$$$): Palmyra Plantation, an 1850s cottage; the Ripley Farmhouse, a classic rural house with a tin-covered roof; and an old barn, renovated to contain nine guest rooms. From Melon Bluff you can visit nearby **Seabrook Village,** a small but growing cluster of rural buildings from an African-American historic community; **Old Sunbury,** whose port made it a viable competitor to Savannah until the Revolutionary War ended its heyday; **Fort Morris,** which protected Savannah during the revolution; and **Midway,** an 18th-century village with a house museum and period cemetery. To reach Melon Bluff, take Interstate 95 south from Savannah (about 30 mi) to Exit 76 (Midway/Sunbury), turn left, and go east for 3 mi. ⊠ *2999 Islands Hwy., Midway* ☎ *912/884–5779 or 888/246–8188* 🖷 *912/884–3046* ⊕ *www.melonbluff.com.*

Mighty Eighth Air Force Heritage Museum. The famous World War II squadron the Mighty Eighth Air Force was formed in Savannah in January 1942 and shipped out to the United Kingdom. Flying Royal Air

Force aircraft, the Mighty Eighth became the largest air force of the period. Exhibits at this museum begin with the prelude to World War II and the rise of Adolf Hitler and continue through Desert Storm. You can see vintage aircraft, fly a simulated bombing mission with a B-17 crew, test your skills as a waist gunner, and view interviews with courageous World War II vets. The museum also has three theaters, an art gallery, a 1940s-era English pub, a 7,000-volume library, archives, memorial garden, chapel, and museum store. ⌧ *175 Bourne Ave., I–95, Exit 102, to U.S. 80, 14 mi west of Savannah, Pooler* ☎ *912/748–8888* ⊕ *www.mightyeighth.org* ⌑ *$10* ⊙ *Daily 9–5.*

☾ **Skidaway Marine Science Complex.** On the grounds of the former Modena Plantation, Skidaway has a 14-panel, 12,000-gallon aquarium with marine and plant life of the continental shelf. Other exhibits highlight coastal archaeology and fossils of the Georgia coast. Nature trails overlook marsh and water. ⌧ *30 Ocean Science Circle, 8 mi south of Savannah, Skidaway Island* ☎ *912/598–2496* ⌑ *$2* ⊙ *Weekdays 9–4, Sat. noon–5.*

Tybee Island. *Tybee* is an Indian word meaning "salt." The Yamacraw Indians came to this island in the Atlantic Ocean to hunt and fish, and legend has it that pirates buried their treasure here. The island is about 5 mi long and 2 mi wide, with seafood restaurants, chain motels, condos, and shops—most of which sprang up during the 1950s and haven't changed much since. The entire expanse of white sand is divided into a number of public beaches, where you can shell and crab, charter fishing boats, and swim. **Tybee Island Lighthouse and Museum** (⌧ 30 Meddin Dr. ☎ 912/786–5801) has been well restored; the Head Keeper's Cottage is the oldest building on the island, and should be on your list. Kids will enjoy the **Marine Science Center** (⌧ 1510 Strand Ave. ☎ 912/786–5917), which houses local marine life such as the Ogeechee corn snake, turtles, and American alligator. Tybee Island is 18 mi east of Savannah; take Victory Drive (U.S. 80), sometimes called Tybee Road, onto the island. Nearby, the misnamed Little Tybee Island, actually larger than Tybee Island, is entirely undeveloped. Contact **Tybee Island Convention and Visitors Bureau** (✉ Box 491, Tybee Island 31328 ☎ 800/868–2322 ⊕ www.tybeevisit.com) for information and maps.

8

SPORTS & THE OUTDOORS

Boating

At the **Bull River Yacht Club Marina** (⌧ 8005 Old Tybee Rd., Tybee Island ☎ 912/897–7300), you can arrange a dolphin tour, a deep-sea fishing expedition, or a jaunt through the coastal islands. **Lake Mayer Park** (⌧ Montgomery Crossroads Rd. and Sallie Mood Dr., Cresthill ☎ 912/652–6780) has paddleboats, sailing, and canoeing, as well as an in-line skating and hockey facility. Capt. Judy Helmley, a long-time and legendary guide of the region, heads up **Miss Judy Charters** (⌧ 124 Palmetto Dr., Wilmington Island ☎ 912/897–4921 or 912/897–2478) and provides packages ranging from two-hour sightseeing tours to 13-hour

NO-HILLS WORKOUT

Savannah is table flat—bad news indeed for any mountaineers who find themselves in coastal Georgia—but great for bicyclists. One favorite spot for local bikers is the 28,000-acre Savannah Wildlife Refuge, where alligators (not that you should poke at them with a stick, but they're really about as dangerous as furniture) bask alongside the trail. Another possibility is Rails-to-Trails, a 3-mi route that starts 1 mi east of the Bull River Bridge on Highway 80 and ends at the entrance to Fort Pulaski. Tom Triplett Park, east of town on U.S. 80, offers three bike loops—3.5 mi, 5 mi, and 6.3 mi. Though much of downtown is fairly unfriendly to bikers, several of the suburbs—Windsor Forest, Ardsley Park, the Isle of Hope—are fine for riding relatively free of traffic hassles.

deep-sea fishing expeditions. **Savannah Islands Expressway** (⊠ Adjacent to Frank W. Spencer Park, Skidaway Island ☎ 912/231–8222) offers boat ramps on the Wilmington River. **Savannah Marina** (⊠ Thunderbolt) provides boat ramps on the Wilmington River.

Golf

Bacon Park (⊠ 1 Shorty Cooper Dr., Southside ☎ 912/354–2625) is a public facility with 27 holes of golf and a lighted driving range. **Henderson Golf Club** (⊠ 1 Al Henderson Dr., at I–95, Exit 94 to Rte. 204, Southside ☎ 912/920–4653) is an 18-hole, par-71 course about 15 mi from downtown Savannah. The **Mary Calder Golf Course** (⊠ W. Lathrop Ave., West Chatham ☎ 912/238–7100) is par 35 for its 9 holes.

Tennis

Bacon Park (⊠ 6262 Skidaway Rd., Southside ☎ 912/351–3850) has 16 lighted asphalt courts. Fees are $3 per person, and you can reserve courts in advance. **Forsyth Park** (⊠ Drayton St. and Park Ave., Historic District ☎ 912/652–6780) contains four lighted courts available until about 10 PM; there's no charge to use them. **Lake Mayer Park** (⊠ Montgomery Crossroads Rd. and Sallie Mood Dr., Southside ☎ 912/652–6780) has eight asphalt lighted courts available at no charge and open 8 AM to 10 PM; until 11 PM May through September.

WHERE TO EAT

Savannah has excellent seafood restaurants, though locals also have a passion for spicy barbecued meats. The Historic District yields a culinary cache, especially along River Street. Several of the city's restaurants—such as Elizabeth on 37th, the Olde Pink House, and Sapphire Grill—are beacons that have drawn members of the culinary upper crust to the region for decades. And there are others, such as Johnny Harris and Mrs. Wilkes' Dining Room, that are treasured mainstays. If you explore a bit, you'll soon discover that such divine dining isn't isolated to Savannah's Historic District, as nearby Thunderbolt, Skidaway, Tybee, and Wilmington islands also have a collection of remarkable restaurants.

WHAT IT COSTS				
$$$$	$$$	$$	$	¢
over $22	$17–$22	$12–$16	$7–$11	under $7

Restaurant prices are for a main course at dinner.

$$$$ ✕ **Elizabeth on 37th.** Regional specialties are the hallmark at this acclaimed
Fodor'sChoice restaurant that goes so far as to credit local produce suppliers on its menu.
★ Although original chef and owner Elizabeth Terry has now retired, the kitchen hasn't faltered one iota. Dishes such as Maryland crab cakes or the plate of roasted shiitake and oyster mushrooms sit comfortably beside Southern-fried grits and honey roasted–pork tenderloin and roasted shiitake and oyster mushroom over dried tomatoes, black-eyed peas, and carrot ragout. The extravagant Savannah cream cake is the way to finish your meal in this elegant turn-of-the-20th-century mansion with hardwood floors and spacious rooms. ✉ *105 E. 37th St., Victorian District* ☎ *912/236–5547* ⌖ *Reservations essential* ▤ *AE, D, DC, MC, V* ☉ *No lunch.*

$$$–$$$$ ✕ **Belford's Steak and Seafood.** In the heart of City Market, Belford's is great for brunch on Sunday, when so many of the downtown venues are closed. A complimentary glass of sparkling wine arrives at your table when you place your order. Brunch entrées include egg dishes, such as smoked salmon Florentine and crab frittatas. The lunch and dinner menus focus on seafood, including Georgia pecan grouper and Lowcountry shrimp and grits. The building used to be a wholesale grocery company; modern tweaks include huge windows, wooden floors, exposed brick walls, and an expansive outdoor patio. ■ TIP➡ **Some have called the crab cakes the best in the city.** ✉ *315 W. St. Julian St., Historic District* ☎ *912/233–2626* ▤ *AE, D, DC, MC, V.*

$$$–$$$$ ✕ **Il Pasticcio.** Sicilian Pino Venetico turned this former department store into his dream restaurant—a bistro-style place gleaming with steel, glass, and tile. The menu changes frequently, but fresh pasta dishes are a constant, and excellent desserts include a superior tiramisu. The signature filet mignon with melted gorgonzola is superb. As the evening progresses—particularly on weekends when live jazz ensembles start up around 10 PM—the scene gets ever more lively and hip. A lower level caters to private parties; the upper level, separate from the restaurant, is a hip-hop club. ✉ *2 E. Broughton St., Historic District* ☎ *912/231–8888* ▤ *AE, D, DC, MC, V* ☉ *No lunch.*

$$$–$$$$ ✕ **The Lady & Sons.** Expect to take your place in line, along with locals, here. Everyone patiently waits to attack the buffet, which is stocked for both lunch and dinner with specials such as moist, crispy fried chicken; crab stew; chicken potpie; the best baked spaghetti in the South; green beans cooked with ham and potatoes; tender, sweet creamed corn; and homemade lemonade. Look for owner Paula H. Deen on the Food Channel or pick up a copy of her cookbook that includes recipes for

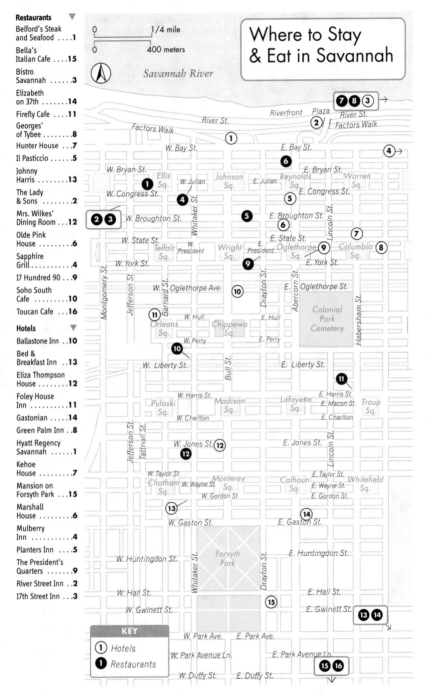

Restaurants ▼

Belford's Steak
and Seafood **1**

Bella's
Italian Cafe **15**

Bistro
Savannah **3**

Elizabeth
on 37th **14**

Firefly Cafe **11**

Georges'
of Tybee **8**

Hunter House ...**7**

Il Pasticcio **5**

Johnny
Harris **13**

The Lady
& Sons **2**

Mrs. Wilkes'
Dining Room ...**12**

Olde Pink
House **6**

Sapphire
Grill **4**

17 Hundred 90 ..**9**

Soho South
Cafe **10**

Toucan Cafe ...**16**

Hotels ▼

Ballastone Inn ..**10**

Bed &
Breakfast Inn ..**13**

Eliza Thompson
House **12**

Foley House
Inn **11**

Gastonian **14**

Green Palm Inn ..**8**

Hyatt Regency
Savannah **1**

Kehoe
House **7**

Mansion on
Forsyth Park ...**15**

Marshall
House **6**

Mulberry
Inn **4**

Planters Inn **5**

The President's
Quarters **9**

River Street Inn ..**2**

17th Street Inn ...**3**

Where to Stay & Eat in Savannah

Savannah River

0 — 1/4 mile

0 — 400 meters

the most popular dishes. She also holds cooking classes year-round here and at her other restaurant, Uncle Bubba's Oyster House. ⊠ *102 W. Congress St., Historic District* ☎ *912/233–2600* ▤ *AE, D, MC, V* ☉ *No dinner Sun.*

$$$–$$$$ ✕ **Sapphire Grill.** Savannah's young and restless pack this trendy haunt nightly. Chef Chris Nason focuses his seasonal menus on local ingredients, such as Georgia white shrimp, crab, and fish. The Grill features succulent choices of steak, poultry, and fish, with a myriad of interesting à la carte accompaniments such as jalapeño tartar, sweet soy-wasabi sauce, and clemson blue-cheese tarragon-dijon mustard. Vegetarians will delight in the elegant vegetable presentations—perhaps including roasted sweet onions, spicy peppers, rice-marinated watercress, or fried green tomatoes with grilled ginger. Chocoholics should try the delicious, potent chocolate flan. ■ TIP➔ **Downstairs the decor is hip with gray brick walls alongside those painted a deep sapphire and a stone bar; upstairs is quieter and more romantic.** ⊠ *110 W. Congress St., Historic District* ☎ *912/443– 9962* ⌁ *Reservations essential* ▤ *AE, D, DC, MC, V* ☉ *No lunch.*

★ **$$$–$$$$** ✕ **17 Hundred 90.** In a rustic structure dating to colonial days, tucked in among ancient oaks dripping with Spanish moss, you'll find a very creative kitchen. Entrées include pan-seared veal medallions with artichoke hearts and capers in lemon butter; roasted half duckling with a port-wine lingonberry sauce; and local shrimp stuffed with scallops and crabmeat and served with a lemon beurre-blanc sauce. ■ TIP➔ **There's a ghost story to go with dinner, so make sure the waiter fills you in.** ⊠ *307 E. Presidents St., Historic District* ☎ *912/237–7122* ▤ *AE, D, DC, MC, V* ☉ *No lunch weekends.*

★ **$$–$$$$** ✕ **Bistro Savannah.** High ceilings, burnished heart-pine floors, and graybrick walls lined with local art contribute to the bistro qualities of this spot by City Market. The menu has specialties such as seared beef tenderloin with fingerling potatoes, portebello mushrooms, red chard in a cabernet sauce, and shrimp and *tasso* (seasoned cured pork) on stoneground grits. Another treat is the crispy roasted duck. ⊠ *309 W. Congress St., Historic District* ☎ *912/233–6266* ▤ *AE, MC, V* ☉ *No lunch.*

$$–$$$$ ✕ **Georges' of Tybee.** There's a romantic ambience in this upscale restaurant with a warmly lighted interior, a lovely stone fireplace, and dark rose-painted walls. Chef Robert Wood puts a refreshing spin on favorites such as a grilled rack of lamb, served with spinach, olives, and mushrooms tossed with Israeli couscous and apricot and fig chutney. The sautéed black grouper is a treat, served over bamboo rice with Asian slaw and coconut curry. ■ TIP➔ **The restaurant's beachfront sister, North Beach Grill, is way more casual, serving burgers by day and jerk chicken and pork in the evening.** ⊠ *1105 E. U.S. 80, Tybee Island* ☎ *912/786–9730* ▤ *AE, MC, V* ☉ *Closed Mon. No lunch.*

$$–$$$$ ✕ **Hunter House.** When owner John Hunter followed the lady he loved to Georgia several years ago, he wasn't expecting to fall in love again— with Tybee Island, let alone create one of the region's finest dining rooms. Built in 1910 as a family beach house, this totally renovated home offers an intimate dining experience with a Victorian ambience. Seafood dominates the menu and includes deliciously creative dishes such as a cognac-laced seafood bisque and baked Chilean sea bass topped with

8

apple bark–smoked bacon and served over Boursin cheese–garlic-chive mashed potatoes. Meat eaters need not despair; chicken and steak options are available and the restaurant boasts a pot roast as the house special. ■ TIP→ **Though the restaurant is the primary business, the house also has a quality B&B with four guest rooms.** ☒ *1701 Butler Ave., Tybee Island* ☎ *912/786–7515* 🖃 *AE, D, DC, MC, V* ☺ *Closed Sun. Nov.–Apr.*

$$–$$$$ ✕ **Olde Pink House.** This pink-brick Georgian mansion was built in 1771 for James Habersham, one of the wealthiest Americans of his time, and the old-time atmosphere comes through in the original Georgia pine floors of the tavern, the Venetian chandeliers, and the 18th-century English antiques. The she-crab soup with sherry is a light but flavorful version of a Lowcountry specialty. Regional ingredients find their way into many of the dishes, including the black grouper stuffed with blue crab and served with a Vidalia onion sauce. ☒ *23 Abercorn St., Historic District* ☎ *912/232–4286* 🖃 *AE, MC, V* ☺ *No lunch.*

$$–$$$ ✕ **Firefly Cafe.** Chef and owner Sharon Stinogel offers a fresh twist on Southern fare at this upbeat neigborhood spot, on the corner of Troup Square, in a cozy residential area. The menu has something for everyone, including vegetarians and vegans, and offers a myriad of salads with intriguing dressings (the lemon chicken is especially good), as well as flavorful pork chops with garlic mashed potatoes. The outdoor tables are often taken by couples with their dogs in tow—perhaps that's because of the homemade dog biscuits. ☒ *321 Habersham St.* ☎ *912/234–1971* 🖃 *MC, V* ☺ *Closed Mon. No dinner Sun.*

$$–$$$ ✕ **Johnny Harris.** What started as a small roadside stand in 1924, across from Grayson Stadium, has grown into one of the city's beloved mainstays, with a menu that includes Brunswick stew, steaks, fried chicken, seafood, and meats spiced with the restaurant's famous tomato-and-mustard sauces. The hickory smoked BBQ pork is a treat, and their sauces are now so famous that they bottle them for take-home and shipping. ■ TIP→ **Originally, the booths had doors and catered to business and romantic tête-à-têtes. The privacy doors have long gone though the old service bell's still there, and they're still the most comfortable seats in the house.** ☒ *1651 E. Victory Dr., Eastside* ☎ *912/354–7810* 🖃 *AE, D, DC, MC, V* ☺ *Closed Sun.*

$$–$$$ ✕ **Soho South Cafe.** Get set to have your palate treated to a palette of sensory delights in this restaurant cum art gallery cum coffee shop cum bakery cum library. If you do have to wait for a table, the time passes by quickly with so much to absorb. The food is great: from Mom's meat loaf sandwich and a portobella "pizza" to jumbo lump crab cakes. If nothing else, try the signature tomato-basil bisque. ☒ *12 W. Liberty St.* ☎ *912/233–1633* ☖ *Reservations not accepted* 🖃 *MC, V* ☺ *Closed Mon. No dinner Sun.*

★ $–$$$ ✕ **Bella's Italian Café.** From its unpretentious spot in a Midtown shopping center, Bella's serves up simple, wildly popular fare, including scampi, ziti, pizza, and panini as well as a particularly good manicotti. Desserts are also standout versions of classics, such as Italian wedding cake, tiramisu, and cannoli. The genial, hospitable service makes this a perfect place to relax over a glass of wine. ☒ *4408 Habersham St., Midtown* ☎ *912/354–4005* ☖ *Reservations not accepted* 🖃 *AE, D, DC, MC, V* ☺ *No lunch weekends.*

★ **$–$$$** ✕ **Toucan Café.** This colorful café is well worth a trip a bit off the beaten path to Savannah's Southside. It's a favorite for Savannahians entertaining out-of-town visitors; no one, it seems, leaves unsatisfied. The menu defines the term "eclectic," with plenty of appealing options for both vegetarians and meat eaters, including wasabi pea–encrusted tuna, tempura portobello, black-bean burgers, spanakopita, Jamaican jerk chicken, and rib-eye steaks. ⊠ *531 Stephenson Ave., Southside* ☎ *912/352–2233* ▤ *AE, D, MC, V* ⊘ *Closed Sun. and Mon.*

★ **$$** ✕ **Mrs. Wilkes' Dining Room.** Folks line up for a culinary orgy of fine Southern food, served family-style at big tables. For breakfast there are eggs, sausage, piping-hot biscuits, and grits. At lunch try fried or roast chicken, beef stew, collard greens, okra, mashed potatoes, and corn bread. Mrs. Wilkes made this place somewhat of a legend, and her grand daughter and great grandson are keeping it a family affair in more ways than one. Menus are a set price; kids under eight years of age eat for half price. ⊠ *107 W. Jones St., Historic District* ☎ *912/232–5997* ⚅ *Reservations not accepted* ▤ *No credit cards* ⊘ *Closed Jan. and weekends. No dinner.*

WHERE TO STAY

Although Savannah has its share of chain hotels and motels, the city's most distinctive lodgings are the more than two dozen historic inns, guesthouses, and B&Bs gracing the Historic District.

If the term *historic inn* brings to mind images of roughing it in shabbygenteel mansions with antiquated plumbing, you're in for a surprise. Most of these inns are in mansions with the requisite high ceilings, spacious rooms, and ornate carved millwork. And most do have canopy, four-poster, or Victorian brass beds. But amid all the antique surroundings, there's modern luxury: enormous baths, many with whirlpools or hot tubs; film libraries for in-room VCRs; and turndown service with a chocolate, a praline, even a discreet brandy on your nightstand. Continental breakfast and afternoon refreshments are often included in the rate. Special seasons and holidays, such as St. Patrick's Day, push prices up a bit. On the other hand, weekdays and the off-season can yield excellent bargains.

WHAT IT COSTS				
$$$$	$$$	$$	$	¢
over $220	$161–$220	$111–$160	$70–$110	under $70

Hotel prices are for two people in a standard double room in high season.

Inns & Guesthouses

★ **$$$$** ▦ **Foley House Inn.** Two town houses, built 50 years apart, form this elegant inn. Most rooms have king-size beds, and all have fireplaces and reproduction antique furnishings; four rooms have whirlpool tubs; three have balconies. A carriage house to the rear of the property has less expensive rooms. ⊠ *14 W. Hull St., Historic District, 31401* ☎ *912/232–*

6622 or 800/647–3708 🖷 *912/231–1218* ⊕ *www.foleyinn.com* ⟿ *17 rooms, 2 suites* ♿ *In-room VCRs* ⊟ *AE, MC, V* ❙⊙❙ *BP.*

★ **$$$$** 🏨 **Gastonian.** The entire inn, built in 1868, underwent an extensive re-modeling in 2005. Guest rooms are lavishly decorated with antiques from the Georgian and Regency periods; all have fireplaces and most have whirlpool tubs. The Caracalla Suite is named for the oversize whirlpool tub built in front of the fireplace. At breakfast you can find such specialty items as lemon cheese or ginger pancakes. Afternoon tea, evening cordials, and complimentary wine are other treats. ⊠ *220 E. Gaston St., Historic District, 31401* 🕾 *912/232–2869 or 800/322–6603* 🖷 *912/ 232–0710* ⊕ *www.gastonian.com* ⟿ *14 rooms, 3 suites* ♿ *In-room DVDs, Wi-Fi* ⊟ *AE, D, MC, V* ❙⊙❙ *BP.*

$$$$ 🏨 **Kehoe House.** A fabulously appointed 1890s B&B, the Victorian Kehoe House has brass-and-marble chandeliers, a courtyard garden, and a music room. Guest rooms have a modern Victorian feel with a mix of antiques and modern linens. On the main floor a double parlor holds two fireplaces and sweeps the eye upward with its 14-foot ceilings, creating an elegant setting for a beautifully served full breakfast. Rates include access to the Downtown Athletic Club. A charming glass armoire displays Victorian and one-of-a-kind artisan jewelry for sale. ⊠ *123 Habersham St., Historic District, 31401* 🕾 *912/232–1020 or 800/820–1020* 🖷 *912/231–0208* ⊕ *www.kehoehouse.com* ⟿ *13 rooms* ♿ *In-room DVDs, Wi-Fi, concierge* ⊟ *AE, D, DC, MC, V* ❙⊙❙ *BP.*

★ **$$$–$$$$** 🏨 **Ballastone Inn.** This sumptuous inn occupies an 1838 mansion that once served as a bordello. Rooms are handsomely furnished, with luxurious linens on canopy beds, antiques and fine reproductions, and a collection of original framed prints from *Harper's* scattered throughout. On the garden level rooms are small and cozy, with exposed brick walls, beam ceilings, and, in some cases, windows at eye level with the lush courtyard. Most rooms have working gas fireplaces, and three have whirlpool tubs. ■ TIP➔ **Afternoon tea and free passes to a nearby health club are included.** ⊠ *14 E. Oglethorpe Ave., Historic District, 31401* 🕾 *912/236–1484 or 800/822–4553* 🖷 *912/236–4626* ⊕ *www.ballastone. com* ⟿ *16 rooms, 3 suites* ♿ *Dining room, in-room VCRs, bicycles* ⊟ *AE, MC, V* ❙⊙❙ *BP.*

$$$–$$$$ 🏨 **Eliza Thompson House.** Eliza Thompson was a socially prominent widow when she built her fine town house around 1847; today the lovely Victorian edifice is one of the oldest B&Bs in Savannah. A peaceful garden courtyard provides a quiet respite. The rooms are luxuriously decorated with marble baths, rare antiques, plush bedding, and other designer accents. A full breakfast, afternoon wine and cheese, and evening desserts are served in the parlor or on the patio, which has a fine Ivan Bailey sculpture. ⊠ *5 W. Jones St., Historic District, 31401* 🕾 *912/236–3620 or 800/348–9378* 🖷 *912/238–1920* ⊕ *www. elizathompsonhouse.com* ⟿ *25 rooms* ♿ *Cable TV* ⊟ *MC, V* ❙⊙❙ *BP.*

★ **$$$–$$$$** 🏨 **The President's Quarters.** You'll be impressed even before you enter this lovely inn, which has an exterior courtyard so beautiful and inviting it has become a popular wedding-reception spot. Each room in this classic Savannah inn, fashioned out of a pair of meticulously restored 1860s town houses, is named for an American president. Some rooms have four-poster beds, working fireplaces, and private balconies. Expect to be greeted with wine and fruit, and a complimentary afternoon tea will tempt you with sweet cakes. Turndown service includes a glass of port or sherry. There are also rooms in an adjacent town house. Breakfast is served in the adjoining 17 Hundred 90 restaurant. ■ TIP→ **Room 204 is said to be haunted by a lady with a broken heart.** ⊠ *225 E. President St., Historic District, 31401* ☎ *912/233–1600 or 800/233–1776* 🖷 *912/ 238–0849* ⊕ *www.presidentsquarters.com* ⇨ *11 rooms, 8 suites* ♿ *Some in-room hot tubs, in-room DVDs, Wi-Fi* ☰ *D, DC, MC, V* ❘❂❘ *BP.*

$$–$$$ ⊡ **Bed & Breakfast Inn.** So called, the owner claims, because it was the first such property to open in Savannah almost 30 years ago, the inn is a restored 1853 federal-style row house on historic Gordon Row near Chatham Square. The courtyard garden is a lovely cluster of potted tropical flowers surrounding an inviting koi pond. All rooms have private baths and retain many elements of the home's original charm, such as beamed ceilings and exposed-brick walls. There are four self-contained cottages, and some rooms also have kitchens. Afternoon pastries, lemonade, coffee, and tea are served. ⊠ *117 W. Gordon St., Historic District, 31401* ☎ *912/238–0518* 🖷 *912/233–2537* ⊕ *www.savannahbnb.com* ⇨ *14 rooms, 2 suites, 4 cottages* ☰ *AE, D, MC, V* ❘❂❘ *BP.*

★ **$$–$$$** ⊡ **Green Palm Inn.** This inn is a pleasing little discovery. Originally built in 1897 but renovated top to bottom, it's now a delightful B&B. The elegant furnishings of the cottage-style rooms were inspired by Savannah's British-colonial heritage. All rooms have fireplaces and a couple even have fireplaces in the bathrooms. Breakfasts are generous and served with style, and in the evening, you'll be treated to homemade desserts. ⊠ *548 E. President St., Historic District, 31401* ☎ *912/447– 8901 or 888/606–9510* 🖷 *912/236–4626* ⊕ *www.greenpalminn.com* ⇨ *4 suites* ♿ *Fans, cable TV* ☰ *AE, MC, V* ❘❂❘ *BP.*

$$–$$$ ⊡ **17th Street Inn.** You're steps from the beach at this Tybee Island inn dating from 1920. The front deck, adorned with plants, palms, and swings, is a gathering place where you can chat, sip wine, and enjoy breakfast. The inn's rooms each offer a queen bed, efficiency kitchen, private bath, and private entrance. A continental breakfast is served each morning. A self-catering, two-bedroom condo next door sleeps six. ⊠ *12 17th St., Box 114, Tybee Island 31328* ☎ *912/786–0607 or 888/909–0607* 🖷 *912/786–0602* ⊕ *www.tybeeinn.com* ⇨ *8 rooms, 1 condo* ♿ *Kitchenettes, cable TV, Wi-Fi* ☰ *AE, D, MC, V* ❘❂❘ *CP.*

Hotels & Motels

$$$$ ⊡ **Mansion on Forsyth Park.** Sophisticated, chic, and artsy only begin to describe this Kessler property, which was purposely built to blend with its historic surroundings. Sitting on the edge of Forsyth Park, its dramatic design, opulent interiors, and magnificently diverse collection of art creates a one-of-a-kind experience. Every turn delivers something unexpected—a canopied patio by the pool that feels like it's out of *Arabian Nights*; a Nordic-looking full-service spa; back-lighted onyx panels and 100-year-old Italian Corona–marble pillars. The 700 Drayton Restaurant offers fine dining and very attentive service. Upstairs, Casimir's Lounge, with live piano and jazz, is one of the city's hot

8

spots. ⊠ *700 Drayton St., 31401* ☎ *912/238–5158 or 888/711–5114* 🖷 *912/238–5146* ⊕ *www.mansiononforsythpark.com* ⇆ *126 rooms* ⚒ *Restaurant, spa, bar, lounge, meeting rooms; no smoking.* ▭ *AE, D, DC, MC, V.*

$$$–$$$$ 🏨 **Hyatt Regency Savannah.** You definitely won't get the feel of old Savannah here, despite the location in the Historic District: the seven-story structure, built in 1981, has marble floors, a towering atrium, and glass elevators. A $10-million renovation, completed in late 2005, upgraded much of the hotel, giving rooms a contemporary look and adding upscale marble bathrooms.Rooms have balconies overlooking either the atrium or the Savannah River. The Vu Lounge is an appealing spot to have a drink and watch the river traffic drift by. Windows Chophouse, the hotel's restaurant, serves a fine pasta and salad buffet on weekdays and specializes in steak and seafood in the evening. ⊠ *2 W. Bay St., Historic District, 31401* ☎ *912/238–1234 or 800/233–1234* 🖷 *912/944–3673* ⊕ *www.savannah.hyatt.com* ⇆ *325 rooms, 22 suites* ⚒ *Restaurant, indoor pool, health club, bar, lounge, business services, meeting rooms* ▭ *AE, D, MC, V* ⚲ *EP.*

$$$–$$$$ 🏨 **River Street Inn.** The interior of this 1817 converted warehouse is so lavish that it's hard to believe the five-story building once stood vacant in a state of disrepair. Today the 86 guest rooms are filled with antiques and reproductions from the era of King Cotton. French-style balconies overlook both River Street and Bay Street. One floor has charming souvenir and gift shops, and the elevator takes you directly down to the buzz and activity of the waterfront. ⊠ *124 E. Bay St., Historic District, 31401* ☎ *912/234–6400 or 800/253–4229* 🖷 *912/234–1478* ⊕ *www. riverstreetinn.com* ⇆ *86 rooms* ⚒ *2 restaurants, cable TV, in-room data ports, Wi-Fi, billiards, 3 bars, shops, business services, meeting rooms* ▭ *AE, D, DC, MC, V* ⚲ *EP.*

★ $$–$$$$ 🏨 **Mulberry Inn.** This Holiday Inn–managed property is ensconced in an 1860s livery stable that later became a cotton warehouse and then a Coca-Cola bottling plant. Gleaming heart-pine floors and antiques, including a handsome English grandfather clock and an exquisitely carved Victorian mantel, make it unique. The pianist hitting the keyboard of a baby grand every afternoon adds to the elegant flair. The café is a notch nicer than most other Holiday Inn restaurants. An executive wing, at the back of the hotel, is geared to business travelers. ⊠ *601 E. Bay St., Historic District, 31401* ☎ *912/238–1200 or 877/468–1200* 🖷 *912/ 236–2184* ⊕ *www.savannahhotel.com* ⇆ *145 rooms, 24 suites* ⚒ *Restaurant, café, some microwaves, some refrigerators, some in-room VCRs, some in-room data ports, Wi-Fi, pool, gym, outdoor hot tub, bar, meeting room* ▭ *AE, D, DC, MC, V* ⚲ *EP.*

$$$ 🏨 **Marshall House.** This restored hotel, with original pine floors, woodwork, and brick, caters to business travelers while providing the intimacy of a B&B. Different spaces reflect different parts of Savannah's history, from its founding to the Civil War. Artwork is mostly by local artists. Guests get free passes to a downtown health club. ⊠ *123 E. Broughton St., Historic District, 31401* ☎ *912/644–7896 or 800/589–6304* 🖷 *912/234–3334* ⊕ *www.marshallhouse.com* ⇆ *65 rooms, 3 suites* ⚒ *Restaurant, lounge, meeting room* ▭ *AE, D, MC, V* ⚲ *EP.*

★ **$$-$$$** 🖼 **Planters Inn.** Formerly the John Wesley Hotel, this inn is housed in a structure built in 1812, and though it retains the regal tone of that golden age, it still offers all the intimate comforts you would expect from an upscale inn. The inn's 60 guest rooms are all decorated in the finest fabrics and Baker furnishings (a 1920s design named for the Dutch immigrant cabinetmaker). ■ TIP→ **According to lore, a (good) ghost inhabits the hotel, floating through the hallways and straightening skewed paintings hanging in the hallway.** ⊠ *29 Abercorn St., Historic District, 31401* ☎ *912/ 232–5678* 🖶 *912/236–2184* ⊕ *www.plantersinnsavannah.com* ⇆ *60 rooms* ⌂ *Cable TV, hot tubs* ▤ *AE, D, DC, MC, V* ⦿ *EP.*

NIGHTLIFE & THE ARTS

Savannah's nightlife reflects the city's laid-back personality. Some clubs have live reggae, hard rock, and other contemporary music, but most stick to traditional blues, jazz, and piano-bar vocalists. After-dark merrymakers usually head for watering holes on Riverfront Plaza or the south side.

Bars & Nightclubs

The **Bar Bar** (⊠ 219 W. St. Julian St., Historic District ☎ 912/231–1910), a neighborhood hangout, has pool tables, games, and a varied beer selection. Once a month at **Club One Jefferson** (⊠ 1 Jefferson St., Historic District ☎ 912/232–0200), a gay bar, the Lady Chablis bumps and grinds her way down the catwalk, lip-synching disco tunes in a shimmer of sequin and satin gowns; the cover is $5. **Kevin Barry's Irish Pub** (⊠ 114 W. River St., Historic District ☎ 912/233–9626) has a friendly vibe, a full menu until 1 AM, and traditional Irish music seven days a week. It's *the* place to be on St. Patrick's Day. The rest of the year there's a mix of tourists and lo-

> **SAVANNAH SOUL**
>
> **Planters Tavern** (⊠ 23 Abercorn St., Historic District ☎ 912/232–4286), in the basement of the Olde Pink House, is one of Savannah's most romantic late-night spots for a martini serenade. Pianist, vocalist, and composer Gail Thurmond has been a fixture here since 1993 and her vast repertoire includes interpretations of favorites from Gershwin, Porter, Ellington, Mercer, Billie Holiday, Ella Fitzgerald, Lena Horne, and others. You name it, and she'll be able to play it.

8

cals of all ages. **Savannah Smiles** (⊠ 314 Williamson St., Historic District ☎ 912/527–6453) is a dueling piano saloon in which the battles heat up the humor. The place promises good fun—though perhaps not for the prudish.

Coffeehouses

Thanks to a substantial student population, the city has sprouted coffeehouses as if they were spring flowers. Tearooms also abound and seem fitting in a city with so many English influences. The **Express** (⊠ 39 Barnard St., Historic District ☎ 912/233–4683) is a warm, unassuming bakery and café that serves specialty coffees along with decadent desserts and tasty snacks. **Gallery Espresso** (✉ 234 Bull St., Historic District ☎ 912/233–5348) is a combined coffee haunt and art enclave, with gallery shows and free Internet access to customers. It stays open until 10 PM. For traditional afternoon high tea, you can't beat the lavishly outfitted **Gryphon Tea Room** (✉ 337 Bull St., Historic District ☎ 912/525–5880) with its expansive range of teas, from English breakfast to Apricot Arabesque to Black Dragon Choicest Oolong. The tearoom also serves specialty coffees alongside a full menu of scones, baklava, biscotti, and healthier salads and sandwiches.

Jazz & Blues Clubs

Bayou Café and Blues Bar (✉ 14 N. Abercorn St., at River St., Historic District ☎ 912/233–6411) has acoustic music during the week and the Bayou Blues Band on the weekend. There's also Cajun food. **Café Loco** (✉ 1 Old Hwy. 80, Tybee Island ☎ 912/786–7810), a few miles outside Savannah, looks like a shack of a place from the outside, but showcases local blues and acoustic acts that make it well worth the trip. **Jazz'd Tapas Bar** (✉ 52 Barnard St., Historic District ☎ 912/236–7777), is a chic basement venue. Gourmet grazing is the vogue and a range of local jazz artists are featured Tuesday through Saturday.

Music Festivals

For four days in October, the free **Savannah Folk Music Festival** (⊕ www.savannahfolk.org) becomes the city's main musical attraction. The **Savannah Jazz Festival** (⊕ www.savannahjazzfestival.org) is a free event held each September in Forsyth Park featuring artists from around the region. The **Savannah Music Festival** (⊕ www.savannahmusicfestival.org), held each March, offers a rich blend of world-class blues, jazz, classical, rock, and zydeco.

SHOPPING

Find your own Lowcountry treasures among a bevy of handcrafted wares—handmade quilts and baskets; wreaths made from Chinese tallow trees and Spanish moss; preserves, jams, and jellies. The favorite Savannah snack, and a popular gift item, is the benne wafer. It's about the size of a quarter and comes in different flavors. Savannah has a wide collection of colorful businesses—revitalization is no longer a goal but an accomplishment. Antiques malls and junk emporiums beckon you with their colorful storefronts and eclectic offerings, as do the many specialty shops and bookstores clustered along the moss-embossed streets.

Shopping Districts

City Market (✉ W. St. Julian St. between Ellis and Franklin Sqs., Historic District) takes its origins from a farmers' market back in 1755. Today it's a four-block emporium in the middle of a renaissance program, and an eclectic mix of artists' studios, sidewalk cafés, jazz haunts, shops, and art galleries. **Riverfront Plaza/River Street** (✉ Historic District) is nine blocks of renovated waterfront warehouses (once the city's cotton exchange) where more than 75 boutiques, galleries, restaurants, and pubs deliver everything from popcorn to pottery, and even voodoo spells! Leave your stilettos at home or you'll find the street's cobblestones hard work.

PARK & SAVE

Drivers be warned: Savannah patrollers are quick to dole out parking tickets. Tourists may purchase two-day parking passes ($8) at the Savannah Visitors Center and at some hotels and inns. Passes are valid in metered spots as well as in the city's lots and garages; they also allow parkers to exceed the time limit in time-limit zones.

Specialty Shops

Antiques

Arthur Smith Antiques (⊠ 402 Bull St., Historic District ☎ 912/236–9701) has 4 floors showcasing 18th-and 19th-century European furniture, porcelain, rugs, and paintings. Near beautiful Monterey Square, the store is both a good destination shop and worth a detour while exploring the neighborhood.

Art Galleries

Compass Prints, Inc./Ray Ellis Gallery (⊠ 205 W. Congress St., Historic District ☎ 912/234–3537) sells original artwork, prints, and books by internationally acclaimed artist Ray Ellis. **Gallery Espresso** (⊠ 6 E. Liberty St., Historic District ☎ 912/233–5348) has a new show every two weeks focusing on work by local artists. A true coffeehouse, it stays open until the wee hours. **Gallery 209** (⊠ 209 E. River St., Historic District ☎ 912/236–4583) is a co-op gallery, with paintings, watercolors, pottery, jewelry, batik, stained glass, weavings, and sculptures by local artists. **Savannah College of Art and Design (SCAD)** (⊠ 516 Abercorn St., Historic District ☎ 912/525–5200), a private art college, has restored at least 40 historic buildings in the city, including 12 galleries. Work by faculty and students is often for sale, and touring exhibitions are frequently in the on-campus galleries. Stop by Exhibit A, Pinnacle Gallery, and the West Bank Gallery, and ask about other student galleries. Garden for the Arts has an amphitheater and shows performance art.

Benne Wafers

Byrd Cookie Company & Gourmet Marketplace (⊠ 6700 Waters Ave., Highland Park ☎ 912/355–1716), founded in 1924, sells picture tins of Savannah and gourmet foodstuffs such as condiments and dressings. It's the best place to get benne wafers, "the seed of good luck" and trademark Savannah cookies, which are also sold in numerous gift shops around town.

Books

E. Shaver Booksellers (⊠ 326 Bull St., Historic District ☎ 912/234–7257) is the source for 17th- and 18th-century maps and new books on regional subjects; the shop occupies 12 rooms. **"The Book" Gift Shop** (⊠ 127 E. Gordon St., Historic District ☎ 912/233–3867) sells all things related to *Midnight in the Garden of Good and Evil,* including souvenirs and author-autographed copies. **V. & J. Duncan** (⊠ 12 E. Taylor St., Historic District ☎ 912/232–0338) specializes in antique maps, prints, and books.

8

SAVANNAH ESSENTIALS

Transportation

BY AIR

Savannah is served by AirTran Airways, Continental Express, Northwest Airlink, Delta, Independence Air, United Express, and US Airways/Express for domestic flights.

Savannah/Hilton Head International Airport is 18 mi west of downtown. Despite the name, international flights are nonexistent. The foreign trade zone, a locus for importing, constitutes the "international" aspect.
🛈 Airport Information **Savannah/Hilton Head International Airport** ✉ 400 Airways Ave., West Chatham ☎ 912/964-0514 ⊕ www.savannahairport.com.

BY BOAT & FERRY

On the Savannah River, the Port of Savannah is the busiest port from New Orleans to New York. Belles Ferry provides a regular service from the City Hall dock in the Historic District to the Westin Savannah Harbor Resort at the Convention Center, on Hutchinson Island. Ferries are part of the transit system and run daily 7 AM to 11 PM with departures every 10 to 15 minutes. The crossing takes two minutes and costs $1 round-trip (in exact change). Guests staying in the convention district ride for free.
🛈 **Belles Ferry** ✉ 900 E. Gwinnett St. ☎ 912/233-5767 ⊕ www.catchacat.org.

BY BUS

Chatham Area Transit (CAT) operates buses in Savannah and Chatham County Monday through Saturday from 6 AM to 11 PM, Sunday from 9 to 7. Some lines may stop running earlier or may not run on Sunday. The CAT Shuttle operates throughout the Historic District and is free. For other Savannah buses, the fare is $1. Savannah and Brunswick are the coastal stops for Greyhound Bus.
🛈 **Chatham Area Transit** ☎ 912/233-5767 ⊕ www.catchacat.org. **Greyhound/Trailways** ✉ 610 W. Oglethorpe Ave., Downtown ☎ 912/232-2135 or 800/231-2222 ⊕ www.greyhound.com.

BY CAR

Interstate 95 slices north–south along the eastern seaboard, intersecting 10 mi west of town with east–west Interstate 16, which dead-ends in downtown Savannah. U.S. 17, the Coastal Highway, also runs north–south through town. U.S. 80, which connects the Atlantic to the Pacific, is another east–west route through Savannah.

BY TAXI

AAA Adam Cab Co. is a reliable 24-hour taxi service. Calling ahead for reservations could yield a flat rate. Yellow Cab Company is another dependable taxi service. Standard taxi fare is $1.50 a mile. The standard flat rate between Savannah's Historic District and the airport is $25, which can rise to as much as $38 if you're staying in Savannah's South Side.
🛈 **AAA Adam Cab Incorporated** ☎ 912/927-7466. **Yellow Cab Company** ☎ 912/236-1133.

BY TRAIN

Amtrak runs its Silver Service/Palmetto route down the East Coast from New York to Miami, stopping in Georgia at Savannah. The station is about 6 mi from downtown.

🚆 Amtrak ☎ 800/872-7245 ⊕ www.amtrak.com.

Contacts & Resources

BANKS & EXCHANGE SERVICES

Bank of America and other major financial outlets have branches in Savannah; most operate normal office hours weekdays, with half days on Saturday. ATM machines are numerous.

🏦 Bank of America ⊠ 22 Bull St., Historic District ☎ 912/651-8250. **Trust Company Bank** ⊠ 702 W. Oglethorpe Ave., Historic District ☎ 912/944-1072.

EMERGENCIES

Candler Hospital and Memorial Health University Medical Center are the area hospitals with 24-hour emergency rooms.

🚑 Emergency Services **Ambulance, police** ☎ 911.

🏥 Hospitals **Candler Hospital** ⊠ 5353 Reynolds St., Kensington Park ☎ 912/692-6000. **Memorial Health University Medical Center** ⊠ 4700 Waters Ave., Fairfield ☎ 912/350-8000.

💊 24-Hour Pharmacies **CVS Pharmacy** ⊠ Medical Arts Shopping Center, 4725 Waters Ave., Fairfield ☎ 912/355-7111.

INTERNET, MAIL & SHIPPING

Savannah provides free wireless services and most hotels and inns offer complimentary access to the Internet. Consequently, although there are some cafés such as Café Espresso that provide customers with access to terminals, such establishments are getting few and far between. The Live Oak Public Library offers free Internet access on a first-come, first-served basis. The main branch is open 9 to 9 weekdays; 9 AM to 6 PM Saturday, and 2 to 6 on Sunday. Postal services in the Historic District include an outlet at Telfair Square. There's also a handy UPS Store in the heart of downtown at W. Bryan and Bull Streets.

💻 Gallery Espresso ⊠ 234 Bull St., Historic District ☎ 912/233-5348. **Live Oak Public Libary** ⊠ 2002 Bull St., Savannah ☎ 912/652-3600. **UPS Store** ⊠ 22 W. Bryan St., Savannah ☎ 912/233-7807. **U.S. Post Office** ⊠ 118 Barnard St., Savannah ☎ 912/232-2952.

MEDIA

Savannah's intriguing socioeconomic profile supports various media from student journals to upscale lifestyle publications. The *Herald* and *Savannah Morning News* are favorites and the *Savannah Magazine* is a nice glossy lifestyle piece that includes listings of various events about town. It publishes bimonthly. *Connect Savannah* is more detailed and youth-oriented, and lists all manner of arts and entertainment with snappy reviews and the lowdown on the current buzz.

📰 *Connect Savannah* ⊠ 1800 E. Victory Dr., Savannah ☎ 912/233-6128. **The *Herald*** ⊠ 1803 Barnard St., Savannah ☎ 912/232-4505. *Savannah Morning News* ⊠ 1375 Chatham Pkwy., Savannah ☎ 912/238-2040. *Savannah Magazine* ⊠ Box 1088, Savannah ☎ 912/652-0293.

TOUR OPTIONS

HISTORIC DISTRICT TOURS

Beach Institute African-American Cultural Center is the headquarters for the Negro Heritage Trail Tour. A knowledgeable guide traces the city's more than 250 years of black history. Tours, which begin at the Savannah Welcome Center, are at 10 and noon and cost $19.

Carriage Tours of Savannah takes you through the Historic District by day or by night at a 19th-century clip-clop pace, with coachmen spinning tales and telling ghost stories along the way. A romantic evening tour in a private carriage costs $85; regular tours are a more modest $20 per person.

Old Town Trolley Tours has narrated 90-minute tours traversing the Historic District. Trolleys stop at 13 designated stops every half hour daily 9 to 4:30; you can hop on and off as you please. The cost is $23.

One of the most fun ways to explore Savannah's history-laden streets is with Kinetic Tours, which offers guided tours on individual electric-propelled Segways (self-balancing, stand-up, two-wheel scooters). Tours are two hours and cost $65.

🚩 **Beach Institute African-American Cultural Center** ☎ 912/234-8000. **Savannah Area Welcome Center** ✉ 301 Martin Luther King Blvd., 31401 ☎ 912/944-0455 🖷 912/786-5895 ⊕ www.savannahvisit.com. **Carriage Tours of Savannah** ☎ 912/236-6756. **Kinetic Tours** ☎ 912/233-5707. **Old Town Trolley Tours** ☎ 912/233-0083.

SPECIAL-INTEREST TOURS

Historic Savannah Foundation, a preservation organization, leads tours of the Historic District and the Lowcountry. Preservation, *Midnight in the Garden of Good and Evil*, the Golden Isles, group, and private tours are also available. In addition, the foundation leads specialty excursions to the fishing village of Thunderbolt; the Isle of Hope, with its stately mansions lining Bluff Drive; the much-photographed Bonaventure Cemetery, on the banks of the Wilmington River; and Wormsloe Plantation Site, with its mile-long avenue of arching oaks. Fees for the specialty tours start at $75 per hour, with a two-hour minimum for a private group of up to five people.

Personalized Tours of Savannah is a small company offering upscale and intimate tours of the city, with customized themes covering movies filmed in Savannah, the city's extraordinary architecture, ghost tours, and a very good Jewish heritage tour. The owner is a longtime Savannah resident, and tours are peppered with history, anecdotes, and insider knowledge. Tours have a two-hour minimum, are highly individualized, and start at $65 per hour.

🚩 **Historic Savannah Foundation** ☎ 912/234-4088 or 800/627-5030. **Personalized Tours of Savannah** ☎ 912/234-0014 or 800/627-5030.

WALKING TOURS

Much of the downtown Historic District can easily be explored on foot. Its grid shape makes getting around a breeze, and you'll find any number of places to stop and rest.

A Ghost Talk Ghost Walk tour should send chills down your spine during an easy 1-mi jaunt through the old colonial city. Tours, lasting 1½ hours, leave from the middle of Reynolds Square, at the John Wesley Memorial. Call for dates, times, and reservations; the cost is $10.

Savannah-by-Foot's Creepy Crawl Haunted Pub Tour is a favorite. According to the true believers there are so many ghosts in Savannah they're actually divided into subcategories. On this tour, charismatic guide and storyteller Greg Proffit specializes in those ghosts that haunt taverns only, regaling you with tales from secret sub-basements discovered to house skeletal remains, possessed gum-ball machines, and animated water faucets. Tours traditionally depart from the Six Pence Pub, where a ghost named Larry likes to fling open the bathroom doors, but routes can vary, so call for departure times and locations; the cost is $15.

🏛 **A Ghost Talk Ghost Walk Tour** ✉ Reynolds Sq., Congress and Abercorn Sts., Historic District ☎ 912/233-3896. **Savannah-By-Foot's Creepy Crawl Haunted Pub Tour** ☎ 912/238-3843. **Six Pence Pub** ✉ 245 Bull St., Historic District ☎ 912/233-3151.

VISITOR INFORMATION

The Savannah Area Convention & Visitors Bureau does a grand job in providing quality information. The welcome center is easily accessed from U.S. 17 and Highway 80. It's open daily weekdays 8:30 to 5 and weekends 9 to 5. The center has a useful audiovisual overview of the city and is the starting point for a number of guided tours. For detailed information about Tybee Island, drop by the island's visitor center, just off Highway 80. It's open daily 10 to 6.

🏛 **Savannah Area Convention & Visitors Bureau** ✉ 101 E. Bay St., Historic District, 31401 ☎ 912/644-6401 or 877/728-2662 🖷 912/944-0468 ⊕ www.savannahvisit.com. **Savannah Area Welcome Center** ✉ 301 Martin Luther King Blvd., 31401 ☎ 912/944-0455 🖷 912/786-5895 ⊕ www.savannahvisit.com. **Tybee Island Visitor Information Center** ✉ Campbell Ave. and Hwy. 80, Tybee Island, 31328 ☎ 912/786-5444 or 800/868-2322 ⊕ www.tybeevisit.com.

8

The Coastal Isles & the Okefenokee

WORD OF MOUTH

"The day I spent on Cumberland Island was one of the best days I've had in my whole life! (And I'm 46.) Seeing several herds of wild horses, deer, wild turkeys, and miles of wilderness was just incredible. How about walking two miles of beach along the ocean and seeing only four other people? It was unbelievable."

—Postal

"If you are interested in nature I think you will like Jekyll. It is much less developed than St. Simons. I enjoyed Driftwood Beach for walking. From there you can get a good view of some marsh, and we saw a lot of birds there, mainly egrets."

—aloha

Updated by
Chris McBeath

GEORGIA'S COASTAL ISLES are a string of lush barrier islands meandering down the Atlantic coast from Savannah to the Florida border. Notable for their subtropical beauty and abundant wildlife, the isles also strike a unique balance between some of the wealthiest communities in the country and some of the most jealously protected preserves found anywhere. Until recently large segments of the coast were in private hands, and as a result much of the region remains as it was when the first Europeans set eyes on it 450 years ago. The marshes, wetlands, and waterways teem with birds and other wildlife, and they're ideal for exploring by kayak or canoe. Though the islands have long been a favorite getaway of the rich and famous, they no longer cater only to the well-heeled. There's mounting pressure to develop these wilderness shores and make them even more accessible.

The Golden Isles—St. Simons Island, Little St. Simons Island, Sea Island, and Jekyll Island—are the most developed of the coastal isles. Although Little St. Simons Island and Sea Island cater primarily to the wealthy looking to get away from it all, St. Simons Island and Jekyll Island are diverse havens with something for everyone from beach bums to family vacationers to the suit-and-tie crowd. Though it has only a few hundred full-time residents, Sea Island is one of the wealthiest zip codes in America. Except for Little St. Simons, the Golden Isles are connected to the mainland by bridges around Brunswick and are the only coastal isles accessible by car. Little St. Simons, a private island with accommodations for a limited number of overnight guests and day-trippers, is accessible by private launch from the northern end of St. Simons.

Sapelo Island and the Cumberland Island National Seashore can only be reached by ferry from Meridian and St. Marys, respectively. Generally unmarred by development, these remote islands with their near-pristine ecology are alluring for anyone seeking an authentic getaway. Both are excellent for camping, with sites ranging from primitive to (relatively) sophisticated. Noncamping accommodations are limited and require booking well in advance. Miles of untouched beaches, forests of gnarly live oak draped with Spanish moss, swamps and marshlands teeming with birds and wildlife combine to make these islands unique. The best way to visit them is on either public or private guided tours.

The Okefenokee National Wildlife Refuge, 60 mi inland from St. Marys near Folkston, is one of the largest wetlands in the United States. Spread over 700 square mi of southeastern Georgia and northeastern Florida, the swamp is a treasure trove of flora and fauna that naturalist William Bartram called a "terrestrial paradise" when he visited in the 1770s. From towering cypress swamps to alligator- and snake-infested waters to prairielike grasslands, the Okefenokee is a mosaic of ecosystems, much of which has never been visited by humans.

Exploring the Coastal Isles & the Okefenokee

Visiting the region is easiest by car, particularly Sapelo and the Okefenokee, because many of the outer reaches of Georgia are remote places with little in the way of transportation options. Touring by bicycle is an option for most of the region, but note that the ferries at Sapelo and Cumberland do not allow bicycles on board.

Coastal Georgia is a complex jigsaw wending its way from the ocean and tidal marshes inland along the intricate network of rivers. U.S. 17, the old coastal highway, gives you a taste of the slower, more rural South. But because of the subtropical climate, the lush forests tend to be dense along the mainland and there are few opportunities to glimpse the broad vistas of salt marsh and islands. To truly appreciate the mystique of Georgia's coastal salt marshes and islands, make the 40-minute ferry crossing from Meridian to Sapelo Island.

The Okefenokee National Wildlife Refuge is a mysterious world where, as a glance at a map will indicate, all roads suddenly disappear. This large, interior wetland is navigable only by boat, and it can be confusing and intimidating to the uninitiated. None of the individual parks within the area give a sense of the total Okefenokee experience—each has its own distinct natural features. Choose the park that best aligns with your interests and begin there.

About the Restaurants

Restaurants range from fish camps—normally rustic dockside affairs connected to marinas where the food is basic but good, plentiful, and reasonably priced—to the more upscale eateries that tend to spawn around the larger towns. A series of restaurants has sprung up in the Golden Isles and Brunswick that are defying the stereotype that equates beach vacations with fast food. And though there's still room for growth, the area now has several menus gaining not only local but nationwide attention. The rising tide of quality has begun to lift all boats.

"Family style" is a dining method you're likely to encounter in this part of the world. It's a traditional, "pass-the-peas-please" approach where diners, both from your group and sometimes others as well, sit together at large tables with courses already set out for you to serve yourself at will.

About the Hotels

Hotels range from Victorian mansions to Spanish-style bed-and-breakfasts to some of the most luxurious hotel–spa accommodations found anywhere. Outside the Golden Isles and Brunswick, some towns have only a few places to stay the night, so if you plan on visiting, book as far in advance as possible. Most hotels offer the full range of guest services but, as a matter of philosophy, many B&Bs do not provide televisions or telephones in the rooms. When that's the case, you'll find them in the common areas.

Lodging prices quoted here may be much lower during nonpeak seasons, and specials are often available during the week in high season.

	WHAT IT COSTS				
	$$$$	$$$	$$	$	¢
RESTAURANTS	over $22	$17–$22	$12–$16	$7–$11	under $7
HOTELS	over $220	$161–$220	$111–$160	$70–$110	under $70

Restaurant prices are for a main course at dinner. Hotel prices are for two people in a standard double room in high season.

TOP 5 REASONS TO GO

The Saltwater Marshes: Fringing the coastline, waist-high grasses transform both sunlight and shadow with their lyrical textures and shapes. This landscape inspired Georgia poet Sidney Lanier to describe the marshes as "a silver-wrought garment that clings to and follows the firm sweet limbs of a girl."

Sapelo Island: When land was set aside as an independent state of freed slaves, it became known as Georgia's Black Republic. Vestiges of that community remain at Sapelo, and have made it an island of contrasts—rich in history and ecowilderness, and home to Hog Hammock, a one-of-a-kind community that echoes the culture and practices of its African slave heritage.

The Horses of Cumberland: Cumberland Island is about as far removed from civilization as you can get, and seeing the majesty of these horses run wild across the shore is worth every effort of planning ahead. There are some 200 feral horses, descendants of those that were abandoned by the Spanish in the 1500s.

Jekyll Island Club: Originally the winter retreat of the exceptionally rich, this Millionaire's Village of mansion-size "cottages" is an elegant exposé of how the royalty of corporate America once played. Once an exclusive club, today you can wander around the community at your leisure.

Go for a ride: The level terrain on all the islands makes for great biking, though the most scenic is Jekyll Island. It offers 20 mi of paved bike paths that traverse salt marshes, maritime forest, and beach, as well as the island's National Historic Landmark District.

9

Timing

Early spring and late fall are ideal for visiting the coastal isles and the Okefenokee. By February, temperatures often reach into the 70s, while nights remain cool and even chilly, which keeps the bugs at bay. Because of the high demand to visit these areas before the bugs arrive and after they depart, you should book ferry reservations to Sapelo Island and Cumberland Island National Seashore months in advance in spring and fall: without a reservation, you risk having to wait days for a cancellation. If you plan to stay in the immediate vicinity of St. Marys or Meridian, the docking points for the Cumberland and Sapelo ferries, or Folkston, the gateway to the Okefenokee, it's advisable to book rooms for these areas well in advance for spring as accommodations are scarce and the demand is high. The Cumberland Island ferry accepts reservations six months in advance. If you go during the warmer months, always remember to bring water because these areas generally offer minimal services.

By May, deerflies and mosquitoes swarm the coast and islands in abundance. Don't underestimate their impact: during peak times in some areas they are so thick they sound like hail hitting your car. And though many localities spray, it's imperative to have a good repellent handy, especially

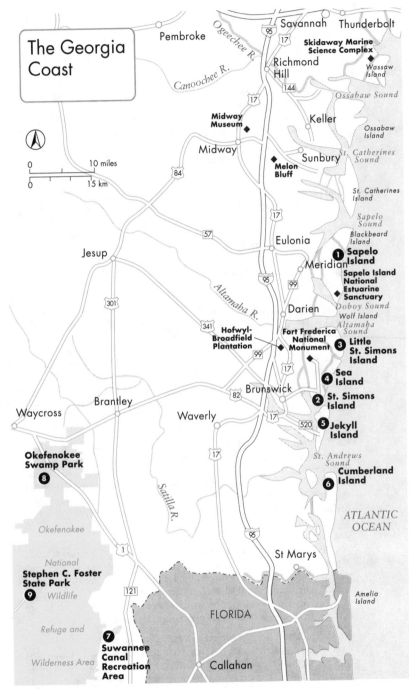

The Georgia
Coast

when traveling to outlying areas. Despite the subtropical heat and humidity, summer is busy and you can count on crowds flocking to the beaches, so you'll want to make reservations at least a couple of months in advance. The season lasts until Labor Day, but you can still count on many travelers making weekend getaways until October or late November, when the weather begins to turn cooler. Hurricane season officially runs from June through the end of November, but August and September are typically the peak months.

THE COASTAL ISLES

Each of the six coastal isles described in this chapter offers a different experience. Sapelo, Little St. Simons, and Cumberland are the least developed and most ecologically intact of all the islands. With their broad range of wildlife and pristine little-used beaches, they're perfect if you want a real getaway. Visiting these isles requires some advance planning: they're only accessible by ferry or private launch, and Cumberland and Sapelo have limited services. Brunswick and most of the Golden Isles are more complete vacation destinations, with a broad range of lodging, dining, and entertainment options. Though they're more developed and more easily accessible, they still offer the best of what Georgia's coastal isles are all about: natural beauty, beaches, and a slower pace of life.

Sapelo Island

❶ *8 mi northeast of Darien.*

The fourth largest of Georgia's coastal isles—and bigger than Bermuda—Sapelo Island is a unique community in North America. It still bears evidence of the early-Paleo-Indians who lived here some 4,500 years ago, and is home to the Geechee, direct descendants of African slaves who speak a creole of English and various African languages. This rapidly dwindling community maintains many traditional African practices, including the making of sweetgrass baskets and the use of herbal medicines made from recipes passed down for generations. It's also a nearly pristine barrier island with miles of undeveloped beaches and abundant wildlife. To take the 40-minute ferry ride from Meridian on the mainland through the expanse of salt marshes to Sapelo Island is to enter a world seemingly forgotten by time.

You can explore many historical periods and natural environments here, but facilities on the island are limited. Note that you can't simply walk up to the dock and catch the ferry—you need to have a reservation for a tour, a campsite, or one of the island's lodgings (or have prearranged plans to stay with island residents). Bring insect repellent, especially in summer, and leave your pets at home. You can rent a bicycle on the island, but you cannot bring a bicycle on the ferry.

Start your visit at the **Sapelo Island Visitor Center** in Meridian on the mainland near the Sapelo Island ferry docks. Here you'll see exhibits on the island's history, culture, and ecology, and you can purchase tickets for a round-trip ferry ride and bus tour of the island. The sights that make up the bus tour vary depending on the day of the week but always included are the marsh, the sand-dune ecosystem, and the wildlife management area. On Friday and Saturday the tour includes the 80-foot **Sapelo Lighthouse**, built in 1820, a symbol of the cotton and lumber industry once based out of Darien, a prominent shipping center of the time. To see the island's **Reynolds Mansion**, schedule your tour for Wednesday or Saturday. To get to the visitor center and Meridian Ferry Dock from downtown Darien, go north on Route 99 for 8 mi, following signs for the Sapelo Island National Estuarine Research Reserve. Turn right onto Landing Road at the Elm Grove Baptist Church in Meridian. The visitor center is about a ½ mi down the road. ✉ *Rte. 1, Box 1500, Meridian* ☎ *912/437–3224, 912/485–2300 for group tours, 912/485–2299 for camping reservations* ⊕ *www.sapelonerr.org.*

Hog Hammock Community is one the few remaining sites on the south Atlantic coast where ethnic African-American culture from the slave era has been preserved. The "Salt Water Geechee," Georgia's sea island equivalent to the Gullah, are descendants of slaves who worked the island's plantations during the 19th century. Hog Hammock's 40 residents are the last members of a disappearing culture with its own distinct language and customs. **The Spirit of Sapelo Tours** (✉ Box 7, Sapelo Island, 31327 ☎ 912/485–2170) provides private guided bus tours led by an island native who discusses island life, culture, and history. **Sapelo Culture Day** (☎ 912/485–2197 ⊕ www.sapeloislandgeorgia.org), a celebration of Geechee folklore, music, food, handcrafts, and art takes place in Hog Hammock every year on the third weekend in October. Reservations are required.

OFF THE
BEATEN
PATH
COLONIAL COAST BIRDING TRAIL – Georgia's vast network of rivers, marshes, and barrier islands provides ideal habitat for hundreds of species of birds, from nesting wood storks to red painted buntings. This "trail" is a string of 18 sites along the coast from the border of South Carolina to Florida, straddling U.S. 17 and Interstate 95. Four of the sites (Harris Neck National Wildlife Refuge, Jekyll Island, Cumberland Island, and the Okefenokee National Wildlife Refuge) have been designated Important Birding Areas (IBAs) by the Georgia Audubon Society. With more than 330 species of birds to watch for, the staffs of visitor centers along the way have maps and plenty of bird-watching suggestions for both skilled and novice birders. ☎ *478/994–1438* ⊕ *georgiawildlife.dnr.state.ga.us.*

Sports & the Outdoors

CANOEING &
KAYAKING
The Altamaha River, the largest undammed river on the East Coast, runs inland from near Darien. You can take expeditions along it with **Altamaha Coastal Adventures** (✉ 112 Witcher Rd., Carlton ☎ 912/437–6010), which rents equipment and conducts guided trips from the waterfront in Darien. With them you can explore tidal swamps, marshlands, and Queen and Sapelo islands.

Where to Stay & Eat

★ $$–$$$ ✕ **Mudcat Charlie's.** This tabby-and-wood restaurant on the Altamaha River sits right in the middle of the Two Way Fish Camp and is a favorite haunt of locals from nearby Darien. The restaurant overlooks the

The Nile of the East Coast

THE ALTAMAHA RIVER IS A NATIONAL TREASURE. Formed by the confluence of the Ocmulgee and Oconee rivers near Hazelhurst, it's the longest undammed river and the second largest watershed in the eastern United States, covering almost 15,000 square mi. After running its 137-mi course, it spills into the Altamaha Sound, between Sapelo Island and Little St. Simons, at a rate of 100,000 gallons every second, or more than 3 trillion gallons a year—a flow comparable to Egypt's Nile.

The Altamaha's greatest value lies in the 170,000 acres of river swamps that shoulder the length of its course, serving as refuge to at least 130 endangered plants and animals, including several freshwater mussels found nowhere else in the world. The swamps are also incubators for life-giving organic matter such as leaves, twigs, and other detritus. Spring floods flush this matter downstream, where it's trapped by the salt marshes that stretch between the mouth of the river and Georgia's barrier islands. This natural fertilizer feeds marsh grasses, which in turn feed fungi and phytoplankton, and so on up the food chain.

boats moored in the marina, and the seafood is local. Crab stew, fried oysters, and shrimp are the specialties, and the peach and apple pies are made in-house. It's 1 mi south of Darien on U.S. 17, just after the third bridge. Look for the Two Way Fish Camp sign. ⊠ *250 Ricefield Way* ☎ *912/261–0055* ▤ *AE, D, MC, V.*

★ **$–$$$** ✕ **Skipper's Fish Camp.** You'll find this upscale take on the fish camp theme at the foot of Skipper's dock on the Darien River, where the working shrimp boats moor. It has a beautiful courtyard pond that uses water from the river and an open-air oyster bar. Popular menu items include Georgia white shrimp, ribs, and fried flounder. There's usually a wait on the weekends, so get there early. At the southern end of Darien, turn right at Broad just before the river bridge, then take the first left down to the docks. ⊠ *85 Scriven St.* ☎ *912/437–3474* ▵ *Reservations not accepted* ▤ *AE, D, MC, V.*

¢–$$ ✕ **The Tabby Cottage.** There are lots of novelties—from sweetgrass baskets to roadkill jewelry—prominently displayed at this tabby souvenir shop in Hog Hammock, but the main attraction is the small dining area in the corner. There Nancy and Ceaser Banks work their magic with fresh local shrimp; smothered pork chops; and slow-cooked, open-pit ribs. The secrets of Sapelo cooking are on full display here, and the "killer bread pudding" is as advertised. The old Wurlitzer jukebox by the bathrooms has everything from James Brown to Marvin Gaye to Harold Melvin and the Blue Notes—and it's still just a quarter. ⊠ *400 E. Autobahn, Hog Hammock* ☎ *912/485–2199* ☉ *Closed Sun. and Mon. No dinner.*

$–$$ ☷ **The Blue Heron Inn.** Bill and Jane Chamberlain's airy, Spanish-style home sits on the edge of the marsh and is only minutes from the ferry at the Sapelo Island Visitors Center. The downstairs dining and living areas have an open, Mediterranean feel, with a large, rustic fireplace and a sweeping view of the marsh. Guest rooms are simply decorated with colorful quilts; most have four-poster beds, and all have a view of the marsh. The proprietor, an Athens native, provides drinks and hors d'oeuvres on the 3rd-floor terrace overlooking the Doboy Sound every evening, and his breakfast specialties include lime French toast and sweet Georgia shrimp omelets. ⊠ *1 Blue Heron La., Meridian 31319* 🕾🕾 *912/437–4304* ⊕ *www.blueheroninngacoast.com* ⇥ *4 rooms, 2 suites* ⚘ *Wi-Fi; no room phones, no room TVs* ▭ *MC, V* ◉ *BP.*

★ **$–$$** 🖼 **Open Gates.** Built by a timber baron in 1876, this two-story, white-frame house on Darien's Vernon Square is filled with antiques and Victorian atmosphere. Each room is beautifully decorated, and the library has an excellent collection of books of local historic interest. Innkeepers Kelly and Jeff Spratt hold master degrees in biology and arrange guided tours of the Altamaha River and surrounding area. A full Southern breakfast and evening cocktails are included in your stay. ⊠ *301 Franklin St., Box 662, Darien 31305* 🕾 *912/437–6985* 🖷 *912/882–9427* ⊕ *www.opengatesbnb.com* ⇥ *5 rooms, 4 with bath* ⚘ *Pool, library; no room TVs* ▭ *MC, V* ◉ *BP.*

¢ 🖼 **The Wallow Lodge.** Cornelia Walker Bailey's memoir of life growing up Geechee on Sapelo, *God, Dr. Buzzard, and the Bolito Man,* has made her a folk hero and focused awareness on the disappearing communities of descendants of African slaves. A stay at Bailey's Wallow Lodge offers a chance to experience the island's distinct culture. Each room is decorated in what Bailey describes as "Sapelo Period" style, with furniture and memorabilia from residents of the island. Cotton chenille, a tradition on Sapelo, and quilted spreads cover the beds. ■ TIP➔ **The lodge has a communal kitchen. Unless you make prior arrangements for meals, you must bring your own supplies from the mainland.** ⊠ *1 Main Rd., Box 34, Sapelo Island, 31327* 🕾 *912/485–2206* 🖷 *912/485–2174* ⊕ *www. gacoast.com/geecheetours* ⇥ *6 rooms, 5 with bath* ⚘ *No room phones, no room TVs* ▭ *No credit cards* ◉ *EP.*

⚠ **Comyam's Campground.** The name of Hog Hammock's only campground comes from the Geechee word meaning "come here." And the marsh-side view is just for backpackers coming for a more rustic taste of the island life. ⌂ *Box 7, Sapelo Island, Tom's Hole, 31327* ⚘ *Flush toilets, showers* ⇥ *30 sites* 🕾 *912/485–2170* 🖷 *912/485–2174* ⊕ *www.gacoast.com/ geecheetours* ⚘ *Reservations essential* ▱ *$10 per person per day, not including ferry.*

Nightlife

It seems appropriate that the only watering hole in Hog Hammock is named **The Trough** (⌂ Box 34, 1 Main Rd. 🕾 912/485–2206). It's a small, bare-bones, belly-up-to-the-bar establishment, but owner Julius Bailey serves his beer ice cold, and there's usually a good conversation going on. It's next to the Wallow Lodge (operated by Julius's wife, Cornelia), right "downtown."

| EN ROUTE | Rice, not cotton, dominated Georgia's coast in the antebellum years, and the **Hofwyl-Broadfield Plantation** is the last remaining example of a way of life that fueled an agricultural empire. The main farmhouse, in use since the 1850s when the original house burned, is now a museum with family heirlooms accrued over five generations, including extensive col- |

lections of silver and Cantonese china. A guide gives an insightful talk on rural plantation life. Though grown over, some of the original dike-works and rice fields remain, as do some of the slave quarters. A brief film at the visitor center complements exhibits on rice technology and cultivation, and links to Sierra Leone, from where many slaves were taken because of their expertise in growing rice. ⊠ *555 U.S. 17N, 4 mi south of Darien* ☎ *912/264–7333* ⊕ *www.gastateparks.org/info/hofwyl* ⊠ *$5* ☉ *Tues.–Sat. 9–5, Sun. 2–5:30.*

St. Simons Island

❷ *22 mi south of Darien; 4 mi east of Brunswick.*

St. Simons may be the Golden Isles' most developed vacation destination: here you can swim and sun, golf, hike, fish, ride horseback, tour historic sites, and feast on local seafood at more than 50 restaurants. (It's also a great place to bike and jog, particularly on the southern end, where there's an extensive network of trails.) Despite the development, the island has managed to maintain some of the slow-paced Southern atmosphere that made it such a draw in the first place. Upscale resorts and the restaurants are here for the asking, but this island the size of Manhattan has only 20,000 year-round residents, so you can still get away from it all without a struggle. Even down in the village, the center of much of St. Simons's activity along Mallory Street, there are un-paved roads and quiet back alleys of chalky white sand that seem like something out of the past.

In the village area, at the more developed south end of the island, you can find shops, several restaurants, pubs, and a popular public pier. For $20 a quaint **"trolley"** (☎ 912/638–8954) takes you on a 1½-hour guided tour of the island, leaving from near the pier at 11 AM and 1 PM in high season and at 11 AM in winter.

☺ Named after St. Simons slave Neptune Small, **Neptune Park** (⊠ 550 Beachview Dr. ☎ 912/638–0305), on the island's south end in the village, has picnic tables, a children's play park, miniature golf, and beach access. The casino swimming pool ($4 per person), is open each summer near the St. Simons Lighthouse. Bathrooms are in the library beside the visitor center.

St. Simons Lighthouse, one of only five surviving lighthouses in Georgia, has become a symbol of the island. It's been in use since 1872; a predecessor was blown up to prevent its capture by Union troops in the Civil War. The **Museum of Coastal History,** occupying two stories of the lightkeeper's cottage, has period furniture and a gallery with photo displays illustrating the significance of shipbuilding on St. Simons, the history of the lighthouse, and the life of James Gould, the first lighthouse keeper. The keeper's 2nd-floor quarters contain a parlor, kitchen, and two bedrooms furnished with period pieces, including beds with rope mattress suspension. ⊠ *101 12th St.* ☎ *912/638–4666* ⊕ *www.saintsimonslighthouse.org* ⊠ *$5* ☉ *Mon.–Sat. 10–5, Sun. 1:30–5.*

At the north end of the island is the **Fort Frederica National Monument,** the ruins of a fort built by English troops in the mid-1730s to protect the southern flank of the new Georgia colony against a Spanish invasion from Florida. At its peak in the 1740s, it was the most elaborate British fortification in North America. Around the fort are the foundations of homes and shops and the partial ruins of the tabby barracks and magazine. Start your visit at the National Park Service Visitors Center, which has a film and displays. ⊠ *Off Frederica Rd. near Christ Episcopal Church* ☎ *912/ 638–3639* ⊕ *www.nps.gov/fofr* ⊠ *$3* ⊙ *Daily 9–5.*

The white-frame, Gothic-style **Christ Episcopal Church** was built by shipwrights and consecrated in 1886 following an earlier structure's desecration by Union troops. It's surrounded by live oaks, dogwoods, and azaleas. The interior has beautiful stained-glass windows, and several of the pews were handmade by slaves. ⊠ *6329 Frederica Rd.* ☎ *912/ 638–8683* ⊠ *Donations suggested* ⊙ *Weekdays 2–5.*

> **WHERE LEGENDS LANDED**
>
> In May 1803 an "Igbo" chief and his West African tribesmen became Geechee folk legends when they "walked back to Africa," drowning en masse rather than submitting to a life of slavery. Captured in what is modern-day Nigeria, the tribesmen disembarked their slave ship at **Ebo Landing** and headed straight into Dunbar Creek, chanting a hymn. Though the site is now private property, it can be seen from the road. ⊠ *From the F. J. Torras Causeway, turn left on Sea Island Rd. After Hawkins Island Dr., look left (north) just before crossing small bridge at Dunbar Creek. The landing is at bend in creek.*

☪ **Maritime History Museum.** At the restored 1936 Historic Coast Guard Station, this new center is geared as much for kids as adults. It features the life of a "Coastie" in the early 1940s through personal accounts of the military history of St. Simons Island and has illustrative displays on the ecology of the islands of the coast of Georgia. ⊠ *East Beach Causeway* ☎ *912/638–4666* ⊠ *$6* ⊙ *Mon.–Sat. 10–5, Sun. 1:30–5.*

Sports & the Outdoors

BIKING   St. Simons has an extensive network of bicycle trails, and you can ride on the beach as well. **Ocean Motion** (⊠ 1300 Ocean Blvd. ☎ 912/638–5225 or 800/669–5215) rents bikes for the entire family, from trail bikes to beach bikes to seats for infants. At **Wheel Fun** (⊠ 532 Ocean Blvd., just off intersection with Mallory St. ☎ 912/634–0606) you can rent anything from multispeed bikes to double surreys with bimini tops that look like antique cars and carry four people.

CRABBING &   There's no simpler fun for the kids than to grab a crab basket or fishing
FISHING   pole and head to St. Simons Island Pier next to Neptune Park. **St. Simons**
☪ **Island Bait and Tackle** (⊠ 121 Mallory St. ☎ 912/634–1888) is near the foot of the pier and is open 364½ days a year. Owners Mike and Trish Wooten have everything from crabbing and fishing gear to snacks and cold drinks. They also sell one-day, weekly, and yearly licenses.

GOLF The top-flight golf facilities at the Lodge at Sea Pines are available only to members and guests, but St. Simons has two other high-quality courses open to the general public. **The Hampton Club** (⊠ 100 Tabbystone St. ☎ 912/634–0255 ⊕ www.hamptonclub.com), at the north end of St. Simons on the site of an 18th-century cotton, rice, and indigo plantation, is a *Golf Digest* "Places to Play" four-star winner. The par-72 course designed by Joe Lee is amid towering oaks, salt marshes, and lagoons. **Sea Palms Golf and Tennis Resort** (⊠ 5445 Frederica Rd. ☎ 912/638–3351 or 800/841–6268 ⊕ www.seapalms.com) on a former cotton plantation, offers 27 holes of golf and a driving range.

KAYAKING & After an instructional clinic, head off to explore the marsh creeks, SAILING coastal waters, and beaches with **Ocean Motion** (⊠ 1300 Ocean Blvd. ☎ 912/638–5225 or 800/669–5215), which has been giving kayaking tours of St. Simons for more than 20 years. If sailing is your thing, try **Barry's Beach Service** (⊠ 420 Arnold Rd. ☎ 912/638–8053 or 800/ 669–5215) for Hobie Cat rentals and lessons in front of the King and Prince Beach and Golf Resort on Arnold Road. Barry's also rents kayaks, boogie boards, and beach funcycles (low, reclining bikes), and conducts guided ecotours.

SCUBA DIVING Gray's Reef, off Sapelo island, is one of only 12 National Marine Sanctuaries, home to Loggerhead turtles, and part of the northern right whale-breeding grounds, all of which make it an attractive place for diving. **Island Dive Center** (⊠ 101 Marina Dr., in Golden Isles Marina on F. J. Torras Causeway ☎ 912/638–6590 or 800/940–3483) is the place to go for scuba and snorkeling instruction, equipment rental, and charter trips. They also have jet skis for rent. ■ TIP➜ **If underwater photography is your thing, this is the place for underwater classes.**

Where to Stay & Eat

★ $$$–$$$$ ✕ **CARGO Portside Grill.** This superb bistro beside the port in Brunswick has a menu that reads like a foodie's wish list, with succulent coastal fare from many ports. Chef and owner Alix Kenagy puts a creative spin on Southern fare and, whether it's the sesame catfish, pork tenderloin with vidalia salsa, or pasta with grilled chicken, smoked tomatoes, poblano peppers, and caramelized onions in a chipotle cream sauce, it's all good here. Save room for the Georgia peach pound cake. ⊠ *1423 Newcastle St., Brunswick 31520* ☎ *912/267–7330* ☐ *AE, MC, V* ☉ *Closed Sun. and Mon. No lunch.*

★ $$$–$$$$ ✕ **Halyards.** When you ask St. Simons restaurateurs which is their pick for the island's best, Halyards gets a nod nearly every time. This polished, elegant restaurant with a laid-back attitude makes everything but the bread and ketchup in-house. Chef–owner Dave Snyder's devotion to quality has earned a faithful following of discerning locals. Headliners are the seared, sushi-grade tuna with a plum wine reduction, the seafood paella containing everything from lobster to calamari, and the filet mignon. There's also a tasting menu with four sample dishes paired with select wines from the restaurants nearly 200 item wine list. Two servers are sommeliers, so if you don't know, just ask. ⊠ *600 Sea Island Rd., in Shops At Sea Island shopping center, intersection of Sea Is-*

land and Frederica roads ☎ *912/638–9100* ⌂ *Reservations essential* ⊟ *AE, D, MC, V* ☺ *Closed Sun. No lunch.*

$–$$$$ ✕ **Bennie's Red Barn.** The steaks are cut fresh daily and cooked over an oak fire in this barn of a restaurant that has been serving St. Simons for 50 years. Though there's room for 200 people, it feels just like family with the checkered tablecloths and the big open fireplace. There's also fresh local seafood. The pies are homemade. And there's music next door at Ziggy Mahoney's Thursday through Saturday until 2 AM. ⊠ *5514 Frederica Rd.* ☎ *912/638–2844* ⊟ *AE, D, MC, V* ☺ *No lunch.*

$–$$$ ✕ **Gnat's Landing.** There's more than a little bit of Margaritaville in this Key West–style bungalow catering to the flip-flop crowd. Seafood is their specialty with a gumbo that's outta sight. Besides being the strangest item on the menu, the fried dill pickle is also the most popular. Sandwiches and salads are also offered. And, of course, there's the "$8,000 margarita," which is about how much owner Robert Bostock spent in travel and ingredients coming up with the recipe. There's live music most Sunday nights and once a year there's "Gnatfest," a party blowout with live bands for all those pesky regulars. ⊠ *310 Redfern Village* ☎ *912/ 638–7378* ⊟ *AE, D, MC, V.*

$–$$ ✕ **The Beachcomber BBQ and Grill.** No shoes, no shirt, no problem in this small, rustic eatery where the walls are covered with reed mats and the barbecue smokes away on a cooker right beside the front door. Despite the name, it doesn't boast a beachfront location. However, it's one of the best barbecue joints on the island, offering everything from sandwiches to pulled pork, ribs, and brisket by the pound. ■ TIP→ **The freshly squeezed lemonade is to die for.** ⊠ *319 Arnold Rd.* ☎ *912/634–5699* ⊟ *AE, MC, V.*

$–$$ ✕ **Mullet Bay.** After 9 PM the older beach bar crowd has this place hopping, and at weekends the bar and wraparound porches can be standing-room only until the wee hours. By day, however, this spacious and casual restaurant is great for families, serving a good selection of burgers, pastas, and salads. The kids' menu starts at $1.95. ■ TIP→ **The platters of fried popcorn shrimp are delicious and perfect for sharing.** ⊠ *512 Ocean Blvd.* ☎ *912/634–9977* ⊟ *AE, D, MC, V.*

$ ✕ **Reynolds Street Deli and Café.** Choose from one of the 18 deli salad selections made in-house and go sit under the 125-year-old live oak out on the deck. This little red deli across the F. J. Torras Causeway in Brunswick is a laid-back, eat-in, or take-out spot with everything from a roasted barley salad to Southwest pasta with chipotle pepper to chicken piccata with grilled asparagus. ■ TIP→ **The two- and three-item samplers and nightly dinner specials are a terrific value.** ⊠ *1402 Reynolds St., Brunswick 31520* ☎ *912/261–2082* ⊟ *D, MC, V* ☺ *Closed Sun.*

★ ¢–$ ✕ **Rafters Blues Club, Restaurant and Raw Bar.** If you're looking for cheap, delicious food and a raucous good time, this is your place. Revelers sit at long picnic tables and heartily partake of the offerings from the prodigious bar and the equally generous kitchen. The restaurant serves ocean fare such as "U-Crak-'em" oysters, baked mussels, and a "sea-style" shrimp quesadilla with caramelized papaya, lime, and molasses. Rafters is open late and presents live entertainment Wednesday through Saturday. ⊠ *315½ Mallory St.* ☎ *912/634–9755* ⊟ *AE, D, MC, V* ☺ *Closed Sun.*

$$$$ ⊡ **The Lodge at Sea Island Golf Club.** Simply put, this small resort over-
FodorśChoice looking the sea is one of the top golf and spa destinations in the coun-
★ try. It has the feel of an elegant English-country manor, with exposed
ceiling beams, walls covered with tapestries, hardwood floors softened
by oriental rugs, and your own private butler, on-call 24 hours a day.
Dashingly decorated rooms and suites have water or golf-course views,
and there are four stellar restaurants. The lodge serves as the clubhouse
for the Sea Island Golf Club (though the name is misleading—all of the
facilities are on St. Simons Island). Seaside, the first of three courses here,
was inspired by St. Andrews in Scotland and has breathtaking panora-
mas of coastal Georgia. ⊠ *St. Simons Island 31522* ☎ *912/638–3611
or 866/465–3563* ⊕*www.seaisland.com* ⌦*40 rooms, 2 suites* ⚘*4 restaurants, in-room VCRs, in-room data ports, Wi-Fi, 3 18-hole golf courses,
tennis court, pool, hot tub, spa, bar, lounge, children's programs (ages
3–19), meeting room* ☰ *AE, D, DC, MC, V* ⫧*EP.*

$$–$$$$ ⊡ **King and Prince Beach and Golf Resort.** This resort is a cushy retreat
with spacious guest rooms and luxurious two- and three-bedroom vil-
las. Guests get golf privileges at the Hampton Club at the Hampton Plan-
tation on St. Simons, as well as access to many outdoor activities such
as sailing and tennis. The villas are all privately owned, so the total num-
ber available for rent varies from time to time. ■ TIP➔ **The historic main
building has been refurbished to include a Starbucks.** ⊠ *201 Arnold Rd.,
31522* ☎ *912/638–3631 or 800/342–0212* ☒ *912/634–1720* ⊕ *www.
kingandprince.com* ⌦ *145 rooms, 2 suites, 41 villas* ⚘ *2 restaurants,
Wi-Fi, golf privileges, 2 tennis courts, 5 pools (1 indoor), 3 hot tubs,
bicycles, bar, lounge* ☰ *AE, D, MC, V* ⫧*EP.*

$$–$$$ ⊡ **Sea Palms Golf and Tennis Resort.** If you're looking for an active get-
away, this contemporary complex could be the place for you—it has golf,
tennis, a fitness center loaded with state-of-the-art equipment, a beach
club, sand-pit volleyball, horseshoes, and bicycling. The guest rooms,
touted to be the largest standard rooms in the Golden Isles, have bal-
conies with views of the Marshes of Glynn and the golf course; the fur-
nishings are somewhat unimaginative. Guests have beach club privileges.
⊠ *5445 Frederica Rd., 31522* ☎ *912/638–3351 or 800/841–6268*
☒ *912/634–8029* ⊕ *www.seapalms.com* ⌦ *112 rooms, 23 suites, 11
villas* ⚘ *2 restaurants, 27-hole golf course, 3 tennis courts, 3 pools, health
club, bicycles, volleyball, bar, meeting rooms* ☰ *AE, DC, MC, V* ⫧*EP.*

$$ ⊡ **St. Simons Inn.** This Spanish-style inn sits in a prime spot by the lighthouse, only minutes by foot from the village and the beaches. Rooms
are basic but clean and comfortable. Suites have whirlpools, and apartments are fully equipped. There's a two-night minimum during high season. Discounts are available for longer stays. ⊠*609 Beachview Dr., 31522*
☎ *912/638–1101* ☒ *912/638–0943* ⊕ *www.stsimonsinn.com* ⌦ *34
rooms, 6 suites* ⚘ *Microwaves, refrigerators, Wi-Fi, pool* ☰ *AE, D, DC,
MC, V* ⫧*BP.*

$ ⊡ **Holiday Inn Express.** With brightly decorated rooms at great prices,
this no-smoking facility is an attractive option in this price category. The
King Executive rooms have sofas and desks. ⊠ *Plantation Village, 299
Main St., 31522* ☎ *912/634–2175 or 888/465–4329* ☒ *912/634–2174*

⊕ *www.HIexpress.com/stsimonsga* ➷ *60 rooms* ♻ *Cable TV, pool, bicycles, laundry service, meeting room* ☰ *AE, D, MC, V* ⭘l *BP.*

Little St. Simons Island

❸ *10–15 min by ferry from Hampton River Club Marina on St. Simons Island.*

Little St. Simons is 15 minutes by boat from St. Simons, but in character it's a world apart. The entire island is a privately owned resort; there are no telephones and no televisions, and the only habitation, a rustic former hunting lodge on the riverfront with a small guest compound, is so at home with its surroundings that deer graze there in the open. "Luxury" on Little St. Simons means having the time and space to relax and get in tune with the rhythms of nature.

The island's forests and marshes are inhabited by deer, armadillos, raccoons, gators, otters, and more than 200 species of birds. As a guest at the resort, you can take part in guided activities, including tours, horseback rides, canoe trips, and fly-fishing lessons, most for no additional charge. You're also free to walk the 7 mi of undisturbed beaches, swim in the mild surf, fish from the dock, and seine for shrimp and crab in the marshes.

From June through September, up to 10 nonguests per day may visit the island for a fee of $100, which includes the ferry to the island, a tour by truck, lunch at the lodge, and a beach walk. Contact the Lodge on Little St. Simons Island for more information.

Where to Stay

★ $$$$ ▦ **Lodge on Little St. Simons Island.** Privacy and simplicity are the star attractions at this rustic island lodge with a capacity of only 30 guests. Staying here is a package deal: you get three meals a day, use of all equipment and facilities, and drinks at the cocktail hour. The friendly, attentive staff includes three full-time naturalists who lead nature talks and tours. Meals, taken family style, feature platters heaped with fresh fish and homemade breads and pies. Transportation from St. Simons Island is also part of the package. ⬠ *Box 21078, 31522* ☎ *912/638–7472 or 888/733–5774* 🖷 *912/634–1811* ⊕ *www.littlestsimonsisland.com* ➷ *14 rooms, 1 suite* ♻ *Restaurant, pool, beach, boating, fishing, bicycles, horseback riding; no room phones, no room TVs* ☰ *AE, D, MC, V* ⭘l *FAP.*

Sea Island

❹ *5 mi northeast of St. Simons Island.*

Tiny Sea Island—with a full-time population of less than 200—is one of the nation's wealthiest communities, and over the years it's played host to presidents, kings, and counts. Most recently, it hosted the 2004 G-8 Summit. Established by Howard Coffin, the wealthy Detroit auto pioneer who also owned Sapelo Island, Sea Island has been the domain of the well-heeled since 1928. The hub of activity is the very swanky Cloister, revamped in 2006 to make it even more exclusive (and expensive: lodgings range from $725 to $5,000). Now a gated community, it's accessible only to registered guests, guests of the Sea Island Resort, and Sea Island Club members.

EN
ROUTE
Heading south toward Jekyll Island on U.S. 17, you cross over the longest spanning bridge in the state, the soaring **Sidney Lanier Bridge,** which rises 185 feet into the air. It's fittingly named for the Macon native and poet who penned "The Marshes of Glynn," a masterpiece of 19th-century American poetry. It was inspired by the breathtaking vistas of the salt marshes surrounding Brunswick, St. Simons, and Jekyll islands.

VACATION RENTALS

Do-it-yourselfers and families on a budget have many options beyond hotels and campsites. For vacation cottage rentals throughout the islands, contact **By the Sea Vacations** (☎ 912/638-6610 or 866/639-6610). In addition to real-estate sales, **Parker-Kaufman Realty** (☎ 912/638-3368 or 888/227-8573 ⊕ www.parker-kaufman.com) also manages a range of rental homes.

Jekyll Island

❺ *18 mi south of St. Simons Island; 90 mi south of Savannah.*

For 56 winters, between 1886 and 1942, America's rich and famous faithfully came south to Jekyll Island. Through the Gilded Age, World War I, the Roaring '20s, and the Great Depression, Vanderbilts and Rockefellers, Morgans and Astors, Macys, Pulitzers, and Goodyears shuttered their 5th Avenue castles and retreated to elegant "cottages" on their wild Georgia island. It's been said that when the island's distinguished winter residents were all "in," a sixth of the world's wealth was represented. Early in World War II the millionaires departed for the last time. In 1947 the state of Georgia purchased the entire island for the bargain price of $675,000.

Jekyll Island is still a 7½-mi playground, but it's no longer restricted to the rich and famous. A water park, picnic grounds, and facilities for golf, tennis, fishing, biking, and jogging are all open to the public. One side of the island is lined by nearly 10 mi of hard-packed Atlantic beaches; the other by the Intracoastal Waterway and picturesque salt marshes. Deer and wild turkeys inhabit interior forests of pine, magnolia, and moss-veiled live oaks. Egrets, pelicans, herons, and sandpipers skim the gentle surf. Jekyll's clean, mostly uncommercialized public beaches are free and open year-round. Bathhouses with restrooms, changing areas, and showers are open at regular intervals along the beach. Beachwear, suntan lotion, rafts, snacks, and drinks are available at the Jekyll Shopping Center, facing the beach at Beachview Drive. Visitors must pay a parking fee of $3 per entry at the island toll gate. The money is used to support conservation of the island's natural and cultural resources.

■ **TIP→** Watch for the Georgia Sea Turtle Center, expected to open in Spring 2007 at the converted 1903 power plant. This museum-style center will offer educational tours, and be a rehabilitation facility for the endangered loggerhead turtles, many of which lay their eggs at Jekyll Island beaches 114 nesting sites May through August.

9

The **Jekyll Island History Center** gives tram tours of the Jekyll Island National Historic Landmark District. Tours originate at the museum's visitor center on Stable Road four times a day. Tours at 11 and 2 include two millionaires' residences in the 240-acre historic district. Faith Chapel, illuminated by Tiffany stained-glass windows, is open for meditation daily 2–4. ✉ *100 Stable Rd., I–95, Exit 29* ☎ *912/635–4036* 🖷 *912/635–4004* ⊕ *www.jekyllisland.com* ✉ *$10, tours at 10 and 4, $17.50, tours at 11 and 2* ⊙ *Daily 9–5; tours daily, 10, 11, 2, and 4.*

OFF THE BEATEN PATH

DRIFTWOOD BEACH – If you've ever wondered about the effects of erosion on barrier islands, head at low tide to this oceanfront boneyard on North Beach, where live oaks and pines are being consumed by the sea at an alarming rate. The snarl of trunks and limbs and the dramatic, massive root systems of upturned trees are an eerie and intriguing tableau of nature's slow and steady power. It's been estimated that nearly 1,000 feet of Jekyll's beach have been lost since the early 1900s. ■ TIP→ Bring your camera; the photo opportunities are terrific and this is the best place to shoot St. Simons Lighthouse. ✉ *Head to far north of Jekyll on Beachview Dr. to large curve where road turns inland. When ocean is visible through forest to your right, pull over and take one of the many trails through trees to beach.*

Sports & the Outdoors

CYCLING   The best way to see Jekyll is by bicycle: a long, paved trail running right along the beach, and there's an extensive network of paths throughout the island. **Jekyll Island Mini Golf and Bike Rentals** (✉ N. Beachview Dr. at Shell Rd. ☎ 912/635–2648) has a wide selection, from the surrey pedal cars, which can hold four people, to lay-down cycles, to the more traditional bikes. **Wheel Fun** (✉ 60 S. Oceanview Dr. ☎ 912/635–9801) sits right in front of the Days Inn and is easy to get to Jekyll's southern beachfront.

FISHING   With 40 years of experience in local waters, Captain Vernon Reynolds of **Coastal Expeditions** (✉ Jekyll Harbor Marina ☎ 912/265–0392 ⊕ www.coastalcharterfishing.com) provides half-day and full-day trips in-shore and offshore for fishing, dolphin-watching, and sightseeing. Aside from his ample angling skills, Larry Crews of **Offshore Charters** (✉ Jekyll Island Marina ☎ 912/270–7474 or 912/265–7529 ⊕ www.offshore-charters.com) also offers his services as captain to tie the knot for anyone who's already landed the big one.

GOLF   The **Jekyll Island Golf Club** (✉ 322 Capt. Wylly Rd. ☎ 912/635–2368) has 63 holes, including three 18-hole, par-72 courses, and a clubhouse. Green fees are $40, good all day, and carts are $17 per person per course. The 9-hole, par-36 **Oceanside Nine** (✉ N. Beachview Dr. ☎ 912/635–2170) is where Jekyll Island millionaires used to play. Green fees are $22, and carts are $7.25 for every 9 holes.

HORSEBACK RIDING   Take a sunset ride through the Maritime forest along the North Beach with **Victoria's Carriages and Trail Rides** (✉ 100 Stable Rd., in stables at Jekyll Island History Center ☎ 912/635–9500). Morning and afternoon rides include visits to the salt marsh and Driftwood Beach, a boneyard of live oaks and pine trees being reclaimed by the sea. Rides leave from the Clam Creek picnic area across from the Jekyll Island Campground.

NATURE CENTER   The **Tidelands Nature Center**, a 4H program sponsored by the University of Georgia, has summer classes for kids and adults on everything from loggerhead sea turtles to live oaks to beach ecology. You can learn how the maritime forest evolves or get a lesson in seining and netting. There are guided nature walks, kayak tours, and canoe and paddleboat rentals. The center also has touch tanks and exhibits on coastal ecology. ⊠ *100 Riverview Dr.* ☎ *912/635–5032* ⊕ *www.tidelands4h.org* 🖼 *$1 for exhibit* ☉ *Mar.–Oct., Mon.–Sat. 9–4, Sun 10–2; Nov.–Feb., weekdays 9–4, Sat. 10–2.*

TENNIS   The **Jekyll Island Tennis Center** (⊠ 400 Capt. Wylly Rd. ☎ 912/635–3154 ⊕ www.gate.net/~jitc) has 13 clay courts, with 7 lighted for nighttime play. The facility hosts six USTA-sanctioned tournaments throughout the year and provides lessons and summer camps for juniors. Courts cost $18 per hour daily 9 AM to 10 PM. Reservations for lighted courts are required and must be made prior to 6 PM the day of play.

WATER PARK   **Summer Waves** is an 11-acre park using more than a million gallons of water in its 18,000-square-foot wave pool, water slides, children's activity pool with two slides, and circular river for tubing and rafting. Inner tubes and life vests are provided at no extra charge. ⊠ *210 S. Riverview Dr.* ☎ *912/635–2074* ⊕ *www.summerwaves.com* 🖼 *$16.95* ☉ *Late May–early Sept., Sun.–Thurs. 10–6, Sat. 10–8; hrs vary at beginning and end of season.*

Where to Stay & Eat

$$$$ ✕ **Courtyard at Crane.** When it was built in 1917, the Crane cottage—actually an elegant Italianate villa—was the most expensive winter home on Jekyll Island. Now, as part of the Jekyll Island Club Hotel, the Courtyard at Crane offers casual alfresco dining. The menu has a Mediterranean flair with plenty of salads at lunch and more substantial dishes into the evening such as marinated grilled rib eye, and a vegetable strudel. ⊠ *375 Riverview Dr., Jekyll Island Club Hotel* ☎ *912/635–2600* ▤ *AE, D, DC, MC, V* ☉ *No dinner Fri. and Sat.*

★ $$$$ ✕ **Grand Dining Room.** The colonnaded Grand Dining Room of the Jekyll Island Club maintains a tradition of fine dining first established in the 19th century. The huge fireplace, views of the pool, and sparkling silver and crystal all contribute to the sense of old-style elegance. Signature dishes are the pistachio-crusted rack of lamb, grouper flamed with hazelnut liqueur, and the filet mignon. The menu also includes local seafood and regional dishes such as Southern fried quail salad. The wine cellar has its own label cabernet, merlot, white zinfandel, and chardonnay, made by Round Hill Vineyards. ⊠ *371 Riverview Dr.* ☎ *912/ 635–2600* ⚑ *Reservations essential* 🏛 *Jacket required* ▤ *AE, D, DC, MC, V.*

$$–$$$$ ✕ **Latitude 31.** Right on the Jekyll Island Club Wharf, in the middle of the historic district, Latitude 31 wins the prize for best location. The menu has everything from Oysters Rockefeller to seafood crepes to bourbon peach- and pecan-glazed pork tenderloin. There's also a kids'

menu. ⊠ *Jekyll Island Club Wharf* ☎ *912/635–3800* ▤ *D, MC, V* ☺ *Closed Mon.*

★ **$–$$$**   ✕ **The Rah Bar.** A tiny swamp shack raw bar right on the end of the Jekyll Island Club Wharf (connected to Latitude 31), the Rah Bar is the place for a hands-on experience. It's elbow-to-elbow dining (unless you eat at the tables outside on the wharf) with "rah" oysters, "crawdaddies," and "u peel 'em" shrimp. As you eat, you look out on the shrimp boats and the beautiful salt marsh sunsets. ⊠ *Jekyll Island Club Wharf* ☎ *912/635–3800* ▤ *D, MC, V* ☺ *Closed Mon.*

$$ ✕ **SeaJay's Waterfront Café & Pub.** A casual tavern overlooking the Jekyll Harbor Marina, SeaJay's serves delicious, inexpensive seafood, including a crab chowder that locals love. This is also the home of the wildly popular Lowcountry boil buffet: an all-you-can-eat feast of local shrimp, corn on the cob, smoked sausage, and new potatoes. There's live music Thursday through Saturday night. ■ TIP→ **Bring the kids, their special menus run from $3.95.** ⊠ *1 Harbor Point Rd., Jekyll Harbor Marina, 31527* ☎ *912/635–3200* ▤ *AE, D, MC, V.*

★ **$$–$$$$**   🏨 **Beachview Club.** Grand old oak trees shade the grounds of this luxury, all-suites lodging. Rooms are either on the oceanfront or have a partial ocean view; some rooms are equipped with hot tubs and gas fireplaces. Efficiencies have either one king-size or two double beds, a desk, and a kitchenette. The interior design reflects an understated island theme, and the unique meeting room in the Bell Tower accommodates up to 35 people for business events. Higher-end suites have full kitchens. ⊠ *721 N. Beachview Dr., 31527* ☎ *912/635–2256 or 800/299–2228* 🖷 *912/635–3770* ⊕ *www.beachviewclub.com* ↪ *38 rooms, 6 suites* ♿ *Some kitchenettes, microwaves, Wi-Fi, pool, hot tub, bicycles, bar, meeting room* ▤ *AE, D, DC, MC, V* ⧆ *EP.*

★ **$$–$$$$**   🏨 **Jekyll Island Club Hotel.** This sprawling 1886 resort was once described as "the richest, the most exclusive, the most inaccessibile club in the world." Not so today. The resort's focal point is a four-story clubhouse, with its wraparound verandas and Queen Anne–style towers and turrets. Rooms, suites, apartments, and cottages are decorated with mahogany beds, armoires, and plush sofas and chairs. Two beautifully restored former "millionaires' cottages"—the Crane and the Cherokee—add 23 elegant guest rooms to this gracefully groomed compound. The B&B packages are a great deal. ⊠ *371 Riverview Dr., 31527* ☎ *912/635–2600 or 800/535–9547* 🖷 *912/635–2818* ⊕ *www.jekyllclub.com* ↪ *138 rooms, 19 suites* ♿ *3 restaurants, cable TV, in-room VCRs, in-room data ports, Wi-Fi, pool, bicycles, croquet, bar, lounge, meeting room* ▤ *AE, D, DC, MC, V* ⧆ *EP.*

$$–$$$ 🏨 **Buccaneer Beach Resort.** If you want to be far from the crowds of the historic district, try this resort where most of the 200-plus rooms and suites have private balconies overlooking the ocean on Jekyll Island's southern shore. Accommodations include one-, two- and three-bedroom suites. Golf and honeymoon packages are available. ⊠ *85 S. Beachview Dr., 31527* ☎ *912/635–2261* 🖷 *912/635–3230* ⊕ *www.buccaneerbeachresort.com* ↪ *200 rooms, 6 suites* ♿ *Restaurant, tennis court, pool, exercise equipment, hot tub, bicycles, shuffleboard, 2 bars, playground, meeting rooms* ▤ *AE, D, DC, MC, V* ⧆ *EP.*

$$–$$$ ☒ **Jekyll Oceanfront Inn.** At the largest oceanfront resort hotel on the island, the buildings, which are completing an upgrade program, are spread across 15 verdant acres. Popular with families, the inn accommodates children under 17 free when they stay with parents or grandparents. Packages include summer family-focused arrangements and romantic getaways. The restaurant offers basic, hearty fare, including an all-you-can-eat Saturday night seafood buffet. ⊠ *975 N. Beachview Dr., 31527* ☎ *912/635–2531 or 800/736–1046* 🖷 *912/635–2332* ⊕ *www.jekyllinn.com* ⊋ *262 rooms, 76 villas* ♻ *Restaurant, refrigerators, pool, spa, volleyball, 2 bars, lobby lounge, children's programs (ages 5–12), playground, laundry service, meeting room* ▭ *AE, D, DC, MC, V* ❢❂❢ *EP.*

⚠ **Jekyll Island Campground.** At the northern end of Jekyll across from the entrance to the fishing pier, this campground lies on 18 wooded acres with more than 200 sites that can accommodate everything from backpackers looking for primitive sites to RVs needing full hookups. Pets are welcome but there's a $2 fee. ♻ *Flush toilets, dump station, guest laundry, showers, electricity, public telephone* ⊠ *1197 Riverview Dr., 31527* ☎ *912/635–3021 or 866/658–3021* ⊕ *www.jekyllisland.com* ▭ *AE, MC, V* ⊠ *$30–$42.*

Cumberland Island

❻ *47 mi south of Jekyll Island; 115 mi south of Savannah to St. Marys*
Fodor'sChoice *via I–95; 45 min by ferry from St. Marys.*
★

Cumberland, the largest of Georgia's coastal isles, is a national treasure. The 18-mi spit of land off the coast of St. Marys is a nearly unspoiled sanctuary of marshes, dunes, beaches, forests, lakes, and ponds. And although it has a long history of human habitation, it remains much as nature created it: a dense, lacework canopy of live oak shades sand roads and foot trails through thick undergrowths of palmetto. Wild horses roam freely on pristine beaches. Waterways are homes for gators, sea turtles, otters, snowy egrets, great blue herons, ibises, wood storks, and more than 300 other species of birds. In the forests are armadillos, wild horses, deer, raccoons, and an assortment of reptiles.

In the 16th century, the Spanish established a mission and a garrison, San Pedro de Mocama, on the southern end of the island. But development didn't begin in earnest until the wake of the American Revolution, with timbering operations for shipbuilding, particularly construction of warships for the early U.S.–naval fleet. Cotton, rice, and indigo plantations were also established. In 1818, Revolutionary War hero Gen. "Lighthorse" Harry Lee, father of Robert E. Lee, died and was buried near the Dungeness estate of General Nathaniel Greene. Though his body was later moved to Virginia to be interred beside his son, the gravestone remains. During the 1880s the family of Thomas Carnegie (brother of industrialist Andrew) built several lavish homes here. In the 1950s the National Park Service named Cumberland Island and Cape Cod as the most significant natural areas on the Atlantic and Gulf coasts. And in 1972, in response to attempts to develop the island by Hilton Head–de-

Georgia's Black Republic

AFTER CAPTURING SAVANNAH in December 1864, General William Tecumseh Sherman read the Emancipation Proclamation at the Second African Baptist Church and issued his now famous Field Order Number No. 15, giving freed slaves 40 acres and a mule. The field order set aside a swath of land reaching 30 mi inland from Charleston to northern Florida (roughly the area east of Interstate 95), including the coastal islands, for an independent state of freed slaves.

Under the administration of General Rufus Saxton and his assistant, Tunis G. Campbell, a black New Jersey native who represented McIntosh County as a state senator, a black republic was established with St. Catherines Island as its capital. Hundreds of former slaves were relocated to St. Catherines and Sapelo islands, where they set about

cultivating the land. In 1865 Campbell established himself as virtual king, controlling a legislature, a court, and a 275-man army. Whites called Campbell "the most feared man in Georgia."

Congress repealed Sherman's directive and replaced General Saxton with General Davis Tillison, who was sympathetic to the interests of former plantation owners, and in 1867 Federal troops drove Campbell off St. Catherines and into McIntosh County, where he continued to exert his power. In 1876 he was convicted of falsely imprisoning a white citizen and sentenced, at the age of 63, to work on a chain gang. After being freed, he left Georgia for good and settled in Boston, where he died in 1891. Every year on the fourth Saturday in June, the town of Darien holds a festival in Campbell's honor.

veloper Charles Fraser, Congress passed a bill establishing the island as a national seashore. Today most of the island is part of the national-park system.

Though the **Cumberland Island National Seashore** is open to the public, the only public access to the island is via the *Cumberland Queen*, a reservations-only, 146-passenger ferry based near the National Park Service Information Center at St. Marys. Ferry bookings are heavy in summer. Cancellations and no-shows often make last-minute space available, but don't rely on it. You can make reservations up to six months in advance. ■ TIP→ Note that the ferry does not transport pets, bicycles, kayaks, or cars.

From the park-service docks at the island's south end, you can follow wooded nature trails, swim and sun on 18 mi of undeveloped beaches, go fishing and bird-watching, and view the ruins of Thomas Carnegie's great estate, **Dungeoness.** You can also join history and nature walks led by park-service rangers. Bear in mind that summers are hot and humid and that you must bring everything you need, including your own food, soft drinks, sunscreen, and insect repellent. There's no public transportation on the island. ⬦ *Cumberland Island National Seashore, Box 806, St. Marys 31558* ☎ *912/882–4335 or 888/817–3421* 🖷 *912/673–7747* ⊕ *www.nps.gov/cuis* ✉ *Round-trip ferry $15, day pass $4* ☉ *Mar.–Sept.,* *ferry departure from St. Marys daily 9 AM and 11:45 AM; from Cumberland, Sun.–Tues. 10:15 AM and 4:45 PM, Wed.–Sat. 10:15 AM, 2:45 PM, 4:45 PM. Oct. and Nov., ferry departure from St. Marys daily 9 AM and 11:45 AM; from Cumberland 10:15 AM and 4:45 PM. Dec.–Feb., Thurs.–Sun., ferry departure from St. Marys 9 AM and 11:45 AM, from Cumberland 10:15 AM and 4:45 PM.*

**OFF THE
BEATEN
PATH**

THE FIRST AFRICAN BAPTIST CHURCH – This small, one-room church on the north end of Cumberland Island is where John F. Kennedy Jr. and Carolyn Bessette were married on September 21, 1996. Constructed of whitewashed logs, it's simply adorned with a cross made of sticks tied together with string and 11 handmade pews seating 40 people. It was built in 1937 to replace a cruder 1893 structure used by former slaves from the High Point–Half Moon Bluff community. The Kennedy–Bessette wedding party stayed at the Greyfield Inn, built on the south end of the island in 1900 by the Carnegie family. ⊠ *North end of Cumberland near Half Moon Bluff.*

Sports & the Outdoors

KAYAKING Whether you're a novice or skilled paddler, **Up The Creek** (⊠ 111 Osborne St., St. Marys ☎ 912/882–0911) can guide you on kayak tours through some of Georgia and Florida's most scenic waters. Classes include navigation, tides and currents, and kayak surfing and racing. Trips include Yulee, the St. Marys River, and the Cumberland Sound. The sunset dinner paddle includes a meal at Borrell Creek Restaurant overlooking the marsh.

WATER PARK If the heat has you and the kids are itching to get wet, head to the **St. Marys Aquatic Center** (⊠ 301 Herb Bauer Dr., St. Marys ☎ 912/673–8118 ⊕ www.ci.st-marys.ga.us/aquatic.htm), a full-service water park where you can get an inner tube and relax floating down the Continuous River, hurtle down Splash Mountain, or corkscrew yourself silly sliding down the Orange Crush.

Where to Stay & Eat

ISLAND ✕⊡ **Greyfield Inn.** Once described as a "Tara by the sea," this turn-of-
★ **$$$$** the-20th-century Carnegie family home is Cumberland Island's only accommodation. Built in 1900 for Lucy Ricketson, Thomas and Lucy Carnegie's daughter, the inn is filled with period antiques, family portraits, and original furniture that evoke the rustic elegance of a bygone era. And with a 1,000-acre private compound, it offers a solitude that seems a thing of the past as well. Prices include all meals, transportation, tours led by a naturalist, and bikes. Nonguests also can dine on the menu ($$$$) that changes daily. The catch of the day might produce a homemade carrot and thyme spaetzl with baked halibut, sautéed local chanterelles, and asparagus in a pearl-onion cream sauce. Dining is family style. ⊠ *8 N. 2nd St., Box 900, Fernandina Beach, FL 32035-0900* ☎ *904/261–6408 or 866/410–8051* 🖶 *904/321–0666* ⊕ *www.greyfieldinn.com* 🛏 *16 rooms, 4 suites* & *Restaurant, bicycles, bar; no room phones, no room TVs* ▭ *D, MC, V* ⫣❍⫣ *FAP.*

⚠ **Hickory Hill, Yankee Paradise, Stafford Beach, Brickhill Bluff, and Sea Camp.** The island has five camping sites in a National Wilderness Area, all of which require reservations usually at least two months in advance. Sea Camp is the ideal spot for first-time campers. It's a half mile from the dock and has restrooms and showers nearby. None of the sites allow pets or fires, and stays are limited to seven days. The other locations are primitive sites and are a 4 to 10 mi hike. ■ TIP→ **Because ferry reservations are mandatory to camp, book the boat at the same time.** ⌂ *Cumberland Island National Seashore, Box 806, St. Marys 31558* ☎ *912/882–4335 or 877/860–6787* 🖷 *912/673–7747* ⊕ *www.nps.gov/cuis* 🖾 *Park access, $4 per person; backcountry sites, $2 per person per day; Sea Camp, $4 per person per day.*

MAINLAND
$–$$$

✕ **Lang's Marina Restaurant.** Everything's made from scratch at this popular waterside restaurant, including the desserts. And the seafood comes fresh from the owner's boats. You can order shrimp, scallops, and oysters, or opt for the Captain's Platter and get some of everything. Fish is available fried, grilled, or blackened. ⌂ *307 W. St. Marys St., near waterfront park, St. Marys* ☎ *912/882–4432* ▤ *MC, V* ⊙ *Closed Sun. and Mon. No dinner Tues. No lunch Sat.*

$–$$

✕ **The Williams' Saint Marys Seafood and Steak House.** Don't let the tabby-and-porthole decor fool you. In a region full of seafood restaurants, this one's full of locals for a reason. The food is fresh, well made, and plentiful, and the price rarely gets so right. The menu includes frogs' legs and gator tail for the more adventurous. ⌂ *1837 Osborne Rd., St. Marys* ☎ *912/882–6875* ▤ *MC, V.*

$$–$$$

▥ **Spencer House Inn.** At this pink Victorian inn, built in 1872, some rooms have expansive balconies (with obligatory rockers), which overlook the neatly tended grounds, and some have antique claw-foot bathtubs. Innkeepers Mike and Mary Neff will prepare picnic lunches if you ask. The inn is listed in the National Register of Historic Places, and is a perfect base for touring the St. Marys and Cumberland Island area. ⌂ *200 Osborne St., St. Marys 31558* ☎ *912/882–1872 or 888/840–1872* 🖷 *912/882–9427* ⊕ *www.spencerhouseinn.com* 🛏 *13 rooms, 1 suite* 🖴 *Cable TV, in-room broadband, Wi-Fi* ▤ *AE, D, MC, V* ⍾ *BP.*

¢–$$

▥ **Cumberland Island Inn and Suites.** Children under 18 stay free at this modern, moderately priced hotel on Osborne Road, 3 mi from the St. Marys waterfront. The spacious suites have complete kitchens, large refrigerators, sleeper sofas, executive work desks with ergonomic chairs, and free high-speed Internet access. Some suites feature Jacuzzis. ⌂ *2710 Osborne Rd., St. Marys 31558* ☎ *912/882–6250 or 800/768–6250* 🖷 *912/882–4471* ⊕ *www.cumberlandislandinn.com* 🛏 *79 rooms, 39 suites* 🖴 *2 restaurants, some kitchens, microwaves, refrigerators, in-room data ports, pool, bar, meeting rooms, business center, laundry facilities* ▤ *AE, D, MC, V* ⍾ *BP.*

¢

▥ **Riverview Hotel.** This circa 1916 tabby hotel has an airy, Dodge City atmosphere that's straight out of the Old West. Among the features are a double veranda, mounted deer heads on the wall, an old camera collection in a glass case, and antique, high-backed typewriters on display. The popular Seagle's Waterfront Café features seafood and steaks; try the rock shrimp. The hotel is across from the Cumberland Island Ferry office. With its reasonable rates, it's something of an econo-resort right on the St. Marys waterfront. ■ TIP→ **The hotel will provide picnic lunches for your Cumberland Island excursion.** ✉ *105 Osborne St., St. Marys 31558* ☎ *912/882–3242* ⊕ *www.riverviewhotelstmarys.com* ⇔ *18 rooms* △ *Restaurant, cable TV, bar* ☰ *AE, D, DC, MC, V* ⵔ⊙ⵔ *BP.*

Nightlife

The closer you get to borders, the more pronounced allegiances become. A case in point is **Seagle's Saloon and Patio Bar** (✉ 105 Osborne St., St. Marys ☎ 912/882–1807), a little watering hole not far from the Florida state line that's festooned with University of Georgia Bulldog memorabilia. Bawdy bartender Cindy Deen is a local legend.

EN ROUTE On your way back from Cumberland Island, stop in at the **St. Marys Submarine Museum** (✉ 102 W. St. Marys St., across from Cumberland Island Ferry office ☎ 912/882–2782 ⊕ http://stmaryssubmuseum.com). This small, fascinating museum is a natural in a town that owes much of its existence to the nearby Kings Bay Naval Base, home of the Atlantic Trident fleet. The museum has an extensive collection of photos and artifacts, including uniforms, flags, scale models, designs, sonar consoles, hatches, working steering positions, and a working periscope.

OKEFENOKEE NATIONAL WILDLIFE REFUGE

Larger than all of Georgia's barrier islands combined, the Okefenokee National Wildlife Refuge covers 730 square mi of southeastern Georgia and spills over into northeastern Florida. From the air, all roads and almost all traces of human development seem to disappear into this vast, seemingly impenetrable landscape, the largest intact freshwater wetlands in the contiguous United States. The rivers, lakes, forests, prairies, and swamps all teem with seen and unseen life: alligators, otters, bobcats, raccoons, opossums, white-tailed deer, turtles, bald eagles, red-tailed hawks, egrets, muskrats, herons, cranes, red-cockaded woodpeckers, and black bears all make their home here. The term *swamp* hardly does the Okefenokee justice. It's the largest peat-producing bog in the United States, with numerous and varied landscapes, including aquatic prairies, towering virgin cypress, sandy pine islands, and lush subtropical hammocks.

During the last Ice Age, 10,000 years ago, this area was part of the ocean flow. As the ocean receded, a dune line formed, which acted as a dam, forming today's refuge. The Seminole Indians named the area "Land of the Quivering Earth." And if you have the good fortune to walk one of the many bogs, you can find the earth does indeed quiver like Jell-O in a bowl.

There are three gateways to the refuge: an eastern entrance at the U.S. Fish and Wildlife Service headquarters in the Suwannee Canal Recreation Area, near Folkston; a northern entrance at the Okefenokee Swamp Park near Waycross; and a western entrance at Stephen C. Foster State Park, outside the town of Fargo. Visiting here can feel frustrating, because none of the parks encompass everything the refuge has to offer; you need to determine what your highest priorities are and pick your gateway on that basis. The best way to see the Okefenokee up close is to take a day trip from whichever gateway you choose. You can take an overnight canoeing-camping trip into the interior, but be aware that access is restricted by permit. Plan your visit between September and April to avoid the biting insects that emerge in May, especially in the dense interior.

Suwannee Canal Recreation Area

❼ *8 mi southwest of Folkston via Rte. 121.*

The east entrance of the Okefenokee near Folkston offers access into the core of the refuge by way of the man-made Suwannee Canal. The most extensive open areas in the park—Chesser, Grand, and Mizell Prairies—branch off the canal and contain small natural lakes and gator holes. The prairies are excellent spots for sport fishing and birding, and it's possible to take one- and two-hour guided boat tours of the area leaving from the Okefenokee Adventures concession, near the visitor center. The concession also has equipment rentals and food at the Camp Cornelia Cafe. The visitor center has a film, exhibits, and a mechanized mannequin that tells stories about life in the Okefenokee (it sounds hokey but it's surprisingly informative). A boardwalk takes you over the water to a 50-foot observation tower. Hikers, bicyclists, and private motor vehicles are welcome on the Swamp Island Drive; several interpretive walking trails may be taken along the way. Picnicking is permitted. *Refuge headquarters* ⊠ *Rte. 2, Box 3330, Folkston 31537* ☎ *912/496–7836* ⊕ *okefenokee.fws.gov* 🖃 *$7 per car* ☼ *Refuge: Mar.–Oct., daily ½ hr before sunrise–7:30 PM; Nov.–Feb., daily ½ hr before sunrise–5:30 PM.*

Sports & the Outdoors

CANOEING & CAMPING Wilderness canoeing and camping in the Okefenokee's interior are allowed by reserved permit only (for which there's a $10 fee per person per day). Permits are difficult to come by, especially in the cooler seasons. Reservations can be made only by phone. You need to call **refuge headquarters** (☎ 912/496–3331 ☼ Weekdays 7 AM–10 AM) within two months of your desired starting date to make a reservation. Guided overnight canoe trips can be arranged by **Okefenokee Adventures** (⊠ Rte. 2, Box 3325, Folkston 31537 ☎ 912/496–7156 ⊕ www.okefenokeeadventures.com). They also do 1- and 2-hour boat tours ($12.50, $20.50) and have boat and canoe rentals.

Where to Stay & Eat

¢–$ ✕**Okefenokee Restaurant.** Everything's home-cooked at this half-century-old, local institution, and from the fried shrimp to the black-eyed peas, it's all good. They open early for breakfast and have a daily lunch buffet from 11 to 2, which includes a drink, for less than $8. ⊠ *103 S. 2nd St., Folkston 31537* ☎ *912/496–3263* ▭ *D, MC, V* ☼ *Closed Sun.*

$$–$$$ ▦ **The Inn at Folkston.** Eight miles from the Suwannee Canal Recreation Area entrance to the Okefenokee, the Inn at Folkston is a minirefuge with a huge front veranda, hot tub, porch swings, and rocking chairs. This beautifully restored, craftsman-style inn is filled with antiques, and each room is uniquely decorated. The romantic Lighthouse Room has

Train-Spotting, Southern Style

THOUGH FOLKSTON IS BEST KNOWN as a gateway to the Okefenokee, it also has a growing reputation as a hot spot for train aficionados. As many as 60 trains a day pass through the "Folkston Funnel," a double track that serves as the main artery for traffic in and out of Florida; just to the north, in Waycross, is the largest rail yard in the southeast.

The Funnel—on Tower Street, just off Main—is decidedly spectator-friendly: it has a covered track-side viewing platform equipped with ceiling fans, a scanner to monitor radio traffic between trains, bathrooms, picnic tables, a grill, and lights that flood the tracks for nighttime viewing. The Folkston chamber of commerce has even put together a Web page (www. folkston.com/trains/trains.htm) for train watchers. Park yourself on the platform and you're likely to see trains carrying everything from automobiles to grain to orange juice. Several Amtrak passenger trains pass daily as well, including the Autotrain.

a king-size bed, a fireplace, and a screened-in porch; the Oriental Room has an Asian theme. And get set for a terrific breakfast; the four-cheese soufflé with artichokes and the classic eggs Benedict with hollandaise sauce are particularly good. ■ TIP→ Ask about midweek business rates for a good deal. ⊠ 509 W. Main St., Folkston 31537 ☎ 912/496–6256 or 888/509–6246 ⊕ www.innatfolkston.com ➾ 4 rooms ⚙ Wi-Fi, hot tub, library; no room TVs, no smoking ☰ AE, D, MC, V ⎱◎⎰ BP.

$–$$ ⊞ **The Folkston House.** This white, two-story B&B built in 1900 has elegantly furnished rooms with antiques and period furniture. Each evening homemade refreshments are served in the parlor and in the morning there's a full Southern breakfast in the Victorian dining room or outside on the dining porch. ⊠ 802 Kingsland Dr., Folkston 31537 ☎ 912/ 496–3455 or 877/312–6726 ⊕ www.folkstonhouse.com ➾ 7 rooms ⚙ No phones, no smoking ☰ AE, D, MC, V ⎱◎⎰ BP.

¢–$ ⊞ **Western Motel.** Though nondescript, this clean, moderately priced hotel is a good base for visiting the Okefenokee. The rooms are spacious, and there are executive suites and a Jacuzzi suite. ⊠ 1207 S. 2nd St., Folkston 31537 ☎ 912/496–4711 ⎙ 912/496–2075 ➾ 30 rooms, 3 suites ⚙ In-room data ports, pool, no-smoking rooms ☰ AE, D, DC, MC, V ⎱◎⎰ BP.

Okefenokee Swamp Park

☾ ❽ *8 mi south of Waycross via U.S. 1.*

This park serves as the northern entrance to the Okefenokee National Wildlife Refuge, offering easy access as well as exhibits and orientation programs good for the entire family. The park has a 1⅓-mi nature trail, observation areas, wilderness walkways, an outdoor museum of pioneer life, and boat tours into the swamp that reveal its unique ecology. A boardwalk and 90-foot tower are excellent places to glimpse cruising gators and birds. A 1½-mi train tour (included in the admission price) passes by a Seminole village and stops at Pioneer Island, a re-created pioneer homestead, for a 30-minute walking tour. ⊠ *5700 Okefenokee Swamp Park Rd., Waycross* ☎ *912/283–0583* 🖶 *912/283–0023* ⊕ *www. okeswamp.com* 💲 *$12, plus $4–$16 for boat tours* ⊙ *Daily 9–5:30.*

Where to Stay & Eat

$ ✕🍴 **Pond View Inn.** Though the pond is long gone, everything else is just as it should be in one of the more elegant dining options ($$–$$$$; closed Sun. and Mon., no lunch) in Waycross. This restaurant in the historic district has 18-foot ceilings, hardwood floors, and white table cloths, and the food makes some interesting variations on a Southern theme. The crab cakes are excellent. For dessert, try the bread pudding with rum butterscotch sauce. Sara and David Rollison's small B&B is just upstairs and has a similar elegance. There's a sense of refinement in these double rooms with views of the downtown historic district. Rooms feature queen beds, private baths, and Jacuzzis. ⊠ *311 Pendleton St., Waycross 31501* ☎ *912/283–9300 or 866/582–5149* ⊕ *www. pondviewinn.com* 💲 *4 rooms* ⚭ *Restaurant, Wi-Fi; no smoking* ☰ *AE, MC, V* ⦿ *BP.*

$ 🍴 **Holiday Inn Waycross.** What makes this chain hotel stand out is its bargain package deal: for $90 you get a double room and two adult admissions to the Okefenokee Swamp Park, including the boat ride, train ride, and attractions. ⊠ *1725 Memorial Dr., 31501* ☎ *912/283–4490 or 800/ 465–4329* 🖶 *912/283–4490* ⊕ *www.ichotelsgroup.com* 💲 *142 rooms, 9 suites* ⚭ *Putting green, pool, exercise equipment, bar, lounge, laundry facilities, car rental, some pets allowed (fee)* ☰ *AE, D, DC, MC, V* ⦿ *BP.*

⚠ **Laura S. Walker State Park.** One of the few state parks named for a woman, this 600-acre park honors a Waycross teacher who championed conservation. The park, 9 mi northeast of the Okefenokee Swamp Park, has campsites with electrical and water hookups. Be sure to pick up food and supplies on the way. Boating and skiing are permitted on the 120-acre lake, and there's an 18-hole golf course. Rustic cabins cost $20 per night, plus $2 parking. ⊠ *5653 Laura Walker Rd., Waycross 31503* ☎ *912/287–4900 or 800/864–7275, 912/285–6154 for golf course* ⊕ *http://gastateparks.org/info/lwalker* 💲 *44 tent, trailer, RV campsites; group campsite sleeps 142* ⚭ *Picnic area, pool, fishing, golf, playground* 💲 *$18–$22.*

Stephen C. Foster State Park

⑨ *18 mi northeast of Fargo via Rte. 177.*

Named for the songwriter who penned "Swanee River," this 80-acre island park is the southwestern entrance to the Okefenokee National Wildlife Refuge and offers trips to the headwaters of the Suwannee River, Billy's Island—site of an ancient Indian village—and a turn-of-the-20th-century town built to support logging efforts in the swamp. The park is home to hundreds of species of birds and a large cypress-and-black-gum forest, a majestic backdrop for one of the thickest growths of vegetation in the southeastern United States. Park naturalists lead boat tours and recount a wealth of Okefenokee lore while you observe alligators, birds, and native trees and plants. You may also take a self-guided excursion in a rental canoe or a motorized flat-bottom boat. Campsites and cabins are available. ⊠ *Rte. 1, Box 131, Fargo 31631* ☎ *912/637–5274* ⊕ *http://gastateparks.org/info/scfoster* ⊠ *$5 per vehicle for National Wildlife Refuge* ⊙ *Mar.–mid-Sept., daily 6:30 AM–8:30 PM; mid-Sept.–Feb., daily 7 AM–7 PM.*

OFF THE
BEATEN
PATH

SUWANNEE RIVER VISITORS CENTER – A high-definition film and exhibits on swamp, river, and timbering history are part of the fare at this visitor center in Fargo. There are also animal exhibits featuring black bears, bobcats, otters, snakes, fish, and birds. The 7,000-square-foot facility is ecofriendly, employing solar-powered fans, composting toilets that use no water, decking made from recycled plastic, insulation from recycled newspapers, and a retaining wall made from recycled dashboards and electrical cables. Guided boat tours are available, as are canoe and boat rentals. ⊠ *125 Suwannee River Dr., at U.S. 441 bridge over Suwannee River, near Fargo* ☎ *912/637–5274* ⊕ *http://gastateparks.org/info/scfoster* ⊠ *Free* ⊙ *Wed.–Sun. 9–5.*

Where to Stay

⚠ **Stephen C. Foster State Park.** The park has sites for all types of camping as well as basically equipped, two-bedroom cottages that can sleep up to eight. Be aware that the gates of the park are closed between sunset and sunrise—there's no traffic in and out for campers, so you need to stock up on supplies before the sun goes down. You can book sites and cabins up to 11 months in advance. ⬠ *Rte. 1, Box 131, Fargo 31631* ☎ *912/637–5274 or 800/864–7275* ⊕ *http://gastateparks.org/info/scfoster* ⬡ *66 tent, trailer and RV sites, pioneer camping, 9 cottages* ⊠ *$17–$90.*

THE COASTAL ISLES & THE OKEFENOKEE ESSENTIALS

9

Transportation

BY AIR

The coastal isles are served by the Brunswick Golden Isles Airport, 6 mi north of Brunswick, and the McKinnon St. Simons Airport on St. Simons Island. McKinnon accommodates light aircraft and private planes.

The Brunswick Golden Isles Airport is served by Delta affiliate Atlantic Southeast Airlines (ASA), with up to four daily flights from Atlanta. ✈ **Atlantic Southeast Airlines** ☎ 800/282–3424. **The Brunswick Golden Isles Airport** ⊠ 500 Connole St. ☎ 912/265–2070 ⊕ www.glynncountyairports.com. **McKinnon St. Simons Island Airport** ⊠ Off Demere Rd. ☎ 912/628–8617.

BY BOAT & FERRY

Cumberland Island, Sapelo Island, and Little St. Simons are accessible only by ferry or private launch. The *Cumberland Queen* serves Cumberland Island and the *Anne Marie* serves Sapelo Island. The Lodge on

Little St. Simons Island operates a private launch that is available only to overnight or day-trip guests by prior arrangement.

🇮 **Anne Marie** ⊠ Sapelo Island Visitors Center, Rte. 1, Box 1500, Darien 31305 ☎ 912/437-3224 ⊕ www.sapelonerr.org. **Cumberland Queen** ☞ Cumberland Island National Seashore ⌂ Box 806, 101 Wheeler St., St. Marys 31558 ☎ 912/882-4336 or 877/860-6787 📠 912/673-7747 ⊕ www.nps.gov/cuis. **The Lodge on Little St. Simons Island** ⌂ Box 21078, Little St. Simons Island 31522 ☎ 912/638-7472 or 888/733-5774 📠 912/634-1811 ⊕ www.littlestsimonsisland.com.

BY CAR

From Brunswick take the Jekyll Island Causeway ($3 per car) to Jekyll Island and the Torras Causeway to St. Simons and Sea Island. You can get by without a car on Jekyll Island and Sea Island, but you'll need one on St. Simons. You cannot bring a car to Cumberland Island, Little St. Simons, or Sapelo.

BY TAXI

Courtesy Cab provides taxi service from Brunswick to and from the islands for a set rate that ranges from $15 to $25 to St. Simons and from $25 to Jekyll Island with a $2 per person surcharge to a maximum of seven persons. Island Cab Service can shuttle you around St. Simons for fares that range between $7 and $15 depending on your destination.

🇮 **Courtesy Cab** ⊠ 4262B Norwich Exit, Brunswick ☎ 912/264-3760. **Island Cab Service** ⊠ 708 E. Island Square Dr., St. Simons 31522 ☎ 912/634-0113.

Contacts & Resources

BANKS & EXCHANGE SERVICES

Brunswick has several major bank branch offices. Bank of America is open weekdays 9 to 6 (the Atama Connector location also opens until 1 PM on Saturday). Sun Trust Bank is open Monday through Thursday 9 to 4, and 9 to 5 on Friday. The drive-in opens at 8 AM.

🇮 **Bank of America** ⊠ 777 Gloucester St., Brunswick 31520 ☎ 912/267-4901 ⊠ 167 Altama Connector, Brunswick 31520 ☎ 912/264-0972. **Sun Trust Bank** ⊠ 2203 Demere Rd., St. Simons 31522 ☎ 912/638-3349.

EMERGENCIES

The main emergency services are part of the S.E. Georgia Health System, at Brunswick Campus a few minutes from downtown Brunswick. There are no emergency dental clinics or 24-hour pharamacies.

🇮 **S.E. Georgia Health System, Brunswick Campus** ⊠ 2415 Parkwood Dr., Brunswick 31520 ☎ 912/466-2000.

INTERNET, MAIL & SHIPPING

Although most hotels have Internet or Wi-Fi access, if you're touring and just want to check e-mail, your best bet is the free service provided to visitors at the Visitor Welcome Centre on St. Simons. Bits, Bytes N Buns, a nifty café-cum-bakery in Brunswick, offers free Wi-Fi access with a $3 purchase and has computer stations to let you blast through a Word document or spreadsheet. It's open 6:30 AM to 6 PM, weekdays. U.S. Postal Services are also available.

🚻 **Bits, Bytes N Buns** ✉ 1178 Chapel Crossing Rd., Brunswick ☎ 912/265-2737. **Brunswick Golden Isles Visitor Center** ✉ 4 Glynn Ave., Brunswick 31520 ☎ 912/265-0620 or 800/809-1790 ⊕www.bgicvb.com. **Brunswick Golden Isles Visitor Center** ✉530 Beachview Dr., St. Simons ☎ 912/638-9014. **U.S. Postal Service** ✉ 18 S. Beachview Dr., Jekyll Island ☎ 912/635-2625 ✉ 620 Beachview Dr., St. Simons ☎ 912/635-2625 ✉ 1501 N. Way, Darien ☎ 912/437-4318.

MEDIA

The *Brunswick News* is the area's only daily community paper; it runs a "what's happening" section on Tuesday.

🗞 **The *Brunswick News*** ✉ Box 1557, Brunswick 31520 ☎ 912/265-3885 ⊕ www.thebrunswicknews.com.

TOUR OPTIONS

St. Simons Transit Company offers year-round bus, boat, and trolley tours from St. Simons Island and Jekyll Island that explore the surrounding marshes and rivers and get you up close and personal with dolphins, manatees, and other marine life. Kayaks and canoes are also a great way to explore the creeks. Tour operators include Southeast Adventure Outfitters, St. Simons Island, and Brunswick.

🚻 **St. Simons Transit Company** ✉ 105 Marina Dr., St. Simons 31522 ☎ 912/638-5678 ⊕ www.saintsimonstransit.com. **Southeast Adventure Outfitters** ✉ 313 Mallory St., St. Simons 31522 ☎ 912/638-6372 ⊕ www.southeastadventure.com.

VISITOR INFORMATION

The Brunswick and the Golden Isles Visitors Center provides helpful information on all of the Golden Isles. For camping, tour, ferry and other information and reservations contact the Georgia State Parks Department.

🚻 **Brunswick and the Golden Isles Visitors Center** ✉ 4 Glynn Ave., Brunswick 31520 ☎ 912/265-6620 ✉ 530 Beachview Dr., St. Simons 31522 ☎ 912/638-9014 ☎ 800/809-1790 ⊕ www.bgicvb.com. **Georgia State Parks** ☎ 800/864-7275 for reservations, 770/398-7275 within metro Atlanta, 404/656-3530 for general park information ⊕ www.gastateparks.org. **Jekyll Island Welcome Center** ✉ 1 Downing Musgrove Causeway, Jekyll Island ☎ 912/635-3636 ⊕ www.jekyllisland.com. **St. Simons Visitors Center** ✉ St. Simons, F.J.Torras, Causeway at U.S. 17, St. Simons Island 31522 ☎ 912/265-6620 ⊕ www.bgicvb.com.

Southwest Georgia

WORD OF MOUTH

"Just south of Atlanta—about an hour away, I think—is a little town in the mountains aptly called Pine Mountain. It is beautiful and full of charm. [Callaway Gardens Resort and Preserve] are great, and there's a butterfly house where you can see thousands of butterflies in one place. Sometimes they land on you."

—doglover888

"If you like old houses and antiques, I don't think you can do much better than Thomasville. It is in extreme southwest Georgia and, in my view, one of the most charming towns in south Georgia."

—Sunshinesue

By Jody Jenkins
Updated by
Chris McBeath

THE ROLLING AGRICULTURAL LANDSCAPES of a slower, older South, where things remain much the same as they were for generations, can be found within a couple of hours' drive of Atlanta's high-rise bustle. Here, scattered along a vast coastal plain that covers much of the southern part of the state, small towns evoke a time when the world was a simpler place where people lived close to the land and life was measured on a personal scale. In southwest Georgia, peanuts, corn, tobacco, and cotton are the lifeblood of the local economies, and you're as likely to see a tractor on a country road as a car.

People here live far from the hassles of modernity—the daily grind of traffic jams and suburban sprawl. The accents are slow and seductive. Small towns and petite country hamlets beckon with their charming town squares and elegant bed-and-breakfasts. In southwest Georgia the inclination simply to relax is contagious—it can saturate you slowly but completely, like syrup on a stack of pancakes. And the southern pride is palpable: sometimes seen in yellow ribbons scattered throughout entire communities or heard in conversation that still refer to "the War between the States" rather than the Civil War.

Despite the quiet pace of life here, this is the land of such greats as President Jimmy Carter, writers Erskine Caldwell and Carson McCullers, singers "Ma" Rainey and Otis Redding, and baseball-legend Jackie Robinson. For a time even Franklin Delano Roosevelt was drawn here; he returned again and again for the healing mineral waters of Warm Springs. Columbus was the birthplace of Coca-Cola, the first product ever to gain truly international fame. And Habitat for Humanity, an international nonprofit organization that builds low-income housing, was also born and is still based here, in Americus.

Exploring Southwest Georgia

Because of the long distances involved, the best way to see southwest Georgia is by car. Between Cordele and Archery, you can opt out of driving duties and hop a ride on the SAM Shortline—a great way to see the countryside.

10

About the Hotels & Restaurants

Columbus has gained renown as the pit-barbecue capital of the world, and indeed this region of Georgia does lovely things by slow-cooking pork over green oak. Barbecue joints in the area, such as Columbus's own Country's On Broad, are homey, hands-on affairs that specialize in lots of high-quality country-style cooking at relatively low prices.

Lodging in the area runs the gamut from elegant, luxurious properties to low-profile but unique B&Bs to reliable and inexpensive chain hotels. RV parks and campgrounds are also available.

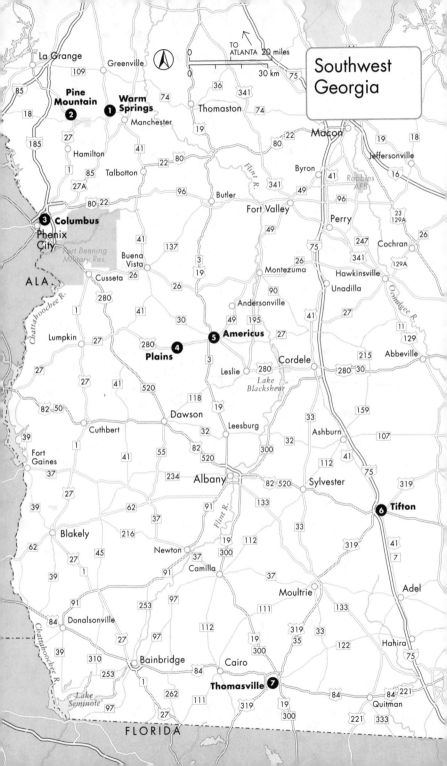

TOP 5 REASONS TO GO

Columbus River Walk: At the heart of the city's renaissance, this 12-mi promenade with its red brick and ironwork follows the banks of the Chattahoochee river before heading inland to the National Infantry Museum. Walking is great as there's an opportunity to take detours to see the Coca-Cola Space Science Center and the Civil War Navy Yard.

Callaway Gardens Resort and Preserve: 14,000 acres of gardens and parkland make this the raison d'être for visiting Pine Mountain. In spring, the rhododendrons and wild azaleas take your breath away. If flowers really aren't your thing, then there's golf, fishing, tennis, a spa, and arts and crafts programs.

Thomasville Plantations: Nowhere is the lore of the deep South better understood than in and around the plantations of Thomasville. Because many have been restored as country inns, or are open to the public, they are almost like living museums. The entire region could be renamed "Tarasville."

Agrirama: If you want to understand the rhythm and heart of the agricultural South, this historical showcase is a sensory experience. You can interact with the region's pioneer settlers as you watch them plough fields by mule or as the local doctor dispenses home-spun remedies.

Yoder's Deitsch Haus: Here's one of the few places to experience an unexpected slice of Mennonite culture through hearty, no-nonsense cooking, crafts, and hospitality. Food is filling—plates full of shredded beef and gravy, shoofly pie, and racks of baked goods—and there are handmade crafts such as quality quilts and baskets.

WHAT IT COSTS					
	$$$$	**$$$**	**$$**	**$**	**¢**
RESTAURANTS	over $22	$17–$22	$12–$16	$7–$11	under $7
HOTELS	over $220	$161–$220	$111–$160	$70–$110	under $70

Restaurant prices are for a main course at dinner. Hotel prices are for two people in a standard double room in high season.

Timing

Because many of the towns in the region are off the beaten path, crowds are rarely a problem, though spring (which comes early) and fall (which comes late) are the most popular seasons. If you're not fond of the heat, March to May and September to December are the best times to visit. During this time, book well in advance for the more popular hotels and B&Bs in Pine Mountain, Warm Springs, and Thomasville.

WESTERN FOOTHILLS & FARMLAND

You won't be able to visit this slice of Georgia without feeling the influence of two generations of American presidents, Franklin Roosevelt and

Jimmy Carter. About a hundred miles south of Atlanta, near the Alabama border, Pine Mountain and Warm Springs are the rural retreats they have always been since FDR used to visit, and have retained much of their ambience from yesteryear. The Little White House is among its historical highlights. Americus and Plains (Jimmy Carter country) are two more towns seemingly cut from the pages of the past; not far from Americus is Andersonville, a poignant site of the Civil War's most notorious prison. In the center of the region is Columbus, Georgia's second-largest city and home to America's largest military complex, Fort Benning.

Warm Springs

❶ *97 mi southwest of Atlanta via I–85 and U.S. 27.*

Renowned for centuries for the supposed healing properties of its thermal waters, Warm Springs is where the Creek Indians brought their wounded warriors when all other treatments had failed. In the early 1920s news spread that a young Columbus native and polio victim, Louis Joseph, had made a dramatic recovery after extensive therapy in the springs. Word reached Franklin Delano Roosevelt (1882–1945), who had contracted polio, and a 20-year relationship began between him and this remote mountain village, where he built a cottage for his visits that came to be known as the Little White House. Roosevelt's experiences here led to the effort to eradicate polio around the world through the founding of the March of Dimes, and his encounters with his poor rural neighbors fueled ideas for his Depression-era New Deal recovery programs. After Roosevelt's death, the town fell on hard times, but an influx of crafts and antiques shops in the 1980s has revitalized Warm Springs.

Fodor'sChoice
★

The **Little White House Historic Site/FDR Memorial Museum,** at the south end of town, contains the modest three-bedroom cottage in which Roosevelt stayed during his visits here. The cottage, built in 1932, remains much as it did the day he died here (while having his portrait painted) and includes the wheelchair Roosevelt designed from a kitchen chair. The unfinished portrait is on display along with the 48-star American flag that flew over the grounds when Roosevelt died. The FDR Memorial Museum includes an interesting short film narrated by Walter Cronkite, exhibits detailing Roosevelt's life and New Deal programs, and some of Roosevelt's personal effects, such as his 1938 Ford, complete with the full hand controls he designed. ■ TIP→ **Admission here allows you to also visit the nearby pools where Roosevelt took his therapy.** ⊠ *401 Little White House Rd.* ☎ *706/655–5870* ⊕ *www.fdrlittlewhitehouse.org* ➿ *$7* ☉ *Daily 9–4:45.*

Where to Stay

$–$$ 🏠 **Grand Wisteria Plantation.** Built circa 1832, this elegant neoclassical plantation home 9 mi north of Warm Springs is listed on the National Register of Historic Places. You're free to wander the 13-acre grounds, on which deer, rabbits, and turkeys roam. You'll also come across structures such as the old smoke house, the original cook house, and spring room. Mahogany period pieces, Victorian settees, sleigh beds, and clawfoot tubs fill the rooms. Candlelight dinners and bistro baskets are available by request, and there are weekend packages and seasonal specials. ✉ *15380 Roosevelt Hwy., Alt. 27, Box 397, Greenville 30222* ☎ *706/672–0072* ⊕ *www.grandwisteria.com* ➩ *5 rooms* ⌂ *Some in-room DVDs, hot tubs, library; no TV in some rooms, no kids under 16* ▭ *DC, MC, V* ⦿ *BP.*

¢–$$ 🏨 **Hotel Warm Springs Bed & Breakfast Inn.** Right in downtown Warm Springs, this old hotel has plenty of character and is a great bargain. The guest rooms have oak furniture and 12-foot ceilings with crown molding. Prices are even cheaper if you opt not to have breakfast, though this means you'll miss out on the "Southern breakfast feast," complete with cheese grits. ■ **TIP→ Whether you stay or not, the Tuscawilla Soda Fountain off the lobby is a treat to visit—it was the town's original drug store and soda fountain, often frequented by FDR himself.** ✉ *47 Broad St., 31830* ☎ *706/ 655–2114 or 800/366–7616* ⊕ *www.hotelwarmspringsbb.org* ➩ *11 rooms, 2 suites* ⌂ *Cable TV* ▭ *AE, D, MC, V* ⦿ *BP.*

Pine Mountain

❷ *14 mi west of Warm Springs via Rte. 18 and Rte. 194.*

Pine Mountain Ridge is the last foothill of the Appalachian chain, and the town of Pine Mountain rests at the same elevation as Atlanta, making it generally cooler than the surrounding communities. The flora and fauna here reflect the town's Appalachian connections. Most visitors are lured by the surrounding area's large-scale attractions—such as Callaway Gardens Resort and Preserve—and are then pleasantly surprised that the small-town berg has a folksy, inviting downtown square. Antiques figure prominently in the area economy and shops abound in the town center.

🔾 Just south of the village lies the area's main draw: **Callaway Gardens Resort and Preserve,** a 14,000-acre, nonprofit, family-style golf and tennis resort with a combination of elaborate, cultivated gardens and natural woodlands. This botanical wonderland was developed in the 1930s by textile magnate Cason J. Callaway and his wife Virginia, who were determined to breathe new life into the area's dormant cotton fields. With more than 1,000 varieties, the **Day Butterfly Center** is one of the largest free-flight conservatories in North America. **Mountain Creek Lake** is well stocked with largemouth bass and bream. **Ida Cason Callaway Memorial Chapel**—a favorite wedding venue—is a lovely stone chapel nestled in the woods alongside a lake and babbling stream. ✉ *U.S. 27* ☎ *706/225–5292 or 800/225–5292* ⊕ *www.callawaygardens.com* ▭ *$14; free to overnight guests* ⊙ *Daily 9–5.*

🔾 At the **Wild Animal Safari,** a few miles northwest of town, you can either drive yourself or ride a bus through a 500-acre animal preserve. You may not believe you're still in Georgia: camels, llamas, antelopes, and hundreds of other exotic animals traipse around freely, often coming close to vehicles. An added plus is the **Old McDonald's Farm,** a petting zoo with jovial monkeys and writhing-reptile pits. ■ **TIP→ The park sells special food for you to offer the animals, and some will scamper over your car to get it. Leave your hot newly painted vehicle at home.** ✉ *1300 Oak Grove Rd.*

10

☎ 706/663–8744 or 800/367–2751 ⊕ www.animalsafari.com ✉ $16
☉ Mar. and Apr., daily 10–6:30; May–Labor Day, daily 10–7:30; Labor
Day–Feb., daily 10–5:30; call to confirm hrs and tour-bus schedule.

Sports & the Outdoors

CANOEING &
KAYAKING
About 45 minutes from Pine Mountain between Thomaston and Columbus is the **Flint River Outdoor Center** (⊠ 4429 Woodland Rd., Rte. 36 at Flint River, Thomaston ☎ 706/647–2633), with 5 mi of river courses where you can test your skills in everything from a float tube to kayaks running Class II rapids. The more daring can try Yellow Jacket Shoals, the Flint's only Class III/IV run—rumored to have destroyed more canoes than any other rapids in the Southeast.

HORSEBACK
RIDING
The mountain terrain makes the Pine Mountain area an interesting place for horseback riding. **Roosevelt Stables** (⊠ 1063 Group Camp Rd. ☎ 706/628–7463 or 877/696–4613), in Franklin D. Roosevelt State Park, has 28 mi of trails and

> ### STRETCH YOUR LEGS
>
> **Pine Mountain Trail** is a favorite of the nearly 40 mi of trails in Franklin D. Roosevelt State Park that are designated only for hikers. Although each part of the trail is interesting in its own right, Dowdell's Knob Loop, near the center, makes a great day hike at 4.7 mi. The 6.5 mi Wolfden Loop is another beautiful part of the trail, traveling past beaver dams, over Hogback Mountain, and along the Mountain Creek Nature Trail, which features all manner of plant life. Trail maps are available at the State Park office and at Callaway Gardens Country Store.

offers everything from one-hour rides to overnight trips complete with cowboy breakfasts.

Where to Stay & Eat

$$–$$$$ ✕ **Carriage & Horses.** International cuisine is served in this Victorian house just north of town and overlooking the horse pastures of Grey Eagle Farm. The eclectic menu includes escargot, alligator with mushroom and lemon sauce, grilled trout (a house specialty), and filet mignon served with garlic mashed potatoes. The restaurant's over-size windows and patio make it a local favorite for sunset dining, and often, local artists play assorted easy-listening '40s and '50s music. ⊠ 607 Butts Mill Rd. ☎ 706/663–4777 ⌂ Reservations essential ⊟ AE, D, MC, V ☉ Closed Mon.

$–$$$ ▦ **Chipley Murrah House B&B.** One mile from the Callaway Gardens entrance and near downtown Pine Mountain, this lavish inn occupies a high-style Queen Anne Victorian dating to 1895. A favorite perch in this period-decorated house is the wraparound porch, decked out with rockers, swings, and wicker chairs. Hardwood floors, 12-foot ceilings, and decorative molding are among the beautifully preserved original details. In addition to the guest rooms there are three cottages, one with two bedrooms and two with three bedrooms. ■ TIP→ **Cottage rentals are a great bet for families.** ⊠ 207 W. Harris St., Box 1154, 31822-1154 ☎ 706/663–9801 or 888/782–0797 ⊕ www.chipleymurrah.com ➥ 4 rooms, 3 cottages ⊟ AE, MC, V ☉ Closed Jan. ⼝⼁ BP.

★ $$ ⊞ **Callaway Gardens Resort and Preserve.** Stay at this sprawling resort, and your room key gains you access to its famous gardens from dawn until dusk. Accommodations range from fairly basic motel-style guest rooms to fully furnished one to four bedroom cottages and villas, all of them with lovely panoramic vistas and verdant garden settings. At this writing, a new spa and spa lodge was scheduled to open in early 2007. A 10-mi paved bike trail meanders through the property. There's great fishing in 13 stocked ponds, and the golf courses are famously impressive. Various meal and recreation packages are available. ⊠ *U.S. 27, 31822* ☎ *706/663–2281 or 800/225–5292* 📠 *706/663–5090* ⊕ *www.callawaygardens.com* ⌨ *323 rooms, 20 suites, 155 cottages, 57 villas* ⌂ *4 restaurants, 2 cafés, kitchenettes, cable TV, 2 18-hole golf courses, miniature golf, 10 tennis courts, lake, health club, spa, beach, water-skiing, fishing, bicycles, Ping-Pong, racquetball, volleyball, 2 bars, lounge, shops* ▤ *AE, D, MC, V* ⊚ *EP.*

$ ⊞ **Days Inn.** There are no surprises at this old standby, but it's clean and close to downtown Pine Mountain and area attractions. Check the Web site for significantly cheaper specials. ⊠ *368 S. Main Ave., Box 1570, 31822* ☎ *706/663–2121 or 800/325–2525* 📠 *706/663–2169* ⊕ *www.daysinn.com* ⌨ *40 rooms* ⌂ *Microwaves, refrigerators, cable TV, Wi-Fi, pool, some pets allowed (fee)* ▤ *AE, D, MC, V* ⊚ *BP.*

CAMPING   ⚠ **Pine Mountain Campground.** This large, well-kept campground just
¢–$ north of town has everything from tent sites to full RV hookups to cabins. "Megasites" are paved sites with patios, grills, and fences for privacy. You can swim in the pool and play miniature golf, volleyball, and horseshoes. Pets on a leash are welcome. ⊠ *8804 Hamilton Rd., U.S. 27, 31822-4711* ☎ *706/663–4329* ⊕ *www.camppinemountain.com* ⌨ *50 full hookups, 98 partial hookups, 2 cabins* ⌂ *Grill, flush toilets, full hookups, partial hookups (water and electric), dump station, drinking water, guest laundry, showers, public telephone, general store, play area, swimming (pool)* ⌸ *Full hookups $25, partial hookups $23, tent sites $20, cabins $85* ▤ *MC, V.*

EN
ROUTE   **LaGrange,** which lies 70 mi southwest of Atlanta via Interstate 85 and 27 mi northwest of Pine Mountain, makes for a pleasant diversion. A major cotton-growing region before the Civil War, the town's relative isolation from the battlefronts made it an ideal location for hospitals and convalescent centers. This was also home to the "Nancy Harts," the only all-female militia unit to serve in the war. Today the inviting town center is set around lovely LaFayette Square. Named for the Marquis de Lafayette, a major-general under General George Washington in the Revolutionary War, here's where to find the small but impressive **Chattahoochee Valley Art Museum** (⊠ 112 LaFayette Pkwy., 1 block off Sq. ☎706/882–3267) and its exhibits by regional contemporary artists. A little farther afield is **Bellevue** (⊠ 204 Ben Hill St. ☎ 706/884–1832), a stately, colonnaded 1850s house, listed on the National Register of Historic Places, and considered one of the finest examples of Greek-revival architecture in Georgia.

10

Columbus

❸ *35 mi south of Pine Mountain via U.S. 27.*

Today one of Georgia's largest cities, Columbus literally rose from the ashes of the Civil War to become a major industrial force in the state. Chartered in 1827 along the falls of the Chattahoochee River as a "trading town," Columbus harnessed the energy of the river to power looms and spinning machines for the growing textile industry being fed by surrounding cotton fields. Because of its location at the head of the Chattahoochee, the town quickly became a prominent inland shipping port, and by the start of the Civil War, it was the largest manufacturing center south of Richmond. The town was second only to Richmond in supplying uniforms, weapons, and other goods to the Confederate army, making Columbus a prime target for Union troops. But because of its distance from the battle lines, it wasn't until April 16, 1865—a week after the war had ended at Appomattox—that the 13,000 cavalrymen known as "Wilson's Raiders" attacked Columbus and nearby West Point and burned all the war industries to the ground. The textile mills soon recovered, however, and grew to a prominence that dwarfed their prewar significance. Textiles still play a major role in the Columbus economy.

Today, Columbus is perhaps best known as the home of Fort Benning, the largest infantry-training center in the world; it's also the site of Columbus College's Schwob School of Music, one of the finest music schools in the South. A project to rejuvenate the downtown area has included the renovation of old manufacturing and ironworks buildings and the creation of the 12-mi **Riverwalk** to highlight the city's river origins; this linear park along the Chattahoochee is ideal for jogging, strolling, biking, and rollerblading.

Heritage Corner consists of several historic buildings that you can visit via a guided walking tour given by the Historic Columbus Foundation, headquartered in an 1870 building. Among these buildings is the 1840 four-room **Pemberton House,** home to Columbus native John Pemberton (1831–88), the pharmacist who created Coca-Cola. Other structures here include the one-room early-19th-century **log cabin** that is said to be the oldest extant structure in Muscogee County, the 1828 Federal-style **Walker-Peters-Langdon House,** and the 1840s **Woodruff Farm House.** ⊠ *708 Broadway* ☎ *706/323–7979 or 706/322–3181* 🎫 *Tours $5 per person, 2-person minimum* ☉ *Tours daily at 2.*

The child of minstrel-show performers, blues singer Gertrude Pridgett (1886–1939), more famously known as "Ma" Rainey, the "mother of the blues," toured in tent shows, levee camps, and cabarets throughout the South and Midwest. She recorded more than 100 songs and entertained with the greats, including Louis Armstrong, Bessie Smith, and Tommy Dorsey. She's buried in **Porterdale Cemetery,** an extension of an old slave cemetery, on 10th Avenue. The **Ma Rainey house** (⊠ 805 5th Ave. ⊕ www.gawomen.org/honorees/raineyg.htm), listed on the National Register of Historic Places, can be viewed from the exterior only. The house is listed with other black-heritage sites on a self-guided driving tour brochure available at the **Convention and Visitors Bureau** (✉ 900 Front Ave. ☎ 800/999–1613 for brochure).

🖔 Military buffs and anybody else with an interest in the nation's Civil War past should make it a point to visit the **Port Columbus National Civil War Naval Museum,** which has been lauded for its interactive approach and high-tech exhibits. This is one of the nation's most innovative Civil War museums, heavily focused on the Confederate navy and its influence on the U.S. navy's subsequent development. You can walk the decks of partially reconstructed Civil War ships, and get a glimpse of what combat was like in a full-scale replica of the CSS *Albermarle,* an ironclad combat simulator. ✉ 1002 Victory Dr. ☎ 706/327–9798 ⊕ www. portcolumbus.org ☞ $4.50 ☉ Daily 9–5.

🖔 Columbus State University's **Coca-Cola Space Science Center,** part of the Riverwalk, houses a multimedia planetarium with different hourly shows, an observatory, a replica of an Apollo space capsule, a space shuttle, and other space-related exhibits, including cool flight simulators. ✉ 701 Front Ave. ☎ 706/649–1470 ⊕ www.ccssc.org ☞ $6, includes 1 planetarium show, additional shows $3 ☉ Tues.–Thurs. 10–4, Fri. 10–8, Sat. 10:30–8.

★ One of the city's most notable attractions, the **Columbus Museum** is the state's largest art and history museum and one of the largest in the Southeast. Collections focus heavily on American art ranging from colonial portraiture to the Ashcan School to provocative contemporary works. Other exhibits concentrate on science and the history of the Chattahoochee Valley. ✉ 1251 Wynnton Rd. ☎ 706/748–2562 ⊕ www. columbusmuseum.com ☞ Free ☉ Tues., Wed., Fri., and Sat. 10–5, Thurs. 10–9, Sun. 1–5.

The **Carson McCullers House Museum** was the childhood home of novelist and short-story-writer Carson McCullers (1917–67), who lived here from 1925 to 1944. Among her best-known works are *The Heart Is a Lonely Hunter* and *Reflections in a Golden Eye.* The house is now the site of Columbus State University's Carson McCullers Center for Writers and Musicians, and tours are available by appointment. ✉ 1519 Stark Ave. ☎ 706/327–1911 ⊕ www.mccullerscenter.org ☞ Free ☉ Tours by appointment.

10

OFF THE BEATEN PATH

NATIONAL INFANTRY MUSEUM – It requires some effort to get here, but if you're a military buff it's worth the trouble. Exhibits in this four-story museum include weaponry, uniforms, and equipment of all kinds, and they examine the history of the U.S. infantry. Among the items displayed are Civil War–era dominoes, a gas mask for a horse, a prisoner-of-war uniform, and a Springfield rifle from World War I. Also here are a 100-seat theater, a gallery of military art, and a gift shop. ■ TIP➔ **Expansion plans are underway to open an IMAX theater in late 2007.** To get to the museum take Interstate 185 south to the Victory Drive exit. ✉ Bldg. 396, Baltzell Ave., 6 mi south of Columbus, Fort Benning ☎ 706/545–6762 ⊕ www.benning.army.mil/museum ☞ Free ☉ Weekdays 10–4:30, weekends 12:30–4:30.

Where to Stay & Eat

$–$$ ✕ **Buckhead Grille.** This upscale American grill is touted as one of the best-value restaurants in Georgia. Beef plays a prominent role on the menu, with Kansas City sirloin and Caribbean rib eye as headliners; Monday is steak night. Seafood is also done well here, in such entrées as grilled salmon marinated in a mouthwatering, house-made teriyaki sauce. The wine list is said to be the most extensive in Columbus. You can dine inside or on the patio. ⊠ *5010 Armour Rd.* ☎ *706/571–9995* ▱ *AE, D, DC, MC, V* ☾ *No lunch.*

★ **¢–$$** ✕ **Country's On Broad.** In a land where barbecue reigns supreme, Country's does it not only with taste but with a certain style as well. You can eat inside the restaurant, a converted bus terminal decorated with '50s flair, or sit at a table in the 1946 bus-turned-diner. The barbecue, cooked over hickory and oak, includes not only pork, but also chicken, beef, turkey, ribs, and brisket; buttermilk fried chicken is also on the menu. Besides the two sides and bread, the plates come with a selection of four sauces of varying heats. There are also options for kids and a semi-low-calorie menu. There's also a Country's Barbecue on 12th Avenue, and a couple of other branches around town. ⊠ *1329 Broadway* ☎ *706/596–8910* ⊠ *2016 12th Ave.* ☎ *706/327–7702* ▱ *MC, V.*

¢ ✕ **Fountain City Coffee.** This bustling little coffee shop in the heart of downtown has everything for the coffee hound, including a low-carb latte. Signature drinks include a "mint mocha," and a "chocolate raspberry cloud." Blended frozen espresso drinks and smoothies are also served here. Breakfast *panini* (grilled sandwiches) are served in the morning, and the lunch menu includes soups, salads, sandwiches, tapas, and other snacks. The pastries are wonderful, and the cheesecakes are the best around. Occasionally local artists provide entertainment from folk music to an open mike. ⊠ *1007 Broadway* ☎ *706/494–6659* ▱ *AE, MC, V.*

$$–$$$$ ✕▢ **Rothschild-Pound House Inn & Village.** If pedigree is any indication of quality, then it's no wonder that this B&B has garnered praise of all sorts. The complex comprises nine houses, four cottages, and an 1870 Second Empire Victorian home with a sweeping veranda. The main inn is an elegant reminder of old Columbus, with four-poster mahogany beds, hardwood floors, and period antiques. Original artwork by owner Garry Pound decorates the walls. Occupying the entire front of the 2nd floor of the main house, the Golden Suite has windows on two sides, a separate sitting room, a balcony with rocking chairs, and a Jacuzzi. The cottages have wood-burning fireplaces with a separate parlor and kitchen. Guests have access to a nearby health club. One of the big local draws is Café 222 ($$$), an 1890's storefront restaurant that serves a full breakfast and a traditional southern style lunch. Save room for the banana pudding—it's about as good as it gets. ⊠ *201 7th St., 31901* ☎ *706/322–4075 or 800/585–4075* 🖶 *706/494–8156* ⊕ *www.thepoundhouseinn.com* ⇨ *21 rooms, 4 cottages* ⚬ *Refrigerators, cable TV, in-room VCRs, Wi-Fi* ▱ *AE, D, MC, V* ⊙|*BP.*

FodorsChoice

★

$–$$$ ▢ **Gates House Inn.** Highlights of this exquisitely restored property, which actually consists of two inns, include lush gardens and beautifully appointed interiors straight out of a Victorian novel. Gates Inn West is an 1880 twin-chimney colonial revival decorated with Oriental rugs and antiques. In warm weather you can breakfast on the front porch. Rooms in the Gates Inn East, with its bamboo-furniture-furnished screened porch, are decorated according to such themes as Versailles and Mardi Gras. The extravagant breakfast at either inn might include homemade sourdough bread and brown-sugar, cinnamon, and pecan French toast. Guests have access to a nearby health club. ⊠ *800 Broadway, 31901* ☎ *706/324–6464 or 800/891–3187* 🖷 *706/324–2070* ⊕ *www.gateshouse.com* ↪ *10 rooms* ⚘ *Cable TV, in-room DVDs, bicycles, free parking* ⊟ *AE, MC, V* ¶⊙¶ *BP.*

$–$$ 🏨 **Marriott Columbus.** On the site of a vast 1860s complex of warehouses, factories, mills, and a Confederate arsenal, this hotel is a key component of the Columbus Ironworks Convention and Trade Center just across the street. The rooms and public areas have been renovated—the lobby has huge skylights that pour in natural light onto the marble floors and the original brickwork of its grist Mill origins. Rooms are simple but tasteful, and many overlook the Riverwalk park. With a terrific location between Broadway's Victorian district and the Riverwalk, and a Houlihan's restaurant, the Marriott is a focal point of the city's downtown revival. ⊠ *800 Front Ave., 31901* ☎ *706/324–1800 or 800/455–9261* 🖷 *706/576–4413* ⊕ *www.marriott.com* ↪ *177 rooms* ⚘ *Restaurant, coffee shop, minibars, microwaves, refrigerators, cable TV, in-room data ports, Wi-Fi, pool, health club, bar, lounge, laundry service, meeting rooms, free parking, no-smoking rooms* ⊟ *AE, D, DC, MC, V* ¶⊙¶ *EP.*

$ 🏨 **Country Inn and Suites.** This is a reliable chain property that's ideal if you're staying for more than a few days. It has a cozy B&B atmosphere with spacious rooms and suites, all with coffeemakers and other helpful amenities. ⊠ *1720 Fountain Ct., 31904–1604* ☎ *706/660–1880 or 800/456–4000* 🖷 *706/243–3473* ⊕ *www.countryinns.com* ↪ *62 rooms, 13 suites* ⚘ *Microwaves, refrigerators, cable TV, in-room data ports, Wi-Fi, pool, gym, laundry facilities, free parking* ⊟ *AE, D, DC, MC, V* ¶⊙¶ *BP.*

Nightlife & the Arts

The 2,000-seat **RiverCenter for the Performing Arts** (⊠ 900 Broadway ☎ 706/256–3600, 888/332–5200 for tickets), home to the Columbus Symphony Orchestra, the third oldest orchestra in the country, always has something interesting on tap. The center has hosted Presidential debates as well as the likes of Itzhak Perlman, the Moscow Boys Choir, Bobby McFerrin, and James Taylor. It has also featured Broadway shows such as *Evita, Riverdance,* and *Miss Saigon.*

Since its opening in 1871, the **Springer Opera House** (⊠ 103 10th St. ☎ 706/324–1100, 706/324–5714 for tours), a National Historic Landmark, has been known as one of the finest opera houses in the South. In its heyday, its stage boasted legends such as Ruth Gordon, Lillie Langtry and Will Rogers. Today the theater hosts musicals, dramas, and regional talent.

Shopping

Columbus Park Crossing (⊠ Off Veterans Pkwy at J. R. Allen Pkwy., Exit 10 off I–185) is the city's main mall, anchored by major stores in ap-

10

parel, electronics, home furnishings, and other smaller boutique outlets. In the heart of the historic district, and very much a part of the riverside renaissance, the **Galleria** (⊠ 11 9th St. ☎ 706/653–1950) is a complex of renovated old warehouses that houses a range of boutique and gift shops all under one roof.

Plains

❹ *55 mi southeast of Columbus via U.S. 27 and U.S. 280.*

This rural farming town—originally named the Plains of Dura after the biblical story of Shadrach, Meshach, and Abednego—is the birthplace and current home of former president Jimmy Carter and his wife Rosalynn. The Carters still live in a ranch-style brick house on the edge of town—the only home they have ever owned, and they still worship at the **Maranathan Baptist Church.** Although it's the hub of a thriving farming community, the one-street downtown paralleling the railroad tracks resembles a 1930s movie set.

Each September the town comes alive with the **Plains Peanut Festival,** which includes a parade, live entertainment, arts and crafts, food vendors, and races. The annual softball game pitting President Carter and Secret Service agents against alumni from Plains High School is always a festival highlight.

★ At the **Jimmy Carter National Historic Site** you can still see the late-1880s **railroad depot** that housed his 1976 presidential-campaign headquarters; in January 1977, the "Peanut Special," an 18-car train filled with supporters, departed from here for Carter's inauguration in Washington. The vintage phones here play recordings of Carter discussing his grassroots run for the White House. A couple of miles outside of town on the Old Plains Highway is the 360-acre **Jimmy Carter Boyhood Farm,** where the Carter family grew cotton, peanuts, and corn; it has been restored to its original appearance before electricity was introduced. Period furniture fills the house, and the battery-powered radio plays Carter's reminiscences of growing up on a Depression-era farm. **Plains High School,** in which the Carters were educated, is now a museum and the headquarters of the historic site. You can visit these places and tour the town by picking up a self-guided tour book at the visitor center or the high school. ⊠ *Plains High School, 300 N. Bond St.* ☎ *229/824–4104* ⊕ *www.nps.gov/jica* 🎟 *Free* ☉ *Daily 9–5.*

Where to Stay

$–$$ 🏨 **Plains Historic Inn.** Each spacious room of this inn, in a turn-of-the-20th-century furniture store directly above the Antiques Mall on Main Street, is decorated to reflect the aesthetics of a particular decade between the 1920s and the 1980s. The street-side rooms have a view across Main Street, where Billy Carter's old gas station still sits along with the railroad depot from which President Carter ran his bid for the White House. ■ TIP➡ **The inn books up fast during the Peanut Festival; reserve six months in advance.** ⊠ *106 Main St., Box 314, 31780* ☎ *229/824–4517* 🖷 *229/824–4529* ⊕ *www.plainsgeorgia.com/Plains_Inn.htm* 🛏 *6 rooms, 1 suite* ☖ *Cable TV; no smoking* 🖃 *AE, D, MC, V* ⓧ *BP.*

**EN
ROUTE**

Warp back in time to the mid-19th century at **Westville Village** (✉ Box 1850, Lumpkin ☎229/838–6310 or 888/733–1850 💲$10 ⊙ Tues.–Sat. 10–5). In Lumpkin, at the junction of Interstate 85 and Highway 27, 7 mi east of Plains, this replica of an 1850s town has more than 30 pre-Civil War buildings, relocated and authentically restored. The village comes alive with hearth-cooked food, mules and wagons, and period-dressed townspeople and tradesmen demonstrating skills such as candle making, quilting, and cotton baling.

> **CALLING YESTERYEAR**
>
> One of the state's most unusual museums, the **Georgia Rural Telephone Museum** (✉ 135 Bailey Ave., Leslie ☎ 229/874–4786 💲$5 ⊙ Weekdays 9–3:30), is housed in a former 1920s cotton warehouse in Leslie, halfway between Americus and Cordele on Highway 280. Featuring more than 1,500 phones, the museum claims to have the world's largest collection of telephones.

Americus

❺ *11 mi east of Plains via U.S. 280.*

Founded in 1832, Americus is the only city in the United States named for explorer Amerigo Vespucci (1454–1512). At one time this was one of the largest cities in Georgia and a major center of cotton production. The four-story Windsor Hotel, a sprawling 1892 Victorian structure that takes up a city block, dominates the downtown business district and is a testament to the town's heyday as a resort. Its dazzling turrets, towers, and verandas are a dramatic and elegant reminder of the city's prestigious past.

Today Americus is best known as the site of the international headquarters of **Habitat for Humanity,** an organization dedicated to building decent, affordable housing for low-income families around the world. You can tour the headquarters and watch videos discussing the group's work. A few blocks farther west on West Church Street is **Habitat's Global Village & Discovery Center,** which examines different housing conditions around the world. You can climb into the Papua New Guinea house on stilts, make compressed-earth blocks, or try your hand at roof tiles, just like Habitat builders in Africa and Asia. ✉ *121 Habitat St.* ☎ *229/924–6935 or 800/422–4828* ⊕ *www.habitat.org* 💲 *Headquarters: free. Global Village: $6 suggested donation* ⊙ *Headquarters: Tues.–Sat. 8–5. Global Village weekdays 9–5, Sat. 10–2.*

★ About 10 mi northeast of Americus via Route 49, you can visit a solemn reminder of the Civil War's tragic toll, the **Andersonville National Historic Site.** This infamous prisoner-of-war penitentiary is the nation's only POW museum. Photographs, artifacts, and high-tech exhibits detail not just the plight of Civil War prisoners, but also prison life and conditions affecting all of America's 800,000 POWs since the Revolutionary War. Some 13,000 Union prisoners died—mostly from disease, neglect, and malnutrition—at Andersonville during its 14-month tenure at the tail of the war. At the conclusion of the Civil War, the Swiss-born commandant

10

of Andersonville, Captain Henry R. Wirz, believed by some to be a scapegoat, became the only person executed for war crimes. Wirz refused a pardon promised if he implicated Confederate president Jefferson Davis and was hanged on November 10, 1865. ⊠ *496 Cemetery Rd., Andersonville* ☏ *229/924–0343* ⊕ *www.nps.gov/ande/index.htm* ⊡ *Free* ☉ *Daily 9–5.*

> ### SOLO SIGHT
>
> Look for the historical market and whimsical statue of Charles Lindbergh (1902–74) along the Airport Road at Souther Field Airport, marking the site of his first solo flight in May 1923.

Amid a long stretch of pecan trees and rolling dairy farmland lining Route 26, about 20 mi north of Americus and 3 mi east of Montezuma, you'll find yourself in the heart of the **Mennonite community,** which relocated here in the 1950s after a military-base expansion prompted the group to leave its land in Virginia. Perhaps the easiest way to glimpse the Mennonite lifestyle is to stop by **Yoder's Deitsch Haus and Yoder's Gift Shop** (⊠ 5382 Rte. 26E, Montezuma ☏ 478/472–2024), closed Sunday and Monday, a roadside restaurant, bakery, and gift shop run by the Mennonite community. The restaurant serves hearty fare and homemade desserts, and the bakery sells delicious pastries and pecan, peanut-butter, and shoofly pies. In the gift shop you'll find crafts, quilts, locally canned goods, and hand-hewn furniture such as bentwood rockers. Monday through Saturday during strawberry season (April to mid-July) you can pick berries and take a tour of the **Kauffman Strawberry Farm** (⊠ 1305 Mennonite Church Rd., Montezuma ☏ 478/967–2115 ⊕ www.kauffmanstrawberries.com). At the farm's Silo Kitchen—possibly the tallest kitchen in the world, as it's actually in a grain silo—you can try homemade strawberry and peach ice cream, pies, and pastries.

Where to Stay & Eat

★ $ ✕⊡ **Windsor Hotel.** This ornate jewel of a hotel has garnered awards from the National Trust for Historic Preservation. Built in 1892, it's a monument to Victorian architecture and remains one of the South's best showcases of American heritage. All of the rooms have 12-foot ceilings, and the circular Carter Presidential Suite takes up an entire floor of the hotel's tallest tower. The elegant Grand Dining Room ($$–$$$$; no dinner Sunday) serves a varied menu with a focus on Southern food: corn chowder, crab cakes, quail in an orange-cream sauce, and pecan-crusted or bourbon-glazed salmon. ■ TIP→ **Browse over a brew at Floyd's pub–it has Wi-Fi in the pub and the atrium.** ⊠ *125 W. Lamar St., 31709* ☏ *229/924–1555 or 888/297–9567* ☐ *229/928–0533* ⊕ *www.windsor-americus.com* ⤶ *53 rooms, 4 suites* ⚭ *Restaurant, fans, spa, bar* ⊟ *AE, D, DC, MC, V.*

$–$$ ⊡ **The 1906 Pathway Inn.** Though Tara-esque in size and style, this Greek-revival inn has reasonable rates. Antiques fill the rooms, which are named for historic figures connected to the region, such as Roosevelt and Lindbergh. A sprawling veranda with rockers and a swing wraps around the house. The sumptuous candlelight breakfasts include everything from pancakes and waffles to French toast stuffed with peaches or cream cheese. Guests also have access to use the local fitness center. ⊠ *501 S. Lee St., 31709* ☎ *229/928–2078 or 800/889–1466* 🖷 *229/928–2078* ⊕ *www.1906pathwayinn.com* 🎝 *6 rooms, 1 cottage* ⚙ *In-room VCRs* ⊟ *AE, D, MC, V* |◎| *BP.*

THE SOUTHWEST CORNER

Tifton and Thomasville are the highlights of Georgia's southwest corner. Both are often cited among the nation's most appealing small towns, thanks to inviting town squares, shaded glens, and an easygoing air; you can also find some fine country inns here.

Tifton

6 *72 mi southeast of Americus via U.S. 280 and I–75; 183 mi south of Atlanta via I–75.*

In 1872 Henry Harding Tift, a Connecticut Yankee, set up a lumbering operation that grew into the present-day town (Tifton and the nearby town of Fitzgerald share the distinction of having been founded by Northerners). Tifton derived its wealth chiefly from tobacco farming. The old downtown (Main Street between 4th and 9th streets) dates to the 1940s and includes an art deco–movie house. Norman Crampton ranked Tifton 54th in his noted book *The 100 Best Small Towns in America.*

Agrirama is the site of the Georgia Living History Museum, which depicts life in 19th-century rural Georgia. Agrirama consists of a traditional farm community from the 1870s, an 1890s progressive farmstead, an industrial-sites complex, and a rural town. Among the 35 restored period structures are traditional houses, a forge, a turpentine still, a gristmill, and a cotton gin. Costumed interpretive guides lead you through the 95-acre site. A logging train takes you through the woods to the village, where you can stroll the main street and visit the feed and seed store, the print shop, the drugstore, and the original Victorian home of Henry Harding Tift. ⊠ *1493 Whiddon Mill Rd., I–75 at Exit 63B* ☎ *229/386–3344 or 800/767–1875* ⊕ *www.agrirama.com* 🎟 *$7* ⊙ *Tues.–Sat. 9–5.*

10

A 1900 Romanesque brick church sparkling with stained-glass houses the **Tifton Museum of Arts & Heritage.** Exhibits of varied media are held year-round. ⊠ *285 Love Ave.* ☎ *229/382–3600 or 229/382–8576* 🎟 *$2–$5 donation requested* ⊙ *Tues.–Fri. 1–5.*

OFF THE BEATEN PATH
JEFFERSON DAVIS MEMORIAL HISTORIC SITE – A small museum filled with flags, uniforms, weapons, and other Civil War items sits near the wooded site where Confederate President Jefferson Davis was captured by Union troops nearly a month after Lee's surrender at Appomattox. A spur worn by Davis at the time of his capture as well as posters advertising the reward for his capture are on display, and there's an interesting short film. It's about 15 minutes north of Tifton on Route 125. ■ TIP➔ Check out the J. D. Nature Trail. Once a part of an old country road, the ⅓-mi easy walk offers great wildlife viewing (there are 47 different species of birds alone) and

leads to a boardwalk over some beautiful wetlands. ⊠ *338 Jeff Davis Park Rd., Fitzgerald* ☏ *229/831–2335* ⊕ *www.gastateparks.org/info/jeffd/* ⊠ *$3* ⊙ *Wed.–Sat. 9–5, Sun. 2–5:30.*

Where to Eat

$ ✕ **Pit Stop Bar-B-Que & Grill.** In addition to barbecue pork, you have a choice of beef, chicken, or turkey dishes, plus Brunswick stew, baked beans, corn on the cob, and cobbler and banana pudding. Locals swear by Pit Stop's "awesome potato," a baked potato stuffed with pork, layered with cheese, and served with coleslaw on the side. It's a meal in itself. ⊠ *1112 W. 8th St., across from Agrirama* ☏ *229/387–0888* ⊟ *AE, D, MC, V.*

Thomasville

❼ *55 mi south of Tifton via U.S. 319; 236 mi south of Atlanta via I–75 and U.S. 319.*

The early fortunes of this appealing small town in the Tallahassee Red Hills paralleled the rise and fall of the antebellum cotton plantations that lined the region's famed "Plantation Trace." Following the Civil War, thousands of Union prisoners who had been evacuated from the nearby Andersonville prison to Thomasville brought home stories of the curative effects of the balsam breezes of the pine-scented air. These stories fueled the second boom in the region's fortunes, during which Northerners fleeing the cold wintered here. The wealthier among them built elegant estates in and around the town.

Although Thomasville's golden era has long since ended and there's little left of the old-growth forests that brought winter vacationers south, the distinct pine-scented air remains, as does the Victorian elegance of the town's heyday. Thomasville retains the rich atmosphere of a bygone era and the stately vestiges of a once-posh resort, but without the crowds. Known as the "City of Roses," it draws thousands of visitors each spring to its annual Rose Festival (the fourth weekend in April). And during the Victorian Christmas, locals turn out in period costumes to enjoy horse-drawn carriage rides, caroling, and street theater.

One of Thomasville's more interesting sights is the **Lapham–Patterson House,** built by Chicago shoe manufacturer Charles W. Lapham. At the time of its construction in 1884, the three-story Victorian house was state-of-the-art, with gas lighting and indoor plumbing with hot and cold running water. Each room was built with at least five or six walls. But the most curious feature of this unusual house is that Lapham, who had witnessed the Great Chicago Fire of 1871, had 45 exit doors installed because of his fear of being trapped in a burning house. The house is now a National Historic

ANTIQUE ANTICS

Toscoga Marketplace (⊠ 209 S. Broad St., Thomasville ☏ 229/227–6777) is home to some 90 antique dealers and, as south Georgia's largest antique mall, is the local sponsor of the greatly heralded *Antiques Roadshow* TV show.

King Cotton's Royal Comeback

SUCH WAS GEORGIA'S PREEMINENCE in world cotton production at the turn of the 20th century that the international market price was set at the Cotton Exchange in Savannah. And the huge plantations of southwest Georgia—which in their heyday required an estimated 20,000 slaves to operate—were major players in the engine driving the state's economic prosperity.

For more than 100 years, from the first time it was planted in Georgia in 1733 until the beginning of the Civil War, cotton was the most commercially successful crop in the state. But because the seeds had to be separated from the lint by hand, production was laborious and output was limited. Slavery was actually on the decline in Georgia until 1793, when a young Yale graduate named Eli Whitney (1765–1825) came to Savannah's Mulberry Grove Plantation as a tutor to the children of Revolutionary War hero Nathaniel

Greene. After watching the difficulty workers were having separating the seeds from the cotton, he invented a simple machine of two cylinders with combs rotating in opposite directions. The "gin," as he called it (short for engine), could do the work of 50 people and revolutionized the cotton industry. So significant was its immediate impact on the U.S. economy that President George Washington personally signed the patent issued to Whitney.

In 1900 a new problem arose. The boll weevil came to the U.S. via Mexico and quickly undermined cotton production. The weevil was a major cause of the onset of the economic depression that spread throughout the South. Cotton production was at an all-time low in Georgia by 1978; in 1987 the state began a boll weevil eradication program that has all but wiped out the threat. And the result is that today Georgia is once again one of the top producers in the nation.

Landmark because of its unique architectural features. ✉ 626 N. Dawson St. ☎ 229/225–4004 ⊕ www.gastateparks.org/info/lapham/ 🖼 $5 ☉ Tues.–Sat. 9–5, Sun. 2–5:30.

🄲 The **Birdsong Nature Center** encompasses 565 acres of lush fields, forests, swamps, and butterfly gardens, plus miles of walking trails. It's a wondrous haven for birds and scores of other native wildlife. Nature programs are offered year-round. ✉ 2106 Meridian Rd. ☎ 229/377–4408 or 800/953–2473 ⊕ www.tfn.net/birdsong 🖼 $5 ☉ Wed., Fri., and Sat. 9–5, Sun. 1–5.

★ For a glimpse of the grandeur of Southern life Tara-style, visit **Pebble Hill Plantation,** listed on the National Register of Historic Places and the only plantation in the area open to the public. Pebble Hill dates to 1825, although most of the original house was destroyed in a fire in the 1930s. Highlights of the current two-story main house include a dramatic horseshoe-shape entryway, a wraparound terrace on the upper floor, and an elegant sunroom decorated with a wildlife motif. Surrounding the house

10

are 34 acres of immaculately maintained grounds that include gardens, a walking path festooned with jasmine, a log-cabin school, a fire station, a carriage house, kennels, and a hospital for the plantation's more than 100 dogs (prized dogs were buried with full funerals, including a minister). The sprawling dairy-and-horse-stable complex resembles an English village. Grab a cup of lemonade from the large thermos under the oak tree opposite the Plantation Store—it's compliments of the house. ⊠ *5 mi south of Thomasville on U.S. 319, just past Melhana Plantation on right* ☎ *229/226–2344* ⊕ *www.pebblehill.com* ☎ *Grounds $3, house tour $7* ☉ *Oct.–Aug., Tues.–Sat. 10–5, Sun. 1–5; last tour at 4.*

Where to Stay & Eat

$$$–$$$$ ✕ **Liam's Restaurant.** With a flair for the unexpected, this bistro turns out a rotating seasonal menu with such updated Southern dishes as Jamaican pork loin with sweet red-onion marmalade, and duck with cottage cheese, pecans, and corn cake with a blueberry sauce. Liam's also serves a full cheese cart of various artisan cheese from Europe, as well as local selections. It's especially proud of its humongous European breakfast served every Saturday. Wine is not on the menu, but you're free to bring your own bottle. An open kitchen, garden dining, and paintings by local artists create a cozy dining room. ⊠ *109 E. Jackson St.* ☎ *229/226–9944* ⊟ *MC, V* ☉ *Closed Sun. and Mon. No dinner Tues. and Wed.*

$$–$$$ ✕ **Mom and Dad's Italian Restaurant.** That's definitely oregano you smell when entering Mom and Dad's—but also expect to hear a Southern drawl. These go together perfectly at this restaurant, a great place for Italian food made with rich cheeses and thick red tomato sauce. The garlic bread is served warm and strong enough to turn your breath into a blowtorch. ⊠ *1800 Smith Ave.* ☎ *229/226–6265* ⊟ *MC, V* ☉ *Closed Sun. and Mon. No lunch.*

$–$$ ✕ **George & Louie's.** The fresh gulf seafood served at this airy Key West–style restaurant is as good as you can find anywhere. Try the broiled shrimp, cooked in olive oil with a smattering of fresh garlic; fresh mullet dinner; or combination platter with homemade deviled crab, shrimp, oysters, scallops, and flounder for one, two, or three people. The fried green tomatoes sprinkled with feta are cooked to perfection, and the burgers are a local favorite. Vintage music from the '40s plays on the sound system, and there's outdoor dining under umbrellas. ⊠ *217 Remington Ave.* ☎ *229/226–1218* ⊟ *No credit cards* ☉ *Closed Sun.*

$$$$ ✕▣ **Melhana Grand Plantation Resort.** The grounds of this sprawling 50-acre plantation—listed on the National Register of Historic Places—are dotted with dozens of buildings, shade trees, gardens, bridal paths, and trails. Most rooms are massive, with gorgeous four-poster beds and antique writing desks. A highlight here is Melhana's Chapin Dining Room ($$$$; jacket requested, reservations required, no lunch). The Southern meals here—including the likes of Atlantic salmon with a black-bean-and-tomato ragout, and grilled beef tenderloin topped with crab—are every bit as exquisite as the surroundings in which they are served. ⊠ *301 Showboat La., 31792* ☎ *229/226–2290 or 888/920–3030* ⊟ *229/226–4585* ⊕ *www.melhana.com* ⇝ *38 rooms, 17 suites, 2 cottages* ⚬ *Restau-*

rant, cable TV, tennis court, indoor pool, health club, horseback riding, library 🍴 *AE, MC, V* ☺ *Closed lunch Mon.–Sat; closed dinner Sun.–Thurs.* 🍽 *BP.*

★ **$$$–$$$$** 🏠 **1884 Paxton House Inn.** Each room is unique in this immaculate property, a stately blue Victorian mansion with a wraparound veranda. Antiques and period reproductions decorate the public spaces and guest rooms. Thoughtful details include designer fabrics, Egyptian-cotton bath towels, goose-down pillows, evening turndown service, and homemade cranberry, orange, or blueberry bread for breakfast. Accommodations are spread among the main inn, a pool house, a garden cottage, and a carriage house. Afternoon tea and lemonade socials are part of the fun of this inn in the downtown historic district. ✉ *445 Remington Ave., 31792* ☎ *229/226–5197* 🖶 *229/226–9903* ⊕ *www.1884paxtonhouseinn.com* ⇆ *9 rooms* ☖ *Fans, in-room DVDs, some in-room data ports, Wi-Fi, pool, hot tubs; no kids under 12* 🍴 *AE, MC, V* 🍽 *BP.*

SOUTHWEST GEORGIA ESSENTIALS

Transportation

BY AIR

Delta Airlines has daily flights into Columbus Metro Airport from Atlanta. Plains, Tifton, Pine Mountain, and other small communities have facilities for small and privately owned aircraft only.

🛈 **Columbus Metro Airport** ✉ 3250 W. Britt David Rd., Columbus 31909-5399 ☎ 706/324-2449 ⊕ www.flycolumbusga.com.

BY BUS

Greyhound Bus Lines serves Columbus, Cordele, LaGrange, Lexington, Thomasville, and Tifton.

🛈 **Greyhound Bus Lines** ☎ 800/231-2222 ⊕ www.greyhound.com.

BY CAR

A car is the best way to tour this part of Georgia. Interstate 75 runs north–south through the eastern edge of the region and connects to several U.S. and state highways that traverse the area. Interstate 85 runs southwest through LaGrange and Columbus. Do explore backcountry roads—they offer the landscapes and ambience of the real South. Just be sure to travel with a good road map and expect detours for photo opportunities.

10

BY TRAIN

A great means of seeing the countryside, the SAM Shortline Southwest Georgia Excursion Train originates in Cordele and runs west through Georgia Veteran's State Park, Leslie, Americus, Plains, and Archery. You can get on or off at any of the stations, stop over for the night, and take the train again the next morning (check the schedule to be sure there's a train running the next day).

🛈 **SAM Shortline Southwest Georgia Excursion Train** ✉ 105 E. 9th Ave., Box 845, Cordele 31010 ☎ 229/276-0755 or 877/427-2457 ⊕ www.samshortline.com.

Contacts & Resources

BANKS & EXCHANGE SERVICES

Banking services in this area are few and far between. Columbus, of course, has many banks and financial institutions, many of which are open for half-days on Saturday. Elsewhere, expect opening hours on weekdays 9:30 to 5.

🏦 Banks **Bank of America** ✉ 200 Main St., LaGrange 30240-3220 ☎ 706/845-6863. **Columbus Bank & Trust** ✉ 1148 Broadway, Columbus 31901-2429 ☎ 706/644-1996. **Commercial Bank** ✉ 101 S. Crawford St., Thomasville 31792-5502 ☎ 229/226-3535. **Sumpter Bank & Trust** ✉ 201 E. Lamar St., Americus 31709-3632 ☎ 229/924-0301. **Sun Trust Bank** ✉ 1246 1st Ave., Columbus 31901-4298 ☎ 706/653-8401.

EMERGENCIES

Although southwest Georgia is largely rural, most communities have hospitals with emergency services. There are no 24-hour pharmacy or emergency dental clinics in the region.

🚑 Emergency Services **Ambulance, fire, police** ☎ 911.

🏥 Hospitals **Columbus Doctors Hospital** ✉ 616 19th St., Columbus ☎ 706/494-4262 ⊕ www.doctorshospital.net. **John D. Archibold Memorial Hospital** ✉ 915 Gordon St., Thomasville ☎ 229/228-2781 7 AM-9 PM, 229/228-2000 after hours ⊕ www.archbold. org. **Sumter Regional Hospital** ✉ 100 Wheatley Dr., Americus ☎ 229/924-6011 ⊕ www.sumterregional.org. **Warm Springs Medical Center** ✉ 5995 Spring St., Warm Springs ☎ 706/655-3331 ⊕ www.warmspringsmc.org.

💊 Pharmacies **CVS Pharmacy** ✉ 4904 River Rd., Columbus ☎ 706/322-5489. **Plains Pharmacy** ✉ 103 Main St., Plains ☎ 229/824-5255. **Pine Mountain Pharmacy** ✉ 145 N. Main St., Pine Mountain ☎ 706/663-2255. **Thomas Drug Store** ✉ 108 S. Broad St., Thomasville ☎ 229/226-2535. **Walgreen Drug Store** ✉ 4808 Buena Vista Rd., Columbus ☎ 706/569-9308.

INTERNET, MAIL & SHIPPING

If the community has a town square, you're likely to find the area supports wireless connectivity, and most hotels take advantage of that service. If you're without your laptop, head for the local library or FedEx Kinko's. Rates vary but you can expect to pay around $3 per hour, though at the Columbus Public Library $3 is the cost of a guest library card that translates into free Internet access for a month.

💻 **Columbus Public Library** ✉ 300 Macon Rd., Columbus 31906 ☎ 706/243-2669. **FedEx Kinko's** ✉ 1605 Bradley Park Dr., Columbus 31904-3072 ☎ 706/320-0511. **LaGrange Memorial Public Library** ✉ 117 Alford St., LaGrange 30240 ☎ 706/882-7784. **U.S. Post Office** ✉ 128 Forsyth St., Americus 31709 ☎ 229/924-8957 ✉ 3916 Milgen Rd., Columbus 31907 ☎ 706/562-1760 ✉ Calumet Center, LaGrange 30241-6703 ☎ 706/883-7126 ✉ 15 Liberty St., Thomasville 31757 ☎ 229/227-9731 ☎ 800/275-8777.

MEDIA

The *Atlanta Journal Constitution* reaches as far as Columbus. Travel farther south, and most national news is obtained in *USA Today* and local daily publications.

📰 *Columbus Ledger-Enquirer* ✉ Box 711, Columbus 31902 ☎ 706/751-8565 ⊕ www. ledger-enquirer.com. *Columbus Times* ✉ 2230 Buena Vista Rd., Columbus 31906 ☎ 706/324-2404 ⊕ www.columbustimes.com. *LaGrange Daily News* ✉ 105 Ashton

St., LaGrange 30240 ☎ 706/884-7311 ⊕ www.lagrangenews.com. *Tifton Gazette* ✉ 211 N. Tift Ave., Tifton 31794 ☎ 229/382-4321 ⊕ www.tiftongazette.com.

VISITOR INFORMATION

You'll find the folks at every visitor center to be exceptionally helpful. All are open 9 to 5 on weekdays. On Saturday most centers (except for LaGrange and Tifton) are open 10 to 4. Most (except for Plains and Americus) are closed Sunday.

🚩 **Americus-Sumter County Welcome Center** ✉ Windsor Hotel, 125 W. Lamar St., Box 275, Americus 31709 ☎ 229/928-6059 or 888/278-6837 ⊕ www.americus-sumterchamber.com. **Columbus Convention and Visitors Bureau** ✉ 900 Front Ave., 31902 ☎ 706/322-1613 or 800/999-1613 ⊕ www.visitcolumbusga.com. **LaGrange-Troup County Chamber of Commerce** ✉ 111 Bull St., Box 636, LaGrange 30241-0636 ☎ 706/884-8671 ⊕ www.lagrangechamber.com. **Pine Mountain Welcome Center** ✉ 101 E. Broad St., Pine Mountain 31822 ☎ 706/663-4000 or 800/441-3502 ⊕ www.pinemountain.org. **Plains Welcome Center** ✉ 1763 U.S. 280, Plains 31780 ☎ 229/824-7477 ⊕ www.plainsgeorgia.com. **Thomasville Welcome Center** ✉ 401 S. Broad St., Thomasville 31792 ☎ 229/228-7977 or 866/577-3600 ⊕ www.thomasvillega.com. **Tifton-Tift County Tourism Association** ✉ 115 W. 2nd St., Box Q, Tifton 31793 ☎ 229/386-0216 ⊕ www.tiftontourism.com. **Warm Springs Welcome Center** ✉ 1 Broad St., Warm Springs 31830 ☎ 706/655-3322 or 800/337-1927 ⊕ www.warmspringsga.com.

10

Atlanta

WORD OF MOUTH

"Atlanta is beautiful and, while it is Southern, it might not feel like the quintessential Southern city. It [has] been built up and modernized and is a real hybrid. If you can make it over to Virginia-Highland, a bit east of the park (short cab ride), you will see funkier older neighborhoods with cool older houses that have been renovated. Walk down Virginia Avenue and you can stroll through the boutiques and interesting restaurants."

—chicagolori

"You should go to Stone Mountain. It's the largest piece of exposed granite in the world (as big as a mountain). You can hike up it or take a tram-like thing. It's awesome."

—takemethere

By Deborah
Geering

Updated by
Michele Foust

A WARM EMBRACE greets visitors to Atlanta. Top-notch shopping and world-class dining top the list of rewards these days. In the past, many of the major draws—Stone Mountain Park, for example—were outside the city limits. Today there's plenty downtown to keep you occupied. The Georgia Aquarium, the largest in the world, draws visitors who want to get up close and personal with a quartet of whale sharks. The Woodruff Arts Center is a cultural hub where you can catch a performance by the Atlanta Symphony Orchestra or gaze on treasures from the Louvre on loan at the High Museum of Art. And the fizzy World of Coke is dedicated to the hometown beverage.

Atlanta is experiencing a period of explosive growth. The latest estimates place the city's population at 442,000. But the 28-county Atlanta Metropolitan Statistical Area counts more than 4.7 million residents. A good measure of the city's expansion is the ever-changing downtown skyline, along with office and residential towers constructed in the Midtown, Buckhead, and the outer perimeter (fringing Interstate 285, especially to the north) business districts. Residents, however, are less likely to measure the city's growth by skyscrapers than by the increase in traffic jams and crowds, higher prices, and the ever-burgeoning subdivisions that continue to push urban sprawl farther and farther into surrounding rural areas.

Originally built as the terminus of the Western & Atlantic Railroad, Atlanta is still a transportation hub. The city now serves the world through Hartsfield-Jackson Atlanta International Airport—now ranked as the busiest in the world. At this writing, it serves nearly 86 million passengers annually. Direct flights to Europe, South America, Africa, and Asia have made Atlanta easily accessible to the more than 50 countries that have representation in the city through consulates, trade offices, and chambers of commerce. Atlanta has emerged as a banking center and is the world headquarters for such Fortune 500 companies as Home Depot, Coca-Cola, United Parcel Service, and SunTrust Banks.

Still viewed by die-hard Southerners as the heart of the Old Confederacy, Atlanta has become the best example of the New South, a fast-paced modern city proud of its heritage. Transplanted Northerners and those from elsewhere account for more than half the population and have undeniably affected the mood of the city, as well as the mix of accents of its people. Irish immigrants played a major role in the city's early history, along with Germans and Austrians. Since the 1980s, Atlanta has seen spirited growth in its Asian and Latin-American communities. Related restaurants, shops, and institutions have become part of the city's texture.

"The city too busy to hate," Atlanta has a strong link to the civil rights movement. It was the home of Dr. Martin Luther King Jr. His widow, Coretta Scott King, founded the King Center after his assassination in 1968. The center is at the heart of the Sweet Auburn historic district, once the home of Atlanta's first black millionaire, Alonzo Herndon, and now a carefully restored and preserved neighborhood that seeks to tell the story of African-American segregation and success. The district in-

TOP 5 REASONS TO GO

The Georgia Aquarium: Wildly successful after its opening in late 2005, the world's largest aquarium draws visitors from all over the globe.

A stroll through the park: April in Paris has nothing on Atlanta, especially when the abundant azaleas and dogwoods are blooming in Atlanta Botanical Garden, Centennial Park, and Piedmont Park.

Following in King's footsteps: Home of Martin Luther King Jr., Atlanta was a hub of the civil rights movement. Not to be missed is a visit to the King Center and a tour

through his childhood home on Auburn Avenue.

Civil War history: Atlanta may have been burned during General William Sherman's march to the sea, but artifacts in the city's museums—as well as at historic sites in nearby Kennesaw, Marietta, and Roswell—give history buffs the chance to relive those difficult times.

Southern cooking, and then some: Good Southern food has always been easy to find in Atlanta, but the richness of its ethnic diversity makes it a great place to sample a wide range of cuisines.

cludes the birthplace and childhood home of Martin Luther King Jr., as well as the Ebenezer Baptist Church and the Jimmy Carter Presidential Library & Museum.

EXPLORING ATLANTA

The greater Atlanta area embraces five counties. The city of Atlanta is primarily in Fulton and DeKalb counties, although its southern end and the airport are in Clayton County. Outside Interstate 285, which encircles the city, Cobb, Gwinnett, and northern Fulton counties are experiencing much of Atlanta's population increase.

Atlanta's lack of a grid system confuses many drivers, even locals. Some streets change their names along the same stretch of road, including the city's most famous thoroughfare, Peachtree Street, which follows a mountain ridge from downtown to suburban Norcross, outside Interstate 285: it becomes Peachtree Road after crossing Interstate 85 and then splits into Peachtree Industrial Boulevard beyond the Buckhead neighborhood and the original Peachtree Road, which heads into Chamblee. Adding to the confusion, dozens of other streets in the metropolitan area use "Peachtree" in their names. ■ TIP➔ Before setting out anywhere, get the complete street address of your destination, including landmarks, cross streets, or other guideposts, as street numbers and even street signs are often difficult to find.

Atlanta proper has three major areas—downtown, Midtown, and Buckhead—as well as many smaller commercial districts and intown neighborhoods. Atlanta's downtown is filled with government staffers and office workers by day, but at night the visiting conventioneers—and, as city improvements take hold, residents—come out to play. Midtown and Buckhead are the best places to go for dinner, nightclubs, and shows, but some intown neighborhoods like Virginia-Highland and Little Five Points have unique characteristics that merit exploration.

The city's public transportation system, the Metropolitan Atlanta Rapid Transit Authority (MARTA), operates bus and rail networks in Atlanta and Fulton and DeKalb counties. The two major rail lines, which run east–west and north–south (there's a northern spur, so consult a map before you jump on board), extend roughly to the edges of Interstate 285. ■ TIP→ **MARTA is best for traveling to and from the airport and within downtown, Midtown, and Buckhead; if you plan to venture beyond those regions, you should call a taxi or rent a car.**

In 2006, MARTA launched the Atlanta Tourist Loop, a shuttle service around the downtown and Midtown areas. Look for specially designed buses on two different circuits marked Atlanta Tourist Loop. Route 100 winds around downtown, while Route 101 circles Midtown. Individual rides between sites—using a Breeze card or cash—are $1.75, and require exact change. Weekend passes are $9, while weekly passes are $13. Children six and under ride for free. The two loops intersect at the Georgia Aquarium and the North Avenue MARTA station. Buses run about every 30 minutes.

MARTA offers a bus route connecting the Georgia Aquarium and Zoo Atlanta. Its single-ride fare is $1.75. Route 97, as it's called, also makes other stops, including one at Underground Atlanta. The bus runs weekdays 8 to 5 and weekends and holidays 9 to 5.

Numbers in the text correspond to numbers in the margin and on the Downtown Atlanta & Sweet Auburn and Atlanta Neighborhoods maps.

Downtown Atlanta

Downtown Atlanta clusters around the hub known as Five Points. Here you'll find the MARTA station that intersects the north–south and east–west transit lines, both of which run underground here. On the surface, Five Points is formed by the intersection of Peachtree Street with Marietta, Broad, and Forsyth streets. It's a crowded area, and traffic can be snarled in the early morning and late afternoon. With the opening of the Georgia Aquarium and the World of Coca-Cola, which join the Imagine it! Children's Museum and the CNN Center, has taken on greater interest for travelers. Lush Centennial Olympic Park—built for the 1996 Olympic Games—is a great place to watch children play in the Olympic Rings fountain or to enjoy a take-out lunch.

Main Attractions

★ ❶ **Atlanta Cyclorama & Civil War Museum.** A building in Grant Park (named for a New England–born Confederate colonel, not the U.S. president) houses a huge circular painting depicting the 1864 Battle of Atlanta, during which 90% of the city was destroyed. A team of expert European panorama artists completed the painting in Milwaukee, Wisconsin, in 1887; it was donated to the city of Atlanta in 1897. On the second level, a display called

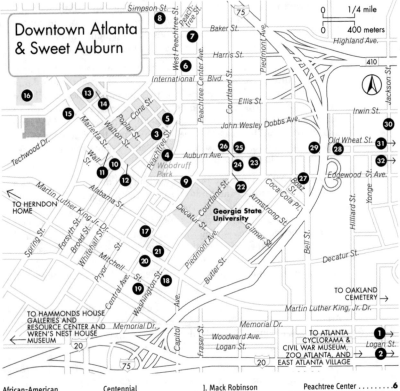

Downtown Atlanta & Sweet Auburn

"Life in Camp" displays rifles, uniforms, and games soldiers played to pass the time. There's also a video detailing the painting's restoration. An outstanding bookstore has dozens of volumes about the Civil War. To get here by car, take Interstate 20 east to Exit 59A, turn right onto Boulevard, and then follow signs to the Cyclorama. The museum shares a parking lot and entrance walkway with Zoo Atlanta. ✉ *800C Cherokee Ave., Grant Park* ☎ *404/658–7625* ⊕ *www. webguide.com/cyclorama.html* 🎟 *$7* ☉ *Daily 9:30–4:30.*

> **SAVE SOME DOUGH**
>
> Atlanta's **CityPass** (☎ 888/330–5008 ⊕ www.citypass.com) offers discount admission to the Georgia Aquarium, the World of Coca-Cola, the High Museum of Art, and the Inside CNN Atlanta Studio Tour. It also includes a choice between the Atlantic Botanical Garden or Fernbank Museum of Natural History. The ticket booklets, which cost $59, can be purchased during your trip at any participating attraction or in advance. Either way, you save a lot of waiting in line.

☾ ⓭ **Centennial Olympic Park.** This 21-acre swath of green was the central venue for the 1996 Summer Olympics. The benches at the Fountain of Rings allow you to enjoy the water and music spectacle—seven tunes are timed to coincide with water displays. The All Children's Playground is designed to be accessible to kids with disabilities. Nearby is the world's largest aquarium and Imagine It! Children's Museum. The park also has a café, restrooms, a playground, and ice-skating in winter. ■ TIP➔ **Don't miss seeing Centennial Olympic Park at night, when eight 65-foot-tall lighting towers set off the beauty of the park. These stylized reproductions represent the kind of markers that led ancient Greeks to significant public events.** ✉ *Marietta St. and Centennial Olympic Park Dr., Downtown* ☎ *404/223–4412* ⊕ *www.centennialpark.com* ☉ *Daily 7 AM–11 PM.*

★ ⓯ **CNN Center.** The home of Cable News Network occupies all 14 floors of this dramatic structure on the edge of downtown. The 55-minute CNN studio tour—difficult for some people because it descends eight flights of stairs—is a behind-the-scenes glimpse of the control room, news rooms, and broadcast studios. You can make reservations by telephone or online. ✉ *1 CNN Center, Downtown* ☎ *404/827–2300* ⊕ *www.cnn. com/studiotour* 🎟 *Tour $12* ☉ *Daily 9–5.*

⓮ **Georgia Aquarium.** With more than 8 million gallons of water, this wildly popular attraction is the world's largest aquarium. The 550,000-square-foot building, an architectural marvel resembling the bow of a ship, has tanks of various sizes filled with more than 100,000 underwater creatures. Dramatic white beluga whales, a favorite with many visitors, share an 800,000 gallon tank. Massive whale sharks Ralph, Alice, Norton, and Trixie swim in the 6.2-million-gallon Ocean Voyager Gallery, the world's largest indoor marine exhibit. The aquarium is slowly growing a living coral reef that is home to a variety of brightly colored fish. But everything you see here doesn't have gills; there are also penguins, sea lions, sea otters, river otters, sea turtles, and giant octopi. Hoards of kids—and many adults—can always be found around the six touch tanks. A cartoon show featuring Deepo, the aquarium mascot, is an extra $6.

FodorsChoice ★

FodorsChoice ★

One-hour behind-the-scenes tours are $50. Cafe Aquaria serves sandwiches, salads, and other light fare. There are often huge crowds, so arrive early or late for the best chance of getting a close-up view of the exhibits. ■ TIP→ Purchase tickets at least a week ahead. Online ticketing is best, as you are e-mailed tickets you can print out at home. ⊠ *225 Baker St., Downtown* ☎ *404/581–4000 or 877/434–7442* ⊕ *www.georgiaaquarium.org* ✆ *$23* ☉ *Memorial Day–Labor Day, daily 8–6; Labor Day–Memorial Day, daily 9–6.*

★ ☾ ❽ **Imagine It! The Children's Museum of Atlanta.** In this colorful and joyfully noisy museum geared to children ages eight and younger, kids can build sand castles, watch themselves perform on closed-circuit TV, operate a giant ball-moving machine, and get inside an imaginary waterfall (after donning raincoats, of course). Other exhibits rotate every few months. ⊠ *275 Centennial Olympic Park Dr. NW, Downtown* ☎ *404/659–5437* ⊕ *www.imagineit-cma.org* ✆ *$11* ☉ *Weekdays 10–4, weekends 10–5.*

☾ ㉑ **World of Coca-Cola.** At this three-story facility, you can sip samples of Coca-Cola Company products from around the world and peruse more than a century's worth of memorabilia from the corporate archives. The gift shop, predictably named Everything Coca-Cola, sells everything from refrigerator magnets to evening bags. At this writing, work was well under way for the new World of Coca-Cola, at Centennial Olympic Park near the Georgia Aquarium. The new facility, twice the size of the old one, will have space to display 1,500 artifacts. ⊠ *55 Martin Luther King Jr. Dr., Downtown* ☎ *404/676–5151* ⊕ *www.woccatlanta.com* ✆ *$9* ☉ *June–Aug., Mon.–Sat. 9–6, Sun. 11–5; Sept.–May, Mon.–Sat. 9–5, Sun. 11–5.*

☾ ❷ **Zoo Atlanta.** This zoo has nearly 1,000 animals living in naturalistic habitats. The gorillas and tigers are always a hit, as are two giant pandas named Yang Yang and Lun Lun. Children can ride the endangered species carousel, meet new friends at the petting zoo; the whole family can take a ride on the Norfolk Southern Zoo Express Train. To reach the zoo by car, take Interstate 20 east to Exit 59A and turn right on Boulevard. Follow the signs to the zoo, which is right near the Atlanta Cyclorama & Civil War Museum. ⊠ *800 Cherokee Ave. SE, Grant Park* ☎ *404/624–5600* ⊕ *www.zooatlanta.org* ✆ *$18* ☉ *Daily 9:30–4:30.*

Also Worth Seeing

⓫ *Atlanta Journal-Constitution.* In its more than a century of continuous publication, the city's—and the state's—dominant newspaper has employed such illustrious writers as Reconstruction-era "New South"–proponent Henry Grady, Uncle Remus–creator Joel Chandler Harris, *Gone With the Wind*–author Margaret Mitchell, and civil rights advocate Ralph McGill. ⊠ *72 Marietta St., Downtown* ☎ *404/526–5151.*

⓳ **City Hall.** When this 14-story neo-Gothic building, designed by Atlanta architect G. Lloyd Preacher, was erected in 1929, critics dubbed it the "Painted Lady of Mitchell Street." The newer wing, with its five-story glass atrium and beautiful marble entryway, houses frequently changing shows of local art. ⊠ *68 Mitchell St., Downtown* ☎ *404/330–6000* ☉ *Weekdays 8:30–5.*

③ Flatiron Building. The English-American Building, as it was originally known, was designed by Bradford Gilbert. Similar to the famous New York City Flatiron Building, built in the early 1900s, this 11-story building dates from 1897 and is the city's oldest skyscraper. ☒ *84 Peachtree St. NW, Downtown* ⊙ *Weekdays 9–5:30.*

> **HELP AT HAND**
>
> Need a helping hand—or simply directions—while exploring downtown? Watch for a member of the **Atlanta Ambassador Force** (⊕ www.atlantadowntown.com). The members, easily recognized by their pith helmets, are a traveler's best friend.

⑯ Georgia Dome. This arena accommodates 71,250 spectators with good visibility from every seat; it's the site of Atlanta Falcons football games and other sporting events, conventions, and trade shows. The white, plum, and turquoise 1.6 million-square-foot facility is crowned with the world's largest cable-supported oval, giving the roof a circus-tent top. Hourlong tours, given Tuesday to Saturday, take you everywhere from the press box to the locker rooms. ☒ *1 Georgia Dome Dr., Downtown* ☏ *404/223–8687* ⊕ *www.gadome.com* ☒ *Tours: $6* ⊙ *Tours: Tues.–Sat. 10–3.*

★ ⑱ Georgia State Capitol. The capitol, a Renaissance-style edifice, was dedicated on July 4, 1889. The gold leaf on its dome was mined in nearby Dahlonega. Inside, the **Georgia Capitol Museum** houses exhibits on its history. On the grounds, state historical markers commemorate the 1864 Battle of Atlanta, which destroyed nearly all of the city. Statues memorialize a 19th-century Georgia governor and his wife (Joseph and Elizabeth Brown), a Confederate general (John B. Gordon), and a former senator (Richard B. Russell). Former governor and president Jimmy Carter is depicted with his sleeves rolled up, a man at work. ■ **TIP→ Fans of Martin Luther King Jr. should visit the governor's wall, where a portrait of the civil rights leader was unveiled in 2006.** ☒ *206 Washington St., Downtown* ☏ *404/656–2844* ⊕ *www.sos.state.ga.us/museum/default.htm* ⊙ *Museum weekdays 8–5; guided tours weekdays at 10, 11, 1, and 2; additional tours at 9:30 and 10:30 during Jan.–Mar. legislative session.*

⑨ Hurt Building. Named for Atlanta developer Joel Hurt, this restored 1913 Chicago-style high-rise is known for its intricate grillwork. The lower level is filled with shops and art galleries. The excellent City Grill restaurant is at the top of a sweeping marble staircase. ☒ *50 Hurt Plaza, Downtown.*

⑫ J. Mack Robinson College of Business. Atlanta architect Phillip Trammel Shutze designed this 14-story edifice, originally known as the Empire Building, in 1901. In 1929 Shutze refashioned the first three floors, bestowing on them a decidedly Renaissance look. This was one of the city's first steel-frame structures, but during the renovation Shutze resheathed the base with masonry. The edifice is also known as the Bank of America Building, the NationsBank Building, the Citizens & Southern National Bank Building, and the Atlanta Trust Company Building. ☒ *35 Broad St., Downtown.*

❺ Margaret Mitchell Square. A cascading waterfall and columned sculpture are highlights of this park named for one of Atlanta's most famous authors, whose masterpiece is *Gone With the Wind.* ⊠ *Peachtree St. at Forsyth St. NW, Downtown.*

★ **❼ Museum of Design Atlanta.** In the Peachtree Center in the Marquis Two Tower, MODA is the only museum in the southeast devoted exclusively to design. It features exhibitions on fashion, graphics, architecture, furniture, and product design. ⊠ *285 Peachtree Center Ave., Downtown* ☏ *404/ 979–6455* ⊕ *www.museumofdesign.org* ☞ *Free* ☉ *Tues.–Sat. 11–5.*

❻ Peachtree Center. John Portman designed this skyscraper complex, built between 1960 and 1992. Across the street from this collection of shops and restaurants, connected by skywalks, is the massive **AmericasMart-Atlanta** wholesale market. Two additional Portman creations, the **Atlanta Marriott Marquis** and the **Hyatt Regency Atlanta** hotels, are also connected by skywalks. A MARTA station is convenient to Peachtree Center. ⊠ *231 Peachtree St. NE, Downtown* ☏ *404/654–1296* ⊕ *www. peachtreecenter.com.*

⓴ Shrine of the Immaculate Conception. During the Battle of Atlanta, pastor Thomas O'Reilly persuaded Union forces to spare his church and several others around the city. That 1848 structure was then torn down to make room for this much grander building, whose cornerstone was laid in 1869. The church was nearly lost to fire in 1982 but has been exquisitely restored. ■ TIP→ **To view the church, contact the rectory for an appointment.** ⊠ *48 Martin Luther King Jr. Dr., at Central Ave., Downtown* ☏ *404/521–1866* ☉ *By appointment only.*

❿ Statue of Henry Grady. Alexander Doyle's bronze sculpture honors Henry Grady, editor of the old *Atlanta Constitution* and early advocate of the so-called New South. The memorial was raised in 1891, after Grady's untimely death at age 39. ⊠ *Marietta and Forsyth Sts., Downtown.*

⓱ Underground Atlanta. Dotted with historic markers, this six-block entertainment and shopping district was created from the web of subterranean brick streets, ornamental facades, and tunnels that fell into disuse in 1929, when the city built viaducts over the train tracks. Merchants then moved their storefronts to the upper level, leaving the original street level for storage. The Atlanta Convention & Visitors Bureau has a visitor center on the upper level. Today the facility houses restaurants, nightclubs, shops, galleries, and a food court. The district continues to have its ups and downs—many of the upper-level shops are currently empty. ■ TIP→ **AtlanTIX, a half-price ticket outlet theater and cultural attractions, is in Underground Atlanta. It's open 11 to 6 Tuesday to Saturday, noon to 4 Sunday.** ⊠ *50 Upper Alabama St., Downtown* ☏ *404/ 523–2311* ⊕ *www.underground-atlanta.com.*

OFF THE BEATEN PATH

HAMMONDS HOUSE – The handsome Eastlake Victorian house that belonged to Otis Thrash Hammonds, as well as his fine collection of Victorian furnishings and his paintings, are the focal point of this museum. The permanent and visiting exhibitions are devoted chiefly to works by African-American artists, although art from anywhere in the African-influenced world can be a focus. ⊠ *503 Peeples St., West End* ☎ *404/ 335–2411* ⊕ *www.hammondshouse.org* ⊠ *$4* ⊙ *Tues.–Fri. 10–6, weekends 1–5.*

WREN'S NEST HOUSE MUSEUM – Joel Chandler Harris, author of the Uncle Remus tales, lived in this rambling cottage in Atlanta's West End from 1881 until his death in 1908. Forty years later Walt Disney filmed *Song of the South,* based on Harris's stories, on the property. ⊠ *1050 Ralph David Abernathy Blvd., West End* ☎ *404/753–7735* ⊠ *$8* ⊙ *Tues.–Sat. 10–2:30.*

❹ Woodruff Park. This triangular park named for the city's great philanthropist, Robert W. Woodruff, the late Coca-Cola magnate, fills during lunchtime on weekdays with business executives, street preachers, university students, and homeless people. Nearby restaurants catering to the office crowd make it an easy place to enjoy a take-out lunch. ⊠ *Bordered by Edgewood and Peachtree Sts., Downtown.*

Sweet Auburn

Between 1890 and 1930, the historic Sweet Auburn district was Atlanta's most active and prosperous center of black business, entertainment, and political life. Following the Depression, the area went into an economic decline that lasted until the 1980s, when the residential area where civil rights leader Reverend Martin Luther King Jr. (1929–68) was born, raised, and later returned to live was declared a National Historic District.

Main Attractions

★ **㉔ African-American Panoramic Experience (APEX).** The museum's quarterly exhibits chronicle the history of black people in America. Videos illustrate the history of Sweet Auburn, the name bestowed on Auburn Avenue by businessman John Wesley Dobbs, who fostered business development for African-Americans on this street. ⊠ *135 Auburn Ave., Sweet Auburn* ☎ *404/521–2739* ⊕ *www.apexmuseum.org* ⊠ *$4* ⊙ *June–Aug. and Feb., Tues.–Sat. 10–5, Sun. 1–5; Sept.–Jan. and Mar.–May, Tues.–Sat. 10–5.*

㉜ Ebenezer Baptist Church. A Gothic revival–style building completed in 1922, the church came to be known as the spiritual center of the civil rights movement. Members of the King family, including the slain civil rights leader, preached at the church for three generations. A tour of the church, which is managed by the National Park Service, includes an audiotape outlining the building's history. The congregation itself now occupies the building across the street. ■ TIP→ **A federally funded restoration project is planned for the original church. Call before visiting.** ⊠ *407 Auburn Ave., Sweet Auburn* ☎ *404/688–7263* ⊠ *Free* ⊙ *Tours: Mon.–Sat. 9–5, Sun. 1–5* ⊕ *www.historicebenezer.org.*

Fodor'sChoice ★

㉚ Martin Luther King Jr. National Historic Site and Birth Home. The modest Queen Anne–style residence is where Martin Luther King Jr. was born and raised. Besides items that belonged to the family, the house contains an outstanding multimedia exhibit focused on the civil rights movement. To sign up for guided tours, go to the **National Park Service Visitor Cen-**

Fodor'sChoice ★

ter (⊠ 450 Auburn Ave., Sweet Auburn), across the street from the Martin Luther King Jr. Center for Nonviolent Social Change. Parking is on the corner of John Wesley Dobbs Street and Boulevard, behind the visitor center. ■ TIP→ **A limited number of visitors are allowed to tour the house each day. Advance reservations are not possible, so sign up early in the day.** ⊠ *501 Auburn Ave., Sweet Auburn* ☎ *404/331–5190 Ext. 3017* ⊕ *www.nps.gov/malu* ⊠ *Free* ☉ *Tours: daily 10–5.*

③① Martin Luther King Jr. Center for Nonviolent Social Change. The Martin Luther King Jr. National Historic District occupies several blocks on Auburn Avenue, a few blocks east of Peachtree Street in the black business and residential community of Sweet Auburn. Martin Luther King Jr. was born here in 1929; after his assassination in 1968, his widow, Coretta Scott King, established this center, which exhibits such personal items as King's Nobel Peace Prize, bible, and tape recorder, along with memorabilia and photos chronicling the civil rights movement. In the courtyard in front of Freedom Hall, on a circular brick pad in the middle of the rectangular Meditation Pool, is Dr. King's white-marble tomb; the inscription reads; Free at last, Free at last, Thank God Almighty I'm Free at last. Nearby, an eternal flame burns. A chapel of all faiths sits at one end of the reflecting pool. Mrs. King, who passed away in 2006, is also entombed at the center. ⊠ *449 Auburn Ave., Sweet Auburn* ☎ *404/526–8900* ⊕ *www.thekingcenter.org* ⊠ *Free* ☉ *Daily 9–5.*

Also Worth Seeing

㉓ *Atlanta Daily World* Building. This simple two-story brick building, banded with a white frieze of lion heads, was constructed in the early 1900s. Since 1945 it has housed one of the nation's oldest black newspapers. Publisher Alexis Scott is the granddaughter of William A. Scott II, who founded the paper in 1928. ⊠ *145 Auburn Ave., Sweet Auburn* ☎ *404/659–1110* ⊕ *www.atlantadailyworld.com.*

㉕ Atlanta Life Insurance Company. The landmark enterprise, founded by former slave Alonzo Herndon, began in modest quarters at 148 Auburn Avenue. It moved to this modern complex in 1980. The lobby exhibits art by black artists from the United States and Africa. ⊠ *100 Auburn Ave., Sweet Auburn* ☎ *404/659–2100* ☉ *Weekdays 8–5.*

OFF THE
BEATEN
PATH

HERNDON HOME – Alonzo Herndon (1858–1927) emerged from slavery and founded both a chain of successful barbershops and the Atlanta Life Insurance Company. He traveled extensively and influenced the cultural life around Atlanta's traditionally black colleges. Alonzo's son, Norris, created a foundation to preserve the handsome Beaux-Arts home as a museum. ⊠ *587 University Pl. NW, near Morris Brown College, Vine City* ☎ *404/581–9813* ⊠ *$5* ☉ *Tours Tues. and Thurs. 10–4, or by appointment.*

㉖ Auburn Avenue Research Library on African-American Culture and History. An extension of the Atlanta-Fulton Public Library, this unit houses a noncirculating collection of about 60,000 volumes dealing with topics of African-American interest. The archives contains art and artifacts, transcribed oral histories, and rare books, pamphlets, and periodicals.

There are frequent special events, all free to the public. ✉ *101 Auburn Ave., Sweet Auburn* ☎ *404/730–4001* ⊕ *www.afplweb.com/aarl* ⊗ *Mon.–Thurs. 10–8, Fri. and Sat. noon–6, Sun. 2–6.*

㉒ **Baptist Student Union.** This restored Victorian building adjacent to the Georgia State University campus once contained the Coca-Cola Company's first bottling plant. ✉ *125 Edgewood Ave., Sweet Auburn* ☎ *404/659–8726.*

㉘ **John Wesley Dobbs Plaza.** John Wesley Dobbs was an important civic leader whose legacy includes coining the name "Sweet Auburn" for this neighborhood. The plaza, which was built for the 1996 Olympic Games, has a life mask of Dobbs himself; children playing here can view the street through the his eyes. ✉ *Auburn Ave. adjacent to I–75/85 overpass, Sweet Auburn.*

OFF THE
BEATEN
PATH

OAKLAND CEMETERY – Established in 1850 in the Victorian style, Atlanta's oldest cemetery was designed to serve as a public park as well as a burial ground. Some of the 70,000 permanent residents include six governors, five Confederate generals, and 6,900 Confederate soldiers. Also here are novelist Margaret Mitchell and golfing great Bobby Jones. You can bring a picnic lunch or take a tour conducted by the Historic Oakland Foundation. The King Memorial MARTA station on the east–west line also serves the cemetery. ✉ *248 Oakland Ave., Sweet Auburn* ☎ *404/688–2107* ⊕ *www.oaklandcemetery.com* ⊗ *Tours: Mar.–Nov., Sat. at 10 and 2, Sun. at 2.*

㉙ **Odd Fellows Building.** The Georgia Chapter of the Grand United Order of Odd Fellows was a trade and social organization for African-Americans. In 1912 the membership erected this handsome Romanesque revival–style building. Terra-cotta figures adorn the splendid entrance. Now handsomely restored, the building houses offices. ✉ *236 Auburn Ave., Sweet Auburn* ☎ *404/525–5027* ⊗ *Weekdays 9–5.*

㉗ **Sweet Auburn Curb Market.** The market, an institution on Edgewood Avenue since 1923, sells flowers, fruits, and vegetables, and a variety of meat—everything from fresh catfish to foot-long oxtails. Vendors also include an Italian deli, an organic coffee shop, and a smoothie shop. Individual stalls are run by their owners, making this a true public market. Don't miss the splendid totemic sculptures by Atlanta artist Carl Joe Williams. ✉ *209 Edgewood Ave., Sweet Auburn* ☎ *404/659–1665* ⊗ *Mon.–Sat. 8–6.*

Midtown

Midtown Atlanta—north of downtown and south of Buckhead—has earned its own place in the Atlanta landscape. Four-miles square, its skyline of gleaming office towers rivals that of downtown. The renovated mansions and bungalows in its residential section have made it a city showcase. The newly expanded Woodruff Arts Center, the nation's largest performing- and visual-arts center, is here, as are 25 other arts and cultural venues. Piedmont Park and the Atlanta Botanical Garden are also here. The neighborhood is the hub for the city's sizeable gay community.

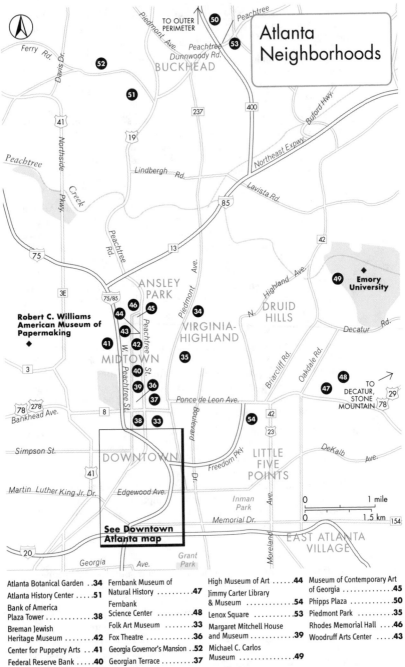

Atlanta Neighborhoods

Main Attractions

Atlanta Botanical Garden. Occupying 30 acres inside Piedmont Park, the grounds contain acres of display gardens, including a 2-acre interactive children's garden; a hardwood forest with walking trails; the Fuqua Conservatory, which has unusual and threatened flora from tropical and desert climates; and the award-winning Fuqua Orchid Center, with a spectacular collection of tropical and high-elevation orchids. A variety of special exhibits take place throughout the year. ✉ *1345 Piedmont Ave., Midtown* ☎ *404/876–5859* ⊕ *www.atlantabotanicalgarden.org* ✄ *$12* ⊙ *Apr.–Oct., Tues.–Sun. 9–7; Nov.–Mar., Tues.–Sun. 9–5.*

Bank of America Plaza Tower. At 1,023 feet, this is the South's tallest building. The 1992 skyscraper's graceful birdcage roof is easily visible from the highway. The elegant marble central lobby is worth a glimpse. ✉ *600 Peachtree St. NE, Midtown* ☎ *404/607–4850* ⊙ *Mon.–Thurs. 8:30–4, Fri. 8:30–6.*

Center for Puppetry Arts. The largest puppetry organization in the country houses a museum where you can see more than 350 puppets from around the world. Make sure to check out the furry and funny creatures from Jim Henson's productions. Elaborate performances, which include original works and classics adapted for stage, are presented by professional puppeteers—youngsters and adults alike are spellbound. In particular, the popular Christmas performance of *The Velveteen Rabbit* is a truly magical experience. ✉ *1404 Spring St., at 18th St., Midtown* ☎ *404/873–3391* ⊕ *www.puppet.org* ✄ *$16* ⊙ *Wed.–Sat. 9–5, Sun. 11–5.*

OFF THE BEATEN PATH

EAST ATLANTA VILLAGE – This earthy outpost of edgy-cool shops and restaurants evolved, beginning in 1996, thanks to a group of proprietors with dreams much bigger than their bank accounts: spurning the high rents of fancier parts of town, they set up businesses in this then-blighted but beautiful ruin of a neighborhood 4 mi southeast of downtown. Soon artists and trendoids came to soak up the ensuing creative atmosphere. East Atlanta, which is centered at Flat Shoals and Glenwood avenues, just southeast of Moreland Avenue at Interstate 20, area has had its ups and downs, but after new streetscapes were installed in 2005, it's seeing a resurgence. The majestic homes have almost all been renovated, and what remains unrestored seems simply to romanticize the area's hint of "fashionable" danger. Check out the delightfully funky gift shop called **Traders Neighborhood Store** (✉ 485-B Flat Shoals Ave., East Atlanta ☎ 404/522–3006).

Fox Theatre. One of a dwindling number of vintage movie palaces in the nation, the Fox was built in 1929 in a fabulous Moorish-Egyptian style. The interior's crowning glory is its ceiling, complete with

---

GARDEN SPOTS

Atlantans love their gardens—and the chance to show them off. **Garden tours** are plentiful in spring, so check the *Atlanta Journal-Constitution* (⊕ www.ajc.com). December brings tours of the inside of many similar houses, all done up for the holidays.

moving clouds and twinkling stars above Alhambra-like minarets. Threatened by demolition in the 1970s, the Fox was saved from the wrecker's ball by community activists. Today it's still a prime venue for musicals, rock concerts, dance performances, and film festivals. ■ TIP→ **Tours, conducted by Atlanta Preservation Center, should be scheduled in advance.** ⊠ *660 Peachtree St. NE, Midtown* ☎ *404/881–2100 for box office, 404/688–3353 for tours* ⊕ *www.foxtheatre.org* ▣ *Tour: $10* ⊙ *Tour: Mon., Wed., and Thurs. at 10, Sat. at 10 and 11.*

★ **㊹ High Museum of Art.** This museum's permanent collection includes 19th- and 20-century American works, including many by African-American artists. It also displays contemporary art. The building itself is a work of art; the American Institute of Architects listed the sleek structure, designed by Richard Meier, among the 10 best works of American architecture of the 1980s. An expansion designed by Renzo Piano opened in 2005. At this writing, a three-year partnership with the Louvre Museum in Paris was scheduled to begin in late 2006, making available hundreds of works from the Parisian museum's collection. ■ TIP→ **On the third Friday of every month, the museum is open until 10 PM.** ⊠ *Woodruff Arts Center, 1280 Peachtree St., Midtown* ☎ *404/733–4400, 404/733–4444 recorded information* ⊕ *www.high.org* ▣ *$15* ⊙ *Tues., Wed., Fri., and Sat. 10–5, Thurs. 10–8, Sun. noon–5.*

㊴ Margaret Mitchell House & Museum. While she wrote her masterpiece, the author of *Gone With the Wind* lived in a turn-of-the-20th-century apartment house she called "the Dump." Volunteers gathered the funds necessary to restore the building in the early 1990s. To many Atlantans, the Margaret Mitchell House symbolizes the conflict between promoting the city's heritage and respecting its roots. The house has been struck by arsonists twice, in 1994 and 1996, the second time within days of a scheduled opening after a major restoration. Some say the city's most famous writer should not be lauded, as her book includes stereotypes of African-Americans during the Civil War. However, her fans point out that she helped to fund medical-school scholarships to Morehouse College for scores of African-American students. The visitor center exhibits photographs, archival material, and personal possessions. ⊠ *990 Peachtree St., at Peachtree Pl., Midtown* ☎ *404/249–7015* ⊕ *www.gwtw.org* ▣ *$12* ⊙ *Daily 9:30–5.*

Also Worth Seeing

㊷ Breman Jewish Heritage Museum. The history of the Jewish community in Atlanta is told through a permanent exhibit called "Creating Community." Other exhibits document the Holocaust and the immigrant experience in America. The facility—the largest archive of Georgia Jewish history—also contains a research library and an education center. ⊠ *1440 Spring St., Midtown* ☎ *678/222–3700* ⊕ *www.thebreman.org* ▣ *$6* ⊙ *Mon.–Thurs. 10–5, Fri. 10–3, Sun. 1–5.*

㊵ Federal Reserve Bank. The exhibits within this grand, monetary museum explain the story of money as a medium of exchange and the history of the U.S. banking system. Items displayed include rare coins, uncut sheets of money, and a gold bar. The self-guided tour includes a video called

The Fed Today. ✉ *1000 Peachtree St. NE, Midtown* ☎ *404/498–8777* ⊕ *www.frbatlanta.org* 🖙 *Free* ⊙ *Weekdays 9–4.*

㉝ Folk Art Park. This open-air exhibit gathers works that reflect the diverse styles of the country's (especially Southern) folk art. Works by more than a dozen artists are on display, among them Harold Rittenberry, Howard Finster, and Eddie Owens Martin. Martin's brightly painted totems and snake-top walls replicate portions of Pasaquan, the legendary visionary environment that Martin created at his farm near Columbus, Georgia. ✉ *Ralph McGill Blvd. at Courtland St., Baker St., and Piedmont Ave., Midtown.*

㊲ Georgian Terrace. The oldest hotel in the city of Atlanta, Georgian Terrace is known as the Grande Dame of the South. Built in 1911, the Beaux-Arts style hotel housed the stars of the film *Gone With the Wind* when it premiered in 1939 at the nearby Loew's Theater (now demolished). Stars of the Metropolitan Opera stayed at the hotel when the Met used to make its annual trek to Atlanta, and according to locals, Enrico Caruso routinely serenaded passersby from its balconies. President Calvin Coolidge is among the other dignitaries who slept here. Renovated in 1991, the building is now a luxury hotel. ✉ *659 Peachtree St. NE, Midtown* ☎ *404/897–1991 or 800/651–2316* ⊕ *www.thegeorgianterrace.com.*

㊺ Museum of Contemporary Art of Georgia (MOCA GA). Georgia's visual artists are showcased in this office-building lobby. More than 400 paintings, sculptures, and other works are part of the permanent collection. ✉ *1447 Peachtree St. NE, Midtown* ☎ *404/881–1109* ⊕ *www.mocaga.org* 🖙 *Free* ⊙ *Tues.–Sat. 10–5.*

☾ ㉟ Piedmont Park. The city's outdoor recreation center, this park has been a popular destination since the late 19th century. Tennis courts, a swimming pool, and paths for walking, jogging, and rollerblading are part of the attraction, but many retreat to the park's great lawn for picnics with a smashing view of the Midtown skyline. Each April the park hosts the popular Dogwood Festival. ✉ *Piedmont Ave. between 10th St. and Monroe Dr., Midtown* ⊕ *www.piedmontpark.org.*

㊻ Rhodes Memorial Hall. This former residence, now headquarters of the **Georgia Trust for Historic Preservation,** is one of the finest works of Atlanta architect Willis F. Denny II. It was built at the northern edge of the city in 1904 for Amos Giles Rhodes, the wealthy founder of a Southern furniture chain. The stained-glass windows in the hall depict the rise and fall of the Confederacy. ✉ *1516 Peachtree St., Midtown* ☎ *404/ 881–9980* ⊕ *www.georgiatrust.org* 🖙 *$5; $8 for Sun. behind-the-scenes tour* ⊙ *Weekdays 11–4, Sun. noon–3.*

Robert C. Williams American Museum of Papermaking. More than 10,000 tools, machines, papers, and watermarks, plus manuscripts and books, trace the history of papermaking from its origins. The museum is housed at the Georgia Institute of Technology's Institute of Paper Science and Technology. ✉ *500 10th St. NW, Midtown* ☎ *404/894–7840* ⊕ *www. ipst.gatech.edu/amp* 🖙 *Free* ⊙ *Weekdays 9–5.*

In Search of the Old South

GONE WITH THE WIND enthusiasts coming to Atlanta for the first time are often disappointed to discover that Scarlett O'Hara's beloved plantation, Tara, was no more real than Scarlett herself. But history buffs can find antebellum treasures in towns like Marietta and Kennesaw (about 20 mi northwest of Atlanta) and Roswell (about 23 mi north of Atlanta).

Marietta was occupied by Union troops in the summer of 1864 as they marched south toward Atlanta. The town square and some other buildings were burned, but many of the gracious old homes remained. The **Marietta Museum of History** (✉ 1 Depot St. NE, Marietta ☎ 770/528–0431 ⊕ www.mariettahistory.org), on the 2nd floor of the historic 1845 Kennesaw House, traces the history of Cobb County. The **Marietta Gone With the Wind Museum** (✉ 18 Whitlock Ave. ☎ 770/794–5576 ⊕ www.mariettaga.gov/gonewind) pays homage to the movie with props and costumes.

A few miles north of Marietta are two sights not to be missed by Civil War buffs. The 2,884-acre **Kennesaw Mountain National Battlefield** (✉ Old U.S. 41 and Stilesboro Rd., Kennesaw ☎ 770/427–4686 ⊕ www.nps.gov/kemo) was the site for crucial battles in 1864. The National Park Service maintains 16 mi of well-used hiking trails. On weekends a shuttle bus to the top of the mountain runs every half-hour. A small museum has uniforms, weapons, and other items from the era. The fascinating **Southern Museum of Civil War and Locomotive History** (✉ 2829 Cherokee St., Kennesaw ☎ 770/427–2117 ⊕ www.southernmuseum.org) is

the home of the General, a locomotive stolen by Union forces from the Confederates during the Civil War. Although the General is hard to beat, don't miss the large Glover Machine Works factory display, which includes the country's only restored belt-driven locomotive assembly line.

Roswell's historic district is listed on the National Register of Historic Places. Like Marietta and other nearby towns, it was occupied by Union forces in 1864. They burned down its mills and charged the 400 women and children who had produced cloth for Confederate uniforms with treason. The Roswell Presbyterian Church served as a hospital during the war. Three of the historic founders' homes, all built in the 1840s, survived the war and are open daily for tours. **Barrington Hall** (✉ 535 Barrington Dr., Roswell ☎ 770/640–3253 ⊕ www.cvb.roswell.ga.us) is widely recognized as one of the nation's best examples of Greek-revival architecture. **Bulloch Hall** (✉ 180 Bulloch Ave., Roswell ☎ 770/640–3253 ⊕ www.cvb.roswell.ga.us) was the childhood home of Mittie Roosevelt, mother of President Teddy Roosevelt and grandmother of Eleanor Roosevelt. It has a nice museum shop. The original furniture of the Archibald Smith family fills **Smith Plantation** (✉ 935 Alpharetta St., Roswell ☎ 770/640–3253 ⊕ www.cvb.roswell.ga.us).

43 **Woodruff Arts Center.** The center includes the world-renowned **Atlanta Symphony Orchestra,** the **High Museum of Art,** and the **Alliance Theatre,** plus the nearby **14th Street Playhouse,** which has several repertory companies. Both theaters present contemporary dramas, classics, and frequent world premieres. ⊠ *1280 Peachtree St. NE, Midtown* ☎ *404/733–4200* ⊕ *www.woodruffcenter.org.*

Buckhead

Many of Atlanta's trendy restaurants, music clubs, chic shops, and hip art galleries are concentrated in this neighborhood. Atlanta's sprawl doesn't lend itself to walking between major neighborhoods, so take a car or MARTA to reach Buckhead. Finding a parking spot on the weekends and at night can be a real headache, and waits of two hours or more are common in the hottest restaurants.

> ### THE BUC STOPS HERE
>
> **The Buc** (☎ 404/812-7433 ⊕ www.bucride.com) is a free bus shuttle service linking two MARTA stations, the Buckhead station and the Lenox station. It also stops at major hotels in central Buckhead, making it an easy way to get to the subway. It runs every day except Sunday. Route maps are available at all stops.

Main Attractions

51 **Atlanta History Center.** Life in Atlanta, the South, and the Civil War are the focus of this fascinating museum. Displays are provocative, juxtaposing *Gone With the Wind* romanticism with the grim reality of Ku Klux Klan racism. Newest on the scene is a two-story addition highlighting the history of the Olympics, focusing on the 1996 Centennial Olympic Games in Atlanta. Also on the 33-acre site are the elegant 1928 **Swan House** mansion and the newly restored plantation house that is part of **Tullie Smith Farm.** The Kenan Research Center houses traveling exhibitions and an extensive archival collection. Lunch is served at the Swan Coach House, which also has a gallery and a gift shop. ⊠ *130 W. Paces Ferry Rd. NW, Buckhead* ☎ *404/814–4000* ⊕ *www.atlantahistorycenter.com* ⊠ *$15* ⊙ *Mon.–Sat. 10–5:30, Sun. noon–5:30.*

Fodor'sChoice
★

Also Worth Seeing

52 **Georgia Governor's Mansion.** This 24,000-square-foot 1967 Greek-revival mansion contains 30 rooms with federal-period antiques. It sits on 18 acres that originally belonged to the Robert Maddox family (no relation to Georgia governor Lester Maddox, who was its first occupant). ■ TIP→ Reservations are necessary for parties of 10 or more. ⊠ *391 W. Paces Ferry Rd. NW, Buckhead* ☎ *404/261–1776* ⊕ *www.gov.state.ga.us/about_mansion.shtml* ⊠ *Free* ⊙ *Tours: Tues.–Thurs. 10–11:30.*

53 **Lenox Square.** Anchored by Bloomingdale's, Neiman Marcus, and Macy's, this mall is a popular shopping destination. It offers more than 250 chain and specialty stores and several upscale restaurants, as well as an extensive food court. A MARTA station sits right across the street. ⊠ *3393 Peachtree Rd., Buckhead* ☎ *404/233–6767* ⊕ *www.lenoxsquare.com.*

⑤⓪ Phipps Plaza. The luxury marble-floor mall is one of Atlanta's premier shopping areas, with nearly 100 upscale chain stores. It also includes a 14-screen movie theater. ✉ *3500 Peachtree Rd., Buckhead* ☎ *404/262–0992 or 800/810–7700* ⊕ *www.phippsplaza.com.*

Virginia-Highland & the Emory Area

Restaurants, art galleries, and boutiques are sprinkled throughout Virginia-Highland/Morningside, northeast of Midtown. Like Midtown, this residential area was down-at-the-heels in the 1970s. Reclaimed by writers, artists, and a few visionary developers, Virginia-Highland (as well as bordering Morningside) is a great place to explore. To the east, the Emory University area is studded with enviable mansions. Near the Emory University campus is Druid Hills, the location for the film *Driving Miss Daisy,* by local playwright Alfred Uhry. The neighborhood was designed by the firm of Frederick Law Olmsted, which also designed New York's Central Park.

> ### THE NAME GAME
>
> Founded in 1837 by the Western & Atlantic Railroad, Atlanta has changed names several times. It was nicknamed Terminus, for its location at the end of the tracks. Marthasville was its first official name, in honor of the then-governor's daughter. It switched soon afterward to Atlanta, the feminine of Atlantic—another nod to the railroad.

Main Attractions

★ ☺ **④⑦ Fernbank Museum of Natural History.** One of the largest natural-history museums south of the Smithsonian Institution in Washington, D.C., holds a permanent exhibit, "A Walk Through Time in Georgia." You can meander through 17 galleries to explore the earth's natural history, or watch a film in the on-site IMAX theater. Another special feature is "Giants of the Mesozoic," which includes an exact replica of the world's largest dinosaur. The café, with an exquisite view of the forest, serves great food. ✉ *767 Clifton Rd., Emory* ☎ *404/929–6300* ⊕ *www.fernbankmuseum. org* ✎ *$12* ☉ *Museum Mon.–Sat. 10–5, Sun. noon–5; IMAX Mon.–Thurs. 10–5, Fri. 10–10, Sat. 10–5, Sun. noon–5.*

★ **⑤④ Jimmy Carter Presidential Library & Museum.** This complex occupies the site where Union General William T. Sherman orchestrated the Battle of Atlanta (1864). The museum and archives detail the political career of former president Jimmy Carter. The adjacent Carter Center, which is not open to the public, focuses on conflict resolution and human rights issues. Outside, the Japanese-style garden is a serene spot to unwind. Both Carter and former First Lady Rosalynn Carter maintain offices here. ✉ *441 Freedom Pkwy., Virginia-Highland* ☎ *404/865–7100* ⊕ *www. jimmycarterlibrary.org* ✎ *$8* ☉ *Mon.–Sat. 9–4:45, Sun. noon–4:45.*

★ ☺ **④⑨ Michael C. Carlos Museum.** Housing a permanent collection of more than 16,000 objects, this excellent museum designed by renowned American architect Michael Graves exhibits artifacts from Egypt, Greece, Rome, the Near East, the Americas, and Africa. European and American prints and drawings cover the Middle Ages through the 20th century. The gift shop sells rare art books, jewelry, and art-focused items for children. The museum's Caffé Antico is a good lunch spot. ☒ *Emory University, 571 S. KilgoCircle, Emory* ☎ *404/727–4282* ☞ *$7* ⊕ *www.carlos. emory.edu* ☉ *Tues.–Sat. 10–5, Sun. noon–5.*

Also Worth Seeing

☾ ➋ **Fernbank Science Center.** The museum, in the 65-acre Fernbank Forest, focuses on ecology, geology, space exploration. In addition to the exhibit hall, there's an observatory with shows on Thursday at 8, Friday at 3 and 8, Saturday at 11, 1:30 and 3, and Sunday at 1:30 and 3. ☒ *156 Heaton Park Dr., Emory* ☎ *678/874–7102* ⊕ *www.fernbanksciencecenter. org* ☞ *$4* ☉ *Mon.–Wed. 8:30–5, Thurs. and Fri. 8:30 AM–10 PM, Sat. 10–5, Sun. 1–5.*

OFF THE BEATEN PATH

INMAN PARK AND LITTLE FIVE POINTS – Since this once-grand neighborhood about 4 mi east of downtown was laid out by famous developer Joel Hurt in 1889, the area has faded and flourished a number of times, which explains the vast gaps in opulence evident in much of the architecture here. Huge, ornate Victorian mansions sit next to humble shotgun shacks. But no matter the exact address or style of home—be it modest or massive—all of Inman Park now commands considerable cachet among all types, from young families to empty nesters to gays and lesbians. Here you'll also find the delightfully countercultural Little Five Points section, ground zero for Atlanta funk. Though many of the storefronts here where Moreland, Euclid, and McLendon avenues intersect defy description, all are delightful. Check out the fascinating **Junkman's Daughter** (☒ 464 Moreland Ave. NE, Inman Park ☎ 404/577–3188), a funky-junky department store. The **Clothing Warehouse** (☒ 420 Moreland Ave., Inman Park ☎ 404/524–5070) is one of the many colorful vintage-clothing stores here. **A Capella Books** (☒ 1133 Euclid Ave. NE, Inman Park ☎ 404/681–5128) stocks some 25,000 new and out-of-print titles.

Other Area Attractions

It's essential to drive to most of these venues, so plan your visits with Atlanta's notorious rush hours in mind.

☾ **Chattahoochee Nature Center.** Birds and animals in their natural habitats may be seen from nature trails and a boardwalk winding through 124 acres of woodlands and wetlands. A gift shop, indoor exhibits, birds-of-prey aviaries, and a picnic area are on the property. ☒ *9135 Willeo Rd., Roswell* ☎ *770/992–2055* ⊕ *www.chattnaturecenter.com* ☞ *$3* ☉ *Mon.–Sat. 9–5, Sun. noon–5.*

Decatur Historical Courthouse. Known as the Old Courthouse on the Square, this charming building was constructed in 1898 and now houses the DeKalb History Center. It's right in the midst of the shops, coffeehouses, and cafés of Decatur's quaint main square. Free concerts are sometimes held in the gazebo behind the Old Courthouse. ■ **TIP→ Getting here is easy, as Decatur has its own stop on MARTA's east–west rail line.** ☒ *101 E. Court Sq., Ponce de Leon Ave., east 8 mi to Decatur Sq. at Clair-*

mont Ave., Decatur ☎ 404/373–1088 🖷 404/373–8287 🌐 www.dekalbhistory.org 🎟 Free ⏲ Weekdays 9–4.

Six Flags Over Georgia. Georgia's major theme park with heart-stopping roller coasters, family rides, and water attractions (best saved for last so you won't be damp all day), is a child's ideal playground. The new Goliath is a giant among roller coasters—at 200 feet, it's the largest in the Southeast. The heart-clenching ride hits speeds of 70 mph. The park also has well-staged musical revues, concerts by top-name artists, and costumed characters such as the Justice League. ■ TIP→ **To get here, take MARTA's west line to the Hamilton Homes station and then hop aboard the Six Flags bus.** ✉ *I–20W at 7561 Six Flags Pkwy., Austell* ☎ *770/948–9290* 🌐 *www.sixflags.com* 🎟 *$50* ⏲ *June–mid-Aug., open daily; mid-Aug.–Oct. and Mar.–May, open weekends; hrs vary.*

HOLDING OUT FOR A HERO

On highways around the city, Georgia Department of Transportation employees can be spotted in yellow trucks emblazoned with the word **HERO.** They can provide enough gas to get to a filling station, fix a flat tire, give your battery some juice, or pull your stranded car to the shoulder. Since 1996, these folks have helped more than 500,000 stranded motorists–and have delivered nine babies. To get roadside help, call *368 on your cell phone or 404/635-6800 from any phone.

★ **Stone Mountain Park.** At this 3,200-acre state park, you'll find the largest exposed granite outcropping on earth. The Confederate Memorial on the north face of the 825-foot-high domed mountain is the world's largest sculpture, measuring 90 feet by 190 feet. There are several ways to see the sculpture, including a cable car that lifts you to the mountaintop and a steam locomotive that chugs around the mountain's base. Summer nights are capped with the **Lasershow Spectacular,** an outdoor light display set to music and projected onto the side of Stone Mountain—attendance is a rite of passage for new Atlantans. Annual events such as the Yellow Daisy Festival and the Scottish Highland Games are popular in the fall. There's also a wildlife preserve, an antebellum plantation, a swimming beach, two golf courses, a campground, a hotel, a resort, several restaurants, and two Civil War museums. Crossroads, an entertainment complex with an 1870s-Southern-town theme, offers costumed interpreters and a movie theater. ✉ *U.S. 78E, Stone Mountain Pkwy., Stone Mountain* ☎ *770/498–5600* 🌐 *www.stonemountainpark.com* 🎟 *$8 per car* ⏲ *Daily 6 AM–midnight.*

★ **Your DeKalb Farmers Market.** This sprawling warehouse store 9 mi east of Atlanta may not be a true farmers' market, but it's truly a market experience to remember. Rows of bins of produce from around the world are perhaps the biggest attraction: root vegetables from Africa, greens from Asia, wines from South America, cheeses from Europe. The store also has one of the largest seafood departments in the country (a few species still swimming) and sizable meat, deli, and wine sections. The reasonably priced cafeteria serves dishes ranging from lasagna to goat stew. ■ TIP→ **The market is accessible by MARTA bus from the Avondale** rail station. ⊠ *3000 E. Ponce de Leon Ave., Decatur* ☎ *404/377–6400* ⊕ *www.dekalbfarmersmarket.com* ☉ *Daily 9–9.*

SPORTS & THE OUTDOORS

At almost any time of the year, in parks, private clubs, and neighborhoods throughout the city, you'll find Atlantans pursuing everything from tennis to soccer to rollerblading. The magazine **Atlanta Sports & Fitness** (☎ 404/843–2257 ⊕ www.atlantasportsmag.com), available free at many health clubs and sports and outdoors stores, is a good link to Atlanta's athletic community.

Baseball

Atlanta's most beloved team, Major League Baseball's **Atlanta Braves** (⊠ 755 Hank Aaron Dr., Downtown ☎ 404/522–7630 ⊕ braves.mlb.com), play in Turner Field, formerly the Olympic Stadium.

Basketball

The **Atlanta Hawks** (⊠ 1 Philips Dr., Downtown ☎ 404/878–3800 ⊕ www.nba.com/hawks) play downtown in Philips Arena.

Biking

Closed to traffic, **Piedmont Park** (⊠ Piedmont Ave. between 10th St. and Monroe Ave., Midtown ⊕ www.piedmontpark.org) is popular for biking, running, dog-walking, and other recreational activities. **Skate Escape** (⊠ 1086 Piedmont Ave., across from Piedmont Park, Midtown ☎ 404/892–1292) rents and sells bikes and in-line skates.

Connecting Atlanta with the Alabama state line, the **Silver Comet Trail** (☎ 404/875–7284 ⊕ www.pathfoundation.org) is very popular with bikers. The trail is asphalt and concrete.

Part of the Atlanta–DeKalb trail system, the **Stone Mountain/Atlanta Greenway Trail** (☎ 404/875–7284 ⊕ www.pathfoundation.org) is a mostly off-road paved path that follows Ponce de Leon Avenue east of the city into Stone Mountain Park. The best place to start the 17-mi trek is the Jimmy Carter Presidential Library & Museum.

Football

The **Atlanta Falcons** (⊠ 1 Georgia Dome Dr., Downtown ☎ 404/223–8000 ⊕ www.atlantafalcons.com) play at the Georgia Dome. In July and August, training camp is held in Flowery Branch, about 40 mi north of Atlanta. There's no charge to watch a practice session.

Georgia Force (⊠ Philips Arena, 1 Philips Dr., Downtown ☎ 404/223–8000 ⊕ www.georgiaforce.com) is part of the Arena Football League, whose season runs February to May.

Golf

Golf is enormously popular here, as the numerous courses attest. The only public course within sight of downtown Atlanta is the **Bobby Jones Golf Course** (⊠ 384 Woodward Way, Buckhead ☎ 404/355–1009), named after the famed golfer and Atlanta native and occupying a portion of the site of the Civil War's Battle of Peachtree Creek. Despite having some of the city's worst fairways and greens, the immensely popular 18-hole, par-71 course is always crowded.

North Fulton Golf Course (⊠ 216 W. Wieuca Rd., Buckhead ☎ 404/255–0723) has one of the best layouts in the area. It's at Chastain Park, within the Interstate 285 perimeter. It has 18 holes and is par 71.

Stone Mountain Park (⊠ U.S. 78E, Stone Mountain Pkwy., Stone Mountain ☎ 770/465–3278 ⊕ www.stonemountainpark.com) has two courses. Stonemont, an 18-hole, par-72 course with several challenging and scenic holes, is the better of the two. The other course, Lakemont, is also 18-hole, par 72.

Hockey

Their name sounds tough, but the National Hockey League's **Atlanta Thrashers** (⊠ 1 Philips Dr., Downtown ☎ 404/878–3300 ⊕ atlantathrashers.com) are named for the state bird, the brown thrasher. They play downtown in Philips Arena.

The **Gwinnett Gladiators** (⊠ Arena at Gwinnett Center, 6400 Sugarloaf Pkwy., Duluth ☎ 770/497–5100 ⊕ gwinnettgladiators.com), a farm team for the Atlanta Thrashers, play in the East Coast Hockey League. Games are played October to April.

Running

Chattahoochee National Recreation Area (⊠ 1978 Island Ford Pkwy. ☎ 678/538–1200) contains different parcels of land that lie in 16 separate units spread along the banks of the Chattahoochee River, much of which has been protected from development. The area is crisscrossed by 70 mi of trails.

Tennis

Bitsy Grant Tennis Center (⊠ 2125 Northside Dr., Buckhead ☎ 404/609–7193), named for one of Atlanta's most well-known players, is the area's best public facility. There are 13 clay courts (6 of which are lighted) and 10 lighted hard courts. Charges per hour are $3 for the hard courts, $4.50 for the clay courts. The courts and clubhouse close at 9 PM.

Piedmont Park (⊠ 400 Park Dr., Midtown ☎ 404/853–3461) has 12 lighted hard courts. Access the tennis center from Park Drive off Monroe Drive; even though the sign says DO NOT ENTER, the security guard will show you the parking lot. Hours are weekdays 10 to 9, Saturday 9 to 6, and Sunday 10 to 6. The cost for out-of-towners is $3 per hour before 6 and $3.50 after 6.

WHERE TO EAT

There's no shortage of urban chic in the dining scene, but traditional Southern fare—including Cajun and creole, country-style and plantation cuisine, coastal and mountain dishes—thrives. The local taste for things sweet and fried holds true for restaurants serving traditional Southern food. Regional favorites include fried chicken and fried catfish. Desserts in the region are legendary. Catch the flavor of the South at breakfast and lunch in modest establishments that serve only these meals. Reserve evenings for culinary exploration, including some of the new restaurants that present traditional ingredients and dishes in fresh ways. The influx of Asian immigrants makes Atlanta the perfect city to sample Thai, Vietnamese, Korean, Japanese, Indian, and the varied Chinese cuisines.

Most restaurants will accept you just as you are; dress codes are extremely rare in this casual city. But that come-as-you-are attitude can work against patrons on busy nights; many popular restaurants operate on a first-come, first-served basis on weekends, accepting only limited reservations. Waits at some hot dining spots can exceed an hour, especially if you arrive after 7 PM.

Prices

Dining in Atlanta and its suburbs can be quite expensive. Fortunately, many of the more expensive restaurants offer early-bird weeknight specials and prix-fixe menus. Ask when you call to make reservations.

A dining option that has become very popular in recent years are counter-service restaurants. These usually casual restaurants require guests to place their order at a counter, which cuts staffing expenses. In general, the food quality remains quite high. Many local restaurant names operate under this system, including Fellini's Pizza, Willy's California-Style Burritos, and Moe's Southwest Grill.

WHAT IT COSTS				
$$$$	**$$$**	**$$**	**$**	**¢**
AT DINNER over $22	$17–$22	$12–$16	$7–$11	under $7

Restaurant prices are for a main course at dinner, excluding sales tax of 6%–8%.

Downtown

American–Casual

$–$$$ ✕ **Max Lager's American Grill & Brewery.** Line up a tasting of the house brews—the pale ale and brown ale are tops—and then order the Gulf Coast gumbo, the "Maximum" T-bone (an 18-ounce steak), or one of the popular specialty pizzas. The pub also brews its own root and ginger beers. This lively place near the city's major high-rise buildings is hopping after business hours. ⊠ *320 Peachtree St., Downtown* ☎ *404/525–4400* ⌕ *Reservations not accepted* ⊟ *AE, D, DC, MC, V.*

$–$$$ ✕ **Ted's Montana Grill.** The Ted in question is CNN founder Ted Turner, who has left a significant mark on this city. That's why Atlantans feel a sense of ownership for this chain specializing in bison meat. Chicken, beef, and trout also play a role on the menu. Ceiling fans, tin ceilings, and mahogany paneling add to the faux mountain decor. ⊠ *133 Luckie St., Downtown* ☎ *404/521–9796* ⌕ *Reservations not accepted* ⊟ *AE, D, DC, MC, V.*

$–$$ ✕ **Sops on Ellis.** The sleek urban decor at this downtown newcomer features avocado-stained furnishings in a setting of gold, burnt orange, and robin's-egg blue. Some regulars on the menu include sautéed tilapia topped with kimchee coleslaw and blackened beef tenderloin covered with crumbled blue cheese and chipotle mustard. The menu also includes lump crab-corn-spinach chowder and other tasty soups and salads. ⊠ *Ellis St. and Carnegie Way, Downtown* ☎ *404/223–7677* ▭ *D, MC, V* ⊗ *No dinner Sun.–Wed. No lunch weekends.*

Contemporary

$$$-$$$$ ✕ **BED.** You can't get breakfast in bed, but you can have dinner there at this newest addition to the high-concept chain. Reserve one of the plush beds for dining and drinking in a contemporary atmosphere. Have an intimate dinner for two, or drinks with eight of your closest friends. (It's pricey, though; you have to spend a *minimum* of $500 to reserve a bed.) The menu is French with a Southern flair; lobster with a coconut-cashew-ginger sauce and crab ravioli are menu standouts. The lobby bar is connected to the second floor by a handsome spiral staircase. A rooftop bar, complete with outdoor beds, overlooks Centennial Olympic Park and the downtown skyline. Drinks range from Pillow Talk to Bed Kitty to the most popular, Pussy Galore. ⊠ *110 Marietta St. NW, Downtown* ☎ *404/222–7992* ⌕ *Reservations essential* ▭ *AE, D, DC, MC, V.*

★ **$$$-$$$$** ✕ **Food Studio.** No less stylish for being a former plow factory, this restaurant gleams with high-tech touches. Food Studio is known for innovative American dishes—such as citrus-glazed black cod with warm soba-shiitake salad, baby bok choy, and vanilla-miso butter—but has added a few more traditional dishes. Desserts range from the parfait-like frozen lemon-basil bombe to the warm cherry tart with pistachio ice cream. ⊠ *King Plow Arts Center, 887 W. Marietta St., Downtown* ☎ *404/815–6677* ⌕ *Reservations essential* ▭ *AE, DC, MC, V* ⊗ *No lunch weekends.*

Eclectic

¢-$ ✕ **Loaf & Kettle.** Downtown workers line up to enjoy a gourmet lunch in the airy atrium of the historic Healey Building. Favorite meals include salads, soups such as lump crab-corn-spinach chowder, and robust sandwiches like blackened turkey breast with mango-cranberry chutney and white-cheddar cheese. The service is as friendly as it is fast. The funky—and fun—decorations at Loaf & Kettle include spoon collages at the front counter and cash register. ⊠ *57 Forsyth St. NW, Downtown* ☎ *404/525–8624* ▭ *D, MC, V* ⊗ *Closed weekends. No dinner.*

Pizza

¢-$ ✕ **Rosa's Pizza.** It takes a bit of courage to shout out your order from the long line that snakes back and forth in the entryway of this New York–style pizza joint. But regulars—mostly students and office workers—are used to the routine and will even gently prod newcomers when it's their turn to speak up. The two-slice-and-a-drink special—a steal at $6—is always a good choice, as are the handmade calzones. ■ TIP→ **Get**

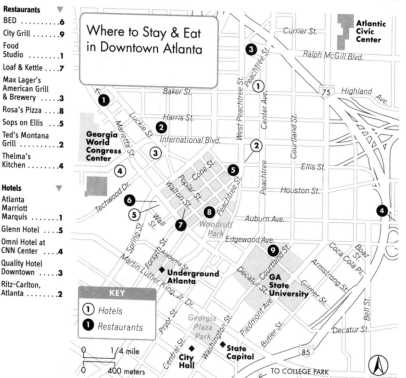

here early, as the place closes at 6 PM. ⊠ *62 Broad St. NW, Downtown* ☎ *404/521–2596* ▭ *No credit cards* ☉ *Closed weekends.*

Southern

$$–$$$$ ✕ **City Grill.** A posh power-lunch spot in Atlanta, City Grill has made the most of its grand location—at the top of a sweeping double marble staircase—in the elegantly renovated historic Hurt Building. Get a load of the hand-painted murals depicting a magical forest. An extensive wine list accompanies the menu, which includes a variety of hickory-grilled meats. Desserts range from peach cobbler to key lime parfait to Coca-Cola cake. ⊠ *50 Hurt Plaza, Downtown* ☎ *404/524–2489* ▭ *AE, D, DC, MC, V* ☉ *Closed Sun. No lunch Sat.*

¢–$ ✕ **Thelma's Kitchen.** After losing her original location to make way for Centennial Olympic Park, Thelma Grundy moved her operation to Auburn Avenue. The new location—more cheerful than the earlier spot—serves favorites like okra pancakes, fried catfish, "cold" slaw, and macaroni and cheese, all of which are among the best in town. Thelma's desserts, including lemon cheese pound cake, sweet-potato pie, red velvet cake, and pecan pie, are worth the trip. ⊠ *302 Auburn Ave., Sweet Auburn* ☎ *404/688–5855* ◬ *Reservations not accepted* ▭ *No credit cards* ☉ *Closed Sun. No dinner.*

Midtown

American

$$$$
Fodor'sChoice
★

✕ **Bacchanalia.** Often called the city's best restaurant, Bacchanalia has been a special-occasion destination since it opened in Buckhead in 1993. Chef-owners Anne Quatrano and Clifford Harrison helped transform an industrial zone west of Midtown when they moved to their current location in 2000. The renovated warehouse, known for its 20-foot ceilings, is decorated in deep, inviting tones. The kitchen focuses on locally grown organic produce and seasonal ingredients. Items on the prix-fixe menu change frequently, but could include crab fritters, wood-grilled beef tenderloin, and warm chocolate cake. ⊠ *1198 Howell Mill Rd., West Midtown* ☎ *404/365–0410 Ext. 22* ⚑ *Reservations essential* ☐ *AE, DC, MC, V* ⊘ *Closed Sun.*

★ $$$–$$$$

✕ **Park 75.** Considered a jewel in the city's culinary crown, swanky Park 75 is the domain of Chef Robert Gerstenecker. He has created a seasonal menu that includes standouts like Beef Two Ways, a combination of Kobe short ribs and filet of Angus beef, served with fingerling potatoes. His made-to-order Sunday brunch, which changes weekly, is also popular. Reserve a table in the middle of the kitchen so you can observe the master at work while sampling a constant stream of delicacies. Each course is paired with an appropriate wine. ⊠ *Four Seasons Hotel, 75 14th St., Midtown* ☎ *404/253–3840* ☐ *AE, D, DC, MC, V* ⊘ *No dinner Sun.*

Café

$$$–$$$$

✕ **Mid City Cuisine.** Contemporary American cuisine, with an emphasis on using the freshest produce, is served at this coolly comfortable café. Chef Shaun Doty prepares everything from gumbo to steak tartare, but whole fish baked in a salt crust is a favorite. Thursday is champagne night, featuring a variety of sparkling wines and specialty cocktails served in the open-air lounge. ⊠ *1545 Peachtree Rd., Midtown* ☎ *404/ 888–8700* ☐ *AE, D, DC, MC, V.*

Contemporary

$$–$$$$

✕ **One Midtown Kitchen.** An unassuming warehouse entrance down a side street near Piedmont Park leads to a seductively lighted, industrial-chic restaurant. The dining room is energetic but can be loud; the back porch, on the other hand, is quieter and offers a serene view of the park and the city skyline. Small plates like the wood-roasted pizza are outstanding, as is the price-tiered wine list. Order a glass or bottle, choose several plates for the table, and share. ⊠ *559 Dutch Valley Rd., Midtown* ☎ *404/892–4111* ☐ *AE, MC, V* ⊘ *No lunch.*

Italian

$$$–$$$$

✕ **Veni Vidi Vici.** Gleaming wood and sleek furnishings create the perfect environment for an indulgent Italian meal. Start with *piatti piccoli* (savory appetizers) before moving on to the mushroom risotto, linguine with white clam sauce, or osso buco. Gnocchi with Gorgonzola is another favorite, as are the fragrant rotisserie meats. ⊠ *41 14th St., Midtown* ☎ *404/875–8424* ☐ *AE, D, DC, MC, V* ⊘ *No lunch weekends.*

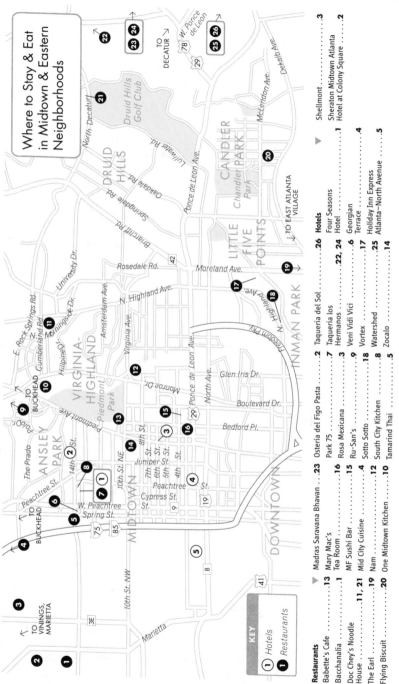

Where to Stay & Eat in Midtown & Eastern Neighborhoods

KEY

① Hotels

① Restaurants

Restaurants

Babette's Cafe **13**
Bacchanalia **1**
Doc Chey's Noodle
House **11, 21**
The Earl **19**
Flying Biscuit **20**

Madras Saravana Bhavan ... **23**
Mary Mac's
Tea Room **16**
MF Sushi Bar **15**
Mid City Cuisine **4**
Nam **12**
One Midtown Kitchen **10**

Osteria del Figo Pasta **23**
Park 75 .... **7**
Rosa Mexicana **3**
Ru-San's **9**
Sotto Sotto **4**
South City Kitchen **8**
Tamarind Thai **10**

Taqueria del Sol **2**
Taqueria los
Hermanos **22, 24**
Veni Vidi Vici **9**
Vortex **17**
Watershed **8**
Zocalo **5**

Hotels

Four Seasons
Hotel **1**
Georgian
Terrace **4**
Holiday Inn Express
Atlanta–North Avenue **5**

Shellmont **3**
Sheraton Midtown Atlanta ... **1**
Hotel at Colony Square **2**

★ **$-$$** ✕ **Osteria del Figo Pasta.** High-quality counter-service restaurants like this one have changed the face of Atlanta dining. In exchange for standing in a short line and paying up front, you can still get excellent food at a reasonable price. That's the concept behind this Italian eatery, which keeps it simple with pasta dishes, salads, and a few desserts. Bring an appetite, as the portions are quite generous. ⊠ *1210 Howell Mill Rd., West Midtown* ☎ *404/351–3700* ⚅ *Reservations not accepted* ☰ *MC, V* ⊗ *Closed Sun.*

Japanese

$-$$$ ✕ **MF Sushibar.** Salsa and techno music keep things lively at this highly regarded Japanese eatery. Whether you take a seat at the bar or at one of the tables, you're going to enjoy some of the best sushi in town. Particularly popular is the Godzilla roll—shrimp tempura topped with smoked salmon, eel, and avocado. The ginger salad is refreshing treat. ⊠ *265 Ponce de Leon Ave., Midtown* ☎ *404/815–8844* ☰ *AE, D, DC, MC, V.*

★ **$-$$** ✕ **Ru-San's.** With sushi chefs who holler greetings, servers who encourage diners to engage in beer-chugging contests, and a boisterous clientele, this storefront sushi joint feels like walking into a party. Locals love the extensive menu, which includes variations on sushi, sashimi, and tempura. Choose from the 24-seat sushi bar, the booths in the dining room, or the bamboo-lined outdoor patio. ⊠ *1529 Piedmont Rd. NE, Midtown* ☎ *404/875–7042* ☰ *AE, D, MC, V.*

Mexican

★ **$$-$$$$** ✕ **Rosa Mexicano.** An 18-foot waterfall greets diners to this upscale Mexican restaurant. The dining room is decorated in vivid colors, especially the trademark pink. Attentive service includes tableside guacamole preparation with the traditional mortar and pestle. Atlantans like the warm corn tacos stuffed with roasted chicken, served in miniature cast iron skillets with pinto beans and crispy corn kernels. The beef filet with a wild mushroom and tequila sauce is also popular. ⊠ *245 18th St. NW, Atlantic Station* ☎ *404/347–4090* ☰ *AE, D, DC, MC, V.*

$-$$$ ✕ **Zocalo.** People come to this restaurant's inviting open-air patio—warmed in the winter by giant heaters—for the city's best Mexican food. Order the guacamole, prepared tableside, as a starter before moving on to dishes like chicken breast simmered in a thick mole sauce or shrimp sautéed in chipotle salsa. The bar has an excellent selection of top-shelf tequilas. ⊠ *187 10th St., Midtown* ☎ *404/249–7576* ⚅ *Reservations not accepted* ☰ *AE, D, DC, MC, V.*

Pan-Asian

¢-$ ✕ **Doc Chey's Noodle House.** Claim your share of bench space at the crowded rows of tables, smile at the folks crammed in next to you, and then dig in to the big bowls of flavorful soups and rice dishes. Entrées such as noodles and eggplant with tomato-ginger sauce and Thai-style curry over rice come with your choice of chicken, tofu, shrimp, or salmon. ⊠ *1424 N. Highland Ave., Virginia-Highland* ☎ *404/888–0777* ⚅ *Reservations not accepted* ☰ *AE, D, MC, V* ⊠ *1556 N. Decatur Rd., Emory* ☎ *404/378–8188* ⚅ *Reservations not accepted* ☰ *AE, D, MC, V* ⊗ *No lunch Sun.*

Taste of the South

GEORGIA IS AN EXCELLENT PLACE to sample Southern food. In Atlanta and Savannah you'll find restaurants that serve the finest traditional cuisine, as well as more innovative cooking. Remember that Southern food varies widely across the region and even within states. Nothing reflects this more than barbecue, and few culinary differences produce as many passionate opinions. Taste as you travel, and add to the debate.

Locals in Georgia and Mississippi generally prefer tomato-based sauces on ribs or chopped meat—but variations abound. In North Carolina barbecue is chopped pork piled on a bun with hand-cut coleslaw on top. Sauces range from vinegar and pepper (and little else) to Lexington style, with some tomato in the mix. In South Carolina mustard-based barbecue sauces are widely savored, whether on chopped meat or on ribs. In eastern Alabama, you'll find a unique white sauce for barbecue. Memphis-style 'cue is famous for its dry rub, although there's also a "wet" style, in which the same spices, moistened, are rubbed on the ribs. In parts of Tennessee, barbecued mutton is traditional.

Gumbo, the spicy soup that is so clearly from this region, is an apt metaphor for the South's demographics because the word reflects all that comes to the Southern table (and to Southern culture) from its people. The term is West African,

from *ngombo*, which meant "okra" in that part of the world. And what would gumbo be without okra? But gumbo is also French: a proper gumbo is based on a *roux*, a sauté of fat and flour cooked to the color of peanut butter. The cook might sauté vegetables for a gumbo, making a kind of *sofrito*, a legacy from the Spanish settlers in the lower part of Louisiana. Using sassafras or filé powder to thicken gumbo is a legacy of Southern Native Americans.

One defining ingredient in Southern cooking is corn—another Native American legacy. Parch the corn with lye, which swells the grains, and you get hominy. Grind the corn, white or yellow, and you have grits. Sift the grits, and you have cornmeal for making corn bread, fluffy spoon bread, corn pone, hoecakes, hush puppies, and johnnycake (or Native American "journey" cake). Ferment the grain, and you get corn whiskey, also known as white lightning or moonshine (and arguably like Southern grappa).

When traveling in Georgia and the rest of the South, you'll find the area's diversity on its tables. Many of the region's chefs use the traditional ingredients to craft "new" Southern dishes as a way of restoring that sense of elegant dining to the region's cuisine. Others wouldn't get near that sort of style, preferring to do the original dishes proud. Take your pick: either way you'll dine divinely.

Southern

★ **$$–$$$$** ✕ **South City Kitchen.** The culinary traditions of South Carolina inspire the dishes served at this cheerful restaurant. This is the place to get fried green tomatoes with goat cheese, she-crab soup, or buttermilk fried chicken. The chef prepares catfish in many intriguing ways. Crab hash, served with poached eggs and chive hollandaise, is a classic. Don't miss the chocolate pecan tart. Within walking distance of the Woodruff Arts Center, the spare, art-filled restaurant attracts a hip crowd. ⊠ *1144 Crescent Ave., Midtown* ☎ *404/873–7358* ☱ *AE, DC, MC, V.*

$–$$$ ✕ **Mary Mac's Tea Room.** Local celebrities and ordinary folks line up for the country-fried steak, fried chicken, and fresh vegetables. Here, in the Southern tradition, waitresses will call you "honey" and pat your arm to assure you that everything's all right. It's a great way to experience Southern food and hospitality all at once. ⊠ *224 Ponce de Leon Ave., Midtown* ☎ *404/876–1800* ☱ *AE, MC, V.*

Tex-Mex

★ ¢–$ ✕ **Taqueria del Sol.** Don't let the long lines outside at this counter-service eatery discourage you. They move quickly, and you'll soon be rewarded with a full bar, a wide selection of tacos and enchiladas, unusual sides like spicy collard greens and jalapeño coleslaw, and a fabulous trio of salsas. Don't pass up the chunky guacamole. ⊠ *1200-B Howell Mill Rd., West Midtown* ☎ *404/352–5811* ⌕ *Reservations not accepted* ☱ *AE, MC, V* ☯ *Closed Sun. No dinner Mon.*

Thai

★ $–$$$$ ✕ **Tamarind Thai.** All that is good about Thai flavors—refreshing lime, spicy basil, hot peppers, and cooling coconut, and smoky fish sauces—is even better at this standout known for excellent service. Favorite dishes include chicken with green curry and sea bass with three-flavor sauce. Meals are served in a simple, subdued, but elegant setting. Parking is limited in the area; you may end up having to make a mad dash across multilane 14th Street. ⊠ *80 14th St., Midtown* ☎ *404/873–4888* ☱ *AE, MC, V* ☯ *No lunch weekends.*

Vietnamese

★ $–$$$$ ✕ **Nam.** Brothers Alex and Chris Kinjo paid tribute to their mother's homeland with this stylish eatery. Gauzy curtains separate the tables, and sleek servers whisk by dressed in black and red. The crab-and-asparagus soup is packed with plenty of meat. Rich caramelized onions add mouthwatering depth to spicy clay-pot catfish. ⊠ *931 Monroe Dr., Suite A-101, Midtown* ☎ *404/541–9997* ☱ *AE, D, MC, V* ☯ *No lunch Mon. or weekends.*

Inman Park, Candler Park & East Atlanta Village

American–Casual

¢–$$$ ✕ **The Earl.** A scrappy yet delightful first stop on the East Atlanta bar scene, the Earl has a hearty menu of classic pub food, as well as a few entrées that are more innovative, such as jerk tuna. Don't let the comically eclectic interior fool you: the food is surprisingly well prepared. There's a stage in the corner, as this is one of the city's favorite rock venues. ⊠ *488 Flat Shoals Ave., East Atlanta Village, East Atlanta* ☎ *404/522–3950* ☱ *AE, D, MC, V.*

¢–$$ ✕ **Vortex.** Talk about disconcerting: you enter this restaurant through the mouth of a massive, spiral-eyed skull. The restaurant's motto, printed on servers' T-shirts, is IT'S NEVER TOO LATE TO START WASTING YOUR

LIFE. But beyond the shenanigans are tasty delights, particularly the hefty burgers. A little-known perk is the bar's amazingly extensive selection of top-shelf liquor, consistently voted "Best in Atlanta" by the city's namesake magazine. ⊠ *438 Moreland Ave., Little Five Points* ☎ *404/688–1828* ⊟ *AE, D, DC, MC, V.*

Eclectic

¢–$$ ⬠ ✕ **Flying Biscuit.** There's an hourlong wait on weekends for the big, fluffy biscuits served with cranberry-apple butter. Other huge hits at this cheery spot include sausage made with free-range chicken and sage, and bean cakes with tomatillo salsa. Fancier dinners include roasted chicken and turkey meat loaf with pudge (mashed potatoes). There are also plenty of vegetarian options. Next door is a bakery serving biscuits to go, as well as freshly baked muffins and cookies. ⊠ *1655 McLendon Ave., Candler Park* ☎ *404/687–8888* ⬡ *Reservations not accepted* ⊟ *AE, MC, V.*

Continental

★ $$–$$$$ ✕ **Babette's Cafe.** Sunny yellow walls and back-porch seating add to the homey charm of this renovated bungalow. The restaurant, which describes its cuisine as European country, offers such seasonal dishes as halibut with potato-leek gratin and beef tenderloin with Gorgonzola sauce. Loyal locals love the Sunday brunch. ⊠ *573 N. Highland Ave., Inman Park* ☎ *404/523–9121* ⊟ *AE, D, DC, MC, V* ☻ *Closed Mon.*

Italian

★ $$–$$$$ ✕ **Sotto Sotto.** This hot spot close to downtown has an adventurous take on Italian cuisine. The former commercial space hops with young, hip patrons dining on wood-roasted duck breast with couscous, spaghetti with sun-dried mullet roe, and utterly perfect *panna cotta* (custard). ⊠ *313 N. Highland Ave., Inman Park* ☎ *404/523–6678* ⊟ *AE, DC, MC, V* ☻ *No lunch.*

Buckhead

American

★ $$$–$$$$ ✕ **Woodfire Grill.** This restaurant, with a relaxed atmosphere reminiscent of the Napa Valley, has gained a reputation as one of the city's finest. Chef Michael Tuohy carefully selects every ingredient, down to the organic greens tucked under chèvre-stuffed fried squash blossoms. Favorites include the cedar plank salmon and wood-grilled hanger steak. ⊠ *1782 Cheshire Bridge Rd. NE, Buckhead* ☎ *404/347–9055* ⊟ *AE, D, DC, MC, V* ☻ *No lunch.*

Contemporary

$$$–$$$$ ✕ **Aria.** The rustic heartiness of Chef Gerry Klaskala's entrées also appeal to the epicurean palate. His talent is best captured by his love of "slow foods"—braises, stews, roasts, and chops cooked over a roll-top French grill. This makes for very weighty plates, but Klaskala lovingly flavors every ounce. For example, pork shoulder is presented with a delicious balsamic reduction and Gorgonzola polenta. Don't miss renowned pastry chef Kathryn King's mouthwatering dessert menu, including Valrhona-chocolate-cream pie with Drambuie sauce. ⊠ *490 E. Paces Ferry*

Fodor'sChoice
★

436 <

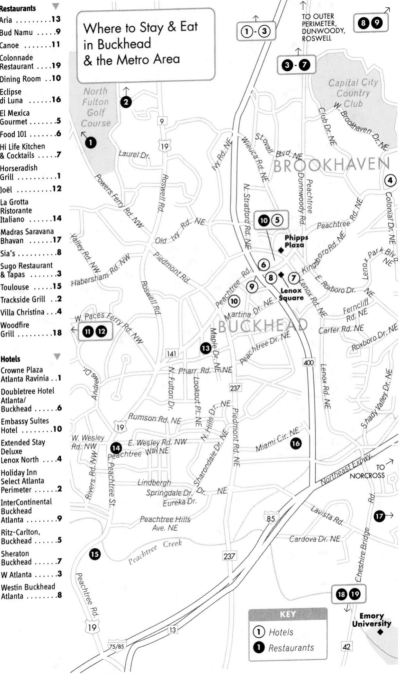

Rd., Buckhead ☎ *404/233–7673* ⌂ *Reservations essential* ▤ *AE, D, DC, MC, V* ☉ *Closed Sun. No lunch.*

$$$–$$$$ ✕ **Canoe.** This popular spot on the banks of the Chattahoochee River overflows with appreciative patrons nearly all day. In nice weather, the outdoor dining spaces allow the best view of the river. The restaurant has built a reputation based on such dishes as crispy pheasant croquettes with brown-butter sweet potatoes and huckleberry sauce; seared mountain trout with smoked salmon ravioli; and slow-roasted rabbit with wild mushroom ravioli and Swiss chard. Sunday brunch—with smoked salmon eggs Benedict, housemade English muffins with citrus hollandaise, and other offerings—is superb. ✉ *4199 Paces Ferry Rd. NW, Buckhead* ☎ *770/432–2663* ▤ *AE, D, DC, MC, V.*

★ **$$$–$$$$** ✕ **Joël.** Chef Joël Antunes, former executive chef at the Ritz-Carlton, spices up the entrées at this chic French brasserie with Mediterranean and Asian influences. The rotating menu may include sautéed veal sweetbreads with endive, dried pears, and a port sauce or seared scallops with leek and tomatoes. ✉ *3290 Northside Pkwy., Berkeley Park* ☎ *404/233–3500* ▤ *AE, D, DC, MC, V* ☉ *Closed Sun. No lunch Sat.–Mon.*

Continental

$$$$ ✕ **The Dining Room.** Chef Arnaud Berthelier 's prix-fixe menu includes
Fodor's Choice dishes such as Four Story Hill Farm lamb, fried spinach and ricotta ravi-
★ olis with apricot chutney and crispy Wild John Dory "pave," morel duxelle, wild asparagus, and chanterelle jus. The menu is served in an elegant dining room featuring apple-green silk walls and floral upholstery with a slight Asian influence. The bronze sculpture that dominates the center of the room is a work by 18th-century French sculptor Paul Comolera, who helped create the Arc de Triomphe in Paris. ✉ *Ritz-Carlton, Buckhead, 3434 Peachtree Rd. NE, Buckhead* ☎ *404/237–2700* ⌂ *Reservations essential* 🏛 *Jacket required* ▤ *AE, D, DC, MC, V* ☉ *Closed Sun. and Mon. No lunch.*

French

$$$–$$$$ ✕ **Toulouse.** Open spaces enclosed by warm, rough-brick walls characterize the attractive dining room at Toulouse. The food is inspired by the cooking of southwestern France, but in execution it clearly draws on some American influences—particularly with dishes like the buffalo meat loaf with roasted tomatoes and wild mushrooms. The country potato soup is a perfect cold-weather meal. Especially wonderful are the roast chicken and the crème brûlée. ✉ *2293B Peachtree Rd., Buckhead* ☎ *404/351–9533* ▤ *AE, DC, MC, V* ☉ *No lunch.*

Italian

★ **$$$–$$$$** ✕ **La Grotta Ristorante Italiano.** Overlook the location in the ground level of a posh condominium—this place is a class act. The burgundy-and-cream interior is elegant, and the staff is excellent. Old northern Italian favorites such as prosciutto with grilled pears and mascarpone cheese and potato-and-herb gnocchi with a wild mushroom sauce are the core of the menu. ✉ *2637 Peachtree Rd., Buckhead* ☎ *404/231–1368* ⌂ *Reservations essential* ▤ *AE, D, DC, MC, V* ☉ *Closed Sun. No lunch.*

Mediterranean

★ $$$ ✕ **Eclipse di Luna.** This hot spot has captured the fancy of twentysome-
things, who flock here on weekends. The lunch menu includes sandwiches
and salads; evening fare consists of tapas such as *patatas bravas* (pota-
toes with olive oil and spicy sauce). The only real entrée is traditional
paella: saffron-flavored rice overflowing with fresh seafood, chicken, and
chorizo. A vegetarian version is available. The restaurant is tucked at
the very end of the Miami Circle design center. ✉ *764 Miami Circle,
Buckhead* ☎ *404/846–0449* ▭ *AE, MC, V* ☾ *Closed Mon.*

Southern

$$$–$$$$ ✕ **Horseradish Grill.** Once a red horse barn, this establishment has arched
windows across the front that brighten the space. It may be a little noisy,
but it's a good spot for authentic, if upscale, Southern dishes. The menu
changes seasonally, with entrées ranging from venison stew to skillet-
fried chicken. ✉ *4320 Powers Ferry Rd., Buckhead* ☎ *404/255–7277*
▭ *AE, D, DC, MC, V* ☾ *No lunch Sat.*

$–$$$ ✕ **Colonnade Restaurant.** For traditional Southern food—fried chicken,
ham steak, and turkey with dressing—insiders head to Colonnade, a local
institution since 1927. The interior, with patterned carpeting and red
banquettes, is a classic version of a 1950s restaurant. ✉ *1879 Cheshire
Bridge Rd., Buckhead* ☎ *404/874–5642* ⚮ *Reservations not accepted*
▭ *No credit cards* ☾ *No lunch Mon. and Tues.*

Metro Atlanta

American

$$–$$$$ ✕ **Hi Life Kitchen & Cocktails.** This hip restaurant 20 mi northeast of down-
town Atlanta presents an eclectic menu of American favorites, but devo-
tees swear by the heaping plate of lobster prepared three ways, depending
on the season. Other favorites include beef tenderloin medallions and
mountain trout picatta. The design is decidedly upscale, with pale wood
and wrought-iron accents. ✉ *3380 Holcomb Bridge Rd., Norcross*
☎ *770/409–0101* ▭ *AE, DC, MC, V* ☾ *No lunch weekends.*

$–$$$ ✕ **Trackside Grill.** This family-owned neighborhood favorite in historic
Kennesaw is not your typical grill. The Southern offerings are all house-
made, including crispy potato chips fried each morning. On busy days,
once they're gone, they're gone. Fried green tomato BLTs—with goat
cheese, red pepper puree, and toasted sourdough bread—are a lunch and
brunch favorite. For dinner there's pecan fried chicken or shrimp and
grits. The cheerful dining room is decorated with railroad memorabilia
in honor of its location, a block away from the Southern Museum of
Civil War and Locomotive History. It's quaint at night when the lights
are dimmed and the candles are lighted. Patio dining is available. ✉ *2840
S. Main St., Kennesaw* ☎ *770/499–0874* ⚮ *Reservations welcome*
▭ *AE, MC, V* ☾ *No dinner Sun.*

Contemporary

$$$–$$$$ ✕ **Sia's.** "Creative American" is how this sleek suburban restaurant de-
scribes its contemporary cuisine, which includes such entrées as pan-seared
wild salmon and cranberry grilled lamb chops. A cozy bar tucked away

from the open circular dining room is a nice place to stop for drinks, too. ⊠ *10305 Medlock Bridge Rd., Duluth* ☎ *770/497–9727* ▭ *AE, D, DC, MC, V* ☽ *Closed Sun. No lunch weekends.*

$$–$$$$ ✕ **Food 101.** This restaurant north of Altanta is a hit, given the gut-filling comfort food—lamb shank with braised vegetables, for example, or meat loaf with mashed potatoes and string beans. Wine drinkers especially love this place for its selection of 50 selections by the glass. ⊠ *4969 Roswell Rd., Sandy Springs* ☎ *404/497–9700* ▭ *AE, D, MC, V* ☽ *No lunch Sat.*

Continental

$–$$$ ✕ **Sugo Restaurant and Tapas.** This very romantic chain restaurant has Spanish-red walls, flowing tapestries, and stone urns filled with fresh tomatoes and breads and pasta. Lamb saltimbocca, a rolled and stuffed lamb tenderloin, is dressed with proscuitto, asiago cheese, fresh basil, and walnut-fig pesto, among other ingredients. All the recipes are derived from the Greek-Italian background of Federico Castellucci, the genial host at the Clock Tower Place branch, who makes it a point to visit every table. As a thank you to guests at the end of the meal with generous servings, waiters provide a toast of Moscato D'Asti (an Italian dessert wine). ⊠ *Park Place Shopping Center, 4505 Ashford Dunwoody Rd., Dunwoody* ☎ *678/320–0320* ⊠ *Clock Tower Place, 408 S. Atlanta St., Roswell* ☎ *770/641–9131* ⊠ *Roswell Crossing, 625 W. Crossville Rd., Roswell* ☎ *770/817–4230* ▭ *AE, D, DC, MC, V.*

Indian

★ $–$$ ✕ **Madras Saravana Bhavan.** This outstanding south Indian vegetarian restaurant is almost always packed with Indian families and other diners happily devouring huge platters of *dosai* (rice- or lentil-flour crepes filled with vegetables) and curries. Service is friendly and helpful, especially for the uninitiated. The restaurant is hidden in a rundown shopping center on the outskirts of Decatur. ⊠ *2179 Lawrenceville Hwy., Decatur* ☎ *404/636–4400* ▭ *AE, D, MC, V.*

Italian

$$–$$$$ ✕ **Villa Christina.** Look no farther for elegant Italian food with a twist. You enter down a lighted path resplendent with gardens, a waterfall, and a stone bridge. The dining room doubles as an art gallery, with two murals depicting a glorious Tuscan landscape. From the kitchen comes seared wild striped sea bass on a bed of spinach, and grilled Tuscan veal chops with a sweet-onion brûlée of Parma ham. The house specialty, seafood *cioppino*, is a medley of succulent shellfish swimming in a saffron-tomato stew. ⊠ *4000 Summit Blvd., Dunwoody* ☎ *404/303– 0133* ▭ *AE, D, DC, MC, V* ☽ *Closed Sun. No lunch Sat.*

Korean

$–$$ ✕ **Bud Namu.** City foodies drive 25 mi into the suburbs for this Korean restaurant's clay-wrapped roasted duck, and stuffed pumpkin (with sticky rice, plums, chestnuts, and pine nuts), both of which must be ordered a few hours—and on weekends a few days—in advance. Friendly, helpful service enhances the experience. ⊠ *3585 Peachtree Industrial Blvd., Duluth* ☎ *770/622–8983* ▭ *AE, MC, V.*

Mexican

$–$$$ ✕ **El Mexica Gourmet.** The authentic fare produced by the kitchen illustrates that Mexican cuisine is not all tacos and enchiladas—though if that's what you're up for, you'll find plenty of that here, too. Alongside those Mexican staples dig into specialties like beef *tampiqueña* (smothered with sautéed onions and peppers) and red snapper *veracruzana* (pan-fried with a tomato and onion sauce). Look for the restaurant behind Applebee's. ✉ *11060 Alpharetta Hwy., Roswell* ☎ *770/594–8674* ▤ *AE, MC, V.*

$–$$ ✕ **Taqueria los Hermanos.** At this tiny storefront restaurant in a shopping center, the Ballasteros brothers serve marinated pork tacos, delicate chiles rellenos, and, occasionally, their mother's handmade tamales. Don't leave without tasting the *tres leches* (three milk) cake. ✉ *Killian Hills Crossing shopping center, 4760 Lawrenceville Hwy., Lilburn* ☎ *678/380–3727* ▤ *AE, D, MC, V* ☾ *No lunch weekends* ✉ *4418 Hugh Howell Rd., Tucker* ☎ *678/937–0660* ▤ *AE, D, MC, V* ☾ *No lunch weekends.*

Southern

★ **$$–$$$** ✕ **Watershed.** Indigo Girl Emily Saliers and three of her friends launched this casual restaurant in a converted gas station. Chef Scott Peacock, coauthor of *The Gift of Southern Cooking,* specializes in elegant takes on classic Southern fare: the planet's best shrimp salad, homemade pimento cheese with sharp cheddar, roasted or fried chicken, an outstanding chocolate cake, and Georgia pecan tart with a scrumptious shortbread crust. Also a wine bar, Watershed sells wine both retail in bottles and by the glass at the comfy bar. When she's not in the recording studio, Saliers makes a fine sommelier and loves to talk about wine. ✉ *406 W. Ponce de Leon Ave., Decatur* ☎ *404/378–4900* ▤ *AE, MC, V* ☾ *No dinner Sun.*

Tex-Mex

★ **¢–$$** ✕ **Taqueria del Sol.** The lines move quickly at this Tex-Mex counter-service eatery serving a wide selection of tacos and enchiladas, unusual sides like spicy turnip greens and jalapeño coleslaw, and a fabulous salsa trio. Also popular is the creamy corn chowder. ✉ *359 W. Ponce de Leon Ave., Decatur* ☎ *404/377–7668* ⌦ *Reservations not accepted* ▤ *AE, MC, V* ☾ *Closed Sun. No dinner Mon.*

WHERE TO STAY

One of America's most popular convention destinations, Atlanta offers plenty of variety in terms of lodgings. More than 76,000 rooms are in metro Atlanta, with about 12,000 downtown, close to the Georgia World Congress Center, Atlanta Civic Center, and Philips Arena. Other clusters are in Buckhead, in the north Interstate 285 perimeter, and around Hartsfield-Jackson Atlanta International Airport.

Prices

Atlanta lodging facilities basically have two seasons: summer and convention (conventions are generally held year-round, though there are fewer in summer).

	WHAT IT COSTS				
	$$$$	**$$$**	**$$**	**$**	**¢**
FOR 2 PEOPLE	over $220	$161–$220	$111–$160	$70–$110	under $70

Hotel prices are for two people in a standard double room in high season, excluding service charges and 6%–8% sales tax, plus a 7% bed tax.

Downtown

★ **$$$–$$$$** 🏨 **Omni Hotel at CNN Center.** Adjacent to the home of the Cable News Network is this sleek hotel with two towers: one with 600 rooms, the other with 467 rooms. The ultramodern marble lobby overlooks Centennial Olympic Park through floor-to-ceiling windows. Creams, browns, and rich red accents decorate the rooms and complement the mahogany furniture. The hotel is at MARTA's CNN Center station. ⌧ *100 CNN Center, Downtown, 30303* ☎ *404/659–0000 or 800/843–6664* 🖷 *404/525–5050* ⊕ *www.omnihotels.com* 🛏 *1,036 rooms, 31 suites* ⌂ *2 restaurants, in-room broadband, in-room data ports, Web TV, cable TV, Wi-Fi, pool, health club, spa, lobby lounge, Internet room, business services, meeting rooms, parking (fee)* ⊟ *AE, D, DC, MC, V* ⏀ *EP.*

★ **$$$–$$$$** 🏨 **Ritz-Carlton, Atlanta.** Traditional afternoon tea—served in the intimate, sunken lounge beneath an 18th-century chandelier—sets the mood. Notice the 17th-century Flemish tapestry when you enter from Peachtree Street. All suites have flat-screen TVs. All rooms have bay-window views of the downtown skyline. The Atlanta Grill is one of downtown's few outdoor dining spots. It's opposite MARTA's Peachtree Center station. ⌧ *181 Peachtree St., Downtown, 30303* ☎ *404/659–0400 or 800/241–3333* 🖷 *404/688–0400* ⊕ *www.ritzcarlton.com* 🛏 *422 rooms, 22 suites* ⌂ *Restaurant, in-room broadband, in-room data ports, Wi-Fi, cable TV, bar, laundry service, Internet room, business services* ⊟ *AE, D, DC, MC, V* ⏀ *EP.*

$$–$$$$ 🏨 **Glenn Hotel.** This boutique hotel is a mix of New York sophistication and Miami sex appeal. Its room are small, but a thoughtful renovation makes the best of the space. Glass walls between the oversize showers and the sleeping areas mean you won't miss a minute of the program on your 32-inch plasma TV. The contemporary decor is sleek and sophisticated. ⌧ *110 Marietta St. NW, Downtown 30303* ☎ *404/521–2250 or 866/404–5366* 🖷 *404/521–2256* ⊕ *www.glennhotel.com* 🛏 *93 rooms, 16 suites* ⌂ *Restaurant, in-room broadband, Web TV, Wi-Fi, gym, bar, meeting rooms, parking (fee)* ⊟ *AE, D, DC, MC, V* ⏀ *EP.*

$–$$$$ 🏨 **Atlanta Marriott Marquis.** Immense and coolly contemporary, the building seems to go up forever as you stand under the lobby's huge fabric sculpture that hangs from the skylighted roof 47 stories above. Guest rooms, which open onto this atrium, are decorated in dark greens and tans. Fresh flowers fill the major suites, two of which have grand pianos and ornamental fireplaces. You don't even have to walk outside to reach the Peachtree Center MARTA station; it's connected via an indoor walkway. Noise from the lobby can carry to the lower floors, so request one above the 10th floor. The view of downtown Atlanta from upper floor rooms is spectacular. ✉ *265 Peachtree Center Ave., Downtown, 30303* ☎ *404/521–0000 or 800/228–9290* 🖷 *404/586–6299* ⊕ *www.marriott.com* ➫ *1,675 rooms, 69 suites* ♿ *4 restaurants, cable TV, in-room broadband, in-room data ports, Web TV, Wi-Fi, indoor-outdoor pool, health club, 2 bars, Internet room, meeting rooms, parking (fee)* ▭ *AE, D, DC, MC, V* ❙⊙❙ *EP.*

$–$$ 🖳 **Quality Hotel Downtown.** This quiet, older downtown hotel two blocks off Peachtree Street is priced reasonably for its location; this, along with the hotel's proximity to the Georgia World Congress Center and the AmericasMart complex, makes the hotel popular during conventions. Note that prices go up when conventions are in town. Sofas and a grand piano fill the marble lobby, and teal and navy decorate the modest-size rooms. ✉ *89 Luckie St., Downtown, 30303* ☎ *404/524–7991 or 888/729–7705* 🖷 *404/524–0672* ⊕ *www.qualityinn.com* ➫ *75 rooms* ♿ *Cable TV, in-room broadband, Wi-Fi, Internet room, parking (fee)* ▭ *AE, D, DC, MC, V* ❙⊙❙ *BP.*

Midtown

★ **$$$$** 🖳 **Four Seasons Hotel.** From the lobby a sweeping staircase leads up to Park 75, the hotel's chic dining establishment. Rose-hue marble creates a warm feeling in the public spaces and lounges. Amenities abound throughout: marble bathrooms with extra-large soaking tubs, lemon or celadon color schemes, comfy mattresses, and brass chandeliers. The hotel prides itself on its immensely courteous staff—it's considered scandalous if a call to reception rings more than twice before it's answered. Stewards and other staff members are on hand the moment you need their help. ✉ *75 14th St., Midtown, 30309* ☎ *404/881–9898 or 800/ 819–5053* 🖷 *404/873–4692* ⊕ *www.fourseasons.com* ➫ *226 rooms, 18 suites* ♿ *Restaurant, cable TV, in-room broadband, in-room data ports, Web TV, in room DVDs, Wi-Fi, Internet room, pool, health club, spa, bar, meeting rooms, parking (fee), some pets allowed* ▭ *AE, D, DC, MC, V* ❙⊙❙ *EP.*

$$–$$$$ 🖳 **Shellmont Inn.** Designed in 1891 by architect Walter T. Downing, this distinctive lodging is on the National Register of Historic Places. The mansion, which is named for its recurring shell motif, has antique stained, leaded, and beveled glass, enhanced by artfully carved woodwork and charming stencils. Victorian-style antiques fill the guest rooms. ✉ *821 Piedmont Ave. NE, Midtown, 30308* ☎ *404/872–9290* 🖷 *404/ 872–5379* ⊕ *www.shellmont.com* ➫ *5 rooms, 2 suites, 1 carriage house* ♿ *Cable TV, in-room DVDs, in-room broadband, Wi-Fi* ▭ *AE, D, DC, MC, V* ❙⊙❙ *BP.*

★ **$$–$$$$** 🖳 **Sheraton Midtown Atlanta Hotel at Colony Square.** The Sheraton's theatrical lobby and overhanging balconies open onto the bright, open mall of Colony Square, a complex of office, residential, and retail buildings. Rooms are modern, with muted tones; those on higher floors have city views. The hotel is two blocks from MARTA's Arts Center station and two blocks from the Woodruff Arts Center and the High Museum of Art. The parking garage is a bit of a maze. ✉ *188 14th St., Midtown, 30361* ☎ *404/892–6000 or 800/422–7895* 🖷 *404/872–9192* ⊕ *www.*

starwood.com 🛏 *467 rooms, 32 suites* ⚒ *Restaurant, cable TV, pool, in-room broadband, Wi-Fi, lobby lounge, Internet room, business services, meeting rooms, parking (fee), some pets allowed* 🗔 *AE, D, DC, MC, V* ⦿ *EP.*

$–$$ 🏨 **Georgian Terrace.** Enrico Caruso and other stars of the Metropolitan Opera once lodged in this 1911 hotel across the street from the Fox Theatre. The fine hotel, which has always housed the rich and famous, is now on the National Register of Historic Places. The columned lobby is striking, and breathtaking terraces traverse the exterior, making it a popular venue for wedding receptions. All the suites are pastel and plush, providing adequate if not luxurious comfort. ⊠ *659 Peachtree St., Midtown, 30308* ☎ *404/897–1991* 🖷 *404/724–9116* ⊕ *www.thegeorgianterrace.com* 🛏 *319 suites* ⚒ *Restaurant, some kitchens, some kitchenettes, cable TV, in-room broadband, Wi-Fi, pool, health club, Internet room, business services, convention center, meeting rooms, parking (fee)* 🗔 *AE, D, MC, V* ⦿ *EP.*

$$ 🏨 **Holiday Inn Express Atlanta–North Avenue.** Across the street from the Georgia Institute of Technology is this no-frills establishment. Forest-green and cranberry accents, floral bedspreads, and striped curtains spice up the neutral decor. ⊠ *244 North Ave., Midtown, 30313* ☎ *404/881–0881* 🖷 *404/874–8838* ⊕ *www.holiday-inn.com* 🛏 *108 rooms, 2 suites* ⚒ *Cable TV, in room broadband, Wi-Fi, laundry service, business services, free parking* 🗔 *AE, D, DC, MC, V* ⦿ *BP.*

Buckhead & Outer Perimeter

$$$$ 🏨 **Ritz-Carlton, Buckhead.** Decorated with 18th- and 19th-century an-
Fodor'sChoice   tiques, this elegant hotel is a regular stopover for visiting celebrities. The
★   richly paneled Lobby Lounge is a respite for shoppers from nearby Lenox Square and Phipps Plaza; afternoon tea and cocktails are popular. The Dining Room is one of the city's finest restaurants, and many of the area's top chefs have passed through its kitchen doors. The spacious guest rooms are furnished with traditional reproductions. The Club Level, with a separate lounge and concierge, showers you with everything from a bountiful continental breakfast in the morning to chocolates and cordials at night. The large gift shop, called the Boutique, sells everything from linens to luggage. ⊠ *3434 Peachtree Rd. NE, Buckhead, 30326* ☎ *404/237–2700 or 800/241–3333* 🖷 *404/239–0078* ⊕ *www.ritzcarlton.com* 🛏 *524 rooms, 29 suites* ⚒ *3 restaurants, in-room broadband, Wi-Fi, pool, health club, hot tub, spa, bar, Internet room, business services, parking (fee)* 🗔 *AE, D, DC, MC, V* ⦿ *EP.*

$$$–$$$$ 🏨 **Doubletree Hotel Atlanta/Buckhead.** If the complimentary fresh-baked chocolate-chip cookies that welcome you don't convince you to stay here, maybe the excellent location, spacious rooms, and reasonable rates will. The hotel, which offers complimentary transportation within 3 mi, is adjacent to the Buckhead MARTA station. ⊠ *3342 Peachtree Rd., Buckhead, 30326* ☎ *404/231–1234 or 800/222–8733* 🖷 *404/231–5236* ⊕ *www.doubletree.com* 🛏 *230 rooms, 1 suite* ⚒ *Restaurant, cable TV, in-room broadband, Wi-Fi, Internet room, business services, meeting rooms, parking (fee)* 🗔 *AE, D, DC, MC, V* ⦿ *EP.*

★ **$$$–$$$$** InterContinental Buckhead Atlanta. Marble bathrooms with separate soaking tubs and glass showers, 300-thread-count Egyptian-cotton linens, plush bathrobes and slippers, and twice-daily housekeeping are some of the highlights of the traditional-style rooms in this hotel, the flagship for the Atlanta-based InterContinental Hotels Group. Bar XO has outdoor terrace seating overlooking Peachtree. ⊠ *3315 Peachtree Rd. NE, Buckhead, 30326* ☎ *404/946–9000 or 800/327–0200* 🖷 *770/604–5305* ⊕ *www.ichotelsgroup.com* ➡ *401 rooms, 21 suites* ♿ *Restaurant, cable TV, in-room broadband, Web TV, Wi-Fi, pool, health club, spa, bar, lounge, shop, Internet room, business services, meeting rooms, parking (fee)* ▭ *AE, D, DC, MC, V* ⦿ *EP.*

★ **$$$–$$$$** W Atlanta. This ultrachic property makes good on its promise to pamper business travelers. Its sage, blue, and cream "living room" is highlighted by candlestick chandeliers covered with glass domes. Guest rooms are sweepingly large and have all the comforts of home—assuming your home is a dazzling showcase furnished with impeccable taste. In your room you'll find a plush robe and a coffeemaker complete with the hotel's own brand of specialty coffee. ⊠ *111 Perimeter Center W, Dunwoody 30346* ☎ *770/396–6800 or 877/946–8357* 🖷 *770/399–5514* ⊕ *www.whotels.com* ➡ *252 rooms, 23 suites* ♿ *Restaurant, cable TV, in-room broadband, Web TV, Wi-Fi, in-room DVDs, pool, gym, hot tub, sauna, lounge, Internet room, parking (fee)* ▭ *AE, D, DC, MC, V* ⦿ *EP.*

$$–$$$$ Crowne Plaza Atlanta Ravinia. If you're visiting one of the many businesses in Atlanta's Perimeter Center, about a 10-minute drive north of Buckhead, you can't beat the convenience of this hotel and conference center. A lushly landscaped atrium lobby echoes the surrounding woodlands. All rooms were refurbished in early 2006. ⊠ *4435 Ashford-Dunwoody Rd., Dunwoody 30346* ☎ *770/395–7700 or 800/227–6963* 🖷 *770/392–9503* ⊕ *www.crowneplaza.com* ➡ *473 rooms, 22 suites* ♿ *3 restaurants, cable TV, in-room broadband, Web TV, Wi-Fi, tennis court, indoor pool, gym, hot tub, lounge, laundry service, Internet room, business services, meeting rooms, free parking* ▭ *AE, D, DC, MC, V* ⦿ *EP.*

$$$ Westin Buckhead Atlanta. Behind the chic glass-and-white-tile exterior of this hotel overlooking Lenox Square is a chic interior. From the sweeping two-level lobby to the rooms, the hotel offers a contemporary but comfortable look. The decor focuses on natural colors—greens, beiges, browns—accented by exotic foliage. The Palm restaurant is noted for its steaks. ⊠ *3391 Peachtree Rd., Buckhead, 30326* ☎ *404/365–0065 or 800/228–3000* 🖷 *404/365–8787* ⊕ *www.westin.com/buckhead* ➡ *349 rooms, 16 suites* ♿ *Restaurant, cable TV, in room broadband, Web TV, Wi-Fi, some in-room DVDs, pool, health club, bar, Internet room, business services, parking (fee), some pets allowed* ▭ *AE, D, DC, MC, V* ⦿ *EP.*

$$–$$$ Embassy Suites Hotel. Just blocks from the shopping meccas of Lenox Square and Phipps Plaza is this modern high-rise. There are several different kinds of suites—from deluxe units with amenities like wet bars to more basic sleeping-and-sitting-room combinations. All of the rooms open onto a sunny atrium that towers 16 stories above the lobby. Rates include afternoon cocktails. ⊠ *3285 Peachtree Rd., Buckhead, 30305* ☎ *404/261–7733 or 800/362–2779* 🖷 *404/261–6857* ⊕ *www. embassysuites.com* ➥ *317 suites* ♨ *Restaurant, cable TV, in-room data ports, Web TV, Wi-Fi, indoor-outdoor pool, gym, parking (fee)* ☐ *AE, D, DC, MC, V* ⦿| *BP.*

$$–$$$ ▦ **Sheraton Buckhead.** This 8-floor hotel has the advantage of being right across from Lenox Square. Contemporary furnishings fill the rooms; some have a desk and chair, others comfortable sofas. All are equipped with amenities such as hair dryers, coffeemakers, and irons and ironing boards. ⊠ *3405 Lenox Rd., Buckhead, 30326* ☎ *404/261–9250 or 800/ 325–3535* 🖷 *404/848–7391* ⊕ *www.sheraton.com/buckhead* ➥ *369 rooms, 3 suites* ♨ *Restaurant, cable TV, in-room broadband, Wi-Fi, pool, gym, bar, Internet room, business services, meeting rooms, parking (fee), some pets allowed* ☐ *AE, D, DC, MC, V* ⦿| *EP.*

$–$$ ▦ **Holiday Inn Select Atlanta Perimeter.** If frills come second to comfort and familiarity, consider this hotel—which generally caters to the brief-case set—with a superb location in the Perimeter business district. Rooms have coffeemakers, hair dryers, and desks. ⊠ *4386 Chamblee-Dunwoody Rd., Dunwoody 30341* ☎ *770/457–6363 or 800/465–4329* 🖷 *770/936–9592* ⊕ *www.hiselect.com/atl-perimeter* ➥ *250 rooms, 2 suites* ♨ *Restaurant, cable TV, Wi-Fi, pool, gym, lounge, laundry service, Internet room, business services, meeting rooms, free parking, some pets allowed* ☐ *AE, D, DC, MC, V* ⦿| *EP.*

$ ▦ **Extended Stay Deluxe Lenox North.** The next-door grocery store is handy at this comfortable hotel with kitchenettes in the studio suites. Earthy tones contribute to the homey feel. The property is 1 mi north of Lenox Square and across the street from the Brookhaven MARTA station. ⊠ *3967 Peachtree Rd., Brookhaven 30319* ☎ *404/237–9100 or 800/ 398–7829* 🖷 *404/237–0055* ⊕ *www.extendedstayhotels.com* ➥ *91 suites* ♨ *Kitchenettes, cable TV, Wi-Fi, in-room DVDs, pool, gym, laundry service, free parking, some pets allowed* ☐ *AE, D, DC, MC, V* ⦿| *BP.*

NIGHTLIFE & THE ARTS

The Arts

For the most complete schedule of cultural events, check the Thursday "Access Atlanta" section of the *Atlanta Journal-Constitution.* Free editions of the Thursday section are available all week at news boxes in the downtown area. The city's lively and free alternative weekly *Creative Loafing* also has cultural and entertainment listings.

AtlanTIX Ticket Services (☎ 678/318–1400 ⊕ www.atlantaperforms. com), at Underground Atlanta and Lenox Square, sells half-price same-day tickets for performances as well as half-price same-day and next-day tickets for cultural events. Tickets are available Monday to Saturday 11 to 6, Sunday noon to 4. **Ticketmaster** (☎ 404/249–6400 or 800/326–4000 ⊕ www.ticketmaster.com) handles tickets for Fox Theatre, Atlanta Civic Center, Philips Arena, and other venues.

Concerts

The **Atlanta Symphony Orchestra (ASO)** (☎ 404/733–5000 ⊕ www.atlantasymphony.org), under the musical direction of Robert Spano, has 23 Grammy awards to its credit. It performs the fall–spring subscription series in the 1,800-seat Symphony Hall at Woodruff Arts Center. In summer the orchestra regularly plays with big-name popular and country artists in the outdoor Chastain Park Amphitheatre.

Emory University (✉ 1700 N. Decatur Rd., Emory ☎ 404/727–5050 ⊕ www.arts.emory.edu), an idyllic campus surrounded by picturesque homes, has five major venues where internationally renowned artists perform.

Georgia State University (✉ Florence Kopleff Recital Hall, Peachtree Center Ave. and Gilmer St., Downtown ☎ 404/651–4636 or 404/651–3676 ⊕ www.music.gsu.edu) hosts concerts that are free and open to the public. The entrance is on Gilmer Street, and there's parking in the lot at the corner of Edgewood and Peachtree Center avenues.

Dance

The **Atlanta Ballet** (✉ 1400 W. Peachtree St., Midtown ☎ 404/873–5811 ⊕ www.atlantaballet.com), founded in 1929, is the country's oldest continuously operating ballet company. It has been internationally recognized for its productions of classical and contemporary works. Artistic director John McFall has choreographed such dance greats as Mikhail Baryshnikov and Cynthia Gregory; only the third director in the company's history, McFall brings a constant stream of innovative ideas and vision to the group. Performances are usually at the Fox Theatre but sometimes take place elsewhere.

Festivals

The **Atlanta Jazz Festival** (☎ 404/817–6815 ⊕ www.atlantafestivals.com), held Memorial Day weekend, gathers the best local, national, and international musicians for free concerts at Atlanta's Piedmont Park.

The **National Black Arts Festival** (✉ 659 Auburn Ave., Sweet Auburn ☎ 404/730–7315 ⊕ www.nbaf.org), celebrating literature, dance, visual arts, theater, film, and music in venues throughout the city, is held the third week in July. Maya Angelou, Cicely Tyson, Harry Belafonte, Spike Lee, Tito Puente, and Wynton Marsalis have appeared at past events. Admission to events varies.

Opera

The **Atlanta Opera** (✉ 728 W. Peachtree St., Midtown ☎ 404/881–8885 or 800/356–7372 ⊕ www.atlantaopera.org) usually mounts four main-stage productions each year at the Boisfeuillet Jones Atlanta Civic Center. Major roles are performed by national and international guest artists; the chorus and orchestra come from the local community.

Performance Venues

Boisfeuillet Jones Atlanta Civic Center (✉ 395 Piedmont Ave., Midtown ☎ 404/523–6275 ⊕ www.atlantaciviccenter.com), christened after the improbably named Atlanta philanthropist, presents touring Broadway musicals, pop concerts, dance performances, and opera.

Chastain Park Amphitheatre (✉ 4469 Stella Dr. NW, Buckhead ☎ 404/233–2227 or 404/733–5000 ⊕ www.classicchastain.com), home to Atlanta Symphony Orchestra's summer series and other pop concerts, feels more like an outdoor nightclub than a typical performance venue. Pack a picnic, bring a blanket if you've snagged some seats on the lawn, and prepare to listen to your favorite performers over the clink of dishes and the chatter of dinner conversation.

The **Coca-Cola Roxy** (✉ 3110 Roswell Rd., Buckhead ☎ 404/233–7699 ⊕ www.atlantamusicguide.com/the_roxy.htm) was once a theater, so its sloped floors make for an ideal concert hall. Shows range from comedy to rock, jazz to hip-hop.

Ferst Center for the Performing Arts (✉ 349 Ferst Dr., Georgia Tech ☎ 404/894–9600 ⊕ www.ferstcenter.org), at Georgia Institute of Technology, hosts performances that run the gamut from classical and jazz to dance and theater. There's ample free parking on weekends.

Fox Theatre (✉ 660 Peachtree St., Midtown ☎ 404/881–2100 ⊕ www.foxtheatre.org), a dramatic faux-Moorish theater, is the principal venue for touring Broadway shows and national productions, as well as the home of the Atlanta Ballet.

Gwinnett Center and Arena (✉ 6400 Sugarloaf Pkwy., Duluth ⊕ www.gwinnettcenter.com ☎ 770/813–7500 or 800/224–6422 ⊕ www.gwinettcenter.com), 30 mi north of downtown Atlanta, houses the 702-seat performing-arts center and the 13,000-seat arena. The arena hosts national touring acts as well as Gwinnett Gladiators minor-league hockey games.

HiFi Buys Amphitheatre (✉ 2002 Lakewood Way, Downtown ☎ 404/443–5090 ⊕ www.hob.com), 4 mi south of downtown Atlanta, draws national popular music acts all summer. There's seating for up to 19,000 in reserved areas and on its sloped lawn.

Mable House Barnes Amphitheatre (✉ 5239 Floyd Rd., Mableton ☎ 770/819–7765 ⊕ mablehouseamphitheater.com), a 2,200-seat venue 6 mi west of downtown Atlanta, stages classical, jazz, and country music.

With a seating capacity of 21,000, **Philips Arena** (✉ 1 Philips Dr., Downtown ☎ 404/878–3000 ⊕ www.philipsarena.com) is the major venue downtown. In addition to hosting the biggest musical acts, it's also the home of the Atlanta Hawks, the Atlanta Thrashers, and the Georgia Force. The Philips Arena MARTA station makes getting here a snap.

Rialto Center for the Performing Arts (✉ 80 Forsyth St. NW, Downtown ☎ 404/651–4727 ⊕ www.rialtocenter.org), developed by Georgia State University in a beautifully renovated and restructured former movie theater, shows film, theater, and dance, as well as musical performances by local and international performers.

★ **Spivey Hall** (✉ 2000 Clayton State Blvd., Morrow ☎ 678/466–4200 ⊕ www.spiveyhall.org) is a gleaming, modern, acoustically magnificent performance center at Clayton State University, 15 mi south of Atlanta. The hall is considered one of the country's finest concert venues. Internationally renowned musicians perform everything from chamber music to jazz.

Tabernacle (✉ 152 Luckie St., Downtown ☎ 404/659–9022 ⊕ www. livenation.com) began its postchurch life as a House of Blues venue during the 1996 Olympics. Now it hosts top acts of all genres in an intimate setting. Seating is limited; the main floor of the former sanctuary is standing-room only.

Variety Playhouse (✉ 1099 Euclid Ave., Little Five Points, Inman Park ☎ 404/521–1786 ⊕ www.variety-playhouse.com), a former movie theater, is one of the cultural anchors of the hip Little Five Points neighborhood. Its denizens don't don fancy frocks to listen to rock, bluegrass and country, blues, reggae, folk, jazz, and pop.

Woodruff Arts Center (✉ 1280 Peachtree St. NE, Midtown ☎ 404/733–4200 ⊕ www.woodruffcenter.org) houses the Alliance Theatre and the Atlanta Symphony Orchestra.

Theater

Actor's Express (✉ 887 W. Marietta St. NW, Downtown ☎ 404/607–7469 ⊕ www.actors-express.com), an acclaimed theater group, presents an eclectic selection of classic and cutting-edge productions in the 150-seat theater of the King Plow Arts Center, a stylish artists' complex hailed by local critics as a showplace of industrial chic. For an evening of dining and theater, plan dinner at the Food Studio, at the King Plow Arts Center.

Alliance Theatre (✉ 1280 Peachtree St. NE, Midtown ☎ 404/733–5000 ⊕ www.alliancetheatre.org), Atlanta's premier professional theater, presents everything from Shakespeare to the latest Broadway and off-Broadway hits. It's in the Woodruff Arts Center.

The **Atlanta Shakespeare Company** (✉ 499 Peachtree St., Midtown ☎ 404/874–5299 ⊕ www.shakespearetavern.com) stages plays by the Bard and his peers, as well as by contemporary dramatists, at the New American Shakespeare Tavern. Performances vary in quality but are always fun. The Elizabethan-style playhouse is a real tavern, so alcohol and pub-style food are available.

14th Street Playhouse (✉ 173 14th St., Midtown ☎ 404/733–4750 ⊕ www.woodruffartscenter.org) is part of the Woodruff Arts Center. Resident companies include Art Within, Atlanta Classical Theatre, and Theatre Gael. Musicals, plays, and sometimes opera are presented.

★ **Georgia Shakespeare** (✉ 4484 Peachtree Rd. NE, Buckhead ☎ 404/264–0020 ⊕ www.gashakespeare.org), a tradition since 1986, brings plays by the Bard and other enduring authors to the 509-seat Conant Performing Arts Center, on the campus of Oglethorpe University, from June to November.

Horizon Theatre Co. (✉ 1083 Austin Ave., Little Five Points, Inman Park ☎ 404/584–7450 ⊕ www.horizontheatre.com), a professional troupe established in 1983, produces premieres of provocative and entertaining contemporary plays in its 175-seat theater.

Nightlife

Atlanta has long been known for having more bars than churches, and in the South that's an oddity. The pursuit of entertainment—from Midtown to Buckhead—is known as the "Peachtree shuffle." Atlanta's vibrant nightlife includes everything from coffeehouses to sports bars, from country line dancing to high-energy dance clubs.

Bars

★ The **Beluga Martini Bar** (⊠ 3115 Piedmont Rd., Buckhead ☎ 404/869–1090) serves its namesake cocktails in an intimate, comfortable space. There's often live music.

You can't get a Budweiser or Coors at the **Brick Store Pub** (⊠ 125 E. Court Sq., Decatur ☎ 404/687–0990), but you can choose from 288 other bottled and draft brews, along with some very good burgers, salads, and sandwiches. The interior is cavelike but comfortable.

If you want to feel like a local—a too-cool-for-school local—stop by the **Euclid Avenue Yacht Club** (⊠ 1136 Euclid Ave. NE, Little Five Points ☎ 404/688–2582). Everyone's welcome at this neighborhood hangout with the ironically preppy name: college kids, punkers, motorcycle riders, and corporate types.

Limerick Junction (⊠ 822 N. Highland Ave., Virginia-Highland ☎ 404/874–7147), a lively Irish pub, showcases singers from the large Atlanta community that ably render traditional Irish music, as well as performers from the old sod itself. It has a rollicking, good-time feeling about it. Parking is dreadful, so consider a cab. A small cover is common on weekends.

Manuel's Tavern (⊠ 602 N. Highland Ave., Virginia-Highland ☎ 404/525–3447) is a neighborhood saloon where families, students, and professionals gather to brainstorm and partake of the tavern's menu of pleasantly upscale pub food—burgers and hot dogs, sure, but also grilled salmon, fried shrimp, and oysters, and a selection of salads. When the Atlanta Braves play, the crowd gathers around the wide-screen TVs.

Vortex (⊠ 878 Peachtree St., Midtown ☎ 404/875–1667) has a friendly style, knowledgeable bartenders, live bands, and hearty pub fare, making it a local favorite.

Comedy

In the Startime Entertainment complex in Roswell, 20 mi north of downtown Atlanta, is **Funny Farm** (⊠ 608 Holcomb Bridge Rd., Roswell ☎ 770/817–4242). Admission usually ranges from $10 to $14.

Punchline (⊠ 280 Hilderbrand Dr., Balconies Shopping Center, Sandy Springs ☎ 404/252–5233), the city's oldest comedy club, books major national acts. The small club is popular, so you need a reservation. Cover charges can be $20 for some acts, but it's usually worth it.

Country

The 44,000-square-foot **Cowboys Concert Hall** (⊠ 1750 N. Roberts Rd., Kennesaw ☎ 770/426–5006) attracts national talent twice a month. On

Thursday to Sunday, line-dancing and couple-dancing lessons bring out the crowds. The cover is $7—more if an unusually high-profile act is slated.

Billing itself as the nation's largest country-music dance club and concert hall, **Wild Bill's** (⊠ 2075 Market St., Duluth ☎ 678/473–1000) has room for 5,000 dancin', drinkin', partyin' cowpokes. The cover is $8 to $10 most nights.

Dance

In a former car dealership, **Compound** (⊠ 1008 Brady Ave., West Atlanta ☎ 404/872–4621) is a cluster of different spaces, all of them sophisticated. One of the bars has sleek white furnishings and is lighted with an otherworldly glow. There are various dance parties, from salsa on Thursday to hip-hop on Friday.

Havana Club (⊠ 247 Buckhead Ave., Buckhead ☎ 404/869–8484) offers free salsa lessons on Friday and and dancing to live music on Saturday.

To make it through the door at **Tongue & Groove** (⊠ 3055 Peachtree Rd., Buckhead ☎ 404/261–2325), you must dress to impress. Covers range from $10 to $20.

The dress code at **Vision** (⊠ 1068 Peachtree St., Midtown ☎ 404/874–4460)—nothing you'd wear to the beach or the ballgame—is intended to kick things up a notch. The music is hip-hop, disco, and R&B, and the dance floor is huge. The cover charge is $10 to $20.

Gay & Lesbian

Most of the city's many lesbian and gay clubs are in Midtown, but a few can be found in Buckhead and the suburbs.

A fixture on the gay scene since 1978, **Bulldogs** (⊠ 893 Peachtree St., Midtown ☎ 404/872–3025) is the place to hang out with friends or dance to hip-hop, house, or R&B. The cover is $3 to $5.

Burkhart's (⊠ 1492 F Piedmont Rd., Ansley Square Shopping Center, Midtown ☎ 404/872–4403) caters to a mostly male clientele with pool, karaoke, and drag shows. It's more of a neighborhood hangout than a dance club.

Hoedowns (⊠ 931 Monroe Dr., Midtown ☎ 404/876–0001) is where gays and lesbians go to two-step to country music. Free dance lessons are offered Tuesday, Wednesday, Thursday, and Saturday.

WETbar is best-known for the downtown views from its rooftop patio bar and backdoor garden for enjoying Atlanta's weather. Watch for its large projection-screen video wall. Thursday night is college night; Friday, dance night with DJs; Saturday, mainstream DJs. Cover charges vary. ⊠ 960 Spring St., Midtown ☎ 404/745–9494.

Jazz & Blues

★ **Blind Willie's** (⊠ 828 N. Highland Ave., Virginia-Highland ☎ 404/873–2583) showcases New Orleans and Chicago blues groups. Cajun and zydeco are also on the agenda from time to time. The name honors Blind Willie McTell, a native of Thomson, Georgia; his original compositions include "Statesboro Blues," made popular by the Georgia–based Allman Brothers. Cover charges run $3 to $10.

Churchill Grounds (✉ 660 Peachtree St., Midtown ☎ 404/876–3030) celebrates jazz with weekly jam sessions and great local and national acts. Cover charges range from $5 to $10 per set.

Resembling a ship, **Dante's Down the Hatch** (✉ 3380 Peachtree Rd., Buckhead ☎ 404/266–1600) is as popular for its music as it is for its sultry sensibility. Most nights music is provided by a jazz trio, which conjures silky-smooth tunes.

A restaurant by day, **Fuzzy's Place** (✉ 2015 N. Druid Hills Rd., Druid Hills ☎ 404/321–6166) transforms into a blues room at night. The finest local talent holds forth on the stage, including the venerable Francine Reed, one of Atlanta's favorite entertainers. There's usually a $5 to $10 cover change.

Sambuca (✉ 3102 Piedmont Rd., Buckhead ☎ 404/237–5299), a lively bar with good blues and jazz music, attracts a young crowd.

Rock

Eddie's Attic (✉ 515B N. McDonough St., Decatur ☎ 404/377–4976) is a good spot for catching local and some national rock, folk, and country-music acts. It has a full bar and restaurant and is near the Decatur MARTA station. Cover charges range from $5 to $20.

Masquerade (✉ 695 North Ave., Virginia-Highland ☎ 404/577–8178) is a grunge hangout playing everything from industrial to techno to disco. The mix of people reflects the club's three separate spaces, dubbed Heaven, Hell, and Purgatory. Basic bar food is available. The cover is $8 to $30.

Smith's Olde Bar (✉ 1578 Piedmont Ave., Midtown ☎ 404/875–1522) schedules different kinds of talent, both local and regional, in its acoustically fine performance space. Food is available in the downstairs restaurant. Covers vary depending on the act but are usually $5 to $15.

Star Community Bar (✉ 437 Moreland Ave., Little Five Points ☎ 404/681–9018) is highly recommended for those who enjoy grunge and rockabilly. Bands play almost nightly, with covers of $5 to $8, depending on the act. The bar used to be a bank—the Elvis shrine in the vault must be seen to be believed.

10 High Club (✉ 816 N. Highland Ave., Virginia-Highland ☎ 404/873–3607), a brick-walled space in the basement of the Dark Horse Tavern, hosts local and regional bands that are guaranteed to be loud. Covers rarely exceed $10.

SHOPPING

Atlanta's department stores, specialty shops, indoor malls, and antiques markets draw shoppers from across the Southeast. Most stores are open Monday through Saturday 10 to 9, Sunday noon to 6. The sales tax is 7% in the city of Atlanta and Fulton County and 6%–7% in the suburbs.

Shopping Neighborhoods

Nostalgic and cutting-edge at the same time, **Atlantic Station** was built to look like it's been around for a while. Actually, this combo of living, working, and recreational spaces opened in 2005. It covers about 10 square blocks, clustered around a green space known as Central Park. Retailers range from IKEA and Dillard's to Banana Republic and Z Gallerie. It's easy to reach by car, but is also accessible by free shuttle buses from the Arts Center MARTA station. An on-site concierge is happy to help you find your way around or make dinner reservations at the more than a dozen restaurants. ⊠ *1380 Atlantic Dr.* ☎ *404/685–1841* ⊕ *www.atlanticstation.com.*

Buckhead, a commercial district with many specialty shops and strip malls, is no minor shopping destination. Boutiques, gift shops, and some fine restaurants line East and West Paces Ferry roads, Pharr Road, East Shadowlawn Avenue, and East Andrews Drive. Cates Center has similar stores. Others are on Irby Avenue and Paces Ferry Place.

Decatur Square, a quaint town quad with a sophisticated, artistic vibe, is teeming with interesting specialty shops and delectable coffeehouses and cafés. Lively downtown Decatur, 8 mi east of Midtown Atlanta, is one of the metro area's favorite spots for sidewalk strolling and window-shopping.

Little Five Points attracts "junking" addicts who find happiness in Atlanta's version of Greenwich Village. There are vintage-clothing emporiums, used record and bookshops, and some stores that defy description.

In the town of **Marietta,** about 20 mi northwest of downtown Atlanta, is home to a charming town square. The surrounding streets offer dozens of antique shops and other shopping opportunities.

Quaint **Roswell,** about 23 mi north of Atlanta, is a great place to shop for antiques, visit art galleries, and enjoy outstanding restaurants.

Virginia-Highland is a wonderful urban neighborhood for window-shopping, thanks to its boutiques, antiques shops, and art galleries. Parking can be tricky in the evenings, so be prepared to park down a side street and walk a few blocks.

Shopping Centers

Lenox Square (⊠ 3393 Peachtree Rd., Buckhead ☎ 404/233–6767), one of Atlanta's oldest and most popular shopping centers, has branches of Neiman Marcus, Bloomingdale's, and Macy's looming next to specialty shops such as Cartier and Mori. Valet parking is available at the front of the mall, but free parking is nearby. You'll do better at one of the several good restaurants in the mall—even for a quick meal—than at the food court.

Peachtree Center Mall (⊠ 231 Peachtree St., Downtown ☎ 404/524–3787) has specialty shops, such as International Records, Touch of Georgia, and the Atlanta International Museum gift shop.

Perimeter Mall (⊠ 4400 Ashford-Dunwoody Rd., Dunwoody ☎ 770/394–4270), known for upscale family shopping, has Nordstrom, Macy's, Dillard's, and Bloomingdale's and a plentiful food court. Its restaurants include the Cheesecake Factory, Goldfish, and Maggiano's Little Italy.

Phipps Plaza (✉ 3500 Peachtree Rd., Buckhead ☎ 404/262–0992 or 800/810–7700) has branches of Tiffany & Co., Saks Fifth Avenue, and Gucci, as well as such shops as Niketown and Teavana.

Underground Atlanta (✉ 50 Upper Alabama St., Downtown ☎ 404/523–2311) has such shops as the Underground Railroad Quilt Gallery; African Pride, with objets d'art from all parts of the continent; and Habersham Winery, a tasting room for Georgia wines. You can ride the Aero Balloon, a tethered balloon that rises high enough to give you a great view of the city. The food court is good for a quick bite.

Outlets

The interstate highways leading to Atlanta have discount malls similar to those found throughout the country. About 60 mi north of the city on Interstate 85 at Exit 149 is a huge cluster of outlets in the town of Commerce.

Discover Mills Mall (✉ 5900 Sugarloaf Pkwy., Lawrenceville ☎ 678/847–5000), 25 mi northeast of downtown Atlanta, has bargain stores like Off 5th Saks Fifth Avenue and Last Call Neiman Marcus.

North Georgia Premium Outlets (✉ 800 Hwy. 400 S, at Dawson Forest Rd., Dawsonville ☎ 706/216–3609) is worth the 45 minutes it takes to get here from Atlanta's northern perimeter. This shopping center has more than 140 stores, including Williams-Sonoma, OshKosh B'Gosh, Bose, and numerous designer outlet shops: Coach, Ann Taylor, and Ralph Lauren.

Specialty Shops

ANTIQUES & DECORATIVE ARTS
Bennett Street in Buckhead has antiques shops, home-decor stores such as John Overton Oriental Rugs-Antiques, and art galleries, including the Bennett Street Gallery. The Stalls on Bennett Street is a good antiques market.

Chamblee Antique Row (☎ 404/606–3367 ⊕ www.antiquerow.com) is a browser's delight. At Peachtree Industrial Boulevard and Broad Street in the suburban town of Chamblee, it's just north of Buckhead and about 10 mi north of downtown.

Buckhead's **Miami Circle,** is an upscale enclave with shops for antiques and decorative-arts lovers.

ART GALLERIES
The city is overflowing with art galleries—some new, some well established. For more information on the Atlanta art-gallery scene, including openings and location maps, consult *Museums & Galleries* (☎ 770/992–7808 ⊕ www.nwpublications.com/publications/museums.php), a magazine distributed free around the city.

Fay Gold Gallery (✉ 764 Miami Circle, Buckhead ☎ 404/233–3843) displays works by regional and national contemporary artists, featuring paintings, sculpture, and photography.

Jackson Fine Art Gallery (⌧ 3115 E. Shadowlawn Ave., Buckhead ☎ 404/ 233–3739) exhibits fine-art photography.

Marcia Wood Gallery (⌧ 263 Walker St., Castleberry Hill ☎ 404/827– 0030) shows contemporary paintings, sculpture, and photography.

Mason Murer Fine Art (⌧ 199 Armour Dr., Midtown ☎ 404/879–1500) has a 24,000 square-foot gallery offering the finest in contemporary and regional art.

Vespermann Glass Gallery (⌧ 309 E. Paces Ferry Rd., Buckhead ☎ 404/ 266–0102) carries lovely handblown glass objects and jewelry.

FOOD **East 48th St. Market** (⌧ Williamsburg Shopping Center, 2462 Jett Ferry Rd., Dunwoody ☎ 770/392–1499) sells Italian deli meats, breads, cheeses, and prepared foods.

Shop at **Eatzi's Market & Bakery** (⌧ 3221 Peachtree Rd., Buckhead ☎ 404/237–2266) for prepared foods, imported cheeses, great breads, and fine wines.

Star Provisions (⌧ 1198 Howell Mill Rd., West Midtown ☎ 404/365– 0410) is a chef's dream, with fine cookware, gadgets, and tableware for sale, plus top-of-the-line cheeses, meats, and baked goods.

The health-wise can take comfort at **Whole Foods Market** (⌧ 77 W. Paces Ferry Rd. NW, Buckhead ☎ 404/324–4100 ⌧ 2111 Briarcliff Rd., Druid Hills ☎ 404/634–7800 ⌧ 650 Ponce de Leon Ave. NE, Midtown ☎ 404/853–1681), with a dizzying amount of pesticide-free produce, hormone-free meats, and fresh seafood.

Your DeKalb Farmers Market (⌧ 3000 E. Ponce de Leon Ave., Decatur ☎ 404/377–6400) has 175,000 square feet of exotic fruits, cheeses, seafood, sausages, breads, and delicacies from around the world. The cafeteria-style buffet, with a selection of earthy and delicious hot foods and salads, is alone worth the trip.

ATLANTA ESSENTIALS

Transportation

BY AIR

Hartsfield-Jackson Atlanta International, the busiest passenger airport in the world, is served by more than 26 airlines, including AirTran, America West, American, Continental, Delta, JetBlue, Midway, Midwest Express, Northwest, United, and US Airways. Although an underground train and moving walkways help you reach your gate more quickly, budget a little extra time for negotiating the massive facility. Because of the airport's size, security lines can be long, especially during peak travel periods. The airport typically suggests arriving 1½ hours before your flight.

The airport is 13 mi south of downtown. There are large parking facilities, which tend to fill up quickly. Check their current capacity, which is available on the airport's Web site. Locals know that MARTA, the regional subway system, is the fastest and cheapest way to and from the airport, but taxis are available. The fare to downtown is $25 for one person, $26 for two, and $30 for three. From the airport to Buckhead, the fare is $35 for one person, $36 for two, and $39 for three. Buckhead Safety Cab and Checker Cab offer 24-hour service.

Atlanta Airport Superior Shuttle vans run daily every 15 minutes between 6 AM and 11:30 PM to Perimeter Center offices, hotels,

> ## CATCHING YOUR FLIGHT
>
> Locals take **MARTA** (☎ 404/848-5000 ⊕ www.itsmarta.com) to and from Hartsfield-Jackson International Airport, which has the traffic snarls common with larger airports. The $1.75 fare is a fraction of the amount charged by shuttles or taxis.

11

and residences. The trip can take 30 to 45 minutes, depending on the traffic. The cost ranges from $27 to $32 one-way. Atlanta Link operates vans every 15 minutes between 6 AM and midnight to downtown, Midtown, and the Buckhead–Lenox area. Vans heading downtown cost $17 for the 20-minute trip. Vans to Midtown cost $19 for the 40-minute trip, and vans to the Buckhead–Lenox area cost $21 for the 45-minute trip.

Airport Metro Shuttle operates shuttles around-the-clock to destinations around the region. Reservation must be made at least 12 hours in advance. Typical fees are $55 for two passengers to Marietta or Roswell.
🛈 Airport Contacts **Hartsfield-Jackson Atlanta International Airport** ⊠ 6000 N. Terminal Pkwy., Hapeville ☎ 404/530-7300 ⊕ www.atlanta-airport.com.
🛈 Taxis & Shuttles **Atlanta Airport Superior Shuttle** ☎ 404/766-5312 ⊕ atlsuperiorshuttle.com. **Atlanta Link** ☎ 404/524-3400 ⊕ www.theatlantalink.com. **Airport Metro Shuttle** ☎ 404/766-6666 ⊕ airportmetro.com. **Buckhead Safety Cab** ☎ 404/233-1152. **Checker Cab** ☎ 404/351-1111. **MARTA** ☎ 404/848-5000 ⊕ www.itsmarta.com.

BY BUS

Amtrak operates its Thruway bus service daily between Atlanta's Brookwood Station and Montgomery and Mobile, Alabama. Other Thruway buses go from the station to Macon and Columbus, Georgia, and to Chattanooga and Nashville, Tennessee. Greyhound provides transportation from numerous points in the country to downtown Atlanta and Hartsfield-Jackson Atlanta International Airport.

MARTA operates more than 100 routes covering more than 1,000 mi. The fare is $1.75, and exact change or a Breeze card is required. Service is limited outside the perimeter of Interstate 285, except for a few areas in Clayton, DeKalb, and north Fulton counties.
🛈 **Amtrak** ⊠ 1688 Peachtree St., Buckhead ☎ 404/881-3060 or 800/872-7245 ⊕ www.amtrak.com. **Greyhound** ⊠ 232 Forsyth St., Downtown ☎ 404/584-1728 or 800/231-2222 ⊕ www.greyhound.com. **MARTA** ☎ 404/848-5000 ⊕ www.itsmarta.com.

BY CAR

The city is encircled by Interstate 285. Three interstates also crisscross Atlanta: Interstate 85, running northeast–southwest from Virginia to Alabama; Interstate 75, running north–south from Michigan to Florida; and Interstate 20, running east–west from South Carolina to Texas.

Some refer to Atlanta as the "Los Angeles of the South" because driving is virtually the only way to get around. Atlantans have grown accustomed to frequent delays at rush hour—the morning and late-afternoon commuting periods seem to get longer every year. Beware: the South as a whole may be laid-back, but Atlanta drivers are not; they tend to drive faster than drivers in other Southern cities.

If you plan to venture beyond the neighborhoods served by MARTA, you will want to rent a car. Many national agencies have branch offices all over the city, as well as at Hartsfield-Jackson Atlanta International Airport.

🚗 **Alamo** ☎ 404/530-2800 ⊕ www.alamo.com. **Avis** ☎ 404/530-2725 ⊕ www.avis.com. **Budget** ☎ 404/530-3000 ⊕ www.budget.com. **Hertz** ☎ 404/530-2925 ⊕ www.hertz.com. **National** ☎ 404/530-2800 ⊕ www.nationalcar.com.

BY SUBWAY

MARTA has clean and safe subway trains with somewhat limited routes that link downtown with many major landmarks. The system's two main lines cross at the Five Points station. MARTA uses a smart-card fare system called Breeze. The cards are available at RideStores and from vending machines at each station by using cash or credit cards. The one-way fare is $1.75, but the cards offer several options, including weekend, weekly, and monthly passes.

Trains generally run weekdays 5 AM to 1 AM and weekends and holidays 6 AM to 12:30 AM. Most trains operate every 15 to 20 minutes; during weekday rush hours, trains run every 10 minutes. Airport travelers should be careful about catching the right train. One line ends up at North Springs station to the north. The other to Doraville station, to the northeast. Daily parking is free at MARTA parking facilities. Long-term parking rates range from $4 to $7 daily. All stations do not have lots, however.

🚇 **MARTA** ☎ 404/848-5000 ⊕ www.itsmarta.com.

BY TAXI

Taxi service in Atlanta can be uneven. Drivers often lack correct change, so bring along plenty of small bills. You can also charge your fare, as many accept credit cards. Drivers may be as befuddled as you may be by the city's notoriously winding streets, so if your destination is somewhere other than a major hotel or popular sight, bring along printed directions.

In Atlanta taxi fares begin at $2.50, than add 25¢ for each additional ⅛ mi. Additional passengers are $2. If you remain within the Downtown Convention Zone, the Midtown Zone, or the Buckhead Zone, a flat rate of $8 for one person and $2 for each additional passenger is charged to any destination.

You generally need to call for a cab, as Atlanta is not a place where you can hail one on the street. Buckhead Safety Cab and Checker Cab offer 24-hour service.

🚕 Taxi Companies **Buckhead Safety Cab** ☎ 404/233-1152. **Checker Cab** ☎ 404/351-1111.

BY TRAIN

Amtrak operates daily service from Atlanta's Brookwood Station to New York; Philadelphia; Washington, DC; Baltimore; Charlotte, North Carolina; Greenville, South Carolina; and New Orleans.

Amtrak ✉ Brookwood Station, 1688 Peachtree St. NW, Buckhead ☎ 404/881-3060 or 800/872-7245 ⊕ www.amtrak.com.

Contacts & Resources

BANKS & EXCHANGE SERVICES

Wachovia, SunTrust, and Bank of America have the largest number of branches in metro Atlanta. Many other banks have branches in the city and suburbs. Most branches have ATMs.

Bank of America ✉ 35 Broad St. NW, Downtown ☎ 404/893-8282 ✉ 3116 Peachtree Rd. NE, Buckhead ☎ 404/262-6340. **SunTrust** ✉ 1175 Peachtree St. NE, Midtown ☎ 404/870-3140 ✉ 1685 North Decatur Rd. NE, Virginia-Highland ☎ 404/728-1200. **Wachovia** ✉ 494 Ponce de Leon Ave. NE, Midtown ☎ 404/897-6010.

EMERGENCIES

For 24-hour emergency rooms contact Atlanta Medical Center, Grady Memorial Hospital, Northside Hospital, and Piedmont Hospital.

Emergency Services Ambulance, fire, police ☎ 911.

Hospitals **Atlanta Medical Center** ✉ 303 Parkway Dr., Downtown ☎ 404/265-4000. **Grady Memorial Hospital** ✉ 80 Jesse Hill Jr. Dr., Downtown ☎ 404/616-4307. **Northside Hospital** ✉ 1000 Johnson Ferry Rd., Dunwoody ☎ 404/851-8000. **Piedmont Hospital** ✉ 1968 Peachtree Rd., Buckhead ☎ 404/605-5000.

24-Hour Pharmacies CVS ✉ 1943 Peachtree Rd., Buckhead ☎ 404/351-7629 ✉ 1554 N. Decatur Rd., Decatur ☎ 404/373-4192 ✉ 2350 Cheshire Bridge Rd., Buckhead ☎ 404/486-7289.

INTERNET, MAIL & SHIPPING

Shipping services are available at all FedEx Kinko's and UPS Store locations in the Atlanta area. Four UPS Store locations in the downtown area, listed below, offer high-speed wireless connections. For other high-speed hubs, try many of the area's coffeehouses, including the more than 100 Starbucks locations.

Post offices in Atlanta are open weekdays 9 to 5.

Post Offices **Buckhead Station** ✉ 3851 Peachtree St., Buckhead ☎ 404/816-9486. **Downtown Station** ✉ 1 CNN Center Mall, Downtown ☎ 404/524-3394. **Midtown Station** ✉ 1072 W. Peachtree St., Midtown ☎ 404/486-7289.

Shipping Companies **FedEx Kinko's** ✉ 3637 Peachtree Rd. NE, Buckhead ☎ 404/233-1329 ✉ 1375 Peachtree St. NE, Midtown ☎ 404/876-4752 ✉ 100 Peachtree St. NW, Downtown ☎ 404/221-0000. **UPS Store** ✉ 2870 Peachtree Rd., Buckhead ☎ 404/814-1771 ✉ 541 10th St. NW, Midtown ☎ 404/733-6797 ✉ 3535 Peachtree Rd., Buckhead ☎ 404/442-8830 ✉ 925B Peachtree St. NE, Midtown ☎ 404/685-8280.

MEDIA

The *Atlanta Journal-Constitution* is the city's daily newspaper. *Creative Loafing,* a free alternative weekly, is available at many bookstores and restaurants. The *Atlanta Daily World,* serving the African-American community, is published weekly.

TOUR OPTIONS

Gray Line of Atlanta has a four-hour "Georgia's Great" bus tour for $48 (includes the Jimmy Carter Presidential Library & Museum, Martin Luther King Center, and the World of Coca-Cola) and a four-hour "All Around Atlanta" tour for $55 (the Margaret Mitchell House and Georgia Aquarium). The MARTA bus system links many of the city's top tourist sites, making do-it-yourself touring a more affordable option for many tourists.

The Atlanta Preservation Center runs several walking tours of historic areas and neighborhoods for $10 each; tours usually last one to two hours. Especially noteworthy are tours of Sweet Auburn, the neighborhood associated with Martin Luther King Jr. and other leaders of Atlanta's African-American community; Druid Hills, the verdant, genteel neighborhood where *Driving Miss Daisy* was filmed; and the Fox Theatre, the elaborate 1929s picture palace.

🎫 **Atlanta Preservation Center** ☎ 404/688-3353, 404/688-3350 for tour hotline ⊕ www.preserveatlanta.com. **Gray Line of Atlanta** ☎ 770/449-1806 or 800/593-1818 ⊕ www.americancoachlines.com.

VISITOR INFORMATION

The Atlanta Convention & Visitors Bureau, which provides information on Atlanta and the outlying area, has several information centers in Atlanta: Hartsfield-Jackson Atlanta International Airport, in the Atrium; Underground Atlanta; and the Georgia World Congress Center.

🎫 Tourist Information **Atlanta Convention & Visitors Bureau** ✉ 233 Peachtree St., Suite 100, Downtown, 30303 ☎ 404/521-6600 ✉ Underground Atlanta, 65 Upper Alabama St., Downtown ☎ 404/523-2311 ✉ Georgia World Congress Center, 285 International Blvd., Downtown ☎ 404/223-4000 ⊕ www.atlanta.net.

Central Georgia

WORD OF MOUTH

"We didn't have a chance to spend too much time in Macon, but we have been hoping to go back soon. It has some restored homes, and the small downtown is beautiful, with nice restaurants, and perfect for strolling. I wish we would have had at least one full day and night there . . . worth a stop, at least."

—amcc

"There's a small town south of Athens, called Madison, that is just so quaint and pretty with a lot of old homes that really look antebellum. We always stop in Madison on our way to Macon."

—mrsd2fan

Updated by
Chris McBeath

TOOL DOWN U.S. 441—the Antebellum Trail—to Macon, and you'll quickly see that the elegance of the Old South is all very new again, with many refurbishments returning historic buildings to their original splendor. Central Georgia, roughly, forms a triangle bordered within Athens, Macon, and Augusta, which together, give you a real flavor of Georgia's elegant past, and vibrant future. Madison epitomizes small-town America with its charming antebellum and Victorian architecture. Eatonton, 20 mi down the highway, also has its share of stately historic houses, although your attention will really be arrested by the statue of the giant rabbit on the courthouse lawn. It's part of the town's tribute to favorite son Joel Chandler Harris, creator of Br'er Rabbit and Uncle Remus.

If possible, make it to Macon in March, when the city's cherry trees are in full, spectacular flower. The annual festival celebrating the trees is a blast. And you can rock year-round at Macon's Georgia Music Hall of Fame, paying tribute to the state's musicians who have contributed so much to America's musical culture. Ray Charles, James Brown, the Allman Brothers Band, Chet Atkins, and Otis Redding are but a few of the legends honored in the hall.

In Athens, you can find remnants of antebellum Georgia. As home of the University of Georgia, it also pulses with college life—especially when the Bulldogs are playing. The birthplace of REM and the B-52s, Athens still has a thriving entertainment scene.

From here, head down U.S. 78 to Washington, a picturesque community that exudes a bustling turn-of-the-last-century charm and is a great stopover en route to Augusta, home of the Masters Tournament. Even if you're not drawn to the tees, Augusta, like so many communities in Georgia, is undergoing a renaissance of its waterfront and historic districts to create a visitor destination outside of the annual Masters bash.

Exploring Central Georgia

Athens, Macon, and Augusta form, roughly, a triangle. The best way to catch everything this region has to offer is to head from Athens down U.S. 441 toward Macon. Be prepared to take your time as you'll pass through smaller towns such as Milledgeville and Eatonton, each of which provide pockets of history and anecdotal stories. For example, Washington, which lies on U.S. 78, 38 mi east of Athens, was the first city chartered in honor of the first president. Continue along U.S. 78 and hit Interstate 20 to get to Augusta.

About the Hotels & Restaurants

Central Georgia isn't the first place to look for haute cuisine—even haute Southern cuisine—but there are plenty of opportunities to eat simply and well at reasonable prices. Things get spiced up a bit in Athens, which presents the greatest variety of choices.

The most attractive lodging options here tend to have been around for a long time; the structures, at least, often date from the 19th century. At such places—most commonly B&Bs, but sometimes larger inns—you're

TOP 5 REASONS TO GO

Small Town, Big Heart: Madison has been called America's Number One Small Town as much for its history as for its charm, much of which you can experience first hand around the town square—there's a restaurant in a converted 1800s bank and a couple of stores that are a hybrid of antiques, funky collectibles, and estate pieces.

The Antebellum Trail: Whether you're a fan of *Gone With the Wind* or not, traveling this picturesque trail between Macon and Athens will cast you back in time and give you a warming perspective as to the elegance of the Old South. Historic homes, plantation lands, and heritage townships are as authentic as you'll find anywhere.

Lovely Lakes: Lake Okone, between Madison and Eatonton, has terrific golf courses and excellent fishing if you're tempted to drop a line. Lake Sinclair, on your way to Milledgeville (the former state capital) is another honey-hole for fish because of its year-round warm waters. And Lake Jackson, the oldest lake in the state, is renowned for its recreational activities.

Sunset Cruise on the Augusta Canal: If you're not into paddling under your own steam, then chugging along at a handful of knots aboard oversize St. Petersburg barges is another way to absorb Augusta's canal history. You pass by historic mills, homes, and gardens, as well as riverbanks teeming with wildlife such as blue herons and egrets.

Marvels of Macon: When a city boasts no less that 5,500 individual structures on the National Register of Historic Places, you know it has more to offer than its two notable museums: Georgia Sports Hall of Fame and the Georgia Music Hall of Fame. Stay a while and explore everything from splendid Hay House, to the quaint charm of Sidney Lanier's childhood home, to the lesser known restored Armory downtown.

likely to find big porches with rocking chairs and bedrooms decorated with antiques. If that's more Southern charm than you're after, you can choose from a smattering of chain hotels.

	WHAT IT COSTS				
	$$$$	$$$	$$	$	¢
RESTAURANTS	over $22	$17–$22	$12–$16	$7–$11	under $7
HOTELS	over $220	$161–$220	$111–$160	$70–$110	under $70

Restaurant prices are for a main course at dinner. Hotel prices are for two people in a standard double room in high season.

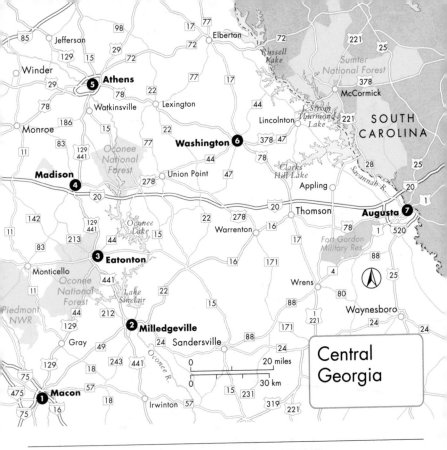

MACON & THE ANTEBELLUM TRAIL

The antebellum South, filtered through the romanticized gauze of *Gone With the Wind*, evokes graciousness, gentility, and a code of honor that saw many a duel between dashing gentlemen. Certainly, the historical architecture along the Antebellum Trail would endorse this picture, and even though many of the white-column mansions were built with the sweat of slaves, there is much to appreciate. Anchored between Macon and Athens, the trail was designated a state trail in 1985, and links the historical communities of Watkinsville, Madison, Eatonton, Milledgeville, and Old Clinton, all of which escaped the rampages of General Sherman's army on his march in 1864 from Atlanta to Savannah.

Macon

 32 mi southwest of Milledgeville via U.S. 441 to Rte. 49; 85 mi southeast of Atlanta via I–75.

At the state's geographic center, Macon, founded in 1823, has more than 100,000 flowering cherry trees, which it celebrates each March with a knockout festival. With 5,500 individual structures listed on the National

12

Register of Historic Places, its antebellum and Victorian homes are among the state's best preserved, and an ongoing program of restoration is revitalizing the downtown core. Following a $1.2 million restoration, the Capitol Theatre (originally founded as a bank in 1897) has reopened for movies and concerts; St. Joseph's Catholic Church has just finished a three-year renovation that makes it more impressive than ever; and the old Armory, complete with its first floor dance hall, is finding new life as an office and retail complex.

★ Among the city's many sites is the **Georgia Music Hall of Fame,** located in Macon as a tribute to the city's extensive contribution to American music. The museum recognizes the Georgians who have helped define America's musical culture. Among the honorees are Ray Charles, James Brown, Little Richard, the Allman Brothers Band, Chet Atkins, REM, and the B-52s. Exhibits also celebrate classical musicians, including Robert Shaw, the late director of the Atlanta Symphony Orchestra; opera singers Jessye Norman and James Melton; and violinist Robert McDuffie. ⊠ *200 Martin Luther King Jr. Blvd.* ☎ *478/750–8555 or 888/ 427–6257* ⊕ *www.gamusichall.com* ⊠ *$8* ☉ *Mon.–Sat. 9–5, Sun. 1–5.*

� There's family fun to be had at the **Georgia Children's Museum** adjacent to the Georgia Sports Hall of Fame. Adults can relax with a cup of hot java in the Lost Parents Café while kids engage in hands-on activities and theater performances. Be sure to check out the evolving model-train diorama about the history and industry of Georgia. ⊠ *382 Cherry St.* ☎ *478/755–9539* ⊕ *www.georgiachildrensmuseum.org* ⊠ *$5 per family weekdays; $5 per person weekends* ☉ *Tues.–Sat. 9:30–5, Sun. noon–5.*

� The **Georgia Sports Hall of Fame,** with its old-style ticket booths, has the look and feel of an old ballpark. Exhibits include a variety of interactive, touch-screen kiosks, and honor sports—including baseball, golf, track and field, and football—at all levels, from prep and college teams to professional. ⊠ *301 Cherry St.* ☎ *478/752–1585* ⊕ *www.gshf.org* ⊠ *$8* ☉ *Mon.–Sat. 9–5, Sun. 1–5.*

★ The unique **Hay House,** designed by the New York firm T. Thomas & Son in the mid 1800s, is a study in fine Italianate architecture prior to the Civil War. The marvelous stained-glass windows and many technological advances, including indoor plumbing, make a tour worthwhile. ■ TIP→ **Hay House was featured on** ***America's Castles* on the A&E Channel.** ⊠ *934 Georgia Ave.* ☎ *478/742– 8155* ⊕*www.georgiatrust.org* ⊠*$8* ☉ *Jan., Feb., July, and Aug., Mon.–Sat. 10–4; Mar.–June and Sept.–Dec., Mon.–Sat. 10–4, Sun. 1–4.*

A REAL FIND

Bag a deal at **Ginger Michelle** (⊠ 466 1st St. ☎ 478/746–3025), a sleek shop featuring contemporary and eclectic clothing, accessories, and shoes. Owners Steve and Ginger Hess are also multi-award-winning furniture designers. Much of their work, Ginger's handbags in particular, is carried in upscale stores across the nation and in Europe at considerably higher prices than you'll find here.

African-American entrepreneur Charles H. Douglass built the **Douglass Theatre** in 1921. Great American musicians have performed here, among them Bessie Smith, "Ma" Rainey, Cab Calloway, Duke Ellington, and locals Little Richard and Otis Redding. It's currently a venue for movies, plays, and other performances. You can take a guided tour of the building. ⊠ *355 Martin Luther King Jr. Blvd.* ☎ *478/742–2000* ⊕ *www.douglasstheatre.org* ⊗ *Weekdays 10–5.*

The **Macon Museum of Arts and Sciences and Mark Smith Planetarium** displays everything from a whale skeleton to fine art. Discovery House, an interactive exhibit for children, is modeled after an artist's garret. ⊠ *4182 Forsyth Rd.* ☎ *478/477–3232* ⊕ *www.masmacon.com* ✉ *$7* ⊗ *Mon. 9–8, Tues.–Sat. 9–5, Sun. 1–5.*

Just 3 mi east of downtown Macon is the **Ocmulgee National Monument**, a significant archaeological site. It was occupied for more than 10,000 years; at its peak, between AD 900 and AD 1100, it was populated by the Mississippian peoples. There's a reconstructed earth lodge and displays of pottery, effigies, and jewelry of copper and shells discovered in the burial mound. ⊠ *1207 Emery Hwy., take U.S. 80 east* ☎ *478/752–8257* ⊕ *www.nps.gov/ocmu* ✉ *Free* ⊗ *Daily 9–5.*

America has more tributes to Sidney Lanier, famous poet and musician of the Old South, than the years he lived. And it all starts at his birthplace, **Sidney Lanier Cottage**, a charming 1840 structure that features much of Lanier's writings among the period furnishings. Even his bride's tiny wedding gown is on show. Lanier died of consumption at 39 years of age after he was captured in 1864 for running the blockade. ⊠ *935 High St.* ☎ *478/743–3851* ⊕ *www.sidneylaniercottage.org* ✉ *$5* ⊗ *Weekdays 9–5, Sat. 10–4.*

★ The **Tubman African American Museum** honors the former slave who led more than 300 people to freedom as one of the conductors of the Underground Railroad. A mural depicts several centuries of black culture. The museum also has an African artifacts gallery. ⊠ *340 Walnut St.* ☎ *478/743–8544* ⊕ *www.tubmanmuseum.com* ✉ *$5* ⊗ *Mon.–Sat. 9–5, Sun. 2–5.*

OFF THE BEATEN PATH

MUSEUM OF AVIATION – This museum at Robins Air Force Base has an extraordinary collection of 90 vintage aircraft and missiles, including a MiG, an SR-71 (Blackbird), a U2, and assorted other flying machines from past campaigns. From Macon take Interstate 75 south to Exit 146 (Centerville/Warner Robins), and turn left onto Watson Boulevard, 7 mi to Route 247/U.S. 129, then right for 2 mi. ⊠ *Rte. 247/U.S. 129 at*

ON THE TRAIL

A meander along the new Ocmulgee Heritage Trail is a delightful diversion. The trailhead is at Gateway Park, at the corner of MLK Boulevard and Riverside Drive. Although only 9 mi of the path have been completed—6 within the Monument area—by 2009 the trail will connect the Ocmulgee National Monument along the river to a park and recreation area underway at the old Macon Waterworks.

Russell Pkwy., 20 mi south of Macon, Warner Robins ☎ *478/926–6870* 🌐 *www.museumofaviation.org* *Free; film $2* ⏲ *Daily 9–5.*

Where to Stay & Eat

$\$$–$\$\$\$$ ✕ **Downtown Grill.** In the heart of a city block of renovated warehouses, this popular restaurant can be hard to find. But it's well worth the search. The old Georgian brick gives a romantic flair to the decor, and the menu has many classic favorites such as pork tenderloin, filet mignon, and a tasty mixed grill with options for fish lovers and vegetarians. ■ TIP→ **Be prepared to walk a block; the approach alleys aren't always accessible by car.** ✉ *562 Mulberry St. Lane* ☎ *478/742–5999* 💳 *AE, MC, V* ⏲ *Closed Sun.*

★ **$\$\$$–$\$\$\$$** ✕ **Henderson Village.** At this resort, 38 mi south of Macon, you can find stunning 19th- and early-20th-century Southern homes and refurbished tenant cottages clustered around a green. Guest rooms have a rustic-style elegance, with fine antiques and access to inviting wraparound porches; suites are even nicer, with fireplaces and whirlpool tubs. The fine 1838 Langston House restaurant ($\$\$$–$\$\$\$$), actually three dining rooms and a glassed-in veranda, is perfect for a meal of Southern-style turbot and pan-seared beef fillet, items that are so popular they never come off the menu. ✉ *125 S. Langston Circle, Perry 31069* ☎ *478/988–8696 or 888/615–9722* 📠 *912/988–9009* 🌐 *www.hendersonvillage.com* *19 rooms, 5 suites* *Restaurant, in-room VCRs, pool, hot tub, fishing, hiking, horseback riding, bar, library, meeting rooms* 💳 *AE, MC, V* 🍽 *BP.*

$\$\$\$$ **1842 Inn.** With its grand white-pillar front porch and period antiques, this inn offers a true taste of antebellum grandeur, and it's easy to see why this place is considered to be one of America's top inns. The rooms have an aristocratic flair, with plush coverlets and embroidered pillows. There are also loveseats, ornate window stoops, and tile fireplaces, as well as period antiques and heirloom-quality accessories. In the morning you can eat breakfast in your room, in one of the parlors, or in the gorgeous courtyard. It's an easy walk to downtown and the historic district. ✉ *353 College St., 31201* ☎ *478/741–1842 or 800/336–1842* 📠 *478/741–1842* 🌐 *www.the1842inn.com* *21 rooms, 1 guest house* *Cable TV, in-room data ports, Wi-Fi, hot tub, laundry service* 💳 *AE, DC, MC, V* 🍽 *BP.*

★ **$\$\$$** **Crowne Plaza.** Its central location is what makes this 16-story, modern and comfortable chain hotel a winner. You can park the car and walk to many historic sites. ✉ *108 1st St., Macon 31201* ☎ *478/746–1461 or 877/227–6963* 📠 *478/738–2460* 🌐 *www.crowneplaza.com* *298 rooms, 9 suites* *Restaurant, in-room data ports, Wi-Fi, pool, sauna, fitness center, bar, meeting rooms* 💳 *AE, MC, V.*

Milledgeville

❷ *20 mi south of Eatonton on U.S. 441.*

Locals believe ghosts haunt what remains of the antebellum homes in Milledgeville. Laid out as the state capital of Georgia in 1803 (a title it held until Atlanta assumed the role in 1868), the town was not as fortunate as Madison in escaping being torched during the Civil War. Sherman's troops stormed through with a vengeance after the general heard hardship stories from Union soldiers who had escaped from a prisoner-of-war camp in nearby Andersonville.

The 1838 Greek-revival **Old Governor's Mansion** became Sherman's headquarters during the war. His soldiers are said to have tossed government documents out of the windows and fueled their fires with Confederate money. The mansion has been home to 10 Georgian governors and has undergone a $10-million restoration. Guided tours of the building, now a museum, are given daily, on the hour. ⊠ *120 S. Clark St.* ☎ *478/445–4545* ⌨ *$5* ☉ *Tues.–Sat. 10–4, Sun. 2–4.*

On West Hancock Street is the Georgia College and State University campus. One of its most famous students was novelist and short-story writer Flannery O'Connor, author of acclaimed novels such as *Wise Blood* and *The Violent Bear It Away*. O'Connor did most of her writing at the family farm, Andalusia, just north of Milledgeville on U.S. 441. The **Flannery O'Connor Room,** inside the **Ina Russell Library,** has many of the author's handwritten manuscripts on display. It also contains O'Connor's typewriter and some of her furniture. ⊠ *231 W. Hancock St.* ☎ *478/445–4047* ⊕ *www.library.gcsu.edu* ⌨ *Free* ☉ *Weekdays 9–4.*

Where to Stay & Eat

$–$$ ✕ **The Brick.** This bar-restaurant has a comfortable, worn-at-the-elbows appeal—which is all-important when you're about to consume massive pizzas with tasty toppings like feta cheese and spinach. Vegetarians will appreciate the "environmentally correct" pizza platter with its all-vegetable-topping. The menu's pasta selection boasts 9,000 combinations, and also offers salads and calzones. ⊠ *136 W. Hancock St.* ☎ *478/452–0089* ⊟ *AE, D, MC, V.*

$–$$ ▦ **Antebellum Inn.** Each room in this pre–Civil War mansion has beautiful period antiques. The Southern breakfasts are fabulous—think gourmet eggs Benedict or orange-essence croissant–French toast with lemon butter curd. The inn is owned and operated by a mother–daughter team, Jane Lorenz and Jo Ann Hicks, and both are bird lovers. In spring, many of the hanging planters have nesting birds. In the morning, birds and woodland creatures flock to the gardens, attracted to the many decorative feeders. ⊠ *200 N. Columbia St., 31061* ☎ *478/453–3993* ⊕ *www.antebelluminn.com* ⇌ *5 rooms* ⛭ *Dining room, Wi-Fi, pool* ⊟ *AE, D, MC, V* ⏅ *BP.*

Eatonton

 ❸ *22 mi south of Madison on U.S. 129/441.*

Right in the middle of the Antebellum Trail, Eatonton is a historical trove of houses that still retains the rare Southern antebellum architecture that survived Sherman's torches. But this isn't the only source of pride for this idyllic town. Take a look at the courthouse lawn; it's not your imagination—that really is a giant statue of a rabbit.

★ ☾ Eatonton is the birthplace of celebrated novelist Joel Chandler Harris, of Br'er Rabbit and Uncle Remus fame. The **Uncle Remus Museum,** built from authentic slave cabins, houses countless carvings, paintings, first-edition books, and other artwork depicting the characters made famous by the imaginative author. It's on the grounds of a park. ⊠ *Turner Park, U.S. 441* ☎ *706/485–6856* ⊕ *www.uncleremus.com/museum.html* ⊠ *$1* ☉ *Mon.–Sat. 10–5, Sun. 2–5.*

The **Eatonton-Putnam Chamber of Commerce** provides printed maps detailing landmarks from the upbringing of Eatonton native Alice Walker, who won the Pulitzer Prize for her novel *The Color Purple*. It also has information on the many fine examples of antebellum architecture in Eatonton, including descriptions and photographs of the town's prize antebellum mansions, and a walking tour of Victorian antebellum homes. ⊠ *105 S. Washington St.* ☎ *706/485–7701.*

Madison

❹ *27 mi south of Athens on U.S. 129/441.*

In 1809 Madison was described as "the most cultured and aristocratic town on the statecoach route from Charleston to New Orleans," and today, that charm still prevails, in large part because General Sherman's Union Army deliberately bypassed the town, thus saving it for posterity. From the picturesque town square, with its specialty shops and businesses, you can walk to any number of antebellum and other residences that make up one of the largest designated historic areas in Georgia. Pick up a Walking Tour Guide at the **Welcome Center** (⊠ 115 E. Jefferson St., on Sq. ☎ 706/342–4454) and it will route you past some 45 Madison homes.

★ Madison is the historic heart of Georgia and although many of the lovely homes are privately owned, **Heritage Hall** is one Greek-revival mansion, circa 1811, that is open to the public. Rooms are furnished to the 19th century and are an elegant insight as to the lifestyle of an average well-to-do family. ⊠ *277 S. Main St.* ☎ *706/342–9627* ⊠ *$5* ☉ *Mon.–Sat. 11–4:30, Sun. 1:30–4:30.*

Where to Stay & Eat

¢–$ ✕ **Ye Olde Colonial Restaurant.** Housed in an old bank, this casual, all-day restaurant is a Madison institution. Food is no-nonsense comfort for the soul—macaroni and cheese, fried chicken, BBQ pork, and squash casserole. For fun, try to grab a seat in the original bank vault; its walls are plastered with money that was used back in 1867 to fund railroad construction after the war. ⊠ *108 E. Washington St.* ☎ *706/342–2211* ⌂ *Reservations not accepted* ▤ *AE, MC, V* ☉ *Closed Sun.*

$$ ▦ **The Farmhouse Inn.** On a sprawling plot, this inn is a great family destination. There are 5 mi of wooded trails to explore, well-stocked ponds to fish, goats and miniature horses to pet, and a grassy picnic area to enjoy beside the Apalachee River. Owner Melinda Hartney even has a scavenger hunt to encourage you to get out and about. Rooms are country fresh—one has a fly-fishing decor, another has decorative quilts, and most adjoin sunny decks. Cottages are set back, away from the more romantic rooms in the main farmhouse. ⊠ *1051 Meadow La., 30650* ☎ *706/342–7933 or 866/253–0023* ⊕ *www.thefarmhouseinn.com* ⊠ *5 rooms, 2 cottages* ▤ *AE, MC, V* ⦿ *BP.*

Athens

❺ *70 mi east of Atlanta via I–85 north to Rte. 316.*

Athens, an artistic jewel of the American South, is known as a breeding ground for famed rock groups such as the B-52s and REM. Because of this distinction, creative types from all over the country flock to its trendy streets in hopes of becoming, or catching a glimpse of the next big act to take the world by storm. At the center of this artistic mêlée is the University of Georgia (UGA). With more than 30,000 students, UGA is an influential ingredient in the Athens mix, giving the quaint but compact city a distinct flavor that falls somewhere between a misty Southern enclave, a rollicking college town, and a smoky, jazz club–studded alleyway. Of course, this all goes "to the Dawgs" if the home team is playing on home turf; although, even then, Athens remains a truly fascinating blend of Mayberry R.F.D. and MTV. The effect is as irresistible as it is authentic.

> ### ROOTED IN HISTORY
>
> In Athens, the large white oak at the corner of Dearing and Finely streets, surrounded by an enclosure of granite posts and an iron chain, is the **Tree That Owns Itself.** The original tree, which fell in 1942, was granted emancipation by Colonel W. H. Jackson, who wrote: "For and in consideration of the great love I bear this tree and the great desire I have for its protection for all time, I convey entire possession of itself and the land within eight feet of it on all sides." The current tree was grown from an acorn of the original.

Although the streets bustle at night with students taking in the coffeehouse and concert life, Athens's quieter side also flourishes. The streets are lined with many gorgeous old homes, some of which are open to the public. Most prominent among them is the **Athens Welcome Center** (⌧ 280 E. Dougherty St. ☎ 706/353–1820 ⊕ www.visitathensga.com), in the town's oldest surviving residence, the 1820 Church-Waddel-Brumby House.

Athens has several splendid **Greek-revival buildings,** including two on campus: the **university chapel** built in 1832, just off N. Herty Drive, and **university president's house** (⌧ 570 Prince Ave.) that was built in the late 1850s. Easiest access to the campus in downtown Athens is off Broad Street onto either Jackson or Thomas streets, both of which run through the heart of the university. Maps are available at the Visitor Center. Another example that gives a fine sense of history is the **Taylor-Grady House** (⌧ 634 Prince Ave.), which was constructed in 1844 and has just reopened for private events after an extensive face-lift. The 1844 **Franklin House** (⌧ 480 E. Broad St.) has been restored and reopened as an office building. **T.R.R. Cobb House** (⌧ 175 Hill St.) is yet another heritage building that has undergone transformation, this time into a museum for Civil War exhibits, which is scheduled to open in 2007.

FodorsChoice
★

Just outside the Athens city limits is the **State Botanical Gardens of Georgia,** a tranquil, 313-acre wonderland of aromatic gardens and woodland paths. It has a massive conservatory overlooking the **International Garden** that functions as a welcome foyer and houses an art gallery, gift shop, and café. ✉ *2450 S. Milledge Ave., off U.S. 129/441* ☎ *706/542–1244* ⊕*www.uga.edu/botgarden* ✆*Free* ☉ *Grounds: Apr.–Sept., weekdays 8–8; Oct.–Mar., weekdays 8–6. Visitor center: Tues.–Sat. 9–4:30, Sun. 11:30–4:30.*

Where to Stay & Eat

$$–$$$$ ✕ **Harry Bissett's.** Get primed to taste the offerings at one of the best restaurants in Athens, where you can expect sumptuous Cajun recipes straight from the streets of New Orleans. Nosh on oysters on the half shell at the raw bar while waiting for a table (if it's the weekend, expect to wait a while). Popular main dishes include fresh-catch Thibodaux (broiled fresh fillet smothered in crawfish étouffée) and chicken Rochambeau (a terrine of chicken breast, béarnaise sauce, shaved ham, and wine sauce). ■ TIP→ Save room for the bread pudding with whiskey sauce. ✉ *279 E. Broad St.* ☎ *706/353–7065* ▤ *AE, D, MC, V* ☉ *No lunch Mon.*

$$–$$$$ ✕ **East-West Bistro.** This popular bistro—one of the busiest spots downtown—has a bar, formal dining upstairs, and casual dining downstairs. The most interesting selections downstairs are the small plates that allow you to sample cuisines from around the world—from wasabi-crusted tilapia to salmon in rice paper to roasted-garlic pork chop. And if you're not a designated driver, the chocolate martini, a blend of Godiva liqueur, ice cream, and vodka, is a must. ■ TIP→ The room upstairs is much quieter, and the booths are very romantic. ✉ *351 E. Broad St.* ☎ *706/546–9378* ⌂ *Reservations not accepted* ▤ *AE, D, MC, V.*

$$ ⌂ **The Foundry Park Inn.** More than a hotel, this boutique village includes luxury rooms, a full service spa, the upscale Hoyt Restaurant, a lively pub and the Melting Point, an intimate night club that features musicians such as Little Feat and Ralph Stanley. The entire inn is built to be a replica of 1820 row houses; the original barn has been converted into stylish meeting rooms. There's really little need to leave, and if you do, you'll find the Classic Center Theater, the University campus, and historic downtown within easy walking distance. ✉ *295 E. Dougherty St., 30601* ☎ *706/549–7020 or 866/928–4367* ⌂ *706/549–7101* ⊕ *www.foundryparkinn.com* ⟿ *119 rooms* ⌂ *Restaurant, Wi-Fi, spa, pub, meeting rooms* ▤ *AE, MC, V.*

$–$$ ⌂ **Grand Oaks Manor.** This lovely colonial-style inn has preserved much of its original design of 1820. Rooms are decorated in rich colors, and furnishings are a mix of antiques and good reproductions. There's a wide front veranda with rocking chairs overlooking extensive acreage, some of which was originally held by William Few, one of Georgia's two signers of the U.S. Constitution. Check out the flat stones, they're remnants of the time when the inn served as a stage coach stop. ✉ *6295 Jefferson Rd., 30607* ☎ *706/353–2200* ⌂ *706/353–7799* ⊕ *www.bbonline.com/ga/grandoaks* ⟿ *5 rooms, 3 suites* ▤ *AE, D, MC, V* ⍾ *BP.*

HEARTBURN IN A HURRY

Varsity Diner (✉ 1000 Broad St. ☎ 706/548–6325) is a Georgia institution. It's where the university MTV crowd meets the Fonz over smothered hot dogs and heaps of fries. To wit, it serves up 2,000 pounds of onions daily, 2 million cups of coke a year, and makes 300 gallons of chili from scratch every day!

¢ ⌐ **Best Western Colonial Inn.** A half mile from the UGA campus, it's a favorite among relatives who come to attend graduation. Don't expect to be blown away by the architectural design, as the hotel building itself, like the rooms it offers, is basic. Rooms, however, are quite comfortable, with thick flowery bedspreads; each room comes equipped with a coffeemaker. Excellent freshly baked cookies are offered every afternoon. ■ TIP→ **Directly across the street is the legendary Varsity Diner, the best food bargain in town.** ⌐ *170 N. Milledge Ave., 30607* ☎ *706/546–7311 or 800/528–1234* ☐ *706/546–7959* ⊕ *www.bestwestern.com* ⇆ *69 rooms* ⌂ *Some microwaves, some refrigerators, in-room data ports, Wi-Fi, pool* ⊟ *AE, D, DC, MC, V* ⌐ *EP.*

EAST TO AUGUSTA

Washington

❻ *38 mi east of Athens via U.S. 78; 100 mi east of Atlanta via I–20 to Exit 154; 100 mi northeast of Macon via U.S. 129 to I–20 to Rte. 47.*

Washington, the first city chartered in honor of the country's first president, is a living museum of Southern culture. Brick buildings, some of which date to the American Revolution, line the lively downtown area, which bustles with people visiting cafés and antiques shops. The Confederate treasury was moved here from Richmond in 1865, and soon afterward the half-million dollars in gold vanished. This mysterious event has been the inspiration for numerous treasure hunts, as many like to believe the gold is still buried somewhere in Wilkes County.

The **Washington Historical Museum** (⌐ 308 E. Robert Toombs Ave. ☎ 706/678–2105) houses a collection of Civil War relics, including the camp chest of Jefferson Davis. The **Robert Toombs House** (⌐ 216 E. Robert Toombs Ave. ☎ 706/678–2226) is furnished with 19th-century antiques, some of which are the personal items of the former U.S. senator for which it is named, who served as secretary of state for the Confederacy during part of the Civil War.

Be sure to stop by historic **Callaway Plantation,** 4 mi west of downtown. Here, at a site dating to 1785, you can experience the closest thing to an operating plantation. Among a cluster of buildings on the estate you can find a blacksmith's house, schoolhouse, and weaving house. An ancient family cemetery is also fun to explore. During the second week of both April and October the estate comes alive with Civil War reenactments and activities such as butter-churning and quilting demonstrations. ⌐ *U.S. 78* ☎ *706/678–7060* ⌐ *$4* ⌚ *Tues.–Sat. 10–5, Sun. 2–5.*

Where to Stay & Eat

$$–$$$$ ✕ **Washington Jockey Club.** It's a bustling place with a terrific bistro atmosphere and an enviable location right on the Courthouse Square in downtown Washington. The menu is a bit pricier than you might expect and runs from excellent salads and sandwiches—try the grilled vegetables on focaccia—to a dinner that's slightly more upscale but stays regional with fried green tomatoes, sweet-potato chips, and fried seafood. ■ TIP→ **The**

12

bar in the back stays open until you go home. ⌧ *5 E. Public Sq.* ☎ *706/678–1672* ⌕ *Reservations not accepted* ▭ *AE, D, MC, V* ⊗ *Closed Sun.*

$–$$ ⊞ **The Fitzpatrick Hotel.** Overlooking the Courthouse Square, this 1898 hotel, originally built by brothers John and Thomas Fitzpatrick, has been beautifully refurbished to its former Victorian elegance. Rooms vary in size, some have private dining nooks in the turret while others have high beds with Napoléon steps and spacious living areas. All have private baths. ⌧ *16 West Sq., 30673* ☎ *706/678–5900* ⎙ *706/678–3018* ⊕ *www.thefitzpatrickhotel.com* ⇗ *17 rooms* ⌕ *Restaurant, in-room broadband, meeting rooms,* ▭ *AE, MC, V* �+◎+ *CP.*

Augusta

❼ *55 mi east of Washington via U.S. 78 and I–20; 150 mi east of Atlanta via I–20; 70 mi southwest of Columbia, SC, via I–20.*

Although Augusta escaped the ravages of Union troops during the Civil War, nature itself was not so kind. On a crossing of the Savannah River, the town was flooded many times before modern-day city planning redirected the water into a collection of small lakes and creeks. Now the current is so mild that citizens gather to send bathtub toys downstream every year in the annual Rubber Duck Race.

The well-maintained multilevel paths of **Riverwalk** (between 5th and 10th streets) curve along the Savannah River and are the perfect place for a leisurely stroll. **Olde Town,** lying along Telfair and Greene streets, is a restored neighborhood of Victorian homes, although many are still very much works in progress.

A converted mill serves as the **Augusta Canal Interpretive Center,** a historical center where imaginative exhibits, including authentic mill equipment and looms, trace Augusta's important role in developing Georgia's textile industry. The Center is still powered by the building's original turbines (which you can see in action), and also uses the power to juice up its Petersburg canal boats. Tours of the **canal,** usually one-hour long, start here and are a fascinating trip through history. Guides are well versed in the passing sights that include assorted wildlife, a working 19th-century textile mill, and two of Georgia's only remaining 18th-century houses. ⌧ *1450 Greene St.* ☎ *706/823–0440* ⊕ *www.augustacanal.com* ⌦ *$6–$10* ⊗ *Tues.–Sat. 9:30–5:30.*

Meadow Garden was the home of George Walton, one of Georgia's three signers of the Declaration of Independence and, at age 26, its youngest signer. It has been documented as Augusta's oldest extant residence. ⌧ *1320 Independence Dr.* ☎ *706/724–4174* ⌦ *$4* ⊗ *Weekdays 10–4, weekends by appointment.*

The **Morris Museum of Southern Art** has a splendid collection of Southern art, from early landscapes, antebellum portraits, and Civil War art, through neo-impressionism and modern contemporary art. ⌧ *Riverfront Center, 1 10th St., 2nd fl.* ☎ *706/724–7501* ⊕ *www.themorris.org* ⌦ *$5, free on Sun.* ⊗ *Tues.–Sat. 10–5, Sun. noon–5.*

☺ Children love the National Science Center's **Fort Discovery,** an interactive high-tech playground with a moonwalk simulator, a bike on square wheels, a hot-air balloon, and a little car propelled by magnets. ⊠ *1 7th St.* ☎ *706/821–0200 or 800/325–5445* ⊕ *www.nationalsciencecenter. org* ⊠ *$8* ⊘ *Tues.–Sat. 10–5.*

Where to Stay & Eat

$$$–$$$$ ✕ **La Maison on Telfair.** Augusta's finest restaurant, operated by chef-owner Heinz Sowinski, presents a classic menu of game, sweetbreads, and, with a nod to the chef's heritage, Wiener schnitzel. The experience is enhanced by the quiet and elegant-styled room. ■ TIP→ **The wine and tapas bar is more casual.** ⊠ *404 Telfair St.* ☎ *706/722–4805* ⚎ *Reservations required* ⊟ *AE, D, DC, MC, V* ⊘ *Closed Sun. No lunch.*

$$–$$$$ ✕ **Le Café du Teau.** You know the place has to be good—when other restaurants close up for the night, the staff come here to chill out. Dinner fare ranges from filet mignon to seafood and pasta. Choose the hors d'oeuvres platter and graze on a variety of tastes such as snails in a yummy mushroom sauce, calimari, crab cakes, and grilled spiced shrimp. On Sunday night, check out the jazz band; it really gets the place movin' into the wee hours of the morning. ⊠ *1855 Central Ave.* ☎ *706/733– 3505* ⊟ *AE, MC, V.*

$$–$$$ ▦ **Partridge Inn.** A National Trust Historic hotel, this restored inn sits at the gateway to Summerville, a hilltop neighborhood of summer homes dating to 1800. There's a splendid view of downtown Augusta from the roof. Rooms are elegant, and have double-line cordless phones and high-speed Internet lines. The hotel's exterior has 12 common balconies and a breathtaking upper veranda accented with shaded architectural porticos over wood-plank flooring, creating a truly lustrous reprieve for a quick coffee and newspaper read. There's also videoconferencing for those who can't bear to be out of sight of their business partners. ⊠ *2110 Walton Way, 30904* ☎ *706/737–8888 or 800/476– 6888* ⧠ *706/731–0826* ⊕ *www.partridgeinn.com* ⊐ *133 rooms, 26 suites* ⚎ *Restaurant, some kitchens, pool, gym, bar, lounge, concierge floor, in-room data ports, Wi-Fi, meeting room* ⊟ *AE, D, DC, MC, V* ▯⊙▯ *BP.*

Sports & the Outdoors

In early April Augusta hosts the much-celebrated annual **Masters Tournament** (⊕ www.masters.org), one of pro golf's most distinguished events. It's broadcast in 180 countries. Tickets for actual tournament play are not available to the general public, but you can try to get tickets for one of the practice rounds earlier in the week—which, for golf addicts, is still hugely entertaining. Tickets are awarded on a lottery basis; write to the Masters Tournament Practice Rounds office, Box 2047, Augusta, GA 30903 by July 15 of the year preceding the tournament.

AN ONION A DAY

Vidalia onions are grown throughout Central Georgia. Because of unique soil conditions, the onions are so sweet you can eat them like apples. Watch for them on menus and at roadside stands.

CENTRAL GEORGIA ESSENTIALS

Transportation

BY AIR

Athens Ben Epps Airport is served by US Airways. Augusta Regional Airport is served by Continental, Delta, and US Airways Express. Middle Georgia Regional Airport is served by Atlantic Southeast Airlines.

Athens Ben Epps Airport ✉ 1010 Ben Epps Dr. ☎ 706/613-3420 ⊕ www.athensairport. net. **Augusta Regional Airport** ✉ 1501 Aviation Way ☎ 706/798-3236. **Middle Georgia Regional Airport** ✉ 1000 Terminal Dr., Rte. 247 at I-75 ☎ 478/788-3760.

BY BUS

Greyhound Bus Lines serves Athens, Augusta, Macon, Madison, and Washington.

Greyhound Bus Lines ☎ 800/231-2222 ⊕ www.greyhound.com.

BY CAR

U.S. 441, known as the Antebellum Trail, runs north–south, merging with U.S. 129 for a stretch and connecting Athens, Madison, Eatonton, and Milledgeville. Macon is on Route 49, which splits from U.S. 441 at Milledgeville. Washington lies at the intersection of U.S. 78, running east from Athens to Thomson, and Route 44, running south to Eatonton. Interstate 20 runs east from Atlanta to Augusta, which is about 93 mi east of U.S. 441.

BY TAXI

Augusta Cab Company provides transportation throughout Augusta-Richmond County. The initial charge ranges $1 to $2.40 depending on your pickup location, plus $1.80 per mi.

Your Cab Company is a reliable 24-hour taxi service in Athens. Rates, based on a grid of designated-area zones, start at $5. The fare to downtown from the airport costs $8.

In Macon, contact Yellow Cab, which covers most of the downtown neighborhoods. $1.50 is the start charge, with $1.50 per mi thereafter.

Augusta Cab Company ☎ 706/724-3543. **Your Cab Company** ☎ 706/546-5844. **Yellow Cab Company** ☎ 478/742-6464.

Contacts & Resources

BANKS & EXCHANGE SERVICES

Banks and ATMs are throughout Central Georgia. Branches of Bank of America are in all major centers.

Bank of America ✉ 1450 Walton Way, Augusta ☎ 706/849-0660 ✉ 110 E. Clayton St., Athens ☎ 706/357-6488 ✉ 487 Cherry St., Macon ☎ 706/744-6400 ☎ 800/432-1000.

EMERGENCIES

Urgent care is available in each of the urban centers, which also serve many of the surrounding communities. Augusta, in particular, is a "medical town"; its Doctors Hospital is noted for its specialty burn unit.

🆘 Emergency Services **Ambulance, police** ☎ 911.

🆘 Hospitals **Athens Regional Medical Center** ✉ 1199 Prince Ave., Athens ☎ 706/475-7000. **Doctors Hospital** ✉ 3651 Wheeler Rd., Augusta ☎ 706/651-3232. **Macon Northside Hospital** ✉ 400 Charter Blvd., Macon ☎ 478/757-8200.

🆘 24-Hour Pharmacies **CVS** ✉ 1271 Gray Hwy., Macon ☎ 478/743-6979 or 912/743-8936.

INTERNET, MAIL & SHIPPING

The three largest towns in Central Georgia (Augusta, Athens, and Macon) offer wireless access in their downtown core, so staying cyber-connected is easier than ever. If you've left your laptop at home, broadband Internet access is available at the Athens Welcome Center in Athens and in Macon at the Macon Library, an impressive building. Because Kinko's is owned by FedEx, locations provide Internet services, plus you can ship your packages, too.

🖥 **FedEx Kinko's** ✉ 2235 W. Broad St., Athens ☎ 706/353-8755 ✉ 262 Robert C. Daniel Jr. Pkwy., Augusta ☎ 706/733-1002 ✉ 181 Tom Hill Sr. Blvd., Macon ☎ 478/474-1246. **Macon Library** ✉ 210 N. Rutherford St., Macon ☎ 660/385-3314. **UPS** ✉ 2803 Wrightsboro Rd., Augusta ☎ 706/736-2901 ✉ 248 Tom Hill Sr. Blvd., Macon ☎ 478/474-8847. **USPS** ✉ 1434 Stovall St., Augusta ☎ 706/738-9822. **USPS** ✉ 115 E. Hancock St., Athens ☎ 706/369-3200 ✉ 451 College St., Macon ☎ 478/752-8400.

MEDIA

Although *USA Today* proliferates most newsstands, each of the major cities covered in this chapter have its own daily newspaper and "what's on" community publication for up-to-the-minute listings. In Augusta, check out the *Augusta Daily Chronicle* and the *Metro Spirit*; in Athens, the *Athens Banner Herald* (daily) and the *Flagpole*; and in Macon, daily news is reported in the *Telegraph*. Macon's the *Georgia Informer* and the upscale *Macon Magazine* are good sources of information on local arts and cultural events.

📰 *Athens Banner Herald* ✉ 1 Press Pl., Athens ☎ 706/549-0123. *Augusta Daily Chronicle* ✉ Box 1928, Augusta ☎ 706/722-5620. *Flagpole* ✉ 112 S. Foundry St., Athens ☎ 706/549-9523. *Georgia Informer* ✉ Box 564, Macon ☎ 478/745-7265. *Macon Magazine* ✉ 2208 Ingleside Ave., Macon ☎ 478/746-7779. *Metro Spirit* ✉ 700 Broad St., Augusta ☎ 706/738-1142. The *Telegraph* ✉ Box 4167, Macon ☎ 478/744-4200.

TOUR OPTIONS

The Augusta Cotton Exchange (also known as the Augusta Visitors Bureau) conducts free tours of its historic brick building, with exhibits from its past as an arbiter of cotton prices. It also has Saturday van tours throughout the historic district of Augusta; the fee is $10 per person.

The Athens Welcome Center runs historic tours of downtown and surrounding neighborhoods daily at 2 PM. Tours are 90-minutes long and $15 per person. Milledgeville Visitor's Bureau offers trolley tours of the town's historic sites at $10 per person.

The Trolley tour is the most compact way of exploring Macon. The price of $17 per person includes admission to key attractions and is fully narrated through its 2½ hour journey. For more information contact the Visitor's Bureau, which is also the departure point. ■ TIP➡ **This tour, as with the other around-the-town combination tours, translates into savings in admissions of up to 20%.**

12

🚹**Athens Welcome Center** ✉ 280 E. Dougherty St., Athens ☎ 706/353-1820 ⊕ www. visitathensga.com. **Augusta Welcome Center** ✉ 5608 Reynolds St., Augusta ☎ 706/ 724-4067 or 800/726-0243 ⊕ www.augustaga.org. **Milledgeville Visitor's Bureau** ✉ 200 W. Hancock St., Melledgeville ☎ 478/452-4687 or 800/653-1804 ⊕ www. milledgevillecvb.com.

VISITOR INFORMATION

Georgia Welcome Center provides maps and brochures about prominent historical and recreational sites around the state. Even small towns usually have a visitor information office.

🚹 Tourist Information **Athens Convention and Visitors Bureau** ✉ 300 N. Thomas St., 30601 ☎ 706/357-4430 or 800/653-0603 🖶 706/549-5636 ⊕ www.visitathensga. com. **Augusta Visitors Bureau** ✉ 560 Reynolds St., 30903 ☎ 706/724-4067 or 800/ 726-0243 🖶 706/262-0287 ⊕ www.augustaga.org. **Eatonton-Putnam Chamber of Commerce** ✉ 105 S. Washington St., Eatonton 31024 ☎ 706/485-7701 ⊕ www.eatonton. com. **Georgia Welcome Center** 🗀 Box 211090, Martinez 30917 ☎ 706/737-1446 ⊕ www.georgia.org. **Macon-Bibb County Convention and Visitors Bureau** ✉ 200 Cherry St., Macon 31201 ☎ 478/743-3401 or 800/768-3401 ⊕ www.maconga.org. **Madison/Morgan County Chamber of Commerce** ✉ 115 E. Jefferson St., Madison 30605 ☎ 706/342-4454 ⊕ www.madisonga.org. **Milledgeville Convention and Visitors Bureau** ✉ 200 W. Hancock St., 31061 ☎ 478/452-4687 ⊕ www.milledgevillecvb.com. **Washington-Wilkes Chamber of Commerce** ✉ 25 E. Sq., Washington 30673 ☎ 706/ 678-2013 ⊕ www.washingtonwilkes.org.

North Georgia

WORD OF MOUTH

"We, too, love the North Georgia mountains. Try Chickamauga Battlefield, if [you're] interested in Civil War history. We find hiking in Fort Mountain State Park to be less crowded and very enjoyable. The waterfall is beautiful at Amicalola State Park, near Ellijay and Blue Ridge. Just hiking and seeing the scenery in North Georgia makes for a great trip."

–BayouGal

"Helen is a tourist trap. The town . . . decided years ago to bring in tourist dollars by remaking their town into a 'quaint German village.' It's actually kind of fun for a few hours, but that's it."

–padams421

By Lan Sluder

Updated by
Michele Foust

AS AN ANTIDOTE to city life, nothing beats the clear skies, cascading waterfalls, and tranquil town squares of North Georgia. Within a few hours drive from metro Atlanta, you can find yourself in the middle of a refreshing cluster of old Southern towns and nature sites that pepper the northern region of the state—the heart of lower Appalachia.

North Georgia is home to one of the largest national forest areas in the East, the 750,000-acre Chattahoochee National Forest. About 15% of the Chattahoochee is designated as wilderness, and of this, the 35,000-acre Cohutta Wilderness is the largest national forest wilderness area in the Southeast. Several bold rivers, including the Chattahoochee, Oconee, Toccoa, and Chattooga, have their headwaters in this forest. Rabun, Burton, Nottley, and Chatuge lakes offer boating and fishing. All over North Georgia are small but enticing state parks, most with cabins for rent and inexpensive camp sites.

In Dahlonega, Blue Ridge, Helen, Clayton, and Ellijay, north and northeast of Atlanta, you can find shops selling handmade quilts, folk-art pottery and antiques. These towns also offer plenty of activities—you can descend into a gold mine, explore a re-created Alpine village, or go apple picking. To the northwest are two of Georgia's most important historic sites: New Echota State Historic Site and the Chickamauga & Chattanooga National Military Park.

Exploring North Georgia

North Georgia is comprised of two fairly distinct areas: the northwest, with modest rolling hills at the edge of the Cumberland Plateau; and the North Georgia mountains, a part of the Blue Ridge Mountains, ranging from a modest 1,000 feet to Brasstown Bald, the highest peak in Georgia at 4,784 feet.

This is a region of small towns, connected by a web of country roads. Public transit is almost nonexistent; you'll need a car to explore. No single main highway gets you to all the points of interest. You'll have to study your maps carefully, and you'll likely end up doubling back here and there. Most of the secondary roads are lightly trafficked, but in the more mountainous areas, you can face steep grades with sometimes treacherous curves.

About the Restaurants

You'll find more fast food than four-star dining in North Georgia. Many small towns may have local diners where the menus run to barbecue and chicken potpie. Here and there you can find a hotel dining room or independent restaurant with local specialties such as mountain trout. North Georgia is also gaining momentum as a second-home and retirement haven. Fine-dining establishments are appearing in many areas to satisfy former city dwellers accustomed to broader fare and higher prices. At a few country-style eateries—such as the Dillard House Restaurant near Clayton and the Smith House in Dahlonega—you'll be served heaping plates of ham, fried chicken, and other Southern dishes.

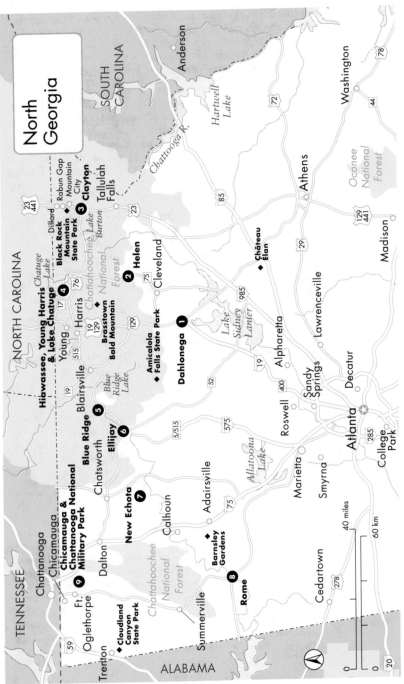

TOP 5 REASONS TO GO

Escape to the wilderness: Hike around, or down, Tallulah Gorge, one of the deepest in the country at 1,000 feet deep; or climb to the top of Amicalola Falls, the tallest cascading waterfall east of the Mississippi, at 729 feet.

Surround yourself in Civil War history: The bloodiest two-day battle of the Civil War was fought at Chickamauga & Chattanooga National Military Park. More than 34,000 Union and Confederate soldiers were wounded or died here.

Take a hike: The starting point of the more than 2,100-mi Appalachian Trail is at Springer Mountain. Even if you're not planning on taking the gigantic hike, the region offers loads of sports opportunities like fishing, kayaking, golfing, day hiking, boating, and camping.

Step back into Georgia's Cherokee past: Visit New Echota, the former capital of the Cherokee Nation. In the late 1830s the government removed about 15,000 Cherokees from their log homes, farms, schools, and stores and gathered them in stockades. They later forced them to walk or ride to Oklahoma in what became known as the "Trail of Tears."

Sample local wine: North Georgia's wine industry is booming. Four wineries are near Dahlonega, but more are scattered in the scenic northeast mountains and connected by the Wine Highway. Some of the European-style wines produced include Cabernet Franc, Touriga Nacional, Merlot, Viognier, and Chardonnay. Tasting rooms are abundant and some of the wineries are adding lunch and dinner options for visitors.

About the Hotels

Chain- and independent motels are found along Interstate 75 and in the suburbs and small towns of North Georgia. In some towns you can find 19th-century homes transformed into small inns or bed-and-breakfasts.

In the mountains are several popular lodges, although the overall number and quality of inns and lodges in the North Georgia mountains doesn't stand up to competition in the neighboring North Carolina mountains. Of special note in North Georgia are the accommodations at state parks, with attractively priced rustic cabins in scenic settings and, in several cases (such as the Lodge at Smithgall Woods and the Amicalola Falls Lodge), gorgeous mountain lodges are run by the state, and at bargain prices to boot. Private owners also offer cabins and cottages for rent, usually by the week. Local chambers of commerce and visitor bureaus usually maintain lists of these cabin rentals.

	WHAT IT COSTS				
	$$$$	$$$	$$	$	¢
RESTAURANTS	over $22	$17–$22	$12–$16	$7–$11	under $7
HOTELS	over $220	$161–$220	$111–$160	$70–$110	under $70

Restaurant prices are for a main course at dinner. Hotel prices are for two people in a standard double room in high season.

Timing

Summer and fall are prime times for travel. Weekends are far busier than weekdays, since many of the visitors to this region come up from nearby Atlanta to beat the heat. For the mountains, the ideal time is October and early November, when fall color is at its peak. Don't arrive at this time of year without reservations and expect traffic, even on secondary roads.

THE NORTH GEORGIA MOUNTAINS

To most Georgians, "North Georgia" means the northeast and north central mountains and foothills—from Clayton and Dillard in the east to Hiawassee and Lake Chatuge in the north, and Blue Ridge and Ellijay and the Cohutta Wilderness to the west. Dahlonega, Helen, and several state parks—Black Rock Mountain, Moccasin Creek, Unicoi, Vogel, and Amicalola Falls—are contained within the broad arc of this scenic mountain region.

Dahlonega

❶ *65 mi northeast of Atlanta via GA 400 and GA 60.*

Fodor'sChoice ★ Hoards of fortune-seekers stormed the town of Dahlonega (pronounced Dah-LON-eh-gah), in the 1820s after the discovery of gold in the hills nearby. The town's name comes from the Cherokee word for "precious yellow metal." But the boom didn't last long. By 1849 miners were starting to seek riches elsewhere. In fact, the famous call "There's gold in them thar hills!" originated as an enticement to miners in the Georgia mountains to keep their minds away from the lure of the gold rush out West. It worked for a while, but government price fixing eventually made gold mining unprofitable, and by the early 1920s Dahlonega's mining operations had halted completely.

Many former mining settlements became ghost towns, but not Dahlonega. Today it thrives as a rustic country outpost with an irresistible town square rife with country stores, art galleries, coffeehouses, gem shops, old small-town businesses, and several sophisticated restaurants. Gold Rush Days, a festival celebrating the first gold rush in 1828, attracts about 200,000 weekend visitors to this small town. The festival is always held the third weekend in October.

The **Gold Museum**, on the main square, has coins, tools, and several large nuggets on display. The courthouse is the oldest public building in North Georgia, and if you look closely at the bricks that form the building's foundation, you'll notice a sprinkling of gold dust in their formation. Along with the exhibits, the museum has a short film celebrating the region's history through interviews with Appalachian old-timers. ⊠ *Public Sq.* ☎ *706/864–2257* ⊕ *www.dahlonega.org* ✉ *$4* ☽ *Mon.–Sat. 9–5, Sun. 10–5.*

★ ☾ At **Consolidated Gold Mine** you can take guided tours of a real mine, which last worked in the early 1980s. With 5 mi of underground tunnels, Consolidated is said to be the largest gold mine east of the Mississippi. You enter the mine (which has been reconstructed for safety), pass through a breathtaking stone passage, and then begin a descent of 120 feet into the mine's geological wonders. Guides, most of them actual miners, expound on historical mining techniques and give demonstrations of tools, such as the "widowmaker," a drill that kicks up mining dust and caused lung disease in many miners. After the tour, you're invited to pan for gold, prospector-style, from a long wooden sluice. Visitors can also pan for minerals and semiprecious to precious gems, such as quartz and sapphire. ⊠ *185 Consolidated Rd.* ☎ *706/864–8473* ⊕ *www.consolidatedgoldmine.com* ✉ *$11* ☽ *Daily 10–5.*

☾ The largest collection of kangaroos outside Australia is at the **Kangaroo Conservation Center,** an 87-acre wildlife park. The center has more than 250 'roos, along with wallabies, blue-winged kookaburras, and a massive blue-crowned pigeon that is as large as a goose. The center has eight species of kangaroos, ranging from a less than two-pound brush-tailed Bettong kangaroo to large varieties that may reach nearly 200 pounds each. Visitors can learn to throw a boomerang, as well as relax in a lush butterfly garden. Guides are knowledgeable about kangaroos and the other Australian animals and plants that live at the center, and they emphasize conservation efforts on site and recycling and conservation at home. Plan on spending at least three hours to do this place justice. Admission is by advance ticket purchase only, and children must be in second grade or beyond. You must take a tour to see the center; times are subject to change. ⊠ *222 Bailey-Waters Rd., 15 mi from Dahlonega via GA 52, Dawsonville* ☎ *706/265–6100* ⊕ *www.kangaroocenter.com* ✉ *$28* ☽ *Mid-Mar.–early Dec., tours Tues.–Sat. 10:15 and 1:15.*

Fodor'sChoice ★

In the Dahlonega area you can find the largest concentration of wineries in Georgia. **Wolf Mountain Vineyards & Winery,** is a 25-acre vineyard on a ridgetop with hillside plantings of cabernet sauvignon, syrah, Mourvedre, and Touriga Nacional. The winery has a collection of early wine-making artifacts. The **Wolf Mountain Vineyards Tasting Room** (⊠ 24 E. Main St. ☎ 706/867–9862) is in Dahlonega. Call for special winery tour or tasting information. ⊠ *180 Wolf Mountain Trail, 5 mi north of Dahlonega* ☎ *706/867–9862* ⊕ *www.wolfmountainvineyards. com* ☽ *Mar.–mid-Dec., Thurs.–Sun. noon–5.*

Three Sisters Vineyards, Dahlonega's first family farm winery, has 15 acres of plantings including Cabernet Franc, merlot, cabernet sauvignon, pinot blanc, Vidal Blanc, and chardonnay, along with American varietals such as Cynthiana-Norton. Picnic fare—deli meats and cheeses, as

The Wine Highway

NORTH GEORGIA MAY NEVER BE AN EASTERN NAPA VALLEY, but wineries are sprouting up all over, producing Merlot, Cabernet Franc, Touriga Nacional, Chardonnay, Viognier, and others. As you travel around the region, especially in northeast Georgia, you'll see burgundy-color signs pointing to vineyard and winery destinations on the **Georgia Wine Highway.** A listing of current wineries is available at ⊕ www.georgiawine.com.

CLAYTON

The boutique, family-owned **Persimmon Creek Vineyards** (⊠ 81 Vineyard La., Clayton ☎ 706/212–7380 ⊕ persimmoncreekwine.com) produces and bottles Riesling, Merlot, Cabernet Franc, and Seyval Blanc wines. **Tiger Mountain Vineyards** (⊠ 2592 Old Hwy. 441, Tiger ☎ 706/782–4777 ⊕ http://tigerwine.com) started in 1995 and is known for

unusual varietals of French and Portuguese grapes such as Touriga Nacional and Petit Manseng, as well as the native Norton grape.

HELEN

Habersham Winery (⊠ 7025 S. Main St., Helen ☎ 706/878–9463 ⊕ www.habershamwinery.com) started producing in 1983 and is one of the oldest wineries in the state. They produce 20 different wines, which are featured at their two restaurants, Nacoochee Grill and Pazzo.

YOUNG HARRIS

Crane Creek Vineyards (⊠ 916 Crane Creek Rd., off Ga. 515, Young Harris ☎ 706/379–1236 ⊕ www.cranecreekvineyards.com) makes 12 regional artisanal wines based on the eight grape varieties it grows. The most popular choices are Vidal Blanc, Seyval, and Cabernet Franc.

well as artisan bread—is available. Special events, including the Georgia Wine Country Festival the first weekend in June, occur monthly. ⊠ *439 Vineyard Way, 8 mi northeast of Dahlonega* ☎ 706/865–9463 ⊕ *www.threesistersvineyards.com* ☉ *Thurs.–Sat. 11–5, Sun. 1–5.*

Frogtown Cellars is a 50-acre vineyard and winery featuring an atypical underground, gravity-flow wine-making facility on three floors. It uses gravity in place of pumps, with wine crush on the first level, fermentation on the second, and storage in wine barrels on the third and lowest level. Lunch is available on days the winery is open; a three-course Sunday brunch and wine-tasting dinners are available by reservation. ⊠ *3300 Damascus Church Rd., 6 mi northeast of Dahlonega* ☎ 706/865–0687 ⊕ *www.frogtownwine.com* ☉ *Feb.–May, Sat. noon–6, Sun. noon–5; June–Oct., Fri. and Sun. noon–5, Sat. noon–6; Nov. and Dec., Sat. noon–6, Sun. noon–5.*

BlackStock Vineyards and Winery, on 90 acres, offers 10 traditional European premium-quality wines. The large outdoor deck overlooks both the vineyards and the mountains. The lodge, built with old barn wood, pulls in elements from the setting, with a stacked stone three-sided fireplace and hand-crafted wrought-iron work replicating the look of the grapevines.

A cascading waterfall is a highlight of the wine cellar. Signature wines are the Viognier and merlot. ⊠ *5400 Town Creek Rd., Dahlonega* ☎ *706/ 219–2789* ⊕ *www.bsvw.com* ⊗ *Mon. and Thurs.–Sat. 10–6, Sun. 12:30–6, Tues. and Wed. by appointment only.*

DRIVE DEFENSIVELY

Motorcyclists and bicyclists have discovered the joys in riding through the mountains of North Georgia. For everyone's safety, be alert on curving, narrow mountain roads.

13

OFF THE BEATEN PATH

AMICALOLA FALLS – This is claimed to be the highest cascading waterfall east of the Mississippi, with waters plunging an eye-popping 729 feet through a cluster of seven cascades. The surrounding 1,021-acre state park is dotted with scenic campsites and cottages strategically situated near a network of nature trails, picnic sites, and fishing streams. The southern starting point of the more than 2,100-mi Appalachian Trail begins near Amicalola Falls. ⊠ *Off GA 52, 18 mi west of Dahlonega, Dawsonville* ☎ *706/265–8888* ⊠ *Parking $3* ⊗ *Daily 7 AM–10 PM.*

Sports & the Outdoors

Appalachian Outfitters (⊠ 2084 S. Chestatee, Hwy. 60 S, Dahlonega ☎ 706/864–7117 or 800/426–7117 ⊕ www.canoegeorgia.com ⊗ Memorial Day–Labor Day, daily 10–3; Apr.–mid-May and early-Sept.–Oct., Thurs.–Sun. 10–3) provides equipment and maps for self-guided canoeing and kayaking trips on the Chestatee and Etowah Rivers. Tube rentals and shuttle service are also available for tubing trips on the Chestatee.

Where to Stay & Eat

$$$–$$$$ ✕ **The Oar House.** Despite being housed in a rustic green building in the woods near the Chestatee River, this fine-dining option brings a bit of Atlanta urbanity to Dahlonega. You can sit on the open-air patio decks while you have oysters on the half shell, shrimp scampi, or rack of New Zealand lamb. ⊠ *3072 E. GA 52, 3½ mi from Dahlonega at MM 18* ☎ *706/864–9938* ☰ *AE, D, MC, V* ⊗ *Closed Sun.*

★ **$$–$$$$** ✕ **Corkscrew Café.** This cozy and intimate restaurant, has rust-color walls covered with original art and a large covered patio. Specialties include hand-carved steaks with a portobello mushroom demi-glaze, seared sashimi-grade tuna, and rack of lamb with a curry-orange sauce. Locals love the curry squash bisque and French onion soup as well as the pecan-crusted trout and eggplant mascarpone. Lunch specials include sandwiches, salads, and soup. ⊠ *51 W. Main St.* ☎ *706/867–8551* ⊕ *www.thecorkscrewcafe.com* ☰ *AE, D, MC, V* ⊗ *Closed Mon.*

$$ ✕ **Smith House.** This popular dining destination serves heaping platters of all-you-can-eat family-style meals that challenge the stamina of the tables and your stomach. Potatoes, fried chicken, peas, cobbler, fried okra, collard greens, pole beans, sweet potatoes—you name a Southern dish, and it's probably offered here. The restaurant is mostly below ground, beneath the main house, which is a hotel. During 2006, work to enlarge the restaurant and hotel uncovered a gold mine—hidden for 100 years—under the structure. ⊠ *84 S. Chestatee St.* ☎ *706/867–7000 or 800/852– 9577* ⊕ *www.smithhouse.com* ☰ *AE, MC, V* ⊗ *Closed Mon.*

$$ [icon] **Historic Worley Bed & Breakfast.** This pristine B&B occupies an 1845 mansion with two garden courtyards. Everyone sits family-style at the large, formally set dining room table; breakfast includes French toast, breakfast casserole, bacon, biscuits, and grits. Often on weekend evenings the proprietors arrange a wine table with cheese and crackers in the entry foyer. Rooms are beautifully furnished, and three have wood-burning fireplaces. The B&B is within walking distance of the Dahlonega town square. ⊠ *168 Main St. West, 30533* ☎ *706/864–7002 or 800/348–8094* ⊕ *www.bbonline.com/ga/worley* ⤶ *7 rooms* ▤ *MC, V* ⓘⓄⓘ *BP.*

$$ [icon] **Len Foote Hike Inn.** No cell phones, Blackberries, or radios allowed! If you really want to get away from civilization and feel up to a 4½ mi hike of moderate difficulty (two to four hours each way), this backcountry pack-it-in-and-pack-it-out inn at Amicalola State Park could be for you. Although the inn has electric lights, there are no electrical outlets, and the showers and bathrooms are in a separate bathhouse. Rustic wood-panel rooms each have two bunk beds and meals are served family-style. In order to have time to hike to the lodge, you *must* check-in no later than 2 PM at the Amicalola Falls State Park visitor center. ■ TIP➔ **The inn is a 4½ mi hike from Springer Mountain, the southern terminus of the Appalachian Trail.** ⊠ *240 Amicalola State Park Rd., 20 mi west of Dahlonega via GA 52, Dawsonville 30534* ☎ *800/581–8032* 🖷 *706/864–4218* ⊕ *www.hike-inn.com* ⤶ *20 rooms without bath* ♨ *Dining room; no a/c, no room phones* ▤ *MC, V* ⓘⓄⓘ *MAP.*

$$ [icon] **Lily Creek Lodge.** This eclectic-looking B&B appears slightly Bavarian on the outside, and some of the rooms echo Venice, Morocco, and Argentina with their decor. The lodge sits on 7 acres and has a pool and outdoor hot tub. Breakfast includes cheese biscuits, granola, and fresh fruit. ⊠ *2608 Auraria Rd., 30533* ☎ *706/864–6848 or 888/844–2694* ⊕ *www.lilycreeklodge.com* ⤶ *10 rooms, 3 suites* ♨ *Some kitchens, Wi-Fi, pool, boccie* ▤ *AE, MC, V* ⓘⓄⓘ *BP.*

$ [icon] **Amicalola Falls Lodge.** One of the most appealing mountain lodges in Georgia is part of the state-park system. As you sit beside a large stone fireplace in the glass-walled lobby, you'll have panoramic views over the mountains. The rooms aren't fancy but you can pay far less than at a private country inn. The park also has 14 cottages for rent and a restaurant serving buffet meals. ⊠ *418 Amicalola Falls State Park Rd., 20 mi west of Dahlonega via GA 52, Dawsonville 30534* ☎ *706/265–8888 or 800/573–9656* 🖷 *706/265–4575* ⊕ *www.amicalolafalls.com* ⤶ *53 rooms, 4 suites, 14 cottages* ♨ *Restaurant, cable TV, meeting rooms* ▤ *MC, V* ⓘⓄⓘ *EP.*

Fodor'sChoice
★

Nightlife & the Arts

The **Historic Holly Theater** (⊠ 69 W. Main St. ☎ 706/864–3759), a classic small-town movie theater built in 1946, stages live theater, movies, and special events.

Mountain music and the arts are the mainstays at the **Buisson Arts Center** (⊠ 199 Choice Ave., Dahlonega ☎ 706/867–0050 ⊕ www.buissonartscenter.com ⊙ Tues.–Thurs. noon–6, Fri. and Sat noon–8, Sun. 1–5). **The Mountain Music and Medicine Show,** featuring bluegrass and gospel music as well as tales from Dahlonega's past, is presented one

Saturday night each month. Many performances, including national acts and Nashville singer-songwriters sessions, take place in the 1897 former church. Studios for resident artists and art classes are on the property.

Helen

2 *6 mi north of Cleveland via GA 75.*

When Helen was founded at the turn of the 20th century, it was a simple little lumber outpost. By the 1960s it was in danger of turning into a ghost town because of a logging bust. Local business leaders came up with a plan to save the town: they transformed the tiny village of 300 into a theme town, and "Alpine Helen," was born. Today businesses along Helen's central streets sport a distinctive German facade, giving you, at least initially, the impression that you've stumbled on a Bavarian vista in the middle of Appalachia. (There's also a scattering of Swiss, Belgian, Danish, Dutch, and Scandinavian facades.) There's no shortage of beer halls, restaurants serving German-style food, steepled roofs, and flowering window boxes. ■ TIP➔ **Don't expect small-town prices.** This is clearly not Bavaria for real, but the effect can be contagious, making you feel as if you've walked into a fairy tale. If it's too touristy for you, move on.

On weekends in summer and fall, Helen's streets approach a traffic gridlock, and parking (most lots in town charge $2 or $3 a day) is at a premium. Despite the ersatz Alpine theme, Helen's elevation of a mere 1,440 feet means it can be hot in the summer. To cool off, consider a tube trip down the Chattahoochee or head to more authentic country towns like Dahlonega in the nearby Blue Ridge Mountains.

Chattahoochee National Forest covers about ¾-million acres of land in North Georgia. It's named after the Chattahoochee River, whose headwaters are in the North Georgia mountains. The forest was created piecemeal, beginning in 1911, from bits and pieces of often environmentally degraded and abused land, and was officially established in 1936. About 15% of the Chattahoochee is wilderness. The national forest supports an estimated 500 species of fish and wildlife, including black bears, white-tailed deer, and wild turkeys. In 1959, 96,000 acres of land in middle Georgia were added, and the combined forests are called the Chattahoochee-Oconee National Forests and total more than 865,000 acres. ✉ *1755 Cleveland Hwy., Gainesville 30501* ☏ *770/297–3000.*

A child-friendly museum, **Charlemagne's Kingdom** recreates sections of Germany, from the North Sea to the Alps, all in HO model-train scale. The Autobahn is depicted, as is the entire walled town of Rothenburg (there are 350 building replicas) and moving hot air balloons. There are six running trains, thousands of hand-painted figurines, and sound effects including the ocean, a carnival, and German music. The shop sells Lionel trains, Thomas the Tank Engine, and John Deere toys. Willi Lindhorst, a native of Oldenburg, Germany, created the train layout and its trappings and owns the shop with his wife Judi. ✉ *8808 N. Main St.* ☏ *706/878–2200* ⊕ *www.georgiamodelrailroad.com* ✈ *$5* ☉ *Mar.–Dec., daily 10–6; Jan. and Feb., call for hrs.*

At the **Nora Mill Granary,** the original 1,500-pound, 48-inch millstones from 1876 are still in working order. The grist mill, on the banks of the Chattahoochee River, utilizes a 100-foot sluice to feed 19th-century turbines. Grain is hauled to the mill in a vintage 1941 Chevrolet dump truck. A gift shop next door sells cornmeal, grits, and other staples ground on the premises. ✉ *7107 S. Main St.* ☎ *800/927-2375* ⊕ *www.noramill.com.*

The Folk Pottery Museum of Northeast Georgia, 4 mi southeast of Helen, showcases a 200-year unbroken tradition of folk pottery in northeast Georgia (especially in nearby Mossy Creek and the Gillsville-Lula area). Part of the 5,000-square-foot facility shows how the pottery was used as essential household items, and the remainder showcases a 200-piece collection donated to the museum. On display are the whimsical face jugs that have become an emblem of Southern folk art. ✉ *GA 255 N, Sautee Nacoochee* ☎ *706/878–3300* ⊕ *www.folkpotterymuseum.com* 🖃 *$4* ⊙ *Weekdays 10–5, weekends noon–5.*

Visit **Unicoi State Park** for a refreshing escape from crowds in downtown Helen. Two miles from town you'll find more than 1,000 acres of relative peace and quiet, 12 mi of hiking trails, a 53-acre lake, and a campground. The park has a lodge and restaurant. ✉ *1788 GA 356* ☎ *706/878–2201 or 800/864–7275* ⊕ *www.gastateparks.org/info/unicoi/* 🖃 *$3 parking fee.*

Sports & the Outdoors

TUBING
"Tube the Hootch" with **Cool River Tubing** (✉ 590 Edelweiss Strasse ☎ 706/878–2665 or 800/896–4595 ⊙ Late May–early Sept.), which shuttles you on a bus upriver to begin the float back to town. You can choose a short (1½ hours) or long (2½ hours) float trip. Prices are $5 for a single trip of either length or $10 all day. Cool River also operates a waterslide. A combination all-day ticket for tubing and waterslide is $10.

Where to Stay & Eat

$$–$$$$ ✕ **Hofbrauhaus Inn.** This beer hall, which shares its name with a famous counterpart in Munich, makes for a convivial and lively bunch, especially during Oktoberfest. The menu is saturated with hearty German-style food, including schnitzel and *bratkartoffeln* (fried potatoes); unfortunately, the food is not memorable, despite its popularity among those who want to eat the "local" cuisine. There are also plenty of options for other international fare, including Hungarian goulash and broiled African lobster tails. ✉ *1 N. Main St.* ☎ *706/878–2248* ⊟ *AE, D, MC, V.*

$$–$$$$ ✕ **Nacoochee Grill.** Beef, chicken, and fish grilled on a live fire are the focus at this casual restaurant set in a cottage in Nacoochee Village, just outside town. A chowder made of roasted corn, trout, and salmon is a specialty. Venison stew, delicious with a side of smashed horseradish potatoes; crab cakes; and pies made from local fruit are available seasonally. ✉ *7277 S. Main St.* ☎ *706/878–8020* ⊟ *AE, D, DC, MC, V.*

$–$$ ✕ **Farmer's Market Café.** This cheerfully decorated eatery, with old wooden floors, old-time photographs, and red-checked tablecloths, has hearty, reasonably priced American fare—seafood, sandwiches, salads, and vegetable plates. A favorite dish is the country-fried steak served with green beans and mashed potatoes. ⊠ *63 Chattahoochee St.* ☎ *706/ 878–3705* ▤ *AE, D, DC, MC, V.*

★ **$$$$** 🏨 **The Lodge at Smithgall Woods.** As part of a 5,600-acre heritage preserve park run by the state of Georgia, the lodge, set in old growth hardwoods, consists of five separate cottages. The centerpiece is a two-story, four-bedroom cabin constructed of Montana lodge-pole pine. Dinner and breakfast, featuring locally grown vegetables and local specialties like mountain trout, are included in the rates. The state park has some of the best trout streams in Georgia, and the lodge is often used as an executive retreat by Atlanta businesspeople. Guests can book an individual room, a cottage (three to five rooms), or the entire lodge. ⊠ *61 Tsalaki Trail, 30545* ☎ *706/878–3087 or 800/318–5248* 🖷 *706/878– 0301* ⊕ *www.smithgallwoods.com* ⇆ *14 rooms in 5 cottages* ⌂ *Dining room, kitchens, cable TV, fishing, hiking* ▤ *AE, D, MC, V* ⟨◯⟩ *FAP.*

$–$$ 🏨 **Country Inn & Suites.** The faux-Bavarian motif carries only to the front door. Inside you'll find a lobby with hardwood floors and fireplace, a modern heated swimming pool, and well-maintained guest rooms. ⊠ *877 Edelweiss Strasse, 30545* ☎ *706/878–9000 or 800/456–4000* 🖷 *706/878–7878* ⊕ *www.countryinns.com/helenga* ⇆ *47 rooms, 16 suites* ⌂ *In-room broadband, indoor pool, exercise equipment, laundry facilities* ▤ *AE, D, DC, MC, V* ⟨◯⟩ *BP.*

$–$$ 🏨 **The Lodge at Unicoi.** Choose either the comfortable mountain lodge, with 100 attractive lodge rooms, or a one-, two-, or three-bedroom cottage (some with a fireplace), at this state-run accommodation. You can fish, canoe, or swim in the 53-acre lake, play tennis, hike on 12 mi of trails, or take part in educational and nature events led by park rangers. In summer and fall reservations are essential and can be made up to 11 months in advance. ⊠ *GA 356, 30545, 4 mi north of Helen via GA 356* ☎ *706/878–2201 or 800/573–9659* 🖷 *706/878–1897* ⊕ *www. unicoilodge.com* ⇆ *100 rooms, 30 cottages, 84 camp sites* ⌂ *Dining room, some kitchens, some cable TV, in-room data ports, Wi-Fi, 4 tennis courts, lake, fishing, hiking, meeting rooms* ▤ *AE, D, MC, V* ⟨◯⟩ *EP.*

Shopping

★ In an old grist mill with beautiful views of the Soque River, **Mark of the Potter** (⊠ 9982 GA 197 N ☎ 706/947–3440) offers an outstanding selection of pottery from more than 30 artisans. The emphasis is on functional pieces, with a great variety of clay and firing techniques and glazes in every imaginable color. Items range from coffee scoops to lamps, mugs to elaborate vases and casserole dishes. ■ TIP➔ Although it's a bit out of the way, the shop is legendary among Georgia pottery-lovers. Children and adults alike will enjoy sitting on the porch and feeding the huge pet trout.

Old Sautee Store (⊠ 2315 GA 17, 5 mi south of Helen, Sautee ☎ 706/ 878–2281) has been operating continuously for more than 130 years. The museum portion displays everything from old-time Lydia Pinkham Tonic for "women's problems" to Octagon, a lye soap often used many decades ago to wash laundry. The retail store, heavily influenced by an earlier owner's Scandinavian heritage, sells amber jewelry, Norwegian flatbread, and Swedish farmer's cheese. You can also pick up old-time candy and gums such as Black Jack and Beemans, a variety of clothing perfect for mountain hiking and visiting, and toys.

The Gourd Place (✉ 2319 Duncan Bridge Rd., Sautee ☎ 706/865–4048) is a unique museum and gourd and pottery store filled with colorful gourd collections from around the world. Owners Priscilla Wilson and Janice Lymburner also produce attractive stoneware and porcelain vases, bowls, and votive candleholders using liquid clay poured into gourds.

EN
ROUTE

Beginning and ending in Helen, the **Russell-Brasstown Scenic Byway** is a 41-mi loop through some of the most dramatic mountain scenery in northeastern Georgia. Start the counterclockwise drive from GA 17/75 north from Helen, turn left on GA 180, left at GA 348, turn left at GA 75 Alt. back to Helen. The loop passes the Raven Cliff Wilderness, wildlife management areas, the headwaters of the Chattahoochee River, a section of the Appalachian Trail, and goes near the state parks of Vogel, Unicoi, Smithgall Woods, and Brasstown Bald mountain.

Clayton

❸ *35 mi northeast of Helen via GA 356, GA 197, and U.S. 76.*

The town of Clayton, with a downtown filled with shops, is a gateway to North Georgia's mountains. It makes a good base to explore Tallulah Gorge State Park and its falls, and Black Rock Mountain State Park. A short drive northwest on U.S. 76 will take you to several of the region's most appealing lakes, including Rabun and Chatuge.

★ **Tallulah Gorge State Park** is home to a 2 mi-long, 1,000-foot-deep canyon, one of the deepest in the country. In the late 1800s this 2,710-acre park was one of the most-visited destinations in the Southeast, with 17 hotels to house tourists who came to see the roaring falls on the Tallulah River. Then, in 1912, to provide electric power, the "Niagara of the South" was dammed, and the falls dried up, along with the tourism. Today the state of Georgia has designated more than 20 mi of the state park as walking and mountain-biking trails. There's also an interpretive center, a 63-acre lake with a beach, a picnic shelter, and 50 tent and RV sites. Occasionally, water is released for experienced canoers and kayakers; a few times a year, aesthetic flows replicate the original river. See Web site for details. ✉ U.S. 441, *Tallulah Falls* ☎ 706/754–7970, 706/754–7979 *for camping reservations* ⊕ *www.gastateparks.org/info/tallulah* ⛃ *$4 parking fee* ☉ *Daily 8 AM–dusk. Interpretive center 8–5.*

> ### HIKING TIPS
>
> Each day, 100 hiking permits are issued at the interpretive center for spectacular **Tallulah Gorge,** considered one of the most stunning gorges in the eastern United States. The hike to the floor of the 1,000-foot gorge with its lush vegetation, scenic waterfalls, and rocky bottom is about 2½ mi round-trip. Tennis shoes, hiking boots, or river sandals are required for the strenuous hike. Damp walkways can be slick; use caution when climbing near waterfalls or on wet days. The trip takes three to four hours. Rim trails to overlooks are also open to visitors.

The **Foxfire Museum** is a collection of 20 log cabins, some authentic, assembled to re-create Appalachian life before the days of electricity and running water. The nonprofit foundation behind Foxfire, established in 1966, has published a dozen Foxfire books on traditional Appalachian life, the most recent in late 2004. ⊠ *200 Foxfire La., off U.S. 441 at Black Rock Mountain Pkwy., Mountain City* ☎ *706/746–5828* 🖃 *$5* ⊙ *Mon.–Sat. 8:30–4:30.*

★ The **Chattooga River** was the first river in the Southeast to be designated a Wild and Scenic River by Congress. It begins in the Whitesides Mountains of North Carolina and forms the border between Georgia and South Carolina. With Class II to Class V rapids, the Chattooga is popular for white-water rafting, especially in spring and summer when water levels are highest. Movie buffs should note that this was one of the locations for the movie *Deliverance.* ⊠ *From Clayton drive east 7 mi on U.S. 76 to Hwy. 76 Bridge at Georgia–South Carolina state line.*

Lake Rabun was built in 1915, the first of six lakes in the state built by Georgia Railway and Power Co. It covers only 834 acres, but its small size is misleading as its narrow fingers dart through mountain valleys. Lightly visited by tourists and populated with weekend cabins and old boat houses, it has a low-key charm. The lake offers boating and fishing, and there's a small beach at Rabun Beach Recreation Area at the east end of the lake. ⊠ *West of U.S. 23/441 via Old Hwy. 441S and Burton Lake Rd., 2½ mi southwest of Clayton* ⊕ *www.lakerabun.com.*

Another of the six lakes built by Georgia Railway and Power Co., the 2,700-acre **Lake Burton** is in the Chattahoochee National Forest. On the lake, at GA 197, is the **Lake Burton Fish Hatchery,** inside Moccasin Creek State Park. It has trout raceways (used to raise trout from fingerlings), and a kids-only trout fishing pool for ages 11 and younger. ⊠ *Off U.S. 76, west of Clayton, Clarkesville* ☎ *706/947–3194* 🖃 *$3 parking fee.*

★ At more than 3,600 feet, **Black Rock Mountain State Park** is the highest state park in Georgia. Named for the black-gneiss rock visible on cliffs in the area, the 1,738-acre park has 10 mi of trails, a 17-acre lake, 64 camp and RV sites, and 10 cottages. ⊠ *Black Rock Mountain Pkwy., off U.S. 441, 3 mi northwest of Clayton, Mountain City* ☎ *706/746–2141, 800/864–7275 for camping and cottage reservations* ⊕ *www.gastateparks.org/info/blackrock* 🖃 *$3 parking fee* ⊙ *Daily 7 AM–10 PM.*

Sports & the Outdoors

WHITE-WATER RAFTING The North Carolina–based **Nantahala Outdoor Center** (⊠ Chattooga Ridge Rd., 13 mi from Clayton off U.S. 76 ☎ 800/232–7238 ⊕ www.noc.com), the largest rafting company in the region, runs part-day, day-long, and overnight white-water rafting trips on the Chattooga River, from $60 per person. **Southeastern Expeditions LLC** (⊠ 7350 U.S. 76 E, 7 mi from Clayton ☎ 800/868–7238) has full-day trips and a limited number of half-day trips starting at $49 a person.

Where to Stay & Eat

★ $$$ ✕🏨 **Glen-Ella Springs Country Inn.** This restored old hotel has a rustic charm, peaceful location, and fine food ($$$–$$$$) emphasizing regional specialties, such as trout pecan and Lowcountry shrimp on grits. Rooms have no TVs but plenty of reading material, and they open onto common porches with rocking chairs. You have to BYOB. ⊠ *1789 Bear Gap Rd., Clarkesville 30523* ☎ *706/754–7295 or 877/456–7527* 🖶 *706/754–1560* ⊕ *www.glenella.com* ⇔ *12 rooms, 4 suites* ⚭ *Restaurant, Wi-Fi, pool, hiking, meeting rooms; no room TVs* ⊟ *AE, D, MC, V* ⊙ *BP.*

★ **$–$$** ✕⊡ **Dillard House.** An inviting cluster of cottages and motel-style rooms, this establishment sits on a plateau near the state border. The extremely popular Dillard House Restaurant ($$$) serves all-you-can-eat platters of Southern favorites such as roasted chicken, barbecue, corn on the cob, and cabbage casserole. Some rooms have vistas of the Blue Ridge Mountains, stone fireplaces, or interior French doors, and many open onto a large front porch with rocking-chairs. All rooms look out onto the beautifully landscaped grounds. ⊠ *768 Franklin St., Dillard 30537* ☎ *706/746–5348 or 800/541–0671* 🖶 *706/746–3344* ⊕ *www.dillardhouse.com* ⇔ *90 rooms, 25 chalets, 4 cottages, 6 suites* ⚭ *Restaurant, some kitchens, some refrigerators, cable TV, Wi-Fi, 2 tennis courts, hot tub, horseback riding* ⊟ *AE, D, DC, MC, V* ⊙ *EP.*

$$ ⊡ **Lake Rabun Hotel.** Set in shady hemlocks across the road from Lake Rabun, this rustic hotel has rough-hewn wood paneling, a fieldstone fireplace, and furniture handmade from mountain laurel and rhododendron. You can take a sunset cruise, rent a pontoon boat, fish, or swim in the lake. The inn, built in 1922, is truly a throwback to an earlier time. ⊠ *35 Andrea La., Lakemont 30552* ☎ *706/782–4946* ⊕ *www.lakerabunhotel.com* ⇔ *9 private suites* ⚭ *Restaurant, Wi-Fi, bar, meeting room; no room TVs* ⊟ *AE, D, MC, V* ⊙ *EP.*

Shopping

Main Street Gallery (⊠ 51 N. Main St. ☎ 706/782–2440), one of the state's best sources for folk art, carries works by regional artists, including Sarah Rakes, O. L. Samuels, Jay Schuette, and Jimmy Lee Sudduth. The store also carries pottery, paintings, and sculpture. A wide variety of quality local arts and crafts items, such as jewelry, stained glass, and wood carvings, are offered at **Georgia Heritage Center for the Arts** (⊠ U.S. 441 ☎ 706/754–5989).

> **CLOSED ON SUNDAY?**
>
> Planning on shopping? Call ahead. Many smaller town shops—such as those in Clayton and Blairsville—are closed on Sunday. But Dahlonega and Helen shops are open daily. Knowing where to shop and when will help you plan your itinerary.

Hiawassee, Young Harris & Lake Chatuge

❹ *26 mi northwest of Clayton, via U.S. 76; 21 mi north of Helen via GA 75/17.*

The little town of Hiawassee, population 750, and nearby Young Harris, population 600, are near the largest lake in North Georgia, Lake Chatuge, and the tallest mountain in the state, Brasstown Bald. The lake has excellent boating and other water-theme recreation. Appealing mountain resorts are nearby as well. A half-hour drive will take you to Brasstown Bald, where temperatures even on the hottest summer day rarely rise above the low 80s. The Georgia Mountain Fair, held annually, has a permanent location on the shores of Lake Chatuge. A number of festivals are held at the fairgrounds every year, including the Rhododendron and Bluegrass festivals in May and the Fall Festival and State Fiddler's Convention in October. The Georgia Mountain Fair claims to be the "Country Music Capital of Georgia."

★ **Brasstown Bald,** in the Chattahoochee National Forest, reaches 4,784 feet, the highest point in Georgia. Below the Bald is Georgia's only cloud forest, an area of lichen-covered trees often kept wet by clouds and fog. From the observation platform at the top of the Bald on a clear day you can see Georgia, North Carolina, South Carolina, and Tennessee. A paved but steep ½-mi trail leads from the parking lot (where there are restrooms and a picnic area) to the visitor center, which has exhibits and interpretative programs. You also can ride a bus ($2) to the visitor center. ⊠ *GA 180 Spur, 18 mi southwest of Hiawassee via U.S. 76, GA 75, GA 180, and GA 180 Spur* ☎ *706/896–2556* ⊕ *www.fs.fed.us/conf/* 🖼 *$3 parking fee, $2 shuttle* ☉ *Late May–Oct., daily 10–6; Nov.–mid-May, weekends 10–6, depending on weather.*

Hamilton Rhododendron Gardens, on the grounds of the Georgia Mountain Fair at Lake Chatuge, display more than 3,000 rhododendrons, native azaleas, and other unique plants, including the rare yellow azalea developed by the garden's founder, Fred Hamilton. ■ TIP→ **The best time to see the rhododendrons and azaleas in bloom is April to June.** ⊠ *Georgia Mountain Fairgrounds, Hiawassee* ☎ *706/896–4191* 🖼 *Free* ☉ *Daily dawn–dusk.*

Where to Stay

★ **$$$–$$$$** 🏨 **Brasstown Valley Resort.** For upscale, lodge-style accommodations, this resort is a great option. The rooms are comfortable and spacious, in an elegant but rustic style. Some have fireplaces and balconies overlooking the valley. The stone fireplace in the lobby is an impressive 70 feet high. The resort also features a variety of sports activities. ⊠ *6321 U.S. 76, Young Harris 30582* ☎ *706/379–9900 or 800/201–3205* 🖨 *706/ 379–4615* ⊕ *www.brasstownvalley.com* 🛏 *102 rooms, 32 cottages, 5 suites* ⚷ *Restaurant, cable TV, in-room broadband, Wi-Fi, 18-hole golf course, 4 tennis courts, indoor-outdoor pool, health club, hot tub, sauna, hiking, horseback riding, bar, convention center* ☰ *AE, D, DC, MC, V* ⏹ *BP.*

$$–$$$ 🏨 **The Ridges Resort and Club.** Many of the beautifully appointed rooms in this lodge are decorated with leather furnishings, stone steps, and rustic wood and have gorgeous views of Lake Chatuge. You can relax in the lobby before a towering fieldstone fireplace and admire the landscape from the floor-to-ceiling window that faces the lake. A nearby marina has boat rentals, including pontoons, paddleboats, sailboats, and kayaks. ■ TIP→ **Winter discounts available.** ⊠ *3499 U.S. 76, Hiawassee 30546* ☎ *706/896–2262 or 888/834–4409* 🖨 *706/896–4128* ⊕ *www. theridgesresort.com* 🛏 *62 rooms, 4 suites* ⚷ *2 restaurants, cable TV, in-room broadband, Wi-Fi, golf privileges, tennis court, pool, exercise*

equipment, boating, marina, convention center ▭ *AE, D, DC, MC, V*
⊙| *EP.*

Blue Ridge

❺ *39 mi southwest of Hiawassee via U.S. 76/GA 515; 66 mi west of Clayton via U.S. 76/GA 515; 53 mi northwest of Dahlonega via GA 52 and
U.S. 76/GA 515*

Blue Ridge, population 1,200, is one of the most pleasant small mountain towns in North Georgia. After you've shopped for antiques or
crafts at Blue Ridge's many small shops, you can ride the revived Blue
Ridge Scenic Railway to McCaysville, a town at the Tennessee line, and
then back through the mountains.

☾ The **Blue Ridge Scenic Railway** makes a 3½ hour, 26-mi round-trip along
the Toccoa River. The trip includes a halfway stop in **McCaysville,
Georgia**, smack on the Georgia–Tennessee state line. Several restaurants,
shops, and artisans there make it a point to be open during the 1 ½-
hour layover. The train, which has open and Pullman cars and is pulled
by diesel engines, is staffed with friendly volunteer hosts. The ticket office, now on the National Register of Historic Places, dates from 1905
and was originally the depot of the L&N Railroad. Children of all ages
enjoy the ride. ■ **TIP→** In summer you may want to consider the closed, air-
conditioned coaches, although many passengers prefer the thrill of open-air
cars. ⊠ *241 Depot St.* ☎ *706/632–9833 or 800/934–1898* ⊕ *www.
brscenic.com* ⊡ *$24–$33, depending on season* ⊗ *Mid-Mar.–late Dec.
Check Web site or call for schedules.*

☾ The **Swan Drive-In Theater** originally opened in 1955 and is one of only
four drive-in movie theaters still operating in Georgia. You can take in
a movie under the stars and fill up on corn dogs, tater wedges, and popcorn from the concession stand. Window speakers have been replaced
by the movie sounds broadcast to your car radio. The name of the drive-
in comes from the swans in the ponds of England that the owner ad-
mired during World War II. ⊠ *651 Summit St.* ☎ *706/632–5235.*

Ellijay

❻ *84 mi west of Clayton via U.S. 76; 37 mi northwest of Dahlonega via
GA 52; 80 mi north of Atlanta via I–75, I–575, and GA 5/515.*

Billed as "Georgia's apple capital," Ellijay is also popular among antiques aficionados. The town, on the site of what had been a Cherokee
village called Elatseyi (meaning "place of green things"), has a colorful
cluster of crafts shops and antiques markets.

The most popular time to visit Ellijay is in fall, when roadside stands
brimming with delicious ripe apples dot the landscape. The annual
Georgia Apple Festival takes place the second and third weekends of
October. In addition to showcasing the many manifestations of the
crisp fruit—apple butter, apple pie, apple cider, and so on—the festival
offers a host of arts and crafts exhibitions.

Buy freshly picked apples (usually August to early November) at 80-acre **Hillcrest Orchards**. Feast on homemade jellies, jams, breads, and doughnuts at the farm's market and bakery. Also on the orchard's premises are a petting zoo, a small museum, and a picnic area. On some September weekends (dates vary), the Apple Pickin' Jubilee features live music, wagon rides, pick you own apples, and other activities. ⊠ *9696 GA 52* ☏ *706/273–3838* ⊕ *www.hillcrestorchards.net* ✍ *$5 for special events including Apple Pickin' Jubilee; $3 for petting zoo* ⊗ *Mid-Aug.–Nov. 30, daily 9–6.*

13

The 3,712-acre **Fort Mountain State Park** has a 17-acre lake with sandy beach, horseback riding (for a fee), 14 mi of hiking trails, and 30 mi of mountain biking trails ($2 trail fee for biking). The gem of the park is a mysterious wall of rock, 855 feet long, thought to have been built by Native Americans around AD500. Tent and RV sites ($20 to $22) and rental cottages ($80 to $120) are also on-site. ⊠ *181 Fort Mountain Park Rd., Chatsworth* ☏ *706/695–2621* ⊕ *www.gastateparks.org* ✍ *Free; park pass fee of $3 vehicle* ⊗ *Daily 7 AM–10 PM.*

Sports & the Outdoors

There are plenty of options for fishing, canoeing, and kayaking on the Cartecay River, which runs through town. **Mountaintown Outdoor Expeditions** (⊠ 122 Adventure Trail, 5 mi east of Ellijay off GA 52 on Lower Cartecay Rd. ☏706/635–2524 ⊕www.mountaintownoutdoorexpeditions. com) arranges outdoor adventures for people of all skill levels.

Where to Stay

$$–$$$ ⊡ **Whitepath Lodge.** From nearly every room you get panoramic vistas of the tranquil North Georgia mountains. The main lodge has eight suites, each with two bedrooms, three baths, and a fully equipped kitchen. The neighboring Shenandoah Lodge has six two-floor suites with fireplaces and multilevel decks overlooking the woods. If you're a sports enthusiast, you'll be happy with all the recreational activities nearby—18-hole golf courses, mountain biking, horseback riding, tubing, seasonal whitewater rafting, boating, canoeing, kayaking, and fishing. ⊠ *987 Shenandoah Dr., Ellijay 30540* ☏ *706/276–7199* ⊕ *www.whitepathlodge. com* ✍ *14 suites* ⋄ *Kitchens, cable TV, tennis court, pool, basketball, hiking, meeting rooms* ▤ *MC, V* ⊙ *EP.*

$–$$ ⊡ **Best Western Mountain View Inn.** This two-story motel sits on a hilltop above East Ellijay. The rooms sport cheerful decor with bedspreads in bright primary colors. Some rooms indeed have mountain views. Suites are oversized rooms with a sitting area, not true suites, but they do have two TVs. ⊠ *43 Coosawattee Dr., East Ellijay 30539* ☏ *706/515–1500 or 866/515–4515* ⊕ *www.bwmountainviewinn.com* ✍ *52 rooms* ⋄ *Cable TV, in-room broadband, Wi-Fi, indoor pool, hot tub* ▤ *AE, D, DC, MC, V* ⊙ *BP.*

$ ⊡ **Cohutta Lodge.** On 150 acres atop Fort Mountain near the Cohutta Wilderness, the views from this lodge are resplendent. Outdoor activities can be arranged through the hotel. ⊠ *500 Cochise Trail, off GA 52, Chatsworth 30705* ☏ *706/695–9601* ☐ *706/695–0913* ⊕ *www. cohuttalodge.com* ✍ *47 rooms, 5 suites, 2 cabins* ⋄ *Restaurant, in-room* *broadband, indoor pool, hiking, horseback riding, meeting rooms* ▤ *MC, V* ▯◎▯ *EP.*

Shopping

Mountain Treasures (✉ 5711 GA 52 E ☏ 706/635–5590) sells mountain home furnishings with a comfortable lodge motif. **Corks & Crumbs** (✉ 5 Southside Sq. ☏ 706/276–7622) has a Frogtown Cellars winery tasting room; a bakery serving scones, cinnamon rolls, cookies, and a handful of different breads; wine accessories; and a few antiques and collectibles.

THE NORTHWEST

Northwest Georgia is rich in history. Chickamauga & Chattanooga National Military Park reminds visitors of the devastation of the Civil War and the determination of both Southern and Northern soldiers participating in its bloodiest two-day battle. The area also pays homage to Georgia's former Cherokee residents, driven by the federal government from their verdant homeland in New Echota—once the capital of the Cherokee nation—to dusty Oklahoma on the Trail of Tears. Thousands lost their lives in military stockades and on the 800-mi journey, which started in 1838. Northwest Georgia lies along the Cumberland Plateau, with its flat-top sandstone mountains.

New Echota

❼ *71 mi northwest of Atlanta via I–75 north to GA 225; 41 mi southwest of Ellijay via U.S. 76 to GA 382 W/GA 136.*

From 1825 to 1838 New Echota was the capital of the Cherokee Nation, whose constitution was patterned after that of the United States. The town was named in honor of Chota, a Cherokee town in present-day Tennessee. The public buildings and houses in town were generally log structures. There was a council house, a printing office, a Supreme Court building, and the *Cherokee Phoenix* newspaper. The first newspaper established (in 1828) by Native Americans, it utilized the 86-character alphabet developed by Sequoyah, who spent 12 years developing the written Cherokee language despite having no formal education. He is the only known person in history to have single-handedly created a written language.

The Treaty of 1835, signed in New Echota by a small group of Cherokee leaders, relinquished Cherokee claims to lands east of the Mississippi. Most Cherokees considered the treaty fraudulent. A few years later 7,000 federal and state troops began removing Cherokee from their homes in Georgia, North Carolina, and Tennessee and put them in stockades, including one in New Echota. About 15,000 Cherokee were then forced to travel west to Oklahoma on foot, horseback, and in wagons, along what is known as the "Trail of Tears." Thousands died along the way. After reaching Oklahoma in 1839, the three principal signers of the Treaty of 1835 were assassinated by Cherokee who considered them traitors.

Following the removal of the Cherokee, New Echota reverted to farmland. Today, one original building remains, some buildings have been reconstructed and furnished, and other structures have been moved to the site. The visitor center has a movie and a variety of books about the Cherokee history. When visiting New Echota you can stay in Calhoun, the nearest town to New Echota, or in Dalton, Rome, Chickamauga, or even in Chattanooga.

★ A small museum and a collection of buildings at **New Echota State Historic Site** detail the site's history. Worcester House, a home and Presbyterian mission station, is an original building, restored in the late 1950s. The Cherokee Council House is a reconstruction of the 1819 building where the legislature met. The Supreme Courthouse is also a reconstruction, as is the print house, where thousands of books translated in Cherokee and the weekly *Cherokee Phoenix* were published. Other buildings—including the 1805 Vann Tavern—and outbuildings were relocated to the site. ✉ *1211 Chatsworth Hwy., GA 225, 1 mi east of I–75 near Calhoun* ☎ *706/624–1321* ⊕ *www.georgiastateparks.org* 🎟 *$4* ☉ *Tues.–Sat. 9–5, Sun. 2–5:30.*

The beautifully restored, three-story brick **Chief Vann House** was commissioned in 1804 by a leader of the Cherokee Nation. Moravian artisans helped construct the intricately carved interior mantles and other woodwork. The well-decorated home is furnished as it would have been when Chief Vann lived there. Of mixed Scottish and Cherokee parentage, Chief James Vann owned numerous slaves who also worked on the construction of the house. His son, Cherokee statesman Joseph Vann, lived in the house until he was evicted by the Georgia Militia in 1835, and forced to move to Cherokee Territory, in what is now Oklahoma. ✉ *82 GA 225 at GA 52, Chatsworth, 17 mi northeast of New Echota* ☎ *706/695–2598* ⊕ *http://gastateparks.org/info/chiefvann* 🎟 *$4* ☉ *Tues.–Sat. 9–5, Sun. 2–5:30.*

Rome

❽ *23 mi southwest of Calhoun via GA 53; 70 mi northwest of Atlanta via I–75 to U.S. 411.*

Like its much larger Italian namesake, Rome, Georgia, population 35,000, is built on seven hills. Indeed, a bronze replica of the Capitoline Wolf, can be seen in downtown Rome, in front of City Hall. The statue was a 1929 gift from the government of Italy.

Rome was an important transportation center during the Civil War, but since then has become better known as the site of remarkable Berry College, where generations of rural Georgians have earned higher educations. Historic downtown Rome has been described as the most intact Victorian city center in Georgia. It was revitalized 25 years ago, and is rich with businesses, small shops, restaurants, and entertainment. In the foothills of the Appalachian Mountains, three rivers—the Ooastanaula, Etowah, and Coosa—run through Rome.

The **Oak Hill and the Martha Berry Museum** has exhibits telling the story of Martha Berry (1866–1942) and the college that bears her name. Founded by Berry in 1902 as a public school for enterprising but poor rural Georgians, Berry College is now considered the largest college campus in America, sitting on a 28,000-acre campus. "Education combines the head, heart, and hands," Berry said, and the school continues its founder's policies of low tuition and a work-study program so that first-generation college students can afford to attend. You can also tour Berry's estate, Oak Hill, with its five gardens, originally designed 1927–33. ✉ *Veterans Memorial Hwy. at U.S. 27* ☎ *706/291–1883 or 800/220–5504* ⊕ *www.berry.edu* 🖭 *$5* ☻ *Mon.–Sat. 10–5.*

Featuring Native American artifacts, art work, and other displays, the **Chieftains Museum & Major Ridge Home,** on the banks of the Oostanaula River, is housed in an 18th-century white clapboard plantation house; the former home of Major Ridge, a Cherokee tribal leader. ✉ *501 Riverside Pkwy. NE* ☎ *706/291–9494* 🖭 *$3* ☻ *Tues.–Fri. 9–3, Sat. 10–4.*

Where to Stay & Eat

$$–$$$$ ✕ **La Scala.** Piero Barba from Capri, Italy, established this outpost of Italian cooking in 1996. The menu is dominated by classic dishes: osso buco, braciola, seafood, and pasta. The wine list includes French, American, and Italian wines. ✉ *413 Broad St.* ☎ *706/238–9000* ▭ *AE, D, DC, MC, V* ☻ *Closed Sun. No lunch.*

★ **$–$$** ▥ **Claremont House.** This beautifully restored 1882 Victorian inn has huge rooms with 14-foot ceilings and is furnished with period antiques. Breakfast is sumptuous, featuring stuffed French toast among its delicious options. ✉ *906 E. 2nd Ave., 30161* ☎ *706/291–0900 or 800/254–4797* ⊕ *www.theclaremonthouse.net* ➶ *4 rooms, 1 cottage* ⟂ *Dining room, Wi-Fi* ▭ *AE, MC, V* ⦿ *BP.*

Chickamauga & Chattanooga National Military Park

❾ *110 mi northwest of Atlanta via I–75 and GA 2; 42 mi north of New*
Fodor'sChoice *Echota State Historic Site via I–75; 12 mi south of Chattanooga, TN,*
★ *via U.S. 27.*

This site, established in 1890 as the nation's first military park, was the scene of some of the Civil War's bloodiest battles. In Chickamauga alone, 34,624 were killed, missing, and wounded in September 1863. Though the Confederates won the battle at Chickamauga, the Union army retained control of Chattanooga. The normally thick cedar groves and foliage covering Chickamauga were trampled and, according to eyewitness accounts, trees were so shot up that a sweet cedar smell mingled with the blood of fallen soldiers.

Some areas around the park now suffer from suburban sprawl, but the 9,000-acre park itself is made up of serene fields and islands of trees. Monuments, battlements, and weapons adorn the roads that traverse the park, with markers explaining the action.

The **Chickamauga Battlefield Visitor Center** has an excellent small museum offering a timeline of the battle, a film on the military strategy that involved 124,000 soldiers, a collection of 346 antique military rifles, and a well-stocked bookstore. There's a 7-mi self-guided auto tour through the park, with numerous spots to stop and view the more than 700 monuments and historical markers in Chickamauga, and mid-June to September you can join a free, 90-minute auto caravan through the park, led by a park ranger. ⊠ *1 mi south of intersection of GA 2 and U.S. 27, Fort Oglethorpe* ☎ *706/866–9241* ⊕ *www.nps.gov/chch* ☎ *Free; $3 for visitors center and multimedia show* ⊙ *Daily 8:30–5.*

The **Walker County Regional Heritage & Model Train Museum,** in a former railroad depot, has a fascinating hodgepodge of items from the attics and garages of Chickamauga residents. You'll see everything from Civil War and World War I artifacts to 1950s lawn mowers and HO–gauge model trains. ⊠ *100 Gordon St., Chickamauga* ☎ *706/375–4488* ☎ *$2* ⊙ *Weekdays 10–3, Sat. 10–4.*

OFF THE BEATEN PATH

CLOUDLAND CANYON STATE PARK – At this 3,845-acre park, you can see firsthand the unusual geology of this remote part of northwestern Georgia. Hike down the canyon, which drops 1,100 feet from the rim, and you're literally walking down millions of years of geologic time. If you make it all the way to the bottom—the trail totals 4½ mi—you'll be rewarded with sights of two waterfalls. ⊠ *122 Cloudland Canyon Park Rd., Rising Fawn* ☎ *706/657–4050* ⊕ *www.georgiastateparks.org* ☎ *$3 parking* ⊙ *Daily 7 AM–10 PM.*

NORTH GEORGIA ESSENTIALS

Transportation

BY AIR

The gateway airports for this region are Hartsfield-Jackson International Airport in Atlanta and Chattanooga Metropolitan Airport in Chattanooga, Tennessee.

🄵 **Chattanooga Metropolitan Airport** ⊠ 1001 Airport Rd., Chattanooga, TN ☎ 423/855-2202 ⊕ www.chattairport.com. **Hartsfield-Jackson Atlanta International Airport** ⊠ 6000 N. Terminal Pkwy., Atlanta ☎ 404/530-7300 ⊕ www.atlanta-airport.com.

BY CAR

A car is by far the best means—and in many areas the only means—of transportation around this region. U.S. 19 runs north–south, passing through Dahlonega and up into the North Georgia mountains. U.S. 129 runs northwest from Athens eventually merging with U.S. 19. GA 75 stems off U.S. 129 and goes through Helen and up into the mountains. U.S. 23/441 runs north through Clayton; U.S. 76 runs west from Clayton to Dalton, merging for a stretch with GA 5/515. GA 52 runs along the edge of the Blue Ridge Mountains, passing through Ellijay. Interstate 75 is the major artery in the northwesternmost part of the state and passes near the New Echota State Historic Site and the Chickamauga and Chattanooga National Military Park.

BY TAXI

Very few North Georgia communities have taxi services as people in the area are almost completely reliant on private cars.

🚖 **American Cab** ✉ Dalton ☎ 706/226-8703. **Grey Cab** ✉ Toccoa ☎ 706/886-2839. **Helen Taxi Service** ✉ Helen ☎ 706/892-4067. **It's Your Trip Transportation** ✉ Blue Ridge ☎ 706/633-3668 ⊕ http://itsyourtriptaxi.com. **Paddy's Taxi** ✉ Dahlonega ☎ 706/300-7143.

Contacts & Resources

BANKS & EXCHANGE SERVICES

Bank service is widely available in North Georgia. Most banks maintain weekday working hours, though some also offer Saturday morning service. A variety of ATM sites are also available.

🏦 **AmSouth Bank** ✉ 1400 Turner-McCall Blvd., Rome ☎ 706/295-7700. **BB&T** ✉ Main and Memorial Dr., Dahlonega ☎ 706/864-3314. **Community Bank & Trust** ✉ 174 N. Hwy. 441, Clayton ☎ 706/782-1010. **United Community Bank** ✉ 214 N. Main St., Blairsville ☎ 706/896-4186 ✉ 558 Industrial Blvd., Ellijay ☎ 706/635-5411 ✉ Main St., Helen ☎ 706/865-2265.

EMERGENCIES

🚨 **Emergency Services Ambulance, police** ☎ 911.

🏥 **Hospitals Chestatee Regional Hospital** ✉ Mountain Dr., Dahlonega ☎ 706/864-6136. **Fannin Regional Hospital** ✉ 2855 Old Hwy. 5 N, Blue Ridge ☎ 706/632-3711. **Mountain Lakes Medical Center** ✉ 196 Ridgecrest Circle, Clayton ☎ 706/782-3100. **North Georgia Medical Center** ✉ 1362 S. Main St., Ellijay ☎ 706/276-4741. **Northeast Georgia Medical Center** ✉ 743 Spring St., Gainesville ☎ 770/535-3553. **Redmond Regional Medical Center** ✉ 501 Redmond Rd., Rome ☎ 706/291-0291. **Union General Hospital** ✉ 214 Hospital Circle, Blairsville ☎ 706/745-2111.

💊 **Pharmacies Blue Ridge Pharmacy** ✉ 793 E. Main St., Blue Ridge ☎ 706/632-2244. **Eckerd Pharmacy** ✉ 566 Main St., Dahlonega ☎ 706/864-7641. **Fred's Pharmacy** ✉ 534 Bell Creek, Hiawassee ☎ 706/896-4302. **Huff Drug Store** ✉ 76 Industrial Blvd., Ellijay ☎ 706/635-7931. **Randy's Helen Pharmacy** ✉ 8016 S. Main St., Helen ☎ 706/878-0066. **Super Wal-Mart** ✉ 450 W. Belmont Dr., Calhoun ☎ 706/625-4274 ✉ 815 Shugart Rd., Dalton ☎ 706/281-2855. **Walgreen's** ✉ 701 Martha Berry Blvd., Rome ☎ 706/295-7787.

INTERNET, MAIL & SHIPPING

UPS has outlets in major towns. Shipping is also available at local post offices. Wireless Internet access is usually available in libraries and visitors centers. In some towns, it's also available in downtown.

🏢 **Dahlonega-Lumpkin Chamber of Commerce and Visitors Center** ✉ 13 Park St. S, Dahlonega ☎ 706/864-3711 or 800/231-5543. **Gilmer County Public Library** ✉ 103 Dalton St., Ellijay ☎ 706/276-4528. **Greater Rome Convention and Visitor's Bureau** ✉ 402 Civic Center Dr., Rome ☎ 706/295-5576 or 800/444-1834. **Helen Public Library** ✉ 90 Pete's Park Rd., Helen ☎ 706/878-2438. **Rabun County Welcome Center** ✉ 232 U.S. 441N, Clayton ☎ 706/782-5113. **The UPS Store** ✉ 420 WalMart Way, Suite B, Dahlonega ☎ 706/867-7555 ✉ 96 Craig St., Ellijay ☎ 706/698-4877 ✉ 3 Central Plaza, Rome ☎ 706/290-9500. **U.S. Post Office** ✉ 118 Main St., Blairsville ☎ 706/745-2541 ✉ 165 Depot St., Blue Ridge ☎ 706/632-7377 ✉ North Main St., Clayton ☎ 706/782-3731 ✉ 72 Alicia La., Dahlonega ☎ 706/864-2517 ✉ 1119 Murray Ave., Dalton ☎ 706/

279-1329 ✉ 801 Industrial Blvd., Ellijay ☎ 706/635-4356 ✉ 7976 S. Main St., Helen ☎ 706/878-2422 ✉ 600 E. 1st St., Rome ☎ 706/290-9729.

MEDIA

There are a number of good bookstores in this region.

🚩 **Barnes & Noble** ✉ 1442 Turner-McCall Blvd., Rome ☎ 706/232-3202. **The Book Nook** ✉ 96 Craig St., Suite 101, E. Ellijay ☎ 706/515-8700. **Ivy Mountain Books** ✉ 2413 Hwy. 76, Hiawassee ☎ 706/781-7902. **Prater's Main Street Books** ✉ 34 N. Main St., Clayton ☎ 706/212-0014.

TOUR OPTIONS

Tours of Helen and White County are available for $50 for a half-day. Dahlonega's Downtown Walking Audio Tour costs $5 per person and features music, as well as information on this gold-rush town. Greater Rome Convention and Visitor's Bureau offers walking and driving tours of downtown Rome, Myrtle Hill Cemetery (where Woodrow Wilson's first wife and Civil War soldiers are buried), and Berry College.

🚩 **Alpine Helen-White County Convention and Visitors Bureau** ✉ 726 Bruckenstrasse, Helen ☎ 706/878-2181 or 800/858-8027 ⊕ www.helenga.org. **Dahlonega's Downtown Walking Audio Tour** ✉ 199 Choice Ave., Dahlonega ☎ 706/867-0050 ⊕ www. buissonartscenter.com. **Greater Rome Convention and Visitor's Bureau** ✉ 402 Civic Center Dr., Rome ☎ 800/444-1834 or 706/295-5576 ⊕ www.romegeorgia.org.

VISITOR INFORMATION

A variety of services—from maps to brochures to directions—are available at tourist offices in North Georgia. All are open during office hours on week days and usually at least one day on weekends.

🚩 Tourist Information **Blairsville & Union County Chamber of Commerce** ✉ 385 Welcome Center La., off Blue Ridge Hwy., Blairsville 30512 ☎ 706/745-5789 ⊕ www. blairsvillechamber.com. **Dahlonega-Lumpkin Chamber of Commerce and Visitors Center** ✉ 13 Park St. S, Dahlonega ☎ 706/864-3711 or 800/231-5543 ⊕ www.dahlonega. org. **Dalton-Whitfield County Convention and Visitors Bureau** ✉ 2211 Dug Gap Battle Rd., Dalton ☎ 706/270-9960 ⊕ www.daltoncvb.com. **Fannin County Chamber of Commerce and Welcome Center** ✉ 3990 Appalachian Hwy., Blue Ridge ☎ 706/632-5680 or 800/899-6867 ⊕ www.blueridgemountains.com. **Gilmer County Chamber of Commerce and Welcome Center** ✉ 368 Craig St., E. Ellijay ☎ 706/635-7400 ⊕ www. gilmerchamber.com. **Greater Rome Convention and Visitors Bureau** ✉ 402 Civic Center Dr., Rome ☎ 706/295-5576 or 800/444-1834 ⊕ www.romegeorgia.org. **Helen Welcome Center** ✉ 726 Bruckenstrasse ☎ 706/878-2181 or 800/858-8027 🖷 706/878-4032 ⊕ www.helenga.com. **Rabun County Welcome Center** ✉ 232 U.S. 441N, Clayton ☎ 706/782-5113 ⊕ www.gamountains.com. **Towns County Tourism Association** ✉ 1411 Jack Dayton Circle, Young Harris ☎ 706/896-4966 ⊕ www.mountaintopga.com.

SMART TRAVEL TIPS

There are planners and there are those who, excuse the pun, fly by the seat of their pants. We happily place ourselves among the planners. Our writers and editors try to anticipate all the issues you may face before and during any journey, and then they do their research. This section is the product of their efforts. Use it to get excited about your trip to the Carolinas and Georgia, to inform your travel planning, or to guide you on the road should the seat of your pants start to feel threadbare.

AIR TRAVEL

If you're flying into the Carolinas or Georgia, chances are you'll pass through Hartsfield-Jackson Atlanta International Airport. It's by far the most popular airport in the region, and is the busiest in the world, at least in terms of number of passengers—more than 85 million annually. (Chicago's O'Hare International Airport claims to be the busiest in terms of number of flights.)

Flying time to Atlanta is 4½ hours from Los Angeles, 2½ hours from New York, 2 hours from Chicago, 2 hours from Dallas, and 9 hours from London. By plane, Charlotte is an hour northeast of Atlanta, Raleigh 75 minutes northeast, Wilmington 1¾ hours east, Asheville 1 hour north, and Charleston, Hilton Head, and Savannah an hour east–southeast.

CARRIERS

Hartsfield-Jackson Atlanta International Airport is the primary hub of Delta Airlines and AirTran Airways. Altogether, about two dozen domestic and international airlines fly into Atlanta. US Airways has a hub at North Carolina's Charlotte-Douglas International Airport, which is also served by more than a dozen other airlines. Raleigh-Durham International is not a hub for any carrier, but is serviced by more than a dozen airlines. Commuter airlines, including US Airways Express, Continental Express, Delta Connection, and United Express have service between many smaller North Carolina airports as well as those in South Carolina and Georgia.

🛪 Major Airlines **Alaska Airlines** ☎ 800/252-7522 or 206/433-3100 ⊕ www.alaskaair.com. **Amer-**

ican Airlines ☎ 800/433-7300 ⊕ www.aa.com.
ATA ☎ 800/435-9282 or 317/282-8308 ⊕ www.ata.
com. **Continental Airlines** ☎ 800/523-3273 for U.S.
and Mexico reservations, 800/231-0856 for international reservations ⊕ www.continental.com. **Delta
Airlines** ☎ 800/221-1212 for U.S. reservations, 800/
241-4141 for international reservations ⊕ www.
delta.com. **jetBlue** ☎ 800/538-2583 ⊕ www.
jetblue.com. **Northwest Airlines** ☎ 800/225-2525
for U.S. reservations, 800/447-4747 for international
destinations ⊕ www.nwa.com. **Southwest Airlines**
☎ 800/435-9792 ⊕ www.southwest.com. **Spirit
Airlines** ☎ 800/772-7117 or 586/791-7300 ⊕ www.
spiritair.com. **United Airlines** ☎ 800/864-8331 for
U.S. reservations, 800/538-2929 for international
reservations ⊕ www.united.com. **US Airways**
☎ 800/428-4322 for U.S. and Canada reservations,
800/622-1015 for international reservations ⊕ www.
usairways.com.

🛪 Smaller Airlines **Air Canada** ☎ 800/776-3000
⊕ www.aircanada.com. **AirTran** ☎ 770/994-8258
or 800/247-8726 ⊕ www.airtran.com. **American
Eagle** ☎ 800/433-7300 ⊕ www.aa.com. **Delta
Connection** ☎ 800/221-1212 or 800/282-3424
⊕ www.delta.com. **Continental Express** ☎ 800/
525-0280 ⊕ www.continental.com. **Fly First Class**
☎ 516/921-0200 ⊕ www.flyfirstclass.biz. **Midwest
Express** ☎ 800/452-2022 ⊕ www.midwestairlines.
com. **Northwest Airlink** ☎ 800/225-2525 ⊕ www.
nwairlink.com. **United Express** ☎ 800/864-8331
⊕ www.united.com. **US Airways Express** ☎ 800/
428-4322 ⊕ www.usairways.com.

CHECK-IN & BOARDING

Double-check your flight times, especially
if you made your reservations far in advance. Airlines change their schedules, and
alerts may not reach you. Always **bring a
government-issued photo ID to the airport**
(even when it's not required, a passport is
best), and **arrive when you need to and
not before.** Check-in usually at least an
hour before domestic flights and two to
three hours for international flights. But
many airlines have more stringent advance
check-in requirements at some busy airports. The TSA estimates the waiting time
for security at most major airports and
publishes the information on its Web site.
Note that if you aren't at the gate at least
10 minutes before your flight is scheduled
to take off (sometimes earlier), you won't
be allowed to board.

Don't stand in a line if you don't have to.
Buy an e-ticket, check-in at an electronic
kiosk, or—even better—check-in on your
airline's Web site before you leave home.
If you don't need to check luggage, you
could bypass all but the security lines.
These days, most domestic airline tickets
are electronic; international tickets may be
either electronic or paper.

You usually pay a surcharge (up to $50) to
get a paper ticket, and its sole advantage is
that it may be easier to endorse over to another airline if your flight is cancelled and
the airline with which you booked can't
accommodate you on another flight. With
an e-ticket, the only thing you receive is an
e-mailed receipt citing your itinerary and
reservation and ticket numbers. Be sure
to carry this with you as you'll need it to
get past security. If you lose your receipt,
though, you can simply print out another
copy or ask the airline to do it for you at
check-in.

Particularly during busy travel seasons and
around holiday periods, if a flight is over-
sold, the gate agent will usually ask for
volunteers and will offer some sort of
compensation if you're willing to take a
different flight. **Know your rights.** If you're
bumped from a flight *involuntarily,* the
airline must give you some kind of compensation if an alternate flight can't be
found within one hour. If your flight is delayed because of something within the airline's control (so bad weather doesn't
count), then the airline has a responsibility
to get you to your destination on the same
day, even if they have to book you on another airline and in an upgraded class if
necessary. Read your airline's Contract of
Carriage; it's usually buried somewhere on
the airline's Web site.

Be prepared to quickly adjust your plans
by programming a few numbers into your
cell: your airline, an airport hotel or two,
your destination hotel, your car service,
and/or your travel agent. Bring snacks,
water, and sufficient diversions, and
you'll be covered if you get stuck in the
airport, on the tarmac, or even in the air
during turbulence.

CUTTING COSTS

It's always good to **comparison shop.** Web sites (aka consolidators) and travel agents can have different arrangements with the airlines and offer different prices for exactly the same flight and day. Certain Web sites have tracking features that will e-mail you immediately when good deals are posted. Other people prefer to stick with one or two frequent-flier programs, racking up free trips and accumulating perks that can make trips easier. On some airlines, perks include a special reservations number, early boarding, access to upgrades, and more roomy economy-class seating.

Check early and often. Start looking for cheap fares up to a year in advance, and keep looking until you see something you can live with; you never know when a good deal may pop up. That said, **jump on the good deals.** Waiting even a few minutes might mean paying more. For most people, saving money is more important than flexibility, so the more affordable nonrefundable tickets work. Just remember that you'll pay dearly (often as much as $100) if you must change your travel plans. Check on prices for departures at different times of the day and to and from alternate airports, and look for departures on Tuesday, Wednesday, and Thursday, typically the cheapest days to travel. Remember to **weigh your options,** though. A cheaper flight might have a long layover rather than being nonstop, or landing at a secondary airport might substantially increase your ground transportation costs.

Note that many airline Web sites—and most ads—show prices *without* taxes and surcharges. Don't buy until you know the full price. Government taxes add up quickly. Also **watch those ticketing fees.** Surcharges are usually added when you buy your ticket anywhere but on an airline's own Web site. (By the way, that includes on the phone—even if you call the airline directly—and for paper tickets regardless of how you book).

🚩 Online Consolidators AirlineConsolidator.com ⊕ www.airlineconsolidator.com, for international tickets. Best Fares ⊕ www.bestfares.com; $59.90 annual membership. Cheap Tickets ⊕ www. cheaptickets.com. Expedia ⊕ www.expedia.com.

Hotwire ⊕ www.hotwire.com is a discounter. lastminute.com ⊕ www.lastminute.com specializes in last-minute travel; the main site is for the U.K., but it has a link to a U.S. site. Luxury Link ⊕ www. luxurylink.com has auctions (surprisingly good deals) as well as offers at the high-end side of travel. Orbitz ⊕ www.orbitz.com. Onetravel.com ⊕ www.onetravel.com. Priceline.com ⊕ www. priceline.com is a discounter that also allows bidding. Travel.com ⊕ www.travel.com allows you to compare its rates with those of other booking engines. Travelocity ⊕ www.travelocity.com charges a booking fee for airline tickets but promises good problem resolution.

ENJOYING THE FLIGHT

Get the seat you want. Avoid those on the aisle directly across from the lavatories. Most frequent fliers say those are even worse than the seats that don't recline (e.g., those in the back row and those in front of a bulkhead). For more legroom, you can request emergency-aisle seats, but only do so if you're capable of moving the 35- to 60-pound airplane exit door—a Federal Aviation Administration requirement of passengers in these seats. Seats behind a bulkhead also offer more legroom, but they don't have under-seat storage. Often, you can pick a seat when you buy your ticket on an airline's Web site. But it's not always a guarantee, particularly if the airline changes the plane after you book your ticket; check back before you leave. SeatGuru.com has more information about specific seat configurations, which vary by aircraft.

Fewer airlines are providing free food for passengers in economy class. **Don't go hungry.** If you're scheduled to fly during meal times, verify if your airline offers anything to eat; even when it does, be prepared to pay. If you have dietary concerns, request special meals. These can be vegetarian, low-cholesterol, or kosher, for example. It's a good idea to pack some healthful snacks and a small (plastic) bottle of water in your carry-on bag.

Ask the airline about its children's menus, activities, and fares. On some lines infants and toddlers fly for free if they sit on a parent's lap, and older children fly for half price in their own seats. Also inquire about policies involving car seats; having one may limit where you can sit. While you're at it, ask about seat-belt extenders for car seats. And note that you can't count on a flight attendant to automatically produce an extender; you may have to inquire about it again when you board.

HOW TO COMPLAIN

If your baggage goes astray or your flight goes awry, complain right away. Most carriers require that you **file a claim immediately.** The Aviation Consumer Protection Division of the Department of Transportation publishes *Fly-Rights,* which discusses airlines and consumer issues and is available online. You can also find articles and information on mytravelrights.com, the Web site of the nonprofit Consumer Travel Rights Center.

▤ Airline Complaints **Office of Aviation Enforcement and Proceedings** (Aviation Consumer Protection Division) ☎ 202/366-2220 ⊕ airconsumer.ost. dot.gov. **Federal Aviation Administration Consumer Hotline** ☎ 866/835-5322 ⊕ www.faa.gov.

AIRPORTS

The sheer number of flights at Hartsfield-Jackson Atlanta International Airport (ATL)—well over 2,000 arriving and departing flights daily—make it an obvious, if sometimes hectic, choice. With some 200 concessionaires at the airport, you won't have trouble finding a bite to eat or something to read. If you have to stay overnight, you'll have plenty of lodging choices—there are at least 30 hotels and motels near the airport, many with free shuttle service. Remember that you're going to have to tackle crowds whether you're waiting to buy a burger, get through security, or board the underground train other concourses. The airport's Web site has regularly updated estimates of waits at security areas, so you can judge when you should get there. Locals say a couple of hours before your flight is about right.

North Carolina's Charlotte-Douglas International Airport (CLT), near the border of North Carolina and South Carolina, is a US Airways hub. Although not as vast as Hartsfield-Jackson, Charlotte-Douglas is

quite large, and its people-moving systems work well. If you get tired, plop down in one of the white rocking chairs in the Atrium, a tree-lined indoor crossroads between airport concourses. A food court, with mostly fast-food outlets, can be found here. Within a few miles are more than a dozen hotels, most with free airport shuttles. In the center of the state, right off Interstate 40, is Raleigh-Durham International Airport (RDU), a prime gateway into central and eastern North Carolina. It sometimes feels like the airport is constantly under construction. Until renovations are completed on Terminal C sometime in 2010, most carriers are using Terminal A. Those who live in the western reaches of the Triangle are just as likely to use the Piedmont Triad International Airport (GSO), at the convergence of four interstates in North Carolina. It primarily serves the Triad area—Greensboro, Winston-Salem, and High Point—as well as some cities in southwestern Virginia. The portal to western North Carolina is Asheville Regional Airport (AVL), which was completely renovated in 2006. It provides easy access to the mountains with nonstop flights not only from regional hubs such as Atlanta, Charlotte, and Raleigh-Durham, but also from more far-flung cities like Detroit, Houston, New York, and Washington. For visits to the North Carolina coast, you can fly into Wilmington International Airport (ILM), a small facility with service by three carriers. Upstate South Carolina has the small but user-friendly Greenville–Spartanburg International Airport (GSP), which often has lower fares than either the Charlotte or Asheville airports.

For the most part, fares tend to be lower at the region's major airports, but you can sometimes find good deals at smaller airports such as South Carolina's Charleston International (CHS), Myrtle Beach International Airport (MYR), and Georgia's Savannah/Hilton Head International (SAV). However, these attractive airports are somewhat off the beaten path for any place but their immediate environs on the coast. Additionally, it can be difficult to find direct flights to the smaller airports in the Carolinas and Georgia if you're flying in from outside the region.

Long layovers don't have to be only about sitting around or shopping. These days they can be about burning off vacation calories. Check out www.airportgyms.com for lists of health clubs that are in or near many U.S. and Canadian airports.

🚹 Airlines & Airports **Airline and Airport Links.com** ⊕ www.airlineandairportlinks.com has links to many of the world's airlines and airports. **Asheville Regional Airport** ⊠ 708 Airport Rd., Fletcher, NC ☎ 828/684-2226 ⊕ www.flyavl.com. **Charlotte-Douglas International Airport** ⊠ 5501 Josh Birmingham Pkwy., Charlotte, NC ☎ 704/359-4000 ⊕ www.charmeck.org. **Charleston International Airport** ⊠ 5500 International Blvd., North Charleston, SC ☎ 843/767-1100 ⊕ www.chs-airport.com. **Greenville-Spartanburg International Airport** ⊠ 2000 GSP Dr., Greer, SC ☎ 864/877-7426 ⊕ www.gspairport.com. **Hartsfield-Jackson Atlanta International Airport** ⊠ 6000 N. Terminal Pkwy., Hapeville, GA ☎ 404/530-7300 ⊕ www.atlanta-airport.com. **Myrtle Beach International Airport** ⊠ 1100 Jetport Rd., Myrtle Beach, SC ☎ 843/448-1589 ⊕ www.myrtlebeachairport.com. **Piedmont Triad International Airport** ⊠ 6415 Bryan Blvd., Greensboro, NC ☎ 336/665-5600 ⊕ www.flyfrompti.com. **Raleigh-Durham International Airport** ⊠ 160 Terminal Blvd., Morrisville, NC ☎ 919/840-2123 ⊕ www.rdu.com. **Savannah/Hilton Head International Airport** ⊠ 400 Airways Ave. West Chatham, GA ☎ 912/964-0514 ⊕ www.savannahairport.com. **Wilmington International Airport** ⊠ 1740 Airport Blvd., Wilmington, NC ☎ 910/341-4125 ⊕ www.flyilm.com.

🚹 Airline Security Issues **Transportation Security Agency** ⊕ www.tsa.gov/public has answers for almost every question that might come up.

GROUND TRANSPORTATION

Of all the airports in the region, only Hartsfield-Jackson Atlanta International is well served by public transportation. The Metropolitan Atlanta Rapid Transit Authority, better known as MARTA, has frequent service to and from the airport. It's the quickest, cheapest, and most hassle-free way into the city. Hop on MARTA's North–South Line and you can get downtown in about 15 minutes, all for just $1.75. MARTA's Airport Station is in the South Terminal building near the baggage claim area. Trains run weekdays 5 AM to 1 AM and weekends and holidays 6 AM to 12:30 AM. Most trains operate every 15 to 20 minutes; during weekday rush hours, trains run every 10 minutes.

Limited bus service—hourly from 5:25 AM to 7:25 PM—is available between the Charlotte Transportation Center in Uptown Charlotte and Charlotte–Douglas International Airport. The Triangle Transit Authority (TTA) has an airport bus-shuttle service that connects to Raleigh-Durham International Airport, but the shuttle does not operate on Sunday. The airport shuttle meets TTA regional buses at the TTA Bus Center in Research Triangle Park.

Most of the airports in the region are served by taxi, limo, and shuttle services. Taxi fares vary, but here are some of the fares from major airports: from Raleigh-Durham International to Raleigh or Durham, $27.50; from Charlotte-Douglas International Airport to the Charlotte city center, $21; from Hartsfield–Jackson Atlanta International to downtown Atlanta, $25. Additional charges may apply for more passengers. Private limousine or van services also serve the major airports—Atlanta alone has some 200 authorized limo services. Generally, these private transfer services have rates that start at about twice what you'd pay for a taxi. In Atlanta, use only authorized vehicles with the airport decal on the bumper, as others may overcharge you or have drivers who have little knowledge of local destinations.

🚹 **Charlotte Area Transit System** ☎ 704/336-7433 ⊕ www.charmeck.org. **Metropolitan Atlanta Rapid Transit Authority** ☎ 404/848-5000 ⊕ www.itsmarta.com. **Triangle Transit Authority** ☎ 919/549-9999 ⊕ www.ridetta.org.

BIKE TRAVEL

Throughout coastal Georgia, South Carolina, and North Carolina, hills are few and the scenery remarkable. You can find extensive, in many cases marked, bike routes throughout North Carolina's Outer Banks, around Savannah and Georgia's coastal islands, and throughout greater Charleston and coastal South Carolina's Lowcountry. Serious enthusiasts, especially mountain bikers, might take to the more precipitous parts of North Carolina and Georgia, which are the Great Smoky Mountains and north Georgia mountains, respectively.

DeLorme's *Atlas & Gazeteer* state maps, usually available in local bike shops and drug stores, contain lots of topographic detail useful for bike riders. The Division of Bicycle and Pedestrian Transportation, part of North Carolina's Department of Transportation, can provide maps of scenic biking routes in the state. Many tourist boards and local bike clubs also distribute bike maps.

Web sites can also be helpful in planning your bike trips. Southeastern Cycling (⊕ www.sadlebred.com) has information on road and trail riding throughout the Southeast, including the Carolinas and Georgia, and has extensive libraries of free ride maps. Mountain Biking in Western North Carolina (⊕ www.mtbikewnc.com) has up-to-date information on the best mountain trails. Trails.com (⊕ www.trails. com), a commercial site, has gathered information on more than 30,000 bike trails, including many in Georgia, South Carolina, and North Carolina. A year's subscription costs $49.95, but a 14-day trial subscription is free.

🚲 Bike Maps **DeLorme** ⊠ 2 DeLorme Dr., Yarmouth, ME 04096 ☎ 800/561-5105 ⊕ www. delorme.com. **Georgia Bikes** ⌂ Box 49755, Atlanta, GA 30359 ☎ 404/441-9355 or 404/634-6745 ⊕ www.georgiabikes.org. **North Carolina Division of Bicycle and Pedestrian Transportation** ⊠ 1552 Mail Service Center, Raleigh, NC 27699 ☎ 919/733-2804 ⊕ www.ncdot.org/transit/bicycle/maps/maps highways.html. **South Carolina Trails Program** ⊠ 1205 Pendleton St., Columbia, SC 29201 ☎ 803/734-0173 ⊕ www.ncdot.org/transit/bicycle/maps/ maps_highways.html.

BOAT & FERRY TRAVEL

Ferries are a common, and necessary, way to get around coastal areas, and especially to visit North Carolina's Outer Banks and Georgia's Sea Islands.

The Ferry Division of the North Carolina Department of Transportation operates seven ferry routes over five separate bodies of water: the Currituck and Pamlico

sounds and the Cape Fear, Neuse, and Pamlico rivers. Travelers use the three routes between Ocracoke and Hatteras Island, Swan Quarter, and Cedar Island; between Southport and Fort Fisher; and between Cherry Branch and Minnesott Beach. Ferries can accommodate any car, trailer, or recreational vehicle. Pets are permitted if they stay in the vehicle or are on a leash. Reservations, which can only be made by telephone, are available for the Cedar Island–Ocracoke and Swan Quarter–Ocracoke routes; on other routes, space is on a first-come, first-served basis. Schedules generally vary by season, with the largest number of departures from May through October.

Ferries are the only form of public transportation to Sapelo and Cumberland islands in Georgia. The Georgia Department of Natural Resources operates a ferry between Meridian and Sapelo. Advance reservations are required, and can be made by phone or at the Sapelo Island Visitor Center in Meridian. From March to November, a privately run passenger ferry runs daily between St. Marys and Cumberland Island. The rest of the year, the ferry does not operate on Tuesday and Wednesday. Reservations are essential, especially in summer.

FARES & SCHEDULES

In North Carolina, the Cedar Island–Ocracoke and Swan Quarter–Ocracoke ferries cost $1 for pedestrians, $3 for bicycles, and $15 to $45 for vehicles. The Southport–Fort Fisher ferry costs $1 for pedestrians, $3 for bicycles, and $5 to $15 for vehicles. Tickets can be purchased with cash, traveler's checks, and credit cards. The other North Carolina ferries are free.

In Georgia, the pedestrian ferry to Sapelo Island costs $1. The pedestrian ferry to Cumberland Island costs $15 round-trip.

🚢 Boat & Ferry Information **Cumberland Island National Seashore** ⌂ Box 806, St. Marys 31558 ☎ 912/882-4335 or 888/817-3421 ⊕ www.nps.gov/ cuis. **North Carolina Department of Transportation Ferry Division** ⊠ 113 Arendell St., Morehead City, NC 28557 ☎ 800/293-3779 ⊕ www.ncdot.org/ transit/ferry. **Sapelo Island Visitor Center** ⊠ Route

1, Box 1500, Meridian, GA 31305 ☎ 912/437-3224
⊕ www.sapelonerr.org.

BUSINESS HOURS

Businesses and government offices in the
Carolinas and Georgia generally are open
the same times as the rest of the United
States, with only a few local differences.
Banks and post offices are usually open
weekdays from 9 to 5 (often to 6 on Friday) and frequently Saturday morning. In
rural areas, post offices often close for
lunch. Liquor stores in all three states are
closed on Sunday. In Georgia, in addition
to national holidays, government offices
are closed on Confederate Memorial Day
(usually the fourth Monday in April) and
Robert E. Lee's Birthday (January 19 but
usually celebrated the day after Thanksgiving). South Carolina also celebrates Confederate Memorial Day, but on May 10.

MUSEUMS & SIGHTS

Museums typically operate Tuesday
through Saturday from 10 to 5, and
Sunday from 1 to 5. Many museums
and state-run tourist attractions are
closed Monday.

SHOPS

From Monday to Saturday, shops in urban
and suburban areas open at 9 AM or 10 AM
and close anywhere from 6 PM to 10 PM;
on Sunday, they frequently don't open
until noon and close at 5 or 6. Many su-
permarkets in urban and suburban communities are open 24 hours; they often
contain pharmacies and banks with extended hours.

BUS TRAVEL

Regional bus service, provided by Greyhound and Trailways, is abundant
throughout the Carolinas and Georgia. It's
a handy and affordable means of getting
around; if it's a simple matter of getting
from one city to another, consider this option. Buses sometimes make frequent
stops, which make the trip much longer
but also let you see towns you might
otherwise bypass. In some communities,
the bus stations are found in marginal
neighborhoods; take a taxi rather than
walk to or from the bus terminal.

Nearly all intercity buses are equipped
with air-conditioning, restrooms, and reclining seats. The age and condition of
buses vary.

CUTTING COSTS

Greyhound offers a variety of discounts
for students, seniors, military personnel,
and veterans, so be sure to ask. Greyhound's North America Discovery Pass
allows unlimited travel throughout the
United States and Canada during any 7-,
15-, 30-, or 60-day period. The cost is
$283 to $645, depending on length of
the pass.
🚍 Discount Passes **Greyhound Discovery Pass**
☎ 214/849-8100 or 800/231-2222 ⊕ www.
discoverypass.com.

FARES & SCHEDULES

You can purchase tickets in advance online, by phone, through a travel agent, or
at a bus terminal, or you can walk up to
the ticket counter and buy a ticket for the
next available bus. As with airline tickets,
you'll usually pay more for last-minute
travel. In-state fares range from $20 to
$70, depending on how far you're going.
For example, Atlanta to Savannah is
about $40, and Asheville to Raleigh is
around $60.

Greyhound and other carriers usually accept cash, traveler's checks, and major
credit cards.

RESERVATIONS

Most carriers don't permit reservations for
a specific departure, and seating is on a
first-come, first-served basis. Boarding
usually begins 15 to 30 minutes before departure. Advance-purchase tickets and
passes don't guarantee you a seat. On popular routes, buses are sometimes full, so
get to the station in plenty of time to
queue up for a seat.
🚍 Bus Information **Greyhound** ☎ 800/231-2222
⊕ www.greyhound.com. **Trailways** ☎ 703/691-
3052 ⊕ www.trailways.com.

CAR RENTAL

Request car seats and extras such as GPS
when you book, and make sure that a con-
firmed reservation guarantees you a car.
Agencies sometimes overbook, particularly

for busy weekends and holiday periods. Rates are sometimes—but not always—better if you book in advance or reserve through a rental agency's Web site. There are other reasons to book ahead, though: for popular destinations, during busy times of the year, or to ensure that you get a certain type of car (vans, SUVs, exotic sports cars).

It's important to **reserve a car well in advance of your expected arrival.** Rental rates vary from city to city, but are generally lowest in larger cities where there's a lot of competition. Economy cars cost between $27 and $61 per day, and luxury cars go for $70 to $198. Weekend rates are generally much lower than those on weekdays, and weekly rates usually offer big discounts. Rates are also seasonal, with the highest rates coming during peak travel times. Local factors can also affect rates; for example, a big convention can suck up most of the rental-car inventory and boost rates for those remaining.

Don't forget to factor in the taxes and other add-ons when you're figuring up how much a car will cost. At Atlanta's Hartsfield-Jackson International Airport, you'll have to add the 7% sales tax, 11.11% concession-recoupment fee, 3% city excise tax, $4 daily customer facility charge, $1.39 daily fleet-tax recovery charge, and $1.15 vehicle license-recovery charge. These "miscellaneous charges" mean that a $138 weekly rental adds up to a whopping $208 when some $68 in taxes and fees are folded in.

CUTTING COSTS
Really weigh your options. Find out if a credit card you carry or organization or frequent-renter program to which you belong has a discount program. And check that such discounts really are the best deal. You can often do better with special weekend or weekly rates offered by a rental agency. (And even if you only want to rent for five or six days, ask if you can get the weekly rate; it may very well be cheaper than the daily rate for that period of time.)

Price local car-rental companies as well as the majors. Also investigate wholesalers, which don't own fleets but rent in bulk

from those that do and often offer better rates (note you must usually pay for such rentals before leaving home). Consider adding a car rental onto your air–hotel vacation package; the cost will often be cheaper than if you had rented the car separately on your own.

Note that airport rental offices often add supplementary surcharges that you may avoid by renting from an agency whose office is just off airport property. Don't buy the tank of gas that's in the car when you rent it unless you plan to do a lot of driving. Avoid hefty refueling fees by filling the tank at a station well away from the rental agency (those nearby are often more expensive) just before you turn in the car.

Some off-airport locations offer lower rates, and their lots are only minutes from the terminal via complimentary shuttle. Also ask whether certain frequent-flyer, American Automobile Association (AAA), corporate, or other such promotions are accepted and whether the rates might be lower the day before or after you had originally intended to travel.

In some cases you can find that the same agency offers a region's cheapest luxury car rates but priciest economy cars, or that the cheapest agency in one city may have high rates in another. It pays to check around. Also, although an economy car is almost always your cheapest option, agencies sometimes offer upgrade specials that cost only a dollar or two more per day. Think carefully about how much and where you'll be using the car before choosing among economy, compact, standard, luxury, and premium; it may be worth the extra few dollars per day for a more substantial vehicle if you're traveling long distances, driving up into the mountains or over rugged terrain, traveling with more than a couple of passengers, or using the car extensively. If you're traveling in winter, you may want to pay a little extra for a four-wheel-drive vehicle.

Local Agencies **Armada** ☎ 770/416-7996 ⊕ www.armadavans.com. **Triangle Rent A Car** ☎ 919/840-3400 ⊕ www.trianglerentacar.com. Major Agencies **Alamo** ☎ 800/462-5266 ⊕ www.alamo.com. **Avis** ☎ 800/230-4898

⊕ www.avis.com. **Budget** ☎ 800/527-0700 ⊕ www.budget.com. **Hertz** ☎ 800/654-3131 ⊕ www.hertz.com. **National Car Rental** ☎ 800/227-7368 ⊕ www.nationalcar.com.

🔂 Automobile Associations U.S.: **American Automobile Association (AAA)** ☎ 315/797-5000 ⊕ www.aaa.com; most contact with the organization is through state and regional members. **National Automobile Club** ☎ 650/294-7000 ⊕ www.thenac.com; membership is open to California residents only.

INSURANCE

Everyone who rents a car wonders about whether the insurance that the rental companies offer is worth the expense. No one—not even us—has a simple answer. It all depends on how much regular insurance you have, how comfortable you are with risk, and whether or not money is an issue.

If you own a car and carry comprehensive car insurance for both collision and liability, your personal auto insurance will probably cover a rental, but read your policy's fine print to be sure. If you don't have auto insurance, then you should probably buy the collision- or loss-damage waiver (CDW or LDW) from the rental company. This eliminates your liability for damage to the car. Some credit cards offer CDW coverage, but it's usually supplemental to your own insurance and rarely covers SUVs, minivans, luxury models, and the like. If your coverage is secondary, you may still be liable for loss-of-use costs from the car-rental company (again, read the fine print). But no credit-card insurance is valid unless you use that card for *all* transactions, from reserving to paying the final bill.

You may also be offered supplemental liability coverage; the car-rental company is required to carry a minimal level of liability coverage that covers all renters, but it's rarely enough to cover claims in a really serious accident if you're at fault. Your own auto-insurance policy will protect you if you own a car; if you don't, you have to decide if you are willing to take the risk.

U.S. rental companies sell CDWs and LDWs for about $15 to $25 a day; supplemental liability is usually more than $10 a day. The car-rental company may offer you all sorts of other policies, but they're rarely worth the cost. Personal accident insurance, which is basic hospitalization coverage, is an especially egregious rip-off if you already have health insurance.

Note that you can decline the insurance from the rental company and purchase it through a third-party provider such as Travel Guard (www.travelguard.com)—$9 per day for $35,000 of coverage. That's sometimes just under half the price of the CDW offered by some car-rental companies. Also, Diners Club offers primary CDW coverage on all rentals reserved and paid for with the card. This means that Diners Club's company—not your own car insurance—pays in case of an accident. It *doesn't* mean your car-insurance company won't raise your rates once it discovers you had an accident.

CAR TRAVEL

A car is your most practical and economical means of traveling around the Carolinas and Georgia. Atlanta, Savannah, Charleston, Myrtle Beach, and Asheville can also be explored fairly easily on foot or by using public transit and cabs, but a car is helpful to reach many of the most intriguing attractions, which are not always downtown.

Although you'll make the best time traveling along the South's extensive network of interstate highways, keep in mind that U.S. and state highways offer some delightful scenery and the opportunity to stumble on funky roadside diners, leafy state parks, and historic town squares. Although the area is rural, it's still densely populated, so you'll rarely drive for more than 20 or 30 mi without passing roadside services, such as gas stations, restaurants, and ATMs.

Among the most scenic highways in the Carolinas and Georgia are **U.S. 78**, running east–west across Georgia; **U.S. 25, 19, 74**, and **64**, traveling through the Great Smoky Mountains of western North Carolina; **U.S. 17** from Brunswick, Georgia, along the coast through South Carolina and North Carolina; and the **Blue Ridge Parkway** from the eastern fringes of the Great Smoky Mountains through western North Carolina into Virginia.

Unlike some other areas of the United States, the Carolinas and Georgia have very few toll roads. Currently, only Georgia State Route 400 in Atlanta, the Cross Island Parkway on Hilton Head, South Carolina, and the Southern Connector in Greenville, South Carolina, are toll roads. As a bonus, gasoline prices in South Carolina and Georgia are consistently among the lowest in the nation (prices in North Carolina are less of a bargain, due to higher state gas taxes.)

RULES OF THE ROAD

State lawmakers set speed limits, even for federal interstate highways. Limits vary from state to state and from rural to urban areas, so **check posted speeds frequently.** Interstate speed limits in the Carolinas and Georgia are generally 65 to 70 mph; the limit is usually 55 mph on other highways and 35 mph in cities and towns, if not otherwise posted.

Currently there are no restrictions on the use of handheld cell phones by adults while driving in the Carolinas and Georgia. As of 2006, a North Carolina law prohibits drivers under 18 from using cell phones except to answer calls from parents or report an emergency. Radar detectors are legal in private vehicles, except on military bases. High-occupancy-vehicle lanes are rare but do exist on some major arteries, especially those through Atlanta. You can use these lanes only if you have a certain number of passengers in your vehicle.

Some towns in the Carolinas and Georgia still raise funds for their civic needs by handing out speeding tickets to unwary motorists. When entering small towns, slow down and check carefully for speed limit signs.

Unless otherwise indicated, you may turn right at a red light after stopping if there's no oncoming traffic. When in doubt, wait for the green. In Atlanta, Asheville, Charleston, Columbia, Charlotte, Savannah, and the Triangle and Triad cities of North Carolina, be alert for one-way streets, "no left turn" intersections, and blocks closed to vehicle traffic.

Always strap children under age 6 or under 40 pounds (regardless of age) into approved child-safety seats. Children must wear seat belts regardless of where they're seated.

CRUISE TRAVEL

Charleston is the only city in the region where cruises embark. Carnival and Norwegian Cruise Line have ships to Bermuda, the Bahamas, and the Caribbean that depart from Charleston in the spring and fall. Charleston and Savannah are the only cities in the Carolinas and Georgia that are regular ports of call for cruise lines, and they attract only a handful of ships. Princess Cruises, Royal Caribbean International, and Crystal Cruises each have one ship that calls occasionally at Charleston, typically in the fall. Charleston and Savannah are spring destinations for a small cruise ship, the *Spirit of Nantucket,* operated by Cruise West.

🚢 Cruise Lines **Carnival Cruise Lines** ☎ 888/227-6482 ⊕ www.carnival.com. **Cruise West** ☎ 800/296-8993 ⊕ www.cruisewest.com. **Crystal Cruises** ☎ 800/804-1500 ⊕ www.crystalcruises.com. **Norwegian Cruise Lines** ☎ 866/234-0292 ⊕ www.ncl.com. **Princess Cruises** ☎ 800/774-2377 ⊕ www.princess.com. **Royal Caribbean International** ☎ 866/562-7625 ⊕ www.royalcaribbean.com.

EATING OUT

The increase of international flavors in the region reflects the tastes and backgrounds of the people who have flooded into the Carolinas and Georgia over the past couple of decades. Bagels are as common nowadays as biscuits, and, especially in urban areas, it can be harder to find country cooking than a plate of hummus. For the most part, though, you can still find plenty of traditional Southern staples—barbecue, fried chicken, greens, and the like.

Atlanta, once a culinary backwater, now has a big-city mix of neighborhood bistros, ethnic eateries, and expense-account restaurants. A new wave of restaurants in Charleston and Savannah serves innovative versions of Lowcountry cooking, with lighter takes on traditional dishes. In North Carolina, you can find some nationally recognized restaurants in

Charlotte, Asheville, and elsewhere. Outside of the many resort areas along the coast and in the mountains, dining costs in the region are often lower than those in the North.

Vegetarians will have no trouble finding attractive places to eat in any of the larger metropolitan areas, although in small towns they may have to stick with pizza. Asheville is a haven for vegetarians; it has been named to many lists of the top vegetarian cities, including being named the most vegetarian-friendly city in the United States by People for the Ethical Treatment of Animals.

The restaurants we list are the cream of the crop in each price category. Properties indicated by ✕⊡ are lodging establishments whose restaurant warrants a special trip.

For information on food-related health issues *see* Health *below.*

MEALS & MEALTIMES

The Southern tradition of Sunday dinner—usually a midday meal—has morphed to some degree, at least in urban areas, to Sunday brunch. For many this meal follows midmorning church services, so be advised that restaurants will often be very busy through the middle of the day. In smaller towns, many restaurants are closed on Sunday.

Southerners tend to eat on the early side, with lunch crowds beginning to appear before noon. The peak time for dinner is around 7. Only in big cities like Atlanta and in college towns like Athens and Chapel Hill will you find much in the way of late-night dining.

Unless otherwise noted, the restaurants listed in this guide are open daily for lunch and dinner.

PAYING

For guidelines on tipping *see* Tipping *below.* As in the rest of the country, only the smallest restaurants don't accept major credit cards.

CATEGORY	COST
$$$$	over $22
$$$	$17–$22
$$	$12–$16
$	$7–$11
¢	under $7

Restaurant prices are per person for a main course at dinner.

RESERVATIONS & DRESS

Regardless of where you are, it's a good idea to make a reservation if you can. In some places (Hong Kong, for example), it's expected. We only mention specifically when reservations are essential (there's no other way you'll ever get a table) or when they're not accepted. For popular restaurants, book as far ahead as you can (often 30 days), and reconfirm as soon as you arrive. (Large parties should always call ahead to check the reservations policy.) We mention dress only when men are required to wear a jacket or a jacket and tie.

For the most part, restaurants in the Carolinas and Georgia tend to be informal. A coat and tie are rarely required, except in a few of the fanciest places. You'll be safe almost anywhere if you show up in business-casual clothes.

WINES, BEER & SPIRITS

Blue laws—legislation forbidding sales on Sunday—have a history in this region dating to the 1600s. These bans are still observed in many rural areas, particularly with regard to alcohol sales. Liquor stores are closed on Sunday in the Carolinas and Georgia, although beer and wine generally can be purchased in grocery stores or convenience stores. In North Carolina and South Carolina, beer and wine can't be sold anywhere on Sunday mornings. There are entire counties in the Carolinas and Georgia that prohibit the sale of alcoholic beverages in restaurants. Some cities and towns allow the sale of beer and wine in restaurants, but not mixed drinks. In North Carolina, bottled distilled spirits are only sold through state-run "ABC" (Alcoholic Beverage Control) outlets; beer and wine, however, are available in most grocery and convenience stores.

Although the Carolinas and Georgia will never be the Napa Valley, the last decade has seen a huge increase in the number of vineyards. North Carolina now has more than 60 wineries, and the Yadkin Valley is the state's first federally recognized American Viticultural Area, with more than 400 acres of vineyards in production. Asheville Biltmore Estate Wine Company is the most popular winery in the United States, with about 1 million visitors each year. Georgia's Wine Highway, which takes you by a number of wineries that are open to the public, runs from just north of Atlanta up through the north Georgia mountains. Muscadine and scuppernong grapes are native to warmer parts of the region; the sweetish wine from these grapes may not impress you, but traditional wine grapes are also widely grown.

Microbreweries are common all over the region, with hot spots being Asheville, Charlotte, and Charleston, as well as the Triangle of Raleigh, Durham, and Chapel Hill. There are more than 40 microbreweries in North Carolina, some two dozen in South Carolina, and about a dozen in Georgia, where state laws on beer distribution have crimped the growth of microbreweries.

Was the service stellar or not up to snuff? Did the food give you shivers of delight or leave you cold? Did the prices and portions make you happy or sad? Rate restaurants and write your own reviews in "Travel Ratings" or start a discussion about your favorite places in "Travel Talk" on www.fodors.com. Your comments might even appear in our books. Yes, you, too, can be a correspondent!

HEALTH

With the exception of the mountains of north Georgia and western North Carolina, in the Carolinas and Georgia it's hot and humid for at least six months of the year. Away from the coast, midsummer temperatures can reach the high 90s, making heat exhaustion and heat stroke real possibilities. Heat exhaustion is marked by muscle cramps, dizziness, nausea, and profuse sweating. To counter its effects, lie down in a cool place with the head slightly lower than the rest of the body. Sip cool, not cold, fluids. Life-threatening heat stroke is caused by a failure of the body to effectively regulate its temperature. In the early stages, heat stroke causes fatigue, dizziness, and headache. Later the skin becomes hot, red, and dry (due to lack of sweating), and body temperatures rise to as high as 106℉. Heat stroke requires immediate medical care.

When you're at the beach or anywhere in the sun, slather on the sunscreen. Reapply it every two hours, or more frequently if you go swimming or are perspiring a lot. Remember that many sunscreens block only the ultraviolet light called UVB, and not UVA, which may be a big factor in skin cancer. Even with sunscreen it's important to wear a hat and protective clothing and to avoid prolonged exposure to the sun.

The coastal areas of the Carolinas and Georgia, especially the swamps and marshes of the Lowcountry, are home to a variety of noxious bugs: mosquitoes, sandflies, biting midges, black flies, chiggers, and no-see-ums. Most are not a problem when the wind is blowing, but when the breezes die down—watch out! Experts agree that DEET is the most effective mosquito repellent, but this chemical is so powerful that strong concentrations can melt plastic. You can buy repellents with 100% DEET, but those containing less than 30% should work fine for adults; children should not use products with more than 10%. Products containing the chemical picaridin are effective against many insects, and don't have the strong odor or skin-irritating qualities of those with DEET. The plant-based oil of lemon eucalyptus, used in some natural repellents, performed well in some studies. Mosquito coils and citronella candles will also help ward off mosquitoes.

For sandflies or other tiny biting bugs, repellents with DEET alone are often not effective. What may help is dousing your feet, ankles, and other exposed areas with an oily lotion, such as baby oil, which effectively drowns the little buggers.

The mountains of western North Carolina and north Georgia generally have few mosquitoes or other biting bugs, but in warm-weather hikers may pick up chiggers or ticks. Use repellents with DEET on exposed skin. Wasps, bees and small but ferocious yellow jackets are common throughout the region.

You can drink tap water everywhere in the region, although in coastal areas it may have a sulfur smell. Many visitors to the beaches prefer to buy bottled water.

INSURANCE

What kind of coverage do you honestly need? Do you even need trip insurance at all? Take a deep breath and read on.

We believe that comprehensive trip insurance is especially valuable if you're booking a very expensive or complicated trip (particularly to an isolated region) or if you're booking far in advance. Who knows what could happen six months down the road? But whether or not you get insurance has more to do with how comfortable you are assuming all that risk yourself.

Comprehensive travel policies typically cover trip-cancellation and interruption, letting you cancel or cut your trip short because of a personal emergency, illness, or, in some cases, acts of terrorism in your destination. Such policies also cover evacuation and medical care. Some also cover you for trip delays because of bad weather or mechanical problems as well as for lost or delayed baggage. Another type of coverage to look for is financial default—that is, when your trip is disrupted because a tour operator, airline, or cruise line goes out of business. Generally you must buy this when you book your trip or shortly thereafter, and it's only available to you if your operator isn't on a list of excluded companies.

If you're going abroad, consider buying medical-only coverage at the very least. Neither Medicare nor some private insurers cover medical expenses anywhere outside of the United States besides Mexico and Canada (including time aboard a cruise ship, even if it leaves from a U.S.

port). Medical-only policies typically reimburse you for medical care (excluding that related to preexisting conditions) and hospitalization abroad and provide for evacuation. You still have to pay the bills and await reimbursement from the insurer, though.

Expect comprehensive travel insurance policies to cost about 4% to 7% of the total price of your trip (it's more like 12% if you're over age 70). A medical-only policy may or may not be cheaper than a comprehensive policy. Always read the fine print of your policy to make sure that you're covered for the risks that are of the most concern to you. Compare several policies to make sure you're getting the best price and range of coverage available.

Just as an aside: you know you can save a bundle on trips to warm-weather destinations by traveling in rainy season. But there's also a chance that a severe storm will disrupt your plans. The solution? Look for hotels and resorts that offer storm–hurricane guarantees. Although they rarely allow refunds, most guarantees do let you rebook later if a storm strikes.

Insurance Comparison Sites Insure My Trip. com ⊕ www.insuremytrip.com. **Square Mouth.com** ⊕ www.quotetravelinsurance.com.

Comprehensive Travel Insurers Access America ☎ 866/807-3982 ⊕ www.accessamerica.com. **CSA Travel Protection** ☎ 800/873-9855 ⊕ www. csatravelprotection.com. **HTH Worldwide** ☎ 610/254-8700 or 888/243-2358 ⊕ www.hthworldwide. com. **Travelex Insurance** ☎ 888/457-4602 ⊕ www.travelex-insurance.com. **Travel Guard International** ☎ 715/345-0505 or 800/826-4919 ⊕ www.travelguard.com. **Travel Insured International** ☎ 800/243-3174 ⊕ www.travelinsured.com.

Medical-Only Insurers Wallach & Company ☎ 800/237-6615 or 504/687-3166 ⊕ www.wallach. com. **International Medical Group** ☎ 800/628-4664 ⊕ www.imglobal.com. **International SOS** ☎ 215/942-8000 or 713/521-7611 ⊕ www. internationalsos.com.

FOR INTERNATIONAL TRAVELERS

CURRENCY

The dollar is the basic unit of U.S. currency. It has 100 cents. Coins are the penny (1¢); the nickel (5¢), dime (10¢), quarter (25¢), and half-dollar (50¢); and the very rare golden $1 coin and even rarer silver $1. Bills are denominated $1, $5, $10, $20, $50, and $100, all mostly green and identical in size; designs and background tints vary. You may come across a $2 bill, but the chances are slim.

CUSTOMS

⚑ **U.S. Customs and Border Protection** ⊕ www.cbp.gov.

DRIVING

Driving in the United States is on the right. Speed limits are posted in miles per hour (mph) along roads and highways (usually between 55 mph and 70 mph). Watch for lower limits in small towns and on back roads (usually 30 mph to 40 mph). Most states require front-seat passengers to wear seat belts; many states require children to sit in the back seat and to wear seat belts. In major cities, rush hour is between 7 and 10 AM; afternoon rush hour is between 4 and 7 PM. To encourage carpooling, some freeways have special lanes for so-called high-occupancy vehicles (HOV)—cars carrying more than one passenger—ordinarily marked with a diamond.

Highways are well paved. Interstate highways—limited-access, multilane highways whose numbers are prefixed by "I–"—are the fastest routes. Interstates with three-digit numbers encircle urban areas, which may have other limited-access express-ways, freeways, and parkways as well. Tolls may be levied on limited-access highways. So-called U.S. highways and state highways are not necessarily limited-access but may have several lanes.

Gas stations are plentiful. Most stay open late (24 hours along large highways and in big cities), except in rural areas, where Sunday hours are limited and where you may drive long stretches without a refueling opportunity. Along larger highways, roadside stops with restrooms, fast-food restaurants, and sundries stores are well spaced. State police and tow trucks patrol major highways and lend assistance. If your car breaks down on an interstate, pull onto the shoulder and wait for help, or have your passengers wait while you walk to an emergency phone (available in most states). If you carry a cell phone, dial *55, noting your location on the small green roadside mileage markers.

ELECTRICITY

The U.S. standard is AC, 110 volts/60 cycles. Plugs have two flat pins set parallel to each other, often with a third round pin that is a ground.

EMBASSIES

⚑ **Australia** ☎ 202/797-3000 ⊕ www.austemb.org. **United Kingdom** ☎ 202/588-7800 ⊕ www.britainusa.com. **Canada** ☎ 202/682-1740 ⊕ www.canadianembassy.org.

EMERGENCIES

For police, fire, or ambulance dial 911 (0 in rural areas).

HOLIDAYS

Major national holidays are New Year's Day (Jan. 1); Martin Luther King Day (3rd Mon. in Jan.); Presidents' Day (3rd Mon. in Feb.); Memorial Day (last Mon. in May); Independence Day (July 4); Labor Day (1st Mon. in Sept.); Columbus Day (2nd Mon. in Oct.); Thanksgiving Day (4th Thurs. in Nov.); Christmas Eve and Christmas Day (Dec. 24 and 25); and New Year's Eve (Dec. 31).

MAIL

You can buy stamps and aerograms and send letters and parcels in post offices. Stamp-dispensing machines can occasionally be found in airports, bus and train stations, office buildings, drugstores, and the like. U.S. mail boxes are stout, dark blue, steel bins at strategic locations in major cities; pickup schedules are posted inside the bin (pull down the handle to see them). Parcels more than 1 pound must be mailed at a post office or at a private mailing center.

Within the United States, a first-class letter weighing 1 ounce or less costs 39¢, and each additional ounce costs 24¢; postcards cost 24¢. A 1-ounce airmail letter to most countries costs 84¢, an airmail postcard costs 75¢; to Canada and Mexico, a 1-ounce letter costs 63¢, a postcard 55¢. An aerogram—a single sheet of lightweight blue paper that folds into its own envelope, stamped for overseas airmail—costs 75¢ regardless of its destination.

To receive mail on the road, have it sent c/o General Delivery at your destination's main post office (use the correct five-digit ZIP code). You must pick up mail in person within 30 days and show a driver's license or passport.

DHL ☎ 800/225–5345 ⊕ www.dhl.com. **Federal Express** ☎ 800/463–3339 ⊕ www.fedex.com. **Mail Boxes, Etc. (The UPS Store)** ☎ 800/789–4623 ⊕ www.mbe.com. **United States Postal Service** ⊕ www.usps.com.

PASSPORTS & VISAS

Visitor visas aren't necessary for citizens of Australia, Canada, the United Kingdom, as well as for most citizens of European Union countries if you're coming for tourism and staying for fewer than 90 days. If you require a visa, the cost is $100 and, depending on where you live, the waiting time can be substantial. Apply for a visa at the U.S. consulate in your place of residence; look at the U.S. State Department's special visa Web site for further information.

Visa Information Destination USA ⊕ www. unitedstatesvisas.gov.

PHONES

All U.S. telephone numbers consist of a three-digit area code and a seven-digit local number. Within many local calling areas, you dial only the seven-digit number; in others, you must dial "1" first and then the area code. To call between area-code regions, dial "1" then all 10 digits; the same goes for calls to numbers prefixed by "800", "888," "866," and "877"—all toll free. For calls to numbers preceded by "900" you must pay—usually dearly.

For international calls, dial "011" followed by the country code and the local number. For help, dial "0" and ask for an overseas operator. The country code is 61 for Australia, 64 for New Zealand, 44 for the United Kingdom. Calling Canada is the same as calling within the United States. Most phone books list country

codes and U.S. area codes. The country code for the United States is 1.

For operator assistance, dial "0." To obtain someone's phone number, call directory assistance at 555–1212 or occasionally 411 (free at many public phones). You can reverse the charges on a long-distance call if phone "collect"; dial "0" instead of "1" before the 10-digit number.

At pay phones, instructions often are posted. Usually you insert coins in a slot (usually 25¢ to 50¢ for local calls) and wait for a steady tone before dialing. When you call long-distance, the operator tells you how much to insert; prepaid phone cards, widely available in various denominations, can be used from any phone. Follow the directions to activate the card (there is usually an access number and then an activation code for the card), then dial your number.

The United States has several GSM (Global System for Mobile Communications) networks, so multiband mobile phones from most countries (except Japan) work here. Unfortunately, it's almost impossible to buy a pay-as-you-go mobile SIM card in the United States—which allows you to avoid roaming charges—without a phone. That said, cell phones with pay-as-you-go plans are available for well under $100. The cheapest ones with decent national coverage are the GoPhone from Cingular and Virgin Mobile, which only offers pay-as-you-go service.

Cell Phone Contacts Cingular ☎ 888/333–6651 ⊕ www.cingular.com. **Virgin Mobile** ☎ No phone ⊕ www.virginmobileusa.com.

LODGING

With the exception of Atlanta, Savannah, Charleston, Asheville, and Charlotte, most lodging rates in the region fall at or below the national average. They do vary a great deal seasonally, however—coastal resorts and mountainous areas tend to have significantly higher rates in summer. All major chains are well represented in this part of the country, both in cities and suburbs, and interstates are lined with inexpensive to moderate chains. It's not uncommon to find clean but extremely basic chains offering double rooms for as little as $25 to $40 nightly along the busiest highways.

In many places you might want to forgo a modern hotel in favor of a historic property. There are dozens of fine old hotels and mansions that have been converted into inns, many of them lovingly restored. Quite a few offer better rates than chain hotels. Bed-and-breakfasts are big in some cities, notably Charleston, Savannah, and Asheville. Each of these cities has two dozen or more B&Bs. There also are loads of B&Bs in many small towns along the coast and in the north Georgia and western North Carolina Mountains.

In many coastal resort areas, vacation home and condo rentals dominate the lodging scene. The North Carolina Outer Banks and Hilton Head are two major rental areas, each with several thousand rental properties. Rental prices vary by season, with peak summer rental rates often three to four times or more higher than off-season rates.

In the North Carolina and Georgia mountains, cabins are popular. These are usually owner-operated businesses with only a few cabins. In Georgia, many state parks rent cabins, and they're often excellent values. In the mountains you'll also find a number of lodges. These vary from simple accommodations to deluxe properties with spas, golf courses, and tennis courts. Many attract families that come back year after year. Mountain lodges are closed for several months in winter.

Thousands of families camp in the Carolinas and Georgia. The North Carolina Outer Banks, the Sea Islands of Georgia, and the Great Smoky Mountains National Park and Pisgah and Nantahala national forests in western North Carolina are especially popular with campers.

The lodgings listed are the cream of the crop in each price category. Properties indicated by ✕⊞ are lodging establishments whose restaurant warrants a special trip. Facilities that are available are listed—but not any extra costs associated with those facilities. When pricing accommodations,

always ask what's included and what costs extra.

Did the resort look as good in real life as it did in the photos? Did you sleep like a baby, or were the walls paper thin? Did you get your money's worth? Rate hotels and write your own reviews in "Travel Ratings" or start a discussion about your favorite places in "Travel Talk" on www. fodors.com. Your comments might even appear in our books. Yes, you, too, can be a correspondent!

CATEGORY	COST
$$$$	over $220
$$$	$161–$220
$$	$111–$160
$	$70–$110
¢	under $70

Hotel prices are for a standard double room in high season.

Most hotels and other lodgings require you to give your credit-card details before they will confirm your reservation. If you don't feel comfortable e-mailing this information, ask if you can fax it (some places even prefer faxes). However you book, get confirmation in writing and have a copy of it handy when you check-in. If you book through an online travel agent, discounter, or wholesaler, you might even want to confirm your reservation with the hotel before leaving home—just to be sure everything was processed correctly.

Be sure you understand the hotel's cancellation policy. Some places allow you to cancel without any kind of penalty—even if you prepaid to secure a discounted rate—if you cancel at least 24 hours in advance. Others require you to cancel a week in advance or penalize you for the cost of one night. Small inns and B&Bs are most likely to require you to cancel far in advance. Most hotels allow children under a certain age to stay in their parents' room at no extra charge, but others charge for them as extra adults; find out the cutoff age for discounts.

Assume that hotels operate on the European Plan (EP, no meals) unless we specify that they use the Breakfast Plan (BP, with full breakfast), Continental Plan (CP, continental breakfast), Full American Plan (FAP, all meals), Modified American Plan (MAP, breakfast and dinner) or are all-inclusive (all meals and most activities).

APARTMENT & HOUSE RENTALS

The far-flung resort areas of the Carolinas and Georgia are filled with rental properties—everything from cabins to luxury homes. Most often these properties, whether part of a huge corporation or individually owned, are professionally managed; such businesses have become an industry unto themselves.

Asheville Cabins, Carolina Mountain Vacations, and Flannery Fork Rentals rent cabins in the high country of North Carolina. Homestead Log Cabins has properties in the Pine Mountain area of Georgia. Intracoastal Realty has long-term as well as off-season rentals on the coast of Cape Fear. Hatteras Realty, Midgett Realty, and Sun Realty, and handle properties on North Carolina's Outer Banks. Island Realty focuses on the Charleston and Isle of Palms area in South Carolina. Hilton Head Rentals and Resort Rentals of Hilton Head Island offer rentals on Hilton Head. Tybee Island Realty handles properties on the tiny Georgia island of the same name.

🏠 **Asheville Cabins** ☎ 800/770-9095 ⊕ www. asheville-cabins.com. **Carolina Mountain Vacations** ☎ 877/488-8500 ⊕ www. carolinamountainvacations.com. **Flannery Fork Rentals** ☎ 828/262-1908 ⊕ www.flanneryfork. com. **Hatteras Realty** ☎ 800/428-8372 ⊕ www. hatterasrealty.com. **Hilton Head Rentals** ☎ 800/368-5975 ⊕ www.hiltonheadrentals.com. **Homestead Log Cabins** ☎ 706/663-4951 or 866/652-2246 ⊕ www.homesteadcabins.com. **Interhome** ☎ 954/791-8282 or 800/882-6864 ⊕ www. interhome.us. **Intracoastal Realty** ☎ 910/256-3780 or 800/346-2463 ⊕ www.intracoastalrentals.com. **Island Realty** ☎ 843/886-8144 or 800/707-6421 ⊕ www.islandrealty.com. **Midgett Realty** ☎ 252/986-2841 or 800/527-2903 ⊕ www.midgettrealty. com. **Resort Rentals of Hilton Head Island** ☎ 800/845-7017 or 843/686-6008 ⊕ www. resortrentalshhi.com. **Sun Realty, Outer Banks** ☎ 800/334-4745 ⊕ www.sunrealtync.com. **Tybee Island Realty** ☎ 912/786-7070 or 800/379-2298 ⊕ www.tybeeislandrealty.com. **Vacation Home Rentals Worldwide** ☎ 201/767-9393 or 800/633-3284 ⊕ www.vhrww.com. **Villas International** ☎ 415/499-9490 or 800/221-2260 ⊕ www. villasintl.com.

BED & BREAKFASTS

Historic B&Bs and inns are found in just about every region in the Carolinas and Georgia and include quite a few former plantation houses and lavish Southern estates. In many rural or less touristy areas, B&Bs offer an affordable and homey alternative to chain properties, but in tourism-dependent destinations you can expect to pay, for a historic inn, about the same as or more than for a full-service hotel. Many of the South's finest restaurants are also found in country inns.

🏠 Reservation Services **Bed & Breakfast.com** ☎ 512/322-2710 or 800/462-2632 ⊕ www. bedandbreakfast.com also sends out an online newsletter. **Bed & Breakfast Inns Online** ☎ 615/868-1946 or 800/215-7365 ⊕ www.bbonline.com. **BnB Finder.com** ☎ 212/432-7693 or 888/547-8226 ⊕ www.bnbfinder.com.

🏠 Local Associations **Asheville Bed & Breakfast Association** ☎ 877/262-6867 ⊕ www. ashevillebba.com. **Association of Historic Inns of Savannah** ☎ 912/233-1833 ⊕ www. historicinnsofsavannah.com. **Romantic Inns of Savannah** ☎ No phone ⊕ www. romanticinnsofsavannah.com. **South Carolina Bed & Breakfast Association** ☎ No phone ⊕ www. southcarolinabedandbreakfast.com.

CAMPING

The Carolinas and Georgia are popular for trailer and tent camping, especially in state and national parks. For more information on parks and other campgrounds, contact the state tourism offices (⇨ Visitor Information).

HOME EXCHANGES

With a direct home exchange, you stay in someone else's home while they stay in yours. Some outfits also deal with vacation homes, so you're not actually staying in someone's full-time residence, just their vacant weekend place.

🏠 Exchange Clubs **HomeLink International** ☎ 800/638-3841 ⊕ www.homelink.org; $80 yearly for Web-only membership; $125 with Web access and two directories. **Home Exchange.com** ☎ 800/877-8723 ⊕ www.homeexchange.com $59.95 for a

1-year online listing. **Intervac U.S.** ☎ 800/756-4663 ⊕ www.intervacus.com; $78.88 for Web-only membership; $126 includes Web access and a catolog.

HOSTELS

Hostels offer barebones lodging at low, low prices—often in shared dorm rooms with shared baths—to people of all ages, though the primary market is young travelers, especially students. Most hostels serve breakfast; dinner and/or shared cooking facilities may also be available. In some hostels, you aren't allowed to be in your room during the day, and there may be a curfew at night. Nevertheless, hostels provide a sense of community, with public rooms where travelers often gather to share stories. Many hostels are affiliated with Hostelling International (HI), an umbrella group of hostel associations with some 4,500 member properties in more than 70 countries. Other hostels are completely independent and may be nothing more than a really cheap hotel.

Membership in any HI association, open to travelers of all ages, allows you to stay in HI-affiliated hostels at member rates. One-year membership is about $28 for adults; hostels charge about $10 to $30 per night. Members have priority if the hostel is full; they're also eligible for discounts around the world, even on rail and bus travel in some countries.

North Carolina has hostels in Asheville, Greensboro, and Pembroke, as well as in Kitty Hawk on the Outer Banks. In South Carolina, hostels are found in two historic properties in Charleston, in the less historic Myrtle Beach, and in Georgetown. Georgia's offerings include hostels in Atlanta and Savannah.

🚩 **Hostelling International–USA** ☎ 301/495-1240 ⊕ www.hiusa.org.

HOTELS

Weigh all your options (we can't say this enough). Join "frequent-guest" programs. You may get preferential treatment in room choice and/or upgrades in your favorite chains. Check general travel sites and hotel Web sites as not all chains are represented on all travel sites. Always research or inquire about special packages and corporate rates. If you prefer to book by phone, note you can sometimes get a better price if you call the hotel's local toll-free number (if one is available) rather than the central reservations number. **Watch out for hidden costs,** including resort fees, energy surcharges, and "convenience" fees for things you won't use. Always verify whether local hotel taxes are or are not included in the rates you're quoted, so that you'll know the real price of your stay.

In summer, especially July and August, hotel rooms in coastal areas and the mountains can be hard to come by unless you book well advance. In the mountains, the autumn leaf-peeping season, typically early October to early November, is the busiest time of the year, and on weekends nearly every room is booked. Lodging in North Carolina's Triad area is difficult during the twice-yearly international furniture shows: in April and October, all rooms are booked within a 30-mi radius of the show's location in High Point.

All hotels listed in this book have private baths unless otherwise noted.

🚩 **Discount Hotel Rooms Accommodations Express** ☎ 800/444-7666 or 800/277-1064. **Hotels. com** ☎ 800/219-4606 or 800/364-0291 ⊕ www. hotels.com. **Quikbook** ☎ 800/789-9887 ⊕ www. quikbook.com. **Steigenberger Reservation Service** ☎ 800/223-5652 ⊕ www.srs-worldhotels.com. **Turbotrip.com** ☎ 800/473-7829 ⊕ w3.turbotrip.com.

MEDIA

NEWSPAPERS & MAGAZINES

There's no major regional newspaper that serves the entire area. The *Atlanta Journal-Constitution* (⊕ www.ajc.com) is Georgia's most influential daily, and the *State* (⊕ www.thestate.com) in Columbia is widely respected in South Carolina. Widely circulated dailies in North Carolina include the *News & Observer* (⊕ www.news-observer.com), headquartered in Raleigh, and the *Charlotte Observer* (⊕ www.charlotte.com). In the North Carolina Mountains, the *Asheville Citizen-Times* covers the western end of the state. Just about every city with a population of greater than 40,000 publishes its own daily paper.

Most major cities have very good alternative weeklies with information on area dining, arts, and sightseeing—these are usually free and found in restaurants, coffeehouses, bookstores, tourism offices, hotel lobbies, and some nightclubs. Of particular note are Atlanta's weekly *Creative Loafing* (⊕ www.cln.com), which has a separate edition for Charlotte, *Mountain Express* ⊕ www.mountainx.com in Asheville, and Raleigh-Durham's weekly *Independent*. Serving the gay and lesbian community are Atlanta's *Southern Voice* (⊕ www.sovo.com) and the Charlotte-based *Q-Notes* (⊕ www.q-notes.com).

The monthly *Southern Living* (⊕ www.southernliving.com) gives a nice sense of travel, food, and lifestyle issues relevant to the region. Local lifestyles magazines include Asheville's *The Laurel* (⊕ www.thelaurelofasheville.com), *Atlanta Magazine* (⊕ www.atlantamagazine.com), *Charleston Magazine* (⊕ www.charlestonmag.com), *Charlotte* (⊕ www.charlottemag.com), *Macon Magazine* (⊕ www.maconmagazine.com), the Raleigh–Durham–Chapel Hill area's *Metro Magazine* (⊕ www.metronc.com), and *Savannah Magazine* (⊕ www.savannahmagazine.com). These publications have colorful stories and dining and entertainment coverage; they're worth picking up prior to your visit, especially if you're planning an extended stay; virtually all have useful Web sites, too.

RADIO & TELEVISION
All the major television and radio networks have local affiliates and channels throughout the Carolinas and Georgia. The CNN empire is based in Atlanta.

MONEY MATTERS
Although the cost of living remains fairly low in most parts of the South, travel-related costs (such as dining, lodging, and transportation) have become increasingly steep in Atlanta. And tourist attractions are pricey, too. For example, a tour of CNN Center is $12, admission to the High Museum of Art in Atlanta is $15, and getting into Georgia Aquarium is a steep $23. Costs can also be dear in resort communities throughout the Carolinas and Georgia.

Prices throughout this guide are given for adults. Substantially reduced fees are almost always available for children, students, and senior citizens. For information on taxes, *see* Taxes.

CREDIT CARDS
Throughout this guide, the following abbreviations are used: **AE**, American Express; **D**, Discover; **DC**, Diners Club; **MC**, MasterCard; and **V**, Visa.

It's a good idea to inform your credit-card company before you travel, especially if you're going abroad and don't travel internationally very often. Otherwise, the credit-card company might put a hold on your card owing to unusual activity—not a good thing halfway through your trip. Record all your credit-card numbers—as well as the phone numbers to call if your cards are lost or stolen—in a safe place so you're prepared should something go wrong. Both MasterCard and Visa have general numbers you can call (collect if you're abroad) if your card is lost, but you're better off calling the number of your issuing bank since MasterCard and Visa usually just transfer you to your bank; your bank's number is usually printed on your card.

🗷 **Reporting Lost Cards American Express** ☎ 800/992-3404 in U.S., 336/393-1111 collect from abroad ⊕ www.americanexpress.com. **Diners Club** ☎ 800/234-6377 in U.S., 303/799-1504 collect from abroad ⊕ www.dinersclub.com. **Discover** ☎ 800/347-2683 in U.S., 801/902-3100 collect from abroad ⊕ www.discovercard.com. **MasterCard** ☎ 800/622-7747 in U.S., 636/722-7111 collect from abroad ⊕ www.mastercard.com. **Visa** ☎ 800/847-2911 in U.S., 410/581-9994 collect from abroad ⊕ www.visa.com.

TRAVELER'S CHECKS & CARDS
Some consider this the currency of the cave man, and it's true that fewer establishments accept traveler's checks these days. Nevertheless, they're a cheap and secure way to carry extra money, particularly on trips to urban areas. Both Citibank (under the Visa brand) and American Express issue traveler's checks in the United States, but AmEx is better known and more widely accepted; you can also avoid hefty surcharges by cashing AmEx checks at AmEx offices. Whatever

you do, keep track of all the serial numbers in case the checks are lost or stolen.

American Express now offers a stored-value card called a Travelers Cheque Card, which you can use wherever American Express–credit cards are accepted, including ATMs. The card can carry a minimum of $300 and a maximum of $2,700, and it's a very safe way to carry your funds. Although you can get replacement funds in 24 hours if your card is lost or stolen, it doesn't really strike us as a very good deal. In addition to a high initial cost ($14.95 to set up the card, plus $5 each time you "reload"), you still have to pay a 2% fee for each purchase in a foreign currency (similar to that of any credit card). Further, each time you use the card in an ATM you pay a transaction fee of $2.50 on top of the 2% transaction fee for the conversion—add it all up and it can be considerably more than you would pay for simply using your own ATM card. Regular traveler's checks are just as secure and cost less.

🖅 **American Express** ☎ 888/412-6945 in U.S., 801/945-9450 collect outside of U.S. to add value or speak to customer service ⊕ www.americanexpress.com.

PACKING

Why do some people travel with a convoy of suitcases the size of large-screen TVs and yet never have a thing to wear? How do others pack a toaster-oven-size duffle with a week's worth of outfits *and* supplies for every possible contingency? We realize that packing is a matter of style—a very personal thing—but there's a lot to be said for traveling light. The tips in this section will help you win the battle of the bulging bag.

Make a list. In a recent Fodor's survey, 29% of respondents said they make lists (and often pack) at least a week before a trip. Lists can be used at least twice—once to pack and once to repack at the end of your trip. You'll also have a record of the contents of your suitcase, just in case it disappears in transit.

Think it through. What's the weather like? Is this a business trip or a cruise or resort vacation? Going abroad? In some places and/or sights, traditions of dress may be more or less conservative than you're used to. As your itinerary comes together, jot activities down and note possible outfits next to each (don't forget those shoes and accessories).

Edit your wardrobe. Plan to wear everything twice (better yet, thrice) and to do laundry along the way. Stick to one basic look—urban chic, sporty casual, etc. Build around one or two neutrals and an accent (e.g., black, white, and olive green). Women can freshen looks by changing scarves or jewelry. For a week's trip, you can look smashing with three bottoms, four or five tops, a sweater, and a jacket you can wear alone or over the sweater.

Be practical. Put comfortable shoes at the top of your list. (Did we need to tell you this?) Pack items that are lightweight, wrinkle resistant, compact, and washable. (Or this?) Try a simple wrinkling test: intentionally fold a piece of fabric between your fingers for a couple minutes. If it refuses to crease, it will probably come out of your suitcase looking fresh. That said if you stack and then roll your clothes when packing, they'll wrinkle less.

Check weight and size limitations. In the United States you may be charged extra for checked bags weighing more than 50 pounds. Abroad some airlines don't allow you to check bags weighing more than 60 to 70 pounds, or they charge outrageous fees for every pound your luggage is over. Carry-on size limitations can be stringent, too.

Be prepared to lug it yourself. If there's one thing that can turn a pack rat into a minimalist, it's a vacation spent lugging heavy bags over long distances. Unless you're on a guided tour or a cruise, select luggage that you can readily carry. Porters, like good butlers, are hard to find these days.

Lock it up. Several companies sell locks (about $10) approved by the Transportation Safety Administration that can be unlocked by all U.S. security personnel should they decide to search your bags. Alternatively, you can use simple plastic cable ties, which are sold at hardware stores in bundles.

Tag it. Always put tags on your luggage with some kind of contact information; use your business address if you don't want people to know your home address. Put the same information (and a copy of your itinerary) inside your luggage, too.

Don't check valuables. On U.S. flights, airlines are only liable for about $2,800 per person for bags. On international flights, the liability limit is around $635 per bag. But just try collecting from the airline for items like computers, cameras, and jewelry. It isn't going to happen; they aren't covered. And though comprehensive travel policies may cover luggage, the liability limit is often a pittance. Your home-owners' policy may cover you sufficiently when you travel—or not. You're really better off stashing baubles and gizmos in your carry-on—right near those prescription meds.

Report problems immediately. If your bags—or things in them—are damaged or go astray, file a written claim with your airline *before you leave the airport*. If the airline is at fault, it may give you money for essentials until your luggage arrives. Most lost bags are found within 48 hours, so alert the airline to your whereabouts for two or three days. If your bag was opened for security reasons in the United States and something is missing, file a claim with the TSA.

WHAT YOU'LL NEED IN THE CAROLINAS & GEORGIA

Except for some high-elevation mountain areas, the Carolinas and Georgia are hot and humid in summer and sunny and mild in winter. Smart but casual attire works fine almost everywhere. A few chic restaurants in the cities prefer more elegant dress, and tradition-minded lodges in the mountains and resorts along the coast still require jackets and ties for men for dinner. For colder months pack a lightweight coat, slacks, and sweaters; you'll need heavier clothing in some mountainous areas, where cold, damp weather prevails and snow is not unusual. Keeping summer's humidity in mind, **pack absorbent natural fabrics that breathe**; bring an umbrella, but leave the plastic raincoat at home. You'll want a jacket or sweater for summer evenings and for too-cool air-conditioning. And **don't forget insect repellent**.

SAFETY

In general, the Carolinas and Georgia are safe destinations for travelers. Most rural and suburban areas have low crime rates. However, some of the region's larger cities have significantly higher crime rates than the national average. Atlanta's robbery and assault rates, for example, are much higher than in cities such as New York or San Francisco. Savannah and Charlotte also have crime rates that top the national average.

In urban areas, follow proven traveler's precautions: don't wander onto deserted streets after dark, avoid flashing large sums of money or fancy jewelry, and keep an eye on purses and backpacks. If you're walking, even around the historic district, ask at your hotel or a tourist information center about areas to avoid; if in doubt, take a taxi to your destination.

Distribute your cash, credit cards, IDs, and other valuables between a deep front pocket, an inside jacket or vest pocket, and a hidden money pouch. Don't reach for the money pouch once you're in public.

GOVERNMENT ADVISORIES

If you travel frequently also look into the Registered Traveler program of the Transportation Security Administration (TSA; www.tsa.gov). The program, which is still being tested in five U.S. airports, is designed to cut down on gridlock at security checkpoints by allowing prescreened travelers to pass quickly through kiosks that scan an iris and/or a fingerprint. How sci-fi is that?

SHOPPING

Beyond the suburban malls, which are usually anchored by national or regional department stores, boutiques, and galleries can be found both in the larger cities and throughout the resort areas. Recognizing the changing demographics of the market, such institutions as Tiffany & Co. have set-up shop here. And thanks to the temperate climate, outdoor arts-and-crafts festivals abound. On most Saturday mornings, bargain hunters can find deals in the ubiquitous flea markets and garage sales.

KEY DESTINATIONS

People travel from afar to furniture outlets in High Point and Hickory, North Carolina, though competition from abroad has meant that some local plants have closed. The dozens of potters clustered around the North Carolina town of Seagrove, in the Sandhills, produce jugs, bowls, mugs, and other functional forms. South Carolina's textile industry carries on, producing the fabrics sold in retail outlets across the central and northern portions of the state. Asheville and the surrounding area has become one of the country's leading arts and crafts centers, with more than 4,000 artisans in residence. Asheville alone has some 100 galleries where you can check out locally made ceramics, textiles, wood carvings, jewelry, and other items.

The Mall of Georgia in Bufford, 30 mi northeast of downtown Atlanta, is the largest mall in the Southeast, with more than 225 stores. Atlanta has many malls, including two large upscale malls, adjacent to each other in Buckhead: Lenox Square Mall and Phipps Plaza. Tanger Outlet Center in Commerce and North George Premium Outlets in South Dawsonville are the two largest outlet centers in the region. There also are many factory-outlet centers along Interstate 95, especially in the Hilton Head and Savannah areas. Note that not all of the stores at outlet centers have great bargains; some are just regular retail stores. Also, some manufacturers produce special lines to be sold only in their outlet stores.

SMART SOUVENIRS

"Face jugs," whimsical pottery pitchers that incorporate caricature-like faces designed to ward off evil spirits, can be found at many of the roadside potteries in the Seagrove area of North Carolina. Prices can be up to several hundred dollars, depending on the size and the artist. In South Carolina, particularly in the Lowcountry, sweetgrass baskets, woven using a technique carried over by African slaves, are both beautiful and utilitarian. The many designs, ranging from small baskets to large clothes hampers, typically cost between $10 and $100.

TAXES

SALES TAX

Sales taxes are as follows: Georgia 4%, North Carolina 4.5%, and South Carolina 5%. Some counties or cities may impose an additional sales tax of 1% to 3%. Most municipalities also levy a lodging tax (usually exempting small inns) and sometimes a restaurant tax. The hotel taxes in the South can be rather steep: more than 10% in Georgia and many counties in North Carolina. Taxes and fees on car rentals, especially if rented from an airport, can easily add 30% or more to your bill.

TIME

Georgia and the Carolinas fall in the eastern standard time (EST) zone, which is the same as New York and Florida, making it three hours ahead of California.

TIPPING

Tipping in the Carolinas and Georgia is essentially the same as tipping anywhere else in the United States. Hotel chambermaids should be tipped $1 to $3 a night for inexpensive and moderate hotels and up to $5 a night per guest for high-end properties. A concierge typically receives anywhere from $5 to $25, depending on the favor requested. Room-service waiters get 10% to 15% (look to see if it's already included on the bill), and $1 to $2 per bag is customary for bellhops, porters, and skycaps. Tips aren't necessary, though they're still accepted, if the hotel includes a service fee in its package price.

In group-tour situations—boat excursions along the coast, for example—the crew will split whatever is left in a communal tip jar; a couple of dollars is appropriate. Museum and tour guides are generally either volunteers or on staff, and therefore don't expect tips. Taxi fares can be rounded up by a couple of dollars. Tips for restaurant servers and bartenders range from 10% to 20%, depending on price and service; gratuities are often included in the bill for large parties. Hairdressers, barbers, and masseuses usually receive a gratuity of 10% to 20%.

TOURS & PACKAGES

GUIDED TOURS

Guided tours are a good option when you don't want to do it all yourself. You travel along with a group (sometimes large, sometimes small), stay in prebooked hotels, eat with your fellow travelers (sometimes included in the price of your tour, sometimes not), and follow a schedule. But not all guided tours are a "If This Is Tuesday, It Must Be Belgium" kind of experience. A knowledgeable guide can take you places that you might never discover on your own, and you may be pushed to see more than you would have otherwise. Tours aren't for everyone, but they can be just the thing for trips to places where making travel arrangements is difficult or time-consuming (particularly when you don't speak the language). Whenever you book a guided tour, find out what's included and what isn't. A "land-only" tour includes all your travel (by bus, in most cases) in the destination, but not necessarily your flights to or even within it. Also, in most cases, prices in tour brochures don't include fees and taxes. And remember that you'll be expected to tip your guide (in cash) at the end of the tour.

The Carolinas and Georgia predominantly attract visitors traveling independently, usually by car. But some areas—notably Savannah, Charleston, Asheville, and the Great Smoky Mountains—get a number of escorted bus tours. Collette Tours has eight-day tours of Atlanta, Savannah, Charleston, and the Georgia Sea Islands. The escorted tours operate in spring and fall, with prices from $1,100 per person. You stay at first-class hotels, such as the Jekyll Island Club on Jekyll Island, and the price includes most breakfasts and dinners. Collette Tours also has an eight-day Great Smoky Mountains tour that includes a visit to the Biltmore Estate in Asheville and stops in Tennessee and Kentucky. Presley Tours has five- to eight-day tours of the Georgia Sea Islands, Charleston, Savannah, Myrtle Beach, and the Great

Smokies. Most tours are $800 to $1,100 per person. A large tour company called Tauck has an eight-day tour of Charleston, Savannah, Jekyll Island, and Hilton Head, staying at such high-end hotels as the Westin Resort on Hilton Head. The cost is $2,080 per person.

🚩 Recommended Generalists **Collette Tours** ☎ 800/942-3301 ⊕ www.escortedcollettetours. com. **Presley Tours** ☎ 800/621-6100 ⊕ www. presleytours.com. **Tauck** ☎ 800/788-7885 ⊕ www. tauck.com.

BIKE TOURS

Discover Adventures has bike tours of the wine country of Georgia and North Carolina. A six-day tour includes visits to six wineries in Georgia and six in North Carolina. The cost is $1,980 per person, and includes bicycle and almost all meals. Overnight stays are at upscale inns and B&Bs, including the Inn at Biltmore in Asheville. The company also offers two- to four-day cycling tours of North Georgia and western and central North Carolina.

🚲 Bike Tour Contacts **Discover Adventures** ☎ 866/442-2848 ⊕ www.discoveradventures.com.

VACATION PACKAGES

Packages *are not* guided tours. Packages combine airfare, accommodations, and perhaps a rental car or other extras (theater tickets, guided excursions, boat trips, reserved entry to popular museums, transit passes), but they let you do your own thing. During busy periods, packages may be your only option because flights and rooms may be otherwise sold out. Packages will definitely save you time. They can also save you money, particularly in peak seasons, but—and this is a really big "but"—you should price each part of the package separately to be sure. And be aware that prices advertised on Web sites and in newspapers rarely include service charges or taxes, which can up your costs by hundreds of dollars.

Note that local tourism boards can provide information about lesser-known and small-niche operators that sell packages to just a few destinations. And don't always assume that you can get the best deal by booking everything yourself. Some packages and cruises are sold only through travel agents.

Each year consumers are stranded or lose their money when packagers—even large ones with excellent reputations—go out of business. How can you protect yourself? First, always pay with a credit card; if you have a problem, your credit-card company may help you resolve it. Second, buy trip insurance that covers default. Third, choose a company that belongs to the United States Tour Operators Association, whose members must set aside funds ($1 million) to cover defaults. Finally choose a company that also participates in the Tour Operator Program of the American Society of Travel Agents (ASTA), which will act as mediator in any disputes. You can also check on the tour operator's reputation among travelers by posting an inquiry on one of the Fodors.com forums.

Most visitors to the Carolinas and Georgia travel independently, usually by car. For many such travelers, package rates aren't available or don't offer enough flexibility. However, visitors planning to fly in and rent a car may want to look at the flight/hotel/rental car packages now routinely offered by online travel companies. These may—or may not—be better deals than buying each one individually. Many of the region's visitor information centers have sections on their Web sites listing local packages; for example, the Atlanta Convention and Visitor's Bureau site lists packages that include hotel rooms and admission to Six Flags over Georgia or tickets to Atlanta Braves baseball games. The American Automobile Association offices—there are 24 in the Carolinas and nine in Georgia—often offer discounted admissions to local attractions to members.

🗐 Organizations **American Society of Travel Agents (ASTA)** ☎ 703/739-2782, 800/965-2782 24-hr hotline ⊕ www.astanet.com. **United States Tour Operators Association (USTOA)** ☎ 212/599-6599 ⊕ www.ustoa.com.

WOMEN'S TOURS

Gutsy Women Travel, a tour company for women who "want to experience the world," offers a six-day tour of Charleston and Savannah for around $1,800 per person. The price includes accommodations at first-class hotels and some meals.

🗐 Women's Tours Contacts **Gutsy Women Travel** ☎ 866/464-8879 ⊕ www.gutsywomentravel.com.

TRAIN TRAVEL

Several Amtrak routes pass through the Carolinas and Georgia; however, many areas are not served by train, and those cities that do have service usually only have one or two arrivals and departures each day. The *Crescent* runs daily through Greensboro, Charlotte, and Atlanta as it travels between New York and New Orleans. Three trains, the *Palmetto*, the *Silver Meteor*, and the *Silver Star* make the daily run between New York and Miami via Raleigh, Charleston, Columbia, and Savannah. The *Carolinian* runs daily from New York to Charlotte, via Raleigh.

CUTTING COSTS

Amtrak offers rail passes that allow for travel within certain regions, which can save you a lot over the posted fare. There are also occasional deals that allow a second or third accompanying passenger to travel for half price or even free. The North American Rail Pass, which grants you unlimited travel in the United States and Canada within any 30-day period, costs $709 most of the year and $999 in peak periods such as summer and the end of December. For non–U.S. residents, Amtrak has several kinds of USA Rail Passes, offering unlimited travel for 5 to 30 days, with rates of $155 to $565, depending on the area traveled, the time of year, and the number of days. Amtrak has discounts for students, seniors, and people with disabilities.

🗐 Train Information **Amtrak** ☎ 800/872-7245 ⊕ www.amtrak.com.

TRAVEL AGENTS

If you use an agent—brick-and-mortar or virtual—you'll pay a fee for the service. And know that the service you get from some online agents isn't comprehensive. For example Expedia or Travelocity don't search for prices on budget airlines like jetBlue, Southwest, or small foreign carriers. That said, some agents (online or not) *do* have access to fares that are difficult to find otherwise, and the savings can more than make up for any surcharge.

A knowledgeable brick-and-mortar travel agent can be a godsend if you're booking a cruise, a package trip that's not available to you directly, an air pass, or a complicated itinerary including several overseas flights. What's more travel agents that specialize in a destination may have exclusive access to certain deals and insider information on things such as charter flights. Agents who specialize in types of travelers (senior citizens, gays and lesbians, naturists) or types of trips (cruises, luxury travel, safaris) can also be invaluable.

A top-notch agent planning your trip to Russia will make sure you get the correct visa application and complete it on time; the one booking your cruise may get you a cabin upgrade or arrange to have bottle of champagne chilling in your cabin when you embark. And complain about the surcharges all you like, but when things don't work out the way you'd hoped, it's nice to have an agent to put things right.

If you're flying into the Carolinas and Georgia, renting a car, traveling to multiple destinations, and staying at several different hotels, you may find that working with a travel agent could save you time, and possibly money. However, if you're visiting only one or two destinations, you may find it preferable to make reservations on your own.

🔒 Agent Resources **American Society of Travel Agents** ☎ 703/739-2782 ⊕ www.travelsense.org. 🔒 Online Agents **Expedia** ⊕ www.expedia.com. **Onetravel.com** ⊕ www.onetravel.com. **Orbitz** ⊕ www.orbitz.com. **Priceline.com** ⊕ www. priceline.com. **Travelocity** ⊕ www.travelocity.com.

VISITOR INFORMATION

Going online is the fastest way to get visitor information. All of the state tourism offices listed below have excellent Web sites, with maps and other travel information that you can browse.

🔒 Tourist Information **Georgia Department of Industry, Trade and Tourism** ⊠ 285 Peachtree Center Ave., NE Marquis Tower II, Suite 1100, Atlanta, GA 30303 ☎ 404/656-3553 or 800/847-4842 📠 404/651-9462 ⊕ www.georgia.org. **North Carolina**

Travel and Tourism Division ⊠ 301 N. Wilmington St., Raleigh, NC 27601 ☎ 919/715-5900 or 800/847-4862 📠 919/733-2616 ⊕ www.visitnc.com. **South Carolina Department of Parks, Recreation, and Tourism** ⊠ 1205 Pendleton St., Suite 106, Columbia, SC 29201 ☎ 803/734-0122 or 888/727-6453 📠 803/734-0138 ⊕ www.travelsc.com.

WEB SITES

We're really proud of our Web site: Fodors.com is a great place to begin any journey. Scan "Travel Wire" for suggested itineraries, travel deals, restaurant and hotel openings, and other up-to-the-minute info. Check out "Booking" to research prices and book plane tickets, hotel rooms, rental cars, and vacation packages. Head to "Talk" for on-the-ground pointers from travelers who frequent our message boards. You can also link to loads of other travel-related resources.

After your trip, be sure to rate the places you visited and share your experiences and travel tips with us and other Fodorites in "Travel Ratings" and "Talk" on www.fodors.com.

In addition to the Web sites listed below, for more information on events in the Carolinas and Georgia try visiting the Web sites of major newspapers and alternative newsweeklies in the area (⇨ Media). Also take a look at the Web sites listed for regional and local tourism offices in the Essentials sections throughout each chapter.

🔒 All About the Carolinas & Georgia **Civil War Traveler** ⊕ www.civilwartraveler.com has information about Civil War sites in the Carolinas and Georgia, as well as in other states. **Doc South** ⊕ docsouth.unc.edu is a vast collection of historical documents and archives on Southern history, culture, and literature. **Dr. Beach** ⊕ www.drbeach.org is Dr. Stephen Leatherman's take on the best beaches in the Carolinas and Georgia and other states. In 2006, North Carolina's Ocracoke Beach was rated the third-best beach in the United States. A wonderful grab bag of information about North Carolina, including information on Eng and Chang Bunker, the "original" Siamese twins who lived in Wilkes County, is available at the **North Carolina Collection** ⊕ www.lib.unc.edu/ncc, part of the University of North Carolina Library. The online edition of **Southern Living** ⊕ www.southernliving.com has many articles on travel, attractions, gardens, and people in the region.

Art & Culture Gullah Culture ⊕ www.pbs.org/now/arts/gullah.html, from the PBS program with Bill Moyers, is a good introduction to Gullah life and culture. **Handmade in America** ⊕ www.handmadeinamerica.org is a community organization whose goal is to establish western North Carolina as the nation's center of handmade objects. **Penland School of Crafts** ⊕ www.penland.org is devoted to the famous crafts school in the North Carolina Mountains, but it also has a wealth of information on crafts in the region. **Southern High Craft Guild** ⊕ www.southernhighlandguild.org represents more than 900 craftspeople in the Southeast.

Southern Literary Review ⊕ www.southernlitreview.com has biographical and bibliographical information on scores of Southern writers, including those hailing from the Carolinas and Georgia.

Several of the region's museums have excellent online information. Atlanta's **High Museum of Art** ⊕ www.high.org is the largest and best art museum in the region. The site for the **Mint Museum of Art** ⊕ www.mintmuseum.org covers the Mint Museum of Art and the Mint Museum of Craft + Design, both in Charlotte. Raleigh's **North Carolina Museum of Art** ⊕ www.ncartmuseum.org is North Carolina's premier art museum.

Golf Georgia State Park Golf Courses ⊕ www.georgiagolf.com has detailed information on Georgia's public golf courses. **Golf Guide** ⊕ www.golfguideweb.com has links to most golf courses in the Carolinas and Georgia. **Golf Link** ⊕ www.golflink.com offers information on nearly all the golf courses in the region. **Golf North Carolina** ⊕ www.golfnorthcarolina.com lets you search a database of North Carolina's 600 golf courses. In addition to the usual course information, this site has sections on golf humor and golf trivia. **North Carolina Golf Trail** ⊕ www.ncgolftrail.com has links to many public golf courses in North Carolina. Public golf courses in South Carolina can be researched on **South Carolina Golf Trail** ⊕ www.scgolftrail.com.

Outdoors The **Appalachian Trail Conservancy** ⊕ www.appalachiantrail.org is dedicated to preserving the nation's longest footpath, which runs from Georgia all the way to Maine. The **Blue Ridge Parkway Association Guide** ⊕ www.blueridgeparkway.org has detailed information on one of the most beautiful roads in America. **Georgia State Parks** ⊕ www.gastateparks.org covers accommodations, recreational activities, and special activities at one of the best state park systems in the United States. **National Forests in North Carolina** ⊕ www.cs.unca.edu/nfsnc is a comprehensive guide to the state's national forests. The **National Park Service** ⊕ www.nps.gov/grsm/ has information on all of the national parks in the region, including the Great Smoky Mountains, the country's most popular national park. Although the site is far from comprehensive, **North Carolina State Parks** ⊕ www.ils.unc.edu/parkproject/main/visit.html has information on state parks. A bit of a hodgepodge, **North Carolina's Outer Banks** ⊕ www.outerbanks.com is a fun source of information on all aspects of the Outer Banks. **South Carolina State Parks** ⊕ www.southcarolinaparks.com is a colorful site with information on accommodations, outdoor activities, and even discounts offered at the parks.

Skiing Ski North Carolina ⊕ www.skinorthcarolina.com has information on skiing and ski conditions at eight North Carolina ski resorts: Appalachian Ski Mountain, Cataloochee Ski Area, Hawksnest Ski Resort, Sapphire Valley Ski Area, Scaly Mountain Snow Tubing, Ski Beech Resort, Sugar Mountain Ski Resort, and Wolf Laurel Resort.

Time Zones Timeanddate.com ⊕ www.timeanddate.com/worldclock can help you figure out the correct time anywhere in the world.

Weather Accuweather.com ⊕ www.accuweather.com is an independent weather-forecasting service with especially good coverage of hurricanes. **Weather.com** ⊕ www.weather.com is the Web site for the Weather Channel.

Wine The excellent site for **Georgia Wine Country** ⊕ www.georgiawinecountry.com has information on more than two dozen wineries in Georgia. **North Carolina Wines** ⊕ www.ncwine.org is a comprehensive site with facts on almost 60 wineries in North Carolina. **Winegrowers Association of Georgia** ⊕ www.georgiawine.com is a guide to touring and tasting Georgia's wineries.

INDEX

NOTES

NOTES

NOTES

NOTES

ABOUT OUR WRITERS

Michele Foust is a native of the Midwest who has learned what keeps Georgia on people's minds. After 16 years of editing business, metro, and feature stories and developing projects for the *Atlanta Journal-Constitution*, she is now a freelance writer, savoring dogwoods and azaleas in the spring, the colorful foliage of the North Georgia mountains in the fall, and everything about Atlanta, a city that balances international flair with world-famous Southern hospitality.

When a love affair brought Chris McBeath to Georgia, little did she realize that it would evolve into an equally compelling love of the Peach State. An award-winning writer with more than 25 years' experience in tourism, Chris has an insider's eye as to what makes a great travel experience. Whether routing through back roads or discovering a hidden-away inn, Chris shares her findings with in-the-know tips and historical anecdotes that truly capture the charm of the South. Chris has written for publications worldwide; her Web site is www.greatestgetaways.com.

A wrong turn as a teenager outside Florence on the way to a family beach vacation was freelance writer Katie McElveen's first experience exploring South Carolina. Twenty-five years later, she hasn't stopped, although she now travels with a map. From her home base in Columbia, Katie has shared her discoveries with locals and visitors alike through her work in such magazines as *Modern Bride*, *South Carolina Smiles*, *Sandlapper*, and *Southern Living*.

Freelance writer Leslie Mizell, who lives in Greensboro, North Carolina, can't tell her left from her right, which makes her a challenging travel companion. She is, however, willing to stop at any roadside stand, shop, or museum because she believes it's not how fast you get there, it's the stories you have when you arrive. For this edition she updated the the Piedmont & the Sandhills and the North Carolina Coast chapters.

Her family's move from Connecticut to South Carolina earned Eileen Robinson Smith the distinction of being Yankee born and Southern raised. Waving goodbye to her apartment on New York City's Park Avenue, she moved into a lakefront home in Charleston in 1982. A former editor of *Charleston* magazine, she has written for local, regional, and national publications such as *Latitudes* and *Sky*. She has been a contributor to *Fodor's Caribbean* for more than a decade. For this guide she returned to her beloved Lowcountry, updating the chapters for Charleston and Hilton Head.

Asheville native and former New Orleans newspaper editor Lan Sluder has written a half-dozen books, including travel guides to Belize and the coast of the Carolinas and Georgia. His articles have appeared in *Caribbean Travel & Life*, the *Chicago Tribune*, the *Charlotte Observer*, the *New York Times*, Canada's *Globe & Mail*, and other publications around the world. He has also contributed to other Fodor's guides, including *Fodor's Belize*. Lan's home base in North Carolina is a mountain farm near Asheville settled by his forebears in the early 1800s.

Fodor's

Georgia and the Carolinas Maps

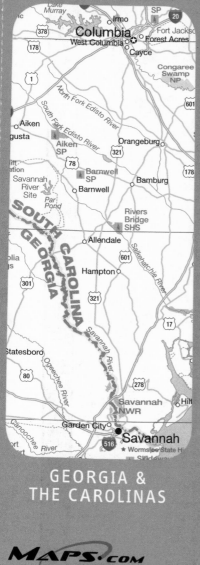

**GEORGIA &
THE CAROLINAS**

ATLANTA &
CHARLESTON

MAPS.COM